Sayyid Jamāl ad-Dīn "al-Afghānī"

A Political Biography

Published under the Auspices of the
Near Eastern Center
University of California
Los Angeles

Sayyid Jamāl ad-Dīn "al-Afghānī"

A Political Biography

by

NIKKI R. KEDDIE

UNIVERSITY OF CALIFORNIA PRESS
Berkeley Los Angeles London
1972

University of California Press
Berkeley and Los Angeles, California

University of California Press, Ltd.
London, England

ISBN: 0–520–01986–5
Library of Congress Catalog Card Number: 74–159671

Designed by Penny Faron
Printed in the United States of America

To David and Arlene;
Leonard, Marion, and Alexa

Preface

I first decided to work on a biography of Jamāl ad-Dīn in the summer of 1964. Until then such research as I had done on Jamāl ad-Dīn was a by-product of a larger study undertaken in 1959 on the Iranian Constitutional Revolution of 1905–1911. The latter subject turned out to have so much source material that it could easily be a lifetime's work or more. In pursuing the background of the Constitutional Revolution while in Iran in 1959–1960, I discovered that several of the revolutionaries and precursors of the revolution who spoke in religious terms were in fact either members of the Azalī branch of the heretical Babi sect or unbelievers. The case of Jamāl ad-Dīn al-Afghānī was a more complex one, as he was neither a Babi nor totally irreligious, but there was considerable evidence, most of it not previously noticed, that he was far from being the pious Sunni Muslim that he often tried to appear. In Iran I was greatly helped by 'Abd al-Husain Zarrinkūb and Sayyid Hasan Taqīzādeh, among others. In London in the summer of 1960 I found the British Foreign Office's special volume on Afghānī, F.O. 60/594.

When in Iran in 1959–1960, I had been convinced by some skeptical Iranian intellectuals that Afghānī was of Afghan birth. Thus, when I went to Hamadan briefly I did not look up Jamāl ad-Dīn's relatives said to be in the area, so convinced was I that he was an Afghan and his relatives could not really be in Iran. Only after meeting and discussing the matter with Albert Hourani in the summer of 1962 did I come to think he might be Iranian, and as I read more primary material about him it became clear, for reasons discussed in the present volume, that there was no doubt that he was born and raised in Iran.

In the summer of 1962 I also met Sylvia Haim and Elie Kedourie who offered great help and encouragement from then on, notwithstanding differences between my view of Afghānī and Kedourie's. It was Elie Kedourie who suggested in the summer of 1964 that I do a biography of Afghānī and convinced me of the feasibility of such a project. In the same summer of 1964 Malcolm Yapp of the University of London School of Oriental and African Studies suggested I look up the "Cabul Diaries" for possible information on Afghānī, a suggestion that turned out to be a most fruitful one.

I also received great help from two persons who were engaged in since-completed doctoral theses on Afghānī—Homa Pakdaman and A. Albert Kudsi-Zadeh, both of whose works are listed in the bibliography of this volume. Both showed and led me to new sources about Afghānī, and helped with interpretations.

Before writing the present volume I wrote a monograph, *Religion and Rebellion in Iran: The Tobacco Protest of 1891–1892* (London, Frank Cass, 1966), which included details on Afghānī's participation in the tobacco movement, and *An Islamic Response to Imperialism: Political and Religious Writings of Sayyid Jamāl ad-Dīn "al-Afghānī"* (Berkeley and Los Angeles, University of California Press, 1968), which translated several of Afghānī's works, with an introduction. I also published several articles incorporating research on Afghānī. Whenever one of these articles is in disagreement with the present work, the latter is to be preferred as incorporating new materials and judgments.

In January 1964, I looked at the Indian archives but found nothing new. In the summer of 1966 I traveled to Istanbul, Tehran, and Cairo. In Istanbul I found one document in the Yıldız Collection (covering the reign of Abdülhamid). I was told that many of the documents of this period had been burned or otherwise removed. In Tehran I saw the complete collection of Afghānī papers to 1891 now in the Majlis Library and received aid from Īraj Afshār and Asghar Mahdavī. In Egypt I saw numerous books and also was helped by Muḥammad Ṣubaiḥ, Shaikh Maḥmud Abū Rayya, and Rashīd Rūstam. Donald Reid, whom I met in Cairo, later copied all the articles he could find by or concerning Afghānī in the newspaper *Mişr*. All the above are thanked for their help.

In Paris I looked at Freemasonic archives. with no results, but found some information in Foreign Ministry and Police Archives—the latter following a lead given by Homa Pakdaman. In London the Public Record Office and the Commonwealth Relations Office turned out to be fruitful sources.

Parts or all of the current manuscript were read by Bernard Lewis, Albert Hourani, Dankwart Rustow, A. Albert Kudsi-Zadeh, Roger Allen, Afaf Lutfi al-Sayyid Marsot, Aziz Ahmad, and Hamid Algar, all of whom made useful suggestions. A series of research assistants were all outstandingly helpful: Shannon Stack, Ali Reza Sheikholeslami, Pamela Smith, Leon Fink of Rochester, and especially Gene Garthwaite who arranged reproduction of Afghānī's papers while in Tehran. Although I have done the extensive reading required by this work in all languages except Urdu, for help in translating difficult documents I have turned to my colleagues Amin Banani, Moshe Perlmann, Abdallah Laroui, Andreas Tietze, and Janos Eckmann, to all of whom are due thanks. For the Urdu translations I am indebted to Ismail Poonawalla and Nasim Jawed.

Thanks also go to the Social Science Research Council for a fellowship in 1959–60 and the Guggenheim Foundation for a fellowship in 1963–64. At the University of California, Los Angeles, Near Eastern Center thanks are especially due G. E. von Grunebaum for his advice and aid, Evelyn Oder for her excellent typing, and Teresa Joseph for eagle-eyed editing. Eugene Genovese at the University of Rochester gave much needed help when I was visiting there in the fall of 1970, as did Virginia Mastroleo. In Iran I was also helped by Mohit Tabataba'i and Mojtaba Minovi. Aid was also given over the years by Niyazi Berkes, William Brinner, Muhsin Mahdi, and Maxime Rodison. Sincere thanks go to them and to all of the persons mentioned in this preface.

Tracing Jamāl ad-Dīn has led me to many lucky hunches on location of material, not all of which are discussed above, and to travels almost duplicating his own. It has been rewarding detective work, and I can only hope that the final product justifies the long search.

Los Angeles
February 1971

Contents

	Note on Transliteration	xii
	Abbreviations	xv
1.	Introduction	1
2.	The First Twenty-seven Years: 1838/39–1866	10
3.	In Afghanistan: 1866–1868	37
4.	Istanbul: 1869–1871	58
5.	Egypt: 1871–1879	81
6.	The Pan-Islamic Appeal	129
7.	India: Late 1879 to Late 1882	143
8.	Propaganda from Paris: 1883–1884	182
9.	The Mahdi and the Sultan: 1884–1885	229
10.	Iran to Russia: 1886–1889	271
11.	Russia to Iran: 1889–1891	306
12.	The Tobacco Protest of 1891–1892	335
13.	The Final Years: Istanbul, 1892–1897	373
	Appendixes	425
	Chronology of Jamāl ad-Dīn	448
	Bibliography	451
	Index	469

Note on Transliteration

Turkish words are transliterated according to the modern Turkish Romanization system and Arabic according to the standard system of the University of California, Los Angeles, Near Eastern Center. Persian and Urdu are transliterated according to a modification of that system whereby vowels are transliterated as in Arabic, but the consonants are given their Persian pronunciation, with no diacriticals on the consonants except for authors and titles in the notes and bibliography. The following table should clarify any ambiguities:

	Persian/Urdu	
Arabic	*Text*	*Notes and bibliography*
ẓ	z	ẓ
ḍ	z	z̤
dh	z	z̲
ṣ	s	ṣ
th	s	s̲
w	v	v

With the exception of ḍ(z̤), dh (z̲), th (s̲), and w (v), consonants are given the same letter value in transliterating from Persian and Arabic. Terminal Persian *eh* equals Arabic *a*.

In modern Turkish Romanization, letters are pronounced much as spelled, except that *c* equals Arabic and English *j*. Thus Jamāl ad-Dīn in Turkish begins with *C*.

Place-names and words whose position in English is attested by their inclusion in recent unabridged dictionaries are spelled without diacriticals, although the sign for *'ain* is retained in the middle of such words: for example, Shi'i, ulama Isma'ili, Babi, Muhammad, Ramadan, Koran.

Abbreviations

A.E.	France. Archives du Ministère des Affaires Étrangères. Perse, 1888–1896.
'Abduh, "Biographie"	'Abduh, Muḥammad. "Biographie d'al-Afghânî," trans. A.-M. Goichon. In al-Afghānī, Sayyid Jamāl ad-Dīn, *Réfutation des matérialistes.* Trans. A.-M. Goichon. Paris, 1942.
Ahmad, *Studies*	Ahmad, Aziz. *Studies in Islamic Culture in the Indian Environment.* Oxford, 1964.
Blunt, *India*	Blunt, Wilfrid S. *India under Ripon.* London, 1909.
"Cabul Diary"	Great Britain. Commonwealth Relations Office. Government of India, Foreign Department. *Proceedings of the Government of India in the Foreign Department, Political.* Calcutta, 1869; "Cabul Diary," Feb., April, Sept.–Dec. 1868, and Jan., 1869.
Cabul Précis	Great Britain. Commonwealth Relations Office. Government of India, Foreign Department. *Narrative of Events in Cabul from the Death of Dost Mahomed to the Spring of 1872. . . . Cabul Précis 1863–74.* Simla, 1866, 1874.

Dīvān-i Furṣat	Furṣat ad-Dauleh Shīrāzī. *Dīvān-i Furṣat.* Tehran, 1337/1958–59.
Documents	Afshār, Īraj, and Aṣghar Mahdavī. *Documents inédits concernant Seyyed Jamāl-al-Dīn Afghānī (Majmū'eh-yi asnād va madārik-i chāp nashudeh dar bāreh-yi Sayyid Jamāl ad-Dīn mashhūr bi Afghānī).* Tehran, 1963.
*EI*²	*Encyclopaedia of Islam.* New ed., Leiden and London, 1960—.
F.O.	Great Britain. Public Record Office. F.O. 60: Original dispatches to and from Persia, especially F.O. 60/594, Djemal ed-Din: Proceedings of and expulsion from Persia, 1883–1897. F.O. 65: Original dispatches to and from Russia, F.O. 78: Original dispatches to and from Egypt. F.O. 248: Archives of the British Embassy in Tehran. F.O. 539: Correspondence relating to Afghanistan, Persia, and Turkestan.
Ḥājji Sayyāḥ	Sayyāḥ, Ḥājji. *Khāṭirāt-i Ḥājji Sayyāḥ.* Ed. Ḥamīd Sayyāḥ and Saifallāh Gulkār. Tehran, 1346/1967–68.
Keddie, *Islamic Response*	Keddie. Nikki R. *An Islamic Response to Imperialism: Political and Religious Writings of Sayyid Jamāl ad-Dīn "al-Afghānī."* Berkeley and Los Angeles, 1968.
Kedourie, *Afghani*	Kedourie, Elie. *Afghani and 'Abduh: An Essay on Religious Unbelief and Political Activism in Modern Islam.* London, 1966.
Kudsi-Zadeh, *Bibliography*	Kudsi-Zadeh, A. Albert. *Sayyid Jamāl al-Dīn al-Afghānī: An Annotated Bibliography.* Leiden, 1970.
Kudsi-Zadeh, "Iranian Politics"	Kudsi-Zadeh, A. Albert. "Iranian Politics in the Late Qājār Period: A Review," *Middle Eastern Studies,* V, 3 (Oct., 1969), 251–257.
Kudsi-Zadeh, "Legacy"	Kudsi-Zadeh, A. Albert. "The Legacy of Sayyid Jamāl al-Dīn al-Afghānī in Egypt." Unpublished Ph.D. dissertation, Indiana University. Bloomington, 1964.

Luṭfallāh	Asadābādī, Mīrzā Luṭfallāh. *Sharḥ-i ḥāl va āsār-i Sayyid Jamāl ad-Dīn Asadābādī ma'rūf bi "Afghānī."* Tabriz, 1326/1947–48. (Rev. ed. of *Sharḥ-i ḥāl-i Sayyid Jamāl ad-Dīn Asadābādī.* Berlin, 1926.)
Makhzūmī, *Khāṭirāt* (Persian) or (Arabic)	al-Makhzūmī, Muḥammad. *Khāṭirāt Jamāl ad-Dīn al-Afghānī.* 2d ed. Damascus, 1965. Partial trans. into Persian [*Khāṭirāt-i Sayyid Jamāl ad-Dīn al-Afghānī*] by Murtaẓā Mudarrisī Chahārdihī. Tabriz, 1328/1949–50.
Mulk Ārā'	'Abbās Mīrzā Mulk Ārā'. *Sharḥ-i ḥāl-i 'Abbās Mīrzā Mulk Ārā',* Ed. 'Abd al-Ḥusain Navā'ī. Tehran. 1325/1946–47.
Pakdaman	Pakdaman, Homa. *Djamal-ed-Din Assad Abadi dit Afghani.* Paris. 1969.
PSHC	Great Britain. Commonwealth Relations Office. Government of India, Foreign Department. *Political and Secret Home Correspondence.* 1882, vol. 51, and 1887, vols. 93–98.
Réfutation	al-Afghānī, Sayyid Jamāl ad-Dīn. *Réfutation des matérialistes.* Trans. A.-M. Goichon. Paris, 1942. (Includes "Réponse à Renan." from *Journal des Débats,* May 18, 1883, and a partial translation of the article "Les materialistes dan l'Inde.") See Nikki R. Keddie, An *Islamic Response to Imperialism* for an English translation of the "Réfutation" and several articles.
Riḍā, *Tārīkh*	Riḍā, Muḥammad Rashīd. *Tārīkh al-ustādh al-imām ash-shaikh Muḥammad 'Abduh.* Vol. 1. Cairo, 1931.
Ṣafā'ī, *Asnād*	Ṣafā'ī, Ibrāhīm, ed. *Asnād-i siyāsī-yi daurān-i Qājāriyyeh.* Tehran, 1346/1967–68.
Ṣifātallāh, *Asnād*	Ṣifātallāh Jamālī Asadābādī. *Asnād va madārik dar bāreh-yi Irānī al-aṣl būdan-i Sayyid Jamāl ad-Dīn Asadābādī.* Tehran. n.d.
Tārīkh al-Afghān	al-Afghānī, Sayyid Jamāl ad-Dīn. *Tatimmat al-bayān fī tārīkh al-Afghān.* Ed. 'Alī Yusūf al-Kirīdlī. Cairo, 1901.

1
Introduction

SAYYID JAMĀL ad-Dīn "al-Afghānī," 1838/39–1897, one of the outstanding figures of nineteenth-century Islamic history, has attracted increasing interest in both the East and West in recent years. Jamāl ad-Dīn, known also as Afghānī, was one of the first important leaders to try to reinterpret traditional Islamic ideas so as to meet the agonizing problems brought by the increasing incursions by the West into the Middle East. Rejecting either pure traditionalism or uncritical imitation of the Christian West, he began what has become a continuing trend among Muslim modernists emphasizing pragmatic values needed for life in the modern world. These included political activism, the freer use of human reason, and efforts to build up the political and military power of Islamic states. By seeking these values within the Islamic tradition instead of openly borrowing them from the hostile West, Jamāl ad-Dīn was able to attain an influence on religious Muslims not possible for those who simply appropriated Western ideas. As the first "Neo-Traditionalist" whose influence spread beyond the borders of a single Muslim country, Afghānī can be regarded as a precursor of various later trends in the Islamic world which reject both pure traditionalism and pure Westernism. Although Afghānī was, during his period of strongest influence, known primarily as an ideologist of Pan-Islam, his style of thought has some affinity with numerous other trends in modern Islam. These trends range from the Islamic liberalism associated particularly with Afghānī's most important disciple, the Egyptian reformer Muḥammad 'Abduh, to the later more conservative Islamic revivalism of Rashīd Riḍā and the Muslim Brethren, and include Pan-Arabism and various other forms of Middle Eastern nationalism. Although Afghānī's direct influence on these movements is often exaggerated, his mode of reinterpreting the Islamic past in modern and nationalist terms displayed an approach that was to become increasingly popular in the Middle East. That Afghānī has been chosen as hero by so many modern Muslims gives his activities and writings an importance that withstands all evidence that his influence during his lifetime was sometimes small. His example of devotion to the cause of liberating Muslims from their Western conquerors has added to his appeal in the contemporary Middle East.

Jamāl ad-Dīn has also attracted interest because of the mysteries and controversies surrounding his life. The two most controversial questions concern his nationality and his religious orthodoxy. Afghānī and his chief Arab disciples maintained that he was born and brought up in Afghanistan, which would have made him, as he claimed to be, a follower of the majority, Sunni, branch of Islam. Yet even during his lifetime there were many Iranians who said he was born and raised in Iran and educated in the minority, Shi'i, branch of Islam which was Iran's state religion. The argument has continued until today, with the Arabs and Afghans generally making him an Afghan Sunni, and the Iranians producing ever more proofs that he was an Iranian Shi'i. The nationality question is tied to the orthodoxy question, which has, however, more dramatic elements. Throughout his life there were incidents pointing to Afghānī's unorthodoxy, and occasionally even irreligion, which his Muslim followers have been at pains to explain away. For example, in 1870 he was expelled from Istanbul on the request of the highest religious officer, the Şeyhülislam, on the grounds that he had given a heretical and unbelieving speech; some later disciples attributed to him skeptical views; and he himself wrote a religiously skeptical article in French in 1883, his "Answer to Renan."[1] Although his views caused him to be attacked during his lifetime, it would seem time to look at

---

1 The incidents are discussed more fully below. The "Answer to Renan" is translated in Nikki R. Keddie, *An Islamic Response to Imperialism: Political and Religious Writings of Sayyid Jamāl ad-Dīn "al-Afghānī"* (Berkeley and Los Angeles, 1968), pp. 181–187 (henceforth called *Islamic Response*).

these views dispassionately as evidence of his advanced and sometimes original mode of thought.

In addition, many other points of Afghānī's biography have remained unclear until now. Biographies of Jamāl ad-Dīn have been written in many languages, but no biographical study written before 1962 is adequate or wholly accurate. A potential biographer of Afghānī is faced with two extraordinary difficulties. First, most of the material for his biography is found most readily in accounts emanating from Afghānī and his disciples, whereas these accounts should in fact be subject to doubt and skepticism. To take only the most obvious instance, Afghānī in Sunni surroundings maintained that he was born and raised in Afghanistan, yet it can now be shown that he was in fact born in the village of Asadabad, near the town of Hamadan in western Iran. In conversation Afghānī also magnified his importance in the governing circles of various countries, and Arabic biographers often repeat stories, first found in newspaper interviews with him, of Nāsir ad-Dīn Shāh's having intended to make Afghānī prime minister of Iran, or of his importance to Russian governing circles, having no basis beyond Afghānī's word. A critical biographer must search for substantiation or refutation of aspects of Afghānī's life and beliefs which rest only on his word or that of his close disciples. This search leads to the second difficulty, the finding of independent documentation. Afghānī spent his life in so many countries that a biographer must travel widely and search through numerous archives in several languages. A biographer is often faced with weighing conflicting accounts—some hostile, some friendly, and a few neutral, all complicating the problems of historical judgment.

Recently there have been encouraging steps toward a more adequate biography of Afghānī based on more than his own words and those of his disciples. In English there have been new appraisals of aspects of Jamāl ad-Dīn's life and activities by (in alphabetical order) Niyazi Berkes, Sylvia Haim, Albert Hourani, Elie Kedourie, A. Albert Kudsi-Zadeh, and others. The most thorough and accurate biography and discussion of Afghānī was published in French in 1969 by Homa Pakdaman. She has made use, among other sources, of the most important new source, the papers that Afghānī left in Tehran in 1891, a catalog of which has been published in Persian along with photographic reproduction of many of the documents (herein called by the shortened title, *Documents*). Another useful biography is found in a 1960 Persian book including genuine Persian governmental correspondence about Afghānī from the generally inaccessible Iranian governmental archives. There is also a more recent collection of Persian documents.[2] Although some of the documents are misidentified in the books that include them, careful work can correct this. There are also other Persian, Turkish, and Arabic sources about Afghānī which are infrequently used, as well as British archival references.

On the basis of such sources it becomes possible to write a biography of Afghānī which, although not definitive, may contribute to a more accurate picture of his life. Afghānī's activities in India, Istanbul, and Russia are still rather obscure, and it is hoped that research by others into archives and papers relating to these countries can establish a picture fuller than is now possible. As of the summer of 1969, the Ottoman archives listed only one document about Afghānī, but it is hoped that more will become available. Russian archival material is not yet available, but it too may appear in the future.

Although Western and Iranian scholars have expressed varying doubts about frequently repeated details of Afghānī's biography, particularly concerning his claimed birth and education in Afghanistan, until now there has not been a systematic critical tracing of the sources on which most of Afghānī's biographers rely, either at first or second hand. Such a search reveals that *virtually all biographies of Afghānī written before the 1960's, trace indirectly or*

---

[2] Ibrāhīm Ṣafā'ī, ed., *Asnād-i siyāsī-yi daurān-i Qajāriyyeh* (Tehran, 1346/1967–68); Khān Malik Sāsānī, *Siyāsatgarān-i daureh-yi Qājār* (Tehran, 1960); Īraj Afshār and Aṣghar Mahdavī, *Documents inédits concernant Seyyed Jamāl-al-Dīn Afghānī (Majmū'eh-yi asnād va madārik-i chāp nashudeh dar bāreh-yi Sayyid Jamāl ad-Dīn mashhūr bi Afghānī)* (Tehran, 1963) (henceforth called *Documents*); and Elie Kedourie, *Afghani and 'Abduh: An Essay on Religious Unbelief and Political Activism in Modern Islam* (London, 1966) (henceforth called *Afghani*). Niyazi Berkes, *The Development of Secularism in Turkey* (Montreal, 1964); Sylvia Haim, *Arab Nationalism* (Berkeley and Los Angeles, 1962); Albert Hourani, *Arabic Thought in the Liberal Age: 1798–1939* (London, 1962); and Keddie, *Islamic Response.* The most complete critical work on Jamāl ad-Dīn, full of useful translations from Persian documents and publications, is Homa Parkdaman's *Djamal-ed-Din Assad Abadi dit Afghani* (Paris, 1969) (henceforth called Pakdaman), with an important preface by Maxime Rodinson. Much new material is also found in A. Albert Kudsi-Zadeh, "The Legacy of Sayyid Jamāl ad-Dīn al-Afghānī in Egypt" (unpublished Ph.D. dissertation, Indiana University, 1968) (henceforth called "Legacy"); Sharīf al-Mujāhid, "Sayyid Jamāl al-Dīn al-Afghānī: His Role in the Nineteenth Century Muslim Awakening" (unpublished M.A. thesis, McGill University, Montreal, 1954); and in various articles cited in the course of the present work.

directly to two almost identical sources, both demonstrably tendentious or misleading. Accounts of his birth and education in Afghanistan, the subsequent trips to India and Mecca, the long involvement in top-level Afghan politics and the 1870 stay in Istanbul almost always stem ultimately from: (1) a biography of Afghānī by Muḥammad 'Abduh published in Beirut in 1885–86, which was prefixed to his Arabic translation of Afghānī's "Refutation of the Materialists," later prefixed to a new edition of *al-'Urwa al-Wuthqā*, and translated into French by A.-M. Goichon in *Réfutation des matérialistes* (Paris, 1942); and (2) a biographical article by Jurjī Zaidān written shortly after Afghānī's death, first published in his periodical, *al-Hilāl*, in 1897 and later in his *Mashāhīr ash-Sharq* (Celebrated Men of the East) in 1903.

'Abduh's and Zaidān's biographies are scarcely ever in conflict, which is not surprising, since Zaidān tells us that most of what he writes is taken from what has been written by 'Abduh and by another disciple of Afghānī's, Adīb Isḥāq.[3] The Isḥāq biography, franker than 'Abduh's, is used less. The most important source for the standard biography of Jamāl ad-Dīn is thus 'Abduh, Afghānī's chief disciple at the time he wrote it. A careful reading of the 'Abduh biography indicates that its primary motive is apologetic, specifically to defend Afghānī against stories of his unorthodoxy and irreligion emanating from some of his former disciples in Egypt.[4] The biog-

[3] Both biographies appeared in several places, at first unsigned, possibly creating the illusion of several independent sources. I have read Jurjī Zaidān's in *al Hilāl*, V (1897), 561–571, and in a Persian translation from Zaidān's book *Tarājim mashāhīr ash-Sharq* (Cairo, 1922). Quotations in E. G. Browne, *The Persian Revolution of 1905–1909* (Cambridge, 1910), p. 7, show that he is quoting from the same 'Abduh biography as that translated by A.-M. Goichon in Jamāl ad-Dīn al-Afghānī, *Réfutation des matérialistes* (Paris, 1942) (henceforth called *Réfutation*). Browne does not mention 'Abduh's authorship, but the internal evidence is clear.

In *al-Hilāl*, p. 563n, Zaidān says "Most of what we present about the biography of this great man is taken from what was written by his eminent learned friend, Shaikh Muḥammad 'Abduh, and the late eloquent writer, Adīb Bey Isḥāq, along with what we have ascertained ourselves or heard from those who were intimate with him or studied under him." The Isḥāq biography is reprinted in Muḥammad Rashīd Riḍā, *Tārīkh al-ustadh al-imām ash-Shaikh Muḥammad 'Abduh*, Vol. I (Cairo, 1931), pp. 39–42 (Vol. I is henceforth called *Tārīkh*).

[4] Cf. the quotations and notes in Goichon's translation of Afghānī's *Réfutation*, pp. 52–57. The offending early biography by Salīm al-'Anḥūrī is reprinted along with other biographical notices about Afghānī in Riḍā, *Tārīkh*. 'Anḥūrī got his information not only from personal contact but also from some of Afghānī's former students.

raphy is distorted and less than frank on many points that 'Abduh actually witnessed. More serious, neither 'Abduh nor Zaidān's informants show any sign of having a source other than Afghānī's word for events before he came to Egypt in 1871 at age of about thirty-three. Also, 'Abduh's biography stops in 1885, and Zaidān's sources are very weak for the years after 1885.

E. G. Browne's biography of Afghānī in the text (as distinct from the notes) of *The Persian Revolution* is essentially a composite paraphrase of the 'Abduh-Zaidān account, with a few additions from another Arab admirer, Rashīd Riḍā. Basically the same account of Afghānī's life is enshrined in both editions of the *Encyclopaedia of Islam,* and has apparently become standard in Urdu as well as French, English, Turkish, and Arabic.[5] By the frequency of its repetition it takes on the appearance of established truth. Some biographies include a long list of sources that all trace back ultimately to the 'Abduh-Zaidān account, and some add new details, embroidery and exaggerations. Frequently, too, one finds several books cited to substantiate a point on Afghānī, all of which trace ultimately to the same inadequate sources.

'Abduh's and Zaidān's accounts are full of exaggerations of Afghānī's importance among government men and scholars in the countries he visited. Zaidān claims, for example, that the Shah sought to make Afghānī prime minister on his first Iranian visit and asked him to plan the reform of the government on his second visit. These stories Jamāl ad-Dīn told to reporters and disciples in his last years, but they are fictions. The 'Abduh-Zaidān account emanates primarily from Jamāl ad-Dīn himself, and, as will be shown, Jamāl ad-Dīn distorted his own biography. The very fact that the standard biography is based on a fictitious account of Afghānī's birth and education in Afghanistan should suffice to raise some doubt about the rest.

As it stands the account has many of the elements of myth, and

---

5 Sharīf al-Mujāhid (*op. cit.*) cites as the best existing biography one written in Urdu by Qāẕī Muhammad 'Abd al-Ghaffār, *Āsār-i Jamāl ad-Dīn Afghānī* (Delhi, 1940). Al-Mujāhid says the author has done original research, but in fact the biography appears to be primarily a wordier version of the standard account supplemented by undocumented Afghan stories about Jamāl ad-Dīn's youth. The only reliable new material seems to be that based on interviews in Hyderabad, discussed below. Most Turkish accounts follow the 'Abduh biography even for the main events of Afghānī's visit to Istanbul in 1870, which they generally take from an unacknowledged partial translation and partial close paraphrase of 'Abduh published by Mehmet Âkif in *Sıratı Müstakim* 90 (May 13/27, 1910), 207–208.

the numerous sources that cite parts of this account from the mouth of Afghānī indicate that he is its main author. In this account, essentially the same thing happens to Jamāl ad-Dīn in nearly every country to which he travels, from his entry into the highest government circles in Afghanistan to his death in Istanbul in 1897. He is first received with the highest marks of welcome by the notables and educated persons of the country, including almost always its rulers. These rulers seek his advice on various important matters and they frequently offer him high office. Then, very suddenly, because of the rulers' unfounded and unjust suspicions, instigated by evil men, or because of machinations by the British, who appear to follow Jamāl ad-Dīn around the world with extraordinary devotion, he is expelled or otherwise forced to leave almost every country he visits. Such a course of events might happen once or twice, but it is hard to believe it could happen as many times as the standard biographies claim. Probing of independent sources shows that the account is somewhat distorted for each of the Eastern places where it is used—Afghanistan, Istanbul (the 1870 visit), Egypt, and Iran. It has plausibility only for the 1892–1897 visit to Istanbul, and even then it is not certain that Afghānī was not plotting against the Sultan as his enemies claimed. What gives the account some verisimilitude, aside from uncritical acceptance of Afghānī's words, is his unusual propensity to seek out people in high office at the same time as he was plotting violent revolutionary or anti-British activity, so that he was sometimes expelled, once his plans were discovered, by the very people with whom he had had amicable contact.

Even when the standard 'Abduh-Zaidān account is supplemented, too often it is by material traceable to Afghānī's utterances, usually as reported to an Arab disciple or later follower such as Rashīd Riḍā. Conflicting accounts in Arabic, like the one by Salīm al-'Anḥūrī suggesting that Afghānī was an unbeliever, which 'Abduh's biography was designed to refute, are largely ignored. Inadequate attention has also been given to the brief biography by Adīb Isḥāq stressing Jamāl ad-Dīn's political and masonic activities in Egypt and his interest in new Western ideas rather than 'Abduh's apologetic religious portrait.[6] Little effort has been made in the past to look into the numerous Turkish, Persian, and British sources that throw doubt on much

---

[6] The Isḥāq and Anḥūrī biographies are reprinted in Riḍā, *Tārīkh*, pp. 39–50. A. Albert Kudsi-Zadeh does use these sources in his publications.

of the standard story and disprove it on numerous points. Only recently have a few scholars used these sources and written more critical accounts.

In view of the wide and continued circulation of the standard account in both East and West, an independent biography of Afghānī at this point must perforce give special attention to sorting out the true and the false in this account. What results is inevitably incomplete and subject to modification by new documents. The biography that follows includes new and important documented facts but, where evidence is uncertain or conflicting, it offers hypotheses, probabilities, and suggestions for further research. The 'Abduh-Zaidān account and those that stem from it are herein called the "standard biography." Many biographical books and articles that contain no documented new information perforce go unmentioned. Accounts that have been rejected are those that are implausible, given a close knowledge of the personalities and circumstances involved, whether these accounts are apologetically or hostilely motivated. Every effort has been made to accept only the most reliable evidence from either apologetic or hostile sources and to pick out the most significant facts from the myriad of available ones.

During Jamāl ad-Dīn's lifetime he and his followers may have had convincing political reasons to claim for him a Sunni origin, and to play down utterances of his that might lessen his influence and reputation among religious Muslims. It now seems time, decades after his death, to reconstruct with newly unearthed evidence a true picture of his life, beliefs, and activities. To say that Jamāl ad-Dīn did not always tell the truth about himself is not to state that he was morally reprehensible, but only that his statements about his life are not an accurate guide for the biographer. His own concerns, unlike ours, were not biographical, but rather with liberating Muslims from European encroachments and reforming their lives and politics, and the stories he told about himself were usually seen as useful for achieving these larger goals.[7]

It is hoped that the following account, for all its lacunae and shortcomings, may help clarify Jamāl ad-Dīn's activities, and may help reorient further research on this crucial figure back to the elementary rules of historical method—back, that is, to a continued search for

---

[7] On Jamāl ad-Dīn's historical greatness despite his frequent untruths see especially the preface by Maxime Rodinson to Pakdaman.

primary documentation—supplemented by a knowledge that Jamāl ad-Dīn's utterances, however interesting and significant, are often not a reliable source for the facts of his own life.[8]

---

[8] For further information about Afghānī in Egypt and India see the more specialized studies by A. Albert Kudsi-Zadeh and Aziz Ahmad, listed in the bibliography.

2

The First Twenty-Seven Years: 1883/39–1866

The Iranian Childhood

THERE IS little reliable documentation about the first twenty-seven years of Sayyid Jamāl ad-Dīn's life. All sources agree that Jamāl ad-Dīn was born in 1838–39 (1254 A.H) and his nephew, Sayyid Lutfallāh Asadābādī, says that Jamāl ad-Dīn was born in the month of Sha'bān, 1254/October-November, 1838.[1]

When the place of birth is mentioned, however, one is on the terrain of violent controversy. Outside Iran Jamāl ad-Dīn usually claimed that he was born in Afghanistan, although in Iran he sometimes admitted his Iranian origin. The evidence for Jamāl ad-Dīn's Iranian birth and childhood is now overwhelming.[2] His main reason for later claiming Afghan birth was probably to avoid identification with the minority, Shi'i, branch of Islam, since virtually all ethnic Persians from Iran were known to be born Shi'is. Afghans and writers from other Sunni countries have generally continued to insist on Jamāl ad-Dīn's Afghan origins, although the weight of evidence is now such that many non-Iranians are coming to accept

1 Mīrzā Luṭfallāh Asadābādī, *Sharḥ-i ḥāl va āṣār-i Sayyid Jamāl ad-Dīn Asadābādī ma'ruf bi "Afghānī"* (rev. ed.; Tabriz, 1326/1947–48), p. 16 (henceforth called Luṭfallāh) *Documents*, pl. 16, photo 40, reproduces a letter from Afghānī applying for admission to an Egyptian masonic lodge in which he gave his age as thirty-seven in 1875, which supports the other sources.

2 For a summary of some of the evidence proving an Iranian birth and childhood, see Appendix I.

the counterclaims put forward originally by Iranians. The place-of-origin name "Afghānī" was adopted by Jamāl ad-Dīn only in 1869, after he was expelled from Afghanistan and began to claim an Afghan birth and upbringing.

Iranians and others who have investigated the details of Jamāl ad-Dīn's origins have established that he was born in the large village of Asadabad near the city of Hamadan in northwest Iran. In this area a large proportion of the population spoke Azerbaijani Turkish, and it is probable that Jamāl ad-Dīn's knowledge of spoken Turkish, which he spoke in the Azerbaijani manner, dates from his childhood in northwest Iran.[3]

There are somewhat conflicting Iranian accounts of Jamāl ad-Dīn's childhood. The most complete one, the general chronology and outline of which have been confirmed by recently published documents, is given by Jamāl ad-Dīn's nephew, Lutfallāh Asadābādī. whose relationship is proven by the recent *Documents* volume. Lutfallāh's biography contains adulatory mythological elements, but many of these stem from Jamāl ad-Dīn himself, who is sometimes quoted directly, and others appear to come from Jamāl ad-Dīn's family and friends, who may have embroidered a basically accurate account. Lutfallāh based his account both on the words of Jamāl ad-Dīn, with whom he spent much time in Tehran between 1887 and 1890, and on family and friends from Asadabad, including Jamāl ad-Dīn's cousin and friend, Shaikh Hādī, who was still alive when Lutfallāh wrote.[4]

Despite the idealized nature of Lutfallāh's accounts it deserves attention both for its basic chronology and itinerary for Jamāl ad-Dīn's early years, confirmed in several spots by independent documentation, and for the picture Jamāl ad-Dīn's projected of his own childhood and adolescence when he was not giving an Afghan account.

---

[3] Jamāl ad-Dīn's use of Azerbaijani rather than standard Ottoman Turkish, and its implications for his childhood location were pointed out in the careful biography by Sayyid Hasan Taqīzādeh in the newspaper *Kāveh* (Berlin), n.s., II, 3 (1921), 6.

[4] Luṭfallāh, p. 18. The date of Luṭfallāh's writing, 1304/1925–26, is given in the introduction, taken from the first edition of this work. Luṭfallāh's younger son, Abū al-Hasan in an interview with me in Tehran, September 10, 1966, stated that Jamāl ad-Dīn was his father's source of information about Jamāl ad-Dīn's adolescent years, and this assertion is also indicated in Luṭfallāh's text. The *Documents* contain numerous family letters and other documents substantiating parts of Luṭfallāh's account, especially the family names and relationships.

Lutfallāh begins by giving a genealogy of Jamāl ad-Dīn's father, who came from a respected branch of Shi'i sayyids (descendants of Muhammad) who has lived in Asadabad for centuries. Jamāl ad-Dīn's father, Sayyid Safdar, is said to have been a modest cultivator but a learned man in contact with many of the outstanding ulama of his time, including the chief *mujtahid* (religious leader) of the Twelver Shi'is, Shaikh Murtazā Ansārī (then living in Ottoman Iraq). (Lutfallāh's son, Sifātallāh claims elsewhere that Safdar also had ties to Shaikh Aḥmad Aḥsā'ī, the founder of the Shaikhi sect of Shi'ism which some Iranians considered heretical.[5]) Lutfallāh records that Jamāl ad-Dīn was born late in 1838, and gives the name and genealogy of Jamāl ad-Dīn's mother, who was, as is frequent in Muslim countries, related to the man she married. Sifātallāh adds a note giving the names of the offspring of Jamāl ad-Dīn's two sisters and brothers whose names he gives elsewhere.[6] Many of these names and relationships were later confirmed by letters in the *Documents.*

From ages five to ten Jamāl ad-Dīn is said to have studied at home with his father and to have quickly learned Arabic and the Koran and its secrets. Jamāl ad-Dīn's fellow pupils, like his cousin Shaikh Hādī, tell amazing stories of his abilities, such as his explaining the secrets of one of the *suras* (chapters) of the Koran to his playmates. Many of Jamāl ad-Dīn's childhood games are said to have been in preparation for his later travels; once he got on a wooden horse, bid good-bye to his parents and sisters, and said he was off for India, Egypt, Turkey, Afghanistan, and other places.[7] He promised his father and mother he would actually make some of his trips. A unique document on Jamāl ad-Dīn's childhood is an adult letter to him from Shaikh Hādī saying his own mother was still awaiting Jamāl ad-Dīn's nomination of her as governor of the province of Khurasan, a promise he had made as a child.[8]

Lutfallāh states that when Jamāl ad-Dīn's father saw how intelligent his son was, he took him, *without his mother's knowledge,* to the city of Qazvin to study, at the age of about ten. Jamāl ad-Dīn is said

---

[5] Introduction by Ṣifātallāh Jamālī Asadābādī to Jamāl ad-Dīn Asadābādī, *Maqālāt-i Jamāliyyeh* (Tehran, 1312/1933–34), p. 7. On the Shaikhis and Jamāl ad-Dīn's connections with them, see below in this chapter.

[6] Ṣifātallāh Jamālī Asadābādī, *Asnad va madārik dar bāreh-yi Irānī al-aṣl būdan-i Sayyid Jamāl ad-Dīn Asadābādī* (Tehran, n.d.), p. 21 (henceforth called *Asnād*). See also Ṣifātallāh's note in Luṭfallāh, p. 16.

[7] Luṭfallāh, pp. 17–18.

[8] *Documents,* photo 45.

to have been so enamored of his studies that he worked hard every day, taking no holidays and refusing to walk around to visit the town.

Toward the end of his second year in Qazvin there was a cholera epidemic there, and dead bodies were placed in the cellar of the *madrasa* (religious school) where Jamāl ad-Dīn lived. Lutfallāh then quotes a story directly from Jamāl ad-Dīn: after he had helped his father prepare the body of a mulla, who had been their friend, and put it in the cellar, Jamāl ad-Dīn determined that he must learn the cause of the dread disease. He took some candles, went for several nights to the cellar, *secretly from his father*, opened the shrouds, and studied the heads and faces of the victims, replacing the shrouds afterwards. When his father discovered what he was doing, he took him to Tehran.[9] This story, which seems to have no strong self-interested motive, may well be a true and vivid recollection.

The next passage, quoted directly from Jamāl ad-Dīn, does have the flavor of his adult accounts of bold encounters with the great and powerful. Jamāl ad-Dīn told his nephew:

> "At the beginning of 1266 [1849–50] we went to Tehran and lived in the Sanglaj quarter in the home of Sulaimān Khān Sāhib Ikhtiyār, who knew my father, was from the same district, and was the governor of Asadabad. The next day I asked people: Who today is the most famous *alim* [religious scholar] and mujtahid of Tehran? They designated Āqā Sādiq [Tabātabā'ī]. The next day, *without my father's knowing*, I went to his mosque school and saw him. The religious students were around Āqā and he was busy teaching. I greeted him and, owing to the lack of places, I sat at the door of the chamber. He had an important Arabic book in his hand (the Sayyid gave its name but I [Lutfallāh] have forgotten it), and he was explaining and interpreting it, but in an abbreviated and unclear fashion. After the completion of the lesson I said: 'Sir, could you restate this problem again in a way that will be useful since full advantage was not derived from these brief explanations?'
>
> "Āqā looked toward me and said with a look sharp and angry with disdain: 'You—what is this impertinence?'
>
> "I said: 'A request to understand intellectual problems has nothing to do with impertinence. The understanding of

9 Luṭfallāh, pp. 19–20.

> knowledge has no relation to greatness or smallness.' And I read and translated the same problem without hesitation to the extent of two pages.
>
> "Āqā when he saw this immediately rose and came to me and I also rose and got ready, thinking that he intended to hit me. When he reached me he kissed my face and, taking my hand, sat me down next to him. He showed great kindness and asked me about my circumstances and origin. I introduced myself, and he immediately sent someone to bring my father and ordered a set of clothes in my size. After introductions and completing the external formalities, he related everything for my father and asked me to put on the clothes. With his own hands he fastened the turban and put it on my head. Until that day I had not put on a turban. . . ."[10] [Italics mine.]

Āqā Sayyid Sādiq is said to have been host to Jamāl ad-Dīn and his father for the next few days. During the same year the boy and his father set out for the holy Shi'i shrine cities in Ottoman Iraq where Jamāl ad-Dīn could continue his education. Other sources indicate that Jamāl ad-Dīn's later servant, Abū Turāb, had served Sayyid Sādiq, possibly confirming some contact between Jamāl ad-Dīn and the latter.[11]

Basically the same chronology for time in Asadabad, Qazvin, and Tehran was given in a brief biography of Jamāl ad-Dīn included in an 1889 publication by the Iranian Minister of Press, I'timād as-Saltaneh, who had known Jamāl ad-Dīn in Tehran from 1887 to 1889.[12] Lutfallāh's son, Sifātallāh, also gives basically the same story, with some new details, but gives a different version regarding the reason Jamāl ad-Dīn's father quit Asadabad for Qazvin which may reflect his further investigations. When Jamāl ad-Dīn was ten years old, Sifātallāh says: "Because of local disagreements and differences that existed among the sayyids of Asadabad, Sayyid Safdar who was a learned, ascetic, and mild man, in order to escape the tumult and disputations, chose to emigrate, and because of the aptitude that he recognized in his child, Sayyid Jamāl ad-Dīn, he took him with him. About 1264 A.H. [1847–48] they entered the city of Qazvin together

10 *Ibid.*, pp. 20–21.

11 Pakdaman, p. 34 n. 50, and the sources cited therein.

12 Muḥammad Ḥasan Khān I'timād as-Salṭaneh, *al-Ma'āṣir va al āṣār* (Tehran, 1889), p. 224.

and remained there four years."[13] Sifātallāh's figure of four rather than two years in Qazvin may be accurate, as most of Lutfallāh's subsequent dates seem to be pushed back two or three years.

In the account given by Lutfallāh, taken primarily from Jamāl ad-Dīn himself, is the striking fact that three of the crucial turning points that helped advance Jamāl ad-Dīn's education and position are recounted as having occurred with the aid of secrecy or stealth. His father is said to have hidden from his wife the fact that he was taking Jamāl ad-Dīn to Qazvin to advance his education; while Jamāl ad-Dīn hid from his father both his cholera investigations, which impressed his own mind and were the cause of the next upward move to Tehran, and his intention to attend the class of Tehran's greatest mujtahid. The last event may be exaggerated; there is no corroboration of the supposed impression made by the twelve-to-fourteen-year-old boy, but the form in which Jamāl ad-Dīn chose to tell the story is significant of his outlook. The virtues of secrecy and dissimulation in appropriate circumstances were taught by Shi'ism, and Jamāl ad-Dīn apparently recalled his own childhood in ways that emphasized the benefits of keeping one's plans secret.

Lutfallāh's account of Jamāl ad-Dīn's stay in the Iraq shrine cities, chiefly the holy city of Najaf, also taken from Jamāl ad-Dīn, repeats the pattern of influence on the powerful, followed by unjust calumniations by jealous and evil men and forced departure, found in so many of Jamāl ad-Dīn's stories of his life. The basic fact of an advanced Shi'i education at the shrine cities is confirmed by three independent sources, showing Jamāl ad-Dīn's account to contain true elements.[14] According to Lutfallāh's account, Jamāl ad-Dīn and his father went to the Shi'i shrine cities of Iraq by way of the Iranian city of Burujird, where a leading mujtahid kept them in his home for three months. After visiting the Shi'i shrines of Iraq they went to see Shaikh Murtazā (Ansārī, the leading Shi'i mujtahid and most important resident of these cities), who was impressed with Jamāl ad-Dīn's keen intelligence and had a house prepared for father and son. Jamāl ad-Dīn is said to have studied with Shaikh Murtazā for four years, while his father returned to Asadabad after two or three months. Shaikh Murtazā gave Jamāl ad-Dīn an *ijāzeh* (certificate of

[13] Ṣifātallāh, *Asnād*, p. 45.
[14] See notes 16 and 17 for these sources.

advanced knowledge) and paid his expenses during these years. Jamāl ad-Dīn's intelligence and perception are said to have become famous among the ulama of the shrine cities, of whom some favored and some opposed him. One group of ulama were envious of him and planned to execute him. Shaikh Murtazā learned of the plot and sent Jamāl ad-Dīn to India with an enlightened sayyid at the age of sixteen, in 1270 (1853–54).[15] Other sources, cited below, indicate the Jamāl ad-Dīn probably left for India two or three years later than Lutfallāh says.

That Jamāl ad-Dīn had a Shi'i education in the shrine cities is confirmed by two letters dating from ca. 1890 in the *Documents* from an Iranian who remembered their studying together for several years at Najaf, and names as their teacher Mullā Husain (Qulī) Hamadanī Darjuzainī. It is also confirmed by the investigations of an Iranian scholar Muhīt Tabātabā'ī, who found another Iranian, Sayyid Habībī, who studied with Jamāl ad-Dīn in Najaf and said they were both students of Mīrzā Rizā Qulī, a professor of philosophy.[16] Muhīt Tabātabā'ī's informant said that Jamāl ad-Dīn was an excellent student, but that he was especially interested in philosophy, and that it was for this reason that many of the mullas opposed him.

Another Iranian, Hājji Sayyāh, relates in his memoirs that when he saw Jamāl ad-Dīn in Isfahan in November 1886, Jamāl ad-Dīn asked to see a certain Mullā Haidar of Isfahan, who had been his friend in Najaf. Mullā Haidar came and he told Hājji Sayyāh that Jamāl ad-Dīn as a youth had had such a good memory that he could retain anything even if he had heard it just once. Mullā Haidar made statements interpreted by Hājji Sayyāh to mean that some persons in Najaf had insisted Jamāl ad-Dīn was the promised Mahdi of the Shi'is, and although Jamāl ad-Dīn had denied any such claim, the claim became the reason for his expulsion from Najaf.[17]

In private conversation Jamāl ad-Dīn's grandnephew, Abū al-Hasān, a son of Lutfallāh's who shows no tendency to downgrade Jamāl ad-Dīn, said that Jamāl ad-Dīn's difficulties with the mullas of Najaf arose largely from his laxness in carrying out his religious

---

15 Luṭfallāh, pp. 21–22.

16 Interview with Muhammad Muhīt Tabātabā'ī, Sept., 1966. *Documents*, pp. 100–101, letter from Āqā Shaikh Muhammad Hasan from Qum to Amīn az-Zarb in Tehran, dating from Jamāl ad-Dīn's second trip to Iran (late 1889–early 1891).

17 Ḥājji Sayyāh, *Khātirāt-i Ḥājji Sayyāh*, ed. Ḥamid Sayyāh and Saifallāh Gulkār (Tehran, 1346/1967–68), pp. 290–291 (henceforth called Ḥajji Sayyāh). On the Mahdi, see the discussion below in this chapter on Twelver Shi'ism.

182946

duties; he even ate during Ramadan, the holy month of daytime fasting. The grandnephew added that Jamāl ad-Dīn chose India as his next destination because he expected more religious freedom there.[18]

These accounts of the reasons for Jamāl ad-Dīn's troubles with some of the Najaf ulama differ in detail, but they all agree that the troubles arose over religious differences. In the light of similar later religious troubles, such reasons seem more plausible than the story, given by Lutfallāh from Jamāl ad-Dīn, of jealousy and murder plots directed against an adolescent. (If there were jealousy and plots, they would be more plausibly explained by mahdist claims than by envy of the young Jamāl ad-Dīn, as cited by Lutfallāh.) The similarity of pattern in Jamāl ad-Dīn's accounts of jealousy and plots as the motives behind his expulsions from Istanbul in 1871 and Egypt in 1879 is striking.

None of the Iranians who remembered studying with Jamāl ad-Dīn at Najaf says that Shaikh Murtazā was his teacher, and two name another individual as his professor. Muhīt Tabātabā'ī doubts that Jamāl ad-Dīn in his teens could have been a student of the greatest of Iranian mujtahids, and there is no record, as there should be, of any *ijāzeh*. It seems likely that this part of Jamāl ad-Dīn's story is exaggerated, although he may well have had some contact with Shaikh Murtazā.[19]

Although the Sifātallāh-Lutfallāh story of Jamāl ad-Dīn's childhood and education has more factual basis than any other account, it is impossible to ascertain at this date exactly how much of it is accurate.

What appears clear about Jamāl ad-Dīn's traditional education, not only from the various accounts of his childhood but even more from later reports by those who knew him, is that he received a thorough grounding in the traditional Islamic disciplines, plus considerable

---

18 Interview with Afghanī's grandnephew, Abū al-Hasan Jamālī, Sept, 1966.

19 Interview with Muhammad Muhīt Tabātabā'ī, Sept., 1966. Khān Malik Sāsānī, *Siyāsatgarān-i daureh-yi Qājār* (Tehran, 1338/1959–60), p. 186 n. 1, states: "It is difficult to accept that the late Shaikh Murtazā Ansārī would give the *ijāzeh* of *ijtihād* to a nineteen-year-old; also if Sayyid Jamāl ad-Dīn had such an *ijāzeh* there should be at least a photograph of such an important document somewhere." The *Documents*, p. 20, reprint a laudatory inscription that Jamāl ad-Dīn wrote in 1865–66 about Shaikh Murtazā on a book authored by the Shaikh. The editors in a note say this may show that Jamāl ad-Dīn was his pupil, and Pakadaman, p. 34 n. 51, takes it as proof that Jamāl ad-Dīn knew Shaikh Murtazā, certainly the most that might be inferred from it.

knowledge of the Islamic philosophers, particularly the Persian ones, including Avicenna, Nasīr ad-Dīn Tūsī, and others, and of Sufism. The *Documents* prove not only that he possessed philosophical and Sufi works, but also that he showed some interest in various esoteric subjects, such as mystical alphabets, numerical combinations, and esoteric treatises. The influence of Islamic philosophy, which was widely taught in Iran, was particularly strong in Jamāl ad-Dīn's later thought.

There is much in Jamāl ad-Dīn's later life and thought that seems to reflect both traditional Iranian influences, and the particular religious and political climate of Iran in the mid-nineteenth century. Twelver Shi'i Islam, the Iranian state religion, holds that the Twelfth Imam, or hereditary infallible leader, disappeared over a thousand years ago, but will return as Mahdi to institute the millenium. The messianic strain in Twelver Sh'ism is a more central element than it is in the Sunni tradition of other Muslim countries. Pending the return of the Twelfth Imam his will is interpreted by mujtahids, religious leaders who exercise *ijtihād* (judgment or endeavor) to interpret his will in religious and legal questions. Whereas for the Sunnis the door of *ijtihād* was closed in the early centuries of Islam, the Twelver Shi'is legitimize variation in the interpretation of law and doctrine. Although the practical difference in rates of change in law and custom between Shi'is and Sunnis has been small, Shi'i doctrine provides a better theoretical basis for the introduction of innovation than does Sunnism. (The relative isolation of Iran and Iraq in the nineteenth century, however, meant that modern ideas in fact developed sooner in Sunni countries with greater Western contact, such as Egypt and Turkey, although in Muslim India Shi'is were prominent among the modernizers.) Both Jamāl ad-Dīn's messianic tendencies and his advocacy of reinterpreting religious doctrine seem to be based partly on Iranian Shi'i traditions.

Another characteristic of Jamāl ad-Dīn, documented below, was his practice of *taqiyya*, or precautionary dissimulation of his true beliefs, and his use of quite different arguments to an elite audience of intellectuals than to a mass audience. These related features are found in various Iranian and Islamic cultural traditions. Shi'ism began as a minority, persecuted religion, and it early legitimized precautionary dissimulation; many Shi'is taught that it was wrong to reveal one's real beliefs to outsiders. The Sufi mystics and the Hellenized philosophers also practiced dissimulation, partly for precautionary reasons, and both believed that men could be divided into an elite of the initiated and a mass for whom unquestioning literalist orthodoxy was most useful. *Taqiyya* also occurs among orthodox Sunnis, but it is not nearly as central to their thought and behavior as it is among Shi'is, Sufis, and philosophers.

Judging both from accounts of his stay at Najaf and from his library and teachings, the Islamic philosophers were a major influence on the young Jamāl ad-Dīn. Unlike the Muslim territories west of Iran, where the Greek-inspired philosophers had for centuries generally been suppressed as heretics and removed from the school curriculum, Iran had a living philosophical tradition, with some of the books of Avicenna and later Iranian philosophers taught even in religious schools. The rationalist interpretation of religion favored by many of these philosophers influenced Jamāl ad-Dīn, and some of the ideas that caused him to be attacked as a heretic in the Sunni world come straight from the philosophers.

In addition Jamāl ad-Dīn was later well acquainted with and influenced by the religio-political ferment experienced by Iran in the late eighteenth and nineteenth centuries manifested particularly in the Shaikhi and Babi movements. A significant new school of Twelver Shi'ism, the Shaikhi school, was founded in the late eighteenth century, and its influence spread in the Shi'i areas of Ottoman Iraq and Iran. Shaikhism, which was regarded as heretical by many of the predominant *uṣūlī* school of Twelver Shi'ism, involved a combination of rationalist philosophy and mysticism typical of Iranian philosophers and also a stronger messianic tension than the usual Twelver Shi'i doctrine.[20] Among the earliest documents copied in the hand of Jamāl ad-Dīn are three treatises at least two of which were written by Shaikhi leaders, while the third also appears to be a Shaikhi work. One of these manuscripts is a short treatise on the crafts by Shaikh Aḥmad Aḥsā'ī (1753–1826), the founder of Shaikhism, whom some mujtahids had excommunicated; and another was *Mir'at al-'Ārifīn* by his second successor, who led the Shaikhis from the 1840's through the 1860's, Hājji Muhammad Karīm Khān Qājār Kir-

[20] On the Shaikhis, see Alessandro Bausani, *Persia religiosa* (Milan, 1959), pp. 403–407; A. L. M. Nicolas, *Essai sur le Cheikhisme*, 4 pts. (Paris, 1910–1914); G. Scarcia, "Kermān 1905: La 'guerra tra Šeihi e Bālāsarī,'" *Annali del Istituto Universitario Orientale di Napoli*, n.s., XIII (1963), 195–238; and H. Corbin, "L'École Shaykhie en Théologie Shi'ite," École Pratique des Hautes Études, Section des Sciences Religieuses, *Annuaire 1960–61* (Paris, 1961), pp. 3–59.

mānī (1809–1870).[21] Although these two texts seem to have been copied by Jamāl ad-Dīn in the 1860's, it is probable that Jamāl ad-Dīn's interest in Shaikhi ideas dates back before then, probably to his time in Najaf. It is unlikely that Jamāl ad-Dīn would have begun to study Shaikhism only after going to Sunni lands where Shaikhi ideas were scarcely known. According to information reaching Muhīt Tabātabā'ī, it was during his time in Najaf that Jamāl ad-Dīn learned of Shaikhi ideas as well as those of the quite clearly heretical messianic Babis.[22] Such interests may help account for the hostility to him of the more orthodox ulama of Najaf.

The Shaikhis stressed both the philosophical and mystical aspects of Shi'ism, developing theories found in earlier philosophers and mystics about the coexistence of the real and spiritual worlds—worlds that the Shaikhis further defined and subdivided. The treatise by Muhammad Karīm Khān copied by Jamāl ad-Dīn is an explication of these varied worlds and of the different levels of meaning and existence of the Koran and of the letters, words, and suras found in it. The idea of the Koran as mystically encompassing an infinity of varied meanings is one that was used later by Jamāl ad-Dīn to attribute new meanings to this Holy Book. Another Shaikhi idea later echoed by Jamāl ad-Dīn was their key difference from other Shi'is—what the Shaikhis called the "Fourth Pillar" of religion—the idea that there is always in the world a perfect Shi'i who can guide men in right ideas and action during the absence of the Twelfth Imam. Whereas the other Twelver Shi'is believed that in the absence of the Twelfth Imam believers must rely on the learned but fallible judgment of one or one of several mujtahids, the Shaikhis, following the ideas of Shaikh Ahmad Ahsā'ī, believed that each epoch had its own ideal guide, whose role was more exalted than that of the mujtahid. Echoes of this Shaikhi idea may be found in

---

21 *Documents*, pp. 14–15, doc. 9, treatises 2, 3, and 4 (treatises in the Majlis Library, Tehran). Thanks to Dr. 'Abd al-Husain Zarrinkūb for identifying treatise 2 from my photograph of the original. Treatise 3, an incomplete fragment apparently on an alchemical topic—changing the composition of bodies—may also be a Shaikhi work.

22 Interview with Muhammad Muhīt Tabatabā'ī, Sept., 1966. Many sources cite Jamāl al-Dīn's good knowledge of Babism, and Buṭrus al-Bustānī in his Arabic encyclopedia cites Jamāl ad-Dīn as the major source of his article on Babism (*Dā'irat al-Ma'ārif*, V [Beirut, 1881], s.v. "Bābī"). After conversations with Jamāl ad-Dīn's grandnephew and others in the summer of 1966, and after seeing evidence that points to Shaikhi rather than Babi interests, I now think it improbable that Jamāl ad-Dīn's family were Babis.

Jamāl ad-Dīn's later life, particularly in the famous talk that brought his expulsion from Istanbul.[23] Shaikhi ideas were well known in the shrine cities during Jamāl ad-Dīn's time there.

As for Babism, in 1844 a young sayyid, 'Alī Muhammad of Shiraz, had declared himself to be the *Bāb*, or gate, to the Twelfth Imam, whose manifestation was expected by some Shaikhis. In later years his claims increased until he said he was the Twelfth Imam himself, bringing a new religious dispensation that superseded the law and teachings of the Koran. He and his disciples quickly gained a wide following throughout Iran for their new dispensation. Babism was somewhat equalitarian regarding social classes and the sexes, favorable to economic enterprise, and in general more in tune with the demands of modern society than the traditional religion, even though it contained primarily traditional elements. Probably the popularity of messianic Babism was tied to the economic and social dislocations brought by the early Western impact in Iran.[24] (In the 1860's most Babis followed into the Bahai religion a leader who continued to honor the *Bāb* but who said he had a new religious dispensation. Bahaism spread far beyond the Middle East, while those who continued to follow the original dispensations, the *Azalīs*, remained a small group, confined largely to Iran.)

Babi struggles and uprisings occurred in Iran during Jamāl ad-Dīn's boyhood there, and a great persecution and emigration of Babis came in 1852 after a group of them had made an attempt on the life of the young Shah, Nāsir ad-Dīn. According to Lutfallāh's biography, made more precise on the basis of further research by Sifātallāh, Jamāl ad-Dīn lived in Tehran at this time, and left for the shrine cities in about 1852. Although an attempt to tie the young Jamāl ad-Dīn or his father with Babism would be speculative, it seems clear from his later writings and words that Jamāl ad-Dīn was well acquainted with both Shaikhi and Babi doctrine.[25] During his adolescent years in the

[23] The resemblance between Jamāl ad-Dīn's talk in Istanbul and Shaikhi doctrine was pointed out to me by Homa and Nasser Pakdaman. See Pakdaman, pp. 47–48, for a discussion of this resemblance.

[24] On Babism as a social movement see Nikki R. Keddie, "Religion and Irreligion in Early Iranian Nationalism," *Comparative Studies in Society and History*, IV, 3 (April, 1962), esp. pp. 267–274, and the sources cited there.

[25] As noted in more detail below, *Documents*, pl. 7, photo 19, has the end of a treatise by Shaikh Ahmad Ahsā'ī, copied by Jamāl ad-Dīn "Istanbūlī" in Baghdad (probably in the early 1860's), where he has written over the word "Baghdad," indicating a desire to hide the fact that he was there in his youth. There is no record of his ever referring to an early stay in Baghdad. For several years after

Shi'i shrine cities in Iraq, and perhaps before, Jamāl ad-Dīn was almost surely exposed to discussions of these new religious doctrines. He grew up in an environment where disputes and doctrinal innovation were more in the air in religious circles than they were in most of the Sunni world, and this probably affected his own propensity to innovate.

The politically activist and meliorist ideas of the Babis may have contributed to Jamāl ad-Dīn's revision of Islam in these directions. Babism was one of several activist religious movements that Jamāl ad-Dīn had a chance to witness in the Muslim world, which probably contributed to his understanding of the power of religious appeals to the Muslim masses. It is not implied that the adult Jamāl ad-Dīn was either a Babi or a Shi'ite.

The Indian Experience

AFTER THE childhood years, the Persian sources converge with the 'Abduh-Zaidān account in saying that Jamāl ad-Dīn left for India in his late teens. Here there exists one of the earliest personal reminiscences that is almost surely authentic, although it has apparently been ignored outside of a few Persian works. In 1921 the Persian nationalist newspaper, *Kāveh,* published in Berlin, printed an article by its editor, Sayyid Hasan Taqīzādeh, about Sayyid Jamāl ad-Dīn. This article made an admirable attempt at scholarly method and objectivity, and the author ended by noting the many obscure and contradictory points in Jamāl ad-Dīn's life, and by requesting authentic information from his readers.

Later in 1921, *Kāveh* printed a letter from a Mīrzā Muhammad 'Alī Khān Sadīd as Saltaneh, which enclosed a letter by Jamāl ad-Dīn to the writer's father. (A photograph of Jamāl ad-Dīn's letter is print-

their expulsion from Iran in 1852 the Babis were centered in Baghdad, and there may be some connection, although most Babis had been forced to leave Baghdad in the early 1860's.

ed in *Kāveh.*) Sadīd as-Saltaneh recalled that Jamāl ad-Dīn had stayed with them in Bushehr (Bushire) in 1885 for about six months when the writer was a boy, and he gives details about this stay. He also writes that in 1272 A.H. (1855–56) Afghānī "came from Hamadan to Shiraz and Bushehr and went to India. He had some recommedations from Hamadan to Hājji 'Abd al-Nabīy . . . a merchant of Bushehr." Sadīd as-Saltaneh also mentions the house where Sayyid Jamāl ad-Dīn stayed on this first trip to India.[26] This story suggests that Jamāl ad-Dīn returned to Hamadan before going to India.

Another event that may help date Jamāl ad-Dīn's stay in Bushehr is his first encounter there, referred to in several independent sources, with Mīrzā Muhammad Bāqir Bavānātī, later to be the great Orientalist E. G. Browne's Persian teacher in England. When Jamāl ad-Dīn spoke of this encounter near the end of his life, he said that it occurred while the British troops were occupying Bushehr, and since the troops were there between December 1856 and March 1857 the end of Jamāl ad-Dīn's stay there was probably in these months. The story of the encounter between Jamāl ad-Dīn and Bavānātī exists in two radically different versions. Both agree that Bavānātī had been expelled from Shiraz for statements against the Islamic religion. According to Jamāl ad-Dīn's story (at a time when he was trying to emphasize his own religiousness), after he had heard Bavānātī's blasphemies and unsuccessfully asked him to stop them, he arranged for a group of young Afghan compatriots to beat up Bavānātī in order to stop this blasphemous behavior. Jamāl ad-Dīn stated that this occurred on his return from Mecca to Afghanistan, a country that he in fact entered for the first time in 1866. Bavānātī himself, however, told a very different story, more consistent with what is known of the young Jamāl ad-Dīn. He said that his life was in danger in Bushehr from those angered by his anti-Islamic words, and that Jamāl ad-Dīn had used his authority as a sayyid to get a threatening crowd to leave the blasphemer with him, assuring them that he would be put to death, but that Jamāl ad-Dīn instead helped him to escape.[27] Both Bavānātī and Jamāl ad-Dīn seem to have varied their stories some, to judge from the several versions that are recorded, but the basic Ba-

26 *Kāveh*, II, 9 (1921), p. 11.

27 Bavānātī's story, in variant versions, is recorded with citations in Irāj Afshār, *Savād va bayāẕ* (Tehran, 1344/1965–66), pp. 1–18. Jamāl ad-Dīn's story, with the statement that it occurred while British troops were occupying Bushehr, is in the recollection of Afghānī's words by 'Abd al-Qādir al-Maghribī, *Jamāl ad-Dīn al-Afghānī* (Cairo, 1948), pp. 54–55.

vānātī story, that Jamāl ad-Dīn aided rather than attacked the young blasphemer, seems plausible. That Jamāl ad-Dīn later presented himself as a promoter of acts of physical violence in defense of orthodoxy is of interest.

The best guess for the date of Jamāl ad-Dīn's first trip to India from Bushehr is thus ca. early 1857/1273, when he was eighteen or nineteen years old. Although Jamāl ad-Dīn reported that he stayed in India only a little over a year, his stay may in fact have been longer. Possibly Afghānī wanted to minimize the amount of time he had spent in India, and this may account for so curious a matter as the Lutfallāh account's making Jamāl ad-Dīn take about two and a half years for a trip from India to Mecca that he undertook after leaving India. Lutfallāh explains that Jamāl ad-Dīn stopped at several places between India and Mecca but even so it seems strange. Also in many biographies is the identical expression that he stayed in India "a year and some months," which may well be Jamāl ad-Dīn's own statement. In normal usage, of course, this implies a year and a few months, but it could mean a year and, say, forty months. In view of the documents now available, Jamāl ad-Dīn's story that he spent several years before 1866 in Afghanistan is so unlikely that it can almost be ruled out. There is no demonstrable date for any other place than India in the 1858–1865 period, and it seems likely that at least part of this period was spent in India. In an autobiographical account written in 1866 Jamāl ad-Dīn says he has been wandering for five years, which also suggests that he stayed put in India for a few years until ca. 1861.[28] Lutfallāh says that Jamāl ad-Dīn spent some months in Calcutta at the home of a Hājji 'Abd al-Kārīm. Otherwise, we know nothing yet of his whereabouts during this significant stay, although it is likely that he landed first in Bombay, where there was a large Persian community.[29]

The really important point may not be how many years Jamāl ad-Dīn spent in India, but that his Indian experience in this period, however long, must have had a more decisive influence on him than either he or his biographers note. There have been a number of books and articles, mostly by Pakistanis and Indians, which discuss and sometimes inflate the influence Jamāl ad-Dīn had in India. All the more curious is the apparent lack of serious discussion of the equally

---

28 For a summary of this account see below, chap. 3, pp. 37–38.

29 The location of Jamāl ad-Dīn in Bombay in 1275/1859 in *Documents*, p. 5, is an error for 1285, corrected in *Documents*, p. 166. *Luṭfallāh*, p. 23.

important question (which should also have an appeal for South Asians)—*the influence India had on Jamāl ad-Dīn*. There are a few perceptive remarks on this question in Sayyid Hasan Taqīzādeh's articles on Jamāl ad-Dīn, but otherwise this point, which seems to hold several keys for the understanding of Jamāl ad-Dīn's later activities and writings, has been generally neglected.

Biographers often note casually that it was in India that Jamāl ad-Dīn first became acquainted with modern Western knowledge. It seems very likely that this knowledge had a major influence on his life and ideas. This influence is discernible upon careful reading of his writings for Islamic audiences, and, much more dramatically, in his writings for Western audiences. Jamāl ad-Dīn never became as Westernized as some of his intellectual contemporaries in the Muslim world, but his words do reflect a considerable interest in and influence of Western ideas, which, to judge from his Westernized appearance in Afghanistan in 1866–1868, must date from this period. Perhaps more important, it seems reasonable to suppose that it was his experiences in India that set Jamāl ad-Dīn on the path of strong opposition to British imperial rule in Muslim lands which characterized so much of his life. Jamāl ad-Dīn constantly decried British territorial conquest of lands ruled until recently by Muslims. Yet there seems to be little in his early Iranian and later Afghan experience which could explain such a special emphasis. Most Iranians who thought about it in this period were at least as afraid of Russian as of British conquest, while Jamāl ad-Dīn was fairly consistently friendly to the Russians. In fact, before 1865, recent British conquest was an experience of Muslims only in India. As seems to have been overlooked, Jamāl ad-Dīn's first stay in India, aroung 1856–1858, was in the period right after the unexpected British conquest of further Indian territory, and he was probably there during the Indian Mutiny in which leading Muslims played a primary role. Jamāl ad-Dīn's later stays in India overlapped the period when British official policy was to disfavor and be suspicious of the Muslims, largely because of their role in the Mutiny. One reaction to the British conquests, the Mutiny, and subsequent British disfavor was that of Sir Sayyid Ahmad Khān, who after the Mutiny turned to a policy of reformist Westernization and tried to end British disfavor, partly by making the Indian Muslims both loyal and Western. But a quite different reaction to these events was possible—indignation at the British conquest and a desire to master Western secrets, not in order to become a loyal British subject but to gain the power needed to oust the British. In any case, Jamāl ad-Dīn's fierce opposition to British rule of Muslim territory would seem almost perforce to have roots in his various stays in India, whether arising from some undocumented experiences or from what he saw, or both. The influence of these stays on Jamāl ad-Dīn has not been given nearly the attention it merits. It is also curious and relevant that the only place where Jamāl ad-Dīn's political program of combined radicalism, modernism, nationalism, and Pan-Islam ever became a serious political program of an active opposition movement was in the Khilāfat movement in India, years after Afghānī's death.[30]

In addition to the dramatic events of the Mutiny, there were other movements of thought and action among Indian Muslims which may have influenced Jamāl ad-Dīn and seem to find echoes in some of his later words. Coming from an Iranian environment, where elements of philosophy, Sufisim, and heresy had often encouraged traditional forms of unorthodoxy, including even religious skepticism, he now entered an Indian environment in which both Western ideas and new movements among Muslims might have a further impact on his ideas. As early as the eighteenth century, Shāh Walī Allāh of Delhi had suggested a continuous modification of the interpretation of Islamic law according to the needs of each age, a reopening of the door of *ijtihād* by qualified experts. He also suggested an evolutionary scheme of historical development, culminating in a caliphate that should now be revived, in terms that, like those of Jamāl ad-Dīn later, often recall the great Muslim thinker, Ibn Khaldūn.[31]

The Indian Muslims were also among the first in the modern world to have to face the problem of the conversion of a former *Dār al-Islām*

---

30 Aziz Ahmad, *Studies in Islamic Culture in the Indian Environment* (Oxford, 1964) (henceforth called *Studies*), chap. 4, which, however, appears to overstate the immediate intellectual influence of Jamāl ad-Dīn in India. Ahmad has corrected this in his *Islamic Modernization in India and Pakistan 1857–1964* (London, 1967), chap. 6. Wilfred C. Smith, *Modern Islam in India* (rev. ed., London, 1946), Part II, chap. 2, seems just in noting that violent anti-British feeling had died down in the late nineteenth century to reappear in a new, middle-class form around 1912, the time of the first important Indian Pan-Islamic publications. On the Indian experience see also Kudsi-Zadeh, "Legacy," pp. 36–39.

31 See Ahmad, *Studies*, chap. 9, and his "An Eighteenth-Century Theory of the Caliphate," *Studia Islamica*, XXVIII (1968), 135–144, on Shāh Walī Allāh and his followers. The caliphate stressed by Shāh Walī Allāh had to be an Arab Quarish caliphate, but the stress on the caliphate as well as on the need for *jihād* in view of the Hindu conquest of Muslim territory may have contributed something to later Pan-Islamic trends.

(abode of Islam), by foreign conquest, into a *Dār al-ḥarb* (abode of War). Hindu conquest of Muslim territory in the eighteenth century already brought calls for holy war, *jihād,* from Shāh Wāli Allāh. According to a strict interpretation of Islamic theory, a foreign conquest of Islamic territory, unless the conquerors left the local Muslim officials and customs intact, should be answered by *jihād.* In addition to this theoretical point the Indian Muslim community suffered particularly from the dislocations caused by British conquest. The Muslim ruling classes of northern India were largely removed from their former positions and were far less apt to go to the secularized schools set up by the British—the only real avenue to service in the new government—than were the Hindus. The authority of the ulama, and even their possibility of having a livelihood, declined with the secularization of education and of judicial institutions. The Muslim lower classes shared with their Hindu counterparts the increased dislocations and pressures brought by the British rule.

In this situation there soon developed a situation of almost chronic religious revolt lasting from the early nineteenth century until its crushing in 1863. Revolt was concentrated in two areas—Bengal and the Northwest Frontier—but warriors for the *jihād, mujāhids,* were recruited from other areas of India too. The revolt began against the Sikhs in the Northwest and was first led by Sayyid Ahmad Brelwī, a favored disciple of Shāh 'Abd al-Azīz, the eldest son of Shāh Walī Allāh. In a celebrated *fatwā* in 1803 Shāh 'Abd al-Azīz had declared that British India was no longer *dār al-Islām.* From this to a call for *jihād* was only a short step, which was soon taken, and a series of religious revolts with purist and messianic overtones followed.[32] Some Muslim leaders also called for *jihād* against the British during the 1857 Mutiny.

Appeals to Central Asian and Afghan rulers to help rid Indian Muslims of infidel rule were made by both Shāh Walī Allāh and Sayyid Ahmad Brelwī. In the first Afghan war the Northwest Frontier religious warriors, *mujāhids,* joined in the fight against the British, while during the Mutiny there was a strong party in Afghanistan which favored joining on the side of the rebels. The idea of some kind

[32] See Ahmad, *Studies,* chap. 9; Ziya-ul-Hasan Faruqi, *The Deoband School and the Demand for Pakistan* (London, 1963); " 'Abd al-'Azīz al-Dihlawī" and (Sayyid) "Aḥmad Brēlwī in *EI*²; Freeland Abbott, "The Jihād of Sayyid Aḥmad Shahīd," *Muslim World,* LII (July, 1962), 216–222; and "The Transformation of the Jihad Movement," *Muslim World,* LII (Oct., 1962), 288–295; and Mahmud Husain *et al.*, eds., *A History of the Freedom Movement,* Vol. I (Karachi, 1957), pp. 556–600.

of alliance between Indian Muslims and helpers who would attack the Northwest Frontier was thus in existence among some Indian Muslims and their rulers, by the time Jamāl ad-Dīn came to India.

Jamāl ad-Dīn in later years put forth programs for an international Muslim alliance along with Hindus to drive the British out of India. That the program was in part inspired by his Indian experience seems highly probable.

The question of what attitude to take toward the *jihād* and, specifically, whether Indian Muslims were duty-bound to carry out *jihād* against the British concerned not only the *mujāhids* and the participants in the Mutiny but many peaceful Indian Muslims as well. It was hotly debated in the Indian Muslim community in the mid-nineteenth century, and if the weight of opinion gradually came to oppose *jihād*, as might have been expected in view of its growing impracticality, this opinion was by no means unanimous. Jamāl ad-Dīn appears after his Indian experience as a frequent advocate of *jihād* but also as a man whose strictly religious or spiritual enthusiasm is suspect. It seems reasonable to suppose that his direct experience and indirect knowledge of religious revolts helped convince him that traditional religious sentiments were the most powerful weapons available to a Muslim who wished to raise a movement strong enough to sweep the foreigners from Muslim lands.

Interest in the *jihād* and bitter opposition to the British thus seem likely to have had their roots in Jamāl ad-Dīn's Indian experience. In addition, there were some trends in India toward greater unity with Muslims outside India in this time of severe hardship for Indian Muslims, and possibly even for alliance with the Ottoman Sultan.[33] All this was natural enough in a time when Muslims were being conquered and despoiled, and it is possible that Jamāl ad-Dīn was influenced in the same direction either by these trends or by the events that set them in motion. The idea of an alliance with the Ottoman Sultan was certainly more apt to arise from Jamāl ad-Dīn's experience in Sunni India, which had friendly feelings toward the Sultan, than from Shi'i Iran, which did not.

In later years Jamāl ad-Dīn also frequently voiced the idea that the

---

[33] For a brief and perceptive analysis of this and other aspects of the trends among Indian Muslims in this period, see W. C. Smith, "The 'Ulamā in Indian Politics," in C. H. Philips, ed., *Politics and Society in India* (London, 1962). On 'Abd al-'Azīz's grandson Mawlānā Muhammad Ishāq, Faruqi (*op. cit.*, p. 19 n. 1) says: "His programme was mainly based on the 2 principles: (1) a strict observance of 'Hanafi mazhab' and (2) an alliance with the Ottoman Sultanate of Turkey."

British were out to destroy Islam and to convert the Muslims to Christianity. Although this is in part simply a reflection of traditional Muslim attitudes to Christianity, the idea seems to have been particularly prevalent among Indian Muslims. The actual appropriation by the British of some of the territory and income entrusted to Muslim educational purposes and its use for schools in which Christians taught, as well as the activities of missionaries in India and the undermining of the position and livelihood of the ulama, lent weight to this feeling.[34]

What else may be said about what Jamāl ad-Dīn learned from the time he spent in India? The standard biographies tell us that while in India (in theory, a bit over a year) he gained some mastery over Western knowledge and science. This idea is usually presented without comment, as if modern Western knowledge were something that could simply be pasted onto a traditional Iranian-Islamic education without causing any cracks in the latter. Yet, as many traditionally educated Middle Easterners who have gone through this process could confirm, the process is frequently a traumatic and fundamental one for a man of intelligence. It often results in a profound modification of former views, though this modification can be made more easily and with less complete rejection of past learning by someone with a heterodox and philosophical background. Islamic philosophers had already suggested that reason was the surest guide to the truth for the philosophical elite, and that this elite should reject a literal interpretation of the Koran when it was found to be contrary to the conclusions of demonstrative reasoning. The conclusions of the medieval philosophers were not those of the modern West, but the philosophers' acceptance of reason as a better guide than a literalist interpretation of revelation might open a mind to even very different conclusions than those reached by the philosophers themselves.

There apparently exists only one substantial account of what Jamāl ad-Dīn actually did learn and come to believe in India, that by Salīm al-'Anḥūrī, a Syrian writer who knew Afghānī in Egypt in the 1870's, and it is against this account that 'Abduh's apologetic biography is largely directed. 'Anḥūrī's account has been generally ignored by later biographers, probably because 'Abduh, disturbed by

34 W. W. Hunter, *The Indian Musulmans: Are They Bound in Conscience to Rebel Against the Queen?* (London, 1871), chap. 4, "The Wrongs of the Musalmans under British Rule"; Faruqi, *op. cit.*, chap. 1. Although Hunter was purposefully overstating the Muslims' woes, his account has a factual base.

'Anḥūrī's attribution to Jamāl ad-Dīn of irreligious ideas, talked 'Anḥūrī into publishing a retraction of it. Yet there is so much resemblance between what 'Anḥūrī says of Jamāl ad-Dīn's views on religion—which 'Anḥūrī says Jamāl ad-Dīn learned in India and retained through the 1870's when 'Anḥūrī and various disciples knew him in Egypt—and the views Afghānī expressed to certain Westerners later, notably in his "Answer to Renan," that 'Anḥūrī's account may well be largely correct. 'Anḥūrī got his story both from his own brief experience in Egypt with Jamāl ad-Dīn in the 1870's and from several former students of Afghānī's, who may have had no reason to try to hide his true beliefs. For them, What Jamāl ad-Dīn came to believe in India was what he still believed in his years in Egypt. 'Abduh, on the other hand, at the time he combatted this story, was engaged with Jamāl ad-Dīn in Islamic and Pan-Islamic activity that might be seriously weakened by 'Anḥūrī's story of Jamāl ad-Dīn's unbelief. The 'Anḥūrī biography does have several factual errors, but they do not necessarily invalidate what he says of Jamāl ad-Dīn's ideas. Jamāl ad-Dīn's documented appearance after India, in Afghanistan 1866–1868, as a man who "apparently, follows no particular religion," and whose "style of living resembles more that of an European than of a Mussulman" lends some weight to 'Anḥūrī's account.[35] 'Anḥūrī says that while Jamāl ad-Dīn was in India

> He excelled in the study of religions, until this led him to irreligion [or atheism—*ilḥād*] and belief in the eternity of the world. He claimed that vital atoms, found in the atmosphere, formed, by a natural evolution, the stars which we see and which revolve around one another through gravity, and that the belief in an omniscient Prime Mover was a natural delusion that arose when man was in a primitive state of evolution and corresponded with the stage that his intellectual progress had reached. This meant that when man was a pure savage and primitive he used to worship the lowest things in existence, like wood and stone, and when he had progressed on the ladder of civilization and knowledge, his

[35] Great Britain. Commonwealth Relations Office. Government of India, Foreign Department. *Narrative of Events in Cabul from the Death of Dost Mohamed to the Spring of 1872. . . . Cabul Précis 1863–74* (Simla, 1866, 1874) (henceforth called *Cabul Précis*), "Descriptive Roll of the Syud Rumi at Cabul, who is suspected to be a Russian Agent in attendance at the Cabul Durbar," p. 47 (113). As noted in chap. 5, below, some others who knew Jamāl ad-Dīn in Egypt write that he was not a believer in the 1870's.

> objects of worship rose correspondingly, and he began to venerate fire, then clouds, then the heavens and their celestial bodies. Man went on progressing on the scale of knowledge and deriving light from the lamp of science; taking the natural course he elevated the object of his worship and raised it in degree of loftiness until he said: "It is free from quality and quantity, free of beginning and end, boundless and incomprehensible, filling everything and in everything, seeing all while none see it." Man's intellectual capacities progressed after that, however, until they reached the knowledge that all these [beliefs] are kinds of delusions and confused dreams, originating from man's fear of death and his desire for immortality. This made him build from air castles of faith and towers of hope, such as had taken root in his imagination to the point that they almost became a fixed belief.
>
> Man began by saying that he would pass on after his death to an eternal life, and that the wood or the stone were what would lead him to this highest place if he showed reverence to it and showered devotion upon it, and there arose from this worship liberation from the bitterness of thought about a death with no life after it. Then it occurred to him that fire was more powerful and greater in benefit and harm, so he turned to it. Then he saw that the clouds were better than fire and stronger, so he adhered to and depended on them. The links of this chain, wrought by the two tools of delusion and desire together with the instinct and nature of man, continued to increase until man culminated at the highest state. The result of natural laws was a reaction leading to the conviction that all the above is idle talk which originates in desires, and that it has no truth and no definition.[36]

Jamāl ad-Dīn's life and words from his first well-documented appearance in 1866–1868, and continuing thereafter, give evidence that he was at least skeptical about existing positive religions, he held an evolutionary view of religion, believing that a simpler prophetic religion was useful for less advanced peoples, and a more rational reformed religion was what most men needed later. It seems likely that, as 'Anḥūrī's account suggests, at least some of these views go back to his Indian experience, which probably reinforced innovative tendencies already noted for his period in Najaf. 'Anḥūrī's suggestion

36 'Anḥūri biography of Afghānī, reprinted in Riḍā, *Tārīkh*, pp. 43–44. Kedourie (*Afghani*, pp. 15–16) translates part of the passage that I translate at greater length.

that Jamāl ad-Dīn was an atheist is, however, belied by his notebooks from the 1860's, discussed below.

1858–1865: The Darkest Years

After the first Indian stay, all sources have Jamāl ad-Dīn next take a leisurely trip to Mecca, stopping at several points along the way. There is as yet no documentation that either confirms or throws doubt on such a trip, which he probably did make. It seems likely, however, that Jamāl ad-Dīn moved back the date of this trip to make it agree with his story of a very short stay in India before it, and long years in the service of the Afghan government after it. The simplest explanation of Jamāl ad-Dīn's probable movements in the years 1858–1865 which is in accord with existing documents and clues is that he most likely spent the first part of this period in India, and after his stay there, went on the slow trip to Mecca later than he claimed (an autobiographical document suggests these travels began about 1861), and then went back via Iraq and possibly Istanbul to Iran. His presence in Iran in 1865 is documented in the Afshār-Mahdavī *Documents* volume.

'Abduh's biography gives a story of almost ten years in the service of the Afghan government which can be rejected out of hand on the basis of the documents cited in the next chapter. Lutfallāh's biography has a story that seems to reflect an attempt to reconcile the facts about Jamāl ad-Dīn's 1865–1866 trip to Iran with his claim to have entered Afghan government service before 1863 and to have spent only "a year and some months" in India. This story has Afghānī take about two and a half years on the route from India to Mecca, then has him return to Iran via Karbala and Najaf, the Shi'i holy cities in Iraq, go to Asadabad briefly in 1277 (1860–61), then to Tehran for several months, then via Khorasan to Afghanistan for five years. The trip across Iran follows the route that Jamāl ad-Dīn actually took in 1865–66, as shown in the *Documents*, but the dates have been moved back.[37] Lutfallāh puts Jamāl ad-Dīn in Afghanistan before 1863, whereas it can now be shown that he first arrived there late in 1866. A notebook entry by Jamāl ad-Dīn says he left the "*makān-i musharraf*," probably the Shi'i shrine cities of Iraq, in September–October, 1865, and dates his travel to Tehran, northeast Iran, and Afghanistan in 1865–66.[38]

Since Jamāl ad-Dīn did not tell the truth about his locations in the period from 1858 to 1865, there are various possibilities as to where he spent these years. In addition to the trip to the Shi'i shrine cities, certain items in the *Documents* suggest stops in Istanbul and Baghdad during these years. Among his earliest notebooks there is a short "Treatise on the Crafts" by the founder of Shaikhism Aḥmad Aḥsā'ī, in Jamāl ad-Dīn's handwriting, at the end of which he wrote, "I wrote this in the Abode of Peace, Baghdad, and I am a stranger in the lands and banished from the homelands, Jamāl ad-Dīn al-Husainī al-Istanbūlī."[39] Internal and external evidence suggests that the inscription was written before Jamāl ad-Dīn reached Iran on his way to Afghanistan. This indicates that Jamāl ad-Dīn began to use the place-of-origin name "Istanbūlī," which he later employed in Afghanistan, even before he reached Afghanistan. Since Jamāl ad-Dīn seems never to have used a place-of-origin name of a place he had not been to, and since it would have been risky for him in Afghanistan to claim to be from a city he had not even seen, one may guess that he had actually been in Istanbul in these years. An autobiographical fragment written in Afghanistan suggests that Jamāl ad-Dīn had visited many countries with different religions in the 1860's, and British representatives in Afghanistan thought he had been in Russian territory.[40]

---

37 Luṭfallāh, pp. 22–23; *Documents*, p. 156, date table.

38 *Documents*, p. 9, doc. 91; photo 8. This notation by Jamāl ad-Dīn says that he had left the *makān-i musharraf* (probably the Shi'i shrine cities in Iraq) in September–October 1865, had entered Tehran in mid-December [1865], left Tehran in May–June 1866, and there lived near the Jām'eh Mosque. He reached Tus [near and probably meaning Mashhad] in June–July 1866, left in September–October 1866, and there stayed in the home of a Mullā Husain in the main street, Khiyābān-e Bālā. He entered Herat, Afghanistan, in October, 1866 and stayed forty days. The remaining dates in the notation deal with Jamāl ad-Dīn's stay in Afghanistan, and are given in the next chapter.

39 *Documents*, p. 15, doc. 9: 4; pl. 7, photo 19.

40 See the documents cited in chap. iii. The complete version of one of the British documents even gives a Russian route to Afghanistan, which is disproved by the *Documents'* evidence that Jamāl ad-Dīn came to Afghanistan from Iran. The autobiographical text is in the *Documents*, pl. 1, photo 2, and is summarized in chap. 3, pp. 37–38.

A curious feature of the Baghdad inscription is that after his trip to Afghanistan Jamāl ad-Dīn not only wrote "Kābulī," over "Istanbūlī" in red ink, but tried to obliterate the word "Baghdad" with the same ink by writing another word over it.[41] This attempted effacement, plus the fact that Jamāl ad-Dīn is never recorded as referring to a youthful stay in Baghdad, suggests that he was perhaps trying to hide this stay. Whether or not this reticence is connected to the fact that some Iranian Babi exiles were located in Baghdad in these years is a matter for speculation. The expression, "a stranger in the lands and banished from the homelands," repeated in later documents from Jamāl ad-Dīn's pen, may confirm an expulsion from the Shi'i shrine cities or may refer to early troubles in Iran that none of Jamāl ad-Dīn's biographers has recorded.

On his way from Iraq to Tehran Jamāl ad-Dīn stopped off for a few days with his parents and two sisters in Asadabad, and Sifātallāh recalls the memories of this brief visit of his father, Lutfallāh, who was then a boy. On this visit Jamāl ad-Dīn's father and other relatives pleaded with him repeatedly to cease his constant traveling and to settle down with his family. Jamāl ad-Dīn refused, and when their entreaties became too insistent he said: "I am like a royal falcon for whom the wide arena of the world, for all its breadth, is too narrow for flight. I am amazed that you wish to confine me in this small and narrow cage."[42] Although there is no proof that these words are accurately recalled, they seem so typical of Jamāl ad-Dīn that they may be given some credence. The comparison of himself to a bird was repeated later, and the horror of being caged up, along with the need to keep moving, are constant themes of his life.

From Asadabad Jamāl ad-Dīn went to Tehran, where the *Documents'* chronology show that he arrived in mid-December of 1865 and stayed until the late spring of 1866. It was apparently in Tehran that his lifelong servant, Abū Turāb, joined him. After this Jamāl ad-Dīn went to Mashhad (Meshed) in northeast Iran and then to Herat, in western Afghanistan, late in 1866. From northeast Iran there remains a draft of a letter from Jamāl ad-Dīn to his friend and cousin, Shaikh Hādī, who had been with him in Tehran. Indicating resentment regarding mistreatment in Iran is a poem of eight verses which Jamāl ad-Dīn wrote while he was still in northeast Iran. In this poem Jamāl

---

[41] *Documents*, p. 15, doc. 9:4; pl. 7, photo 19. I have seen the original.
[42] Preface by Ṣifātallāh Jamālī to *Maqālāt-i Jamāliyyeh*, pp. 11–12.

ad-Dīn says "Iranian demons and beasts of prey have burnt my body and soul," and hence he is quitting Iran for Turkish soil. He says that he will seek justice at the court of the Sultan, and if he does not receive it he will seek justice from God. He refers to his desire to go to Bukhara, also voiced in another early poem, and it appears that he wished to go to Bukhara before seeing the Sultan. What oppression Jamāl ad-Dīn had experienced in Iran, why he wished to go to Bukhara, and what he expected of the Sultan are all matters for speculation. [43] The desire to go to Bukhara is referred to again during Jamāl ad-Dīn's stay in Afghanistan.

Substantial contemporary documentation of Jamīl ad-Dān's activities begins only with his arrival in Afghanistan late in 1866. Despite the dearth of documentation regarding Jamāl ad-Dīn's first twenty-seven years, however, some points may now be regarded as certain. Among these are: (1) Jamāl ad-Dīn was born in Asadabad, a large village near Hamadan in northwest Iran, into a family of sayyids. (2) He received his early education and upbringing in Iran. (3) He went via Bushehr to India around 1856 or 1857. (4) He then spent some time in India. (5) In 1865–66 he spent several months in Tehran, and then went to Herat via Mashhad. In addition, it may be regarded as virtually certain that Jamāl ad-Dīn as an adolescent was educated in Najaf, one of the Shi'i shrine cities in Iraq. It is highly probable that after his trip to India he went to Mecca, the Shi'i shrine cities, and Baghdad. It also seems probable that he spent some time in Istanbul. Jamāl ad-Dīn's stay in Iran in 1865–66 is documented in the *Documents*, where it is also shown that he had strong grievances concerning his treatment in Iran even in these early years, and that he regarded himself as expelled from his homeland. Some of the documents regarding Jamāl ad-Dīn's stay in Afghanistan suggest that he had spent time in Russian territory; this is possible but thus far unconfirmed.

As for Jamāl ad-Dīn's ideas, education, and experiences in his first

[43] *Documents*, pl. 2, photos 3, 5–6; and pp. 81–82. Padkaman, pp. 36–37, states that *makān-i musharraf* (the sacred place), which Jamāl ad-Dīn's notebook states that he left in September, 1865, is a title referring to the audience chamber of the Sultan in Istanbul. Although Iranian scholars I have consulted suggest this title refers rather to the Shi'i cities, Dr. Pakdaman's view may perhaps be an alternative possibility. It is at least conceivable that Jamāl ad-Dīn had some mission taking him from Istanbul toward Afghanistan and Bukhara. After translating part of Jamāl ad-Dīn's poem about his mistreatment in Iran, Dr. Pakdaman asks if it may suggest his implication in the Babi movement. She states that the poem implies that Jamāl ad-Dīn was forced to leave Iran at this point.

twenty-seven years, we must judge mainly from later indications. In the immediately subsequent years, 1867–1872, we find him in command of traditional religious knowledge and of Islamic philosophy, but not as someone concerned to appear orthodox. Various documents in this later period show him to have innovating and rationalist ideas. His main concerns in 1867–1872 are already political. In 1867 and 1868 he espouses strongly anti-British schemes that appear to reflect Indian ideas and experiences. In Afghanistan he has already adopted some Western ideas and practices, while in Istanbul in 1870 he appears as an advocate of modernized education as a means of self-strengthening for Eastern countries. And so even for the dark period before 1866 enough can be determined about Jamāl ad-Dīn's life to show a picture far different from that of the standard biographies.

3

In Afghanistan: 1866–1868

JAMĀL AD-DĪN's notebooks, reproduced in the *Documents,* show us that, after traveling from Tehran to northeast Iran, he reached Herat in western Afghanistan in October 1866. He spent forty days in Herat, and then went to Qandahar (Kandahar) for eight months, from December 1866 through July 1867. From there he went via the town of Ghazni to the Afghan capital, Kabul, which he entered in late October 1867.[1] Other documents, cited below, tell us of Jamāl ad-Dīn's political activities from early 1867 through 1868. There is little indication of what he did before this, during his forty days in Herat and at the beginning of his stay in Qandahar. The *Documents* do, however, include some significant writings by Jamāl ad-Dīn done in Herat and Qandahar.

During his stay in Herat in the fall of 1866 Jamāl ad-Dīn wrote an autobiographical text, which, for all its striking resemblance to other spiritual autobiographies, such as that of the great Iranian medieval theologian, al-Ghazālī, probably reflects his actual mental history. He says that for years he had devoted himself to the traditional sciences, which wasted his time and taught him nothing about this world or the other world. At the age of nineteen, he continues, he was obliged to frequent formalist and superficial ulama, and came to understand

---

[1] See the table of dates in *Documents* and the documents referred to in it, especially p. 9, doc. 91, photo 8, where Jamāl ad-Dīn notes both his dates and his dwelling areas in each city he visited through 1868.

that the ulama of each religious group were captives of inadequate doctrines. He goes on to say that he has spent five whole years traveling in many parts of the world and talked with the leaders of every religion and followers of every school. (This would date his extensive travels from 1861, and mean an Indian stay of several years before that.) He concludes, after noting his disappointment with men of every religion and station of life:

> I saw that this world was only an unreal mirage and appearance. Its power was precarious and its sufferings unlimited, hiding a venom in every delight, an anger in every benefit. Thus I was inevitably led to remove myself from these tumults and to break all my ties of attachment. And thanks to God and all those who were near him, I was saved from the world of shadows and penetrated the universe of devotion, resting on the sweetness of the cradle of lights. Today I have chosen for company the Prophet and his companions.[2]

The paradoxical combinations of a Sufi mystical streak with extraordinary political activism has considerable precedent in Islamic history. The form of these memoirs is so conventional as to raise some doubt about their value as a biographical source, but judging from Jamāl ad-Dīn's later life one can believe the combination of religious questioning, skepticism, and somewhat mystic temperament which they reveal. These memoirs do tend to contradict 'Anḥūrī's suggestion that Jamāl ad-Dīn was an atheist.

Also showing Jamāl ad-Dīn's ties to mysticism of a Neoplatonic philosophical type is a twelve-page treatise on *'irfān* (gnosticism) copied in his handwriting in a notebook and dated April 7, 1867, in Qandahar. The treatise, as noted above, was by Hajjī Muhammad Khān Kirmānī, the third leader of the Shaikhis, and Jamāl ad-Dīn's interest is shown not only by his writing it out but by notes inscribed by him at the end dating from Istanbul and from his teaching of philosophy in Cairo in 1875.[3] Jamāl ad-Dīn's copying and carrying about for years of this and another Shaikhi treatise suggest the continued appeal for him of this school's combination of philosophy, mystical ideas, and religious innovation.

Beginning in 1867, there exists not only personal material but also the first well-documented information about Jamāl ad-Dīn's political

2 *Ibid.*, pl. 1, photo 2.

3 *Ibid.*, p. 14, doc. 9; pl. 7, photo 18. I have read the original in Tehran.

activities. Before turning to this information, it is useful to look at the Afghan political situation in which he had to operate.

After the death of the powerful Afghan Amir, Dūst Muhammad Khān, in 1863, he was succeeded by the heir-designate, Shīr 'Alī Khān. There followed a series of complex civil wars among Dūst Muhammad's sons and grandsons, with Shīr 'Alī's half brother A'zam Khān, as a leading pretender. When the latter was defeated he was given asylum by the Government of India from May 1864, until April 1865. A'zam Khān had hitherto been rather pro-British but, objecting to British treatment of him in India, he now became anti-British.

A'zam Khān returned to Afghanistan to resume the fight in 1865 and captured Kabul in February 1866, while Shīr 'Alī kept control of part of the country. The British refused to recognize the new government as long as Shīr 'Alī had such control. A'zam Khān now began to voice threats to the British Indian newswriter at Kabul, who was temporarily the only Government of India representative there, that he would seek a Russian alliance.

A'zam Khān won a major victory in May 1866, taking Ghazni and releasing his imprisoned older brother, Afzal Khān, who was now named Amir, although real power remained with A'zam Khān. A'zam Khān won a further victory against Shīr 'Alī in January 1867, near Qandahar. He stayed with his army in Qandahar until September 1867, then went for a short time to Ghazni, and then returned to Kabul. Afzal Khān died in October and A'zam Khān now took the title of amir. His rule was apparently most unpopular with both masses and notables, as he tried to strip the latter of their lands and priviliges, and was extortionate in collecting taxes. A'zam Khān in 1867–68, when Jamāl ad-Dīn was advising him, was preoccupied with the question of retaining his throne against the always threatening Shīr 'Alī, and was putting out unsuccessful feelers for both British and Russian aid. There is no indication that he tried any reforms that might assure him some popular loyalty. The standard Afghānī biography repeats a widespread misconception when it says that in this period the British were aiding Shīr 'Alī; although they did not hide their preference for him they in fact gave him no military aid until he recaptured Kabul in 1868.[4]

---

[4] The events of this period are described at first hand in the *Cabul Précis* and in Government of India, Foreign Department, *Proceedings of the Government of India in the Foreign Department, Political* (Calcutta, 1869), "Cabul Diary" (hence-

To return to Jamāl ad-Dīn: Once A'zam Khān took Qandhar in January 1867, Jamāl ad-Dīn's activities are documented. The Government of India's "Cabul Diaries" and its *Narrative of Events in Cabul from the Death of Dost Mahomed to the Spring of 1872* (*Cabul Précis*) include the earliest substantial independent documents about Afghānī, and date from his appearance in Afghanistan in 1866–1868, years later than the standard account suggests. They contain the reports of the British government news reporter who was responsible for informing the Government of India about events in Afghanistan and who had been placed on the scene to report on happenings. The British were concerned about the sudden appearance in 1866 in the high counsels of the then Amir of Afghanistan, A'zam Khān, of a foreign Sayyid, who was advising the Amir to follow an anti-British course. The British thus had their own representative in Kabul and various local informants find out what they could about this man. That the man was Jamāl ad-Dīn can easily be seen by reading the documents. There is no possible doubt about it because: (1) The dates of his presence in Qandahar, Ghazni, and Kabul, and his association with the Amir A'zam Khān in 1866 to 1868 given in these documents correspond exactly to the dates in these three cities and the contact with the Amir independently documented by entries in Afghānī's personal notebooks catalogued in the *Documents*. (2) He is accompanied by his lifelong faithful servant, whose name is given as Abu T[u]rab, as it is elsewhere later. (3) His anti-British words and his mode of expression are characteristic of Afghānī. (4) There were no other persons in the entourage of A'zam Khān who could re-

forth called "Cabul Diary") (both sources are "confidential prints" available in the Commonwealth Relations Office of Great Britain). The period is analyzed by men who had access to primary information in John Wyllie (Undersecretary to the Foreign Department of the Government of India and writer of the first part of the *Cabul Précis*), *Essays on the External Policy of India*, ed. W. W. Hunter (London, 1875); and Stephen Wheeler, *The Ameer Abdur Rahman* (New York, 1895), chap. ii. The latter work translates and comments upon an early autobiography of 'Abd ar-Rahmān Khān covering this period. The period is also discussed in H. B. Hanna, *The Second Afghan War*, Vol. I (London, 1899); *The Life of Abdur Rahman, Amir of Afghanistan*, ed. Mir Munshi Sultan Mahomed Khan, Vol. I (London, 1900); William Habberton, *Anglo-Russian Relations Concerning Afghanistan, 1837–1907* (Urbana, Ill., 1937); M. A. Terentyef, *Russia and England in Central Asia*, trans. F. C. Daukes, 2 vols. (Calcutta, 1876); A. P. Thornton, "The Reopening of the 'Central Asian Question,' 1864–69," *History*, XI, 141–143 (1956), 122–136, and "Afghanistan in Anglo-Russian Diplomacy, 1869–73," *Cambridge Historical Journal*, XI, 2 (1954), 204–218. On British relations with Shīr 'Alī see the *Cabul Précis* for these years; also Wheeler, *op. cit.*, pp. 38–46; and Wyllie, *op. cit.*, "Masterly Inactivity."

motely be taken for Sayyid Jamāl ad-Dīn. (5) He uses the name Sayyid Rūmī (meaning "from Turkey"), and claims to be from Istanbul: the *Documents* show this use of the name "Rūmī," and that in Afghanistan he often used the (place-of-origin) name "Istanbūlī," and never one showing an Afghan or Iranian origin. (6) He is known to have come recently from Iran, also documented independently in the *Documents*. (7) He signs two letters "Jamāl ad-Dīn." (8) He is expelled, as he admitted, by Amir Shīr 'Alī late in 1868.

Combining the *Documents* and Government of India documentation we know that he sayed with A'zam Khān in Qandahar, moved with him for a short stay in Ghanzi, and went to Kabul when A'zam Khān returned to that capital to become amir in October 1867. The first references in the Government of India documents to Jamāl ad-Dīn appear shortly after his arrival in Kabul, late in 1867. The account comes from the Government of India's *Précis* of events in Afghanistan since 1863, which was based on several sources and informants in Afghanistan. The *munshī* (Moonshee), or newswriter referred to, was an Indian who for several years had been the British representative and informant at Kabul, and who was well informed about happenings at the Afghan court.

On Jamāl ad-Dīn, the *Précis* begins:

> The often-roused apprehensions of the Moonshee, lest the Affghan Rulers should seek foreign assistance if none came from the side of India, were increased by the appearance about this time of a mysterious personage who is styled the Syud Rumi. The following extracts from the [*munshī*'s] diary relate to this personage:—
>
> "A Syud of Constantinople has, for some time past, been at Cabul. He gives out that he is there for pleasure on his travels, and he is constantly granted private interviews with the Ameer, who allows him Rupees 200 per mensem subsistence or guest money. It is not known who he really is; some suspect him to be an Agent of some Government."

The next entry in the munshī's diary reads: "Just at present the Constantinople Syud (referred to in a former diary) receives such distinguished consideration from the Ameer, that no one about the Court can be held to receive as much, and constantly remains in private attendance on the ameer. Many people suggest, as not unlikely, that he is a Russian emissary. . . ." A later entry speaks of the visits of important persons to Jamāl ad-Dīn, and of his late night secret audiences with the Amir. It concludes: "A person of reliability informs me that this Syud has brought a promise of a 'crore' of money in cash from the Russian Government to cement their alliances with assurances of further assistance. . . ."[5]

The British were naturally interested in this personage, and supplemented their knowledge about him with information from other informants, presumably Afghans. In March 1868, one of these wrote about him:

> The Hajee Syud Rumi, a secret Agent of the Russian Government of Toorkistan, is now the most influential and leading member of the Ameer's Privy Council. He is believed to have traveled from Tiflis to Bokhara, through Sherwan and Tabrez, in Persia and Urgunj, and thence to Herat, through the Turkoman Steppes. In 1866 he visited Candahar, *where he met Ameer Mahomed Azim Khan, presenting to him some Secret papers that he had brought for him.* He has since been with the Ameer, who always keeps him about his person. [Italics mine throughout these documents.]
>
> One of the Hajee's followers is a man who goes by the name of Abutrab, with short eyes, red complexion, and light hair, apparently a native of Tiflis.[6]

For some of the diary entries, one must go directly to the "Cabul Diaries," reports that were sent in regularly by the munshī or other representative and translated into English and printed by the British in India. In late February 1868, the munshī reported: "The Constantinople Syud affects to be annoyed with the Ameer, and to desire to leave shortly for Bokhara. Probably he has some mission."[7] This report may be connected with an undated letter from the Amir photographed in the *Documents* which reluctantly grants Jamāl ad-Dīn permission to leave, although the city referred to is not Bukhara but Peshawar. One poem written by Afghānī in eastern Iran just before this period had alluded repeatedly to his desire to go to Bukhara, and another expressed this desire once.[8]

---

5 *Cabul Précis,* p. 46 (p. 112 on the supplementary numbering system of the *Précis;* these page numbers are henceforth listed in parentheses).

6 *Ibid.*

7 "Cabul Diary," Feb. 11–20, 1868, p. 13.

8 *Documents,* pp. 81–82; and pl. 40, photo 89. The printed transcriptions of these poems mistakenly transcribe "if I do not go to Bukhara" as "if I go to Bukhara."

"Cabul Diaries" written in March 1868 note that the Amir has shown the Sayyid Rūmī a translation of a paper from the British Government in India proposing to develop trade and open the Khyber route, and also papers regarding the case of the murder by an Afghan of a certain Mr. Bean. A more important entry comes in April: "It is said that the Syud Roomee has presented some Russian notes to the Ameer, who has with great secrecy been endeavoring to cash the notes through Syud Jan, a Cabullee merchant, who has agents at Bokhara, Tashkend, and in Hindustan; also through the Gomashtesh [*sic* for Gomashteh] Niaz Juhood (or Yahoodee), a Bokhara merchant."[9]

Later in April, the Amir was reported worried over the Russian military advance in Bukhara and its threat to Afghanistan, but at the same time to be trying to get recognition and aid from Russia, without definite result. A private newsletter extracted in the "Cabul Diary" without naming the author (who was someone other than the British agent) dated April 20, 1868, said:

> The Ameer is believed to have received assurances of friendship on the part of the Russian Government from the Syud Rumi, who further informed him that the Russian Government had arranged with the Ameer of Bokhara to have a Russian Resident and four Commercial Establishments at Bokhara, and Cantonments at Charjoee and other places. He suggested that if the Ameer allied himself with the Russian Government, like the Ameer of Bokhara, the advantages to his Government would be great; he could then hope to receive assistance both in arms and money from them, while he had in vain been applying to the British Government for protection ("sarparasti") and aid. The British Government, he added, was now despaired [*sic*] of retaining its hold on Afghanistan, and was only thinking of strengthening its position on the Indus. He would accordingly advise the Ameer to give up all hopes of friendship and protection from the British Government, and sow the seed of affection towards the Russians in his heart, and, avoiding all neutrality, stick fast to only one side, that of the Russians. . . . Now that the Russian influence had been extended to the Oxus, the Ameer need not be afraid of the anger or vengeance of the British Government.

---

9 April 14–16, 1968, pp. 430–431.

> *20th April.* The Ameer accordingly sent for the British Agent, and told him that he had now lost all hopes in the British Government; that he felt sure that Government would not take Cabul under its protection, "sarparasti," that the Russians having made satisfactory arrangements in Toorkistan, and extended their influence to the Oxus, he feared for the security of his own Government, and must now make his own arrangements, but wanted to know if the British Government would yet take the Cabul Government under its protection.[10]

The British Agent referred to was a regular British Indian representative or *vakīl* who had been sent to Kabul after some years when only the munshī had been present.

The *Cabul Précis* has further information on the Amir's consultation with Jamāl ad-Dīn on the British request to open the Khyber Pass for trade. The British did not at this time give any particular importance to the question, but one of the British informants wrote in March 1868:

> "The Hajee [Jamāl ad-Dīn] has led the Ameer to believe that the British Government, in wishing for an opening out of the Khyber Pass, have some other object in view than that professed by them, *viz.*, the promotion of the Indian and Toorkistan trade. He argues that the best policy to conquer a foreign country is to open out new communications by means of trade.
>
> "He stated that the trade between India and the Western countries had existed ever since the time of Darius by only three routes . . . that there now existed no depression of trade sufficient to necessitate the opening out of a new channel . . . that when the Russians had advanced through the Kirghiz Steppes against Khiva and taken possession of the territory around about the Sea of Aral, the English apprehended a Russian invasion of India, sent secret spies, Burnes, Stoddart, and Conolly, etc., to Affghanistan and Bokhara; and though their territory did not then adjoin either Affghanistan or Herat, they aimed at securing possession of both those countries by all the means in their power . . . that now that the Russians had advanced to the Oxus, the anxiety of the

10 "Cabul Diary." "Extract from a Private News-letter, dated Cabul, April 20. 1868," p. 24.

English could well be imagined; and that they had no doubt some special reasons for requiring an opening out of the Khyber Pass.

The Hajee has accordingly advised the Amir to write to the British Government to say that the Indian trade with Affghanistan and Bokhara had reached its climax, and is not capable of expansion . . . that if the British Government have some other object in view than the promotion of trade, the Ameer would be glad to know it.

"The Hajee is averse to the Khyber Pass being opened to all. *The Russian Government . . . he says . . . never deprives its allies and feudatories of their possessions, and alludes to the case of Khudayar Khan of Khokand as an instance.*"[11]

The same facts were reported by the newly arrived Muslim vakīl, who added that the Sayyid had advised the Amir to subsidize certain tribes to keep the Pass closed. The Amir followed the Sayyid's advice, refusing to open the Pass. The Amir's government was reported to be convinced that the request for its opening was part of a British attempt to interfere further in Afghanistan. On another question on which the Amir had consulted Jamāl ad-Dīn, the British were also rebuffed with a refusal to execute the murderer of Mr. Bean and with an offer only of blood money.[12]

An important report came in June 1868, from a man who, from internal evidence, must have been an Afghan of governmental rank, not suspected of being a British informant. The report below is headed "Descriptive Roll of the Syud Rumi at Cabul, who is suspected to be a Russian Agent in attendance at the Cabul Durbar [Court]":

> Pale complexion, open forehead, azure eyes, has a goat-beard, with some red hairs in it, moustache small, slender make, head shaved, age about 35 years [in fact ca. 30]. Is dressed like a Noghai, drinks tea constantly, and smokes in the Persian style. *Is well versed in Geography and History, speaks Arabic and Turkey* [*sic*—probably Turkī in the original] *fluently, talks Persian like an Irani (Persian). Apparently, follows no particular religion. His style of living resembles more that of an European than of a Mussulman.*
>
> He is attended by an Irani (Persian) by the name of *Abutrab.*

[11] *Cabul Précis,* pp. 47–48 (113–114).

[12] "Cabul Diary," April 23, 1868, enclosed abstract translation of letter from A'zam Khān to the British Agent.

There follows an account of what the Sayyid said in the presence of the writer about Russia and England, revealing anti-British feeling and the use of inaccurate arguments calculated to bring a given end, both of which recur throughout Jamāl ad-Dīn's life. There is also the first mention of the theme of a Russian invasion of India:

> The Syud Rumi's feelings towards the Russians and the English will best be understood from the following remarks gratuitously made by him in course of conversation during the two hours the writer was in his company:—
>
> *Firstly.*—The Emperor of Russia has sent his uncle with two lakhs Russian soldiers, and one lakh Cossacks and Kalmucks, etc., to Toorkistan, with the ultimate object of advancing on India by Herat, and conquering that country. The English cannot cope with the Russians in open field.
>
> *Secondly.*—The English first gave out that it was in conformance to their own wishes that the Russians had advanced on and taken Toorkistan, and that there being a Treaty of friendship between the Russian and the English Governments, the former would never interfere with India. Then they wanted to make out that the Russians were hostilely inclined towards them. By such rumours they tried to test the feelings of the Princes of India, with whom they have left secret spies, in connection with the present advance of Russia.
>
> *Thirdly.*—The Emperor of Russia is the master of 18 lakhs of "Khanazzadugan" [*Précis* adds, "Soldiers born and bred at home. (Serfs?)"], who consider it their duty to sacrifice their lives, if need be, in his cause.
>
> *Fourthly.*—The English Government never abide by their Treaty; they are not known to have adhered to any of their agreements for a period exceeding ten years. They secure possession of countries by fraud. But the Russian Government strictly keep their word. *The English are thieves of unknown extraction, who have lately sprung up, and owe all that they have gained to their intrigues. The Russian State has existed since the time of Alexander the Great.*
>
> *Fifthly.*—The Russians are generous and lenient, even to their foes; for instance, the Russian Emperor had allowed 30 years' grace to Sultan Mahomed, father of Abdool Majed Khan, the Sultan of Turkey, at a time when he (the Sultan) having, from suspicious motives, destroyed 40,000 men of his army, expressed his inability to resist a contemplated Russian invasion upon his territory; and it was after the expira-

> tion of this period (30 years) that the Russian Government took 70 cities from the Sultan.
>
> *Sixthly.—The Sovereign of England is devoid of all power in the State, being at the mercy of her Parliament, but the Emperor of the Russians, though having a Parliament* [*Council of State?*] *is all-powerful.*
>
> Talking of Indian affairs, he remarked that he considered Nana Rao to have been a fool, inasmuch as he cut off the hands of certain butchers before he had seized Cawnpore, thereby prejudicing the minds of Mussulmans against himself; that 300 English soldiers had succeeded in taking the Bailey Guard at Lucknow and seizing upon the house of the Oudh King's General; that thousands of the Hindoostani (mutineers) threw themselves down in the Goomtee River and were drowned, etc., etc.[13]

The last remarks would seem to indicate an interest in Indian affairs in general and in the Mutiny, as an anti-British war, in particular.

Jamāl ad-Dīn appears in these documents as a purely political agent, possibly having ties to Russia or at least carrying papers from someone outside Afghanistan. Presumably it was these papers and/or arguments by Jamāl ad-Dīn which convinced the Amir to take this young foreigner almost immediately into his highest counsels, possibly in the hope of getting the foreign military aid in the Afghan civil war. The exclusive influence that Jamāl ad-Dīn came to have with the Amir is the first of many such relations indicating the enormous persuasive and even charismatic powers of his personality and discourse. The only religious reference suggests unconcern with presenting a religious posture. This point may seem surprising only because of the subsequent success of the religious view of Jamāl ad-Dīn. As noted below, even in the years right after this. in Istanbul and Egypt, Jamāl ad-Dīn did not take a particularly religious position.

In the summer of 1868 A'zam Khān's military situation was deteriorating and his unpopularity increasing. Shīr 'Alī recaptured Qandahar in June and took Kabul in September, reestablishing himself as amir. A'zam Khān at first continued fighting, but then fled to Mashhad in the hope of getting Iranian support. He died, however, in the summer of 1869 on his way to Tehran. After Shīr 'Alī's capture of Kabul the British abandoned their policy of benevolent neutrality toward him and began to give him military and financial aid.

---

13 *Cabul Précis*, p. 47 (113).

The British documents indicate that Jamāl ad-Dīn made no attempt to stay with, or to rejoin, A'zam Khān, as the standard biography claims. Rather, he tried to regain as much as he could of his former stipend, position, and influence with the new amir, Shīr 'Alī. He apparently hoped to win over Shīr 'Alī to his anti-British program, a hopeless task in view of the new amir's British support.

Right after Shīr 'Alī's recapture of the capital in early September 1868, the "Cabul Diary" of the vakīl reported: "Syud Roomi has been taken and brought to the Ameer, who reproached him for having served a master like Azim Khan who was utterly regardless of religion. The Syud replied that he had never served Azim Khan willingly, and was now glad that the connection was severed. The Ameer provided him with a house and clothes, and ordered that he should have a monthly stipend."[14] Later in September. the vakīl noted, "Syud Roomi, who has hitherto made no progress, or gained no stability in the Ameer's Court, has now begun to gain the friendship of the courtiers." In a report at the end of September, 1868, the "Diary" included a translation of the first letter from Jamāl ad-Dīn to enter this narrative:

> From the day that the Amir returned to Cabul, Sayad Rumi . . . by reason of his friendliness to the cause of Amir Mahomed Azim Khan, has been staying as a guest with Sirdar Zulfiqar Khan. . . .
>
> He has now forwarded a letter to the Amir, of which the following is a copy:—
>
> "Oh! Amir of the Faithful, God be praised that you are a person of perception and sagacity. You know that Zulfiqar Khan is not a Hatim Tai or myself 'dust soiled and disheveled' . . . nor were you like Mahomed Azim Khan a breaker of promises. My day has extended into a month, and yet I have no settled post. You are a sea of courage. If from any cause you are suspicious of me, and your action is the result of observation, pray inform me. Hospitality is limited to days, not to months. One for a few days is a guest, beyond that he becomes dishonoured."[15]

It thus seems that the Amir Shīr 'Alī did not provide the house and stipend that he had reportedly promised.

---

14 "Cabul Diary," Sept. 8–10, 1868, p. 139.
15 *Ibid.*, half week to Sept. 28, pp. 38–39.

By the end of October Jamāl ad-Dīn was evidently fed up with waiting for his house and stipend, and, one may assume from his letters, for a post with some influence with the new Amir. He then wrote two letters of complaint, one to the Amir and one to the Amir's brother, on the basis of which the Amir became more suspicious of him and decided to expel him from Afghanistan. The "Diary," with its typical transliteration errors, gives the signature "Jumaludin" for each letter. Jamāl ad-Dīn's letter to the Amir's brother, Sardār Muhammad Aslam Khān, reads:

> "I beg to state that some time previous to this I presented a petition to you; but, owing to your attention towards the English, you did not acquaint the Ameer. The English are a people whom you have seen.
>
> "I beg to state my cash and property and necessaries of life have been expended in this business, and now neither the Ameer dismisses me that I may go whither I will, nor will he give me a house and subsistence. I am bewildered in the house of another, such a one as you know, neither can I trade in this country so as to provide means to set up house with: my means small, the object of my desire distant. As you know best, kindly acquaint the Ameer, so that he may either dismiss me or give me a fixed residence. Please God, in time he will see good service from me. I hope you will tear up this petition.
>
> "Farewell, Jumaludin, etc."[16]

The letter to the Amir in the same days is translated twice in the British documents, once in the "Cabul Diaries," and once in the *Cabul Précis*, with some minor variation. Below is the translation of the *Cabul Précis*:

> "Oh! Ameer of the faithful! Oh! Sutan of the Moslems! I beg to state I am fleeced. In this business I have spent 716 golden libras, each equal to 10½ Cabuli, and 240 golden majurs, each equal to 5 Cabuli. By this reason, I am now helpless, and have moved to the house of another; and if my means had not been expended, I should have purchased a house for myself. *Neither the Ameer will speak a word in regard to the appointed object*, nor will he appoint a res-

16 *Ibid.*, half week to Nov. 1, second enclosure, p. 55.

> idence or allowance for my support. I have not asked for crores or lakhs; after a month I can still speak a word on this matter, but without a resting place I cannot delay a moment. If you neither appoint me a residence nor pension (allowance), be so kind as to dismiss me, and grant me two lines just stating that so and so has been dismissed by me. Farewell."[17]

The "Cabul Diaries" translation, unlike the *Précis* one gives the signature, again as "Farewell, Jumaludin, etc." It also has this additional sentence in the translation: "Zurficar Khan has already refused me point blank 40 times."[18] Reporting on the letters and the Amir's consequent decision to expel Jamāl ad-Dīn, the vakīl writes: "The Ameer after perusing both letters has come to the decision that this person has an object of his own in view, and therefore considers his residence in Afghanistan to be full of hazard to the country; he has given him 12 tomans for road expenses, and ordered his immediate dismissal to Persia by way of Candahar and Herat."[19]

The two final entries in the "Cabul Diaries" on Jamāl ad-Dīn come in November 1868. The first tells of two further letters from him to the Amir and his consequent immediate expulsion:

> The arrangement which had formerly been made for the expulsion of Syud Roomee from Cabul (by the Government of Cabul) being still in abeyance, that individual has written two more letters to the Ameer, couched in very unbecoming words; consequently the Ameer being very much annoyed, has given the Governor of Cabul most peremptory orders for his immediate expulsion. Accordingly, he has this day been expelled, and is forwarded stage by stage towards Candahar under the charge of four sowars. On arrival there, the people are to expel him from their country to foreign territory.[20]

Finally, in late November, comes the last, and most interesting, report in which it is stated that Jamāl ad-Dīn had revealed himself to be a Russian agent and again requested leave to go to Bukhara. Since this apparently all rests on the word of one courtier it is far from be-

---

17 *Cabul Précis*, p. 65 (131).
18 "Cabul Diary," half week to Nov. 1, first enclosure, pp. 54–55.
19 *Ibid.*, half week to Nov. 1, p. 54.
20 *Ibid.*, half week to Nov. 12, 1868, pp. 505–507.

ing certain, but it is not out of line at all with information reaching the British from other sources. (As noted above, the desire to go to Bukhara is seen in an earlier British report and in two poems by Jamāl ad-Dīn in the *Documents*):

> It has been ascertained from one of the courtiers that Syud Roomee has plainly discovered himself to the Ameer as a Russian Agent and expressed a desire to make an alliance between the Russian and Afghanistan Governments. The Ameer told him: "I perfectly know my neighbours, and am well acquainted with the circumstances of the Russian Government; your further residence in this country is contrary to my pleasure." And he has, rejecting his request to be allowed to go to Bokhara, forwarded him stage by stage towards Candahar, from which place he is to be expelled from the country.[21]

These documents, which give much information not even hinted at in any of the biographies, provide enough material for several new conclusions and even more new questions.

Although the documents imply that Jamāl ad-Dīn was a Russian agent, we know both that the British representatives in Afghanistan were all too keen on finding such agents, and that Jamāl ad-Dīn on other occasions exaggerated his ties to foreign governments, so this point cannot be considered as settled. It is plausible that Jamāl ad-Dīn, who already evinced a strong hostility to the British, was simply trying to marshal all the persuasive power he could to turn the Amir to an anti-British policy. Since the Amir needed military aid from the outside just to maintain his internal position, Jamāl ad-Dīn would have done all he could to encourage him to turn to the Russians and break with the hated British. The possibility that Jamāl ad-Dīn had had contact with some Russian officials and had been encouraged by them cannot be dismissed, however.

The documents show that Jamāl ad-Dīn in 1866 was already concealing his Iranian origin. Perhaps he wished to present himself as a Sunni, or as a representative of the most powerful Muslim state, the Ottoman Empire. It is also possible that there was something in his Iranian past that he was concerned, now as later, to keep hidden, or that he had other reasons to claim to be from Istanbul.

---

[21] *Ibid.*, half week to Nov. 23, 1868, pp. 417–418.

The documents discredit Jamāl ad-Dīn's story, repeated by later biographers, that he was an adviser to Dūst Muhammad Khān and was in Afghanistan from 1863 or earlier. Neither the munshī, who had been at the court for several years, nor the other governmental informants had seen him before his arrival at court. His sudden influence with A'zam Khān may be explained by the papers he is reported to have brought with him, and/or by the extraordinary personal magnetism and mental ability that continued throughout his life to gain him access to men of power and intelligence.

The documents show that Jamāl ad-Dīn presented himself as a political adviser, rather than as a reformer or as a religious personage. Although the phrase in the English report, "apparently, follows no particular religion," may be a mistranslation from a Persian phrase meaning that he followed no particular school or sect, even the latter would indicate no particularly religious posture. The Afghan documents are among the many sources that suggest that at least until 1881, the date of the "Refutation of the Materialists," Jamāl ad-Dīn was not particularly concerned to present himself as a religious figure. On the other hand, his references to God and the Prophet in notebook entries, cited above, suggest that he believed in them and identified as a Muslim.

It is also significant that Jamāl ad-Dīn's first appearance in the light of history should involve not only political plans, but unsuccessful ones. Throughout his career he was frequently involved in complex political schemes. Despite his undoubted intelligence, he often exaggerated what one Muslim leader might accomplish in affecting powerful Western governments, and he was understandably impatient for dramatic results. An alliance of the Afghans with the Russians to fight the British was a typical goal, indicating not only some unrealism but also that his experience with the British had already made him see them as the main danger to Muslim independence and had moved him to search for almost any way to weaken British power over Muslims.

The Persian *Documents* provide additional information on the Afghan period of a more private and personal nature. The notebook entry by Jamāl ad-Dīn that records his dates of travel from the time he left the "makān-i musharraf," probably the Shi'i shrine cities of Iraq, in September–October 1865, through his stays in Tehran, Tus, Herat, Qandahar, and Kabul, the last of which he entered on October 24, 1867, and left on November 6, 1868, also gives the date of his final exile from Qandahar as December 11, 1868. (From Qandahar, the *Documents* confirm, Jamāl ad-Dīn went to Bombay.)[22]

More substantial material comes from Jamāl ad-Dīn's stay in Kabul from October 1867 through November 1868. There is a letter to the new Amir A'zam Khān at the time Jamāl ad-Dīn entered Kabul, saying that the Amir's call to him has arrived, that he is under the banner of the Amir's justice, and that he hopes the Amir will appoint for him a residence near his own—a request A'zam Khān soon met with lodgings in the castle compound of Bālā Hisār. There is a petition from Jamāl ad-Dīn to the Amir asking him to free a certain individual, unnamed, whom he says has been imprisoned through the enmity of some troublemaking ulama.[23] A petition that may refer to the same man is also photographed, from persons other than Jamāl ad-Dīn, asking the Amir to expel a certain man, called "Wahhābī," who is accused of being a corrupter of religion, and whom, it is said, the Amir's father had imprisoned and ordered expelled.[24] An incomplete photograph is included of a letter from A'zam Khān in answer to a letter from Jamāl ad-Dīn. The *Documents* describe the Amir's answer as one expressing sadness at Sayyid Jamāl ad-Dīn's proposed departure.[25] Very likely this refers to the period of coolness between the two and to Jamāl ad-Dīn's proposed leave, mentioned in the British documents. On the same subject is another answer to a letter of request from the Sayyid, written by the Amir. It says that the Sayyid's letter asking leave to go to Peshawar had arrived, that the Amir could not be happy in the Sayyid's absence, and if the Sayyid wished to sever their ties, the Amir would give permission under duress.[26] Why the Sayyid wanted to leave, and if and why he wanted to go to Peshawar, we do not know.

Finally, there are some notes written in dejection in the month of the Sayyid's expulsion from Kabul. One ends with a phrase he had used before and was to use again in the future, "the stranger in the land and the man exiled from the homeland, Jamāl ad-Dīn al-Hu-

---

22 *Documents*, p. 9, doc. 91; photo 8, and the date table.

23 *Ibid.*, pl. 3, photo 7; p. 5 and pl. 2, photo 4.

24 *Ibid.*, unnumbered photograph between numbers 89 and 90, pl. 41. The Wahhābīs were a strict puritanical sect who arose in Arabia in the eighteenth century and whose influence spread to India and beyond. According to an autobiographical fragment quoted below, some persons accused Jamāl ad-Dīn of Wahhābism.

25 *Ibid.*, p. 32, letter 123; pl. 40, photo 88.

26 *Ibid.*, p. 32, letter 124; pl. 40, photo 89.

sainī al-Istanbūlī." And another, "This was written in the home of Sardār Zū al-Faqār Khān in the utmost distress of mind and dejection of heart in the city of Kabul."[27] Many of the documents are signed with the place-of-origin name "Istanbūlī," and none with a name indicating either an Iranian or an Afghan origin.

A week before Jamāl ad-Dīn left Kabul, when he was under expulsion orders, he wrote an interesting statement in rhymed prose, showing that then as later his beliefs were a subject of confusion and controversy to others:

> . . . .
> The English people believe me a Russian (*Rūs*)
> The Muslims think me a Zoroastrian (*Majūs*)
> The Sunnis think me a Shi'i (*Rāfiḍi*)
> And the Shi'is think me an enemy of 'Alī (*Nāṣibī*)
> Some of the friends of the four companions have believed me a Wahhābī
> Some of the virtuous Imamites have imagined me a Bābī
> The theists have imagined me a materialist
> And the pious a sinner bereft of piety
> The learned have considered me an unknowing ignoramus
> And the believers have thought me an unbelieving sinner
> Neither does the unbeliever call me to him
> Nor the Muslim recognize me as his own
> Banished from the mosque and rejected by the temple
> I am perplexed as to whom I should depend on and whom I should fight
> The rejection of one requires affirmation of the other
> The affirmation of one makes the friends firm against its opposite
> There is no way of escape for me to flee the grasp of one group
> There is no fixed abode for me to fight the other party
>
> Seated in Bālā Hisār in Kabul, my hands tied and my legs broken, I wait to see what the Curtain of the Unknown will deign to reveal to me and what fate the turning of this malevolent firmament has in store for me.[28]

Although the use of rhyme may account for some of the charges mentioned by Afghānī, their range and similarity to later suspicions is striking.

---

27 *Ibid.*, p. 10 (notebook 1, p. 97); pl. 3, photo 10.

28 *Ibid.*, pl. 3, photo 9.

The documents from this period also provide an example of the difference between Jamāl ad-Dīn's private views and those he expressed in public for specific political ends. In a document photographed from a personal notebook, most of the contents of which date from Jamāl ad-Dīn's 1870 trip to Istanbul, Jamāl ad-Dīn expresses negative views about the Afghan leaders of the period which are similar to those expressed by some other observers. It is unclear whether the document was written for himself or as a private report to someone else, but in any case its contents contrast with his frequent praise many years later of Afghan courage, high principle, and spirit of independence. The item reads as follows (the passages in quotation marks are in Arabic, from the Koran or hadiths; [Traditions of Muhammad] the rest is Persian):

A Summary of the Condition of the People of Afghanistan

As it became clear to this writer: The case of the claimants to power in the land of the Afghans is like the case of the Jewish rabbis and divines, whose followers consider them as divinely appointed masters, and have recourse to them and supplicate them in all their needs, and consider all their possessions and wealth the property of that group, including even life and death, wealth and poverty, glory and baseness. The claimants to power also consider themselves to be divinely appointed, and with their corrupt understanding and faulty opinion they sometimes bequeath land to one, and sometimes expropriate land from another, "And those who consider themselves masters appointed by God, verily they are the lost ones."

And the case of the ignorant ones of that land who claim to have knowledge (*'ilm*) and the seekers after worldly goods (*tālibān-i dunyā*) of that land who imagine themselves to be seekers of knowledge [the ulama and religious students are intended], is like the case of wine and intoxicants. Although these persons have limited usefulness, such as instruction in the daily necessities of fast and prayer, nevertheless their harm is greater than their benefit, because they make many inroads and numerous changes, on their own account, in the laws of God, and they promulgate many orders for their personal desires. If someone says anything against the wishes of that group they issue the verdict of unbelief (*kufr*) upon him. "And those who do not order what God has revealed and ordered, they are the oppressors."

And the case of the *sardārs* and the officers and the officials

> of that land is like the case of the propped up things of wood, and the idols of the Quraish, "They have no power over anything, they do not live and they do not die." They do not have the common sense to unravel difficulties; nor are they possessed of bravery and courage, so that in the battlefields they could wield the sword. Like opportunistic Sufis they are time-servers; on whichever side they see a powerful one they quickly head their horse in that direction. Neither do they have a generous hand to give a coin to a poor one, nor a charitable tongue to say a decent word on behalf of a stranger. In vanity they are like Pharoah and Haman and in treachery they are Satan himself. "Those who sow evil in the land and are overbearing toward the people, they are the ones cursed by God and the ones who curse."[29]

This statement of Jamāl ad-Dīn's view of the Afghans shortly after his contact with them tallies quite well with what the British and Indians in Afghanistan during this period were reporting about the unreliability of many Afghan leaders. It contrasts, however, with the various idealized pictures of the Afghans as proud upholders of and fighters for independence which Jamāl ad-Dīn penned publicly at subsequent times, as in his *History of Afghanistan*, written in Arabic in 1878.

Internal evidence and a reference in the Egyptian newspaper, *Miṣr*, in January 1879 to the newly completed manuscript prove that Jamāl ad Dīn's *History of Afghanistan* was written shortly after the beginning of the Second Anglo-Afghan War of 1878–1880, whose outbreak is the last event mentioned in the book.[30] In 1878 Jamāl ad-Dīn was in Egypt, then threatened by growing British and French power, and it was natural for him, in his introduction to this *History*, to focus on the courage of the Afghans in resisting British demands, and to call upon other Muslim rulers to emulate the Afghans' anti-British resistance.[31]

---

29 *Ibid.*, pl. 4, photo 13–14. Pakdaman, p. 43, believes that the form and style of the original indicate that it is a report addressed to authorities outside Afghanistan.

30 Jamāl ad-Dīn Afghānī, *Tatimmat al-bayān fī tārīkh al-Afghān*, ed. 'Alī Yusūf al-Kirīdlī (Cairo, 1901), pp. 135–137 (henceforth called *Tārīkh al-Afghān*), where Jamāl ad-Dīn refers to 'Abd ar-Rahmān Khān as still living in Samarkand, a city he left in 1880; gives the date of the outbreak of war as 1295 (1878), but fails to note the flights of Shīr 'Alī from Kabul early in 1879 or of his death later that year. This proves the writing dates before 1880 and strongly suggests late 1878. This date is confirmed in *Miṣr* (Alexandria), II, no. 28, Jan. 9, 1879.

31 *Tārīkh al-Afghān*, pp. 11–12.

At the end of the historical part of his book, Jamāl ad-Dīn speaks very highly of Shīr 'Alī (the Amir who had expelled him), calling him beloved of the people for his good character and lack of oppression of his subjects. By 1878 Shīr 'Alī had broken with the British, and he was still ruler of Afghanistan when the Second Afghan War broke out, so Jamāl ad-Dīn's praise is not surprising. Jamal ad-Din also praises Shīr 'Alī's rival of the 1860's, A'zam Khān, as wise, experienced, and a lover of justice who was forced to commit oppression and injustice by necessity and uncontrollable events. Jamāl ad-Dīn does write of some of the military leaders during the Afghan civil wars as being treacherous and unreliable which, he says, forced A'zam to the error, fatal to his rule, of entrusting the leadership of the Qandahar army to his young son. Jamāl ad-Dīn adds that A'zam in matters of belief followed the Sufi path, believing in the unity of all existence.[32] This entire description probably reflects Jamāl ad-Dīn's experience with A'zam, although in his book Jamāl ad-Dīn says nothing of his own role or even presence in Afghanistan during that period.

One may surmise that, whatever his private reservations about the character of Afghan leaders, Jamāl ad-Dīn came in later years to admire them for their warlike qualities and especially for their resistance to British encroachments, both of which he hoped to see emulated elsewhere in the Muslim world. It was thus natural for him to focus in his public writings on those Afghan qualities that he wanted to inspire in others.

Enough is now known to give quite a clear picture of Sayyid Jamāl ad-Dīn's activities in Afghanistan. These activities are seen to involve anti-British plans, perhaps with the cooperation of the Russians, and not the religious and reform activities with which Jamāl ad-Dīn's name has come to be associated. The contrast between the actual Afghan period and what Jamāl ad-Dīn told his followers indicates a gap between his words, as repeated in the standard biography, and the historical record. The power of Jamāl ad-Dīn's personality, as indicated in his influence of Amir A'zam Khān, and his deep concern to rid the East of British imperialist influence are recurrent features of Jamāl ad-Dīn's life already appearing in bold relief in the real story of his Afghan stay.

32 *Ibid.*, pp. 130–136.

4

Istanbul: 1869–1871

THE *Documents* show us that after leaving Qandahar in December 1868, Jamāl ad-Dīn went to Bombay, where he was in March–April 1869 and that he was in Cairo in July 1869. The standard biography says, probably accurately, that he went from India to Cairo, where he stayed for forty days, and then to Istanbul late in 1869. On his activities in Bombay and Egypt in 1869 there is so far only the word of the standard biography. It says, after wrongly stating that Jamāl ad-Dīn left Afghanistan voluntarily to go on a pilgrimage to Mecca, that he was received in India with much honor but was not allowed by the British authorities to meet with the ulama, except under their surveillance. Then it states that in Cairo he frequented the leading Muslim university, al-Azhar, and also gave lessons to students.[1] Some biographies have more detailed accounts of this period and state that the British asked or forced him to leave India, but since all seem to rest on the word of Jamāl ad-Dīn and his disciples it is now impossible to say how accurate they are.

For Jamāl ad-Dīn's stay in Istanbul in 1869–1871 the standard biography is closer to the truth than for the preceding years, but is

[1] M. 'Abduh, "Biographie," in Jamāl ad-Dīn al-Afghānī, *Réfutation des matérialistes,* trans. and ed. A.-M. Goichon (Paris, 1942), p. 38 (henceforth called 'Abduh, "Biographie"), and E. G. Browne, *The Persian Revolution of 1905–1909* (Cambridge, 1910), p. 6. *Documents,* pp. 16, 20.

still characterized by a distortion of uncomfortable facts. There are contemporary Turkish sources that provide a better record of events. and these have been used effectively by Niyazi Berkes.[2] On the basis of Berkes's work, the sources he used, some additional Ottoman documents, and the few items on this period in the *Documents,* one may reconstruct some of Jamāl ad-Dīn's words and actions in this Istanbul period. Compared with later periods, however, little reliable documentation is yet available, even in Istanbul itself.

We do not know why Afghānī, as he now began to call himself, went to Istanbul at this time. It may be guessed from the reformist and modernizing tone of his talks and actions there that he was impressed by Istanbul as the center of strength and modernization in the Islamic world. His stay in Istanbul coincided with the last stage of the *tanzimat* reform period. In these years major reforms in education and law were launched, and the two leading reforming ministers reached the end of their lives—Fuad Paşa in 1869 and Âli Paşa in 1871. Afghānī's membership in the modernizing official Council of Education, his ties to the new university, the Darülfünun, and the content of his speeches show this aspect of his interest in Istanbul.

It may also be true that he was attracted to Istanbul as the foremost capital of the Islamic world. By 1869 Pan-Islamic ideas were already beginning to be in the air, although they came forward with strength only after the death of Ali Paşa in 1871 and the subsequent accession to direct rule of the reigning Sultan, Abdülaziz. Appeals to the Ottoman Sultan for help in the face of conquering unbelievers, it will be recalled, had already been voiced earlier by Indian Muslims. The Muslim states of Central Asia, when faced by Russian conquest, responded even more strongly in the direction of the Sultan. In the 1860's, as the Russians conquered Central Asian Muslim lands, their rulers began to send envoys to Istanbul for aid, and Sultan Abdülaziz was encouraged to put forth claims to a caliphal position of the early Islamic type, implying some kind of sovereignty over all Muslims. How far such movements, still in their early stages, affected Jamāl ad-Dīn at this time it is as yet impossible to state. It

[2] Niyazi Berkes, *The Development of Secularism in Turkey* (Montreal, 1964), pp. 181–188; the most important passages are quoted below. Berkes limits himself to discussing Jāmal ad-Dīn's relations to the university and the attacks made on it, since this is the topic relevant to his narrative. I read several primary Ottoman sources before Professor Berkes's book appeared and came to conclusions similar to his about Afghānī's 1869–1871 stay in Istanbul.

should be noted, however, that all his known associations on this trip to Istanbul were with Westernizers and modernizers who were not especially tied to Pan-Islam. If Pan-Islamic ideas did appeal at all to Afghānī this early, it was probably in the way they were soon to appeal to the "Young Ottoman" liberal constitutionalist and modernizer Namık Kemal—as a means to cut down oppressive Western influence and encroachments in Muslum lands, but not as a bar to Western-inspired ideas.[3] Such activities and speeches as have come down to us have no reference to Pan-Islam at this time or for many years thereafter.

Afghānī, although not as important at this time as the standard biographies claim, does seem to have entered quite soon into some fairly high educational circles. We find him giving a speech at opening ceremonies of the new university in February 1870, only a few months after his arrival. The other speakers were all men of importance in the field of modern education—Safvet Paşa, Minister of Education; Münif, President of the Council of Education; Tahsin, director of the University; and Jean Aristocles, member of the Council of Education. How Afghānī rated such an invitation is unclear, or should be to those who look critically at his biography. The standard biography tells us that Afghānī was famous at the time of his arrival. Yet, in view of what is now known about Afghānī's earlier years, what could he have been famous for at this time? As a man who in Afghanistan claimed to be from Istanbul and only now began to call himself an Afghan? Hardly. The fact that he expected acceptance as an Afghan shows that his past history must have been unknown to most of those he now dealt with.

It seems, however, that Afghānī soon after his arrival made contact with some fairly prominent men in Istanbul. The standard biog-

[3] On Namık Kemal—a figure in some ways parallel to Afghānī as a modernizer, Pan-Islamist, and defender of Islamic traditions—see Şerif Mardin, *The Genesis of Young Ottoman Thought* (Princeton, 1962), chap. x; and Berkes, *op. cit.*, pp. 209–222. There is no evidence of direct interaction between his ideas and Afghānī's, but it might have occurred. On the development of Pan-Islamic feeling from the 1860's onward and its connections with Central Asia, see especially Roderic H. Davison, *Reform in the Ottoman Empire 1856–1876* (Princeton, 1963), pp. 270–279, and the sources cited therein. As Davison notes on pp. 274–275; "Pan-Islamism was, in part, manufactured in the Muslim world outside of the Ottoman Empire. Some Muslim Turks, threatened by Russia and looking to the sultan for aid, hoped he would declare a jihad. Some Indian Muslims, wistfully longing for their vanished glory, also wanted a jihad, but directed against Britain. Among them were a group of exiles living in Istanbul, on stipends granted by the Ottoman government, who had fairly wide Muslim connections."

raphy's story of an early meeting with Âli Paşa is so far unconfirmed, but may be true. More certain is his close contact with Tahsin Efendi, the director of the new university. This scientist, materialist, and freethinker faced constant attacks as an unbeliever, particularly after the growing Islamic reaction in Istanbul which began about 1871.[4] Another advanced modernizer with whom Afghānī had contact both on this trip and later was Münif Efendi, President of the Council of Education, to which Afghānī was appointed in July 1870. Jamāl ad-Dīn was also known to the reformist Minister of Education, Safvet Paşa. The *Documents* include a poem by Afghānī, "A Panegyric to Rüşdi Paşa, the Ottoman Minister of the Interior," and give the name of Afghānī's host in Istanbul as Ismail Bey Vahbi, Inspector at the Ottoman Mint.[5]

In the absence of decisive evidence one may speculate that Afghānī's eloquence, intelligence, and charismatic personality had much to do with his relatively rapid advance—an advance that was paralleled in many of the countries he visited. It is also likely that as a self-styled member of the Sunni ulama Afghānī could assist the modernizers as a man who might help give religious sanction to their educational innovations.[6] What is most clearly demonstrable about

---

[4] On Tahsin Efendi and the University, see Mardin, *op. cit.*, pp. 222–224; and Davison, *op. cit.*, pp. 249–250. These books are most useful for background to Afghānī's stay, although on Afghānī himself they follow the stories given by Turkish and other secondary authors. A summary of Tahsin's life stressing the radical and materialist ideas of this close colleague and backer of Jamāl ad-Dīn is in Berkes, *op. cit.*, pp. 180–181.

[5] *Documents*, pp. 11–12 and 86–87, include the poem to Rüşdi Paşa and one other entry regarding this stay in Istanbul, an entry in Afghānī's personal notebook that reads, "I am residing in the city of Istanbul in the Sulṭan Fātiḥ quarter in the house of Hājji Bek Vahbī and I am studying a book of *jafr* [cabalistic letter divination], Jamāl ad-Dīn al-Husainī al-Afghānī." Investigation of the papers of men known to be in contact with Jamāl ad-Dīn, if such papers exist, might add to our limited information about this stay. Unfortunately, the Ottoman Archives do not yet list any documents about Jamāl ad-Dīn during these years.

[6] In a private letter of December 31, 1964, Professor Berkes writes: "I will not be surprised if one day you come across documents showing that A. was in Turkey before he went to Afghanistan. There does not seem to be much mystery in how A. succeeded to be received by Ali Paşa. We have the example of Vambery. We must also discount A.'s boastings. . . . As to how A. made himself so easily known and distinguished in Turkey in 1870? Did he? We must, at least for the time being, free ourselves from the conventional belief that A. was received enthusiastically and given high honors as soon as he arrived. Was this true? I doubt it. He must have struggled inch by inch to make himself known, and he seemed to have a gift for this, just as a gift to lose it after a while. He seemed to become acquainted with Tahsin, and of course with many others. Tahsin was Bektashi and a known zindiq. Men like Saffet, Münif needed men to side with themselves as what I call "pseudo-

this period is Afghānī's connection with efforts to promote modernized education as a means of self-strengthening.

Afghānī's interest in the strengthening of Islamic countries lasted throughout his life. His concentration on the educational aspect of this problem in Istanbul in 1870 may have been an adaptation to circumstances of the late *tanzimat* period of government-sponsored reforms. In 1870 the type of anti-British militancy Afghānī had promoted in Afghanistan had little chance of influencing official Ottoman circles. On the other hand, a new law for modernized education had just been passed, a modern university, the Darülfünun, was being formed under it, and educational reform might have seemed the best area for Afghānī to promote some of his convictions and also bring himself into a position to influence official policies.

What is clear from Afghānī's words in this period is that he was impressed by the power of the West; that he saw this power as largely due to Western scientific and educational advances; and that he thought the Muslim world must revive its former openness to intellectual innovation, including borrowing from non-Muslims, if it was to revive. With his own knowledge of philosophy and of heterodox ideas it was easier for him to make the transition between his education and an advocacy of science and reason as man's best guides than it was for someone with a more traditionally orthodox background. The Islamic philosophers, with whom Afghānī was well acquainted, had spoken out for science and reason as the best guides for intelligent men, and it was easy for Afghānī to see in the long stifling of philosophy and science in the Islamic world the prime cause of its decline. Afghānī may also have seen the practical advantages of a modern education while in India. His interest both in Muslim self-strengthening and in rationalist philosophy could have turned him to concern with modern and advanced education.

Afghānī's first recorded speech, at the opening ceremonies of the new university in Istanbul, the Darülfünun, reveals him as a man already dedicated to Westernization for self-strengthening ends. On

---

ulema". Until then no one could be called Ulema unless he was in the official ledgers of the Shaikhul Islam. Tahsin was one stolen from this closed guild. (He was dismissed from the ledgers later.) Jamal would be an ideal person to play the role of this pseudo-ulema which Tanzimatists badly needed. . . . If he is not an Ottoman alim, he is an alim of international Islam. He removes his Persian attire, puts on a Turkish turban and a gown, and here you have a modern enlightened real Islamic alim. In the opening ceremony his Arabic speech certainly impresses the people and makes the official ulema green with envy and rage."

this occasion, in February 1870, after praising the Sultan and his ministers, he went on:

> My brothers: Open the eyes of perception, and look in order to learn a lesson. Arise from the sleep of neglect. Know that the Islamic people (*milla*) were [once] the strongest in rank, the most valuable in worth. They were very high in intelligence, comprehension, and prudence. They faced up to the most difficult things with respect to work and endeavor. Later this people sank into ease and laziness. *It remained in the corners of the madrasas and the dervish convents; to such a degree that the lights of virtue were on the point of being extinguished; the banners of education were about to disappear.* [Italics mine] The suns of prosperity and the full moon of perfection began to wane. Some of the Islamic nations came under the domination of other nations. The clothes of abasement were put on them. The glorious *milla* was humiliated. All these things happened from lack of vigilance, laziness, working too little, and stupidity. But now, thanks be to God, and thanks to the Commander of the Faithful, the Shadow of the Lord of the Worlds—may God strengthen religion and the state through him and through his prudent and mature ministers—the Islamic *milla* is beginning to awaken in this country; there is light on every side. Before long this light will dazzle the eyes. The glorious sun of the Muhammadan Sultanate rose from the West; its light spread over all countries.
>
> Brothers, the Commander of the Faithful and his ministers, who walk on the right path, opened for us schools, houses of wisdom (*ḥikma*), homes of education, and universities. As for us, let us learn all branches of science. Let us mount the ladder of humanity. Let us free ourselves from ignorance and animal qualities. Because of these good actions [of our leaders] it is our duty to pray for them and thank them. We must endeavor to acquire perfect knowledge leading us to glory and honor. Let us take care not to waste our lives uselessly. Let us not miss opportunities. Let us not spend our lives on useless things by putting aside things which are useful to us and to our *milla*. Let us not lose the glory of past and the rights of future generations. We must turn all our attention to elevating with honor our *milla* and the sons of our race. We must go to the paths leading to the stages of wisdom. Let us endeavor to raise the honor of the *milla*.

> My brothers, are we not going to take an example from the civilized nations?[7] Let us cast a glance at the achievements of others. By effort they have achieved the final degree of knowledge and the peak of elevation. For us too all the means are ready, and there remains no obstacle to our progress. Only laziness, stupidity, and ignorance are obstacles to advance. These things I say openly. Finally I thank God for the grace of allowing me to find refuge and to settle in this just country. Let [Him] make you and me appreciate the value of the good fortune and qualities of this state. May He never withdraw his grace from all of us. May He never allow this state to decline.[8]

The speech already shows a feature that was to typify Afghānī, as it did certain other contemporary modernizers of Islam, such as Namik Kemal—the interpretation of the Islamic *milla* in almost nationalist terms. This single *milla* is seen as one that should follow the example of the various "civilized *millas*," that is, the Christian nations of Europe. This transition from traditional Islamic ideas to a kind of nationalist appeal, including nationalist reminders of the original glorious golden age from which the community had declined, was facilitated by the traditional concern of Islam with questions of power and politics. During his life Afghānī was able to move back and forth in his appeals to local and Islamic "nationalisms," and it seems quite possible that he was not aware of any contradiction between them—a contradiction that came to the fore as a practical question only with the development of separate Arab and Turkish nationalisms early in the twentieth century.

Despite the use of traditional and ornate phraseology, the speech is essentially an appeal for modern education, for taking an example from the only "civilized nations," those of the West. and for an abandonment of the centuries-old concentration in religious institutions such as madrasas and dervish convents. This picture of Afghānī as a Westernizer is supported by his membership in the Council on Education, a secular body devoted largely to the implementation of a new law for modernizing educational institutions

[7] The use of the word "civilized" to distinguish Western from Islamic nations marks a Westernizer. The word was apparently translated from nineteenth-century Western usage, in which it was similarly limited to advanced Western nations.

[8] *Takvim-i Vekayi* (Istanbul), 22 Zilkade, 1286/Feb. 23, 1870, translated from Arabic into Turkish in Osman Keskioğlu, "Cemâleddin Efgânî," *İlahiyat Fakültesi Dergisi*, X (1962), on pp. 96–97.

of all levels. He probably knew less of modern education than the other members, but was perhaps useful to them as an alim (religious scholar). A personal check indicates that Afghānī's name was not included as a member of the Council in the official Ottoman Yearbook (*Salname*), but the fact that Afghānī was a member for only a few months probably explains the omission. The Ottoman official gazette, *Takvim-i Vekayi*, announced the appointment of "Cemal [Jamāl] Efendi" to the Council in August 1870, and he was apparently removed late in 1870 following an incident at the university when a talk there by Afghānī brought on attacks by the religious authorities.[9]

Afghānī's talk late in 1870 at the Darülfünun which resulted in his expulsion from Istanbul has been subject to increasing distortions by his biographers. The basic standard story is found in 'Abduh's biography, which claims that the chief Ottoman religious leader, the Şeyhülislam, Hasan Fehmi, was so jealous of Afghānī for reasons of self-interest that he was waiting to seize upon his words and distort them to force his expulsion. Other biographers add that Afghānī was feared as a religious rival by the Şeyhülislam, and several Turkish sources attribute the closing of the university soon afterward to this incident.[10] The reality, as revealed by contemporary documents, and recently independently unraveled by Berkes, is somewhat different.

The standard biographies generally speak of Jamāl ad-Dīn's lecture at the Darülfünun in the late autumn of 1870 as if it were an important public event. In fact, it was one of a long series of public lectures announced for the month of Ramadan of that year as part of the public educative functions of the university. There is no evidence that Jamāl ad-Dīn had any widespread fame before the lecture, or that his lecture was well attended by notables, as the standard stories

---

9 Ali Canib, "Cemaleddin Afghanî," *Hayat* (Ankara), III, 77 (May, 1928), 3–6, notes both the absence of Jamāl ad-Dīn's name from the official yearbooks (*Salnames*), which I have checked at the Cambridge University Library, and the *Takvim-i Vekayi* report of Cemal [Jamāl] Efendi's appointment on 26 Jumada I, 1287/August, 1870. On his removal, see Safvet Paşa's letter below.

10 The common Turkish view, including the erroneous statement that the university (Darülfünun) was closed in December, 1870, is repeated in Mardin, *op. cit.*, p. 223, and n. 106. Ali Canib, *op. cit.*, investigated the question of the University's closing in contemporary Turkish newspapers; his conclusions are given below. Most of the relevant parts of this article and of many other Turkish writings on Jamāl ad-Dīn and the University are reprinted in Mehmed Zeki Pâkalın, *Son Sadrâzamlar ve Başvekiller*, Vol. IV (Istanbul, 1944), pp. 140–156, as part of the section on Safvet Paşa.

claim. Nor is there any evidence that the lecture was approved beforehand by various high individuals, including Safvet Paşa the Minister of Education, as is often said.

The official gazette, *Takvim-i Vekayi,* announced the series of lectures two months before they were to be given, noting that their aim was to give elementary knowledge of the sciences to the general public. The series was a continuation of a series undertaken the preceding Ramadan, before the university had opened. The original announcement also asked for qualified volunteers to deliver the scheduled lectures, covering the sciences of physics, chemistry, meteorology, astronomy, biology, medicine, natural history, geology, and agronomy among the natural sciences. Among the social and humanistic disciplines there were scheduled lectures on economics, jurisprudence, ethics, and literature, as well as one on "Progress of the Sciences and Industries," which was presumably the heading under which Jāmal ad-Dīn either volunteered or (as the standard biography states), was requested by Tahsin to talk. The original plan by those scheduling the lecture was for a practical lecture on modern industries and inventions (subtopics listed included "new inventions . . . military equipment, mathematics, weights and measures")—not at all the purview of that part of Jamāl ad-Dīn's talk which can be reconstructed. He may have been unable to talk technically on modern industry and science, and in any case changed the subject into a more traditional one, with unfortunate consequences.[11]

---

11 Ali Canib, *op. cit.,* quotes in full the long announcement of the forthcoming lectures from the *Takvim-i Vekayi* of 1 Rejeb, 1287/Oct. 8, 1870, two months before the lectures were to be given, along with the request for volunteers to give the lectures. Professor Berkes wrote me in a private letter of Dec. 31, 1964: "As you know the Afghani biographers never forget to mention the fact that A. submitted his text to Saffet and Münif. I doubt that this is true. They seem to mention this with particular purpose. At any rate, Saffet in this letter [see below] appears not well acquainted with A. And I tend to believe this. Well, then, we may still ask how had he been chosen to lecture if he was not known even to Saffet Paşa. Yes, it was possible. There were public open lectures, and it was announced that not only the series were open to listeners but also to those who would like to give a lecture. It is conceivable that A. himself applied for lecturing and certainly Tahsin encouraged that. It would be an opportunity not to be missed by A. to bring himself into the public. The outlines of the lecture were already published, perhaps long before A. applied for lecturing. It sounds very modern and Western. Probably Tahsin prepared it. It would be a survey of the progress of modern sciences and the role of this progress in recent technological developments. How could a young man who had not seen a thing about these sciences and a bit of its technological wonders lecture on such a subject. Did he improvise? Did he read? Did he write in Persian and talk in Turkish? All con-

Jamāl ad-Dīn was thus scheduled to give one of a series of fourteen originally planned public lectures, and since his talk came near the beginning of Ramadan, it must have been one of the first talks of that year. What Jamāl ad-Dīn said and what followed has generally been taken from apologetic accounts, notably 'Abduh's biography. 'Abduh gives a text of a small part of Jamāl ad-Dīn's talk. Some later authors, like E. G. Browne and the Turkish Islamist poet, Mehmet Âkif, not indicating that 'Abduh's biography is their source, repeat 'Abduh's story and translate 'Abduh's text as a direct quotation from Jamāl ad-Dīn, as do various more recent Western and Turkish authors. The standard story, taken largely from 'Abduh, but with additional errors taken mostly from Zaidān, appears as follows in Browne, from where it goes forth, often in more elaborate and distorted form:

> Instead of proceeding to Mecca, Sayyid Jamālu'd-Dīn decided to visit Constantinople, where he was well received by 'Ālī Pasha, the Grand Wazīr, and other notables of the Ottoman capital. Six months after his arrival he was elected a member of the *Anjuman-i-Dānish*, or Turkish Academy [untrue], and in Ramadān, A.H. 1287 (Nov.–Dec., 1870) he was invited by Taḥsīn Efendi, the director of the *Dāru'l Funūn* or University, to deliver an address to the students. [Also untrue, it was a lecture for the public.] At first he excused himself, on the ground of his inadequate knowledge of Turkish, but ultimately he consented. He wrote out his speech in Turkish and submitted it to Ṣafvet Pasha, who was at that time Minister of Public Instruction, and also to Shirvānī-Zāde, the Minister of Police, and Munīf Pasha, all of whom approved it. [Almost certainly untrue.] Unhappily the Shaykhu'l-Islām, Hasan Fehmī Efendi, was jealous of the Sayyid, whose influence he was eager to destroy [almost certainly untrue; see below], and when the latter de-

jecture. At any rate, inevitably A. did only the one thing that he was able to do: a traditional disputation on reason vs. revelation. If he had given a survey of the new sciences from astronomy to psychology and had said something about the importance of these for those countries who were in need of material strength against the Europeans it would not create a ripple among the Ulema, because this kind of talk they had already been subjected to for many years. But A. gave a beautiful pretext by his tactlessness and by his ignorance of the subject he undertook. Saffet Paşa, in his regrets over mixing men like A., 'a man of unknown ideas and of unknown activities' into the efforts of establishing a new institution, is well reflecting what I imagine to be the picture."

> livered his address to a large and distinguished audience, which included many eminent Turkish statesmen and journalists, he was watching carefully for some expression on account of which he might be able to impugn the speaker's orthodoxy. Now the Sayyid in his address compared the body politic to a living organism, of which the limbs were the different crafts and professions, and he described the king, for instance, as corresponding to the brain, ironworkers to the arms, farmers to the liver, sailors to the feet, and so on. Then he said: "Thus is the body of human society compounded. But a body cannot live without a soul, and the soul of this body is either the prophetic or the philosophic faculty, though these two are distinguished by the fact that the former is a divine gift, not to be attained by endeavour, but vouchsafed by God to such of his servants as He pleases . . . , while the latter is attainable by thought and study. They are also distinguished by this, that the prophet is immaculate and faultless, while the philosopher may go astray and fall into error. . . ."[12]

Jurjī Zaidān, C. C. Adams, and others go further with this story, saying that the Şeyhülislam was jealous of the growing popularity of Afghānī, whose modern ideas on education were threatening his income and position—a point implied by 'Abduh. In addition to the points in the above standard story already disproven, two important ones remain: What did Afghānī actually say, and what caused religious leaders in Istanbul to attack him so violently that he was ordered to leave the country? For it is true that the religious authorities reacted strongly and the Şeyhülislam declared him a heretic.

The closest thing to a contemporary text of part of Afghānī's talk is found in a book written shortly afterward by an alim, Halil Fevzi,

---

[12] Browne, *op. cit.*, pp. 6–7. Recent Turkish authors often take Afghānī's words from an article by Mehmet Âkif in the newspaper *Sıratı Müstakim* (Istanbul), no. 90, May 13/27, 1910, p. 207. Among other places this article is quoted as definitive by Osman Ergin in *Türkiye maarif tarihi*, Vol. II (Istanbul, 1939), p. 466, who claims that Âkif after great effort had established the true text of Afghānī's talk. Since Âkif's entire article is a close paraphrase of 'Abduh, and Âkif's quotation from Afghānī's talk is identical to the small part of the talk that 'Abduh cites in his biography of Afghānī, and lacks the sections given in the more complete citations below, it is clear that 'Abduh is Âkif's source as well as Browne's. Although 'Abduh's brief citation may be essentially accurate as far as it goes, it does not, as it pretends, cover those parts of Afghānī's talk which caused the trouble. For a translation of 'Abduh's apologetic version see his "Biographie," pp. 40–41.

to refute Afghānī. The words quoted from Afghānī in Persian, probably the language in which Afghānī drafted his talk, do include the ideas cited by 'Abduh, but have important points that he omits. The genuineness of Fevzi's quotations is indicated by their compatibility not only with 'Abduh's version but with partial contemporary reports of Afghānī's words and with Afghānī's known views. A summary of the longer quoted passages follows: The highest crafts are those of the prophet, philosopher, caliph, doctor, and jurisconsult. Not all epochs have need of a prophet, for a single religion and law can nourish many ages and peoples. But each age has need of an especially experienced and learned man, without whom human order and survival will be deranged. This learned man can dominate his period.

"The noblest crafts," Fevzi quotes Afghānī as saying, are those of the prophet and the philosopher. The philosopher's mission is equal to that of the prophet. The two differ only on three points, which Fevzi quotes from Afghānī as follows:

> "Firstly, whereas for the prophet, the truth of things is attained by the paths of inspiration and revelation, for the philosopher it is attained by means of arguments and proofs. Secondly, whereas the prophet cannot commit errors, the philosopher can. Thirdly, the teachings of the philosopher are universal, and do not take into account the particularities of a given epoch, whereas those of a prophet are conditioned by the latter. That is why the prescriptions of prophets vary: they prescribe one order for one time and establish another in a different circumstance in conformity with what circumstances permit, whereas the teachings promulgated by the philosopher do not change either because of a change in situations or of men, or because of the passage of time. . . ."[13]

Afghānī's talk, despite its statement that the prophets are infallible, points to the intellectual superiority of the philosophers, whose statements have universal validity, over the prophets, whose statements are colored by the circumstances of an epoch. Jamāl ad-Dīn's argument that every age needs an especially learned man, without whom human order and survival may be endangered, goes beyond

---

13 Afghānī's words are cited in Persian in the Turkish translation of Halil Fevzi, *Suyūf al-qawāṭi'* (Istanbul, 1872). Thanks to Homa Pakdaman for showing me her microfilm and translation of these passages which she summarizes or quotes in Pakdaman, pp. 47, 197. She points to possible Shaikhi influences on pp. 46, 196.

the statements of most Muslim followers of rationalist philosophy and may, as noted above, reflect the influence of the Shaikhi idea that every age has need of a perfect and learned man in the absence of the infallible imam.

Professor Berkes, who has read and analyzed all of Halil Fevzi's difficult book about Afghānī's talk, argues:

> Although Jamal had indicated three differences between prophethood and philosophy, these distinctions were inconsistent with his view of prophecy as an art like philosophy or science. By his own definition, every art is acquired by experience, and the revealed truths of religion are not in contradiction to those of reason but are merely expressed by different methods or in different terms. Therefore his thesis amounted to the old view of the philosophers that, because the common people were incapable of reason, the prophetic art is needed to convey truths through irrational symbolism. In other words, the prophet interprets the Book and its laws in terms of his own time, by means of an art acquired through experience and not through the open or hidden inspiration of God. According to such a view, the Prophet Muhammad's *shari'a* was neither God-given nor immutable since, as the lecturer said, "There is no need for law-giving prophets in every age because God's *shari'a* is sufficient for several ages; but men need rational regulators of life in every age." Since he also asserted that man's survival was possible by means of technology and the arts and sciences of civilization, there seemed to be no need for prophets.[14]

Berkes may be wrong to discount Afghānī's statement that prophets are divinely inspired, but the point is at least ambiguous. In any case, many Islamic philosophers believed that the intellectual and educated elite could in effect forego prophecy, whatever the prophet's inspiration, since a literal observance of the words and laws brought by the prophets was intended only for the uneducated masses, while the elite's symbolic interpretation of the prophets' words was identical to the conclusions of human reason.[15]

It seems clear that Jamāl ad-Dīn equated philosophy and prophecy as the souls of knowledge, and that, though he made a distinction im-

14 Berkes, *op. cit.*, pp. 185–186.

15 See Nikki R. Keddie, "Symbol and Sincerity in Islam," *Studia Islamica*, XIX (1963), 27–63, and the sources cited in it.

plying that prophecy was infallible, this distinction was implicitly contradicted by his other arguments, particularly the notion that prophets' words differed with time and circumstance. That the main charge against him by Halil Fevzi and other religious enemies, that he said prophecy was a craft, is true is indicated also by the contemporary letters of the Minister of Education, Safvet Paşa. Safvet may or may not have been present at the talk, but was concerned to determine what had been said, since Jamāl ad-Dīn's talk was used by many of the ulama as an excuse for fierce and ultimately successful attacks on the university and its director. Safvet Paşa was himself a strong proponent of the university and Westernization.

Already a few weeks after the talk, in December 1870, when Tahsin Efendi was removed as director of the university, Safvet Paşa wrote to his son, Re'fet Bey:

> The director of the university, Tahsin Efendi, was removed from his office of director last week, because of his foolish utterances made at various places, and his name was also erased by the office of the Şeyhülislam from the register of those learned in religious law. As to Jamāl ad-Dīn al-Afghānī, because his lecture at the University, in which, dividing the crafts into two classes, inspired and acquired ones, he included prophecy in the first class, gave rise to arguments, his discharge from membership in the Council [on Education] was also decided upon.[16]

In a later letter, Safvet Paşa reiterates the statement, saying that the University was closed partly because "an Afghan of unknown ideas and circumstances" had called prophecy a craft.[17]

---

16 Quoted in Pâkalın, *op. cit.*, pp. 155–156.

17 This letter, whose difficult text is often quoted but not explicated in Turkish works, was, according to Pâkalın (*op. cit.*, p. 150), written by Safvet Paşa in 1878, when he was ambassador in Paris, to his friend, Sadullah Paşa; Pâkalın gives a more complete text than do most references (pp: 150–155), including Safvet Paşa's bitter reflections about the lack of progress in modern education. Pâkalın names as his source the Istanbul newspaper *Servetifünun*, nos. 78–1553, 79–1554. The part of the letter dealing with Jāmal ad-Dīn may be translated as follows (the sudden transition from an incident at the inaugural ceremonies at the University to Afghani's talk on the crafts is in the original): "The affair of the prayer which occurred during the inauguration of the University had entirely slipped from my mind. Your reminding me of it has once again caused grief. How could it be otherwise when a person who became the chief of the Murad Mulla Convent (*tekke*) in order to enlighten people; who inherited the various books of his father, a Mesnevi-reader and educated man; who [the son], with a rather long beard and

It appears certain that Afghānī did call prophecy a craft, and that his argument would put philosophy on the same level of importance as prophecy, and would imply that the elite could, even without prophecy, reach the higher realms of reason and science. Over a decade later Afghānī was to express himself to an elite French audience in a manner largely hostile to religion and entirely favorable to science and reason in his "Answer to Renan." He did not go nearly so far on the earlier occasion, but his opponents among the ulama grasped the danger to them of his argument.

It is difficult to reconstruct exactly how much of a stir was caused by Afghānī's talk and the resultant controversy, but enough is known to show that the talk was a matter of some public dispute. In 1928

---

with the Uzbek (dervish-) crown on his head, had his hands kissed by people; taking the Turkish words read that day by me, by Müni Efendi, and Jamāl ad-Dīn Afghānī for Koran verses and for noble hadiths, raised his hands [as a sign of prayer]. But no sooner had he said: 'What in this meeting attended by angels [too] has been read,' than the late Şirvanizade said: 'You are doing this solely in order to insult religion,' and reproached your servant [the writer] with staring eyes. This and the fact that the ignorant shaikh took things read in Turkish for Arabic, are they not strange? If we consider, the late [Şirvanizade] above-mentioned ought to have trampled him under foot and to have expelled him after breaking the crown on his head. I was not acquainted or on friendly terms with the above-mentioned [head of Murad Mulla Tekke]. Nor did I know that the late Shaikh of Murad Mulla had such a bearded son who took over his place after his death. His invitation occurred only on Cevdet Paşa's suggestion. You see, dear Sir, that the evil act of a shaikh who, taking the Turkish words for Arabic, asked God to accord the audience heavenly reward, and the fact that an Afghan of unknown views and circumstances said that prophecy is a craft (*ṣan'at*), having intended to say that it is of God's making (*ṣun'*), were the causes of the closing of a new educational institution after it was created with the utmost difficulty. Really, as you have put it, education in our country is very backward. On the other hand, our Christian subjects are miles ahead of us in matters of education. If it goes on in this way our subjects will make still more progress thanks to the new institutions, and we will remain in the darkness of ignorance. . . ."

In his letter of December 31, 1964, Professor Berkes explains the above letter as follows: "Saffet claims that upon Cevdet's recommendation or invitation the young successor-son of Murad Molla was among the invited dignitaries. Apparently, Saffet, Münif and Tahsin had decided to avoid the traditional *dua* for which they would need an official alim. However, it seems that the arif instinctively raised his hands, probably during Afghānī's Arabic speech, for a *dua* and *Amin's.* Saffet and others become embarrassed, exchange angry looks, one of them, Shirvanizade Rushdi Pasha murmurs and says: you have done all these mockeries to insult Islam, etc. . . . [Saffet] seems to have purposefully spoken in a vague manner in connection with the accusation made later that he was responsible for Afghani's blunders because he should have seen A.'s text. . . . Saffet Paşa, in his regrets over mixing men like A., 'a man of unknown ideas and of unknown activities' into the efforts of establishing a new institution, is well reflecting what I imagine to be the picture.

the Turkish writer Ali Canib, reporting the words of someone who had spoken to a Mahmud Kâmil Efendi (who heard Afghānī's talk), wrote that there was a considerable disturbance during the talk. Mahmud Kâmil Efendi is also reported as saying, as do other sources, that the Şeyhülislam Hasan Fehmi was not present, but that those who were present were summoned to the Şeyhülislam because of the disturbance and were asked what Jamāl ad-Dīn had said. The man reporting Mahmud Kâmil's words says that Afghānī had not said a word against religion. Ali Canib also reports that those who knew Jamāl ad-Dīn said he was very excitable, that he wanted his dispute with the Şeyhülislam to be adjudicated; and refused to keep silent as some of his friends advised—this last point is identical to one made by 'Abduh and may emanate from his biography.[18]

Halil Fevzi's book gives further information on the controversy. According to Fevzi's book, after Afghānī's speech was made, a commission of scholars assembled and discussed how to show up Jamāl ad-Dīn's heresy, and the Fevzi book was a result of this discussion. The book's introduction claims that the book was written by imperial-caliphal order to wipe out harmful traces left among simpleminded Muslims by the absurd and provocative statements of Jamāl ad-Dīn. The two chief charges in the book are that Jamāl ad-Dīn had called prophecy a craft and that he had indicated that prophets were equal in rank to what Fevzi calls "the despicable philosophers." Fevzi says that Jamāl ad-Dīn's opinions—that philosophy is a craft, that it is sufficient to make a man blessed in this world and the next, and that the wisdom of the Prophet agrees with philosophy—mark him as an unbeliever and apostate who, if he does not repent, must immediately be killed. The Fevzi book also includes the text of the Şeyhülislam's anathema against Afghānī and of the dismissal order issued by (or in the name of) Sultan Abdülaziz.[19]

Among Afghānī's papers are copies of two Istanbul newspapers that comment on the incident. One is the Turkish language *Basiret*

---

[18] Ali Canib, *op. cit.*, also reprinted in Pakalın, *op. cit.*, pp. 141–142; and 'Abduh, "Biographie," p. 42.

[19] According to Ergin, *op. cit.*, p. 466, the Sultan's decree *(irade)* is reprinted on p. 5 of Halil Fevzi's book, and the Şeyhülislam's order *(emir)* on p. 6. Fevzi's work was published after Jamāl ad-Dīn's expulsion, but since the work argues for his execution it seems reasonable to assume that it was at least begun while Jamāl ad-Dīn was still in Istanbul. Passages from the book are reprinted in Ergin, *op cit.*, pp. 465 ff. and Ali Canib, *op. cit.*, both also reprinted in Pakalin, *op. cit.*, pp. 142–149.

of 13 Ramadan 1287/December 7, 1870. It contains a brief announcement that Tahsin Efendi and the Afghan, Cemal Efendi, "having voiced some abhorrent expressions in a form entirely against and contrary to the Islamic religion and the illustrious shari'a," have been dismissed from their positions, and that the prime minister has named as director of the Darülfünun Kâzım Efendi, who is possessed with religious firmness and other qualities.[20] The other newspaper contains the only contemporary defense of Jamāl ad-Dīn against his accusers that has yet been unearthed. It comes from the Arabic language Istanbul newspaper *al-Jawā'ib* of December 14, 1870. It states, in its entirety:

> It was noted in the Turkish [language] newspapers that the eminent personages Tahsin Efendi, the director of the Dār al-Funūn, and Shaikh Jamāl ad-Dīn al-Afghānī, one of the members of the Council on Education, stated things that are forbidden in their talks at the Dār al-Funūn, and therefore they were dismissed from their duties. Some people claim that the aforementioned Shaikh denied prophecy. I learned from a letter that reached us from someone who heard [both] their talks that this is untrue, and that the talk of the Shaikh was clear on the superiority of prophecy over philosophy, and from lack of space we are delaying the quotation of this letter until a future time.[21]

The last sentence may suggest fear of censorship, and it is unlikely that the letter was published. If the letter was printed, neither Afghānī nor anyone else has provided us with a copy. In any case, it is evident from the reconstruction of Afghānī's talk above that Afghānī was circumspect enough that he might be reported to have clearly stated the superiority of prophecy to philosophy, as the letter of defense states, while at the same time others might have caught implications derogatory to prophecy.

These two newspapers, as well as Ali Canib's article and an additional contemporary treatise against Afghānī, indicated that the standard biography is correct in reporting that there was some public disagreement and disputation over Afghānī's talk. On the other

---

20 This entry and the following one are among a group of the Jamāl ad-Dīn papers in the Majlis Library, Tehran, which were omitted from the *Documents* catalog.

21 *al-Jawā'ib*, no. 484, 20 Ramadan 1287 Dec. 14, 1870.

hand, the standard biography appears to exaggerate the scale of this disputation, as the newspaper articles are very brief and in all the hostile articles yet unearthed, including one quoted below, the dismissal of Jamāl ad-Dīn is subordinated to that of Tahsin. There seems no reason to accept 'Abduh's picture of general public excitement over Jamāl ad-Dīn's talk and widespread argumentation in the newspapers, with some of them lining up with Jamāl ad-Dīn and others with the Şeyhülislam.[22]

There remains a question: Why should the ulama have chosen to launch such violent attacks on Jamāl ad-Dīn, and, through him, on the university at a time when more radical, scientifically educated, and enlightened Westernizers than he occupied positions of power and influence and were not subject to such violent attacks. Much evidence shows that three of Afghānī's fellow speakers at the opening of the University—Safvet Paşa, Tahsin, and Münif—were all more radical Westernizers than Jamāl ad-Dīn at this time, yet Afghānī was subject to the earliest and fiercest attacks. How can this be explained? One might first be tempted to return to the standard biography's claim of jealousy on the part of the Şeyhülislam. But, looking at the actual situation of that time, Berkes has denied this argument most effectively:

> The story of the Şeyhul-Islam's jealousy probably originated with Jamal. His belief that Fehmi feared him as a possible successor may merely reflect a far-fetched ambition. In the history of the Ottoman Empire there had been only one case of a non-Ottoman Persian appointed to this office; this was an exception which had occurred four centuries earlier. Until the twentieth century the Şeyhul-Islams were chosen from among the members of the Ulema corps who had attained the highest rank (frequently in the judiciary). Jamal was a foreigner, a young man of about thirty-three, who had not yet achieved prominence, and did not belong to the Ulema corps in Turkey or elsewhere. The very fact that he was considered for an appointment to the High Council of Education . . . one of the new, eminently secular institutions, and not to a body traditionally representing the religious institution, indicates that he was not regarded as belonging to the Ulema category.

22 Abduh, "Biographie," p. 42. The additional manuscript mentioned was by the father of 'Abd al-Qādir Maghribī, who names it in his *Jamāl ad-Dīn al-Afghānī* (Cairo, 1948), p. 30.

> That Afghani invited protest because of his proposals to make education more general is also highly unlikely. The members of the High Council of Education were far ahead of him in their liberal views. It does not seem that he had yet been made a permanent member of the Council or had had time to acquire an intimate knowledge of educational problems. As the opening address of the Minister of Education shows, the founders of the university were far more radical than Jamal al-Din gave any suggestion of being.[23]

Berkes goes on to show that Jamāl ad-Dīn was essentially an incidental figure in a dispute that allowed the religious conservatives to get at their real target—the new university. Most Arabic and Western biographies do not mention that the successful attacks on Jamāl ad-Dīn were accompanied by equally successful attacks on the university's director and finally the university itself. Afghānī is linked to the university's director in several references in contemporary Istanbul newspapers to the events mentioned above, however. The English-language *Levant Times* wrote on December 10, 1870, that Jamāl ad-Dīn and the University's director, Tahsin Efendi, had been dismissed, and quoted a Turkish newspaper, referred to as the *Ruzname* [*Ceride-i havadis*?] as saying:

> "Several times in different circumstances the Turkish director of the Darul Funun as well as Jemalledin Efendi have been uncircumspect enough to preach atheism publicly in their teachings and to deny publicly the possibility of divine inspiration in a man chosen by God—which is contrary to the faith of Islam so they have been dismissed by order of the Grand Vizier, who has named Kasim Efendi director of Darul Funun. This measure, which appears to be a little severe, is in conformity with good order."[24]

Continuing the quotation from the *Ruzname*, the French-language Istanbul newspaper, *La Turquie*, went on:

> "When a man is officially charged with teaching in public doctrines in conformity with the State Religion, by virtue of freedom of conscience he can undoubtedly think and be-

23 Berkes, *op. cit.*, pp. 183–184.

24 *Levant Times* (Istanbul), Dec. 10, 1870. Thanks to Professor Stanford Shaw for this reference.

> lieve what he wants, but it is not permissible for him, without abusing the confidence with which the Authorities have honored him, to substitute his own views for the teaching with which he is entrusted, or else he must withdraw and not receive a salary for saying white, when he is being paid to say black."[25]

Sacrificing the two men most under attack did not appease the conservatives, however, who were most concerned when an institution of higher education presumed to preempt fields hitherto reserved to religious institutions, such as law and philosophical subjects which touched on religious areas. As long as the secular institutions had been purely technological or scientific they aroused no outcry, but the university posed a new kind of threat. While it is not true, as some of Afghānī's Turkish biographers maintain, that the university was closed because of Afghānī—such a statement overrates his importance at that time—his talk did give the conservatives a handle with which to attack more effectively the hated institution. That Afghānī's talk was not the immediate cause of the university's closing is shown by the fact that the university was not, as is often said, closed right afterward, but existed for at least a year longer, and its final closing was not connected with any known incident.[26] It was probably part of the general reaction following the death of Âli Paşa in September 1871.

There still remains the question of why Afghānī's words in particular, among all those who had positions in higher education and held advanced views, were singled out for virulent attack by the ulama, to the point that government officials felt forced to remove him from the university and from the Council on Education and to exile him from the country. Why should this talk have caused such trouble in a country that had been undergoing a fairly rapid process of secularization and Westernization for over forty years, and where men with even more advanced views than Afghānī were holders of far higher posts than his? Here again, Berkes appears to have provided the most convincing answer, namely, that as long as the Westernizers spoke of modern ideas in purely secular terms and did not reopen old dogmatic controversies, the ulama found difficulty in at-

[25] *La Turquie* (Istanbul), Dec. 9, 1870.

[26] Berkes, *op. cit.*, p. 185. Details from contemporary Turkish newspapers showing that the Darülfünun was not, as some later writers said, closed right after the incident involving Jamāl ad-Dīn are given by Ali Canib, *op. cit.*

tacking them, while Afghānī, by openly adopting a position already marked as heretical and discussing prophecy itself in philosophical terms, gave the ulama an ideal wedge to attack him and the university as heretical institutions. In summary, Berkes says:

> The incident served, in reality, as a denunciation by the Ulema of the attempt to establish a university which would be the secular duplicate of the *medrese*. Afghani was an incidental figure in the conflict. By discussing the problem of modernization in the familiar language of scholastic philosophy and theology, he gave the Ulema a chance to state their position in their own terms. . . . when the monsieurs of science began to talk of teaching humanistic studies such as history, philosophy, economics, law, and even Roman law, that was too much! To the men of the *medrese*, the Dar-ul-funun showed its real intentions by daring to include even *fiqh* and *kalam* among its godless and blasphemous arts. If once established, the university would be the *medrese*'s real rival—in subject matter, in its human material, in intellectual function—in everything. Here, not in the imaginary fame of the "man of unknown parts" [Safvet Paşa's phrase] from Afghanistan, lay the source of the Şeyul-Islam's crusade. If there was any reason why a particular issue was made of Jamal al-Din's lecture, it was because he presented a thesis which had been well refuted since the time when *kalam* triumphed over philosophy. By using this age-old controversy and its terminology, he unknowingly served the purposes of the Şeyhul-Islam, who welcomed a pretext to attack the new institution.[27]

The religious aura that Jamāl ad-Dīn carried as a turbaned Sunni alim probably also increased the hostility to him of religious conservatives, and moved the Şeyhülislam to demand more extreme treatment than he would have for a non-alim.[28]

Since some of the ulama in both Iran and India discussed and even taught ideas propounded by Muslim philosophers, Jamāl ad-Dīn's past experience in the Eastern Islamic world might not have prepared him for the strong reaction his words aroused from the religious establishment. His contacts largely with modernizers and

---

27 Berkes, *op. cit.*, p. 187.

28 Personal note from Professor Bernard Lewis. See his article, "Ḥasan Fehmī," *EI*², Vol. III, fasc. 43–44, pp. 250–251.

his appreciation of the high level of modernization in the Ottoman Empire may have rendered him all the more surprised at the conservative reaction to his talk. There is no doubt, either, that some of Jamāl ad-Dīn's enemies exaggerated his derogation of the Prophet, seizing upon one part of his words and ignoring those that spoke of the Prophet's infallibility and divine inspiration. Nevertheless, in the Ottoman context of a centuries-old rejection of the Muslim philosophers by the ulama, one can understand the Turkish newspapers' reference to Jamāl ad-Dīn as "uncircumspect" and Safvet Paşa's dismay. The point was not that Jamāl ad-Dīn's views on religion were so radical or unheard of in the Ottoman Empire, but rather that the modernizers had generally got their way partly by avoiding open attacks on established religious beliefs of which the unique position of the Prophet was one of the most important. Yet, while seeing Berkes's point that Jamāl ad-Dīn's speech actually played into the hands of the reviving traditionalist powers, one must also add that Jamāl ad-Dīn's vulnerability on this occasion was to be one of his strengths in the future. One reason for his strong influence with both intellectuals and masses at many points in his life was surely the fact that he could voice new ideas and needs in traditional and Islamic terms. It was nothing very new for someone to express the need to learn from the West. One of Jamāl ad-Dīn's many new contributions was to reconcile this call with a system of thought that, though not orthodox according to most Sunni scholars, had a traditional means of appearing orthodox, was considered Islamic by its proponents, and was developed indigenously in the Islamic world, rather than being brought in by foreigners who were widely hated as infidels, conquerors, and oppressors.

The system of thought to which Jamāl ad-Dīn attached his new teachings came largely from the Islamic philosophers, who had provided a way to reconcile rationalist and even scientific notions with a positive role for revealed religion. They had also provided a justification for precautionary dissimulation in public, a lesson that Jamāl ad-Dīn was to apply more thoroughly after his Istanbul experience than before, although even before this he had sometimes disguised his origins and experience. To understand Jamāl ad-Dīn's appeal in the Islamic world to both the "masses" and the "elite" one must take into account various Islamic and Iranian traditions of precautionary dissimulation of which he was a master. If one cannot accept the mythical view of Jamāl ad-Dīn as a pure hero, one must also avoid judging him, on the basis of a political morality worked out to suit nineteenth-century Western liberalism, as a dishonest opportunist. Afghānī had a genuine and passionate concern with self-strengthening and independence for the Islamic world, and he took considerable risks and made numerous sacrifices for these ends. The means he chose to bring about his ends were, however, somewhat special—characteristic not only of a certain type of visionary leader, but also of important traditions in his background to which not enough attention has hitherto been given.[29] Realizing from bitter experience in Istanbul and possibly even before then that the conservative ulama, who regarded innovation as heresy, would attack him severely for his rationalist view of religion, he sometimes adopted precautions sanctioned by his tradition in order more effectively to arouse Muslims to the need for intellectual revival and political activity to achieve independence, unity, and strength.

The exact date of Jamāl ad-Dīn's enforced departure from Istanbul is not yet known, but his own notations, reprinted in the *Documents*, show that he was still in Istanbul some time in Shawwal 1286/January–February 1871, and that he returned to Cairo in Muharram 1287/April–May 1871.[30] Some biographers say that he went to the Hijaz on his way from Istanbul to Cairo, and one document suggests that this may be true. This is a Turkish letter dating from Istanbul in early March 1871, and if, as seems likely, Jamāl ad-Dīn carried it with him, he must still have been in Istanbul then, but about to leave. It is signed with a seal by a certain "Sayyid Ḥasan," and the beginning of the letter, perhaps including the recipient's name, has been torn off. It says that Sayyid Jamāl ad-Dīn, ex-member of the Council of Education, who has been dismissed by imperial order wishes to make the pilgrimage [to Mecca], and is going there with this aim. The letter praises the intelligence and achievements of Jamāl ad-Dīn, says he should be given every consideration, and asks that he be introduced to the honored amir [the sharif of Mecca].[31] No other details about this intended trip are available, the Afghānī is next encountered in Egypt in the spring of 1871, at the beginning of his eight-year stay in Cairo.

[29] On these traditions see Keddie, "Symbol and Sincerity," and *Islamic Response*.

[30] *Documents*, p. 18. Muhammad 'Abduh (*Mudhakkirāt al-imām Muḥammad 'Abduh*, ed. Tāhir at-Ṭināḥī [Cairo, 1963], p. 34), dates Afghānī's entry into Egypt slightly earlier, which is possible, as Afghānī's own note refers only to the date of his entry into Cairo.

[31] *Documents*, p. 71, doc. 236.

5

Egypt: 1871–1879

Afghānī as Teacher: 1871–1876

For Afghānī's fruitful eight-year stay in Egypt from 1871 to his expulsion in 1879 the biographer has long been provided with several firsthand accounts in Arabic and supplementary information in Western languages. Yet even here there has been some distortion of Afghānī's activities, resulting partly from too much reliance on the words of a small number of Afghānī's disciples and admirers, especially on 'Abduh's biography. Herein are given the main outlines of Afghānī's life in this period as revealed in a variety of memoirs and documents.

Afghānī's firsthand biographers agree that he returned to Egypt, where he had spent about forty days in 1869, largely because he had made a favorable impression on Riyāḍ Pāshā, the prominent Egyptian politician. Riyāḍ offered Afghānī a stipend that came out of official rather than personal funds, and it was apparently on this that Afghānī lived while in Egypt. The Egyptian stipend seems to have involved no specific duties. Afghānī reached Cairo in the spring of 1871, and lived in that city during his eight-year stay. There is disagreement in the early accounts as to whether Afghānī taught for a short time at the traditional Muslim university, al-Azhar.[1]

---

[1] Abduh insists ("Biographie," p. 43) that Afghānī never taught at the Azhar, but later acquaintances, such as 'Anḥūrī, say that he did. Adīb Isḥāq (in Riḍā, *Tārīkh*, p. 40) unlike 'Abduh, says that the government paid Afghānī a stipend in

Afghānī lived in Egypt during a period that became increasingly propitious for his agitation against Western, and particularly British, encroachments into Muslim lands, and for the awakening of Muslims. Without going into the details of this much-discussed period, a few generalizations can be made. The 1870's saw the culmination of the contradictory activities of the Egyptian ruler, the Khedive Ismā'īl, which on the one hand helped modernize Egyptian society, and on the other reduced Egypt to virtual bankruptcy and Western control. The prodigious loans of the Khedive were spent partly on modernization, and the new schools and cultural institutions that marked his reign helped spread enlightenment and modern ideas, as did the theater, literature, and newspapers that began to flower with or without his direct encouragement. On the other hand, the machinations of European lenders and the Khedive's improvidence meant a skyrocketing and ultimately unmanageable debt, which, along with the newly opened Suez Canal, gave the European Powers increasing interest in the control of Egyptian government and finances.[2] This situation reached crisis proportions only in the late 1870s, and in that period Afghānī, among others, was moved to come forward as a political agitator and proponent of change. Up to about 1878 he seems to have concentrated on teaching and encouraging his disciples to form newspapers to propagate his ideas.

One of the earliest documents from Afghānī's Egyptian stay is a passport from the Iranian consul for a trip to Istanbul.[3] This trip was apparently never carried out, but the document indicates that Jamāl ad-Dīn believed or hoped that his exile from Istanbul was to be a brief one.

---

order that he be a teacher, but that he retired to teaching in his home after a quarrel with some of the Azhar ulama. Afaf Lutfi al-Sayyid Marsot informs me that she found in the Egyptian archives a document authorizing the payment of 10 Egyptian pounds a month to Afghānī out of government funds, but it did not indicate that this money was being paid for teaching or for any specific service.

2 Among the works on this period are Georges Douin, *Histoire du règne du Khédive Ismaīl*, 3 vols. (Rome and Cairo, 1933–1941); A. Sammarco, *Histoire de l'Egypte moderne*, Vol. III, *Le Règne du Khedive Ismaīl* (Cairo, 1937) (an apologetic account); David S. Landes, *Bankers and Pashas* (Cambridge, Mass., 1958); Lord Cromer (Evelyn Baring), *Modern Egypt*, Vol. I (London, 1908); M. Sabry, *La genèse de l'esprit national égyptien (1863–1882)* (Paris, 1924), and *L'empire égyptien sous Ismaīl et l'ingérence Anglo-Française (1863–1879)* (Paris, 1933). Cromer (pp. 58–59) notes the increased financial oppression brought by contact of an Oriental ruler like Ismā'īl with Western lenders and adventurers. See also P. J. Vatikiotis, *The Modern History of Egypt* (London, 1969), Pt. I.

3 *Documents*, p. 76, doc. 295, and photo 149.

Muḥammad 'Abduh, Afghānī's closest Egyptian disciple and later a prominent Muslim reformer, has provided memoirs relating to the beginning of Afghānī's stay in Cairo, partly written by 'Abduh himself, and partly told to his own disciple and biographer Rashīd Riḍā. These memoirs are more accurate than 'Abduh's biography of Afghānī. According to the memoirs, Jamāl ad-Dīn arrived in Egypt in March 1871, a date compatible with Afghānī's notation that he reached Cairo in Muharram/April, the month 'Abduh says he met him. 'Abduh says he then began to take lessons from Afghānī in mathematics, philosophy, and theology, and brought other people to take such lessons. The shaikhs of al-Azhar University and the masses of their students, says 'Abduh, began to speak out against Afghānī and his followers, and to claim that the teaching of certain subjects led to the upsetting of true beliefs and introduced errors that would bar the soul from happiness in this world and the next. 'Abduh writes that Afghānī first of all drew to him a group of young students, that later officials and notables also frequented his gatherings, and that the differing reports of his teaching made people eager to meet him and know what he was like. Afghānī taught mainly at his own home, concentrating on the rational sciences.[4]

The religious controversy aroused by Afghānī's teachings during his first years in Egypt is confirmed in memoirs by Ibrāhīm al-Hilbāwī, another Egyptian disciple and later a prominent lawyer. Hilbāwī says that he was an Azhar student no older than sixteen when Afghānī landed, and that he had come to hate Afghānī's name because he believed, along with most of the Azhar shaikhs, that Afghānī was an apostate (or atheist—*mulḥid*) who had come to Egypt to lead people into error and create a party to spread atheism. Hilbāwī recounts first meeting and hearing Afghānī in 1873, after which he completely changed his negative opinion and became one of Afghānī's pupils and admirers.[5]

In Egypt Afghānī apparently took his disciples at whatever point he found them and was able in many cases to lead them to his own combination of Islamic philosophy, concern with self-strengthening via religious and other reforms, and hostility to Western encroach-

---

4 Muḥammad 'Abduh, *Mudhakkirāt al-imām Muḥammad 'Abduh*, ed. Ṭāhir aṭ-Ṭināhī (Cairo, 1963), pp. 34–46.

5 Ibrāhīm Hilbāwī, "Ahamm ḥadīth aththara fī majrā ḥayatī," *al-Hilāl*, XXXVIII, I (Dec., 1929), 138–140. Also reprinted in Anwar al-Jundī, *ash-Sharq fī fajr al yaqẓa* (Cairo, 1966).

ments. That he was not at this time teaching primarily a *defense* of Islam is shown in numerous sources. It is also suggested by the character of many of his closest disciples in Egypt—Syrian Christian writers, themselves often unorthodox, like Adīb Isḥāq, Salīm al-'Anḥūrī, and Louis Ṣābūnjī; a Jewish author, Ya'qūb Ṣanu' (James Sanua); and the young Muḥammad 'Abduh, who in this period was first inclined to Sufi monism and then, under Afghānī's influence, toward a rationalist and philosophical interpretation of Islam. These and other students and disciples of Afghānī were to play a prominent role in journalism and politics, inspired to effective public activity largely by their experience with Afghānī, who may be credited with influencing many of the most important young writers and political activists in Egypt, including also the nationalist leader of the early twentieth century, Sa'd Zaghlūl. The originality and nonconformity of Afghānī's teachings aroused some of the conservative ulama, although Afghānī seems to have been more circumspect in his public statements on religious matters in Egypt than he had been in Istanbul. According to A. Albert Kudsi-Zadeh, who has made a special study of Afghānī's Egyptian period: "When Sa'ad Zaghlūl joined the circle in 1875, for some time he and Hilbāwī kept their association with Afghānī a secret in order to avoid the dangers of the campaign being directed against him and his supporters."[6]

In addition to teaching at his home, Afghānī used to spend long hours holding forth at cafés, especially at Matātyā Café, at that time one of the best cafés of Cairo, where he would drink tea, smoke cigarettes, and gather around him large groups of disciples and curious onlookers as he expounded his ideas.

From 'Anḥūrī, Adīb Isḥāq, 'Abduh, and others who knew Afghānī in Egypt we can get some idea of the nature of Afghānī's teaching during this period, a knowledge that is supplemented by the *Documents*. When these sources are approached without a preconception that Afghānī was known for religious appeals and Pan-Islamic teaching, it can be seen that neither of these features characterized Afghānī's words before 1879.

Salīm al-'Anḥūrī, who knew Afghānī for a time in Egypt and spoke to several of his other disciples before writing his brief biogra-

---

[6] Kudsi-Zadeh, "Legacy," quoting Jundī, *op. cit.* Kudsi-Zadeh here and in recent articles, listed in the bibliography gives further information on Afghānī's disciples, as do Irene Gendzier, *The Practical Visions of Ya'qub Sanu'* (Cambridge, Mass., 1966), and Kedourie, *Afghani.*

phy of Afghānī, states that Afghānī's Pan-Islamism and religious appeals in the 1880's represented a change in policy. After describing the freethinking notions that 'Anḥūrī says Afghānī learned in India and continued to teach in Egypt, 'Anḥūrī says that after Afghānī was expelled from Egypt (by order of the new Khedive Taufīq in 1879): "News of him was withdrawn from this author until there appeared in Paris the paper *al-'Urwa al-Wuthqā* under his name . . . and ['Anḥūrī] realized from its method that he had returned to adherence to the true Islamic religion and *had gone over to a new course which would gain him the favor and approval of the Islamic world* [italics mine]."[7]

Although the change of policy may not have been quite as dramatic as 'Anḥūrī states, it did take place. Afghānī was always a defender of Islamic countries against British physical encroachments, but this defense did not take on a strongly religious and Pan-Islamic guise until Pan-Islamic notions were already much in the air for reasons largely independent of Afghānī's influence.

If it was not Pan-Islam that Afghānī taught in Egypt, what was it that made his home such a popular gathering place for young Egyptian and Syrian intellectuals? To a large degree his popularity must have been a tribute to his eloquence and charismatic personality. 'Abduh and several others refer to him in worshipful terms, even in private correspondence, evincing an emotional and almost religious attachment that cannot be attributed simply to the intellectual content of his teaching. From the time of his first appearance on the historical scene in his relations with the Afghan Amir A'zam Khān, Afghānī evoked this type of adoration. Such personal devotion and discipleship, though it had some unusual aspects with Afghānī, was no unique phenomenon in the Islamic world, and was particularly characteristic of the esoteric, Sufi, and philosophical trends that had influenced Afghānī. Islamic heterodoxy has often ascribed divine, quasi-divine, or mysterious powers to its leaders. Also, the frequent necessity for secret oral teaching of heterodox, Sufi, and philosophical views has made the teacher or Sufi elder occupy an especially exalted role—such a teacher is no mere expositor of texts that might be perfectly understood without his help by an intelligent disciple. He can be, rather, the revealer of a hidden truth, of the secret meaning behind the literal words of many texts, which he alone may be capable

---

7 'Anḥūrī in Riḍā, *Tārīkh*, p. 48.

of expounding. Such guides have often called forth a total and seemingly idolatrous devotion from their disciples in the Islamic world. A similar exaltation of teachers was sometimes found among Sunnis (and among non-Muslims), but was particularly characteristic of the mystically oriented among them. Jamāl ad-Dīn's magnetism was, many sources say, particularly expressed through his striking and penetrating eyes.

Why, aside from personal magnetism, should Jamāl ad-Dīn have been capable of arousing this enthusiastic reaction among young Syrians and Egyptians, who themselves had notable traditions in both the religious and educational fields, and who had other channels to the modern world than this mysterious self-styled Afghan? Rashīd Riḍā has alluded to what seems to be a crucial answer: In the Persian culture area of the Islamic world, the philosophical tradition remained alive until modern times, whereas in the Arabic-speaking world it had virtually died out centuries before.[8] Both the words of Afghānī's disciples and the books of philosophy which the *Documents* show he taught in Cairo demonstrate his concentration on the ideas and methods of the Islamic philosophers. To the Muslims among his disciples at least, one of Afghānī's appeals was that he could point a path to rationalism, science, and fresh interpretations of Islam—a path indigenous to the Islamic world and not involving a wholehearted acceptance of the superiority of the aggressive and threatening foreigner. To both the Muslim and the non-Muslim he sometimes spoke of the glories of ancient Egypt, just as later in India he spoke of the glories of ancient India, and in Iran of ancient Persia. In all three instances he found within the local tradition alternatives to complete acceptance of the culture of the foreign unbeliever who was threatening physical conquest. This sort of argument has subsequently been characterized as apologetic, but in Afghānī its motives seem different from those of later apologists. Subsequent apologetic writing was usually concerned with defending the virtues of Islam before an increasingly Westernized and skeptical audience. Afghānī, at least with his most intimate disciples, tended rather to lead men away from traditional beliefs toward an open-mindedness and rationalism that had an indigenous pedigree. This pedigree made his

[8] Riḍā, *Tārīkh,* p. 79. Riḍā notes, probably accurately, that Jamāl ad-Dīn's outlook was a mixture of ancient and modern philosophy and Sufism. He also notes the closeness of Jamāl ad-Dīn's views and methods to those of the Bātinīs (esoterics) in religion.

philosophy easier to accept than unadorned Westernism, partly because it provided a framework for rationalist interpretations of the Koran and of religious dogma. The esoteric tradition had practical value for Jamāl ad-Dīn and other Muslim intellectuals and activists. It reinforced pride in their own tradition, which was shown to contain much more than dogmas unrelated to modern scientific needs, and it provided a model for creating a fresh interpretation of Islam which might have as much claim to legitimacy as various past interpretations. For activists like Jamāl ad-Dīn and many of his disciples, the esoteric tradition also formed a bridge between the elite and the masses, uniting them in one common effort to defend the abode of Islam against Western imperialist unbelievers. Much as esoteric Ismā'īlī doctrines had in earlier centuries provided different levels of interpretation of the same texts, binding masses and elite in a common program, so Jamāl ad-Dīn's practice of different levels of teaching could weld the rationalist elite and the more religious masses into a common political movement. Jamāl ad-Dīn's wedding of Islamic and Iranian philosophical and esoteric traditions to practical political goals thus provided something that could be given neither by the true traditionalist nor the pure skeptic and Westernizer.

In addition, Jamāl ad-Dīn's hatred for Western and particularly British encroachments in Muslim lands coincided with a growing mood in the Middle East. From about 1871 on the Ottoman Empire entered a period of reaction against the West which culminated in the reign of Sultan Abdülhamid II, who came to power in 1876. In North Africa and Egypt the profiteering and aggressiveness of some Westerners were producing their own reactions. For those who wanted to advance scientifically and technically in order to combat the West without adopting purely Western attitudes, Jamāl ad-Dīn's practice of introducing new ideas through a new interpretation of tradition had a special appeal.

Another of the reasons for Jamāl ad-Dīn's success seems to have been his ability to take a disciple when he found him—in Sufi ideas, Christianity, skepticism, or whatever—and to lead him from there up to the point the teacher deemed prudent and possible. Partly because of this practice we have many different assessments of Jamāl ad-Dīn's true thought and teachings, even from a single period such as the Egyptian one.

Some insight into this teaching process is given by the story of the closest and later the most important of Afghānī's disciples in this period, Shaikh Muḥammad 'Abduh. Before meeting Afghānī 'Abduh had already been repelled by the sterile religious education of his time, and had been won over to a Sufi interpretation of religion. The *Documents* and evidence from Afghānī's disciples show that Afghānī too was acquainted with and influenced by Sufism. Jamāl ad-Dīn must first have encouraged and deepened 'Abduh's Sufi interests, and only later have led him to more radical ideas. As 'Abduh's biographers, Michel and 'Abd al-Rāziq put it:

> Jamāl ad-Dīn exercised on Shaikh 'Abduh a very great influence . . . making him aware of his own strength and opening a new world; which was no longer that of mystic dreams but that of realities. At the moment of their meeting Shaikh 'Abduh was completely given over to Sufism; endowed with that psychological intuition that leaders of men possess and, thanks to his encyclopediac knowledge, Jamāl ad-Dīn knew how to capture the young scholar on his own terrain and lead him bit by bit not only to a more rational conception of religion, but also to problems of a more immediate interest, those that arose for the Orient out of its relations, each day closer, with the West.[9]

Rashīd Riḍā has published 'Abduh's later account to him of his first meeting with Afghānī, almost immediately after the latter's arrival in Egypt. 'Abduh, says Riḍā, recounted that,

> he learned of the arrival of Jamāl ad-Dīn from a Syrian fellow student; the latter told him that there had just arrived in Egypt a great Afghan savant who was staying at Khān Khalīl. This news made Shaikh 'Abduh very happy, and he told his professor Shaikh Ḥasan aṭ-Ṭawīl and proposed to him that they go together to visit the new arrival. This they did, and they found him dining. He graciously invited them to share his meal, but they declined the invitation; he then set to questioning them on certain verses of the Koran and on the explications of these verses by the commentators and the Sufis. Then he commented on these verses himself, and his explication filled Shaikh 'Abduh with admiration and with sympathy, because explication of the Koran and Sufism

[9] B. Michel and M. Abdel Razik, trans., Mohammed Abdou, *Rissalat al Tawhid* (Paris, 1925), Introduction, p. xxiii.

> were the two delights of his eyes, or, as he used to say himself, the two gates of his happiness.[10]

'Abduh then read under Afghānī's tutelage various works of theology, Sufism, philosophy and science. At first Afghānī apparently did not lead 'Abduh away from Sufism, since 'Abduh's first written work, the *Treatise of Mystic Inspirations*, published in 1874, is pervaded with Sufi monism. In its preface 'Abduh gives a glimpse of the profound effect Afghānī had on him, an effect other disciples often echo:

> I, the servant of the servants of science, had freed myself from the grammatical and dialectical doctrines, and had thrown off the chains imposed by the different schools in order to throw myself more freely into the pursuit of science. I was occupied in searching for knowledge, and while I wandered in its prairies I fell on the tracks of the true science; I developed a great love for it, but I did not find a guide who could lead me to it and that troubled me; my mind was full of it but, every time I posed questions about it I was told that it was a sin to devote oneself to it and that those who taught dogma forbade its consideration. This threw me into the depths of stupefaction and what astonished me most was the restricted mentality of these professors who only repeat mechanically what has been transmitted to them; I began to reflect and I understood that he who does not know a thing becomes hostile to that thing. . . .
>
> And while I found myself in this state, with the arrival of the perfect sage, of truth personified, of our venerated master Sayyid Jamāl ad-Dīn al-Afghānī, who does not cease to garner the fruits of science, there arose for us the sun of truths which explained for us the most subtle problems. I turned to him for some of the questions which tormented me and he clarified them for me, for which I give glory to God.[11]

The work to which these words form part of the preface expressed a mystical and pantheistic monism. 'Abduh's relation to Jamāl ad-Dīn seems that of a mystic disciple to an exalted master, and similar terminology reappears in later words of 'Abduh addressed to Jamāl

---

[10] Quoted in *ibid.*, p. xxiv.
[11] Quoted in *ibid.*, p. xxi.

ad-Dīn, even after 'Abduh had passed beyond his mystic stage.[12] Such adulation also appears in many of the letters from 'Abduh and others reproduced in the *Documents,* showing that the worship by Jamāl ad-Dīn's disciples, many of them intelligent men, was quite real and not simply part of the later myth.

Beyond this adulation, what can be said about what 'Abduh was learning from Afghānī at this stage? We know from 'Abduh's autobiographical accounts that he was strongly inclined toward Sufism when he met Afghānī. It seems that Afghānī deepened and expanded his knowledge of Sufism, probably introducing into it that blend of Neoplatonic mysticism and philosophy which had characterized Iranian philosophy for centuries. The philosophical emphasis of what was taught 'Abduh must soon have become stronger, to judge by 'Abduh's second work, advocating a rationalist philosophical interpretation in Islam, instead of his former mystical one.[13] 'Abduh's insistence in this work that where the literal sense of the Koran did not conform to reason an interpretation must be found which did so conform is a commonplace of the Muslim philosophers.

That the rationalist 'Abduh, who was soon to become the political activist and journalist 'Abduh, was following the path of his master and closest confidant seems hardly open to doubt. Witnesses agree that one of Sayyid Jamāl ad-Dīn's chief novelties in his Egyptian teaching consisted in his expositions of the Islamic philosophers. Afghānī's Egyptian library catalogued in the *Documents* concentrates on Iranian philosophy, with several works by Ibn Sīnā and Nasīr ad-Dīn Tūsī, and includes some works of Sufism, alchemy, science, and history, as well as an Arabic translation of Auguste Mariette's very popular and influential history of Egypt.[14] Several of the philosophic works include Afghānī's annotation of when he began teaching them in Cairo. There are few modern and Western works, but other sources, such as Adīb Isḥāq's rather frank biographical notice, tell us that Afghānī did keep up with Western ideas, so this absence should not be taken as proof of lack of interest in, or awareness of, more modern ideas.[15]

---

[12] Cf. 'Abduh's letter translated in Kedourie, *Afghani,* Appendix I. The original of this letter is reproduced in *Documents,* pls. 63–64, photos 134–137.

[13] Michel and Abdel Razik, *op. cit.,* pp. xxv–xxvi.

[14] *Documents,* pp. 14–21.

[15] Isḥāq in Riḍā, *Tārīkh,* p. 42, says: "One of his peculiar excellences is that he used to follow the movement of European knowledge and scientific discoveries and acquaint himself with what scientists discovered and what they had recently in-

Jamāl ad-Dīn's method of teaching was also largely responsible for his popularity and influence. Although he was not in fact the first person to reintroduce the teaching of Islamic philosophy into modern Egypt, he was apparently the first to apply the methods of philosophy to living contemporary problems. Instead of rote repetition and memorization Jamāl ad-Dīn gave new interpretations of the texts he discussed, and asked that his students do the same. His lively and original didactic methods helped attract students and followers.

The existence of different levels of meaning and interpretation both in the texts Afghānī taught and in the way he spoke of them to different audiences, helps account for the different reports made of his teachings by those present. Among them, however, it is important to note that only 'Abduh insists on Jamāl ad-Dīn's religious orthodoxy. Several others, even discounting men hostile to Afghānī or to any deviation from the teachings of the ulama, report rather differently. Salīm al-'Anḥūrī has already been quoted to the effect that Afghānī was irreligious ever since his trip to India. Less extreme and probably more accurate views come from other eyewitnesses. One of these, Luṭfī Jum'a, says, "His beliefs were not true Islam although he used to pretend they were, and I cannot judge about the beliefs of his followers."[16] Dr. Shiblī Shumayyil, a Syrian admirer of Afghānī who helped introduce Adīb Isḥāq to him, writes that when he heard, after Afghānī's Egyptian stay, that Afghānī had written a treatise against the materialists, "I was amazed, because I knew that he was not a religious man. It is difficult for me after my personal experience of the man to pass a definite judgment regarding what I heard about him afterwards, but I am far more inclined to think that he was not a believer."[17] It seems that Afghānī appeared neither religious nor orthodox to many of those who listened to him, and that his teachings centered on religious matters essentially to the degree that they could be given practical or worldly application.

Regarding Afghānī's personal life, we know little beyond his close ties to disciples. While in Egypt Afghānī had no known ties to any

---

vented as if he had studied science in some European higher school." Although this may be exaggerated, the general honesty of Isḥāq's biography makes it worthy of some credence. In some of the articles in *Miṣr*, cited below, Afghānī refers not only to Western concepts of republicanism and constitutionalism, but to telephones and phonographs, invented only about a year before Afghānī mentioned them in an article in *Miṣr* (Alexandria), II, no. 20, Nov. 15, 1878.

[16]Luṭfī Jum'a memoirs of Afghānī reprinted in Jundī, *op. cit.*, p. 20.

[17] Shiblī Shumayyil memoirs of Afghānī, reprinted in *ibid.*, p. 27.

women, and Luṭfī Jum'a states regarding Afghānī's attitude toward women that "he used to abhor them and did not speak well of them."[18] In one speech quoted below, however, he stressed the importance of women's education.

Afghānī's Political Activities: 1876–1879

The *Documents* corroborate and help to date Afghānī's membership and activity in the freemasons in Egypt. Freemasonry in the Middle East in the late nineteenth and early twentieth centuries was sometimes associated with religious heterodoxy, anticlericalism, and interconfessionalism and also with secret political activity. One reason for the popularity of freemasonic organizations among Middle Eastern modernists was their provision of a ready-made structure of secret societies; another was probably that these societies had features familiar to Islamic heterodoxy, such as oaths, mysterious initiations, and the symbolic use of language. The possibility that European members could protect local ones may also have helped. Freemasonry had been brought to Egypt decades earlier by the French, and for a long time remained primarily the preserve of Europeans, but in the 1860's and 1870's Egyptians entered some lodges in considerable numbers and a few branches came to be used largely for political purposes. Even here, however, Jamāl ad-Dīn was not as much an innovator as is sometimes claimed, as he was preceded in the Egyptian political use of masonry by Prince Ḥalīm and his followers. This Prince, the last son of the great Egyptian ruler of the early nineteenth century, Muḥammad 'Alī, had been suddenly excluded from succession to the khedivate by a law that Ismā'īl succeeded, with the help of a large bribe, in extracting from Sultan Abdülaziz in 1873. Ḥalīm's masonic activity was probably part of a plan to get back suc-

[18] Luṭfī Jum'a in *ibid.*, p. 21.

cession rights, and he was exiled for a time and his lodge dissolved because of his political plotting.[19] According to an 1882 letter from Afghānī to Riyāḍ, quoted below, Ḥalīm retained a following among the Egyptian masons in the late 1870's.

Most discussions of Afghānī's masonic activity begin it in 1877 or 1878, but the *Documents* include a letter from him applying for membership in a masonic lodge which dates from the spring of 1875 and a note saying he had entered a lodge in Muḥarram 1293/February 1876. Unfortunately the name or rite of the lodge is not included. The *Documents* also include invitations to sessions of Italian lodges from early 1877 through 1879 and documents beginning in January 1877, from the Eastern Star Lodge, which was affiliated with the Grand Lodge of England. There are also invitations to other lodges' special sessions. It seems probable that Afghānī belonged to an Italian lodge at the same time as he belonged to the Eastern Star Lodge, since the *Documents* catalog an invitation from an Italian lodge as late as February 1879, to a session to elect two new members.[20]

Afghānī's interest in freemasonry may have been in part religious but was much more political. It may be, as M. Sabry says, that it was a British vice-consul, R. Borg, who attracted Afghānī to the Eastern Star Lodge.[21] The 1877 date often given for his masonic affiliation may relate to the Eastern Star affiliation and his attachment of Egyptian disciples to that lodge. The lodge, with Afghānī as its leader, was to become an important political instrument in the growing Egyptian crisis of 1878 and 1879.

Before coming to the events of those years, however, it is worth returning to Afghānī's activities before those dates. In the years before 1878 Afghānī continued his teaching and widened his circle of acquaintances—revealing to some of his disciples, as Adīb Isḥāq noted, his full opinions, while from others he hid his liberal opinions but tried to help them out of superstition and ignorance.[22]

Afghānī's political bent, which had little outlet in the relatively quiet and unpromising state of Egyptian public opinion in the early 1870's, was able to find field for positive action in the changed state of society and public opinion in Egypt beginning about 1877, to which he and his disciples contributed something. As described by

---

19 Douin, *op. cit.*, II, 88–100.
20 *Documents*, pp. 24–25, and the plates referred to therein; also photo 12.
21 Sabry, *Genèse*, p. 142.
22 Isḥāq in Riḍā, *Tārīkh*, p. 40.

'Abduh in his memoirs, with a bit of exaggeration, the change was quite dramatic:

> The Egyptians before 1293 A.H. [1877] in their public and private affairs put themselves completely under the will of the sovereign and his functionaries . . . None of them dared to hazard an opinion on the way in which their country was administered. They were far from knowing the state of other Muslim or European countries, despite the great number of Egyptians who had studied in Europe from Muḥammad 'Alī's time until that date, or who had gone into neighboring Muslim countries, under the reign of Muḥammad 'Alī and Ibrāhīm.
>
> Even though Ismā'īl had instituted in 1283 A.H. [1866], a representative assembly, which should have taught the Egyptians that they were concerned in the affairs of their country and that their will should be consulted, in fact none of them, even within the Chamber, realized that he possessed this inherent right of representation, whether because the law stipulated expressly that the Chamber of delegates would not formulate its opinions except in the strict limits of the prerogatives of the government, or that the mode of work was ruined by the Khedive, who had the habit of letting the members know in advance, through an emissary, his will, and they, after a *pro forma* deliberation, took decisions in conformity with the will of the head of state.
>
> Besides, who would have dared to show his opinion? Nobody, since one could, on the least word, be exiled from one's country or despoiled of his goods or even put to death.
>
> Amid this darkness arrived Jamāl ad-Dīn. He was soon surrounded by students, then by numerous functionaries and by personages curious to know new ideas and doctrines which were being vigorously debated. His students and listeners propagated them in the Egyptian towns, and helped arouse minds, especially in Cairo.
>
> But this feeble ray would never have been able to reach the powerful sovereign in his high sphere except that it continued to grow, slowly and indefinitely in all directions, until war broke out between Turkey and Russia in 1293 [1877]. The Egyptians, strongly interested in the fate of their suzerain power, followed attentively the march of events, on which they were informed by foreigners who got the European newspapers. The few Egyptian newspapers, of recent date, which had only published facts of no importance, be-

> gan to describe the vicissitudes of the war, and there grew up a movement of opinion and a sort of polemic, hitherto unknown, between the partisans of these newspapers and the malcontents. New newspapers were immediately founded to rival the old ones in publishing news and to combat their tendencies. An irresistible desire pushed people to subscribe, with a force more powerful than despotism.
>
> With time, the newspapers touched on political and social questions concerning foreign countries and then set boldly to dealing with the question of Egyptian finances, which embarrassed the government.[23]

The year 1877 marked a turning point in the press and in public opinion, and Jamāl ad-Dīn and his followers were in the forefront of the development of newspapers critical of the government and of foreign activities in Egypt. It was only from about 1877 that Jamāl ad-Dīn's activities began to have significance beyond a very limited circle, and even then the reality of his influence must be separated from later myths. As was often true, his influence on disciples in moving them toward activism, journalism, and new ideas was the successful part of his activity, while his directly political schemes ended in failure.

Jamāl ad-Dīn took advantage of the newly awakened state of public opinion, to which he had contributed something, to further his program for strengthening Egypt against increasing foreign encroachments, opening people's minds to more modern ideas, and advancing his own influence. His contemporaries tell us that he kept abreast of translations of Western works, and that his fondness for the historical writings of François Guizot dates from this period. From later references it can be seen that what most attracted him in Guizot's writings was Guizot's belief in reason and social solidarity as sources of progress and civilization, and also the emphasis on the Protestant movement as a decisive break leading Europe toward material progress and reform. There is evidence that Jamāl ad-Dīn saw himself as something of an Islamic Luther, and was moved by the conviction that religious reform was the only way to introduce material reform and self-strengthening into the Islamic world.[24] Using Islamic philosophy

---

23 Quoted in Sabry, *L'empire égyptien*, pp. 331–332.

24 Cf. the conversation between Jamāl ad-Dīn and Shaikh 'Abd al-Qādir Maghribī in Istanbul, quoted in Riḍā, *Tārīkh*, pp. 82–84. Kudsi-Zadeh ("Legacy," p. 115) notes that Guizot's *Histoire de la civilisation en Europe* was translated into Arabic in 1877. The influence of Guizot's ideas of civilization and progress on Af-

to open Islam to broader and more rationalistic interpretations than were then current, he managed, like many leaders and thinkers, to leave contradictory impressions on his contemporaries in Egypt. Some who knew him well wrote of him as a freethinker or a man of political ambition, while others viewed him largely as a religious reformer. His continual occupation in politics, however, should make one wary of the view that his primary motive was a religious vision, even were there not other evidence against this. He was one of the first reformers seriously to confront the problem of adapting Muslim traditions to new problems, not being content to separate reform and religion into two discrete spheres.

One of the most important factors in Egypt's newly awakened public opinion was the development of political journalism. A degree of freedom of the press under Ismā'īl helped make of Egypt the center of Arabic journalism from about 1875 on, with many Syrians contributing and finding it possible to write more independently in Egypt than they could in their own territory, then under direct Ottoman rule. Afghānī played no role in the first important newspaper of this era, *al-Ahram*, founded in 1875 by the Syrian Taqlā brothers and still in existence, but he did help inspire nearly all the other political journals of the late 1870's, and he helped get government licenses for many of them.

The first of these journals was *Abū Naẓẓāra Zarqā'*, founded by Afghānī's Jewish disciple, Ya'qūb Sanu', in March 1877. Sanu' already had a considerable reputation as a satirical playwright, and he continued his pioneering use of satire and of writing in colloquial Egyptian Arabic in his newspaper. There is disagreement about the degree of Afghānī's inspiration of this newspaper, although Afghānī in general encouraged his disciples to publish newspapers. The actual content of the newspaper seems to have been entirely characteristic of Sanu', rather than Afghānī, not only in its use of colloquial Arabic, which Afghānī never advocated, but also in its partisanship of Prince Ḥalīm, a favorite of Sanu' but not of Afghānī. This partisanship for Ḥalīm and criticism of the Khedive Ismā'īl help account for the suppression of the paper after two months and fifteen issues, and Sanu' himself was banished from Egypt in June 1878.[25] From there he went to Paris, where Afghānī was to rejoin him in 1883.

ghānī is discussed in Albert Hourani, *Arabic Thought in the Liberal Age 1798–1939* (London, 1962), pp. 114–115.

25 Gendzier, *op. cit.*, pp. 49–65; Kudsi-Zadeh, "Legacy," p. 133.

More directly under Afghānī's influence were the papers edited by Afghānī's Syrian Christian disciples Adīb Isḥāq and Salīm an-Naqqāsh. When Isḥāq came from Lebanon to Alexandria in 1876 he was only twenty years old, but even before this he had achieved some fame as a writer, editor, and translator in Lebanon. Then, as summarized by A. Albert Kudsi-Zadeh:

> In 1876, he arrived in Alexandria where he joined his countryman Salīm Naqqāsh in producing theatrical plays under the patronage of Ismā'īl. According to 'Anḥūrī, Isḥāq was unsuccessful in his attempt to present plays in Alexandria and was jobless when the historian Ḥusayn al-Khūrī sent him to Cairo with a letter of recommendation to Afghānī. There he fell under the powerful influence of the Sayyid and soon became one of his staunchest followers. Afghānī encouraged him to start a newspaper and helped him to get the necessary concession. . . . Thus the famous weekly journal *Miṣr* came into being in July 1877. . . .[26]

Miṣr, published first in Cairo and then in Alexandria, had considerable success, and was the main publisher of Afghānī's ideas. Several sources indicate that Afghānī hated to write and that his own articles, both in the Egyptian period and afterward, were dictated to disciples who wrote them down from his oral presentation. In *Miṣr* there were several articles written from such oral presentations, some under Afghānī's own name, and some under a pseudonym.

Continuing his account of the journalistic activity of Afghānī's disciples, Kudsi-Zadeh says:

> In 1878, Isḥāq returned to Alexandria—the hub of diplomatic and commercial life in Egypt—where he could have access to fresh news. Jamāl ad-Dīn suggested that Isḥāq collabo-

[26] Kudsi-Zadeh, "Legacy," p. 134, based on several Arabic citations. On Afghānī's active encouragement of journalism see also 'Anḥūrī in Riḍā, *Tārīkh*, pp. 45–46, 48–49. Ḥusain al-Khūrī's letter of introduction of Adīb Isḥāq to Afghānī is in the Majlis Library collection catalogued in *Documents*, p. 70, doc. 232. It is dated 16 Jumādā al-ūlā, 1294/May 29, 1877. After praising Afghānī and describing Adīb Isḥāq, Khūrī writes that when "Adīb Efendi prepared to leave, he asked me to supply him with a letter to you. He desires to meet you because of the many things that charmed him in the description of your qualities. He was bent on presenting this letter, and I gave it to him with pleasure. Your slave still laments separation, and envies the bearer for the great luck he will find in being near to the leader of intellects and eloquence, until, please God, I make the pilgrimage to the Ka'ba of your eloquence and the abode of your imamate."

> rate with Salīm al-Naqqāsh, and so the two jointly produced the weekly *Miṣr* from Alexandria. He also helped them obtain a permit for a daily newspaper, *al-Tijāra,* which made its debut in June 1878. Although it began as a commercial paper, it soon widened its coverage to include political news and editorials. An agreement signed with Reuters made it the first Egyptian newspaper to subscribe to a worldwide news agency.
>
> In addition to Afghānī, many members of his circle, including Muḥammad 'Abduh, 'Abd Allāh al-Nadīm, and Ibrāhīm al-Laqqānī, contributed to *al-Tijāra.* Its attacks on the "European Ministry" of Wilson and de Blignières forced its suspension for two weeks early in 1879, but its strong political tone continued until it was finally banned by the Khedive Tawfīq later in that year. The Egyptian scholar Ibrāhīm 'Abdu, who had an opportunity to consult the few extant issues, believes that it was Afghānī who caused the paper's closure because he filled it with his revolutionary articles.[27]

Another Syrian Christian emigré influenced by Afghānī was the writer Salīm al-'Anḥūrī, who reached Egypt in 1878. Jamāl ad-Dīn helped him obtain a permit for the newspaper *Mir'āt ash-Sharq,* which first appeared in February 1879. A few months later 'Anḥūrī relinquished his editorship and returned to Syria either because of political dangers or because of ill health, and Afghānī asked another disciple, Ibrāhīm al-Laqqānī, to take over the editorship. When, in August 1879, Afghānī was expelled by the Khedive Taufīq, *Mir'āt ash-Sharq* defended him, and it was then shut down by government order.[28]

Although Muḥammad 'Abduh did not edit a newspaper during Afghānī's Egyptian stay, he did contribute articles to *al-Ahrām* and to other newspapers reflecting Afghānī's influence. Some of Afghānī's disciples, especially Adīb Isḥāq, edited the Alexandria newspaper *Miṣr al-Fatāt* (*Jeune Egypte*) written in both Arabic and French, which promoted an advanced program of constitutionalism and reform in 1879 and 1880.

Afghānī's appreciation of the importance of newspapers in helping

---

27 Kudsi-Zadeh, "Legacy," pp. 136–137, citing Ibrāhīm 'Abduh, *Taṭawwir aṣ-ṣaḥāfa al-miṣriyya, 1798–1951* (Cairo, 1951), and other Arabic sources.

28 Kudsi-Zadeh, "Legacy," citing Ibrāhīm 'Abduh, *op. cit.,* and 'Anhūrī in Riḍā, *Tārīkh,* p. 48.

to create and arouse public opinion was one of his major contributions to the revival of the Middle East. According to 'Abduh, in the middle and late 1870's, Afghānī was running a virtual school for those he encouraged toward journalism, and it is clear than this school was productive of rapid results.[29] The newspapers inspired by Afghānī constituted the majority of the independent press in Egypt in the late 1870's, and helped awaken the first politically informed public opinion in these crucial years.

In the late 1870's Afghānī undertook a large variety of political activities, encouraged by the political ferment of these years. The situation then which gave rise to complex political currents was, in general, as follows. Outside events, including the deposition of Ottoman Sultan and the introduction of the Ottoman constitution of 1876, followed by the Russo-Turkish War and the 1878 Congress of Berlin, with its losses of Ottoman territory, helped agitate opinion within Egypt, itself still technically under the Ottoman Sultan. In addition, in April 1878 Khedive Ismā'īl was forced by outside pressure to agree to a Commission of Inquiry into Egypt's finances. Ismā'īl was also made to agree to the recommendation of the commission in August that he cede his estates to the state, accept the principle of ministerial responsibility, and appoint a British and a French Minister in his cabinet. Ismā'īl chafed under this regime, however, and on February 18, 1879, almost certainly with his complicity, a mob of officers assaulted Prime Minister Nūbār Pāshā and Sir Rivers Wilson, the Minister of Finance in this peculiar regime. Nūbār then resigned, and Ismā'īl apparently turned against Riyāḍ, who had participated in the Commission of Inquiry and was now Minister of Interior. There was public agitation against Riyāḍ, probably stirred up by the Khedive, and Riyāḍ was forced to leave for Naples in April, where he remained until after Ismā'īl was deposed by British and French pressure and Taufīq succeeded him in June, 1879. A group of constitutionalists, led by the prominent statesman Sharīf Pāshā and the opposition forces in the Chamber of Deputies, were working during this crisis to extend the powers of the Chamber and limit those of the Khedive.

By 1877 Afghānī began to enter directly into politics, mainly in three ways—through the Eastern Star masonic lodge; through speeches both to the educated elite and to the masses, who had hitherto ap-

29 'Abduh, "Biographie," p. 44.

parently been unaware of his existence; and through journalism.

The nature of Jamāl ad-Dīn's masonic and political activity is still not entirely clear. 'Abduh leaves out all mention of the suspect masons in his apologetic biography, although on other occasions he admitted the affiliation but played down its importance. The *Documents,* however, prove that Afghānī was a mason from 1876 through 1879 and applied for reaffiliation in Paris in 1884. They also include a notice of his election to chairmanship of the Eastern Star Lodge in January 1878. This Cairo lodge had been chartered by the Grand Lodge of England in 1871.[30] Afghānī may also have been expelled from a masonic lodge as early as 1876 because of attempts to politicize it.[31]

Most sources indicate that it was the Eastern Star Lodge that Afghānī succeeded in using for political purposes. The most detailed account of Afghānī's masonic activities appears in an article by M. Sabry, who stated orally that his information came from direct sources, including one of the involved Muwailihī family. According to Sabry, Afghānī and a group of his followers first joined an Italian lodge in Alexandria, but were influenced by English Vice-Consul Ralph Borg to join an English lodge, whose number reached 300, including many leaders of the nationalist movement of 1878–1882. Sabry claims that some members of this lodge whom he names were also involved in a secret society that planned to assassinate Ismā'īl. Sabry states that Afghānī inaugurated Crown Prince Taufīq into the lodge.[32] The membership number of about 300 and the claim that Taufīq sought admission to the lodge are also found in Adīb Isḥāq.[33]

It is unclear whether Taufīq was a member of the lodge, though it

[30] *Documents,* pp. 24–25, docs. 57, 62, 71, and their photographs. As Kudsi-Zadeh ("Legacy," p. 151 n. 29) notes, the *Documents* editors incorrectly read the transcription of the Italian "Gennaio" as "June" instead of "January." A. G. Mackey, *Encyclopedia of Freemasonry,* Vol. I (Chicago, 1929), s.v. "Egypt."

[31] Kudsi-Zadeh ("Legacy," pp. 155–157) cites stories given by Riḍā (from Abduh) and Makhzūmī to this effect, including Afghānī's objection to obeisance to the Princes of Wales, who visited Egypt in 1875–76.

[32] M. Sabry, "A Page from the History of Jamāl ad-Dīn al-Afghānī," *Revue de l'Institut des Etudes Islamiques,* I, 1 (Cairo, 1958), esp. pp. 190–191 (in Arabic). A shorter version of this story is found in Sabry's two French books cited in n. 2, above. Interview with M. Sabry, Cairo, September, 1966.

[33] Isḥāq in Riḍā, *Tārīkh,* pp. 40–41. Isḥāq states that Afghānī's lodge was affiliated with the French [Grand] Orient rite of masonry—possibly, as suggested by Kudsi-Zadeh ("Legacy," pp. 160–161), referring to a lodge evidently set up by Afghānī and his followers after they broke with another lodge, probably the Eastern Star Lodge. On this break, see below in this chapter.

seems clear that Afghānī and his masonic followers were in contact with Taufīq in this period, and expected positive things from him when he acceded to power.

'Anḥūri states that Jamāl ad-Dīn's increased political importance from 1878 was based on his entry into political activity and his leadership of an Arab masonic group. By this time, 'Anḥūrī and others tell us, among Afghānī's patrons were such important men as Maḥmud Samī Pāshā Bārūdī (later known as a planner of the nationalist acts of Colonel Aḥmad 'Urābī); the leader of the parliamentary opposition 'Abd as-Salām Muwailihī; and his brother Ibrāhīm. The oppositional orator 'Abdallāh Nadīm, as well as the writers and intellectuals who had joined Afghānī earlier, continued to follow his lead. In this period, says 'Anḥūrī, Afghānī began giving public speeches in which he spoke in a new way. He started drawing the common people to his talks and telling them that they, the Egyptians, had submitted to centuries of despotism and submission and their oppressive governments had taken from them what they had created with the sweat of their brows. They had permitted this and remained docile under all conquerors. Afghānī exhorted them to look at the ancient monuments of Egypt which showed the greatness of their ancestors; to awaken from their sleep of intoxication, shake off the dust of stupidity and unworthiness, and either live like free people or die as martyrs. According to 'Anḥūrī, such speeches by Jamāl ad-Dīn were a cause for the awakening of dissatisfaction among the Egyptians with their government, and the first spark that led ultimately to the 'Urābī movement.[34] (Colonel Aḥmad 'Urābī and other nationalist military officers, with the backing of some civilian nationalists, took increasing control of the Egyptian government beginning in 1880, became de facto rulers in 1882, and were defeated by the British invasion and occupation of Egypt in September 1882.)

In addition to the nationalist speeches by Afghānī to the Egyptian masses reported by 'Anḥūrī, there are available a number of other speeches and articles confirming Afghānī's active efforts to arouse Egyptians to patriotic ideas and actions, and to awaken their interest in new political and scientific ideas.

In a speech in Alexandria, Afghānī is reported to have said: "Oh! you poor fellah! You break the heart of the earth in order to draw sustenance from it and support your family. Why do you not break

---

[34] 'Anḥūrī in Riḍā, *Tārīkh*, pp. 46–47.

the heart of your oppressor? Why do you not break the heart of those who eat the fruit of your labor?"[35]

Besides such speeches reported in memoirs, there have now been unearthed a few dictated articles and speeches by Afghānī from 1878 and 1879 that shed further light on his political ideas in this period. In the autumn of 1878, Afghānī published a long article in *Miṣr* on the English and the Afghans, "al-Bayān fī al-Inglīz wa al-Afghān," which was translated into English in the *Homeward Mail.* Parts of the English translation were reprinted in Louis Ṣābūnjī's Arabic-English newspaper *The Bee/an-Naḥla,* published in London, where Ṣabūnjī then lived. In this article Afghānī reiterates the strongly anti-British position he had taken over a decade before in Afghanistan, citing the American Revolution and the Indian Mutiny of 1857 as examples of British oppression. Afghānī adds, after affirming the unity during the Mutiny of all religious sects and groups in India:

> Their rancour and enmity [toward the British] still subsist, and have attained such a pitch that there is not an Indian living who does not pray for the advance of the Russians to the frontier of India, and who does not anxiously await the joyful tidings of their approach in order that they may have the opportunity of freeing themselves from English domination. Here, again, it is clear that if this people, the English, had not appropriated to themselves exclusively the benefits which belonged to others, and degraded themselves by seizing what was not theirs, an alliance of sects like this, holding such extremely opposite views that, under other circumstances, they would gladly have drank one another's blood, could not have been possible. . . .
>
> How widely different is this policy from that of the Russians. . . . That Government has not occupied one Muslim country . . . where it has not succeeded in attracting the affection of the people, from among whom it has promoted many to high posts, and chosen generals and officers of their army, whereas in India you find none who have been advanced to such offices. . . . Hence it is that in the different countries above-named, you do not meet with one malcontent, one who is not grateful for Russian rule. . . .
>
> What a wide difference there is, moreover, between the

[35] Quoted in Aḥmad Shafīq, *Mudhakkirātī fī niṣf qarn,* Vol. I (Cairo, 1934), p. 109; translated in Sylvia Haim, *Arab Nationalism* (Berkeley and Los Angeles, 1962), p. 8.

> policy of the English and that of the French in Algeria! The people of the latter country are infinitely more contented and happy than the people of India. . . . Look at Egypt. . . . Do you find there any useful establishment, any traces of disinterested liberality of English origin? No. Whatever indications of such exist are referable to the French. You will not find there a single school of learning or science, instituted since the time of the late Muhammad-'Aly Pasha, of which the founder, the organizer, the director was not a Frenchman. All hail to the nation whose works bespeak its praise, and to whose virtue as well as to the purity of its garments, unsullied by the pollution of covetousness, the whole world bears witness.[36]

Afghānī then goes on to describe the causes of the second Afghan-British war which began in 1878, and which he attributed to British covetousness.

Miṣr on November 23, 1878, reprinted a statement by Ṣabūnjī in *an-Naḥla* that he had shown a summary of Afghānī's criticism of British policy, especially in Afghanistan, to several British statesmen, and *Miṣr* also reported that British writers and Ṣābūnjī himself had written against what Afghānī said about British policy. In response, Afghānī now wrote that the derogatory things he had written in his article about the English were in proportion of one to a thousand among their bad deeds. The history books to which his opponents refer to refute him are written by the English, and "marked by the hands of English self-love, with the pens of conceit and the pencils of deception, and inescapably they do not relate the truth and do not report reality, and how could they desire to reveal the truth of their deeds when they know that their happiness lies in delusion and deceit and fraud; and the snare of ambiguity and the trap of duplicity."[37]

---

36 *The Bee/an-Naḥla* (London), Dec. 15, 1878. Thanks to A. A. Kudsi-Zadeh for sending me a photocopy of this article. He has published it in French along with another article by Afghānī and an introduction noting Afghānī's differential assessment of British, French, and Russian colonialism in his "Les idées d'Afghânî sur la politique coloniale des Anglais, des Français et des Russes," *Orient*, XII/3–4, 47–48 (1968), 197–206. The Arabic original of this article is not available to me (see next note).

37 *Miṣr* (Alexandria), II, no. 21 (?), Nov. 22, 1878. Many thanks to Donald Reid for copying by hand all the articles he could find in Egypt by or about Afghānī in *Miṣr*, 1878–79. *Miṣr*, II, no. 23, Dec. 6, 1878 says that Afghānī's original article (partly quoted above from an English translation), entitled "al-Bayān fī al-Inglīz

The Second Afghan War of 1878–1880 and the rising foreign threat to Egyptian independence evidently moved Afghānī to resume his strong public attacks on the British, whom he now, as throughout most of his life, saw as the chief foreign threat to Muslim independence and dignity. His book on the history of Afghanistan, *Tatimmat al-bayān fī tārīkh al-Afghān,* was apparently written late in 1878 and its last reference is to the beginning of the Anglo-Russian War in 1878. This book contains chapters on earlier Afghan history, genealogy, and ethnology, but its main aim, as indicated in its first pages, is to point to the courage of the Afghans in resisting militarily British attacks, and to use the Afghan story both to point up the covetousness of the British and the possibility of fighting off their encroachments. In the introduction to this book Afghānī belies the negative views he earlier expressed on Afghan leaders and praises the Afghans for the greatness of soul and high purpose, which keep them from submitting to the insatiable expansionists who, not content with the Thames and the Ganges, must swallow the Nile and other lands and rivers. Using one of his frequently used phrases of praise, he says of the Afghans, "Nobility of soul leads them to choose a death of honor above a life of baseness under foreign rule." The Amirs, he says, choose ministers who reject English influence. The book does not mention Jamāl ad-Dīn's role in Afghanistan.[38]

Miṣr of January 9, 1879, announced that it would soon publish *Tatimmat al-bayān fī tārīkh al-Afghān,* a book by Afghānī on the history of Afghanistan, of which the manuscript had recently reached the editors. In the same volume it would reprint Afghānī's long article on England and Afghanistan, "al-Bayān fī al-Inglīz wa al-Afghān," and another article that had also been printed earlier in *Miṣr,* "The True Reason for Man's Happiness."[39] The latter article

wa al-Afghān," was printed separately in no. 16 of *Miṣr*. Whether this means that the whole issue was devoted to the article, or that it appeared as a special supplement is unclear. Unfortunately, no. 16 was missing from the collection of *Miṣr* found by Mr. Reid, and I have located no other collections of *Miṣr*. Since *Miṣr* was numbered consecutively and appeared at exact weekly intervals, no. 16 should date from October 1878.

38 See the longer discussion of *Tatimmat al-bayān fī tārīkh al-Afghān* in the last pages of chapter 3, above. It can now be dated with certainty by an article in *Miṣr*, II, no. 28, Jan. 9, 1879, saying that the mauscript had recently arrived, describing the contents of each chapter, and announcing plans for early publication. On the book's partial debt to a European writer, see Kudsi-Zadeh, "Legacy," pp. 16–17.

39 *Miṣr*, II, no. 28, Jan. 9, 1879. Rashīd Riḍā later reprinted "The True Reason for Man's Happiness," and in a note said that it was the introduction of a *book* by Afghānī entitled *al-Bayān fī al-Inglīz va al-Afghān* printed at the *Miṣr* press in

begins with a long philosophic introduction stating that the foundation of human happiness comes from the fulfillment of his proper duty by each man in a society, including its rulers. Afghānī goes on to suggest that people owe obeisance only to rulers who safeguard the people and observe just laws, and not to those who are greedy or oppressive. Afghānī next cites the British claims to have improved and benefited India through building cities, railroads and other means of communication, and schools. To this the Indians reply that the British ruined glorious cities in India, and that they built transport and communications

> only in order to drain the substance of our wealth and facilitate the means of trade for the inhabitants of the British Isles and extend their sphere of riches; other than this, what has brought us to poverty and need, with our wealth exhausted, our riches ended, and many of us dead, consumed by hunger? And if you claim that that is due to a defect in our nature, and narrowness in our mental powers, it is surprising from the sons of Brutus, who suffered for long ages and wandered in wild and barbaric valleys, that they should believe in the deficiency and unpreparedness of the sons of Brahma and Mahadiv, the founders of human *sharī'as* and the establishers of civilized laws.[40]

As for the schools established by the British in India, they were built only in order to teach the English language so that Indians could be employed in government offices. The British claim that they ended the oppression of local Indian rulers is laughable, as oppression used to be confined to a few areas, and these rulers spent their wealth in India, but now oppression is general, and the British suck the Indians' blood and skin their flesh in order to take it home as spoils. The strong impression made on Afghānī by his early stays in India is indicated in this article.

Kings, Afghānī continues, always claim that justice is on their side.

Alexandria in 1878 ("al-'Illa al haqīqiyya li sa'āda al-insān," *al-Manār,* XXIII [Jan. 28, 1922], 37n). The date 1878 is either an error for 1879, or else it refers to the special issue no. 16 of *Miṣr.* As for the *History of Afghanistan,* whether the book was originally called by the title of one of its articles rather than that of its major section, the history of Afghanistan, I do not know. Indeed, I know of no one who has actually seen the 1879 book. The Cairo, 1901, edition of the *Tārīkh al-Afghān* does not contain the two articles from *Miṣr.*

40 *Miṣr,* II, no. 20, Nov. 15, 1878; also reprinted in *al-Manār,* XXIII (Jan. 28, 1922), 37–45.

For example, the Russian tsar justified the Ottoman war by the oppression of Ottoman Christians, but the Ottomans refute this, saying if the Russians were moved by compassion, why not have compassion for peoples within their own borders, like the Poles? And the Ottomans add that if they were in fact oppressors of Christians, they could long ago have forced conversion on their Christian subjects.

Afghānī goes on to say that each man, even the most unjust, finds justifications for his evil deeds. A man when poor may be just and compassionate, censure venality, and love patriotism and liberty. When he rises to a high rank, however, the same man will treat the poor harshly, act unjustly, be greedy, sensual, and venal, indifferent to public interests, and a traitor to his homeland, satisfied that the people are not worthy of liberty because they are unprepared for it and would be ruined if they attained it. Such a man will justify his own evil deeds because of *self-love,* which is the cause of hardship and misfortune. Man cannot be free of misfortune except by referring to *reason* in all his affairs, and "emerging from the noose of enslavement to egotistical sultans and rejecting their orders." Afghānī ends by saying that there is one beneficial type of self-love—that which calls men to commit commendable acts for the public interest, and turns reason to love.[41]

This rather diffuse article is notable not only for its anticipation of anti-imperialist arguments that were generally brought forth only some decades later, but also for its demonstration of Afghānī's application of traditional philosophical categories in calling for patriotism, liberty, and opposition to autocratic rulers.

Also indicating Afghānī's application of traditional philosophical categories to current problems are two reports of Afghānī's lectures printed as articles by Muḥammad ʿAbduh which stress the need for education and for industrial development.[42] In the same vein is his review of Buṭrus Bustānī's new Arabic encyclopedia which appeared in *Miṣr* in April 1879, and was also printed in the Bustānī family's Syrian paper *al-Jinān* in the same year. Here Afghānī says that man is divided into a rational enlightened essence and a dark animal

---

41 *Ibid.*

42 "Falsafat at-tarbiyya," and "Falsafat aṣ-ṣināʿa," reprinted in Riḍā, *Tārīkh,* II, 2–14. Dr. Mangol Bayat Philipp translated these articles into English as part of a seminar's work. They are of less interest than the articles summarized above. Riḍā, *op. cit.,* p. 2n, says that the first of these articles was printed in *Miṣr* in early June 1879.

form. In most men the *animal* nature prevails, whereas in a minority the *rational* is dominant. Most men strive only for bodily pleasures; while among rational men there are also two groups. One consists of rulers who use their reason wrongly for killing, plunder, and coercion. The second group is composed of sages, scholars, and inventors. These men cleanse themselves of the "vile animal qualities," improve their minds with true knowledge and rational studies, and strive to spread this knowledge. If one looks at the Greeks, Romans, Persians, and Chaldeans of old, one will see that the names of their rulers have been erased from the human mind, while their great scholars and philosophers remain alive and influential. Bustānī's encyclopedia advances the important work of spreading knowledge. Afghānī concludes:

> O, sons of the East, don't you know that the power of the Westerners and their domination over you came about through their advance in learning and education, and your decline in these domains? . . . Are you satisfied after your past achievements, after you had reached the acme of honor through learning and education, to remain in that wretched state into which you were plunged by ignorance and error. . . . Make the effort to obtain knowledge and become enlightened with the light of truth so as to recoup glory and obtain true independence.[43]

As this review indicates, education and the use of reason were intimately connected with the political independence and justice that Afghānī wished to attain.

Regarding the specifics of Afghānī's political ideas, thus far the most persuasive evidence for his views on government in this period appears in an article entitled "Despotic Government" that he published in *Miṣr* in February 1879. In it he begins by saying that many reasons prevent an Easterner from discussing republican government, among them being the arbitrary rule of despots which deprives their subjects of their rights, people's superstitions, and their persistence in opposing the true (philosophical) sciences. These prevent an Easterner from writing about republican government, "to reveal its true nature, its merits, the happiness of those who have achieved it, and

[43] *Miṣr*, II, no. 43, April 25, 1879. The same article, "Kitāb *Dā'irat al-Ma'ārif*," was also printed in *al-Jinān*, X (1879), 306–308. Thanks to A. A. Kudsi-Zadeh for sending a photocopy of the latter.

the fact that those governed by it enjoy a higher state and loftier position than the other members of the human race." The same reasons restrain him from an exposition of the nature of constitutional government "which would set forth its beneficial results and show how those governed by it have been aroused by original human nature and stimulated to emerge from the lowly estate of animality, to ascend to the highest degree of perfection and to cast off the burdens that despotic government lays upon them." Afghānī then goes on, much in the manner of al-Fārābī and other traditional Muslim philosophers, to distinguish between types of despotism and to define each at some length: the Cruel Government of plundering conquerors, the Oppressive Government characteristic of past and present Eastern governments, of past Western governments, and of the British in India; and Compassionate Government, whose highest subtype is the Enlightened Government. The latter is described and praised at length for promoting economic life, commerce, science, education, human rights, just taxation, and a balanced budget, with the help of learned specialists. The article ends with a thinly veiled warning to oppressive Eastern rulers.[44]

The article suggests that Afghānī thought that republicanism and constitutionalism were the best forms of government (indicating an advanced and open mind, since he had not witnessed such governments directly). Either through fear of censorship or because he felt, with considerable justification, that the actions of a government were more important than its form, he concentrated on describing the ways that an enlightened despotism should act. Since Afghānī felt that both enlightened despotism and constitutional government were far superior to existing Eastern governments, it is understandable that among his disciples were advocates of both paths.

Also showing Afghānī's political views is the only complete contemporary record yet found of a speech by Afghānī in Egypt—a report in *Miṣr* on May 24, 1879, of a talk just given by Afghānī on a visit to Alexandria. The article is entitled "Ḥakīm ash-Sharq" (The Sage of the East), a laudatory title under which Afghānī had come to be known to his admirers in Egypt. Like most of the *Miṣr* articles reporting Afghānī's words, it begins with high praise of Jamāl ad-Dīn. It then details the enthusiastic reception given him on his recent

---

44 "al-Ḥukūma al-istibdādiyya," *Miṣr*, II, no. 33, February 14, 1879. The article is translated and analyzed by L. M. Kenny, "al-Afghānī on Types of Despotic Government," *Journal of the American Oriental Society*, 86, 1 (1966), 19–27.

visit to Alexandria. It says that the enlightened young men of Alexandria asked him to give a speech, and he agreed to talk in Ziziniyya Hall, provided that entry should be by tickets whose price should go to the poor of Alexandria. The reporter says he will give a report of Afghānī's speech as he took it down. (The circumstances of this speech, in a hall with paid tickets, indicate that it was addressed to higher social classes than some of his speeches, reported above.)

Afghānī, after praising the quest for knowledge, says that the spirit of nationality (*jinsiyya*) of the Eastern peoples has been weakened, and this has caused the weakness of all classes and of the body politic. Afghānī states that the members of the audience are descended either from the ancient Egyptians or (referring to the Syrians) from the Phoenicians or Chaldeans. The ancient Egyptians made major original achievements in engineering and mathematics, and taught philosophy, agriculture, and manufacture to the Greeks. The Phoenicians were advanced seafarers who carried civilization to distant colonies and taught the Greeks the art of writing, while the Chaldeans founded stonework, astronomy, and other sciences. Afghānī names the ruins of ancient monuments as a living reproach to those who say Orientals are inferior and incapable of outstanding deeds.

In the present, Afghānī continues, foreigners have divided up Eastern lands, whose backwardness must have a cause. If we examine realities philosophically "we find for our backwardness only two basic causes: fanaticism (*ta'aṣṣub*) and tyranny (*istibdād*)." Fanaticism means the misuse of religion. If we look carefully at the founders of religion, from Mahadiv to Zoroaster, Moses, Jesus, and Muhammad, "we find in their precepts only the call for the recognition of the origin of truth, and that is God, and the call to virtues and the practice of good, coupled with the avoidance of evils." Many of the founders' followers, however, misused their precepts to split thir community and incite divisions and animosities.

As for tyranny, it means tying a nation to the chain of one will and acting only to please that one. Afghānī adds that this obstacle ended when we (the Egyptians) attained a parliamentary regime, and now this regime must be supported if it is to continue. The only thing that will help us emerge from our present difficulties is *zeal*. Zeal is possessed by only some citizens "who know that their honor is only in their race (*jins*), their power is only in their community (*umma*), and their glory is only in their fatherland (*waṭan*)." Afghānī continues:

> That is why I hope that you gentlemen will establish a national [or patriotic] party (*ḥizban waṭaniyyan*) which will protect the rights of your country and will guard its splendor. . . . I hope that you will support the cause of the fatherland and will strengthen in it parliamentary rule, through which the cause of justic and equity may be established, and you may no longer need any foreign protection. . . .
>
> No doubt you know that the national party (*al-ḥizb al-waṭanī*) has no power or permanence as long as the people of the country have no common language, developed with good style. . . .
>
> Should one ask how is it possible to spread zeal, establish the national party, and revive the language, we would say: The most important factor to attain this goal is establishing a hall of oratory where gifted speakers will stand and speak of zeal and enthusiasm, to explain to us rights and duties, and remind us of the glory of our ancestors and the humiliation of our children, showing us the position of the foreigners, their strength, wealth, glory, and power, so we should learn the causes and characteristics of decline. This should be followed by the founding of free newspapers of a patriotic type which will tell the truth, and should in concise style bring distant things near, explain the great events of the past, clarify the state of our neighbors, and show us what is beneficial and what harmful in order that we may follow the former and shun the latter. . . . The difference between them can only be established by the eloquence that moves the blood of the speaker, the power of delivery, and discussion in the newspapers influencing minds as they consider what has been said in the press.[45]

Afghānī went on, in his only recorded words in favor of greater rights for women, to say:

> I am warning you gentlemen against thinking that you will attain the qualities of civilization, acquire knowledge, and advance toward progress and happiness . . . if knowledge among you is confined to men; I am warning you that you should not ignore that it is impossible for us to emerge from stupidity, from the prison of humiliation and distress, and from the depths of weakness and ignominy as long as women are deprived of rights and ignorant of their duties, for they are the mothers from whom will come elementary education

[45] "Ḥakīm ash-Sharq," *Miṣr*, II, no. 47, May 24, 1879.

> and primary morality. No doubt the first thing carved on the tablet of a man's mind is the strongest and hardest to erase. It has been said that what one learns in childhood is like something carved in stone. I say that this image is the basic cause of the differences of beliefs and the variety of tenets. . . . If the mothers are educated, know human rights, and what the precepts of honor and civilization require, there is no doubt that their children will adopt their characters and will acquire from them these virtues. I think that when women's education is neglected, then even if all the males of a nation are learned and high-minded, still the nation is able to survive in its acquired stage only for that generation. When they disappear, their children, who have the character and educational deficiencies of their mothers, betray them, and their nation returns to the state of ignorance and distress.[46]

The articles and speeches quoted or summarized give an idea of Afghānī's major concerns in 1878 and 1879. He attacked British imperialism in the strongest terms, but showed a more benevolent attitude toward French and Russian policies in the East. He recalled the glories of ancient Egypt and its neighbors as a model to show modern Egyptians their capabilities. He attacked religious fanaticism and political despotism, and asked for a strengthening of modern education and of parliamentary rule. He called for orators and newspapers to spread new ideas among the populace and to awaken in them patriotism and zeal for the national interest. In Alexandria in May 1879, he asked specifically for the establishment of a national party, which was in fact beginning to be established in Cairo at about the same time.

That Jamāl ad-Dīn was helping arouse Egyptians against governmental and foreign oppression by making influential and sometimes fiery public speeches in 1878 and 1879 is stressed by various sources, including the London *Times* correspondent, quoted below. More obscure is the actual nature of his political activities and goals, which may have been secret at the time, and have become further obfuscated by later legends. The years 1878 and 1879 and after were years of extremely complex political activity and intrigue in Egypt, in which many groups were involved, and those later stories that try to make of Afghānī the inspirer of all of them have no documentary justification. As described, his role seems to have been to help awaken first the

[46] *Ibid.*

intellectuals and then the masses to opposition to the policies of the Khedive Ismā'īl and the growth of Western control of Egypt, and also to plot political change, largely through his masonic group in Cairo. This plotting probably involved plans for the assassination or deposition of the Khedive and an elevation to important roles of Afghānī and his followers upon the accession of Ismā'īl's son Taufīq. Although Afghānī probably helped to inspire constitutional ideas among his followers in the Chamber of Deputies or in societies like the 1879–80 Alexandria group, Young Egypt, there is no evidence that Afghānī himself gave any particular attention to working out constitutional plans. Afghānī's chief disciple, 'Abduh, preferred, during Taufīq's regime, reform from above carried out by Afghānī's patron Riyāḍ rather than constitutional and other oppositional movements supported by others among Afghānī's disciples.[47] Stories making Afghānī responsible for *all* the opposition currents, including the army officers, the constitutionalists, and the National Party that eventually combined these two groups, are distorted.

Some of Afghānī's biographers exaggerate his direct influence on the nationalist movement of 1879–1882 that culminated in the government of Colonel 'Urābī and his followers. Afghānī and his disciples were not originally closely connected with the officers' group that made up one stream of the later National Party. These officers in the months before mid-1879, were generally working with Ismā'īl, whereas Afghānī was working against him. When 'Urābī and his fellow Egyptian officers first took power after Afghānī's exile, 'Abduh and most of Afghānī's other disciples had contempt for them, considering them ignorant and inept, and only later was there cooperation between Afghānī's disciples and the 'Urābī government.[48] As

---

47 Osman Amin (*Muhammad 'Abduh*, trans. from the Arabic by Charles Wendell [Washington, D. C., 1953], pp. 33–34) quotes 'Abduh's favorable views on the rule of Riyāḍ, whom he served in 1880–81. "Muhammad 'Abduh was a supporter of Riyad Pasha's reform ministry, and preferred this type of government to a representational form, so long as the people were unprepared for it. In the person of Riyad Pasha he saw a good example of the enlightened despot who could 'accomplish in fifteen years what reason unaided could not accomplish in fifteen centuries.' He went into this subject in a famous article entitled, 'Should a Benevolent Despot Rise in the East.' " In this article 'Abduh states that a despot can educate the people in fifteen years to prepare them first for local councils, and then for parliament.

Since others among Afghānī's followers worked for constitutionalism and against Riyāḍ, no absolute conclusion can be based on his followers' actions.

48 Kedourie, *Afghani*, pp. 26–34, and the 1883 letters from 'Abduh and others in Beirut to Afghānī in the *Documents*.

for the other, "constitutionalist," stream of the so-called National Party of 1879–1882, which helped lead the nationalist movement of those years, its earliest origins were apparently independent of Afghānī. In 1879, however, Afghānī was in contact with leaders of the opposition in the Chamber of Deputies and began to cooperate with the chief figure in the civilian nationalist movement, the constitutionalist politician Sharīf Pāshā. In the same year Afghānī also called for the formation of a national party. Afghānī was in touch with Maḥmud Samī Pāshā al-Bārūdī, later 'Urābī's chief political adviser, but stories that link Afghānī to the officers around 'Urābī appear doubtful.[49] One may reasonably conclude that Afghānī in 1879 had ties to constitutionalist politicians and was trying to form a patriotic party, but was not in close contact with the officers who were to be the main force behind the nationalist government of 1881–82.

If Afghānī was not closely involved with the nationalist Egyptian army officers, who in 1878–79 were generally working with rather than against Ismā'īl, what were his immediate political goals and activities in this period? All the direct evidence shows that he was working for the deposition of Ismā'īl, despite the latter's last-minute conversion to the national cause, and the accession of Taufīq. Contemporary reports tell us that Afghānī led a delegation of Egyptians in the spring of 1879 to the French Consul, Tricou (who arrived in May), to urge this change of rulers, and that Afghānī there claimed that he spoke in the name of a national party.[50] This intervention of Afghānī's with the French Consul—not the only example of Afghānī's propensity to deal with foreigners to get rid of foreign control—was not considered important enough by Tricou for him to report home. Indeed there is no mention of Afghānī in the French diplomatic documents on Egypt in this period, and the only English mention comes at the time of Afghānī's expulsion from Egypt, of which the British appear to have been ignorant until informed by Khedive Taufīq. 'Abduh says that Afghānī was in close contact with Taufīq,

49 Kedourie, *Afghani*, pp. 26–34, and Kudsi-Zadeh, "Legacy," pp. 167–169, have differing versions of Afghānī's relationship to the National Party; my conclusions lie in between theirs. Sabry (*Genèse*, pp. 142–143) places two prominent officer nationalists in Afghānī's masonic lodge, but their names are not given by earlier and more direct sources.

50 The earliest version of the story, by Adīb Isḥāq (in Riḍā, *Tārīkh*, p. 41), speaks only of "a large party," but the word "national" may have been included, since the phrase does appear in Afghānī's Alexandria speech, quoted above. The phrase "a national party" comes from 'Abduh's unpublished account of the 'Urābī movement quoted in Riḍā, *Tārīkh*, p. 75.

and that Afghānī and a group of notables helped persuade Sharīf to ask Ismā'īl to abdicate.[51] Ismā'īl's abdication in June, 1879 however, and the accession of Taufīq, were primarily owing to British and French pressure.

In addition to making suggestions to the French Consul, Afghānī's ideas probably encompassed at least an embryonic plot to assassinate Khedive Ismā'īl. 'Urābī in 1903 told Wilfrid Blunt: "The deposition of Ismail lifted a heavy load from our shoulders and all the world rejoiced, but it would have been better if we had done it ourselves as we could then have got rid of the whole family of Mohammed Ali, who were none of them, except Said, fit to rule, and we could have proclaimed a republic. Sheykh Jemal-ed-Din proposed to Mohammed Abdu to kill Ismail at the Kasr-el-Nil Bridge and Mohammed Abdu approved."[52] Commenting on this story, which he probably would never have raised himself, 'Abduh told Blunt:

> As to what Arabi says of his having proposed at that time to depose Ismail, there was certainly secret talk of such action. Sheykh Jemal-ed-Din was in favour of it, and proposed to me, Mohammed Abdu, that Ismail should be assassinated some day as he passed in his carriage daily over the Kasr el Nil bridge, and I strongly approved, but it was only talk between ourselves, and we lacked a person capable of taking lead in the affair. If we had known Arabi at that time, we might have arranged it with him, and it would have been the best thing that could have happened, as it would have prevented the intervention of Europe. It would not, however, have been possible to establish a republic in the then state of political ignorance of the people.[53]

Various contemporary stories make it clear that Jamāl ad-Dīn had been on good terms with the new Khedive Taufīq, who may have been a member of his masonic lodge, and that he expected Taufīq to favor him and to follow his program for reform and lessening Western control. He was soon disillusioned, though, and the violent speeches against foreigners that he had been making since 1878 he apparently resumed in the summer of 1879—indicating that whatever

---

51 *Ibid.*, p. 74.

52 Wilfrid Scawen Blunt, *Secret History of the English Occupation of Egypt* (new ed.; New York, 1922), p. 369.

53 *Ibid.*, p. 375.

understanding he thought he had with Taufīq was not working out. Taufīq was now complaisant to the foreigners who had installed him and hostile to his fiery former colleague.

Some of Afghānī's followers were evidently in part inspired by him to help found the Young Egypt society in Alexandria in 1879, which submitted to Taufīq a project for reform and lessening foreign influence, and whose newspaper, *Miṣr al-Fatat,* (Young Egypt) agitated for these causes until it was banned by Riyāḍ Pāshā, then prime minister, early in 1880. The advanced and detailed constitutional program of Young Egypt may reflect, in part, Afghānī's influence in favor of reform, although there is no direct evidence that he had advocated this specific program.[54]

Afghānī's fiery antiforeign speeches were a danger to the new Khedive, who leaned heavily on his foreign patrons. Taufīq's hostility to an effective orator and leader whose aims were contrary to his own is not surprising. One cannot be sure to what extent Taufīq had promised to give Jamāl ad-Dīn power or to implement his policies—such promises may have been made in order to encourage Jamāl ad-Dīn's support for Taufīq's accession and Ismā'īl's deposition. As often happened, however, Jamāl ad-Dīn, instead of being able to outsmart the foreigners and political leaders whom he hoped to use to

---

54 The *Documents* (pp. 47–51) have a Persian translation of a letter from Ibrāhīm al-Laqqānī to Afghānī, and a photo of the original is included. The letter gives interesting information about the Young Egypt group which supplements that found in Jacob Landau, *Parliaments and Parties in Egypt* (Tel Aviv, 1953), pp. 101–103. It also tells of the role of Afghānī's followers in 'Urābī's government, attributing to them a decisive influence. As a letter from a disciple to a master it appears to exaggerate the master's influence.

Landau notes that 'Abdallāh Nadīm, Salīm an-Naqqāsh, and Adīb Isḥāq (all followers of Afghānī) were members of Young Egypt (most of whose members were Christians and Jews), and that several of the Muslim members left on Nadīm's instigation to form an open Muslim organization instead. He also describes two reform plans of the group, saying, "These two programmes were well expressed and vehemently attacked the evils from which the people suffered. The measures which they suggested [ministerial responsibility, separation of powers, equality before the law, inviolability of person, freedom of religion and press, only lawful taxes, an independent parliament with well-defined powers and free elections, etc.] . . . seemed to offer a judicious solution to many of Egypt's problems. It would appear that the leaders of Young Egypt were not content with asking for some paltry improvements; what they desired was sweeping reform in almost every branch of life in Egypt. Their aspirations were higher and their demands more specific than those of the National Party" (p. 103). There is no evidence that Jamāl ad-Dīn had as clear a reform program in mind as did the writers of this program; nevertheless, since many of these young men were his disciples his influence cannot be discounted.

forward his program, was instead defeated—a feat not too difficult here as in other cases, since it was the foreigners and rulers, and not Jamāl ad-Dīn, who had real power in the situation. According to 'Anḥūrī, Taufīq believed that Jamāl ad-Dīn was working for a constitutional republic, headed by himself, and for this reason had him suddenly arrested and deported in late August of 1879,[55] an event discussed in more detail below.

Jamāl ad-Dīn's political importance just before his expulsion is corroborated in a dispatch from a London *Times* correspondent in Cairo, dated August 20, 1879. Headed "The National Party in Egypt," the dispatch notes the sudden development in the past few years of a nationalist press. The author continues:

> The parliamentary leader of the National party—I must use this term in default of a better—is a certain Salem Bey Miwelhy [Muwailihī]. . . . The first time I saw him was the day before the deposition of the late Viceroy [Ismā'īl], and he spoke lengthily, if not forcibly, on the necessity of giving Ismail Pasha time to carry out his suddenly developed ideas of representative reform, hinting darkly at regrettable results to the European population. . . . But behind this not very formidable individual is a far more characteristic personage. The name of Gamad-el-Din [*sic*] had become recently familiar as attached to a considerable but unknown power in Egypt. The *ipse dixit* of this mysterious being has almost obtained the weight of a Median law among the lower and less educated classes. An Afghan from Cabul by birth, he seems to have been successively expatriated from his own country, from British India, and from Constantinople, to find at Cairo a field for his intrigue and fascination . . . he passes the greater part of the day in a *café* surrounded by his disciples, to whom he lays down such law as he deems expedient for the time. Availing myself of my brotherhood as a mason, of the friendly introduction of Salim Bey Miwelhy, and most important of all, of a perfect Arabic and Persian scholar in the person of the English Director of Egyptian Telegraphs . . . I interviewed this Egyptian Cleon, and, after all that I had heard, found him, much to my surprise,
>
> "the mildest mannered man
> That ever scuttled ship or cut a throat."

---

55 'Anḥūrī in Riḍā, *Tārīkh,* p. 48.

> There was, certainly, no striking originality in his views, nor did he give expression to that fanaticism with which he is credited. But certain well-defined ideas he possessed and he knew how to express them with force. For European interference he had no toleration. The cry of "Egypt for the Egyptians" he maintained to its utmost conclusions, and when I tried to contest his statement that the Wilson-Blignières Ministry had produced no good result whatever, by referring to the cessation of taxation during that period, he stoutly insisted that that result had been produced by the expression of native public opinion and would have equally been effected under a native Ministry chosen from the proper elements. When I pressed him to assume himself Viceroy and to name the Ministry he would choose, he had a string of names ready. Cherif Pasha, he said might be tolerated, but for a time only until young Egypt had gathered strength. Altogether his views were crude and general, but I am not trying to expound the platform of a new party. I have said enough to show that a native opinion exists, has means to find expression, and therefore is not to be utterly ignored.[56]

A second dispatch, apparently from the same correspondent was dated August 30, and printed on September 8. After saying that Riyāḍ Pāshā was planning to return from the exile into which he had been forced by Ismā'īl, in order to help in Egypt's administration, the dispatch continues:

> Meanwhile, the Khedive has already given proof that he will not be made the tool of any party movement.
>
> A certain Gamad ed-Din, an Afghan of doubtful antecedents, has recently acquired a considerable influence over the lower and more fanatical native classes. Supported by Cherif Pasha, he for some time deemed it expedient to conceal his more pronounced views, but on the fall of the late Ministry [of Sharīf] he seems to have lent himself more openly to a propaganda against the introduction of the European element in any form into the administration of the country. Tewfik Pasha, however strongly he may have been opposed to the establishment of a European Ministry, has always been the first to admit the fact that Egyptian regeneration must come from the West, and ignoring *the fulsome compliments lavishly applied to him personally*, placed the Afghan under

56 *The Times*, Aug. 30, 1879.

> arrest and summarily deported him to Djeddah. This measure may not seem consonant with English ideas as to the free expression of opinion, but the peculiar circumstances of the country must be considered, and perhaps sufficient justification for the measure may be found in the fact that Gamad ed-Din was similarly expatriated from British India [italics mine].[57]

The *Times*'s association of Jamāl ad-Dīn with Sharīf Pāshā and with the leadership of the parliamentary opposition in the late summer of 1879 is confirmed elsewhere, and it is interesting that Afghānī stepped up his attacks on the regime in the few weeks between Sharīf's fall and his own expulsion in late August. Sharīf's fall occurred primarily because of Taufīq's refusal to accept the former's proposed constitutional plan. One may conclude from Afghānī's actions, writings, and speeches that in this period Afghānī was, along with Sharīf and the parliamentary opposition, in favor of a constitutional regime, which he had reason to expect to be more of a bar to foreign control and domestic oppression than was the pliable Khedive. He may also have been using his masonic followers to influence the various ministries and to criticize their unjust treatment of native Egyptians.[58] The dismissal of Sharīf meant both the fall of a protector for Afghānī and an end to his hopes that Taufīq might institute a constitutional regime, in which Afghānī and other nationalists might be expected to play a leading role. This could explain Afghānī's apparent turn to strong public speeches shortly before his expulsion, at the very time when the loss of a protector in power might make these tactics more dangerous. According to the *Times*, he increased the violence of his attacks after Sharif's fall. Afghānī, having despaired for the moment of gaining his aims through men in power—Taufīq and Sharīf—must have increased his strong and emotional appeals to the population with a hope of pressuring or overthrowing those in power. That such a hope was not fantastic is indicated by the subsequent success of the 'Urābī movement in taking over real control of the government in 1882, even while Taufīq remained Khedive.

Afghānī, however, had no such force as the Egyptian army or its officers behind him, and thus it was quite easy, as well as natural, for Taufīq to decide upon his sudden expulsion without apparent

[57] *Ibid.*, Sept. 8, 1879.

[58] Muḥammad al-Mahkzūmī, *Khāṭirāt Jamāl ad-Dīn al-Afghānī* (Beirut, 1931), pp. 44–47.

fear of the consequences. In expelling Jamāl ad-Dīn, Taufīq was not moving either irrationally or because of foreign demands, but probably because Jamāl ad-Dīn's influential oratory against the foreigners was a serious embarrassment to him, and because he suspected him of planning to increase his own power at the expense of the khedival power. It is also possible that Taufīq wanted to dispose of him before the return from abroad of Afghānī's patron Riyāḍ. In an 1882 letter to Riyāḍ, quoted below, Jamāl ad-Dīn blames malicious Egyptian enemies for his expulsion, but Taufīq also had his own reasons.

It is unclear how Jamāl ad-Dīn's break with a masonic group in this period fits into the picture. In an Arabic letter of late 1882 to his former patron, Riyāḍ, written when Afghānī stopped at Port Said on his way from India to England, he gives an account of these events which may be summarized from the draft Afghānī kept.[59]

After saying that he was in the [Suez] Canal on his way to London, and then to Paris, Jamāl ad-Dīn states that he and the Khedive [Taufīq] had been true friends, and that he had always been a friend to the Khedive's friends and an enemy to his enemies. A group of masons, to which Afghānī belonged, was working for the accession of Ḥalīm, but Afghānī writes that he opposed them out of friendship for Taufīq and quit their lodge, relinquishing its chairmanship, even though he had been their companion for many years. These masons then feared and opposed him.

The foreign masons and their [Egyptian] followers then went to Tricou, the French Consul, and told him the Egyptians wanted Ḥalīm to rule, and said there would be disturbances if another were chosen. When Jamāl ad-Dīn heard this report, he says, he and the men of his party rushed to the Consul and exposed the falsity of what he had been told. The masons, with whom Jamāl ad-Dīn had been on good terms, now accused him of being associated with the nihilists or the socialists and spread other lies about him, saying he intended to kill both the Khedive [Ismā'īl?] and the consuls. Jamāl ad-Dīn did not think anyone would believe such nonsense, but some did.

After Taufīq became khedive, continues Afghānī, a group of masons of Ḥalīm's party went to the [new] Khedive with accusations against Afghānī to get revenge. These masons were helped by all supporters of Ḥalīm, and by the chief of police, 'Uthmān Pāshā [al-

---

59 *Documents*, pls. 13–15, photos 34–37. See Appendix II for a complete translation.

Ghālib].[60] Sharīf Pāshā [the prime minister] stopped them from their slanders, and 'Uthmān complained to Afghānī after his arrest, "Sharīf tried to dismiss me because of you." After Sharīf resigned, Jamāl ad-Dīn was suddenly seized early in Ramadan while walking home at 2 A.M. When he asked the reasons, one time he was told that the ulama did not want him to remain in Egypt; another time that the foreign consuls were afraid of him; and another that Taufīq had been unable to sleep for three nights for fear of him. The true, hidden reason, says Afghānī, was what was recounted above, and Afghānī stresses the opposition of the chief of police 'Uthmān Pāshā to those who had supported Sharīf as the reason for his expulsion. Afghānī goes on to discuss his mistreatment before deportation (a summary of this section of the letter is given below).

It is difficult to evaluate this letter—unknown until the *Documents* published a photograph of Afghānī's draft—as it contains allegations that appear nowhere else. Clearly, Afghānī was trying to justify himself to Riyāḍ, then a high official in Taufīq government, but he was also dealing with a man who could check on many elements of his story. The impression given by the letter is that it gives Afghānī's beliefs about what happened to him with a bit of expedient editing. He speaks of breaking with one masonic lodge, most of whose members were partisans of Ḥalīm, and of relinquishing its chairmanship. This was probably the Eastern Star Lodge, of which Afghānī had been elected chairman in 1878. It is clear both from this letter and from other stories, summarized below, that Afghānī did not remain in accord with a large number of his former masonic followers, and that a political split with, or expulsion from, a lodge occurred in 1879.

It is known that Ḥalīm in 1879 was working to accede to the khedivate, and that Sultan Abdülhamid, who still had theoretical ultimate sovereignty over Egypt, wanted to withdraw the law issued by Sultan Abdülaziz in 1873 changing succession to the khedivate from the khedive's eldest male relative to his oldest son, an action that would have returned succession to Ḥalīm, the oldest living male in the khedival family. There is some evidence that the French may have been, for a time, inclined to allow this change by the Sultan, but ultimately British opposition to it prevailed. Ḥalīm had been

60 Rashīd Rūstam, in an interview in Cairo, Sept. 15, 1966, said that the 'Uthmān must be 'Uthmān Pāshā al-Ghālib, who was chief of police in Cairo in 1879. See the translation of this letter, Appendix II, where 'Uthmān Pāshā is called *al-Maghlūb* ("the conquered"), a play on al-Ghālib ("the conqueror").

the leader of Egypt's masons, and some of them were still his partisans. The basic story given by Afghānī of the reasons for breaking with a masonic lodge—his and his followers' partisanship for Taufīq and opposition to Ḥalīm—may thus be true. More doubtful is his attribution of his own expulsion from Egypt to false rumors spread by vengeful individuals. Such rumors may have been spread, but Taufīq had potent political reasons to fear and oppose Afghānī.

The report by Adīb Isḥāq that Afghānī and his followers set up a national, politically oriented masonic lodge affiliated to the French (Grand) Orient may refer to the months between the break with a lodge including Ḥalīm's followers and Afghānī's expulsion from Egypt. This new lodge at first worked with Taufīq and favored his accession.[61] Later, however, Taufīq came to fear Afghānī and some of its other members.

A less credible account of Afghānī's break with the masons relates it to religious unbelief. This one is found in a dispatch by the British Counsel, Lascelles, from Cairo on August 30, which also confirms the *Times*'s picture of the reasons for Afghānī's expulsion from Egypt as primarily his violent public preachings. This dispatch is the first notice the British officially took of Afghānī, with whom they seem not yet to be well acquainted. As is the case with Afghānī's later expulsion from Iran, however, the story that became common of British responsibility for his exile from Egypt may have been current among the local population at the time, and Afghānī's followers may really have believed it. Lascelles wrote on August 30:

> The Khedive has informed me that for some time past his attention has been called to the proceedings of an Afghan named Gamal El-Deen who has been inciting the people to rebellion and had been attempting to propagate Nihilism in Egypt.
>
> In spite of frequent warnings from the police, Gamal El Deen had persisted in holding meetings and preaching subversive doctrines, and the Khedive had been obliged to exile him from Egypt at 24 hours notice.
>
> Gamal El Deen, it appears, is a man of considerable capacity and great power as an orator, and he was gradually obtaining an amount of influence over his hearers which threatened to become dangerous. Last year he took an active part in stirring up ill-feeling against the Europeans, and more

61 Isḥāq in Riḍā, *Tārīkh*, pp. 40–41, and Kudsi-Zadeh, "Legacy," pp. 160–161.

> especially the English, of whom he seems to entertain a profound hatred. He was recently expelled from the Free Mason's Lodge at Cairo, of which he was a member, on account of his open disbelief in a Supreme Being.
>
> I have been informed that Gamal El Deen has been successively exiled from his native country, from Madras, from Algiers and from Constantinople and has been forbidden to live in any portion of the Ottoman Empire.[62]

To begin with the masonic part of this story, it seems unlikely that Afghānī's break with a masonic lodge should really have occurred over a theological issue at a time when his ever present concern was politics. This story may reflect Afghānī's reputation in Egypt for unorthodoxy, and there might conceivably be some connection with the Grand Orient's recent controversy removing belief in a Supreme Architect as a condition for membership.[63] More probable seems a political break with a lodge, with the religious story a rumor spread by Afghānī's enemies. This conclusion is supported not only by Afghānī's letter to Riyāḍ, but also by certain other accounts. Adīb Isḥāq and some others speak of the British Consul's spreading British agents in the lodge who wreaked havoc in it. Muḥammad al-Makhzūmī, basing himself on what Afghānī said many years later, gives purported texts of Afghānī's talks disagreeing with members of a Scottish lodge who had said the masons should not participate in politics.[64] These supposedly came at the time of a break with a Scottish lodge, a time that preceded the placing of the Eastern Star under Afghānī's leadership; but the story appears to relate to a lodge's expulsion of Afghānī, which may have occurred later (although there might have been two breaks with lodges—one about 1876, and another in 1879). In any case, the story confirms Afghānī's political view of masonry. There are thus several independent and conflicting accounts of the reasons for Afghānī's quarrel with one or more masonic lodges, but the weight of evidence seems to be that a split occured for political

---

62 Great Britain, Public Record Office, Documents, Foreign Office (henceforth called F.O.) 78/3003, Lascelles to Salisbury, no. 498, Cairo, Aug. 30, 1879.

63 Kedourie, *Afghānī*, p. 21. Kudsi-Zadeh ("Legacy," pp. 157–160), however, gives reasons for rejecting both such a connection and the British Consul's story.

64 Makhzūmī, *op. cit.*, pp. 44–47. Kudsi-Zadeh, "Legacy," pp. 155–157, supports Makhzūmī's chronology and also the view that Afghānī's break was political. The primary accounts on Afghānī's masonic activities are often conflicting and confusing.

reasons, at a time when Afghānī was advocating a political course with which other masons disagreed.

Afghānī's power and persuasion as a mass orator as well as his ties with the elite both among young intellectuals and among the leaders of the National Assembly made him a power to be reckoned with in 1879. If the new Khedive were to persist in his policy of complaisance toward the French and British, who had brought him to power, he had to fear further public attacks by Afghānī on this policy and possibly plots against himself. It is probably significant of Afghānī's considerable influence that the Khedive chose to expel him very suddenly and without warning, before any protests could be made, and also that he chose the period in the interregnum between two powerful politicians, Sharīf and Riyāḍ, each of whom had protected Afghānī. As noted, the expulsion occurred after the fall of Sharīf Pāshā's Ministry, and before Riyāḍ had returned to Egypt to take up office again.

Afghānī and his disciples tell of his rude expulsion from Egypt in late August 1879 when he had no more than the clothes on his back, and also tell a story emanating from the Iranian consul at Suez, who says he offered Afghānī some money for his trip, but Afghānī refused.[65]

In his letter to Riyāḍ late in 1882, Afghānī dwells upon the details of his ill treatment. He says that 'Uthmān Pāshā, who he claims was the key source of Taufīq's suspicions, said to him: " 'I exaggerated about you, but you must go to Hell, either via Iran or India.' However much I sought to be sent to Istanbul or Paris or the Hijaz, he insisted on sending me to Hell. He did not even give me two days, under police guard, to sell what I could not take." Afghānī continues that he was taken from Cairo and kept for two days at Suez, where he was not allowed to eat, and that the local police chief took the money, beads, and handkerchiefs from his and his servant's pockets, claiming that Taufīq had ordered this. "All this came from the activity of Ḥalīm's party and their falsehood. . . . On top of everything, I realized that Ḥalīm's supporters would laugh, since I supported the Khedive and they knew the truth." Jamāl ad-Dīn goes on to tell Riyāḍ that the recent disasters that had overcome Egypt

[65] Isḥāq and 'Abduh in Riḍā, *Tārīkh*, pp. 42, 74–77. 'Abduh claims it was foreign representatives who frightened Taufīq of Afghānī, but, as indicated above, it is likely that foreign suggestions or pressures, which may have occurred, were scarcely necessary.

['Urābī's rule and the fighting that had just culminated in the British occupation of Egypt] were "Divine Retribution" for the government's mistreatment of him, Jamāl ad-Dīn.[66] The same theme of divine retribution visited on powerful men who mistreat him recurs later in Jamāl ad-Dīn's correspondence, particularly regarding his treatment in Iran.

In the same letter Afghānī rejects the reason for his expulsion published in the official gazette, *al-Waqā'i' al-Misriyya* (Cairo, August 31, 1879), that he belonged to a society aiming at the "ruin of religion and the world." The total text of the letter to Riyāḍ indicates that Afghānī regarded his expulsion as a result of betrayal by his Egyptian political enemies, specifically by the masonic and other partisans of Ḥalīm, and by 'Uthmān Pāshā al-Ghālib, both of whom influenced Taufīq against him. Although Afghānī, later in the same letter, shows no hesitation in complaining bitterly about the British for their treatment of him in India, he does not implicate the British in his Egyptian expulsion. 'Uthmān Pāshā is said to have mentioned opposition by the foreign consuls and by the Egyptian ulama as reasons for Afghānī's expulsion, but Afghānī himself here gives no weight to these reasons.[67] It is quite possible that foreign consuls and local ulama had made complaints about Afghānī, but there is no credible evidence that their influence was decisive. Taufīq, despite Afghānī's disclaimers, had reason to fear a powerful and influential orator and agitator who was asking for action against the British and in favor of a strengthened parliamentary regime—two courses opposed by Taufīq. Afghānī's expulsion was thus a logical act from Taufīq's viewpoint.

To summarize Afghānī's position in the late 1870's: Although his immediate political plans, which probably involved a leading role for himself in the independent government he wanted to set up in Egypt, came to naught, there is no denying his influence. If one disregards the words of men who wrote much later, even the *Times* correspondent shows his importance, while those Egyptians and

---

66 *Documents*, pls. 13–15, photos 34–37. See Appendix II.

67 *Ibid.* Kudsi-Zadeh ("Legacy," pp. 180–181) gives his reasons for accepting the Arabic accounts implicating the foreign, and particularly British, consuls, While some of the consuls may have complained about Afghānī, the main point remains that contemporary documents give no reason to believe that such complaints were crucial; Taufīq and Afghānī's official enemies had strong enough motives of their own.

Syrians who wrote and spoke of him only a few years afterward also assert his major role. According to Rashīd Riḍā, 'Abduh even said to him once that Afghānī did worthwhile work only in Egypt.[68] (It is evident from other sources that 'Abduh became disillusioned with Afghānī's methods after 1885.) As argued above, Afghānī was able to inspire young intellectuals largely because he provided a bridge between their traditional culture and the acceptance of various more liberal, rational, and modern approaches—a bridge that came largely from his own philosophical and esoteric Islamic background.

Various accounts of Afghānī's effects on his Egyptian disciples indicate this path. Among them is an account by the Arabophile British author and amateur politician, Wilfrid S. Blunt, of going to Egypt late in 1880 and taking as an Arabic instructor a young Azhar Shaikh, Muḥammad Khalīl. Although this man's account of Afghānī's role given by Blunt in his *Secret History of the English Occupation of Egypt* is a bit exaggerated, the general tone is typical enough. After noting his own delight with Muḥammad Khalīl's broad and tolerant religious views, supported with citations from Islamic texts, Blunt says of him:

> He gave me, too, an account of how this school of enlightened interpretation had sprung up almost within his own recollection at the Azhar.
>
> The true originator of the Liberal religious Reform movement among the Ulema of Cairo was, strangely enough, neither an Arab, nor an Egyptian, nor an Ottoman, but a certain wild man of genius, Sheykh Jemal-ed-din Afghani. . . . Hitherto all movements of religious reform in Sunnite Islam had followed the lines not of development, but of retrogression. There had been a vast number of preachers, especially in the last 200 years, who had taught that the decay of Islam as a power in the world was due to its followers having forsaken the ancient ways of simplicity and the severe observance of the law as understood in the early ages of the faith. On the other hand, reformers there had been of a modern type recently, both in Turkey and Egypt, who had Europeanized the administration for political purposes, but these had introduced their changes as it were by violence, through decrees and approvals obtained by force from the unwilling Ulema, and with no serious attempt to reconcile them with

---

68 Riḍā, *Tārīkh*, p. 79.

> the law of the Koran and the traditions. The political reforms had been always imposed from above, not suggested from below, and had generally been condemned by respectable opinion. Jemal-ed-din's originality consisted in this, that he sought to convert the religious intellect of the countries where he preached to the necessity of reconsidering the whole Islamic position, and, instead of clinging to the past, of making an onward intellectual movement in harmony with modern knowledge. His intimate acquaintance with the Koran and the traditions enabled him to show that, if rightly interpreted and checked the one by the other, the law of Islam was capable of the most liberal developments and that hardly any beneficial change was in reality opposed to it.[69]

Afghānī's importance in integrating Islamic traditions and modern needs is here indicated.

It is apparent that Afghānī was concerned with much more than his own advancement, which, with his intelligence and abilities, he could have achieved better by means other than those he chose to follow. He manifested a consistent concern for the self-strengthening of each Muslim country he visited, and for the achievement of its independence from the encroaching West, and particularly from the British. In Egypt he was also cencerned to spread a more liberal interpretation of Islam, largely as an instrument toward modernization and self-strengthening. In general Afghānī's concern with religion was in part as an instrument in achieving those ends, as will be seen in the analysis below of the "Refutation of the Materialists," (so-called in Arabic, but not in its original Persian) written shortly after his expulsion from Egypt. Even in this instrumental view of religion, however, Afghānī was working within certain Islamic traditions and precedents, since the separation of religion from politics scarcely exists in Islam, and the philosophers in particular had views about the political use of religion which were quite similar to Afghānī's. Here again his innovation was to adapt the philosophical view to pressing nineteenth-century political needs, and to a political activism among the masses which had been more characteristic of the heterodox sects than of the philosophers. The use of speeches and newspapers to politicize public opinion was also a significant innovation.

Afghānī's exact political goals in Egypt are still unclear, and this

---

69 Blunt, *op. cit.*, pp. 76–77.

question must await the appearance of further evidence. Although he made appeals to the masses and wanted Egypt's parliament strengthened, it cannot yet be asserted confidently that he had any specific constitutional program.

The goal that he most clearly and constantly stated was independence from Western encroachments, and this was probably the most important point for him. Some of his followers, specifically those in the Young Egypt party in Alexandria in 1879–80, did work out advanced programs for independence and constitutional reform. Afghānī was an advocate of reform and an attacker of the injustice of the khedival government, but there is no indication of a definite program for a better governmental structure. It is unsafe to extrapolate his views from the programs and activities of his immediate disciples, since, though some of them advocated increased power to the elected representative of the people, 'Abduh was rather an advocate of a preparatory period of enlightened despotism. 'Abduh was exiled to his village at the time of Afghānī's expulsion, but was later recalled to serve Riyāḍ's ministry, and he seems to have felt that a program of slow reform under Riyāḍ was preferable to the nationalist 'Urābī movement that followed.[70]

---

[70] Amin, *op. cit.*, pp. 33–44. Amin quotes 'Abduh on 'Urābī: " 'As for 'Arabi, it had occurred to him neither to reform the government nor to change its head. Such matters were above his powers of imagination. All his thoughts, and his only dominant motives, were fears for his position, a violent hatred of his Circassian colleagues, and his detestation of 'Uthman Pasha [Rifqī]. He had no interests apart from making his position secure, revenging himself on his enemy, and breaking the stranglehold of the Circassians on military appointments. His intention was to enjoy the salaries and influences they had monopolized, since he and the other Egyptian officers had a greater right than strangers to such privileges." After that . . . 'Arabi wanted 'to make use of the army to attempt the formation of a parliament with the same rights as the parliaments of Europe. He imagined that if this parliament were to be created, its members and the people it represented would be grateful to the man who had brought it into existence and that they would make it their concern to preserve his life and his power. He was confident that he could use the members of parliament just as he did the officers of the army. . . . it did not enter his mind that if he did this, both he and the power he appealed to would fall into a bottomless pit; for if he made a plaything of it, he would pave the way for others to hold it in contempt, and it would become a simple matter to abandon all respect for its authority' " (pp. 39–40). Amin adds, " 'Abduh's ideas up to the day of the Abdin demonstration were different as can be imagined from those of 'Arabi, as Mr. Broadley, counsel for the defense of the 'Arabi Party, has remarked. From the very inception of the rebellion, the Sheikh had been a supporter of Riyad Pasha, since he felt that the aims of 'Arabi and his group were not those of the nation as a whole, but of a purely military clique. He considered their actions illegal . . ." (pp. 41–42). After quoting 'Abduh's memoirs on these points, he says that 'Abduh only added his strength to the 'Urābī party

There is no question that Afghānī had an important influence on a small but important group of Egyptians and Syrians, many of whom became outstanding writers of political figures, and, for a shorter time, on a much wider circle. Afghānī's immediate disciples had little direct role in the rise of 'Urābī's nationalist movement, but they did help to arouse nationalist ideas and feelings. They also entered in the later work of the 'Urābī government, when 'Abduh and other disciples of Afghānī had governmental posts. In general, however, Afghānī's contribution to the effective development of Egyptian nationalism in this period is to be found in his influence on a small group of disciples and then on the press and public, more than in direct impact on the course of events between 1879 and 1882. The nationalist movement in these years was led largely by men whose ideas and plans were not primarily shaped by Afghānī. Those stories that attribute the major events of these years to Afghānī's influence are in the realm of glorifying myths. Even after these myths are stripped away, however, Afghānī remains a major figure in the history of the political awakening of Egypt.[71]

---

after it became clear that the Europeans and the Khedive were trying to destroy the national movement.

[71] Kudsi-Zadeh ("Legacy") goes into more detail than I have on the role and influence of Afghānī in Egypt. In this work he stresses Afghānī's influence more than I, but we are not now in major disagreement. The problem of evaluating conflicting sources is so acute for Afghānī biographers that identical conclusions are not to be expected even from those who stress a critical reading of primary accounts. Professor Kudsi-Zadeh is now publishing a paper entitled "Jamāl al-Dīn al-Afghānī and the National Awakening of Egypt: A Reassessment of His Role," *Actes de Ve Congrès d'Etudes Arabes et Islamiques, Bruxelles, 1970* (in press). In a private letter he says, "my conclusions in Brussels paper . . . are quite similar to yours." Professor Kudsi-Zadeh and I have drawn closer together in the years since our first work, both of us having moved some from our original views.

6

The Pan-Islamic Appeal

FROM EGYPT, Afghānī was sent to India, where he remained until late 1882. Before Afghānī's Indian stay is discussed, a long undated Pan-Islamic letter from Afghānī to an Ottoman statesman written apparently in the 1870's is analyzed. Prior to the last years of Afghānī's Egyptian stay, there is no documentation tying him to the nascent Pan-Islamic movement, with which he was later so prominently associated. From what is known of his teachings in Egypt, they consisted of a combination of Islamic philosophy, reformism, and strong antiforeign preachings with nationalistic overtones. Although he apparently tried to show that the roots of the reforms he suggested could be found in Islam, he made no particular efforts as a Muslim apologist, and was under attack for unorthodoxy, in Egypt as well as for his political activities. Beginning with the publication of the "Refutation of the Materialists" in India in 1881, however, and continuing through the later years, Afghānī presents himself to Muslims more and more as a defender both of Islam and of Pan-Islam. This chapter suggests that Afghānī sometimes used Pan-Islamic arguments in the late 1870's. How can this development be accounted for?

In large measure, Afghānī was apparently responding, with his always sharp antennae, to the developing mood of the times in the Muslim world. As Niyazi Berkes and others have shown, the Pan-

Islamic and anti-European policies adumbrated from 1871 to 1876 under the Ottoman Sultan Abdülaziz and carried out by Sultan Abdülhamid from 1876 on, represented not merely a personal whim, but a change in the mood of Ottoman subjects. All the vaunted reforms and Westernizing efforts of the preceding *tanzimat* period had not served either to hold the aggressive West back from attacks or to defeat the infidels once battle was joined. The Russo-Turkish War of 1877–1878, followed by the European imposition of terms at the Congress of Berlin along with the growing financial difficulties of the Ottoman Empire, led to a reaction against the Westernizing program which appeared to have brought on such disastrous results.[1] Elsewhere there were similar reactions against the increasingly aggressive encroachments of Europeans, which were being felt in the 1870's and which culminated in the French occupation of Tunisia in 1881, the British occupation of Egypt in 1882, and the Russian conquest of Merv in 1884. The examples of German and Italian unification also suggested to many Muslims the potency of movements for unity of divided territories behind a single government.

Just as Pan-Islamic ideas had got their first impetus from British aggression in India and Russian aggression in Central Asia, so they were now given a strong further thrust by the stepped-up pace of European financial penetration and conquest in the Ottoman Empire and adjacent lands. How easy and natural it was for one whose primary concern had been reform within the Islamic world to turn also to appeals to Pan-Islamic unity is seen in the case of the Ottoman Turkish reformer, Namık Kemal, who, in the early seventies, was already calling for the unity of Islam.[2] Pan-Islam had the advantage, already seen in some of Jamāl ad-Dīn's teachings, of appealing both to traditional and new needs. Calls for holy war or defense of Islam had a strong traditional basis, as did the notion of restoring a single Islamic state under a revived caliphate. Both ideas, however, could also appeal to a kind of nascent nationalist sentiment. Like more secular nationalisms, this looked back to early traditions of cultural greatness and military prowess and worked for their revival. The ideal of independence from foreign control also had a nationalist element. The contradictions between Pan-Islam and local national-

---

1 Niyazi Berkes, *The Development of Secularism in Turkey* (Montreal, 1964), pp. 253–271.

2 *Ibid.*, pp. 262–268; Şerif Mardin, *The Genesis of Young Ottoman Thought* (Princeton, 1962), chap. and pp. 59–61.

isms which were eventually to smother the former did not appear significant until the early twentieth century.

Although it is impossible to know Afghānī's thought processes, it is clear enough from the "Refutation of the Materialists" and later writings that beginning in the early 1880's he presented himself more decisively to the Islamic public as a defender first of Islam and then of Pan-Islam. More specifically, as is discussed below, he put forth considerable effort to get himself into the good graces of Sultan Abdülhamid. We have already seen Afghānī's propensity—natural enough given the limits of political processes at the time—to enter into relations with those in high position and work through them. His contacts with A'zam Khān, his efforts to advance himself in *tanzimat* circles in Istanbul, and his ties with Taufīq, Riyāḍ, and others in Egypt are typical. At some point Afghānī got the notion of establishing relations with Abdülhamid, who must have seemed to represent the wave of the future, and of trying to become involved in the Sultan's Pan-Islamic program. The idea presented in the standard biography that Afghānī was seduced by Abdülhamid's blandishments in 1892 is contrary to fact. As noted below, Jamāl ad-Dīn initiated dealings with Abdülhamid in 1885, and some of the contents of the "Refutation" made it seem possible that one of its secondary motivations was to appeal to Abdülhamid and those around him.[3]

Finally, the *Documents* present a most significant photograph of a letter by Afghānī to a high Ottoman statesman which presents an appeal that Afghānī be used as a Pan-Islamic emissary. Although the recipient is unnamed, it would seem most probable that it was one of the Ottoman officials whom Afghānī had met or had had some ties with during his stay in Istanbul in 1869–1871. The appeal is clearly directed ultimately to the Sultan, whose approval would be needed for the plans Afghānī suggests. And although the document is most unfortunately undated, and there seems no way to date it with certainty, the most probable date would appear to be ca. 1877–1878. This date appears probable for the following reasons, arising from internal evidence in the document:

1. The projected action suggested by Afghānī—to arouse Muslims bordering on or within Russia to rise against the Russians—suggests that the document dates from the period of the Russo-Turkish war

[3] Cf. chaps. 9 and 11 below.

of 1877–1878. Specifically, Afghani asks for an Ottoman mission to such Muslim peoples, and says that he will "emphasize Russia's aims and convey with an eloquent tongue that if, God forbid, a calamity befalls the Ottoman Government, neither will permanence remain to Mecca nor majesty to Medina." This and other passages in the petition would most plausibly refer to the period 1877–1878.

2. The itinerary suggested by Afghānī for himself suggests a period close to and no later than 1879. In the letter he expresses a willingness to go to Istanbul first, and gives India as his first other destination, indicating he was not yet in India. In his 1882 letter to Riyāḍ (translated in full in Appendix II) Afghānī speaks of his desire in 1879 to go to either Istanbul or Paris, and he in fact went to India for a few years in preference to Iran, where the Egyptians by his own testimony were willing to send him.

3. It does not seem likely that Afghānī would have made this type of pro-British appeal subsequent to the publication of his newspaper, *al-'Urwa al-Wuthqā*, in 1884 where his violent anti-British sentiments were so widely publicized. The similar Pan-Islamic appeal to the Ottoman authorities dating from years later (1891 or 1892) published by Jacob Landau makes quite a different international argument, based on the Sultan's changed sentiments. There all European powers are seen as equally hostile to the Ottoman Empire.[4]

4. The modest language in relation to himself in the original, that is, "an unknown and insignificant person" and other such expressions, going beyond mere formalities, implies that the letter dates from a time when Jamāl ad-Dīn was not well known; again indicating that the letter probably preceded publication of *al-'Urwa al-Wuthqā.*

It must be admitted that logic does not always reveal the truth where Afghānī is concerned, and it is possible that the appeal is somewhat earlier or later than suggested here.[5] Because of the doubt

---

[4] Jacob M. Landau, "Al-Afghani's Panislamic Project," *Islamic Culture*, XXVI, 3 (July, 1952), 50–54.

[5] Discussions with Homa Pakdaman and further study have led me to change my earlier opinion that the letter dates from the mid-1880's. On the other hand I am not convinced by Dr. Pakdaman's view that the letter dates *at the latest* from the beginning of Afghānī's eight-year stay in Egypt and is probably connected with the unexplained passport from the Persian consul in Cairo issued to Afghānī for travel to Istanbul dated July 1871 photographed in the *Documents* (Pakdaman, pp. 50–55). Mrs. Pakdaman's view is not impossible, and should it come to be supported by further evidence it would indicate that Pan-Islamic ideas were expressed by Afghānī much earlier than any dated source indicates, and that he was more an innovator in Pan-Islam than this chapter suggests. Dr. Pakdaman's

surrounding the date of this document, a chapter is here devoted to it alone near its most likely date, without forcibly tying it to any definite chronological sequence. The main line of action and thought suggested by the letter is in accord with Afghānī's words and deeds from the time he left Egypt until the end of his life, and whatever the letter's date, it provides evidence of his trend of thought in his Pan-Islamic phase.

This Persian letter, in its entirety, reads:

> To the Firm Pillar of the Kingdom and the People and the Impregnable Fortress of the Eternal Lofty Government, the Glory of the Ottoman Race and Soul of the Body of All the Muslims, the Pivot of the State and the Glorious One:
>
> I respectfully submit:
>
> Although some of the people of the Porte have wronged this unfortunate one and followed the path of oppression, nevertheless from the nation (*milla*) I have not seen oppression and I have not experienced the bitterness of tyranny from Islam. And since I am counted a part of the nation and a piece of that community (*umma*), if a calamity befalls them or the thorn of humiliation pricks their foot, there is no doubt that I will be steadfast in self-sacrifice, and will choose my death over such a life of humiliation. Consequently, when I looked at the state of the lofty Ottoman Government in this age, and when I considered the condition of the Islamic nation (*millat-i islāmiyyeh*) it rent the shirt of my patience and I was overcome by fearful thoughts and visions from every side. Like a fearfully obsessed man day and night, from beginning to end, I have thought of this affair and have made the means of reform and salvation of this *milla* my profession and incantation. In order to find a means of delivery from these terrible difficulties, I have studied the condition of former peoples and states and the cause of their ascent and decline and their rising and setting, and I have considered the great deeds that have emanated from individual men which are worthy of strong wonder and awe: Until my attention fell in passing on the life of Abū Muslim of Khurasan, who with high purpose and skill extirpated, root and branch, a government like the government of the Banī Umayya, at the peak of power

dating would put the letter in the reign of Abdülaziz, not Abdülhamid, and would demonstrate Pan-Islamic concerns by Afghānī in 1871 which he did not write of again until the 1880's. Thanks to D. A. Rustow for first suggesting the 1877–1878 date.

and the height of fortune, and who scraped their proud face into the dust of baseness. And also at the time of the ranging of my thoughts in this field, the life of Peter the Hermit passed before my perception: The zeal of that indigent hermit and the resolution of that poor monk; how he took a cross on his back and traversed deserts and mountains and entered city after city of the Franks, and in every kingdom raised the cry: "On to battle"; so that he became the cause of the Crusades and the kindler of those horrendous events. The flame of emulation was lit in my heart, and the devotion and skill of the Khurasanian made life and ease forbidden (*harām*) for me. I knew that to consider deeds difficult is nothing but meanness of spirit and baseness and vileness of nature, and that every difficult thing is simple to possessors of resolution and every trouble is accepted by those with zeal. And since that magnificent pivot of the state [i.e., the addressee] is known in all climes for complete resolution, and is praised on all tongues of the people of the cities and has chosen patriotism (*hubb-i milla*) and has seen his honor in the perpetuation of this holy people (*ummat-i muqaddaseh*); therefore I will with full freedom express my thoughts to Your Excellency, without regard for the fact that I am an unknown and insignificant person, and Your Excellency is a famous amir; since the sages of the world on questions of service to the *milla* and love for the government and *umma* pay no attention to rank but always keep their eyes on the goals, from wherever it may come and from whomever it may be.

And these thoughts are:

FIRST: Since the Muslims of India, with their great numbers are mostly holders of property and wealth, and are extremely firm in Islam and are devoted in the defense of the faith and the *milla,* despite the frailty of their bodies; and although these rich men always boast of their equity and liberality and are happy to give, especially in support of the faith, and wish for praise and fame in the path of religion and the protection of the faith, and seek glory; nevertheless they have slept the sleep of neglect and reposed on the bed of ignorance; and they have not understood the benefits of unity and harmony and they do not perceive the harm of division and discord. Therefore, this humble one [i.e., I] desires for the love of the community (or patriotically—Arabic, *ḥubban fī al-milla*) to proceed to that kingdom and to meet with all the *navvābs* and princes and ulama and grandees of that land and explain to them one by one the results that are manifested from unity and solidarity in the whole world and the injuries that have appeared from division and disunity; and to caress their ears with the mystery of the *ḥadīth,* "the faithful are brothers"; and to express inspiring and prudent words and to attract the friendship and cooperation of the learned and the eloquent; and to breathe into them *the new spirit of love of nationality* [*rūh-i jadīd-i hubb-i milliyyat*—an indication that Afghānī recognized the novelty of this spirit] and to rend the curtain of their neglect; to explain to them the place of the luminous Sultanate in the world of Islam; and to reveal and make manifest to this group the fact that the perpetuation of religion depends on the perpetuation of this government. And in all the mosques of the famous cities I shall light a flame in their inner hearth by means of appealing sermons and *ḥadīths* of the Best of the Prophets, and I shall altogether burn out their patience and long-suffering. And I shall dispatch some of the eloquent ulama among them to some of the distant cities and I shall call all the Muslims of India to contribute money, and I shall not follow another road but this, without encroaching upon the policy of the English Government or speaking a word against them. Indeed I shall lay the foundation of my case on the intentions of the Russians [against the Muslims] and will speak eloquently on this subject. And there is no doubt that the English nation (*tā'ifeh*) will be made happy by this wise movement, which will be the cause of the repulsion of the Indians from the Russians; and it is possible that the English, when they recognize that this movement is in harmony with their policy, they too will encourage them [the Indians] to contribute financially, and will become a true partner in this affair. When the movement takes place in India it will have several advantages: *first,* I have no doubt that incalculable financial aid will be forthcoming; *second,* strong friendship and cooperation, perhaps complete Unity of Islam (*ittihād-i tāmm-i islāmiyyeh*) will come about among the Muslims; *third,* when the Unity of all the Muslims becomes understood by the English nation of course they will always maintain a firm policy [in support of] the Ottoman Government; *fourth,* a fine point which is not hidden from those of perception [?implying a revivified and expanded Muslim empire under the Sultan].

SECOND: I wish after the completion of the Indian affair to go to Afghanistan and invite the people of that land, who like a wild lion have no fear of bloodshed and do not admit hesitation in war, especially religious war, to a religious struggle and a national endeavour [*muhārabeh-yi dīniyyeh va mujāhadeh-yi milliyyeh*].[6] I shall emphasize Russia's aims and convey with an eloquent tongue that if, God forbid, a calamity befalls the Ottoman Government, neither will permanence remain to Mecca, nor majesty to Medina, and not even the name of Islam or a rite of the faith will survive. And that afterward they will neither hear the voice of the *mu'azzin* nor see the Koran reader. They will be as low as the Jews of Bukhara, and like sheep without masters a prey to the rapacious wolf. I shall strike the call, "Arise to battle," and raise the sound, "O, sacrifice for Islam." And I shall send the good eloquent ulama to all the people, to the valleys and the mountains, and I shall sponsor alliances with the princes and nobles and warriors and khans. And in all religious sermons I shall make clear the advantages of zeal and ardor and will make a general call to the *millī* war to all, young and old, weak and strong. And I will send some of the experienced, informed, and wise ulama secretly to Kokand and Bukhara to explain conditions for the people of those lands, and make them *await the time and the hour and the arrival of the end of the period* [*muntazir-i vaqt va sā'at va hulūl-i muddat*—the exact terminology often used to herald the advent of the Mahdi].

And after finishing the call in Afghanistan I will go to Baluchistan with the greatest speed and call the people of that land, who are continually employed in brigandage and raiding and plunder, to [join] the general war, with religious exhortation and the lure of worldly profit, and will bring to bear on them the old tricks of diplomacy. And I will head to the Turkomans—those unfortunates who were always known for bravery and daring, and celebrated in all tongues for bloodshed and rebelliousness, but recently have worn the hat of shame on their head and the shirt of disgrace on their breast, and thrown their fame of so many years to the wind, and submit to the subjection of the commands of Russia—and I will call them to revenge and incite the pride of their Turkish race [*jinsiyyat-i turkiyyeh*—another modern thought]

---

6 This phrase is an interesting indication of the admixture of secular and religious "nationalism" in Afghānī; the secular word for war is modified by "religious" while the "holy war" word is defined as "national," though at this time *milliyyeh* could still also have a religious meaning. Both meanings were probably intermixed in Afghānī.

and carry the banner of Unity of Islam (*ittihād-i islāmiyyeh*) on my shoulder into those regions also and call to religious war, and as usual not overlook any strategem or ruse, and plant the seed of ardor and zeal within them, always working with the wisest ulama. And I shall send missionaries of sharp tongue to Kashgar and Yarkand to call the believers of those lands to the unity of the people of the faith. And it is obvious that, when the people begin to fight, the amirs perforce will enter the field without delay. Since I know the customs and temperament of those people and have insight into their nature and habits, I have no doubt that all the Muslims will attack the Russians enthusiastically. They will conquer the Russians on that side, and even altogether destroy them. And no one can deny the immediate advantages of such an event, and its far-reaching benefit, which is the unity of Islam and the union of the community (*ittihād-i islāmiyyeh va ittifāq-i ummat*). And along with this when the people of Afghanistan, who are really the wall and buttress of India, attack Russia, the English will inevitably and forcibly devote their whole efforts to the fight, and will be mired up to their necks and give up the thoughts of domination. [There is an ambiguity, probably deliberate, as to whether the Russians, the English or, by implication, both, will be so distracted by this fight as to give up attempts at domination of the Muslims and Ottomans.]

And if someone should object to this plan, saying: The people of Kokand and Bukhara and Shahr-i Sabz and the Turkomans, are they not the very ones who did not bring the ardor to resist the Russians, and who did not carry honor from the field, and who chose a dishonorable life over an honorable death, and committed that kind of dishonor, therefore what benefit can come from asking their aid; *I say that those wars which occurred were entirely for the sake of tyrannical amirs or oppressive governors*; and when does a man give his life for the sensual pleasures of this kind of amir and governor, and why should he place the foot of firmness and manliness into the field? *But if they fight for the defense of religion and the preservation of the faith they would either have a crown of martyrdom on their heads or the robe of honor on their breasts. For in that time everyone for the sake of his beloved object alone will seek to step into the battlefield and seek battle for the glory of religion.*

And after explaining the plan I respectfully submit that this humble one in no way wishes either a dirham or a dinar from the government. Rather I will arise to this dangerous cause for the love of Islam.

Yes—After getting financial aid in India it occurs to this humble one that I would like some medals for the Afghan, Baluch, and Turkoman amirs. The commission of such an important, weighty affair without permission and authorization from the government would be considered a presumption and an unacceptable act. Also, since those lands are extremely far from the center of politics, and their people are cut off from news of the world and of the Ottoman Government at this time, if I carry out this work without authorization perhaps the amirs of those lands will not like it, and from the seeking of unity discord will arise. Therefore I beg that this letter be passed before your perceptive eyes and its suggestions be weighed one by one by the eyes of your unerring mind, without regard for the fact that the writer is a low and insignificant man, who has no high rank and who has not achieved exalted office; because to that fortunate one [i.e., you] it is apparent that in every age great deeds of this sort issue from a man like me, wandering and with rough garments, knowing cold and heat, bitter and sweet, and having traversed many mountains and deserts and experienced the ways of men. For the men of position are apprehensive about their station, and the owners of wealth and possessions fear for their wealth and property, and possessors of luxury have not been able to endure hardship.

Therefore, if this supplication is accepted by the firm judgment and discriminating mind of that lord of wisdom and intelligence, invest me with a letter of authorization and fortify this humble one with a clear permit, so that with the utmost speed, before time is lost, I may set to work, and in this arena may sacrifice my life for the sake of the *milla*. And if for the purpose of receiving instructions it should be necessary for this humble one to come to Istanbul, I am wholly submissive to the order. The rest is the command of that lord of commands [i.e., the addressee].[7]

---

[7] *Documents*, photos 26–27.

Brief Analysis of the Appeal

WHAT DOES this document reveal about Afghānī? First of all, particularly in conjunction with the document published by Landau and other efforts of Afghānī to approach Abdülhamid II, it casts doubt on the frequent assertion that Afghānī had no special interest in working with or for the Ottoman government. In fact Afghānī was the initiator of this relationship, and made some efforts to get himself employed by that government.

Second, Afghānī says that he was depressed and fearful because of the state of the Islamic nation and was searching for a means of its reform and salvation when he thought of the example of two great men of the past who had rallied their peoples together in holy war against heavy odds. Whether Afghānī is giving an exact account of his actual thought process is not too important. What is important, and is substantiated by later words and deeds, is that Afghānī often felt that the Islamic world could best be saved from the growing menace of European encroachments by an appeal from a charismatic leader, himself, to holy war. Afghānī places side by side Abū Muslim, the Iranian hero who rallied the pro-Abbasid forces against the hated "impious" Umayyads, and Peter the Hermit, a formidable opponent of Islam. For him they were both valid examples of the utility of religious appeals for political purposes. Afghānī then specifically compares himself with Abū Muslim, whom he wishes to emulate.

The strong emphasis on holy war as the way to achieve Pan-Islamic goals is significant. Afghānī on this point is not simply adapting himself to the official Ottoman Pan-Islamic program, but is putting forth a scheme more rash than anything the Sultans ever countenanced. Afghānī, influenced both by Muslim and Christian history, saw in holy war with messianic overtones a sure means for arousing the world's Muslims to action and re-creating a strong Islamic state.

It is probable that he was not quite so unrealistic as the explicit content of the letter would suggest, and that what he had in mind then, as at other times, was to encourage a war between Russia and England, which he hoped would lead to Muslim uprisings. Indeed, this is strongly suggested in the letter itself. But Afghānī was unrealistic throughout his life in not appreciating to what extent the vast technological and military superiority of the West made so aggressive a Pan-Islamic program impossible for the Ottoman government. What Abū Muslim, or, more recently, the rulers of Prussia and Piedmont, could do militarily, the Ottoman Sultan simply could not.

The use of not only holy war but even messianic terminology—the exact words that herald the advent of the Mahdi—is surely no accident. It goes along with other indications that Afghānī and some of his followers saw him as playing a messianic role. The letter has the quite typical mixture of messianism, religion, and pragmatic politics—the first two to be used for goals that are Islamic only in the sense that they will increase the strength of the Islamic peoples. This was certainly a legitimate goal from the point of view of the Islamic tradition, but it was not unually pursued with such an avowed instrumental utilization of messianic and other appeals.

In one sentence alone, that on the appeal projected for the Turkomans, there is the whole mixture, typical for Afghānī, of nationalism, Pan-Islam, holy war, scheming, and use of the ulama for political goals: "I will call them to revenge and incite the pride of their Turkish race and carry the banner of Unity of Islam on my shoulder and call to religious war, and as usual not overlook any strategem or ruse, and plant the seed of ardor and zeal within them, always working with the wisest ulama."

Afghānī includes a criticism of "tyrannical amirs and oppressive governors," and notes that people would rather fight for the defense of the faith than for such men. He does not, however, express any program of reform—probably partly because he did not expect the Sultan to be interested in such suggestions. This is one of many indications that Afghānī generally gave priority to the independence of Muslim countries from European control over reform, however sincere he was in concern with reform. Throughout Afghānī's life, in fact, such political actions as are clearly documented concern primarily the problem of getting out the foreigners, and particularly the British. This is already true in the 1860's and 70's, when Afghānī was in Afghanistan and Egypt, and to some degree the Pan-Islamic program is simply a logical adaptation of this primary goal. He was reasserting the importance of political power in Islam and, like nationalists elsewhere, stating that independence was a prerequisite to meaningful reform.

That Afghānī was a man with a vision can hardly be doubted—what must be doubted is that this vision consisted primarily of a reform of Islam and a revival of a purified religion. Even some of the conversations of Afghānī quoted in Arabic make it clear that Afghānī's interest in a religious reformation, sincere as it may have been, was primarily instrumental. Religious reform, he thought, had been the key to subsequent European progress and power, and such a reformation was also needed for the Islamic world to achieve the same goals.[8]

Afghānī's actual vision seems to have been something rather different—that of a strong Islamic state that would be able to beat back the foreigners and also to emulate them in progress, religious and other reforms and power. The difference in his program which seems to have its origins about 1878 is that he no longer stresses only appeals to the single nation in which he happens to find himself (although he continues to make such appeals to the Indians). In Afghanistan in 1867–68, the Ottoman Empire of 1870, and Egypt in the 1870's the evidence we have of his words indicates that his appeals were rather to local and national feelings than to any idea of unification of all the Islamic peoples. The rise of Pan-Islam gave Afghānī the possibility of trying to fill a more important role than that of the power behind the ruler of a single Muslim country. He could now fit in with the Pan-Islamic aspirations of Sultan Abdülhamid and his entourage, adding a propensity to military adventurism, based on a belief that the faith and numbers of the Muslims would outweigh the technological advantage of the West, which Afghānī apparently still underrated.

To say all this does not imply, nor does the document, that Afghānī was unprincipled. Quite the contrary: he was genuine in his expression of willingness to undergo hardship and his disdain for money. The whole pattern of Afghānī's life is that of a single-minded visionary, driven by a cause—it would only be a little too modern to call him a "professional revolutionary," and the pattern of various

[8] See the relevant citations in chap. 13, below, and the words to this effect from Afghānī quoted in Riḍā, *Tārīkh*, pp. 82–83.

European revolutionary exiles is similar enough to his.[9] The real confusion has been over the nature of his vision. There is ample evidence, and the above document is one more indication, that Afghānī, like some modern nationalists, saw himself as a kind of "secular messiah," who would awaken in his people unexpected sources of strength through his dramatic speeches and intelligent planning. This vision had probably already appeared in earlier years, but it was given wider scope by the Pan-Islamic climate of the 1880's and 1890's

This climate also was probably responsible for Afghānī's increasing concern to present himself in an orthodox Islamic guise and to utilize the ulama for the achievement of his goals. Although there is abundant evidence that Afghānī did not become any more religious in the later period of his life, he found it useful to take on a more religious posture than he had in the past. Afghānī's esoterism made it possible for him to continue to show his closest disciples that his outward show of religiosity was aimed at reformist goals. There is evidence that he continued to have such reformist goals and to speak of them to his followers and sometimes to write of them. When his major political activities are examined, however, they are nearly always found to concern not reform but the strengthening of the Muslim world against Western, and particularly British, encroachments, which he saw as the most important task of his age and the precondition of meaningful reform.

During his stay in India in 1880–1882, Afghānī did not mention Pan-Islamic ideas in any of his numerous published writings and speeches. If ca. 1878 is a correct date for the document translated above one must assume that Afghānī was able easily to swing back and forth between Pan-Islamic and local nationalist appeals, depending upon which was a more appropriate anti-imperialist weapon in the local situation. In appealing to an Ottoman statesman or to an international Muslim audience Pan-Islamic ideas were useful, while in a mixed Muslim-Hindu area like India linguistic or cultural nationalism might be more appropriate than Pan-Islam. What in the twentieth century appear to be contradictory ideas could easily be seen by Afghānī as alternate and mutually reinforcing points of emphasis, with one or the other to be stressed or ignored depending on the local situation and the audience being addressed.

---

9 Cf. the description in Sylvia G. Haim, *Arab Nationalism* (Berkeley and Los Angeles, 1962), p. 6, wherein Afghānī is called "the very type of revolutionary conspirator and activist so well known in Europe in modern times."

7

India: Late 1879 to Late 1882

FROM SUEZ, Egypt, Afghānī was sent on a boat to Karachi in September 1879, Thus far, the main sources about Afghānī's three-year stay in India are British documents and Afghānī's writings and statements. His last days in Egypt and the trip to India are described from his own viewpoint in a letter he wrote from Port Said to his patron, Riyāḍ Pāshā, late in 1882. In this letter, after detailing the harsh treatment given him by his Egyptian captors, including the taking of his money and possessions, Afghānī says that he was sent directly to the port of Karachi, was under guard the whole time, and was interrogated harshly by British authorities upon his arrival in Karachi.[1] According to Government of India documents, Afghānī stayed a short time in Bombay at the home of Muhammad Ali Rogay (a prominent Bombay Muslim).[2]

Afghānī then went to the large princely state of Hyderabad in south India, possibly attracted to it as a Muslim center free of direct British rule. There is little documentation of his stay in Hyderabad, but since Afghānī wrote several articles and his major treatise during

---

1 *Documents*, pls. 13–15, photos 34–37.

2 F.O. 60/594, "Memorandum" on Jamāl ad-Dīn, described in n. 6, below. On Rogay, see several references in Wilfrid S. Blunt, *India under Ripon* (London, 1909) (henceforth called *India*).

this stay, one may surmise that writing was his most important activity.

The activities of Jamāl ad-Dīn in India were not considered significant enough by the British authorities to be mentioned in any of the voluminous materials they regularly sent home to the India Office in London. A report about Afghānī was sent from India to the India Office only in the summer of 1883, after Afghānī had gone to Paris and had begun sending newspapers with anti-British articles to India. At this point the British Resident in Hyderabad, Cordery, sent the Government of India a report on Jamāl ad-Dīn, written by a "Syed Hussein" of Hyderabad. That part of Sayyid Husain's letter which deals with Jamāl ad-Dīn's stay in Hyderabad reads as follows:

> About three years ago a man came here from Egypt who alleged that he had been turned out of the country by the orders of H. H. the new Khedive Towfik Pasha for preaching doctrines distasteful to the authorities. I gathered from his conversations that he was a freethinker of the French type, and a socialist, and that he had been got rid of by the authorities in Egypt for preaching the doctrine of "liberté, fraternité, egalité" to the students, and the masses in that country. I found him to be a well informed man for a Herati (he is a Herati by birth) though rather shallow in his acquirements. He could "hold forth" in Persian and Arabic with great easiness and purity of idiom. He talked a little French and used to say that it was his purpose to go and make Paris his headquarters for some time in order to get justice out of Towfik through the French.
>
> I also understood from Capt. Clerk that he was the author of a violently anti-English article in the periodical "Nahla" that used to be published in London. H. Ex. the late Minister gave him a couple of thousand rupees to enable him to leave the country; but I know that he did not leave the country; but continued to live a rather retired life in the city, spending his time in teaching and philosophical discussions. When, however, the imbroglio in Egypt made a stir in the papers, the Sheikh, Jamal-ud-din (for such was his name) suddenly disappeared from Hyderabad, and I was given to understand that he was gone to Burmah. I felt quite sure, however, that he was gone to no such place, and that either Cairo or Paris was his destination.
>
> Some months ago I was startled by having an Arabic pe-

> riodical sent to me from Paris, and on opening it I found that it was conducted by no other than the quondam philosopher of Hyderabad. . . .[3]

The personages involved in this report from Sayyid Husain via Cordery can be identified from other sources, including the diaries published by Wilfrid S. Blunt, who visited Hyderabad late in 1883 with letters of introduction from Sayyid Jamāl ad-Dīn. The only prominent Sayyid Husain in the Hyderabad government, and the only man who was identified simply by this name to the Resident, was Sayyid Husain Bilgrāmī, a liberal Shi'i from Delhi who had been brought to Hyderabad by the great Hyderabad prime minister, Sir Sālār Jang, and was his private secretary until Sālār Jang's death. Other sources identify him as a moderate liberal, known especially for his work in education. Captain, later Major, Clerk, was the tutor of Sālār Jang's son, also something of a reformer.[4]

Sayyid Husain's picture of Afghānī as "a freethinker of the French type" is reiterated in a report on Afghānī made by the Government of India Thagi and Dakaiti Department in 1896, which contains further information about Afghānī's stay in India. Although the date for the beginning of Afghānī's stay in India, given in this report as 1881, is an error, there seems no reason to doubt most of the report about his behavior in Hyderabad, which contains considerable detail. The bulk of this document is identical with an earlier report made by the Thagi and Dakaiti Department in 1887, when the Government of India was concerned about Afghānī's anti-British activities in Russia.[5] The Department presumably made an investigation in 1887 to find out all it could about Jamāl ad-Dīn's past, and those parts of the resultant biography that deal with India are probably the most reliable ones, since they could be taken from recent eyewitnesses. That part of the 1896 report which concerns Afghānī's time in India reads as follows:

---

3 Syed Husein to Cordery, June 20, 1883, enclosed in F.O. 60/594, Cordery to Grant, June 25, 1883.

4 Blunt, *India*, pp. 60–61, 64–65, 335–336. There are also other references to these persons in Blunt's book, which is indexed. On Sayyid Ḥusain and Sir Sālār Jang see also Anonymous, *Eminent Mussalmans* (Madras, 1926).

5 Government of India, Foreign Department, *Political and Secret Home Correspondence*, vol. 97 (1887), file 1111 (henceforth called *PSHC*). This report, headed "Syad Jamal-ud-Din," was printed and is signed by an Aziz-ud-Din not otherwise identified. It is dated October 13, 1887, and follows several reports from earlier in the same year describing Jamāl ad-Dīn's anti-British activities and writings in Russia that year.

> In Hyderabad he formed the friendship of the Arab Jemadar, Sultan Newaz Jang, through whom he had an interview with the late Sir Salar Jang. He was in Hyderabad for about 20 months, and during his stay he associated chiefly with the rising generation of freethinkers, the followers of Sayad Ahmed of Aligarh. But in spite of all their kindness and hospitality towards him, he published a book in Persian against their doctrines. He seemed to hold strong views on such subjects as 'Revival of Islam' and 'Union is Strength.' His story about his expulsion from Egypt was that he was a Mason, and that the Khedive mistook him for a conspirator, and thus had him suddenly deported.
>
> He received Rs. 5,000 from the late Sir Salar Jang and some small pecuniary help from the other noblemen of Hyderabad. With this money he left the Nizam's capital, and after visiting Bhopal on the way, he reached Calcutta early in 1882, where he remained for about five months and gave some lectures in Persian at the Madrasa on 'Islam.' *While here he offered his services to Government* but they were declined with thanks. In September 1882 he was found expounding his religious views in Madras, and in November of the same year, sailed for England per S.S. '*India*,' where he remained for a short time as Mr. W. Blunt's guest in London [italics mine].[6]

The story attributed to Afghānī about his expulsion from Egypt is exactly the one he wrote to Riyāḍ in 1882 in a letter that also documents his offer to the British government. In a section not quoted, the 1896 report above gives an erroneous date of 1881 for Afghānī's arrival in Hyderabad. In fact, Afghānī was in Hyderabad at least as early as March–April 1880, the earliest date with a Hyderabad location given in Afghānī's personal notebooks.[7]

Sultān Nawaz Jang, named in the Thagi and Dakaiti report as Afghānī's friend, who introduced him to Sir Sālār Jang, is identified further in Blunt's *India under Ripon* and in Government of India documents. He was prince of a coastal state of Arabia, and there are conflicting reports on his political views.[8] Blunt also states that Sālār

---

[6] F.O. 60/594, "Memorandum," signed A. S. Lethbridge, General Superintendent, Thagi and Dakaiti Department, printed and sent to the Foreign Office, confidential, 1896. It contains the information held by the Department regarding Jamāl ad-Din.

[7] *Documents*, photos 34–37, and p. 12, doc. 5.

[8] Blunt, *India*, pp. 59, 65–66; *PSHC*, vol. 51 (1882), list of names said to be in

Jang's son said that Afghānī had been a friend of his father's.

Although Government of India evaluation of Afghānī's views cannot be considered decisive, the picture of Jamāl ad-Dīn as a religious and political radical given by the Government of India documents is confirmed for the Indian stay by Blunt in his *India under Ripon.* Visiting Hyderabad soon after Afghānī had left, Blunt records some conversations with Indians who had known him there. One of them, Sayyid 'Alī Bilgrāmī (the brother of the Sayyid Husain who reported to Cordery on Jamāl ad-Dīn) is quoted as follows: "Of Sheykh Jemal-ed-Din, whom he had known here, he said he was too much of a socialist and firebrand to carry through a reformation." One of the Hyderabad ulama, Rasūl Yār Khān, is described by Blunt as "liberal, socialistic, and an enthusiastic disciple of Jemal-ed-Din's."[9]

According to Blunt's book, largely a transcription from his diaries, Jamāl ad-Dīn in India seems to have made an impression largely as an oral teacher. Thus Rasūl Yār Khān is quoted as saying "In all India you would not find a teacher like Jemal-ed-Din." And Calcutta disciples of Afghānī's suggested that Jamāl ad-Dīn would be the best professor for Blunt's proposed Indian Muslim university.[10]

Further information regarding Afghānī's stay in Hyderabad is in Qāzī Muhammad 'Abd al-Ghaffār's Urdu biography, *Āsār-i Jamāl ad-Dīn Afghānī,* published in 1940. 'Abd al-Ghaffār says that the only reliable information he could get about this period came from an old man in Hyderabad, who had been present during Jamāl ad-Dīn's stay, and gives the following summary of what the old man said: When the Sayyid came to Hyderabad, he stayed at the home of Nawwāb Rasūl Yār Jang (the Rusūl Yār Khān referred to by Blunt). He usually spoke Persian or Arabic, but also knew Turkish and French. The Sayyid was short-tempered. Many learned people of Hyderabad attended his gatherings, and discussions often took place between the Sayyid and religious scholars (whose names are given, as is the title of one dispute). The Sayyid spoke so well that everyone was highly impressed. Afghānī, the old man continued, was very much against the naturalist sect (the followers of Sayyid Ahmad Khān), and he once wrote an article against them entitled "The Aghūrīs with Pomp and Show." When he was about to write this

---

contact with Pan-Islamic and anti-British party at Constantinople. Here the name is given as "Koovat Nawas Jung."

[9] Blunt, *India,* p. 97.

[10] *Ibid.,* pp. 63, 136.

article, he asked his friends what group in the area was the least respected and was told that the least respected caste was called the Aghūrīs. He then chose this appellation for the "naturalists," and used it in the title of his article. The Sayyid's knowledge and intellect became so famous in Hyderabad that Sālār Jang asked to meet him. The Sayyid went to see him, and this meeting had such an effect on Sālār Jang that he tried to get prominent men of Hyderabad to persuade the Sayyid to stay in Hyderabad and take up a position there. The Sayyid, however, said that he was too stubborn to be employed there, and later added that jealousy was rampant in Hyderabad. People would become jealous if he were promoted to a high post, and he would then have to leave Hyderabad; envious men would also try to turn the British against him. For these reasons, the Sayyid declined a position. The Sayyid's servant, 'Ārif (a name used by Abū Turāb), was also an educated man. The Sayyid said his prayers in the Sunni manner and had Sunni beliefs. Rasūl Yār Jang asked him to prepare a dictionary of Arabic. He started work on it, but could not complete it.[11]

Most of the old man's story is credible, with the probable exception of the offer of a governmental position in Hyderabad, referred to nowhere else.

After leaving Hyderabad late in 1881, Jamāl ad-Dīn went via the princely state of Bhopal to Calcutta, where he arrived in early 1882 and stayed for several months. According to Blunt, Jamāl ad-Dīn made a good impression on Maulvi 'Abd al-Latīf, a leader of moderately reformist Muslims of the Indian capital, Calcutta. The latter told Blunt that Muslims were afraid to visit him, Blunt: "He knew, however, that I had the Mohammedan cause at heart, for he had heard from Sheykh Jemal-ed-Din what I had done, and he thought it best to tell me all frankly, and put me on my guard.[12]

Jamāl ad-Dīn's chief disciples at Calcutta, as described by Blunt, were not influential men, but young anti-British students who, like Jamāl ad-Dīn, identified neither with the pro-British liberal followers of Sayyid Ahmad Khān nor with the traditional party. As was

---

[11] Qāẕī Muḥammad 'Abd al-Ghaffār, *Āṣār-i Jamāl ad-Dīn Afghānī* (Delhi, 1940), pp. 122–123. Thanks to Nasim Jawed and Ismail Poonawala for translating the relevant pages of this book for me. The draft of Afghānī's uncompleted Arabic dictionary is in the Majlis Library collection, catalogued in *Documents*, p. 12, doc. 4.

[12] Blunt, *India*, p. 97; pp. 12–13, 79–80. Aziz Ahmad tells me that Blunt's characterization of this man as conservative is incorrect.

true of so many of his disciples, these young students "professed something like worship" for Jamāl ad-Dīn.[13] One Calcutta newspaper editor also admired Afghānī, and translated several of his works into Urdu.[14]

'Abd al-Ghaffār says that Afghānī refrained from participation in politics in India because of his recent bad experience in Egypt, and because he knew the British were watching him in India. He adds that in Calcutta Afghānī was kept under house arrest or surveillance at the house of a friend, Hājji Mīrzā 'Abd al-Karīm Shīrāzī.[15]

In the 1882 letter to Riyāḍ Afghānī says that while he was in Calcutta (then the capital of British India), the British feared an uprising in India and believed that he was an envoy from 'Urābī to incite the Muslims against the British government in India. The British thus held, threatened, and interrogated him, and as 'Urābī's strength grew the British government increased its strictness. Finally, Afghānī writes, because of the severity of the government and its hatred toward him, he asked the British to send him to the Khedive, and gave this request to the viceroy (*ḥakīm*) of India. While the viceroy had the request, and Afghānī was awaiting an answer, the government continued to harass him until the trouble (in Egypt) ended, whereupon the British government released Afghānī, but continued to observe all his movements.[16]

Afghānī's offer to go to the Khedive is nowhere clarified, but the context of the letter indicates that at least one of its motives was to obtain release from British harassment in Calcutta. Presumably this offer is the one referred to in the Thagi and Dakaiti Department's 1896 report of Afghānī (quoted above) when it notes that Afghānī when in Calcutta offered his services to the Government but they were declined with thanks. Neither reference is specific enough to indicate just what services were offered. As Afghānī's activities in 1884–85 demonstrate, however, he was not averse to working with British officials when he thought it might help him to achieve his goals.

---

13 Blunt, *India*, p. 112.

14 Aziz Ahmad, "Afghānī's Indian Contacts," *Journal of the American Oriental Society*, 89, 3 (1969), 476–491, esp. pp. 486–488. In this article Ahmad gives details about Afghānī's various stays in India and summarizes the letters from Indian correspondents in the Majlis Library collection catalogued in the *Documents*. He also proves that later writers have inflated Afghānī's influence in India in the 1880's, and traces the origins of Afghānī's later reputation there.

15 'Abd al-Ghaffār, *op. cit.*, pp. 138–139.

16 *Documents*, pls. 13–15, photos 34–37.

In summary, the limited information from the 1879–1882 Indian stay, his last there, indicates that Afghānī was at this time involved mostly in speaking and writing, and that he impressed some Hyderabadis who knew him as a radical, a freethinker, and a firebrand. The most important result of his Indian stay was certainly his writings, particularly his major book, the so-called "Refutation of the Materialists." In addition to the latter, he wrote a series of articles in Persian first published in a Hyderabad periodical, *Mu'allim-i Shafīq,* edited by Muhibb Husain, which began publication late in 1880. A single letter from Afghānī to an Iranian friend has also been attributed to the period of Afghānī's stay in India.[17]

The *Documents* include copies of Jamāl ad-Dīn's published works which give some useful details about their time and place of publication. Since Jamāl ad-Dīn's first Indian article, "The Benefits of Newspapers," appeared in the very first number of *Mu'allim-i Shafīq,* it is possible that he had been influential in bringing about the publication of this journal.

What must be the first edition of the "Refutation of the Materialists," a lithographed edition of 1298/1881 in Persian, is also included, without indication of city, though it must have been Hyderabad. It is entitled *Haqīqat-i mazhab-i naichirī va bayān-i hāl-i naichiriyyān* (*The Truth of the Naichirī Sect and an Explanation of the Condition of the Naichirīs*). (The common name "Refutation of the Materialists" is taken from the Arabic translation, *ar-Radd 'ala ad-dahriyyīn,* trans. Muḥammad 'Abduh and Abū Turāb [Beirut, 1886]). In the year of its publication 1298/1881, there appeared a second edition at Bombay. There was also an Urdu translation of this book, under its original Persian title, dated Calcutta, 1883.[18]

Sayyid 'Abd al-Ghafūr Shahbāz who translated the "Refutation" into Urdu, gathered together Afghānī's Persian articles for the first time under the title *Maqālāt-i Jamāliyyeh,* and published them in Calcutta in 1884. These consisted of the six articles published in

17 "Nāmeh-yi Sayyid Jamāl ad-Dīn Asadābādī," *Āyandeh* (Tehran), II, 5–6 (1927), 395–401. An Arabic translation of this letter appeared in *al-Muqtaṭaf* (Cairo), 66, 5 (May, 1925), 494–496. The letter is addressed to a Sayyid Ḥājji Mastān Dāghistānī, who is called wrong to blame the ulama for Iran's backwardness, when the Iranian government has been the greatest cause of oppression and ignorance. Although the letter's date is given as December 1881, the letter shows such intimate knowledge of Iranian conditions at the time of writing that my guess is that it was actually written shortly after one of Afghānī's trips to Iran—perhaps from Russia where he went between 1887 and 1889, after a trip to Iran.

18 *Documents,* p. 26; p. 30, doc. 113.

Mu'allim-i Shafīq of Hyderabad, plus five additional items, three of which were in fact brief sections of the "Refutation of the Materialists." Another item is listed as a lecture given in Albert Hall, Calcutta, on November 8, 1883, which must be an error for 1882.[19]

Thus Afghānī from late 1880 until he left India had published eight articles or speeches, plus the "Refutation." It is the latter work that has often been taken in both East and West as proof that Afghānī was a strong defender of orthodox Islam. The Government of India documents, Wilfrid Blunt's reports in *India under Ripon,* and especially "The Refutation of the Materialists" all suggest that during his Indian stay of 1879–1882 Afghānī for the first time presented himself publicly as a strong defender of religion against free thought. The Government of India reports claim a sudden switch from friendship with the followers of Sir Sayyid Ahmad Khān to written attacks on them. This may be exaggerated; Aziz Ahmad has shown that Afghānī was not close to any prominent disciple of Sayyid Ahmad Khān. Nevertheless his association with advanced modernizers seems clear.[20] The "Refutation of the Materialists" is the *first* of Afghānī's writings in which he presents himself as a champion of Islam against heretical and Western liberal tendencies. At the same time, however, he was continuing to write reformist articles. What can be said from the scanty evidence concerning this Indian stay about the reasons for this dual approach?

First, Afghānī was following a trend already strong in the Muslim world. Western physical incursions and Western deprecation of Islam and of Muslims had strengthened anti-Western and Pan-Islamic feelings throughout the Muslim world, and many Muslim liberals were moved to defend Islam. Namık Kemal and some of his fellow "Young Ottomans" are good examples.

Second, Afghānī, as he told Blunt, had noticed a rise in positive feeling toward the Ottoman Sultan in India, which is also noted in the Government of India documents as having occurred particularly during the Russo-Turkish War of 1887–88. Blunt says, recording in his diary a conversation with Afghānī in 1883 about Blunt's projected Indian trip: "I asked him about the language I should most prudently hold regarding the Sultan, and he advised me to say nothing against the Sultan in India or about an Arabian Caliphate; it had been spread about that the English were going to set up a sham

19 *Ibid.*, pp. 26–27.
20 Ahmad, "Afghānī's Indian Contacts," *passim.*

Caliphate in Arabia, under a child, whom they would use to make themselves masters of the holy places; the Sultan's name was now venerated in India as it had not formerly been."[21] "The Refutation of the Materialists" includes some remarks likely to please the Sultan.[22] Both the Pan-Islamic letter discussed in the preceding chapter and Afghānī's correspondence with friends in Istanbul in 1884–85, discussed below, indicate that he thought of working with the Sultan long before 1892.

Third, and most important, Afghānī saw in India that the most strongly Westernizing group among the Indian Muslims, the followers of Sir Sayyid Ahmad Khān, were the partisans of his enemies, the British. According to Blunt, for example, the Calcutta Muslims were divided into two groups; the Westernized followers of Sayyid Amīr 'Alī, identified with Sayyid Ahmad Khān's group and with loyalty to the British; and the conservatives [in fact moderate modernists] under 'Abd al-Latīf. Neither of these groups seems to have appealed to Afghānī—he evidently preferred 'Abd al-Latīf to his more pro-British rivals, and gave Blunt a letter of introduction to him. But 'Abd al-Latīf told Blunt that he had not seen Jamāl ad-Dīn "for he was afraid of compromising himself with one under Government ban."[23] According to one of Jamāl ad-Dīn's young disciples in Calcutta, Jamāl ad-Dīn was trying to point a third path—clearly one that would appeal to the traditionalist majority of the Muslims, be anti-British, and also have an appeal for the younger intellectuals. Speaking of this young disciple of Afghānī's whose name is given only as "Mulvi A.M.," Blunt says:

> He gave me a clearer account of the parties in Calcutta than I have yet received. Amir Ali and his friends have put themselves out of the pale of Mohammedan society by their English dress and ways, while Abd-el-Latif and the body of the Mulvis (Ulema) are too strictly conservative. He had been converted to the large idea of a Mohammedan reform and Mohammedan unity by Jemal-ed-Din, and there were many now of his way of thinking who held a middle position be-

---

21 Blunt, *India*, p. 13.

22 Niyazi Berkes, *The Development of Secularism in Turkey* (Montreal, 1964), pp. 266–267.

23 Blunt, *India*, p. 100. This contradicts the earlier statement that they had seen each other—either Blunt misreports or 'Abd al-Latīf meant he had not wanted to see Jamāl ad-Dīn frequently.

> tween the rival parties. . . . He told me Jemal-ed-Din had been disappointed with the Mohammedans of Calcutta, who were afraid of listening to him on account of the Government. He had found them selfish and unpatriotic. Of Amir Ali he has a poor opinion. Abd-el-Latif he thinks timid, and the rest of the Mulvis are intensely ignorant.[24]

Although the characterizations of Amīr 'Alī and 'Abd al-Latīf may be unfair, the role of Jamāl ad-Dīn is suggested. A somewhat similar situation existed elsewhere in India—the minority of liberal-minded and Westernized Muslims often held governmental posts, and were either-pro-British or shy of attacking them. Since Afghānī believed political independence from the British had to precede true political reform, it was natural for him to work to attract the religious majority of the Muslims to his anti-British and revolutionary program.

During Jamāl ad-Dīn's stay in India the Government of India was beginning to overcome its suspicions of the Muslims, which had resulted from the disaffection of many of them during the Indian Mutiny of 1857. The special difficulties of the Muslim community in India, however, continued into this period. There were still many grievances over the elimination of Muslims from their former governmental and army posts as a result of special recruiting policies. Traditionally, the Muslims in India had not been merchants, and in the nineteenth century the fortunes of their landlords, rulers, and military men apparently declined. Educated Muslims were still largely dependent on the Government for employment, but religious Muslims hesitated to send their sons to government schools, where they were taught by Hindus or Christians. In view of these grievances, it might have seemed that Jamāl ad-Dīn's anti-British program should have soon increased its appeal to the Indian Muslims. In fact, however, the Government of India increasingly reversed its former policy and favored the Muslims as a conservative counterweight to the more nationalist middle-class Hindus. Sayyid Ahmad Khān helped convince the British that the Muslim community could help them in India. Partly because of this change in British policy Sayyid Ahmad Khān's program of giving Muslims a British-style education and encouraging them to enter government service in growing numbers

---

24 *Ibid.*, pp. 104–105. Aziz Ahmad informs me that 'Abd al-Latīf was in fact a moderate reformer.

far overshadowed Afghānī's anti-British program among the Indian Muslims of the late nineteenth century.

It was only in the first decades of the twentieth century that anti-British feeling rose again among the Indian Muslims, and the inadequacies of Sayyid Ahmad Khān's program were again stressed by Muslim intellectuals. Then it was that a program like Afghānī's—in favor of support to the Ottoman Caliphate, cooperation with the Hindu nationalists against the British, and Muslim reform—again came to the fore. This program seems to have had many local and immediate roots and to have owed little to Afghānī's direct influence.[25]

Afghānī's last Indian stay, like the rest of his life, has been highly productive of mythology, although in this case much of it stems from later writers rather than from Afghānī himself. Some recent writers have tried to make much of Afghānī's influence on the Indian Muslim community. Yet even Blunt's admiring report reveals not one Muslim prominent in 1883 or afterward who regarded himself as a disciple of Afghānī's. Aside from Rasūl Yār Khān all the disciples mentioned are young students, and if any of them had later become prominent, Blunt would surely have followed his usual practice of reporting this fact when he published his diaries (in this case in 1909). Any influence Afghānī did have stemmed mainly from his writings, many of which were first published in India, and in some cases soon translated into Urdu. (The *Documents* show his relations with one Calcutta editor, 'Abd al-Ghafūr Shāhbāz.[26]) Only after Afghānī's death did a few Indian Muslim leaders turn to his ideas for inspiration.

A second myth is that Afghānī originated the idea of a Muslim Indian state. Reference to Afghānī as the spiritual father of the idea of an Indian Muslim state is sometimes made with a citation to a chapter by I. H. Qureshi in *Sources of Indian Tradition.* Yet

---

25 Cf. Wilfred C. Smith, "The Pan-Islamic Khilāfāt and Related Movements," in *Modern Islam in India* (Lahore, 1943), pp. 225–240. On p. 226 Smith notes, "even Jamāl al Dīn al Afghānī had only a few isolated Indian disciples."

26 See the items from *Documents* discussed in Ahmad, "Afghānī's Indian Contacts." Ahmad (*Studies,* chap. 4) formerly exaggerated Afghānī's Indian influence. For example, Ahmad says (p. 61). "The Muslims of Calcutta professed for al-Afghānī something like worship.' " The citation is to Blunt. In fact, however, Blunt ascribed this sentiment only to a small group of Muslim students in Calcutta who were hostile to the main groups and leaders there, as indicated above. Ahmad has corrected his own former view in the very informative chapter vi of his *Islamic Modernism in India and Pakistan 1857–1964* (London, 1967), and also in "Afghānī's Indian Contacts."

all that Qureshi actually says, without documentation, when writing of the later movement for an Indian Muslim state, is: "Earlier the famous pan-Islamist thinker, Saiyid Jamāl-u'd-dīn al-Afghānī . . . had written that the destiny of the Muslims of Central Asia was to form a state with Afghanistan and the Muslim majority area in northwestern India."[27] Afghānī had so many ephemeral schemes that this may have been one of them but it is clear from the whole tenor of his talks in India that he was an advocate of Hindu-Muslim cooperation against the British. Indeed, the prominent Indian Muslim leader whose debt to Afghānī has been proven by both Aziz Ahmad and Wilfrid Smith—Maulānā Abū al-Kalām Āzād—was always an advocate of Hindu-Muslim cooperation in the nationalist cause.[28] Indian Pan-Islam as a whole, in its brief period of strength early in the twentieth century, particularly in the Khilāfāt Movement during and after World War I, worked similarly for Hindu-Muslim cooperation in the nationalist cause. In this, however little or much they were influenced by Afghānī, the Indian Pan-Islamists of the twentieth century were following Afghānī's course. Far from advocating a split between the Hindus and the Muslims, Afghānī opposed any breach in the anti-British front. Just as he helped awaken Egyptian nationalism by appeals to the ancient glories of Egypt and to all Egyptians of whatever religion to unite against the foreigner, so in India, even when talking to a Muslim audience, he appealed to the glory of the Indian Hindu past.[29] Although the Pan-Islamic program, if taken to its ultimate logical conclusion, might seem to imply a break with the Hindus, Afghānī was never one to go to such conclusions when they conflicted with his aim of fighting against British control in the East.

An examination of the evidence about Afghānī's Indian stay underlines the fact that Afghānī's most important activity there was his writing. The evidence also shows some change in Afghānī's image during this stay to an apparent defender of Islam against the Westernizers. Both reformist and Muslim apologetic ideas appear in his

---

27 W. T. de Bary, ed., *Sources of Indian Tradition* (New York, 1958), chap. xxvii, by I. H. Qureshi, p. 827. Aziz Ahmad asked Qureshi his source, and Qureshi named a book by Tufayl Aḥmad which similarly quotes no source.

28 Cf. Smith, *op. cit.*, pp. 226–228, 245–247, and *passim*, and the sections on Āzād in Ahmad, *Studies* and *Islamic Modernism*. Muḥammad Iqbāl also cites Afghānī in his writings, but as an advocate of Muslim revival and solidarity, not a separate Indian Muslim state, which Iqbāl came to favor.

29 See below, pp. 159–160.

Indian writings, discussed below, and only a close analysis of these writings can explain the apparent contradictions between his liberal articles and his attacks on various forms of liberalism in the "Refutation of the Materialists."

Jamāl ad-Dīn's Indian Articles

AFGHĀNĪ'S INDIAN articles, written in Persian, include six first published in the Hyderabad journal, *Mu'allim-i Shafīq* from its first issue in December 1880, through its tenth issue in October 1881, with some articles extended over more than one issue. The translated titles of these articles, in the order they appeared, are: "The Benefits of Newspapers," "Teaching and Education," "The True Causes of Man's Happiness and Distress," "The Philosophy of National Unity and the Truth about Unity of Language," "The Benefits of Philosophy," and "A Description of the Aghūrīs with Pomp and Show." The first edition of the collected Persian-language articles by Afghānī, *Maqālāt-i Jamāliyyeh* (*Jamāl's Articles*), was published by 'Abd al-Ghafūr Shāhbāz in Calcutta in 1884. This volume included the six articles listed above plus another article, "Commentary on the Commentator," and a "Lecture on Teaching and Learning" delivered in Albert Hall, Calcutta, in November 1882. The remaining three items in this edition of *Maqālāt-i Jamāliyyeh* are simply sections of the "Refutation of the Materialists."[30]

All Afghānī's Indian articles were in the Persian language and have received little notice from those who do not read Persian; yet

[30] The articles that appeared in *Mu'allim-i Shafīq* and also the Calcutta, 1884, edition of *Maqālāt-i Jamāliyyeh* are in the Majlis Library collection of Afghānī documents in Tehran, catalogued in *Documents*, pp. 26–27. The translations here are from the edition of *Maqālāt-ī Jamāliyyeh* edited by Afghānī's grandnephew, Ṣiftātallāh Jamālī (Tehran, 1312/1933–34). This edition omits the three excerpts from the "Refutation of the Materialists" and adds items that Jamāl ad-Dīn dictated during his visits to Tehran between 1887 and 1890 and one additional Persian article whose first appearance is not dated.

these articles shed important light on Afghānī's mode of thought and discourse at this transitional period of his life. These articles contrast with some of his later writings, and are interesting for what they omit as well as for what they contain. There is no mention of Pan-Islam or of uniting the Muslims behind one leader, the ideas with which Afghānī was to be associated after he left India. On the contrary, there are local nationalist ideas that appear at variance with Pan-Islam. Such local nationalism had also appeared in Afghānī's Egyptian writings and speeches. There is also very little of the Islamic apologetic that was to be associated with Aghānī; there is much more defense of science and philosophy than of Islam. The defense of Islam usually comes in only as part of an attack on Sir Sayyid Ahmad Khān. If ca. 1878 is a correct date for the Pan-Islamic letter translated in chapter 6, then in the years 1878 to 1881 Afghānī was varying his arguments greatly according to his audience and purpose.

Three striking themes of Afghānī's Indian articles are: (1) advocacy of nationalism of a linguistic or territorial variety, meaning unity of Indian Hindus and Muslims, rather than unity of Indian Muslims with foreign Muslims; (2) stress on the benefits of philosophy and modern science, (3) attacks on Sir Sayyid Ahmad Khān as a tool of the foreigners.

On the nationalistic theme, there are two striking articles. One is "The Philosophy of National Unity and the Truth about Unity of Language." It starts with an Arabic heading: "There is no happiness except in nationality, and there is no nationality except in language, and a language cannot be called a language except if it embraces all affairs that those in manufacture and trade need for explanation and use in their work." Afghānī begins by trying to show the significance of his subject for man and the world, much in the manner of medieval Islamic philosophers. He notes that a common language is necessary to bring together scattered individuals, tribes, and groups into one unified nation. He expresses a preference for linguistic over religious ties as factors that are durable in the world:

> In the human world the bonds that have been extensive . . . have been two. One is this same unity of language of which nationality and national unity consist, and the other is religion. There is no doubt that the unity of language is more durable for survival and permanence in this world than unity of religion since in contrast with the latter it does not change in a short time. We see that a single people with one

> language in the course of a thousand years changes its religion two or three times without its nationality, which consists of unity of language, being destroyed. One may say that the ties and the unity that arise from the unity of language have more influence than religious ties in most affairs of the world.[31]

After giving examples to show that linguistic ties are more important than religious ones, Afghānī says that a language can play its unifying function only if it has the terms needed for the practical knowledge and arts of civilization. If these terms are lacking they should be invented, preferably from one's own linguistic stock. Teaching should be in the national language encouraging ties to the national past and making learning accessible to more people than if it is in a foreign language. The encouragement of a national language is a requisite to national unity and patriotism, and Indians should translate modern knowledge into their own languages, especially Urdu.

At the end of this article Afghānī attacks two of the main targets of his Indian writings—on the one hand the religious conservatives who oppose Western learning, and on the other hand Sayyid Ahmad Khān and his followers, or the Naichiriyya. (*Naichiriyya* was a new coinage meaning believers in "nature.") He says that anyone who refers to the principles of the *sharī'a* knows that the spread of science and learning is in no way against religion; on the contrary useful knowledge strengthens religion, since it strengthens its adherents. On the other hand, if some "Indian ropedancer" (i.e., a *naichirī*) says that the English must be followed in everything, including language, it will undermine India's nationhood and bring about complete conquest by the English. English arts and industries should be spread through translation into one's own language.

The purpose of this article, like that of nearly all Afghānī's writings, is pragmatic rather than abstract. In India Afghānī's primary anti-imperialist, and especially anti-British, purpose was best served by emphasizing those factors that united Indians of different religions and distinguished them from the British. Afghānī is not writing a theoretical tract on the relative weights of religion and language in human affairs, but rather an appeal to the Indians to utilize their

31 *Maqālāt-i Jamāliyyeh* (Tehran, 1312/1933–34), pp. 75–87. This article has been partially translated into French by Mehdi Hendessi, "Pages peu connues de Djamal ad-din al-Afghani," *Orient*, 6 (1958), 123–128. The translations here are done by me from the Persian original.

own languages as the vehicle to spread modern knowledge. He mentions Urdu as the language to be especially utilized in translating new knowledge, and he probably hoped that Indians could unite around one major indigenous language. He is arguing both against traditionalists who wished to maintain traditional learning in the old classical languages, and against modernizers who supported British higher education and the spread of modern ideas through the medium of English. Afghānī wished to see Indians of all religions united against the British. Nowhere in his writings does Afghānī appear as Muslim communalist or separatist in relation to India.

Afghānī's pragmatic approach to the problem of encouraging effective anti-imperialist activities frequently involved him in apparent contradictions. The best argument for a mixed Muslim-Hindu audience in India might be quite different from the arguments he used in his Pan-Islamic writings from Paris, directed at the entire Muslim world. Thus, in an article written in his Paris newspaper, *al-'Urwa al-Wuthqā* in 1884, entitled "Nationality and the Muslim Religion," Afghānī makes points almost directly opposed to those on nationality and religion in his Indian articles. Using the same word for nationality, *jinsiyya*, as in India, he now finds it something to blame, not praise. He sees nationalism as a phase of tribalism that the Muslims have overcome. Muslims, having passed this tribal stage, are bound by more universal ties, and have no more concern about racial and ethnic questions.[32]

Afghānī's appeal while in India to Indian unity rather than to Pan-Islamic sentiment is clearly shown in a talk he gave in Calcutta in 1882, the "Lecture on Teaching and Learning." This lecture was directed to a primarily Muslim audience, but its opening passages resemble the assertions of later Hindu nationalists. After saying that he was happy at the presence of Indian youth at his lecture, Afghānī went on:

> Certainly I must be happy to see such offspring of India, since they are the offshoots of that India that was the cradle of humanity. Human values spread out from India to the

[32] "Pages choisies de Djamal ad-din al-Afghani: La nationalite (djinsiya) et la religion musulmane," trans. M. Colombe (from *al-'Urwa al-Wuthqā*, no. 2, March 20, 1884), *Orient*, 22 (1962), 125–130. Bernard Lewis has told me of a similar argument put forth by the Young Ottoman Ali Suavi, referred to in Şerif Mardin, *The Genesis of Young Ottoman Thought* (Princeton, 1962), p. 372; and Bernard Lewis, *The Middle East and the West* (London, 1964), p. 88.

> whole world. These youths are from the very land where the meridian circle was first determined. They are from the same realm that first understood the zodiac. Everyone knows that the determination of these two circles is impossible until perfection in geometry is achieved. Thus we can say that the Indians were the inventors of arithmetic and geometry. Note how Indian numerals were transferred from here to the Arabs, and from there to Europe.
>
> These youths are also the sons of a land that was the source of all the laws and rules of the world. If one observes closely, he will see that the "Code Romain," the mother of all Western codes, was taken from the four *vedas* and the *shastras*. The Greeks were the pupils of the Indians in literary ideas, limpid poetry, and lofty thoughts. One of these pupils, Pythagoras, spread sciences and wisdom in Greece and reached such a height that his word was accepted without proof as an inspiration from heaven.
>
> [The Indians] reached the highest level in philosophic thought. The soil of India is the same soil; the air of India is the same air; and these youths who are present here are fruits of the same earth and climate.[33]

This appeal to Indian Muslims to take pride in the Hindu past was no stranger than Afghānī's earlier appeal to Egyptian Muslims to take inspiration from pre-Islamic Egyptian greatness. In both cases Afghānī was appealing to an effective basis for solidarity against the foreigner. In Egypt, and even more in India, a stress on Muslim unity alone would have been more divisive than uniting a factor in the antiforeign struggle.

The encouragement of nonreligious nationalism is not the only element in Afghānī's Indian articles which sheds light on his thought different from that coming from his better-known Arabic writings. The second striking theme is Afghānī's stress on the benefits of modern science and philosophy. Here the picture of Afghānī that emerges is quite different from that given by a surface reading of the "Refutation of the Materialists" and other "pro-Islamic" writings. When Afghānī speaks of Islam in these articles—unless it is as a source of anti-imperialist solidarity—he tries to prove that true Islam is favorable to philosophy and science. His effort is to convince religious conservatives that they should favor modern science and

[33] "Lecture on Teaching and Learning," translated from *Maqālāt-i Jamāliyyeh* in Keddie, *Islamic Response*, pp. 101–108.

philosophy, not, as in superficially similar articles written by later apologists to convince modern Westernizers that Islam is in accord with their scientific values. Afghānī's arguments, however close to those of modern apologetics, have a vastly different goal. In India Islamic philosophy was taught more than in the Muslim West, and Afghānī may have been less hesitant to *publish* a defense of philosophy here than in Egypt.

In his 1882 lecture in Calcutta, "On Teaching and Learning," whose opening was cited above, Afghānī stresses the importance of modern science and philosophy. After praising the Indian past, Afghānī states "If someone looks deeply into the question, he will see that science rules the world. There was, is, and will be no ruler in the world but science."[34] Afghānī goes on to state that all great empires have been supported by science, up to and including contemporary European conquerors. Ignorance is always subjugated by science, which is the foundation of advanced technology in all fields. Afghānī then takes up the medieval philosophers' concept of philosophy as the organizing soul of the sciences:

> Thus a science is needed to be the comprehensive soul for all the sciences, so that it can preserve their existence, apply each of them in its proper place, and become the cause of progress of each one of those sciences.
>
> The science that has the position of a comprehensive soul and the rank of a preserving force is the science of *falsafa* or philosophy, because its subject is universal. It is philosophy that shows man human prerequisites. It shows the sciences what is necessary. It employs each of the sciences in its proper place.
>
> If a community did not have philosophy, and all the individuals of that community were learned in the sciences with particular subjects, those sciences could not last in that community for a century. . . . That community without the spirit of philosophy could not deduce conclusions from these sciences.
>
> . . . I may say that if the spirit of philosophy were found in a community, even if that community did not have one of those sciences whose subject is particular, undoubtedly their philosophic spirit would call for the acquisition of all the sciences.

[34] *Ibid.*, p. 102.

> The first Muslims had no science but, thanks to the Islamic religion, a philosophic spirit arose among them, and due to that philosophic spirit they began to discuss the general affairs of the world and human necessities. This was why they acquired in a short time all the sciences with particular subjects that they translated from the Syriac, Persian, and Greek into the Arabic language at the time of Mansūr Davānaqī [the Abbasid caliph al-Manṣūr].
>
> It is philosophy that makes man understandable to man, explains human nobility, and shows man the proper road. The first defect appearing in any nation that is headed toward decline is in the philosophic spirit. After that deficiencies spread into the other sciences, arts, and associations.[35]

Islam is praised here only because it prepared the way for science and philosophy, the real sources of knowledge. In another passage the modernized schools erected by the Ottomans and Egyptians are criticized, not for being irreligious, but for lacking a philosophical basis for the sciences they teach.

Afghānī goes on to a strong criticism of the Muslim ulama for their blindness and hostility toward modern science and technology:

> The strangest thing of all is that our ulama these days have divided science into two parts. One they call Muslim science, and one European science. Because of this they forbid others to teach some of the useful sciences. They have not understood that science is that noble thing that has no connection with any nation, and is not distinguished by anything but itself. Rather, everything that is known is known by science, and every nation that becomes renowned becomes renowned through sciences. . . .
>
> How very strange it is that the Muslims study those sciences that are ascribed to Aristotle with the greatest delight, as if Aristotle were one of the pillars of the Muslims. However, if the discussion relates to Galileo, Newton, and Kepler, they consider them infidels. The father and mother of science is proof, and proof is neither Aristotle nor Galileo. The truth is where there is proof, and those who forbid science and knowledge in the belief that they are safeguarding the Islamic religion are really the enemies of that religion. The Islamic religion is the closest of religions to science and

[35] *Ibid.*, pp. 104–105.

> knowledge, and there is no incompatibility between science and knowledge and the foundation of the Islamic faith.[36]

To support his appeal to science, Afghānī cites the great theologian, al-Ghazālī (d. 1111) although he does not mention Ghazālī's hostility to philosophy. Afghānī concludes by saying that no reform is possible in Muslim countries until Muslim leaders and ulama have reformed their outlook, and states that the decline of Muslim countries began with these leaders.

In an article in *Mu'allim-i Shafīq* entitled "The Benefits of Philosophy" Afghānī is even more forthright in his praise of philosophy above religion, and his view of Islamic revelation as a step on the road toward the higher truth of philosophy. Afghānī begins with a series of questions about the meaning and aims of philosophy, ending with an interesting list of names that one may assume were included in his own philosophical knowledge: "Is complete satisfaction to be found in the works of Fārābi, Ibn Sīnā, Ibn Bājja, Shihāb ad-Dīn the Martyr, Mīr Bāqir, Mūlla Sadrā, and the other treatises and notes concerned with philosophy, or is it not?"[37] He says that the difficulties and special terminology of classic philosophic texts have rendered them unknown to most people. He then states that, renouncing these traditional modes, he will say that:

> Philosophy is the escape from the narrow sensations of animality into the wide arena of human feelings. It is the removal of the darkness of bestial superstitions with the light of natural intelligence; the transformation of blindness and lack of insight into clearsightedness and insight. It is salvation from savagery and barbarism, ignorance and foolishness, by entry into the virtuous city of knowledge and skillfulness. In general, it is man's becoming man and living the life of sacred rationality. Its aim is human perfection in reason, mind, soul, and way of life. Perfection in one's way of life and welfare in livelihood are the chief preconditions for the

---

36 *Ibid.*, p. 107.

37 al-Fārābī, d. A.D. 950, and Ibn Sīnā (Avicenna), d. 1037, were two of the greatest masters, commentators, and developers of Hellenistic philosophy in Eastern Islam, as were Ibn Bājja (Avempace), d. 1138, and Ibn Rushd (Averroes), d. 1198, in Muslim Spain. Shihāb ad-Dīn Suhrawardī "the Executed," d. 1191, was the Persian founder of a more mystical "illuminationist" philosophy; while the seventeenth-century Persian philosophers Mīr Bāqir, better known as Mīr Dāmād, and his pupil, Mullā Sadrā, tried to reconcile mysticism, rationalism, and Shi'i beliefs.

> perfection of mind and soul. [Philosophy] is the first cause of man's intellectual activity and his emergence from the sphere of animals, and it is the greatest reason for the transfer of tribes and peoples from a state of nomadism and savagery to culture and civilization. It is the foremost cause of the production of knowledge, the creation of sciences, the invention of industries, and the initiation of the crafts.[38]

The revelation brought by Muhammad is seen as a necessary stage in bringing the Arabs from the ignorance and bestiality of their pre-Islamic savagery to a phase in which they were prepared to accept the higher truths of philosophy.

Significant and striking is Afghānī's criticism of traditional Islamic philosophy. Although his terminology and detailed arguments are often obscure, the main points are clear enough. He criticizes the Muslim philosophers for accepting the arguments of the Greeks as absolute and final, which the Greeks themselves did not do. Muslim thinkers thus accepted blind imitation, whereas, Afghānī states, philosophy and science are continually growing and developing subjects. In an earlier passage he bases this infinite growth of philosophy on the mystical idea of the infinity of meanings in the Koran.[39] Further, the Muslim philosophers incorporated into their books some ideas that are not really philosophical, but come from the polytheistic cosmogony of the ancients, and they also incorporated some defective and incomplete arguments.

Afghānī's chief concern in this article is to appeal to the ulama to apply rational methods to burning modern problems, instead of continuing their traditional scholastic discussions. Addressing the Indian ulama, he says:

> Why do you not raise your eyes from those defective books and why do you not cast your glance on this wide world? Why do you not employ your reflection and thought on events and their causes without the veils of those works? Why do you always utilize those exalted minds on trifling problems? . . .
>
> Yet you spend no thought on this question of great importance, incumbent on every intelligent man, which is: What is the cause of the poverty, indigence, helplessness, and dis-

---

38 "The Benefits of Philosophy," translated in Keddie, *Islamic Response*, pp. 109–122.

39 *Ibid.*, p. 114.

> tress of the Muslims, and is there a cure for this important phenomenon and great misfortune or not? . . .
>
> There is no doubt or question that, if someone does not spend his whole life on this great problem, and does not make this grievous phenomenon the pivot of his thought, he has wasted and ruined his life, and it is improper to call him a philosopher, which means one who knows the essential conditions of beings. . . .
>
> Is it not a fault for a percipient sage not to learn the entire sphere of new sciences and inventions and fresh creations, when he has no information about their causes and reasons, and the world has changed from one state to another and he does not raise his head from the sleep of neglect? Is it worthy of an investigator that he speak in absolute ignorance and not know what is definitely known? He splits hairs over imaginary essences and lags behind in the knowledge of evident matters.[40]

This article is one indication that Afghānī had adopted a progressive notion of the evolution of human knowledge. Islam is incorporated into this notion by saying: first, that it raised the Arabs from a state of barbarism and ignorance to one of civilization and rationality; second, that it encouraged the development of philosophy among them; and third, that since the meanings of the Koran are infinite and encompass all potential knowledge, no one stage of philosophy is final and perfect. Afghānī criticizes his contemporaries for assuming such perfection for a state of knowledge that has now been superseded.

In defending rationalism, reform, and science, while attacking on nationalist grounds some of the main defenders of these modern virtues among Indian Muslims, Sayyid Ahmad Khān and his school, Afghānī had to walk a thin and easily misinterpreted line. Like other Islamic modernists, his general line for defending Islam, nationalism, and modernism at the same time was to try to show that modern virtues originated with Islam, and that the Muslims who rejected them were acting against the principles of their religion. Like the early modernists of many cultures, Afghānī apparently hoped that the rational attiudes and scientific innovations necessary to self-strengthening could be adopted without the foreigners' cultural

---

40 *Ibid.*, pp. 120–122.

and linguistic baggage, whose acquisition could disrupt national and religious unity and encourage passive admiration for foreign conquerors.

In one of his Indian articles, "The True Causes of Man's Happiness and Distress," Afghānī includes both a call to nationalist zeal and a warning against rejection of foreign science and innovation. Commenting on the virtues of patriotic and religious zeal, and the dangers of their excess, Afghānī says:

> The desire to protect fatherland and nationality (*vatan va jins*) and the wish to defend religion and coreligionists, that is, patriotic zeal, national zeal, and religious zeal, arouse men to compete in the arena of virtues and accomplishments. They cause the adherents of religions and the members of nations, tribes, and peoples to strive to raise themselves. They make each of them employ his own effort and strive to attain the bases of greatness and glory and the means to power and majesty.
>
> It is this desire that leads nations and the followers of religions to climb the steps of nobility, and to acquire, through striving, all the distinctions of the human world. . . . It calls man to the preservation of public rights and rouses him to the protection of the fatherland and the defense of the honor of religion. . . .
>
> Having reached this point, I wish to say with a thousand regrets that the Muslims of India have applied the desire to defend religion, or religious zeal, in a very bad way. For they have carried zeal, through misuse, to a point where it has become a cause of hatred for knowledge and the sciences, and a reason for aversion from industries and innovation. They believed they must, out of religious zeal, hate and abominate what was connected with the opponents of faith, even though these things were sciences and arts.
>
> Whereas, what was incumbent upon them from a religious zeal was, whenever they saw a virtue, an accomplishment, a science, or a piece of knowledge, knowing themselves to be the first and rightest, to strive and make efforts to acquire it, and not to allow the opponents of the Islamic true religion to take precedence over them in any one among the virtues and accomplishments. A thousand regrets for this misuse of religious zeal, which finally will result in destruction and overthrow! I fear that the misuse of religious zeal by the Muslims of India has reached the point that the Muslims

will, entirely washing their hands of life, abandon living because the opponents of the Islamic faith live in this world![41]

In addition to recommending simultaneous attachment to one's own culture and willingness to borrow when useful, this article is interesting for its explicit equivalence between patriotism and religious faith, which lead to the same virtues. After the first paragraph which implies equivalence between the "desire to protect fatherland and nationality and the wish to defend religion," both aspirations are treated as a single antecedent in subsequent references to "this desire." Here is one indication of why it was easy for Afghānī to pass back and forth among the defense of local nationalism, Pan-Islam, and zeal for the defense of the Islamic religion.

Within the context of Afghānī's anti-imperialist nationalism on the one hand, and his philosophic rationalism on the other, the import of his attack on Sir Sayyid Ahmad Khān, the third point stressed in his Indian articles, can be understood. The attack was not really on Sayyid Ahmad Khān's rationalism, reformism, and scant orthodoxy—all qualities that also characterized Afghānī. It was rather on Sayyid Ahmad Khān's belief in cooperation with the British instead of nationalist opposition, and his willingness to borrow heavily from the British and openly to abandon much of the Indian Muslim heritage, thus depriving Indian Muslims of a source of national, anti-imperialist pride.

The nationalist and anti-imperialist thrust of the attack on Sayyid Ahmad Khān is clear from Afghāni's articles about him. Afghānī's longest Persian article about Sayyid Ahmad Khān was called "A Description of the Aghūrīs with Pomp and Show." The Aghūrīs were a small, despised caste with special religious practices. and Afghānī applied the name to the followers of Sayyid Ahmad Khān as a term of vituperation.

In this article, after saying that the blind, ignorant, and traitorous consider themselves clearsighted, wise, and courageous, Afghānī attacks those who harm their brothers in the interest of foreigners. "Why should someone who destroys the life spirit of a people be called their well-wisher; why should a person who works for the decline of his faith be considered a sage? What ignorance is this?"[42] he asks.

---

41 *Maqālāt-i Jamāliyyeh*, pp. 130–131.

42 "Sharḥ-i ḥāl-i Aghūriyān bā shaukat wa sha'n," in *ibid.*, p. 28.

In an oblique attack on followers of the British path in education, Afghānī then asks whether one whose interests lie in the ignorance, corruption, and blindness of someone else would try to educate him and cure his blindness. Afghānī goes on to say that there are three types of education. First, a man can be educated to be part of a nation (*qaum*) and to serve its social order. Second, education can be based on the interests of the individual, with no regard for the nation. Finally, education can be geared to the interests of foreigners, of benefit to a group of which he forms no part. In the last case, can one imagine that a man would learn to serve his nation and community? It would be a thousand times better to have no education than to have one that harms one's own nation. Only from the first kind of education can national unity be produced. In view of this it is impossible to imagine that foreigners (i.e., the British rulers of India) would support the first, national, type of education; they have certainly not come in order to strengthen the nationalism and community feeling (*jinsiyya* and *qaumiyya*) of others.

Returning to his attacks on Sayyid Ahmad Khān's group, never named directly, Afghānī says that someone who embraces the killers of his brothers is the worst type of man. Such men put out great efforts to strengthen the Christians by confirming the truth of the Torah and the Gospel.[43] Students should be taught patriotism, and to sacrifice themselves for their nation. The "Aghūrīs," however, teach slavery instead of freedom, and hence are obstacles to the progress of their people. They have no religion and no interest other than to fill their own bellies. They use education only as a means to worldly goals. Here as elsewhere, Afghānī exaggerates the irreligion of Sayyid Ahmad Khān's school and vilifies them as "materialists" in the vulgar as well as philosophic sense.

In a passage that recalls Ibn Khaldūn and some of the Muslim political philosophers, Afghānī goes on to say that when a community or nation is healthy, it is under unified government, and all classes contribute their talents to the whole, like the members of the human body. When that community's unity of thought is weakened, however, discord, division, vices, and corrupation ensue, and the society becomes prey to foreign conquest and rule. Men who sow the seeds of disunity must thus be dealt with harshly.[44]

---

[43] *Ibid.*, p. 33. The reference is to Sayyid Ahmad Khān's unorthodox effort show that the Bible was not, as Muslim doctrine stated, falsified.

[44] *Ibid.*, pp. 38–40.

Afghānī then states that good habits can only be inculcated in a people through centuries of continuous education, and that the interruption of this education with foreign ways can never produce the virtues found among the foreigners, but can only be disruptive. The Aghūrīs teach the abandonment of virtues, disunity of the community (*umma*), and breaking the laws of humanity. They open the way of slavery to foreigners. One of them, referred to only by a pejorative nickname, is particularly attacked in the article. He is like a dog who goes to a stranger rather than to his own master just to get a bone. It is no wonder that the Aghūrīs act this way, but it is strange that others do not understand their base aims. They call to the road of perdition, claiming it is the way to salvation.[45]

In this article the nationalist basis of the attack on Sayyid Ahmad Khān's school is clear. The group is attacked for undermining the unity of the community, and often it is even unclear whether the Indian community as a whole or the Indian Muslims are intended. The defense here is not of religion but of local customs as a shield against submission to foreign ways and rulers. With almost no change of wording the article could apply to any group favoring the wholesale introduction of foreign ways in any colonial country—there is little reference to religion, much less specifically to Islam.

Similar conclusions result from reading Afghānī's shorter Indian article, "Commentary on the Commentator," directed more specifically against Sayyid Ahmad Khān as an individual, rather than simply against his school. In it Afghānī speaks of the need for a sage and renewer who will save the Muslims from their current condition of decline and corruption:

> There is no doubt that in the present age distress, misfortune, and weakness besiege all classes of Muslims from every side. Therefore every Muslim keeps his eyes and ears open in expectation—to the East, West, North, and South—to see from what corner of the earth the sage and renewer will appear and will reform the minds and souls of the Muslims, repel the unforeseen corruption, and again educate them with a virtuous education. Perhaps through that good education they may return to their former joyful condition.[46]

---

[45] *Ibid.*, pp. 42–52.

[46] "Commentary on the Commentator," translated in Keddie, *Islamic Response*, pp. 123–129.

Although Afghānī claims to have looked to Sayyid Ahmad Khān (not named, but clearly implied) as such a potential renewer, it is probable that he pictured himself in this role. Afghānī is no doubt being frank when he then objects to Sayyid Ahmad Khān's high evaluation of human nature; Afghānī stands here with the Muslim philosophical tradition. So does he in his main point, that there are social benefits that can only be assured by religious belief on the part of the masses:

> Even stranger is the fact that this commentator has lowered the divine, holy rank of prophecy and placed it on the level of the reformer. He has considered the prophets to be men like Washington, Napoleon, Palmerston, Garibaldi, Mister Gladstone, and Monsieur Gambetta. . . .
>
> Does he not understand that if the Muslims, in their current state of weakness and misery, did not believe in miracles and hell-fire, and considered the Prophet to be like Gladstone, they undoubtedly would soon abandon their own weak and conquered camp, and attach themselves to the powerful conqueror. For in that case there would no longer remain anything to prevent this, nor any fear or anxiety. And from another standpoint the prerequisites for changing religion now exist, since being like the conqueror and having the same religion as he are attractive to everyone.[47]

Anything that undermines faith in Islam will thus lead Indian Muslims to identify with their British conquerors, which Afghānī wants to avoid at all costs. Convinced of the political evils that would arise from the Muslims' following Sayyid Ahmad Khān on his pro-British path, Afghānī could easily believe that all means, including the exaggerated rhetoric permitted by his tradition were legitimate to discredit Sayyid Ahmad Khān and his school.

The two remaining Indian articles, "The Benefits of Newspapers," and "Teaching and Education," are of less intellectual interest than those analyzed above. The former lists the practical contributions of newspapers, while latter says that the Orient must learn once more to honor science and men of learning if it is to escape from its present decline and misery.[48]

---

47 *Ibid.*, p. 127.

48 Pakdaman, pp. 255–267, translates into French these two Persian articles.

The "Refutation of the Materialists"

WITH THIS background in mind, it is possible to take a look at the "Refutation." The main point to be noted is its thoroughly pragmatic and this-worldly defense of religion; the virtues claimed for religion are social ones. Afghānī repeatedly claims that religion is good for the people because it supports the social fabric, while the Naichirīs like other sectarians, bring dissension and finally political ruin to the community.

Afghānī's first summary of his position toward the Naichirīs is so close to the views and even the language of some Muslim philosophers on the utility of orthodoxy for the majority, and the harm brought by sects, that it is worth quoting at length:

> The materialists, or Naichirīs, have appeared in numerous forms and various guises among the races and peoples, and under different names. Sometimes they have become manifest under the name of "sage," sometimes they have appeared adorned as those who remove oppression and repel injustice. Sometimes they have stepped into the arena dressed as those who know the secrets and uncover the mysteries of truth, and as the possessors of esoteric knowledge. Sometimes they have claimed that their goal is the removal of superstitions and the enlightenment of peoples' minds. For a time they came forth as the lovers of the poor, protectors of the weak, and well-wishers of the unfortunate. Sometimes to fulfill their evil aims they have laid claim to prophethood like other false prophets. Sometimes they called themselves the educators, teachers, and benefactors of the community. But among whatever people they appeared, and whatever guise or name they bore, they became—because of their evil premises and false principles, their harmful teachings, deadly views, and fatal sayings—the cause of the decline and collapse of that people and the annihilation of that community. They de-

> stroyed the social order of those peoples and scattered their members.
>
> For man is very cruel and ignorant. And to this treacherous, greedy, bloodthirsty creature there were supplied beliefs and qualities in the earliest period by means of religions. Tribes and peoples learned these beliefs and qualities as an inheritance from their fathers and grandfathers, and they adjusted their behavior accordingly, avoiding the evil and corruption that are the destroyers of the social order. As a result they enlightened their minds with that knowledge which is the cause of happiness and the foundation of civilization. Thus there was produced for them a kind of stability and continuity.
>
> The sect of Naichirīs, among whatever people they appeared, tried to nullify those beliefs and corrupt those qualities. From them destruction penetrated the pillars of the social order of that people and headed them toward dissolution, until they were suddenly destroyed.[49]

The subsequent pages make clear that the heterodox sects are grouped with the materialists, as similar in nature and equally harmful to the community. The points of the above statement, shared by the Islamic philosophical tradition, are that: (1) Those who spread religious doubts among the people, by whatever means, are the same in their effects because they undermine the social structure. (2) Most men are by nature evil and can be directed to virtue and social stability only by religion.

Afghānī goes on to discuss three important beliefs and three virtues brought by religions, "each of which is a firm pillar for the existence of nations and the permanence of the social order." The first is the belief that man is the noblest of creatures. The second is each man's certainty "that his community is the noblest one, and that all outside his community are in error and deviation." Afghānī was surely not blind to the fact that not every community could be the noblest; again, it is the utility of this view, not its truth, that is important. Then, in a description of the afterlife that is more in line with Neoplatonic philosophy than orthodox ideas, Afghānī goes on:

> The third is the firm belief that man has come into the world in order to acquire accomplishments worthy of trans-

[49] "Refutation of the Materialists," translated from the Hyderabad, 1881 edition in Keddie, *Islamic Response*, pp. 130–174. The quotation is on pp. 140–141.

> ferring him to a world more excellent, higher, vaster, and more perfect than this narrow and dark world that really deserves the name of the Abode of Sorrows.
>
> One should not neglect the important effect of each of these three beliefs on the social order, their great advantages for civilization, and their many contributions to order and the relations among peoples.[50]

None of the three beliefs has much connection with what is usually considered religion, and none of them concerns God: both their nature and utility are human and social.

Afghānī then discusses the virtues arising from each of the three beliefs. Out of the first belief, that man is the noblest creature, comes intellectual perfection for the chosen few, again described in terms recalling the philosophers. Man ascends the ladder of civilization and "proceeds in proportion to his progress in the intellectual sphere, until he becomes one of those civilized virtuous men whose life with brothers who have reached this rung of civilization is based on love, wisdom, and justice. This is the ultimate goal of sages and the summit of human happiness in the world."[51]

Just as the first belief leads to an essentially philosophic conclusion, so too do the second and third. Afghānī may have had an essentially evolutionary view of religion (an assumption supported by some of his other writings and talks that more openly express such a view), in which revealed religion helped lead men from barbarism to civilization and gave them an important impetus to social cohesion and material progress. From the religiously based community there then could arise philosophic and scientific ideas that comprehended the true nature of the world more than did literalist belief in revealed religion. Just as the "Islam" that is praised at the end of the "Refutation" is not the Islam that had existed for many centuries, so the "religion" that is praised in the earlier parts of the essay means something special to Afghānī.

The second belief, the knowledge of every man that his own community is the noblest, pushes nations to achievement in civilization, science, and the arts and to competition in knowledge and progress. Again religion is seen as culminating in a philosophical virtue, by inculcating communal pride and a desire to keep ahead of others. Here

---

50 *Ibid.*, p. 141.
51 *Ibid.*, p. 142.

Afghānī may have had in mind an idealized picture of the early Islamic community, and must have been aware that the Muslim world of the nineteenth century presented no such picture.

The third belief, in rewards and a future life, is described, both when first mentioned and in relation to the results flowing from it, in the philosophical and intellectualist terms that had been rejected for centuries by Muslim orthodoxy. Even Afghānī's terminology is of the Aristotelian and Neoplatonic type used by the philosophers:

> One of the inevitable consequences of the [third] belief, that man has come into the world in order to attain the perfections needed to transfer him to a higher and vaster world, is that when someone acquires this belief he will of necessity always strive to improve and enlighten his mind with true science and sound knowledge. He will not leave his intellect idle, but will bring out of concealment and into the light of the world what has been deposited in him of active power, lofty sentiments, and great virtues. In all stages of his life he will try to rid his soul of impure features and will not stint in the adjustment and improvement of his habits. . . .
>
> Thus this belief is the best impulse toward civilization, whose foundations are true knowledge and refined morals. It is the best requisite for the stability of the social order, which is founded on each individual's knowledge of his proper rights, and his following the straight path of justice. It is the strongest motive for international relations, which are based on truthful and honest observation of the bounds of human intercourse. It is the best basis for the peace and calm of the classes of humanity, because peace is the fruit of love and justice, and love and justice result from admirable qualities and habits. It is the only belief that restrains man from all evils, saves him from the values of adversity and misfortune, and seats him in the virtuous city on the throne of happiness.[52]

The "virtuous city" is the terrain of al-Fārābī and of later Muslim philosophers, as is the effort to rid the soul of impure qualities and to expand the sparks of virtue and knowledge that have been deposited in man. The description before the above passage of the superior world for which men are preparing themselves comes from the philosophers—a world of the intellectually and spiritually per-

[52] *Ibid.*, pp. 143–144.

fect; and it is unclear whether or not this world is achieved on earth through intellectual perfection.

In discussing the three beliefs and the results that flow from them, Afghānī thus says that religion is good both because it leads to human and social virtues and because it leads some men to philosophical and scientific conclusions. This is either an evolutionary view of religion which really has the Islam of the earliest centuries in mind or the attribution to religion of virtues that his enlightened readers would see were really rather the attributes of philosophy.

Afghānī next goes on to the three virtues produced by religion: Shame, Trustworthiness, and Truthfulness. Again he shows not how these three arise from religion but how necessary they are to the proper functioning of the social order. His description of the good social state produced by their presence, and the ruin brought by their absence, seems more likely to point up the lack of these qualities in any existing state with Muslim rulers than the superiority of such states.

Afghānī then specifies the social harm brought by the materialists. They undermine the belief that one's own religion is better than others, thus leading men to evil acts. They attack each of the three beliefs and three habits brought by religion, teaching that all religions are false. This discourages men from practicing virtue, encourages the most bestial vices, and undermines the social order. They attack belief in the Day of Judgment and the habit of shame, which are the foundations of trustworthiness and truthfulness. They also spread a harmful egalitarianism, which will make the lower classes unwilling to perform menial jobs:

> In addition, this group has placed the foundation of their belief on license and communism, and has considered that all desirable things should be shared, and has regarded privileges and distinctions as unsurpation, as shall be noted.
>
> ... The final goal and ultimate object of this group is that all men should share in all desires and delights; that privileges and distinctions should be abolished; that nobody should have superiority or a surplus of anything over another; and that all should be absolutely equal. If it becomes like that, naturally every person will refuse to perform hard and menial tasks and economic life will be disordered; the wheel of dealings and relationships will stop moving; and

> finally this weak species will be brought to the vale of perdition and will disappear completely. . . .
>
> The real cause of the superiority of man is his love for privilege and distinction. When privilege and distinction are removed, souls are stopped from the movement toward eminence and minds neglect to penetrate the truth of things and to discover the subtleties of life. Men would live in this world like beasts of the desert, were it possible for them.[53]

This traditional belief in the utility of social distinctions, which must be bolstered by religious teachings, is consistent with Afghānī's intellectual elitism and his pessimism about human nature, both of which he shares with the philosophers.

When materialism spreads, egoism overcomes individuals and social solidarity is lost:

> The quality of *egoism* consists of self-love to the point that if a personal profit requires a man having that quality to let the whole world be harmed, he would not renounce that profit but would consent to the harm of everyone in the world. This quality makes man put his personal interest above the general welfare, and makes him sell his nation for a paltry profit. Gradually, because of this base life, fear and cowardice overtook man, and he became content and happy with meanness, baseness, slavery, and abasement in his life.
>
> When the state of individuals reached this point, the bond of fusion and interdependence was broken; the unity of the species was annihilated; the power of preservation and the means of survival were lost; and the throne of greatness, glory, and honor was overthrown.[54]

The resemblance of these ideas to those of Ibn Khaldūn, who also, as Mushin Mahdi has shown, had his roots in the Neo-Aristotelian philosophical tradition, is striking. Religion promotes solidarity and its decline is accompanied by harmful individualism.[55]

There follows an account of the "materialist" sects in East and West that have caused the decline of nations, in which the main Is-

---

[53] *Ibid.*, pp. 149–150.

[54] *Ibid.*, pp. 151–152.

[55] See Muhsin Mahdi, *Ibn Khaldûn's Philosophy of History* (London, 1957). Sylvia Haim (*Arab Nationalism* [Berkeley and Los Angeles, 1962], p. 13 n. 14) notes the similarities of Afghānī's and Ibn Khaldūn's views on solidarity.

lamic sects are included. The Islamic sects attracted men into illegitimate allegorical interpretations and denial of the sacred law and of religious duties. Their teachings drew men away from the general interests of the community toward their selfish desires and prepared the way for foreign invasions. Afghānī then criticizes Ottoman modernists as traitors in the recent Ottoman war against the Russians. In Europe materialism has culminated in the evil doctrines of socialism, nihilism, and communism.[56]

Afghānī reiterates his arguments in a discussion of Oriental materialists, and goes on to an interesting discussion of the possible ways of enforcing justice in the world. One of these is to count on the nobility of the human soul, but, he says, in passages again recalling the philosophers, each nation and class has its own standards of nobility, and the higher classes consider themselves bound only by what they can get away with. After refuting the other means of securing justice, Afghānī says:

> Thus, no force remains for restraining men of passions from their transgressions and oppression other than the fourth way. That is the belief that the world has a Creator, wise and powerful; and the belief that for good and evil deeds there is a fixed recompense after this life. If truth, these two beliefs together are the firmest foundation for the suppression of passions and the removal of external and internal transgressions.
>
> . . . For the final cause of all acquired qualities and free acts, as was said above, is man himself; and when a person does not believe in recompense and requital, what else will bar blameworthy qualities to him and call him to good behavior? Especially when a man realizes that being characterized by bad qualities will not result in any loss for him in the world, nor will having good qualities bring him any benefit. . . .
>
> Thus, from all we have expounded, it becomes clear . . . that religion, even if it be false and the basest of religions, because of those two firm pillars—belief in a Creator and faith in rewards and punishments—and because of the six principles that are enshrined in religions, is better than the way of the materialists, or *naichirīs*. [It is better] in the realm of civilization, the social order, and the organization

[56] Translated in Keddie, *Islamic Response*, pp. 160–163.

> of relationships; indeed in all human societies and all progress of mankind in this world.[57]

As in the article "Commentary on the Commentator" Afghānī is here relatively indifferent to the truth of a religion—it is its social utility that concerns him.

Most of Afghānī's tract consists of a defense of religion as such, and only in the last few pages does he argue the superiority of Islam among religions. Islam is superior for several reasons: First, its insistence on the unity of the Creator, which excludes incarnation or any sharing of divine powers; second, its lack of inherent race or class distinctions; and third, its rejection of beliefs that do not rest on proofs.

In this section Afghānī is, without saying so, speaking of his ideal Islam, which may have existed in the past, but which he knew was far from the Islam of his own day. Under the second point, the lack of class distinctions, he speaks critically of the power of the priesthood in Christianity, probably with an eye to the power of the ulama in later Islamic history. On the third point, the necessity for proofs for religious beliefs, Afghānī's characterization of Islam is in the sharpest contrast with what he said about it elsewhere, notably in the "Answer to Renan." The presentation of Islam here surely represents a *desideratum* and not what Afghānī believed existed in his time. The whole passage is more an implied criticism than the encomium it appears to be on the surface:

> [The third foundation of human virtues] is that the members of each community must found their beliefs, which are the first things written on the slates of their minds, on certain proofs and firm evidence. In their beliefs they must shun submission to conjectures and not be content with mere imitation (*taqlīd*) of their ancestors. For if man believes in things without proof or reason; makes a practice of following unproven opinions; and is satisfied to imitate and follow his ancestors, his mind inevitably desists from intellectual movement, and little by little stupidity and imbecility overcome him—until his mind gradually becomes completely idle and he becomes unable to perceive his own good and evil; and adversity and misfortune overtake him from all sides.

57 *Ibid.*, pp. 166–168.

It is no wonder that Guizot, the French Minister, who wrote the history of . . . civilization of the European peoples, said as follows: One of the greatest causes for European civilization was that a group appeared, saying: "Although our religion is the Christian religion, we are seeking the proofs of the fundamentals of our beliefs." The corpus of priests did not give permission, and they said that religion was founded on imitation. When the group became strong their ideas spread; minds emerged from their state of stupidity and dullness into movement and progress; and men made efforts to achieve the perquisites of civilization.

The Islamic religion is the only religion that censures belief without proof and the following of conjectures; reproves blind submission; seeks to show proof of things to its followers; everywhere addresses itself to reason; considers all happiness the result of wisdom and clearsightedness; attributes perdition to stupidity and lack of insight; and sets up proofs for each fundamental belief in such a way that it will be useful to all people. It even, when it mentions most of its rules, states their purposes and benefits. (Refer to the Holy Koran.)[58]

The argument that the Koran enjoins logical proofs and demonstrative reasoning is a favorite one of the Muslim philosophers. The favorable reference to the founders of Protestantism is one of several such references by Afghānī, who seems to have hoped to play the role of a Muslim Luther. He was convinced by Guizot's attribution of much of the West's progress to Protestantism, and his interest in Protestant reform was far more worldly and pragmatic than theological. The above passage, as other of Afghānī's words show, is really an injunction to the Muslims to turn away from a stultifying imitation of their predecessors and toward a more rational and less restrictive faith that would allow room for progress and innovation. That Afghānī is talking not about the Islam he knew in his own day, but as he believed it to have been in ideal and in its early days, is indicated at the end of his treatise: "If someone says: If the Islamic religion is as you say, then why are the Muslims in such a sad condition? I will answer: When they were [truly] Muslims, they were what they were and the world bears witness to their excellence. As for the present, I will content myself with this holy text: "Verily, God

58 *Ibid.*, pp. 171–172.

does not change the state of people until they change themselves inwardly."[59] Afghānī was apparently the first to cite this Koranic text as an admonition to modern change and progress. It has since become a favorite of the modernists.

The "Refutation" has not seemed to Western readers to be a particularly convincing argument, yet it has had and continues to have considerable reputation among Muslims. With it Afghānī seems to have accomplished several goals simultaneously: (1) He suggested to intellectuals the dangers of going too far in their open criticisms of Islam, since religion had the practical virtues of tying together the community and keeping men from vice. (2) To the same group he suggested a way of reform through stressing certain passages of the Koran and certain parts of the Islamic tradition. (3) He combated the pro-British influence of Sayyid Ahmad Khān and his followers by identifying them with the harmful materialists. (4) He suggested certain limits to politico-economic as well as religious reform. (5) He reinforced pride in Islam as the best religion, providing Muslims with a useful counterweight to the British claims of cultural superiority. It would seem that Western disappointment in the book stems from an expectation of finding in it what we would call a "religious" document. It appears rather to be primarily an expedient, political tract; not necessarily even expressing the real opinions of the author, but written in order to accomplish certain goals.

In the ordinary sense of the word, the "Refutation" should not even be classified under "Apologetics." What Afghānī was concerned about, as his whole activity shows, was not to awaken passive admiration of Islam, but to harness Islamic sentiment to certain goals. In the course of time, however, as more and more people began to doubt traditional Islam, the book began in fact to be read as an apologetic tract. The "Refutation" is certainly not an attempt to "rethink" Islam, and any consistent public rethinking might in itself become sectarian, which was just what Afghānī wanted to avoid.

Taken together, the "Refutation" and the Indian articles and lectures illustrate well Afghānī's main approaches to a mass public just before he became known as an ideologist of Pan-Islam. His main theme is unity against the foreign, and particularly British, imperialists. In India it is not Muslim unity against the British that is stressed, but rather the unity of all Indians. For this goal, Indian Muslims

---

59 *Ibid.*, p. 173.

should take pride in the Hindu past, Indians should use their own languages as the media of instruction, and Indian Muslims should not be seduced by those like Sayyid Ahmad Khān who would co-operate with the British and copy British ways. It was only after he left the mixed Hindu-Muslim context of India, and especially beginning in London and Paris in 1883–84, that Afghānī came forth publicly as the champion of Pan-Islam, which might unite Muslims all over the world in cultural pride and anti-imperialist action.

Afghānī left India voluntarily late in 1882 to head for Paris, from where he hoped to be able to work more freely and effectively in propagandizing against British imperialism in Egypt and elsewhere in the Muslim East.

8

Propaganda from Paris: 1883–1884

ACCORDING TO the report by the Government of India's Thagi and Dakaiti Department, Jamāl ad-Dīn left India in November, 1882, via the S.S. *India*.[1] On his way to England, from where he intended to go to Paris, he stopped briefly at Port Said. Here he sent letters to former friends and patrons in Cairo; short notes to Sharīf Pāshā and 'Abdallāh Pāshā Fikrī, and a long letter to Riyāḍ Pāshā. Afghānī's drafts of these letters (photographed in the *Documents*), ask the addressees to give their protection to Abū Turāb, whom Afghānī was sending to Cairo to recover the books and possessions that had been confiscated from him at the time of his expulsion from Egypt. The letter to Riyāḍ, parts of which were quoted in chapters 5 and 7 above, blames the machinations of enemies for Afghānī's expulsion from Egypt and details his bad experiences in India with British interrogations. The tone and detail of Afghānī's letter to Riyāḍ indicate that Afghānī saw him as the closest to him of the prominent men he now addressed. On his reasons for heading for Paris rather than remaining in an Eastern country, Jamāl ad-Dīn wrote to Riyāḍ:

> I know that if I returned to my land while my eyes are all tears, my voice all complaint, and my heart all fire, I would

[1] F.O. 60/594, "Memorandum" by A. S. Lethbridge, General Superintendent, Thagi and Dakaiti Department, 1896.

> not find there any Muslim ready to sympathize with my affliction when I recounted to him my story. For Muslims . . . do not revolt against tyranny and have no pity for its victims. I therefore, even without money, have decided to travel toward lands whose inhabitants enjoy sound minds, attentive ears, and sympathetic hearts to whom I can recount how a human being is treated in the East. Thus will be extinguished the fire that so many sufferings have lit in me and my body will be freed from the burden of sufferings that have broken my heart.

In the same letter Afghānī mentions his plan to go first to London and then to Paris. He also asks Riyāḍ to protect his pupils, especially Muḥammad 'Abduh and Ibrāhīm al-Laqqānī, who were being tried for participation in the 'Urābī movement. If they behaved wrongly, says Afghānī, it was only out of ignorance. Afghānī adds that he is sending letters to Sharīf Pāshā and 'Abdallāh Pāshā Fikrī. To both Riyāḍ and Sharīf, Afghānī wrote that 'Ārif [Abū Turāb] was to collect the monthly salary owed Afghānī by the Egyptian government (meaning that it was in arrears at the time of Afghānī's expulsion from Egypt). In 1883 Abū Turāb transferred the large sum of 2,530 francs to Afghānī in Paris, almost surely obtained from his Egyptian mission.[2]

The stop in Port Said occurred in December 1882, and by January 19, 1883, an Arabic newspaper announced Afghānī's presence in Paris, so that Afghānī's brief stay in London must have occurred in early January 1883. Wilfrid Blunt is mistaken in recording that Afghānī, whom he met for the first time on this trip to London, arrived in London in the spring of 1883, and that he had come from spending a few months in America.[3]

Afghānī reached Europe shortly after the defeat by the British of the 'Urābī movement in Egypt and the beginning of the supposedly temporary British occupation of that country. In his hostility to the

---

[2] The drafts of the letters are photographed in *Documents*, pls. 12–15, photos 32–38. I have been helped by the translation in Pakdaman, p. 76. Abū Turāb speaks of sending money in a later letter in *Documents*, and *Documents*, p. 76, doc. 301, is a letter from the Anglo-Egyptian Banking Company to Afghānī telling him that "Aref" (Abū Turāb) has transferred 2,530 francs to him.

[3] Wilfrid S. Blunt, *Gordon at Khartoum* (London, 1911), p. 40; see also Blunt's letter in Edward G. Browne, *The Persian Revolution of 1905–1909* (Cambridge, 1910), p, 401. Blunt appears to be the only original source for the untrue story that Afghānī spent time in the United States.

British occupation of Egypt Afghānī could find considerable support in Europe. notably in France, and also in the Ottoman Empire. The question of the future of the Sudan, where the self-proclaimed Mahdi, Muḥammad Aḥmad, increased his power during 1883, was another matter where Afghānī's concerns were shared by some of the European public. Afghānī arrived in Europe, then, at a time when his attacks on British policy in the Muslim world were welcome to some Europeans.

During Afghānī's brief stay in London, Louis Ṣābunjī's London newspaper, *an-Naḥla* published an article signed by Afghānī entitled "English Policy in Eastern Countries," and another article whose content makes it seem almost certain that it was also by Afghānī, "The Reasons for the War in Egypt." The first article was a strong attack on British policy in India and in Egypt. The second says that the true reason for the British invasion of Egypt was that the British knew that Sultan Abdülhamid had been striving with success to have all Muslims adhere to the firm bond (*al-'urwa al-wuthqā*) of the caliphate. The British feared for their rule over Indian Muslims, and awaited the right occasion to tear apart the Islamic solidarity (*'aṣabiyya*) that Europeans call "Pan-Islamism." The British thus sent in boats and troops to suppress 'Urābī's movement primarily as a move against the rising Muslim solidarity that the British knew would endanger their influence in the East and their rule in India.[4]

This is the first of Afghānī's published articles in which he speaks favorably of Pan-Islamism and of Sultan Abdülhamid II. The connection of support for the Sultan and for Pan-Islam with opposition to British encroachments on Muslim territory is here made explicit. The article also marks Afghānī's first recorded use of the words *al-'urwa al-wuthqā* (the firmest bond) to apply to the Sultan's caliphate.

The first mention of Afghānī's presence in Paris comes in James Sanua's newspaper, *Abu Naddara Zarka* (a simplified transliteration that appeared in each issue), on January 19, 1883, under the heading "Important News." The item says that the great Jamāl ad-Dīn, who has passed his life working for mankind and who loves the Egyptians, has arrived in Paris, and has immediately begun to write for *Abu*

---

[4] "as-Siyāsa al-injiliziyya fī mamālik ash-sharqiyya" and "Asbāb al-ḥarb bi Miṣr," *al-Manār*, (Cairo) XXV (1925, 756–760, reprinted from *The Bee/ an-Naḥla*, (London) V, 3, without an exact date but only a statement that they date from Afghānī's stay in London in late 1882 or early 1883.

Naddara. The next issue, dated February 9, 1883, has a lithographed drawing of Jamāl ad-Dīn on the first page, along with a lead article by him, "ash-Sharq va ash-sharqiyyīn" (The Orient and Orientals).[5]

Another Paris Arabic newspaper, *al-Baṣīr* edited by a liberal Maronite refugee from the Ottoman Empire, Khalīl Ghānim, wrote on January 25 that Jamāl ad-Dīn had arrived in Paris the week before. The story goes on with extravagant praise of his fame and knowledge, and tells of his stays in India and London. The editor concludes that it is supposed "that he will remain here for a considerable period."[6] This statement, along with the Hyderabad report from Sayyid Husain that Afghānī used to talk of spending time in France in order to get justice from the Khedive Taufīq through the French, indicates that in coming to France, Afghānī had some political plan in mind. In view of French bitterness over the British single-handed occupation in Egypt, it is easy to conclude that Afghānī had hopes of French support against the British in Egypt. His friend, Sanua, was already working for this.[7]

Al-Baṣīr of February 8, 1883, has on its front page an open letter from Afghānī asking the paper's editor, Ghānim, not to criticize the Ottoman Government so much in his paper. Afghānī says that Ghānim's important newspaper should avoid any calumniation of Orientals, who are the target of foreign conquest. Easterners can escape this humiliation only by uniting under a single banner to defend themselves and by supporting their existing government. Ghānim is accused of inadvertently weakening the Muslim community (*umma*) by opposing the Ottoman government, which is the protector of the Eastern peoples from division and ruin. These peoples can try gradually to reform their government, but if the Ottoman government is overthrown and each of its peoples becomes independent they will all become the prey of foreigners. Thus all Ottoman subjects should unite to strengthen their government.[8] This article was one of Af-

[5] *Abu Naddara Zarka,* (Paris) Jan. 19 and Feb. 9, 1883. Henceforth I use the paper's own (colloquial) rather than the scientific transcription of this title, and the Western spelling of Sanua's name which he adopted in France.

[6] *al-Baṣīr,* (Paris) Jan. 25, 1883.

[7] Cf. Irene L. Gendzier, *The Practical Visions of Ya'qub Sanu'* (Cambridge, Mass., 1966).

[8] *al-Baṣīr,* (Paris) Feb 8. 1883. In the Feb. 15, 1883, issue of *al-Baṣīr* Ghānim defends his view that reform and constitutional rule are prerequisites to a strong Ottoman state. Afghānī reiterates his theme of the importance of unity around a common cause in creating a strong state in "The Benefits of Union and the Harm of Disunion" in *al-Baṣīr,* April 26, 1883.

ghānī's first published works favoring the unity of Muslims and Ottomans behind the Ottoman government and its Sultan. It is one of several indications that when forced to choose between advocacy or reform or self-strengthening for the Muslim world, Afghānī gave priority to the latter. In his turn toward Pan-Islam and support for the Sultan, Afghānī was following a path also traversed by other Muslim reformers and nationalists in the late nineteenth century to whom unity and independence of the Muslim world came to appear as the primary goal. To many Muslim reformers outside Ottoman territory, unity behind the Sultan came to seem the best defense against the encroaching West.

Afghānī's early 1883 Paris articles were seen by those of his former Egyptian disciples who were now in exile in Beirut because of their part in the 'Urābī government. Afghānī had apparently not written to them while he was in India or afterward.[9] Now his articles gave his former disciples Adīb Isḥāq and Ibrāhīm Laqqānī news of his whereabouts and inspired them to write him long letters from Beirut. Adīb Isḥāq's first letter, dated February 10, 1883, tells Afghānī of his political and other activities in the past three years, and also tells him that Abū Turāb had recently been exiled from Egypt to Beirut for distributing copies of *Abu Naddara* containing an article by Afghānī, despite Sharīf Pāshā's efforts to free him.[10]

On February 15, 1883, Ibrāhīm al-Laqqānī wrote a long letter to Afghānī, beginning with a page of worshipful praise. The letter includes considerable detail about how Laqqānī and other disciples of Afghānī had participated in the awakening of Egypt and in political events there. Laqqānī also describes his suffering in jail after the British occupation, the attempted intervention by Sharīf in his behalf, and his unexpected meeting with Abū Turāb in an Alexandria jail. They arrived together in Beirut but had been ordered to leave Ottoman territory, an order that they had appealed.[11] In a letter of February 27, 1883, Laqqānī writes that since the Ottoman govern-

---

9 Riḍā (*Tārīkh*, p. 282) reproduces a letter from Afghānī in Port Said to 'Abduh, which Riḍā dates in 1882; both its September date and its contents show that it actually dates from 1891, when Afghānī was on his way from Basra to London.

10 *Documents,* pp. 54–55, no. 171, gives a Persian translation of this Arabic letter, which is not photographed.

11 *Documents,* pp. 46–51, no. 165, is a Persian translation of the letter; the original is on pls. 49–55, photos 106–117. These letters and the reports by Ibrāhīm al-Muwailihī noted below are important new sources for events concerning Egypt, 1879–1885.

ment itself had not ordered the group to leave, they are staying in Beirut.[12]

Among the initial letters reestablishing contact between Afghānī's Egyptian disciples and Afghānī as a result of their hearing of his whereabouts, is a letter from 'Abduh written in terms of mystical admiration, dated March 14, 1883. This letter has been reprinted by Rashīd Riḍā, and its passages of mystic adoration have been translated by Elie Kedourie.[13] In addition to these passages, the letter is interesting for its accusation of treachery against some of Afghānī's followers—Adīb Isḥāq, Salīm Naqqāsh, Sa'īd Būstānī, and another—though no details are given. 'Abduh says that if he had not his wife and children with him he would be the first man to join Afghānī in Paris. In an intriguing reference, 'Abduh says that he is not offended by what Afghānī had said in his letter to Abū Turāb against the Egyptians and in reproach of Ibrāhīm Laqqānī and of 'Abduh himself. He says that Afghānī considers the Egyptians faithless, but that 'Abduh and his friends are not that sort. 'Abduh concludes by asking for a new photograph of Afghānī—he had had two but one had been taken from his house by the police when he was jailed, along with a masonic book in Afghānī's writing, while the other had been taken by Sa'd Zaghlūl. He asks Afghānī to send copies of any articles he writes, as they are preparing notebooks of these articles and had already put in the first article in *al-Baṣīr* and what was in the newspaper *Naḥla*. 'Abduh concludes that the leading Muslims of Beirut have received them, and that 'Abd al-Qādir al-Jazā'īrī (the famous leader of the Muslim revolt against the French in Algeria, who was in exile in Syria, where he died in May 1883), had ordered his son to see 'Abduh. He had come, and he and other leading Muslims all spoke in praise of Jamāl ad-Dīn. A letter from Abū Turāb notes that he and 'Abduh were translating the *Naichiriyyeh* treatise.[14]

Unfortunately, Jamāl ad-Dīn did not habitually keep copies of his own letters, and so we do not have his answers to Beirut, but can

---

12 *Documents*, pp. 51–52, no. 166, is a Persian translation; the original is on pls. 55–57, photos 118–121.

13 Kedourie, *Afghani*, Appendix I, pp. 66–69. Kedourie notes that the version of the letter in Riḍā, *Tārīkh*, II (2d ed.), 599–603, must be 'Abduh's draft, while the version received by Afghānī is in *Documents*, pls. 63–64, photos 134–137.

14 *Documents*, pls. 39, 63–64, photos 86, 134–137. It is this translation that became known as the "Refutation of the Materialists," and, despite its divergencies from the original, became standard in Arabic and was the basis of Goichon's French translation (cited in n. 21, below).

only infer some of his remarks from the letters of his followers. Those disciples who had known Afghānī in Egypt often speak badly of each other in their letters to Afghānī, and these reports may be one source of the negative remarks that 'Abduh's letter ascribes to Afghānī regarding himself and Ibrāhīm [Laqqānī]. In the period right after Afghānī's expulsion from Egypt, his disciples had followed different political paths. Adīb Isḥāq's newspaper, *Miṣr,* had been shut down by Riyāḍ and he then went to Paris where he published a paper on behalf of Sharīf's constitutionalist group, possibly also supported by the ex-Khedive Ismā'īl, which attacked Riyāḍ. Ibrāhīm al-Muwailihī was tied to the ex-Khedive Ismā'īl, was his private secretary after his forced abdication, and promoted propaganda on Ismā'īl's behalf while he was in exile. Muḥammad 'Abduh, on the other hand, following an exile to his village, worked with the Riyāḍ government that came in after Afghānī's exile. Although 'Abduh, Adīb Isḥāq, and others among Afghānī's disciples worked together in the later stages of the 'Urābī movement, their earlier differences may help account for their harsh words about one another to Afghānī.[15] Their letters indicate that they were vying with one another for Afghānī's favor, and it is clear from 'Abduh's going to Paris and his collaboration with Afghānī there in 1884 that, whatever negative remarks about him Afghānī may have written, 'Abduh remained the most favored disciple and collaborator.

Afghānī's activity in Paris in 1883 and 1884 seems to have been primarily journalistic—at least this is the activity of which by far the most information has remained. In 1883 he wrote not only for Ghānim's and Sanua's Paris-based Arabic newspapers, but also for various French papers. British Foreign Office documents speak of him as co-editor of *Abu Naddara.* Although this does not seem to be true in a formal sense, Wilfrid Blunt's diaries make it clear that Afghānī and Sanua were extremely close in this period,[16] and Afghānī probably influenced the contents of Sanua's paper. In any case, they both shared an anti-British, pro-Ottoman, and pro-Egyptian nationalist viewpoint, so that it would be fruitless to try to disentangle the exact amount of Afghānī's influence on Sanua's journal. It is clear

---

15 Cf. Kedourie, *Afghani,* p. 32, *Documents,* pp. 34–69, and the photos referred to therein. Roger Allen is working on a biography of Ibrāhīm al-Muwailihī and his son Muḥammad which will have details on their relations with the ex-Khedive Ismā'īl and Sultan Abdülhamid.

16 Blunt, *Gordon at Khartoum,* diary entries on Sanua, *passim.*

from the British Foreign Office documents that Afghānī expanded the distribution of *Abu Naddara*, particularly in India.[17]

The Exchange with Ernest Renan

The best known of Afghānī's newspaper writings in French is his "Answer to Renan" of May 18, 1883, written in response to a lecture by Ernest Renan on "Islam and Science," first given at the Sorbonne, and published on March 29, 1883, in the *Journal des Débats*. As Renan himself wrote in rejoinder to Afghānī on May 19, 1883, he had met Afghānī about two months previously through Ghānim, who, like Renan, wrote for the *Journal des Débats*. Renan stated, "Few people have produced on me a more vivid impression. It is in large measure the conversation which I had with him that decided me to choose as a subject for my lecture at the Sorbonne the relations between the scientific spirit and Islam."[18] Renan went on, as noted below, to praise Afghānī as a fellow rationalist thinker.

The exchange between Afghānī and Renan has been distorted by some who have not read Afghānī's response to Renan and assume that, since Renan had called Islam hostile to science, Afghānī must have said that Islam was friendly to the scientific spirit. No part of Afghānī's actual argument can be remotely construed in this sense, as a reading of the whole answer shows. Afghānī in his "Answer" was just as categorical as Renan about the hostility of the Islamic religion to the scientific spirit; his quarrel with Renan rested on quite different points, points that were in large measure accepted by Renan in his rejoinder.

Renan in his lecture had stated that early Islam and the Arabs who professed it were hostile to the scientific and philosophic spirit, and that science and philosophy had entered the Islamic world only

---

17 F.O. 60/594, correspondence dated 1883, *passim*.

18 Ernest Renan, *Oeuvres complètes*, Vol. I (Paris, 1947), p. 961.

from non-Arab sources. The science and philosophy that are often called Arab, he went on, are really Greek or Persian. Only one of the great Islamic philosophers was an Arab by birth, and to call their philosophy Arab, just because they wrote in Arabic, makes no more sense than to call medieval European philosophy Latin. Renan's argument, as Afghānī noted in his "Answer," has two major points. One is a racial one: the Arabs by nature and temperament are hostile to science and philosophy, and these subjects were advanced in the Islamic world only by non-Arabs (in fact, though Renan does not here say this, mainly by people of Indo-European or "Aryan" origin). The second is that Islam is essentially hostile to science. This essence was dominant when the Arabs ruled, and later when the Turks did, and it was temporarily and precariously overcome only during the short period when Greek and Persian influences were strong. Although it is true that Renan was hostile to all religious dogma and not only to Islamic dogma, it is not true, as has been claimed, that he was only saying of Islam what he would have said of any other religion. On this he is explicit. Islam, because it unites the spiritual and temporal realms and makes dogma rule in both, is "the heaviest chain that humanity has ever borne."[19]

Afghānī's "Answer to Renan" was apparently written first in Arabic and then translated into French.[20] We must assume the same of all his French articles, or assume at least that their style was corrected, since there are numerous witnesses to the fact that his written and spoken French was imperfect. There is no reason to think the French translation inaccurate, however, since Afghānī soon came to read French quite well, and never made any recorded complaint about the way the "Answer" was translated.

A remarkable point about Afghānī's answer is that in most ways it seems *more* in line with twentieth-century ideas than Renan's original argument. It rejects Renan's racial argument and puts in its place an evolutionary or developmental view of peoples. Renan, says Afghānī, states that the Muslim religion is opposed to science. But, Afghānī points out, no people in its earliest stages accepts science or philosophy. This modern evolutionary view is then buttressed by arguments coming from the most skeptical of the philosophical thinkers of the Islamic world. All peoples in their first stages were incapable of being guided by pure reason, or of distinguishing good from evil

[19] Ernest Renan, *l'Islamisme et la science* (Paris, 1883), p. 17.
[20] Kedourie, *Afghānī*, p. 41.

so as to achieve their own welfare. There then arose prophets—here called "teachers" or "educators"—who, unable to make such primitive peoples follow the dictates of pure reason, found a means to civilize men and make them obedient to authority by attributing their own ideas to a supreme God:

> And, since humanity, at its origin, did not know the causes of events that passed under its eyes and the secrets of things, it was perforce led to follow the advice of its teachers and the orders they gave. This obedience was imposed in the name of the Supreme Being to whom the educators attributed all events, without permitting men to discuss its utility or its disadvantages. This is no doubt for men one of the heaviest and most humiliating yokes, as I recognize; but one cannot deny that it is by this religious education, whether it be Muslim, Christian or pagan, that all nations have emerged from barbarism and marched toward a more advanced civilization.[21]

Continuing the evolutionary argument, Afghānī goes on to recognize the superiority of the modern Western intellectual climate, but attributes it to the fact that Christianity had an evolutionary head start on Islam:

> All religions are intolerant, each one in its way. The Christian religion, I mean the society that follows its inspirations and its teachings and is formed in its image, has emerged from the first period to which I have alluded; thenceforth free and independent, it seems to advance rapidly on the road of progress and science, whereas Muslim society has not yet freed itself from the tutelage of religion. Realizing, however, that the Christian religion preceded the Muslim religion in the world by many centuries, I cannot keep from hoping that Muhammadan society will succeed some day in breaking its bonds and marching resolutely in the path of civilization after the manner of Western society. . . . I plead here with M. Renan, not the cause of the Muslim religion, but that of several hundreds of millions of men, who would thus be condemned to live in barbarism and ignorance.
>
> In truth, the Muslim religion has tried to stifle science and stop its progress.

21 "Réponse de Jamal ad-Din al-Afghani à Renan," in *Réfutation*, pp. 176–177.

Christianity has done the same, and the Catholic Church still tries to do so. On the justness of Renan's view of the believing Muslim as a slave to dogma Afghānī has no quarrel—if anything he expresses himself in even stronger terms:

> A true believer must, in fact, turn from the path of studies which have for their object scientific truth. . . . Yoked like an ox to the plow, to the dogma whose slave he is, he must walk eternally in the same furrow that has been traced for him in advance by the interpreters of the law. Convinced, besides, that his religion contains in itself all morality and all sciences, he attaches himself resolutely to it and makes no effort to go beyond. . . . What would be the benefit of seeking truth when he believes he possesses it all? . . . Wherefore he despises science.[22]

Afghānī then notes, very briefly, that Muslims, at one time, had had a taste for science and philosophy.

On Renan's second point, the innate hostility of the Arabs to science and philosophy, it would appear today that Afghānī gets the better of the argument. He notes justly that the Arabs assimilated with amazing rapidity the Greek and Persian sciences that had been developed over several centuries, and that under Arab rule science and philosophy continued to develop and were later passed to the Christian West. While granting that people who spoke and wrote another language, like the Persians, should not be called Arabs, Afghānī notes that to deny the name Arab to those whose first spoken and written language was Arabic, and to identify them instead with remote ancestors, would be contrary to all usual or sensible practice. Afghānī also notes that many of the Hellenized, philosophically minded peoples conquered by the Arabs were Semites and hence related to the Arabs even before they became Arabized.

If Afghānī rejects the racist side of Renan's argument, and brings in an evolutionary argument, he is, nonetheless, at least as severe as Renan on the hostility of the Islamic religion to science and reason. He points out, however, that all religions share this hostility. In conclusion, Afghānī states:

> It is permissible, however, to ask oneself why Arab civilization, after having thrown such a live light on the world,

22 *Ibid.*, pp. 177–178.

> suddenly became extinguished, why this torch has not been relit since, and why the Arab world still remains buried in profound darkness.
>
> Here the responsibility of the Muslim religion appears complete. It is clear that wherever it became established, this religion tried to stifle science and it was marvelously served in its designs by despotism.
>
> Al-Siuti [sic] tells that the Caliph al-Hadi put to death in Baghdad 5,000 philosophers in order to extirpate sciences in Muslim countries up to their roots. Admitting that this historian exaggerated the number of victims, it remains nonetheless established that this persecution took place, and it is a bloody stain for the history of a religion as it is for the history of a people. I could find in the past of the Christian religion analogous facts. Religions, whatever names they are given, all resemble one another. No agreement and no reconciliation are possible between these religions and philosophy. Religion imposes on man its faith and its belief, whereas philosophy frees him of it totally or in part. How could one therefore hope that they would agree with each other? . . . Whenever religion will have the upper hand, it will eliminate philosophy; and the contrary happens when it is philosophy that reigns as sovereign mistress. As long as humanity exists, the struggle will not cease between dogma and free investigation, between religion and philosophy; a desperate struggle in which, I fear, the triumph will not be for free thought, because the masses dislike reason and its teachings are only understood by some intelligences of the elite, and because, also, science, however beautiful it is, does not completely satisfy humanity, which thirsts for the ideal and which likes to exist in dark and distant regions which the philosophers and scholars can neither perceive nor explore.[23]

This article is one of the most striking of the many indications that Afghānī was far from being the orthodox believer that some of his biographers claim. The "Answer" also contains within itself the explanation of why Afghānī sometimes chose to put on orthodox religious guise. The masses are moved only by religious arguments, while the more truthful rational and scientific arguments can appeal only to a small elite (and hence not be politically efficacious). Reflecting the views of the medieval Islamic philosophers, Afghānī

---

23 *Ibid.*, pp. 183–185.

presents traditional religion as useful to keep the masses moral and obedient. It was Afghānī's genius to be able to adapt Islam to radically new needs and conditions and to introduce modern ideas without renouncing or breaking with those with a more traditional outlook.

Adumbrated in the "Answer" is Afghānī's knowledge of the fate of the medieval Islamic philosophers. Even though they were willing to grant the utility of orthodoxy for the masses, they were not permitted to pursue truth, but were attacked by rulers, theologians, and the orthodox. Afghānī is thus pessimistic about the ultimate triumph of pure freedom of investigation. It is persecuted by those who place faith above reason and by their temporal allies, and it is understood only by the elite, while the masses will always want to speak of otherworldly things that are inaccessible to reason. It can be hoped, however, that the Muslim religion can eventually be reformed as was Christianity to lessen the stifling power of antiscientific dogma, while the masses presumably will be left with enough religious faith and injunctions to satisfy their cravings and keep them in line.

This is not to say that Afghānī was entirely consistent. Even within the "Answer" there is some variation between the optimism of the reformer or revolutionary in the early passages, and the pessimism of the Muslim philosophers about the very restricted circle who can understand truth and science at the end of the article. But contradictory tendencies within one complex individual facing problems that were probably insoluble in his own time, and thrust from the medieval into the modern period, are not to be wondered at, and can themselves be explained. If Afghānī was pessimistic about the possibility of appealing to the masses in the name of anything except religion, and like the philosophers thought that rational demonstrative argument could be understood only by the "few," it helps explain why he made what were essentially political appeals in the name of religion. The "Refutation of the Materialists" stresses the worldly achievements of early Islam, while the "Answer" stresses another aspect—its later dogmatic rigidity. In a sense, it might be said, Afghānī is giving a one-sided presentation in each which is, however, correct within its limits. It seems true that the religious-ideological impetus given by early Islam was an important factor in the early flowering of its civilization, but that, on the other hand, the rigidification of dogma helped bring about decline and later stagnation.

Until very recently nearly all discussions of Afghānī have ignored, or treated as a temporary lapse, this "Answer to Renan," and have sought Afghānī's true beliefs in his writings aimed at a broad Muslim public or in 'Abduh's apologetic biography. It is true that Afghānī's writings in defense of Islam have a much greater total bulk than items like the "Answer to Renan." Yet, as has been seen in analyzing the "Refutation of the Materialists." even the writings that defend Islam have very little content that can justly be called religious, and are designed rather to create political unity and solidarity. Besides this, it should be sufficiently proved by now that for Afghānī, as for many philosophers and heterodox thinkers in the Muslim world, it was proper to speak and write something other than one's true beliefs if this would lead to a desirable goal. It is in the spoken words to his closest followers and disciples and in writings directed at an elite audience that the true beliefs of such a man are to be sought. The "Answer to Renan" was directed at precisely such an elite Western audience, and it is significant that it is frequently misrepresented in Eastern languages as a defense of the Islamic religion. If the "Answer to Renan" does not represent Afghānī's true beliefs, it is almost impossible to imagine why he should have opened himself up in print to possible further attack from orthodox Muslims. Afghānī could quite easily have limited himself to noting the glory of Muslim Arab scientific achievement in the past and to maintaining that true Islam had been distorted in more recent centuries, but he chose rather to attack the Muslim religion. The "Answer to Renan" shows the work of an advanced mind in its evolutionary view of history, its balanced defense of Arab and Muslim achievements, and its appreciation of the conflict between science and religion.

Renan's rejoinder to Afghānī, published in the *Journal des Débats* on May 19, 1883, indicates the personal impression Afghānī made on this eminent rationalist and freethinker as a man of his own stripe. Renan granted the improvement that Afghānī had made on his argument by ridding it of the implication that Islam was an even worse religion than Christianity. Eastern writers often quote only a few sentences of praise of Afghānī from this rejoinder; but it is far more instructive to quote Renan's remarks almost in their entirety. (The first line is from the publication of Renan's *Islam and Science* in book form.)

> A remarkably intelligent Afghan Sheikh, having presented observations on the above lecture, I answered the next day, in the same journal, as follows:
>
> We read yesterday with the interest they merited the very

> judicious reflections that my last lecture at the Sorbonne suggested to Sheikh Jemmal-Eddin. There is nothing more instructive than studying the ideas of an enlightened Asiatic in their original and sincere form. It is by listening to the most diverse voices coming from the four corners of the globe, in favor of rationalism, that one becomes convinced that, if religions divide men, Reason brings them together; and that there is only one Reason.

Renan says that he met Afghānī about two months before, which would have been in March 1883, shortly after his arrival in Paris. He goes on, expressing more explicitly his racial view that only the "Aryans" among the Muslims had a scientific and philosophic spirit:

> Few people have produced on me a more vivid impression. It is in large measure the conversation that I had with him that decided me to choose as a subject for my lecture at the Sorbonne the relations between the scientific spirit and Islam. Sheikh Jemmal-Eddin is an Afghan entirely divorced from the prejudices of Islam; he belongs to those energetic races of Iran, near India, where the Aryan spirit lives still so energetically under the superficial layer of official Islam. He is the best proof of that great axiom which we have often proclaimed, namely, that religions are worth the same as the races that profess them. The liberty of his thought, his noble and loyal character, made me believe while I was talking with him, that I had before me, restored to life, one of my old acquaintances—Avicenna, Averroes, or another of those great infidels who represented for five centuries the tradition of the human mind. For me there was an especially vivid contrast when I compared this striking apparition with the spectacle presented by the Muslim countries this side of Persia—countries in which scientific and philosophic curiosity is so rare. Sheikh Jemmal-Eddin is the best case of ethnic protest against religious conquest that one could cite. . . .
>
> In the learned article of the Sheikh I see only one point on which we are really in disagreement. . . . Everything written in Latin is not the glory of Rome; everything written in Greek is not Hellenic; everything written in Arabic is not an Arab product; everything done in a Christian country is not the effect of Christianity; everything done in a Muslim country is not a fruit of Islam. . . .These sorts of distinctions are necessary if one does not wish history to be a tissue of approximations and misunderstandings. . . .

> One point on which I may have appeared unjust to the Sheikh is that I did not develop enough the idea that all revealed religions manifest themselves as hostile to positive science, and that Christianity in this respect is not superior to Islam. This is beyond doubt. Galileo was no better treated by Catholicism than Averroes by Islam.

Renan thus appears, under Afghānī's influence, to retract his singling out of Islam for dispraise, although his prior remarks reflect a continued anti-Muslim prejudice. Renan then says that he has often stated that

> the human mind must be freed of all supernatural belief if it wishes to work on its essential work, which is the construction of positive science. This does not imply violent destruction or brusque rupture. The Christian does not have to abandon Christianity nor the Muslim Islam. The enlightened parties of Christianity and Islam should arrive at that state of benevolent indifference where religious beliefs become inoffensive. This has happened in about half of the Christian countries, let us hope it will happen in Islam. Naturally on that day the Sheikh and I will agree in applauding. . . . There will be distinguished individuals (though there will be few as distinguished as Sheikh Jemmal-Eddin) who will separate themselves from Islam, as we separate ourselves from Catholicism. Certain countries, with time, will more or less break with the religion of the Koran; but I doubt that the movement of renaissance will be made with the support of official Islam.

Finally, Renan notes justly that Afghānī has provided additional arguments in favor of his own basic points:

> Sheikh Jemmal-Eddin seems to me to have brought considerable arguments for my two fundamental theses—During the first half of its existence Islam did not stop the scientific movement from existing in Muslim lands;—in the second half it stifled in its breast the scientific movement, and that to its grief.[24]

Equally significant in suggesting that Afghānī's "Answer" represented his true beliefs is a letter from 'Abduh in Beirut to Afghānī

24 Renan, *Oeuvres complètes,* I, 960–965.

written on June 14, 1883—a month after the "Answer." It has been summarized and partially translated by Elie Kedourie, who writes:

> The letter begins with those expressions of idolatry of which I have given . . . a characteristic specimen. Then 'Abduh goes on to say that news had reached him of Afghānī's answer to Renan in the *Journal des Débats*; he had thought that a translation would serve to edify the believers and had asked a man of religion (*ba'd al-diniyyin*) to be ready to undertake it on receipt of the French text. But immediately afterwards, 'Abduh writes, he received two numbers of the *Journal* (presumably of 18 and 19 May 1883, containing Afghānī's comentary and Renan's observations), together with a letter from Afghānī. He goes on: "We then praised Almighty God that the numbers of the *Débats* had not been available before the receipt of your letter. We acquainted ourselves with these two numbers. . . . We then dissuaded our first friend from making the translation, alleging that Arabic text [*sic*] was going to be sent, that it would be published then, and that therefore there was no need for a translation. Thus misfortune was averted (*fa'ndafa'a al-makruh*), God be praised. . . . We regulate our conduct . . . according to your sound rule: we do not cut the head of religion except with the sword of religion . . ."[25]

'Abduh's letter envinces no doubt that the French text correctly gives Afghānī's thought, and 'Abduh's statement of relief that the *Débats* had not been available before Afghānī's letter arrived suggests that Afghānī's letter warned against an Arabic translation. 'Abduh goes on to say that Afghānī's followers observe external religious practices (in accord with Afghānī's sound rule only to cut the head of religion with the sword of religion). Whatever 'Abduh's exact meaning may have been in using such a phrase, there is little wonder that 'Abduh was upset by the proposed translation as he later was by Salīm al-'Anḥūrī's 1885 biography of Afghānī. This attributed to Afghānī a skeptical, rationalist, and evolutionary view of religion, which 'Anḥūrī, having heard of it in and from Egypt, describes in terms very similar to those used by Afghānī in the "Answer to Renan." Just as 'Abduh hastened in 1883 to stop a translation

[25] Kedourie, *Afghani*, pp. 44–45. The ellipses represent Kedourie's words; the letter is continuous as quoted. An alternative reading of the last sentence is, "Do not cut . . ." The original is in *Documents*, photos 138–140.

that would have damaged Afghānī's religious reputation, so he hastened in 1885 to talk 'Anḥūrī into retracting his account, and to publish his own, highly apologetic biography, which stressed Afghānī's devotion to the Muslim religion.[26]

Afghānī's "Answer to Renan" is strikingly different from the Turkish work on the same subject written by the Young Ottoman author, Namık Kemal, whose *Refutation of Renan* was an apologetic work defending Arab and Muslim scientific and philosophical achievements, and criticizing the West. The strong negative reaction of religious Muslims who did read Afghānī's "Answer" in the 1880s is recorded in contemporary documents.[27] The "Answer" did not become widely known in the Muslim world, however, and Afghānī's deeds and writings in favor of Muslim unity and independence understandably overshadowed negative rumors about him for most of his Muslim audience.

Afghānī and the British Foreign Office in 1883

IN THE spring and summer of 1883, much later than the standard biographies suggest, Afghānī for the first time came to the serious attention of the British Foreign Office and its representatives abroad. This was primarily a result of Afghānī's anti-British journalistic activity in Paris, especially his writing for, and extending the distribution of, James Sanua's *Abu Naddara*, which was reported to the Foreign Office by the Government of India in the summer of 1883, on the basis of a report from Sayyid Husain and the British resident at Hyderabad, Cordery, partly quoted above in chapter 7.

26 Riḍā, *Tārīkh*, pp. 49–51.

27 Documents quoted in Pakdaman, p. 83. Niyazi Berkes (*The Development of Secularism in Turkey* [Montreal, 1964], pp. 262–263) and Şerif Mardin (*The Genesis of Young Ottoman Thought* [Princeton, 1962], pp. 324–325) discuss Namık Kemal's *Refutation of Renan*.

Somewhat earlier the Foreign Office had been requested by its chief representative in Egypt, the British consul Edward B. Malet, to watch Afghānī. On May 22, 1883, Malet wrote home to the Liberal Government's Foreign Secretary, Granville, enclosing copies of two anonymous letters addressed to himself and Sir Evelyn Wood, head of the Egyptian Army, containing threats of assassination; similar letters had also been received by Sharīf Pāshā and the Khedive Taufīq. The letters were believed to have come from Paris and from Jamāl ad-Dīn, whom Malet identifies as an associate of James Sanua in Paris and a writer for *Abu Naddara*. The attribution of the letters to Jamāl ad-Dīn is presented as a surmise based on the letters' contents and Jamāl ad-Dīn's beliefs. The letters claim to emanate from the "Egyptian Patriotic League," and the letter to Sharīf "states that the members of the League are brothers of the Nihilists and Socialists." Malet suggests that the Foreign Office try to find out about Afghānī's activities in Paris and keep an eye on him.[28] Malet encloses the threatening letter, which has an indication, not mentioned by Malet, that it might emanate from the Sanua-Afghānī circle—namely, the use of masonic symbols and slogans, including the masonic triangle and dots drawn onto the letter.

A translation from the French of the letter to Malet reads as follows:

> Ligue Patriotique Egyptienne Liberté . Civilization . Prosperité
>
> Sir Edward Malet
>
> You are warned in order that you warn your Government, that the league gives you up to August 14, 1883 in the evening to evacuate Egyptian territory. After this the league takes it upon itself my means other than war to evacuate by itself Her Majesty; to obstinacy the league will oppose ruse.
>
> Do not forget that formerly in another country the energy of a humble peasant girl was enough to reawaken an entire sleeping people and to shake off the apathy of an effeminate monarchy.
>
> Do not invoke international law any more in your favor. Beyond this fixed term our motto is: "All means are good to save the country from the greed of the foreigner."
>
> (Signed) The head of the league
>
> (Signed in Arabic) "One who wishes to avenge himself."

---

28 F.O. 60/594, Malet to Granville, no. 174, Confidential, Cairo, May 22, 1883.

And the letter to General Wood reads as follows, after a similar heading:

> The League orders General Wood to resign from the position which he holds in the Egyptian army and to warn his co-nationals to act in the same way.
>
> The people do not want a foreigner to command or to govern them. And you have been promoted without anyone's asking the people's advice.
>
> The League, representing and supported by the Egyptian people, gives you up to August 14 to carry out its will. Beyond this, the League will take steps for forced resignations.
>
> See and reflect.
> Long live liberated Egypt.
> Death to the British.
> The Heads of the League
> "To revenge myself"[29]
> (Signed in Arabic)

Following up a suggestion in Malet's letter home, the Foreign Office asked their Ambassador in Paris, Lord Lyons, to inquire of the French Police what information they had on Afghānī. Lyons wrote back from Paris on June 19, 1883, saying that in the present state of French feeling over England (presumably meaning French hostility over the unilateral British occupation of Egypt), it would be useless to approach the French Police directly. It would be necessary to go through the Minister for Foreign Affairs, and even then Lyons did not consider it politic to raise such a question at that time. He promised to try to obtain information about Jamāl ad-Dīn from other sources, however.[30] Despite this response, somebody in the Foreign Office did make inquiries of the French Police, who responded on July 6, 1883. The French Police acknowledged the inquiry about Jamāl ad-Dīn as supposed author of the menacing letters to Egypt, and said they were giving what information they had on him. The police said he was a man of letters, forty-five years old, a bachelor, and living, since February 17, at 16, Rue de Sèze, at a monthly rental of 50 francs. They said this was his first visit to Paris, and that he arrived from Calcutta. They added:

---

29 Enclosure in *ibid.*

30 F.O. 60/594, Lyons to Granville, no. 393, Secret, Paris, June 19, 1883.

> He passes as very well educated, and, although he expresses himself in French with difficulty, he commands eight languages.
>
> He has written in collaboration with James Sanua, teacher of Arabic and Editor in Chief of a journal written in that language which is published in Paris, 48 Avenue de Clichy, many articles hostile to England.
>
> He receives many visits and appears to be in comfortable circumstances.
>
> His habitual conduct and his morality do not give rise to any unfavorable remark.[31]

The letter was signed by the Prefect of Police, and addressed to the "Director of Criminal Affaires [*sic*]," London, who had presumably made the inquiry.

In the same summer of 1883, the Foreign Office was getting reports of Jamāl ad-Dīn's anti-British journalistic activity from another source—the India Office. The latter forwarded a notice from "Syed Hussein" of Hyderabad, who had known Jamāl ad-Dīn there, and whose comments regarding Hyderabad have already been given. After describing Jamāl ad-Dīn's stay in India, Sayyid Husain continues about his journal (identified in the covering letter from the Hyderabad Resident as *Abu Naddara,* Sanua's paper):

> Some months ago I was startled by having an Arabic periodical sent to me from Paris, and on opening it I found that it was conducted by no other than the quondam philosopher of Hyderabad. Since then I have continued to be favoured with copies of it, as have also many others in Hyderabad. It is printed on a double sheet of paper, and within the limits of the four pages it contains nothing that is not anti-English. The paper in my humble opinion is not fit to be allowed into India, although fortunately there are not many in this country who can read Arabic. It is certainly still less suitable for Egypt where even the lower orders will be able to read it—of this however the authorities in Egypt are the best judges. I only send you this account of the man, and the enclosed copy of the paper together with a translation of portions of it, thinking it my duty to let you know that such a paper finds its way to Hyderabad.

---

31 *Ibid.,* enclosure in Liddell to F.O., Secret, Whitehall, July 10, 1883.

> I may add that to my knowledge the man is penniless, and must therefore have some kind of support at Paris. Whether he is or is not countenanced by the French Government it is not for me to say, perhaps the strained relations between France and England may account for his existence in Paris.[32]

Jamāl ad-Dīn's financing for both his living expenses and his journals, which were distributed free, has been something of a mystery. The suggestion of French support is conceivable, but personal checks at the French Foreign Ministry and Police Archives turned up no evidence of it. Other sources of money that do have documentary support are discussed below. As noted, Afghānī did receive via Abū Turāb 2,530 francs, presumably from Egypt, in 1883, and, given his reported monthly rent of 50 francs, this could have supported him for many months. Also, *Abu Naddara* was financed by Sanua, and the only new expense involved sending out more copies to India and possibly to Egypt.

One of the translated articles enclosed in Sayyid Husain's letter, supposedly addressed to the paper by a resident of Egypt, reads, in the original translation:

> Oh for succour! Oh for deliverance. We are in a despicable condition. Could death be purchased, we would purchase it, and find relief from what the like of which we had never suffered in our lives. The Khedive eats, and drinks, and sleeps, and those around him of our kind are mean and despicable. Power is in the hands of the Europeans who have purchased us through traitors and today we are led by them like donkeys. We walk the streets with our eyes cast down, and our notables kiss the hands of the English, and if you ask, oh reader, regarding our armies we will tell you that the General, namely General Wood, who has been imposed upon us, is an Englishman sent to override us. He is turning out the sons of Cairo and Alexandria from high places and appointing Englishmen in their places, etc.
>
> Ye youth of Egypt, you ought to grave the words of Shaikh Jamal-un-din or your hearts, one of our poets has written a long eulogy on him, a copy of which I will send you. Let the Shaikh know that our hearts were delighted when we heard

---

32 *Ibid.*, Syed Hussein [Bilgrāmī] to Cordery, in Cordery to Grant, Hyderabad, June 25, 1883.

> that he was received with honor by the notables of Paris, and by her Poets and men of learning, and that when he was staying in London, the English Government trembled for their supremacy in India. We conjure him to send us his lucubrations which inspire a new soul into us since they open our hearts to national honor and patriotism and incite us to unfurl the standard of liberty.

Of another article, Sayyid Husain says: "This seems to be a kind of prophecy in which the English are called a race of monkeys, and it is prophesied that there are to be great troubles after the year 1299, and that Islam and the Arab cause is to triumph. This Article and others in this and other numbers of the paper contain many words written in cipher which it is difficult for me to understand. Perhaps they have no difficulty for the initiated in Egypt."[33]

Sayyid Husain's letter implies, though it does not state absolutely, that the enclosed articles are by Jamāl ad-Dīn. Another enclosed article expresses a pro-French view. This was Sanua's attitude and it is likely that Afghānī also held it, especially since there still existed a great deal of anger among Frenchmen of all shades of opinion regarding the British occupation of Egypt in 1882, after which the French no longer had power there.

The reference to troubles to begin after the year 1299/1882, after which Islam and the Arab cause are to triumph, raise a theme that was to be particularly strong in Afghānī's writings in Paris—that of messianism or mahdism. Traditional Islamic mahdist thought among both Sunnis and Shi'is had expected the appearance of the Mahdi, or messiah, to come after a time of great troubles and calamities. It was also common to expect the Mahdi to appear in the first year of a new Islamic century. By coincidence, a series of troubles and calamities had indeed befallen Muslim peoples in the years shortly before the new Islamic century began in November, 1882—The Russo-Turkish War and its aftermath of additional partition of the Ottoman Empire; the French occupation of Tunisia; and the British occupation of Egypt. In addition to these specific calamities for the Muslims, there were growing dislocations in social, economic, and cultural life brought about by the impact of the West such as might have given rise to increasing cultural tensions and messianic

---

33 *Ibid.*, enclosures.

expectations. Already in 1881–82 'Urābī had inspired considerable popular messianic feeling, and in fact there was in 1300/1882–83 a man who claimed to be the Mahdi—the Mahdi of the Sudan. Messianic expectations were spreading in various parts of the Middle East, and Afghānī apparently hoped to utilize them to help unite Muslims and turn back British power.

Afghani in *l'Intransigeant*: Mahdism

AMONG THOSE whom Afghānī met in Paris were the newspaper editors, Georges Clemenceau, then editor of *La Justice*, and Henri Rochefort. The theme of mahdism comes to the fore in a three-part article that Afghānī wrote for Rochefort's leftist Paris newspaper, *l'Intransigeant*, in December 1883. On April 24 of that year Afghānī had contributed to that paper a "Letter on India." In it he said that the dominant aim of the British in recent years had been to become masters of all the routes to India. The British knew that all Indians, of whatever caste, class, or religion, hated them, and that a single shot fired by a foreign power on or near the Indian frontier would suffice to set off a nationwide uprising. Afghānī says, on a theme documented at length by later Indian nationalists and Marxists, that the English have ruined native Indian trade and industry by the importation of English factory goods. He adds that the British have broken the good relations between India and Afghanistan in the recent second Afghan War. As a result of the latter, the Afghans have also turned completely against the English, and are allying with the Russians in order to act together with them at the proper moment. Afghānī then indicates his hope for a Franco-Russo-Ottoman alliance against British expansive designs.[34]

This article puts forth the idea, found again and again during Afghānī's lifetime, of encouraging an outside attack on India, which could only mean a Russian attack, as a means of provoking a mass uprising which Afghānī argues would follow immediately. More specific to the 1880's is the idea of a vast anti-British alliance, hopefully to embrace France, Russia, the Ottoman Empire, and Afghanistan. Afghānī's belief in Hindu-Muslim unity and not in separate Muslim action in India is again shown in this article, and is entirely consistent with his general desire to unite the opponents of Great Britain and to try to liberate India from the British. Another point to be noted in this article, as in the "Answer to Renan" and other articles written for Western audiences, is the logical nature of Afghānī's arguments directed toward an educated Western audience as compared with his articles written in a more rhetorical style for a mass Eastern public. Such rhetorical arguments were more respected in the traditional Middle East than in modern France, and Afghānī was able to change even his manner of writing and speaking in accordance with the level and expectations of the different audiences whom he addressed. He could, when he wished, speak or write in a manner close to that utilized by Westerners with a modern education.

A series of articles in the same socialist newspaper, *l'Intransigeant*, on "The Mahdi" also gives more insight into Afghānī's policies than do many of his better-known Arabic articles. These French articles were occasioned by the sudden rise of the Mahdi of the Sudan, Muḥammad Aḥmad, to international prominence after he defeated an expedition sent out against him by the British General Hicks late in 1883. Europeans now became concerned about the threat of this man, about the meaning of the title, Mahdi, and whether he would appeal to Muslims outside the Sudan. To answer these questions in a way that would encourage the kind of European action he wanted, Afghānī wrote his long, three-part article.

Elie Kedourie has called attention to this long article, and has seen in it an unorthodox and purely instrumental view of Mahdism. The article implies that mahdism is primarily a tool, useful for

---

34 "Lettre sur l'Hindoustan," *l'Intransigeant* (Paris), April 24, 1883. This article and "Le Mahdi" are in Kedourie, *Afghani*, App. II, pp. 70–86. On Afghānī's relations with Rochefort and Clemenceau see Pakdaman, pp. 78–80.

getting Muslim believers to rally round a leader in order to build a political empire. In the first installment of his article, Afghānī cites from Islamic history a whole series of mahdist movements that succeeded in building up powerful states. It is clear that Afghānī had great admiration for this effective use of religious beliefs to mobilize the believers around a program of political conquest. In the view of a true believer, none of these previous "mahdis" could possibly have been the true, unique Mahdi, since their rise to power was not followed by the other eschatological events that mark the advent of the Mahdi. But it is the worldly success, and not the ultimate religious nullity of these individuals, which here interests Afghānī. After listing the empire-building achievements of many Muslim "mahdis" of the past, Afghānī says:

> In a word, under this name, how many Muslims have accomplished brilliant and considerable acts, and have they not brought about a very serious change in the world of believers! . . .
>
> In brief, however diverse these beliefs may be from the point of view of form, it is no less true that every Muslim awaits a Mahdi, ready to follow him and to sacrifice his life to him, along with all he possesses. The Indian Muslims especially, given the infinite sufferings and cruel torments they endure under English domination, are those who await him with the most impatience.
>
> Finally, the prestige of the Mahdi, in the eyes of the Muslims, will depend only on the final success which he may obtain.
>
> Such was, moreover, the case with all his predecessors.[35]

Afghānī's reiterated statement that the position of the present Mahdi is dependent purely on his military success is scarcely a religious one.[36] There seems little doubt, however, that he was stating a psychological truth, and that for many Muslims, if for instance

---

35 "Le Mahdi," *l'Intransigeant* (Paris), Dec. 17, 1883.

36 Cf. Kedourie, *Afghani*, pp. 48–54. I disagree with Kedourie's view that Afghānī here asserts the primacy of the Mahdi over the Caliph and presents himself as a partisan of the Mahdi, although the article is less friendly to the Sultan-Caliph than are Afghānī's Arabic writings. See Menahem Milson, "The Elusive Jamāl al-Dīn al-Afghānī," *The Muslim World*, 58, 4 (Oct. 1968), 295–307; Elie Kedourie "'The Elusive Jamāl al-Dīn al-Afghānī' A Comment," and Milson's "Rejoinder" in *The Muslim World*, 59, 3–4 (July–Oct., 1969), 308–316.

Blunt's account from India at this time are to be trusted, it was precisely this criterion of military success which was regarded as crucial in testing the claims of the Mahdi of the Sudan.

Afghānī goes on to predict that another major military success by the Sudanese Mahdi would raise Muslims all over the world to revolts on his side, and that even many of the Arabs of the Ottoman Empire would join in his favor, against the Ottoman Sultan-Caliph, because in their eyes the Mahdi has precedence over the Caliph. In these articles Afghānī is not concerned mainly with putting forth an abstract religious theory, orthodox or unorthodox, but with frightening the Europeans with the prospect of general Muslim revolt, and hence trying to bring them to some kind of terms with the Muslims. Afghānī nowhere in his article presents himself as a partisan of the Mahdi, or of the general Muslim revolt that he predicts will come if the Mahdi has another victory. He rather tries to present in the most vivid and even exaggerated terms the tremendous effects a further mahdist victory would have on bringing the Muslim world to arms both against the Europeans and against the Ottoman Sultan. He hopes to get some conciliatory acts toward the Muslims from the Western world before this force descends upon it. Particularly, he would like to see the French insist on making the British reach a conciliatory settlement with the Egyptians and the Sudanese. As he concludes his third article:

> Another serious victory of the Mahdi—which would incontestably pass, in the eyes of the Muslims, for a second miracle—would have as a fatal consequence not only the provocation of an insurrection in the Islamic countries under Turkish domination, as well as in Baluchistan, Afghanistan, Sind, India, Bukhara, Kokand, Khiva—but also lead to troubles in Tripoli, Tunis, Algeria, and as far as Morocco. For all Muslims await the Mahdi and consider his arrival an absolute necessity.
>
> The only remedy, I believe, in order to stop the illness before it spreads to the whole body, does not consist, as some important English journals believe, in the abandonment of the Sudan and the conclusion of peace between the Mahdi and the Egyptian government, but rather in Turkish intervention, or yet in the association of the French with the English, in order to prevent a disaster. . . .
>
> Why does not England wish to hear of Turkish interven-

tion in this affair? Is it because she fears Turkey, or because she fears that this power will close the road to India? I believe neither hypothesis. Did not Turkey, in fact, when she was much stronger than she is today, and before the digging of the Suez Canal, let English soldiers cross Egypt to go to fight her coreligionaries, the Muslim Indians, and dispossess them of their goods? The reason for England's attitude can only be, in my opinion, the hatred vowed against the Muslims by the English, and especially by Mr. Gladstone, a fervent Protestant and skilled theologian.

If France and England do not deploy all their energy to prevent certain eventualities, there will result from the action of England alone, in this grave question, considerable disasters for these two powers.

As for the two men who want the Egyptian Khedivate, the ex-Khedive Ismail and Halim Pasha, who profit from the occasion furnished them by the Mahdi to enter into England's good graces, I will limit myself, for the moment, in order not to tire the reader, to speaking of one of them as briefly as possible.

Without doubt the elevation of Halim Pasha to the Khedivial throne would cause great pleasure to all those who desire the aggrandisement and consolidation of Ottoman power. Halim is, in fact, a courtier of the Sultan, he would allow him to place the government of Cairo in absolute dependence to the Divan of Constantinople, as are the vilayets of Syria, Aleppo, etc., etc. But Halim has no party in the valley of the Nile; he is very little known, and the few people who know him consider him an atheist.

It can easily be understood that a man accused of impiety by the Egyptians, who are profoundly religious, would be unable to hold his own against Muḥammad Aḥmad, who appears to the population with the prestige of his religious title of *Mahdi.* It is true that Arabi Pasha has spoken the name of Halim Pasha; he has even declared he would accept him as Khedive; but one should not conclude from this that he is a partisan of Halim or that the latter has a party in Egypt.

It was only when Arabi was driven to the wall and called upon to pronounce for one of the pretenders to the Khedivial throne that he, in order to strengthen his situation in Egypt, declared himself in favor of Halim.

As for the ex-Khedive Ismail, I will consecrate to him a special article, where I will compare the unpleasant conse-

> quences and the good results which his restoration to the Khedivate might have.[37]

Afghānī's remarks about Ḥalīm indicate Afghānī's belief that an effective political leader in the Islamic world must take on a religious coloring. In fact, at least until 1881, Afghānī had more reputation for irreligion than did Ḥalīm. The latter, a son of Muḥammad 'Alī popular with some liberals and Egyptian nationalists, and closely tied to Sultan Abdülhamid, had been a leader of the freemasons in Egypt and had used them to further his own political goals. Afghānī had acted similarly. In opposing Ḥalīm, Afghānī was differing from Sanua, 'Urābī, and some other Egyptian nationalists. To judge by his final remarks, Afghānī neither wholly commended nor condemned the candidacy of Ismā'īl. Various articles in *al-'Urwa al-Wuthqā* the following year are rather favorable to Ismā'īl. It seems that Afghānī was refusing to commit himself on the Egyptian question beyond wanting the English to leave. Thus, when Blunt wrote him about the question, Afghānī carefully refused to say what internal solution and leader he wanted for Egypt.[38] As evidence cited below suggests, Afghānī may have been trying to open negotiations with various parties to try to assure influence for himself and his program if there was a change in the Egyptian government, and may have been refusing to approve strongly of any proposed solution, beyond the departure of the British, pending the results of such negotiations.

Afghānī seems impressed by the prospect of the Mahdi's possible success, and sees it in relation to his own dreams of a strong and reunited Muslim world brought to rebel against imperialist encroachment by religious appeals.[39] Afghānī would clearly like to imitate the success of the Sudanese Mahdi, but he gives no indication that he would like to join him. One may guess that Afghānī hesitated to back any Muslim movement, and especially one emanating from so "backward" a part of the Muslim world, unless he had some assurance that he and his ideas could have some influence over the movement. Despite his late tales to Blunt and others, there is no indication that Afghānī had any contact with the Mahdi of the Sudan. Afghānī's

---

37 "Le Mahdi," *l'Intransigeant*, Dec. 17, 1883.

38 Blunt, *Gordon at Khartoum*, letter from Afghānī to Blunt, p. 546: "You ask me by whom Taufiq must be replaced. I answer that when the time comes it will not be difficult for you, me, or anyone else to know him. It will be necessary to name that man whom the *Egyptian nation* wants and not another."

39 Kedourie, *Afghānī*, p. 49.

main hope for the mahdist movement was that it could be utilized to get the British out of Egypt.

Afghānī's article is interesting both for its immediate political purpose—frightening Europeans into conciliating the Muslim world through the threat of a mass Muslim uprising—and for its relation to Afghānī's own secular messianism. That Afghānī at times saw himself as a messianic savior of the Muslim world is suggested by a variety of evidence. Among this evidence is the letter quoted above in which he compares himself with Abū Muslim. And the socialist editor of *l'Intransigeant,* Henri Rochefort, says of Afghānī in his own autobiography that one of 'Urābī's ex-officers in Paris, "introduced me to another *proscrit,* known through the whole of Islam as a reformer and a revolutionist, the sheik Djemal-ed-Din, a descendant of Mahomet, and himself regarded as somewhat of a prophet."[40] That Afghānī had for many of his followers the aura of a minor prophet, or Mahdi, is indicated by the adoring religious tone of his followers. And Afghānī's disciple, Mīrzā Rizā Kirmānī, almost certainly refers to Jamāl ad-Dīn as the Mahdi in his testimony after killing Nāsir ad-Dīn Shāh in 1896. The key word has been omitted for religious reasons in the transcript, but is clear enough from the mahdist terminology that precedes it. Speaking of Jamāl ad-Dīn, Mīrzā Rizā says: "Whoever appears with these signs and tokens is . . . himself."[41]

Another point that emerges from Afghānī's article on the Mahdi is his view, shared by some but having scant documentation, that the British aimed at forming an Arabian caliphate at Mecca. In the second installment of his article Afghānī says: "Great Britain has the design of forming a small Caliphate at Mecca, in favor of the family of the Bani-Aun, one of whose members is at present the Sharif of Mecca, in order to be able to dispose through him of an all-powerful means of domination over all Muslims." The Muslim revolt against the Sultan that Afghānī predicts will not, he says, have this result desired by the British, as it will either bring the intervention of other European Powers, or, if this intervention is avoided, the Arabs will create not the weak caliphate desired by the British, but "an important caliphate."[42] This statement is apparently the first recorded by

---

40 Henri Rochefort, *The Adventures of My Life,* English trans. by E. W. Smith and H. Rochefort, Vol. II (London, 1897), p. 279.

41 Browne, *Persian Revolution,* p. 82 (part of Browne's translation of Mīrzā Rizā's testimony).

42 "Le Mahdi," *l'Intransigeant,* Dec. 11, 1883.

Afghānī regarding an Arabian caliphate, an idea dear to the heart of the anti-Turkish and Arabophil Wilfrid Blunt, who claims to have gotten it from certain Arabs. As noted below, Sultan Abdülhamid, probably on slender evidence, connected Afghānī with a supposed British plot to form an Arabian caliphate.

Reference by Afghānī to an idea, supposedly current among Indian Muslims, that the British wanted to support an Arabian caliphate is also found in Blunt's diary for 1883. On his way to India in September 1883, Blunt went with his wife to Paris mainly to see the Egyptian exiles there. Blunt's diary, reprinted in his *India under Ripon,* has the following entry about Afghānī:

> When I saw the Sheykh in London in the spring, he wore his Sheykh's dress. Now he has clothes of the Stambouli cut, which, however, sit not badly on him. He has learned a few words of French, but is otherwise unchanged. Our talk was of India, and of the possibility of my being able to get the real confidence of the Moslems there. He said that my being an Englishman would make this very difficult, for all who had any position to lose were in terror of the government, which had its spies everywhere. He himself had been kept almost a prisoner in his house and had left India through fear of worse. Any sheykh who gained notoriety in India was tracked and bullied, and if he persisted in an independent course he was sent on some charge or other to the Andaman Islands. People, he said, would not understand that I wished them well, and would be too prudent to talk. The poorer people might, not the Sheykhs or the Princes. He thought Hyderabad would be my best point, as there were refugees there from every province of India, and they were less afraid of the English Government. . . . I asked him about the language I should most prudently hold regarding the Sultan in India, or about an Arabian Caliphate; it had been spread about that the English were going to set up a sham Caliphate in Arabia, under a child, whom they would use to make themselves masters of the holy places; the Sultan's name was now venerated in India as it had not formerly been.[43]

An interesting sidelight of this entry concerns Afghānī's change of dress. Through most of his life, Afghānī wore the flowing robes and turban that characterized sayyids and members of the ulama. In

---

[43] Blunt, *India,* pp. 12–13.

Paris, however, he adopted a form of dress characteristic of the westernized civil service of Istanbul, and not at all of its religious classes. As Blunt later states, he was followed in this change of style by Shaikh Muḥammad 'Abduh when the latter came to Paris. Nearly all extant photographs of Afghānī show him in robe and turban, but the *Documents* include two photographs of him in his nonreligious Parisian costume, complete with stiff white collar, necktie, buttoned coat, and fez.[44]

Muḥammad 'Abduh joined Afghānī in Paris late in 1883. On January 18, 1884, 'Abduh and an associate wrote a long letter to prince Ḥalīm in Istanbul. In it 'Abduh and his associate, Shūbāshī, say that they came to Paris, leaving their families, in accord with Ḥalīm's wishes and with a promise of money from him, and that they will be able to fulfill their common patriotic goals if Ḥalīm gives them his promised support. They then strongly criticize Ḥalīm's supporters in Europe, Sanua and Muḥammad Bey Wahbī, as, respectively, self-interested and inexperienced. They say that these men are responsible for the (negative) things that Ḥalīm may have heard that Jamāl ad-Dīn had written about him in *l'Intransigeant* (cited above). Although Ḥalīm has described Jamāl ad-Dīn as excitable and careless, Jamāl ad-Dīn is a leader of a strong new society formed to rescue Egypt, which is based in Paris and has branches in Egypt and the East. This society has ties with important statesmen in France and England. Only the lack of funds hinders their work, and, having faith in Ḥalīm's promise, they request £100 for travel and other work to liberate their fatherland.

In his answer Ḥalīm denies that he had asked them to go to Paris and says he had only given Shūbāshī money because he had insisted. Ḥalīm says he will work neither with them nor with Sanua and Wahbī, and that he is surprised that they are putting personal interests above national ones.[45] The overture to Ḥalīm thus seems to have been abortive.

There is thus far no evidence that Afghānī met any prominent politicians in France, but he does record a meeting with Victor Hugo. He also came in touch with some revolutionaries and socialists, including Rochefort and the socialist Olivier Pain, whom Afghānī

44 *Documents*, pl. 71, photos 154–155.

45 *Ibid.*, p. 77, doc. 308, catalogs the exchange with Ḥalīm; the texts are in the Majlis Library, Tehran. P. 69, 230, includes a Persian translation of Ḥalīm's answer, although the editors misread Ḥalīm's name.

evidently led to believe that he was in touch with the Mahdi of the Sudan, whom Pain wished to contact. The *Documents* also include two letters to Afghānī from Egypt, from the Irish nationalist, James O'Kelly, who hoped to reach the Mahdi as correspondent for the *New York Herald* and had letters of introduction from Afghānī, whom he met through Rochefort. O'Kelly's letters voiced the views, also held by Afghānī, that Egypt was on the verge of revolt, that the Mahdi was gaining tremendous prestige among Muslims everywhere, and that if England annexed Egypt she would have to fight France, Russia, and perhaps face a revolt in India.[46] Afghānī was thus not alone among anti-British revolutionaries in overestimating the perils faced by the British Empire in the early 1880s.

al-'Urwa al-Wuthqā

DESPITE THE rebuff from Ḥalīm, Afghānī and 'Abduh were able to procure money from somewhere to launch their most important joint venture in 1884—the publication in Paris and wide free distribution in the Muslim world of the newspaper *al-'Urwa al-Wuthqā* ("The Firmest Bond"—a phrase referring to the Koran first used by Afghānī in 1883 to refer to the caliphate of the Ottoman Sultan). A total of eighteen isseues of this paper were published between March and October 1884 after which the paper suddenly ceased publication, probably because of lack of funds to continue its publication and free distribution. The reason usually cited for the paper's abrupt end—British prohibition of its entry into India and Egypt—seems insufficient in view of its widespread distribution outside those two countries.

The *Documents* include a notebook with the names of the persons to whom each issue was sent without charge. In Cairo, 10 copies of

---

46 *Ibid.*, p. 73, docs. 247, 248, catalogs these letters, which are at the Majlis Library, Tehran. Plate 68, photo 148, is a card fixing the visit to Hugo, which Afghānī spoke of later. See also Rochefort, *op. cit.*, II, 279–281; and "Pourquoi les Anglais ont arreté O'Kelly," *Tribune de Genève* (n.d.), in Pakdaman, pp. 366–367.

each issue were sent to the immediate entourage of the Khedive, 38 to pāshās, including Riyāḍ and Sharīf, 27 to beys, including 'Abd as-Salām al-Muwailiḥī, 57 to efendis, 16 to religious authorities, including four al-Azhar professors, and 8 to other journals. Large quantities were also sent to other cities in Egypt, for a total of 551. On a list concerning Istanbul appear the names first of Sultan Abdülhamid, then of other important personages including Münif Paşa (who, when head of the Council of Education, had known Afghānī in Istanbul); Khair ad-Dīn Pāshā, the Tunisian reformist minister; Shaikh Abū al-Hudā, the Sultan's chief religious confidant; Mu'īn al-Mulk, the Iranian ambassador in Istanbul; Ismā'īl Jaudat, police chief in Cairo under 'Urābī and now a client of Ḥalīm; and others. Among the 88 copies sent to Istanbul were some destined for reviews and newspapers. The list of persons to whom the newspaper was sent includes about nine hundred names, many of important persons, spread throughout the Muslim world. Beirut received 114 issues, 23 went to Damascus, 20 to North Africa, 11 to Tripoli, 7 to Baghdad, 5 to Mecca, and 2 to Medina. Yet the list is incomplete, including no names in Tehran or Asadabad, where other documents show that it was sent.[47]

Contemporary evidence regarding the source of funds for the printing and wide free distribution of *al-'Urwa al-Wuthqā* had been lost from view until recently unearthed by Homa Pakdaman. The evidence appears in two articles published in the newspaper *Paris* of December 3 and 12, 1884, which include letters from an anonymous correspondent from Livorno who is obviously well acquainted with, and hostile to, Afghānī and his circle. In his first letter, the correspondent claims that an intermediary obtained a large sum of money from the ex-Khedive Ismā'īl which enabled Afghānī to bring 'Abduh to Paris and to begin their newspaper. The writer continues that the paper's claim that it was supported by a society with members in all Eastern countries was fictitious. Although Ismā'īl refused to subsidize the journal, Afghānī succeeded in taking another 2,000 francs from him. A wealthy Tunisian general, Ḥusain Pāshā, also gave at least 11,000 francs to the journal. The writer claims that Afghānī and his associates were involved in another scheme to get money from Ismā'īl, which misfired and ended in the expulsion from

[47] Pakdaman (pp. 100–101) summarizes the list, which is catalogued but not photographed in *Documents*, p. 12, doc. 6.

France of Afghānī's associate and Ismā'īl's former secretary, the Egyptian Ibrāhīm al-Muwailihī.

Jamāl ad-Dīn replied to this letter in *Paris* of December 5, 1884. In his reply, Afghānī denied personal accusations by the correspondent, who had stated that Afghānī claimed the title of "prince" and aspired to be the Mahdi. Afghānī also denied certain statements about Ḥusain Pāshā, and was ambiguous about Ismā'īl, saying only, "I never found myself in need of having recourse to the purse of Ismā'īl Pāshā." Afghānī claimed that the correspondent was one of his former interpreters, whom he had fired and who was taking petty revenge.

On December 12, 1884, the Livorno correspondent replied. In a footnote, the editor of *Paris* noted that Jamāl ad-Dīn's reply had scarcely touched the substance of what the correspondent wrote. Regarding Ismā'īl, the correspondent asked if Jamāl ad-Dīn had forgotten the frequent approaches to Ismā'īl made in Afghānī's behalf by an Egyptian, now director of the Bank of Alexandria, which culminated in an interview in January 1884, after which an envoy of Ismā'īl, M. Lavizon, brought Afghānī 1,000 francs to his domicile, and another envoy, Ali Bey "Cheftaky" (Şefkati—a reformist Ottoman former official now in exile who was serving Ismā'īl) was sent to explain to Afghānī that this money was not in order to subsidize a journal. The correspondent also asks whether Afghānī has forgotten his vain trip to Turin, or his visit a month later to the former Khedive Ismā'īl at the Grand Hotel, from which he brought back 2,000 francs. The correspondent asks if Afghānī has forgotten a number of other facts, which he lists, among them "the letters, anonymous or signed with a pseudonym, addressed to high personages in a nihilist style, threatening death to the recipients if they oppose the restoration of Ismail Pāshā." The correspondent adds that Wilfrid Blunt, who is very rich, helped Afghānī and 'Abduh financially. "But his last gift was accompanied by these words: 'It is impossible for me to subsidize a journal hostile to my country.' "[48] No rebuttal to this letter is recorded.

Despite the hostile tone of these letters, which deal also with the expulsion of Ibrāhīm al-Muwailihī from France (discussed in the next chapter), they clearly emanate from someone with detailed in-

---

48 Pakdaman (pp. 357–365) reprints these articles. The trip to Turin is mentioned in one of Afghānī's letters, but not the purpose attributed to it by this writer.

formation about Afghānī, and, along with confirming items in the *Documents* cited below, they contain the only plausible contemporary information thus far on the source of funds for *al-'Urwa al-Wuthqā*. The words attributed to Blunt ring true, and the consequent exhaustion of funds may help account for the abrupt demise of the newspaper after only a few months' publication.

General Ḥusain Pāshā at-Tūnisī, named in the *Paris* articles as a chief financial contributor to *al-'Urwā al-Wuthqā*, was a wealthy Tunisian associated with the reform efforts in Tunisia of the prominent statesman, Khair ad-Dīn, and with attempts to head off the French protectorate in Tunisia established in 1881. In the 1880's General Ḥusain was living in Italy, and had friendly relations with the former Khedive Ismā'īl. The *Documents* include a series of unidentified letters from General Ḥusain in Italy to Afghānī in Paris confirming that he gave money to Afghānī. In his first letter, in March or April 1884, the General promises to come to Paris very soon. In the next letter, in May, 1884, General Ḥusain says he has sent Afghānī a check for 1,000 francs, for which he had to borrow money and squeeze his own expenses. Further correspondence does not resume until December 1884, indicating that General Ḥusain may have been in Paris in the interim. In these later letters, General Ḥusain again refers to money he has sent Jamāl ad-Dīn. It is possible that General Ḥusain helped make contacts in Tunisia for Afghānī and 'Abduh, since 'Abduh chose to travel to Tunisia at the end of 1884, and there was able to raise additional money, as is noted below. In one letter, however, General Ḥusain expresses surprise that 'Abduh had gone to Tunis without telling him.[49]

The *Documents* also include two letters and a visiting card from Ali Bey Şefkati, an Ottoman statesman named in *Paris* as an intermediary between Ismā'īl and Afghānī. Şefkati, a former Ottoman official fled Istanbul in 1878 and edited anti-Abdülhamid newspapers from European exile after 1879. He served for a time as Ismā'īl's

---

49 Documents in the Majlis Library, Tehran, catalogued in *Documents*, p. 62, docs. 204–210. The editors of *Documents* do not identify the writer, and refer to the letters as unreadable, presumably because they are in a North African handwriting style. I identified their author and got the help of Abdallah Laroui in reading them. Thanks are due to him and also to Arnold Green, who supplied further identifying information on General Ḥusain. *Documents*, p. 77, doc. 305, also catalogs an Arabic poem by Rizqallāh b. Ḥusain about a "loan" sent to General Ḥusain at-Tūnisī, dated Oct. 10, 1877.

private secretary. In Şefkati's first letter to Afghānī from Rome, postmarked April 14, 1884, he praises the first issue of *al-'Urwa al-Wuthqā* and says he will have the honor of seeing Afghānī in eight to ten days. The second, from London and dated May 14, 1884, says he has been delayed in London by the current (political) crises, but will leave London soon and have the honor of seeing Afghānī in Paris. They did meet in Paris, since Shefketi left a visiting card saying that he was leaving for London and hoped to see Afghānī again soon.[50] The card is undated and might date either between the two above letters or, more likely, after the second one. The *Documents* do not, however, indicate whether or not Şefkati acted as an intermediary between Ismā'īl and Afghānī, but in view of Şefkati's stint as Ismā'īl's secretary, this is probable.

The difficulty of determining Afghānī's exact sources of financial support is compounded by the fact that Afghānī tried at the same time to be in touch with a series of opposing parties—hoping to use them in his larger goal of ousting the British from Muslim lands. Not only did he back the Sultan at the same time as he presented himself as an agent of the Sudanese Mahdi, whose claims were opposed to those of the Sultan (as discussed in the next chapter), but he also had contact with different claimants to Egypt's rule. Among his associates during the period he was editing *al-'Urwa al-Wuthqā* were two who had ties with one claimant to the khedivate, the ex-Khedive Ismā'īl: namely, General Ḥusain Pāshā at-Tūnisī and Ibrāhīm al-Muwailihī, formerly secretary to Ismā'īl. These two were hostile to each other, however, as is indicated in letters summarized below in which General Ḥusain defends Ismā'īl (whom Afghānī seems to have blamed) from responsibility for the articles in *Paris* against Afghānī and his followers, and attributes the articles rather to Muwailihī, saying that Muwailihī wrote bad things about himself (Muwailihī) in these articles only to hide his responsibility for them.[51]

Among Afghānī's associates were also partisans of Ḥalīm, the Sultan's candidate for the khedivate: namely, James Sanua and

---

50 Turkish language documents in the Majlis Library collection; summarized in *Documents*, pp. 71–72, docs. 238–240. I have referred to the originals with the help of Andreas Tietze. Thanks to Sabri Sayari and D. A. Rustow for finding Turkish sources regarding Şefkati, who is briefly identified in Şerif Mardin, "Libertarian Movements in the Ottoman Empire, 1878–1895," *Middle East Journal*, XVI, 2 (Spring, 1962), 169–182.

51 Majlis Library, Tehran, collection, catalogued in *Documents*, p. 62, docs. 207–210; summarized in chap. 9 n. 22 below.

Ismā'īl Jaudat, who had been in 'Urābī's government, went to live with Ḥalīm in Istanbul after 'Urābī's overthrow, and was sent by Ḥalīm to London in 1884. There he entered into relations with Afghānī and Muwailihī (see next chapter). The unsuccessful attempts of Muḥammad 'Abduh and Shūbāshī to raise money from Ḥalīm have already been noted. On the whole, the evidence suggests no support to Afghānī from Ḥalīm, but possible support from Ismā'īl, and certain support from General Ḥusain, a friend of Ismā'īl's.

Another story of aid from Ismā'īl appeared in the *Journal des Débats* on May 9, 1896, after the assasination of Nāsir ad-Dīn Shāh, After describing Afghānī's earlier life, the *Journal* says, "He was found then in Paris, editing an Arab journal called *The Straight Road* [an erroneous translation of *al-'Urwa al-Wuthqā*], with a subvention from the Khedive Ismā'īl. Certain articles of the journal having displeased the Khedive, the subvention was suppressed and the journal ceased to appear." Lending possible support to this theory is the favorable tone of *al'Urwa al-Wuthqā* toward Ismā'īl and the claimed participation in the newspaper by Ismā'īl's secretary and propagandist, then in Paris, Ibrāhīm al-Muwailihī. On the other hand, the Pan-Islamic tone of *al-'Urwa al-Wuthqā* was more favorable to the Sultan, who had ties to Ḥalīm as a pretender to the khedivate, than to Ismā'īl, and Muwailihī later claimed that Ismā'īl was angered by his, Muwailihī's, contributions to the paper.[52] The earlier story that Ismā'īl gave money to Afghānī for some purpose, but not to support a newspaper, and that Ḥusain Pāshā and Blunt were the newspaper's direct supporters seems to be the most plausible one thus far.

The first issue of *al-'Urwa al-Wuthqā,* dated March 13, 1884, included an article entitled, "The Newspaper and its Program," saying that the paper would serve Easterners by explaining the causes of their decline and what must be done to regain strength. The paper will refute those who say that Muslims cannot advance toward civilization as long as they follow their own principles, and will show that they must, in fact, follow the principles of their ancestors in order to be strong. It will be sent free to all who wish to receive it. Another introductory note to the first issue says that the designs of

---

52 See the autobiographical statements by Muwailihī in the next chapter, taken from the *Documents,* photos 101–105. For favorable references to Ismā'īl see *al-'Urwa al-Wuthqā* (Cairo, 1958), pp. 273 and 409 ff. This book, reprinting in subject order the articles from the newspaper, does not date the articles.

the imperialists were long hidden, but have since been revealed. The Muslim peoples have been oppressed by the West, but now a reaction is growing, and the Muslims will become very strong when they unite against the foreigner. In many countries, especially India and Egypt, societies have been set up to further Muslim unity. One group is said to have met in Mecca and to have asked for a newspaper in Arabic to emanate from a free city like Paris, with Sayyid Jamāl ad-Dīn as its founder. He took it as his duty to his religion and nation, and asked Muḥammad 'Abduh to edit the paper.[53] The list of persons to whom it was sent, in the *Documents*, shows how much money and effort went into its circulation.

This extensive circulation was partly responsible for the considerable reputation and influence of *al-'Urwa al-Wuthqā* in the Muslim world, which were also furthered by the paper's expression in arresting terms of the growing protective and Pan-Islamic mood in that world. The main themes of the paper in its short seven month's existence were hostility to British imperialism, advocacy of Islamic unity, and interpretation of Islamic principles to demonstrate their applicability to urgent contemporary needs. The newspaper combined articles giving detailed analyses of the positions of Great Britain and the other great powers in various parts of the Muslim world, especially Egypt, the Sudan, and India, with more general philosophical articles. Although Muḥammad 'Abduh is said to have done the actual Arabic composition of most of the articles, the tone throughout, and especially in the more political pieces, is so typical of Afghānī that one is justified in regarding them as reflections of the views he wished to put forth before a wide Muslim public.

According to the paper itself and to later comments by its editors, *al-'Urwa al-Wuthqā* was produced and subsidized by a society of the same name, but there is no evidence that this society went beyond Afghānī, 'Abduh, and some of their close associates, or that it carried on any significant activity beyond producing the newspaper.[54] One may imagine, however, that plans regarding the Sudan and Egypt and attempts to influence the great Powers, treated in the next chapter, were discussed secretly by a society consisting of Afghānī and his friends in Paris.

---

53 *al-'Urwa al-Wuthqā*, no. 1, March 13, 1884. Complete sets are at the Bibliothèque Nationale in Paris and in F.O. 78/3682, Baring to Granville, no. 1199, Secret, Cairo, Dec. 31, 1884.

54 Cf. "Djam'iyya," by A. H. Hourani in *EI*2, II, 428–429.

The first issue of *al-'Urwa al-Wuthqā* ran an article entitled "British Policy in the East" reiterating some of the points Afghānī made in his 1883 French-language articles. He here warns that the British will be unable to extinguish the mahdist movement, which threatens to spread beyond the Sudan, and only the Ottomans and liberated Egyptians would be able to put down this movement. He claims that the Turkomans and Afghans will increasingly incline toward Russia, thus causing a danger to the British in India. Other articles in the first issue discuss the evils of British rule in Egypt, and the inevitable failure of Gordon in the Sudan.[55]

Similar themes reappear in the political articles throughout the life of the paper. The last issue, dated October 16, 1884, includes an article claiming that an uprising is feared in Egypt, partly as a result of the Mahdi's victories in the Sudan. It also claims that the Indians are turning against the British and toward the Russians, and that some of the Indian princes are sending representatives to Russian Central Asia to declare their loyalty to the Russians. If the Mahdi should advance and get the support of the courageous people of Upper Egypt, concludes the article, then uprisings would break out in India, and Russia would advance and free the Indians from the yoke of slavery, thus finishing Great Britain as a Power.[56] Another article in the same issue deals with the blindness of some people regarding British designs in Egypt. Whoever has traveled in British colonies like India learns that their people are reduced to hopeless poverty by the burden of taxes. The article says that under Riyāḍ Pāshā Egypt met her financial obligations without undue burdens on the people, but that Britain's pretended benevolent measures are only in her own self-interest. The article shrewdly notes the unlikelihood that the British will leave Egypt soon, despite their claims to the contrary. As they have done elsewhere, the British are using Egyptian collaborators to spread their own dominion on the excuse of restoring tranquillity. The banners of courage, national zeal, and patriotism must be raised in order to destroy the designs of the British and eject those who assist them, who are traitors who can only be saved by repentance and a return to the patriotic path.[57]

Also directed against collaboration with the British is the article "The Materialists in India," which treats Sir Sayyid Ahmad Khān

---

55 *al-'Urwa al-Wuthqā*, no. 1, March 13, 1884.
56 *Ibid.*, no. 18, Oct. 16, 1884.
57 *Ibid.*

and his Indian followers as traitors who have sold out to the British in return for petty favors.[58]

The political articles of *al-ʿUrwa al-Wuthqā* are thus overwhelmingly directed against British imperialism in Muslim lands and combine a realistic if partisan account of the grievances of many of those under British rule with an overestimation of the forces menacing the British. In 1884–85 the British were threatened by the Mahdi in the Sudan and by the Russians in Central Asia, but the chances of widespread and successful revolt in Egypt or India against British rule were not nearly as great as Afghānī seemed to imagine. Overestimation of one's own forces is common among revolutionaries and others who dislike the idea that the changes they hope for cannot occur in their own lifetimes. More unusual is Afghānī's belief, partly expressed in *al-ʿUrwa* and partly elsewhere, that he could help forge an alliance that might include Russia, France, the Ottoman Empire, and Afghanistan, as well as a disaffected mass in India and Egypt which could bring about the expulsion of the British from those countries. The idea of a Russian attack on India which would result in a mass Indian uprising is one that occurs again and again.

In addition to its political articles, largely directed against British imperialism, *al-ʿUrwa al-Wuthqā* included a number of more philosophical articles, primarily devoted to a reinterpretation of Islamic ideas and to the virtues of unity among the Muslims. An article entitled "Nationality and the Muslim Religion" indicates once again how Afghānī changed his arguments for different audiences. While addressing an Indian audience, Afghānī had said that national and linguistic ties were more important and more enduring than religious ones, but now, to an international Muslim audience, Afghānī wrote that Muslims had gone beyond the stage of tribalism that considered nationality primary and would unite together in a larger unit based on their shared religion.[59] The divisions to be found among Muslim states are caused by the deviation of their leaders from true Islamic principles as followed by the first generations of Muslims. If they return to the ways of the first orthodox caliphs, God will soon give them comparable power.

In this and other articles in this more philosophical group, the re-

[58] *Ibid.*, no. 15, Aug. 28, 1884 (pp. 382–387 in the Cairo, 1958, edition). This is translated in full in Keddie, *Islamic Response*, pp. 175–180.

[59] *al-ʿUrwa al-Wuthqā*, no. 2, March 20, 1884; trans. into French by Marcel Colombe (who also translated the articles discussed below) as "La nationalité (djinsiya) et la religion musulmane," *Orient*, 22 (1962), 125–130.

turn to early Islam has for Afghānī primarily a political and military meaning—a return of all classes, nations, and leaders in the Muslim world to unity, which is seen as the key to the revival of the military strength of the early Muslims. The political importance of reviving Muslim unity is stressed again in such articles as "The Causes of the Decadence and the Inertia of the Muslims," and "Islamic Unity."[60] The greed and rivalry of Muslim princes and rulers is blamed for the breakup of Islamic unity, which should be restored.

In an interesting article entitled "Fanaticism" (or solidarity—*ta'aṣṣub*), Afghānī says that those who follow Western ways blame fanaticism for all the evils in the Muslim world. In fact, however, *ta'aṣṣub* is the practice of *'aṣabiyya* (solidarity), and is the key to the defense of one's own people. *Ta'aṣṣub* can be exaggerated, but in proper proportion it is the source of unity, rectitude, and character in a nation, and unity is the source of national strength. Those who imitate the West are opposed to stressing religious ties among people, but the author thinks they are wrong, since any tie that unites people so that they can defend themselves and strive for perfection has the same value, whether it be religious or national in origin. Europeans have seen that religion is the strongest tie of unity among Muslims and thus have tried to break this religious tie before patriotism could develop to replace it. The Indian Naichirīs are English agents, working to weaken Islam. The author is surprised at those Muslims who, by attacking all *ta'aṣṣub*, help destroy Muslim unity and put the community in the hands of foreigners. Westerners who attack Oriental fanaticism while supporting their own missionaries are even stranger. This article again indicates the instrumental use by Afghānī of religious appeals as the strongest available force against Western encroachments at a time when modern nationalism and patriotism were not yet strong sentiments in the East, but Islamic identification was very powerful. It also contrasts with Afghānī's 1879 Alexandria speech listing *ta'aṣṣub* and despotism as the two causes of Islamic decline.[61]

Also pragmatic and political in their implications are the articles attacking fatalism in Islam. One of these, "Christianity, Islam, and Their Followers," notes that the early Muslims were advanced mili-

---

[60] *Ibid.*, no. 5, April 10, 1884, and no. 9, May 22, 1884; trans. in *Orient*, 22 (1962), 131–147.

[61] *al-'Urwa al-Wuthqā* (Cairo, 1958), pp. 39–48. Thanks to Marcel Colombe for showing me his unpublished translation of this article. Afghānī's negative assessment of *ta'aṣṣub* in 1879 is quoted in chap. 5, above, from the newspaper *Miṣr*.

tarily and technically. Then, however, there appeared men who innovated in Islam, introducing the foreign doctrine of fatalism which gradually turned men away from action. The profound study of religion remained confined to small private circles (probably the philosophers are intended). The Koran, in fact, orders Muslims to defend their sovereignty, fight their enemies, and seek power by all means. Thus true Muslims should surpass non-Muslims in the sciences of war, including offensive war, in order to safeguard their rights and protect their religion.[62]

In another article on "Predestination" (or "Divine Decree," *al-Qaḍā' wa al-qadar*), Afghānī says that this Muslim doctrine has been wrongly confused with fatalism, whereas what it means in fact is that everything has its ultimate source and cause in the Creator. Freed of the false doctrine of fatalism, it can be a source of strength and inspiration, as it was for the earliest Muslims. The greatest heroes in history have believed that the Creator was on their side. Fatalism came into the Muslim world with foreign conquest, but the Muslims are now awakening from it.[63]

The overwhelming theme of the general articles in *al-'Urwa al-Wuthqā* is the urgent need to return the Muslim world to its early unity and activism. In discussing the original virtues of Islam, Afghānī again and again points to the military conquests and strength and the political unity of the first Islamic period. With appropriately interpreted quotations from the Koran he identifies military strength, political unity, and the protection of Muslim territory as the leading principles of the Islamic faith, and says that Muslims have only declined since their rulers have abandoned these principles of their religion. He blames Islamic decline largely on the selfishness of individual Muslim rulers and the deviation from original principles by the ulama. Corruption in Islam began with these leaders and subsequently spread to the lower orders of society. In order to fend off its increasingly threatening non-Muslim enemies, the Muslim world must return to its original unity and reverse the innovation of having separate states and sovereigns within the Islamic community. Muslim rulers who have given way to non-Muslim influence and infiltration in their countries, like the Indian princes, are traitors to their religion. Only belief in a religion or nationality

---

62 *al-'Urwa al-Wuthqā*, no. 4, April 3, 1884; trans. in *Orient*, 21 (1962), 89–97.

63 *Ibid.*, no. 7, May 1, 1884; trans. as "La prédestination *(al-kada' wa'l-kadar)*," *Orient*, 21 (1962), 98–109.

can unite people, and in the Muslim world unity must come on a religious basis.[64] Once again there is the pragmatic political interpretation of Islam and the call for a revival of unity as the key to warding off the non-Muslim imperialist threat. Russia is given as an example of a large nation that has defended itself effectively despite its economic and technical backwardness through political unity around one sovereign.[65]

There are contemporary reports of the great influence of *al-'Urwa al-Wuthqā* despite its short life of seven months. It was widely circulated by its editors among leaders all over the Muslim world and also widely read. In a time that followed numerous defeats of Muslims by Europeans, but also saw the victories of the Sudanese Mahdi against British forces, it brought an essentially simple but inspiring message, akin to the message of the early nationalists in various European countries. It called on Muslims to end the fatalism that allowed European powers to conquer their territory piece by piece, and to work for Muslim unity and military strength. It identified these practical goals with true Islam, thus bringing religious as well as nationalist feelings into the service of the self-strengthening cause. The great efforts Afghānī took to publish and distribute it indicate again his appreciation of the efficacy of the new mass media. There is no word in the paper's theoretical articles favoring political democracy or parliamentarianism, or even advocating specific political reforms. One article speaks rather of corruption as springing from bad and selfish rulers, whereas the good society can be assured by wise and virtuous rulers, who understand the needs of their people.[66] Although in Egypt Afghānī had favored constitutional reforms, it is striking that he does not advocate such reforms in his writings after 1879, and if he did favor constitutional reforms, he must have given them a low priority or considered them a distant goal, to be subordinated temporarily to political independence, strength, and unity. The article regarding despotic rulers does begin with an elliptical reference to nations living without consultative powers,

---

64 Nearly all the general and philosophical articles from *al-'Urwa al-Wuthqā*, where these points are found, have been translated into French by Marcel Colombe under the general title, "Pages choisies de Djamal al-din al-Afghani," in *Orient*, 21–25 (1962–1963).

65 "Islamic Unity," *al-'Urwa al-Wuthqā*, no. 9, May 22, 1884, trans. in *Orient*, 22 (1962), 139–147.

66 "The Nation and Absolutism," in *ibid.*, no. 14, Aug. 14, 1884; trans. in *Orient*, 22 (1962), 149–150.

but then suggests not reform but forceful action to extirpate a bad ruler, called a sickened tree, before it can poison the whole nation, and to plant in its place a healthy tree.[67] This is one of several clues that Afghānī plans, at least in the 1880's, envisioned not so much constitutional changes as the overthrow of individual rulers who were lax or subservient to foreigners, and their replacement by strong and patriotic men. Here he was probably influenced by the tendency of both orthodox Muslim writers and Islamic philosophers to overestimate the virtues of the ruler as the chief source of a powerful, healthy, and harmonious polity. On the other hand, the prior and subsequent bad experience with constitutions of Egypt and several other Muslim countries gives some support to Afghānī's downgrading of constitutionalism and his stress on the behavior of a government rather than its form.

There is no stress in Afghānī's articles on the tremendous technological, scientific, and educational advances that would have to be made in order to make the Islamic world capable of resisting Western incursions. Rather, the assumption is, as the example made of Russia indicates, that once the Muslim world is unified and under a ruler devoted to its defense, the technical means may be obtained, even from abroad, for defense. Various reports about Afghānī indicate that he did have some appreciation of Western technology, but he thought, perhaps with some justification, that the first step in the Muslim world would be to change the attitude of both masses and leaders before technology could mean anything. Again, however, there is an overestimation of moral and political attitudes, and an underestimation of economic, political, and technological realities, as moving forces influencing the relationships between the Western and Islamic worlds.

The authorities evidently stopped the entrance of *al-ʿUrwa al-Wuthqā*, as well as *Abu Naddara*, into India and Egypt.[68] This

67 *Ibid.* This article is the one referred to in L. M. Kenny, "Al-Afghānī on Types of Despotic Government," *Journal of the American Oriental Society*, 86 (1966), 19–27, on p. 20 and n. 3, which appears to suggest that the article advocates constitutionalism; a reading of the original shows that it does not. (Kenny is not incorrect—only slightly ambiguous.)

68 There are numerous reports of this, the most direct of which, regarding Egypt, is in F.O. 78/3682, Baring to Granville, no. 1199, Secret, Cairo, Dec. 31, 1884, which encloses sets of both *al-ʿUrwa al-Wuthqā* and *Abu Naddara*, and refers to them as "seditious Arabic journals which have been stopped by the Egyptian Postal Authorities in conformity with the order of the Egyptian Government forbidding their introduction into this country." Both papers "are hostile

action is usually given as the reason for the sudden termination of the paper in October 1884, just seven months after it began, but, as noted, this closing was probably attributable more to the withdrawal or drying up of its financial base. In any case, the simple but inspirational message of the paper had been amply expressed during its short life, and this message had brought Afghānī's name and views to a much wider Muslim public than had heard of him before.

At the end of 1884, Muḥammad 'Abduh made a trip to Tunis in the hope of raising funds. From Tunis he wrote to Afghānī in Paris on December 24, 1884, saying that he had been well received by scholars and religious authorities, and that he had told them that *al-'Urwa al-Wuthqā* was not really the name of a journal but of a society that Afghānī had created in Hyderabad which had branches in different countries, none of which knew of another, and that it was desirable to form a branch in Tunis. 'Abduh said he had formed this branch, promising not to tell the names of its members to anyone but Afghānī. 'Abduh wrote that most of the members of the Tunisian branch were ulama, and names two of them. He added that he had failed to raise money, but that people in Tunisia believed that they (Afghānī and 'Abduh) had a large treasury. 'Abduh reported that he had been reassuring Tunisians by telling them of (fictitious) letters he had recently received from Afghānī. 'Abduh added that he had promised that *al-'Urwa al-Wuthqā* would be published again, and that people in Tunis did not realize that the journal had ceased publishing.[69] A later letter, discussed in the next chapter, from Ibrāhīm al-Muwailihī in Istanbul to Afghānī claims that Khair ad-Dīn Pāshā, the great Tunisian-Ottoman reforming statesman, had told him that he and others had given large sums to 'Abduh, and suggests that 'Abduh might not have reported all the money he had received.[70] The accuracy of this suggestion is unclear.

---

to the present Khedive and to the English occupation." Although most accounts speak of the British as responsible for the stopping of these papers' entry in Egypt, the Khedive Taufīq must have been equally eager to see them stopped.

[69] A Persian translation, but not the original, is in *Documents*, pp. 63–64. Pakdaman, pp. 103–105, translates the Persian version and notes 'Abduh's purposeful misstatements to the Tunisians. My own summary is from the original Arabic, in the Majlis Library collection.

[70] *Documents*, photos 98–99. The Persian translation of this letter in the *Documents*, utilized by Pakdaman, p. 106, goes slightly beyond the original in its accusation against 'Abduh.

After 'Abduh left for Tunis, he and Jamāl ad-Dīn never saw each other again, although Jamāl ad-Dīn continued to express friendly feelings toward his former disciple, and wrote him a letter during a brief stop at Port Said in 1891, when Afghānī was on his way to London from Basra. (This letter is wrongly ascribed to Afghānī's 1882 stop in Port Said by Riḍā and others.)[71] There is no record in the *Documents* of a continuing correspondence between Afghānī and 'Abduh, however, and there are first-hand reports that 'Abduh, who increasingly believed in gradual and educational paths to reform, lost much respect for Afghānī's methods, while Afghānī in the 1890's accused his former disciple of political timidity.[72] For all their later falling out, however, the influence of Afghānī on 'Abduh remained crucial and fruitful, and such collaborative products as 'Abduh's translation (with Abū Turāb's help) of the "Refutation of the Materialists," and his composition of *al-'Urwa al-Wuthqā* under Afghānī's guidance had an important influence on the intellectual and political development of Arabic-speaking Muslims.

After the demise of *al-'Urwa al-Wuthqā* Afghānī remained in Paris, where he was increasingly occupied with political plans involving the Sudanese Mahdi, the British, and the Ottoman Sultan, to which attention is now turned.

---

71 See the discussion on p. 350 below.

72 Riḍā, *Tārīkh*, pp. 894–898, quotes 'Abduh as criticizing Afghānī for sticking to political activity instead of going into education, as Abduh had asked him to do, and also for trying the impossible task of reforming evil rulers. Afghānī is quoted as replying from Istanbul to a letter from 'Abduh, and criticizing 'Abduh for selfish cowardice in having written him in an indirect way and not signing his letter. Riḍā also quotes 'Abduh as saying of Afghānī: "How much his anger destroyed that which his intelligence had built up."

9

The Mahdi and the Sultan: 1884–1885

Jamāl ad-Dīn, Blunt, and the Mahdi

In addition to journalism in Paris, Afghānī in 1884–85 was involved in political plans concerning the Sudanese Mahdi and the British. The continued strength of the Sudanese Mahdi, culminating in his capture of Khartoum and the death of General Gordon in January 1885, provided a background for attempted negotiations on the Sudanese question by Great Britain in which Wilfrid Blunt tried to involve Afghānī. Blunt had ties, through birth and background, with important men in both the Liberal and Conservative parties. He was a friend of Sir Edward Hamilton, Gladstone's private secretary, through whom he sometimes sent messages to Gladstone when he was Liberal Prime Minister. Blunt was also friendly with Randolph Churchill, who had opposed the British occupation of Egypt, regarding which he had presented in Parliament many charges based primarily on Blunt's evidence of British wrongdoing. Blunt knew Sir Henry Drummond Wolff, diplomat and member of Parliament, who along with Churchill was a member of a parliamentary group of Conservatives known as the Fourth Party, which sometimes criticized the foreign policy of the Liberal government on grounds more radical than those of their fellow Conservatives. When the Conservatives took over the British government in the summer of 1885, Churchill became Secretary of State for India, and Wolff was put in charge of a special mission to Istanbul and

Egypt to try to solve the Egyptian question. Both men were thus important figures in Conservative foreign policy, and Blunt tried to influence them toward his own ideas.[1]

Blunt's involvement of Jamāl ad-Dīn and 'Abduh in plans for intervention with the Mahdi led to a series of complex maneuvers, with scant result, which are known so far only through Blunt's *Gordon at Khartoum.* The *Documents* provide more information on these schemes, and also show how Afghānī used them to establish relations with Sultan Abdülhamid—perhaps their only important outcome. Since these maneuvers, and Afghānī's supposed relations with the Mahdi, are often referred to in exaggerated terms that appear to have no factual basis, it is worth trying to reconstruct what actually happened, for all the paucity of results. This is a rare case where sufficient documentation exists for a detailed reconstruction of a political plan involving Afghānī.

Neither the *Documents* nor, apparently, any other primary source gives evidence that Afghānī was actually in touch with the Mahdi, as he claimed. In fact, if Afghānī had any contact with the Mahdi, it would seem strange that there should not be even one letter indicating this in the voluminous correspondence catalogued in the *Documents.* Blunt evidently believed Jamāl ad-Dīn to be in contact with the Mahdi, but he gives no evidence of it beyond Afghānī's own word, and shows that when Afghānī was asked to do something that would prove him to be in toch with the Mahdi, he refused, presenting a plausible excuse. The record is equally negative on the Sudanese side.[2]

On one occasion when Afghānī apparently did something that might prove his relations with the Mahdi, the results were more than dubious. As reported by the French socialist, Henri Rochefort, who writes in the 1890's of the trip to the Sudan in 1884 by a fellow socialist, Olivier Pain:

> The omnipotence of Djemal-ed-Din over his co-religionists made itself felt when it became a question of surmounting the difficulties Olivier Pain was certain to encounter in reaching the Mahdi's army. He did not beg the all-powerful master of the Soudan; he simply ordered him to organize a

[1] Wilfrid S. Blunt, *Gordon at Khartoum* (London, 1911), and *India, passim,* references to Churchill and Wolff; Winston S. Churchill, *Lord Randolph Churchill* (London, 1952), pp. 206–207.

[2] Conversation with Professor P. M. Holt, August 1965, London.

> caravan of sham merchants to cross the desert to join Pain on the frontiers of Upper Egypt and take him to the camp. Djemal's instructions were carried out to the letter. Olivier Pain placed himself under the guidance of the Mahdi's envoys, and safely reached the Soudanese army, then numerous and victorious.
>
> But from that moment I received no further news of fellow-fugitive.[3]

One must wonder at Rochefort's statement that Jamāl ad-Dīn's instructions to the Mahdi with regard to Pain were carried out to the letter. The accounts of two Europeans who were present when Pain reached the neighborhood of the Mahdi make it clear that neither the Mahdi nor any of his followers had any advance notice of Pain's arrival. He was suspected of being an English spy and kept under close guard, and his ill treatment may have contributed to the illness he developed, which culminated in his death. Neither of the European eyewitnesses suggests that Pain ever raised the question of Jamāl ad-Dīn's letter to the Mahdi—his claim to good treatment was based on entirely different points.[4]

Rochefort also quotes a letter from Afghānī referring to "my former pupil at the El-Azhar university who is now the Mahdi."[5] If accurately quoted, this claim is a more extravagant one than Afghānī usually made, since it was easy enough to ascertain that the Mahdi had never studied at al-Azhar. Usually, Afghānī said, as to Blunt, that some of the important followers of the Mahdi had studied under him in Egypt, which also appears doubtful.

Blunt's attempt to involve Afghānī in Sudanese negotiations, as recorded in Blunt's published diary, began on April 18, 1884, when two of Blunt's acquaintances asked him if he would help to save the life of General Gordon, then besieged at Khartoum. Blunt records saying to the two: "If it came to sending an Embassy to the Mahdi, I might be able to help them, and I advised them to put this idea forward, rather than the other. I have written to Jemal-ed-Din to ask him what he thinks of it."[6] Blunt's *Gordon at Khartoum* contains

---

[3] Henri Rochefort, *The Adventures of My Life* English trans. by E. W. Smith and H. Rochefort, Vol. II (London, 1897), pp. 280–281.

[4] Rudolf C. Slatin, *Fire and Sword in the Sudan* (London, 1896), pp. 306–319; Father Joseph Ohrwalder, *Ten Years' Captivity in the Mahdi's Camp* (London, 1892), pp. 172–175; Elie Kedourie, "Further Light on Afghani," *Middle Eastern Studies*, I, 2 (Jan., 1965), 194.

[5] Rochefort, *op. cit.*, p. 281.

[6] Blunt, *Gordon*, p. 221.

not his own letter, but Jamāl ad-Dīn's reply in French from Paris on April 21. Jamāl ad-Dīn begins by saying that he does not consider Gordon a friend of liberty and of Islam (which Blunt must have implied), but, given his confidence in Blunt, he joins in regretting his unhappy situation. Afghānī goes on:

> "I do not hide from you that it would have been easy for me, in view of the confidence which the Mahdi appears to have in me as well as that of his principal partisans of whom a large number are my Soudanese students, to prevent this disaster which threatens Gordon Pasha, if the latest battles between Graham and Osman Digna had not taken place; but after these bloody battles which have cost so much Arab blood, I believe that the Mahdi and his partisans are reduced to seeing that the only means of regaining lost territory and consolidating their prestige would be to take Khartoum and arrest Gordon, if not to take his life."[7]

Having thus armed himself against probable failure, Afghānī goes on to say that if Blunt would write in detail the bases of the peace he wished, Afghānī would do all he could, and advise him on how it might be possible to save Gordon. This letter evidently inspired Blunt to write to Gladstone for the first time on this subject. Blunt's diary records that when the two men who had suggested his mediation returned on April 23, "I read the draft of a letter I had written to Gladstone proposing to act as mediator for the relief of Gordon. This was suggested by one I received this morning from Jemal-ed-Din to the effect that for my sake he would do what he could with the Mahdi to save Gordon't life."[8] Blunt also reprints his letter to Gladstone, and Gladstone's negative reply to his suggestion on April 30.[9]

Meanwhile, Blunt had written again to Jamāl ad-Dīn, whose letter in reply asserted that any settlement must return Egypt to the Egyptians. A peace mission, to be successful, must be made up primarily of Muslims, who must represent the Egyptian nation rather than the present Egyptian government. He suggests also that Blunt should be on any such mission.[10] In this letter Jamāl ad-Dīn refuses

---

7 *Ibid.*, p. 542.
8 *Ibid.*, p. 223.
9 *Ibid.*, pp. 583–585.
10 *Ibid.*, p. 545

to commit himself on Blunt's question of who the next ruler of Egypt should be, and says that he should be the one desired by the Egyptian nation.

In May Jamāl ad-Dīn answered another letter from Blunt with expressions of deep admiration.[11] Jamāl ad-Dīn may have exaggerated Blunt's influence as much as Blunt exaggerated Jamāl ad-Dīn's. There is, for example, a letter translated by Blunt from Jamāl ad-Dīn to him dated May 12, 1885, which says: "I am not alone in gratitude for your distinguished efforts which have forced the Government to evacuate the Soudan.[!] No, be certain that all Moslems, especially the Arabs, will be grateful for this your action to the end of time and they will write your name on tablets inlaid with precious stones and titles of glory and honour for your zeal and courage."[12] This expression of gratitude may be merely polite hyperbole, however.

Jamāl ad-Dīn was attracted by the idea that he or one of his followers would get a major role in negotiations between the British and the Mahdi. Blunt seems not to have sent him any indication of Gladstone's April 30 rejection of his mediation proposal.

A different aspect of the question opened in June 1884 when Labouchere (a leading radical member of Parliament) suggested that Blunt bring Muḥammad 'Abduh from Paris to England as a representative of the Egyptian National Party.[13] Blunt did so, and 'Abduh arrived in London on July 21. Blunt introduced 'Abduh to various prominent people, including several members of Parliament, among them Parnell, the leader of the Irish Home Rulers.

On July 23 Blunt records that Randolph Churchill, after meeting 'Abduh, promised to try to get him an audience with Gladstone. Evidently nothing came of this, beyond an introduction of 'Abduh by Churchill to Lord Hartington, the Minister of War.[14] 'Abduh published his version of the conversation in *al-'Urwa al-Wuthqā*, saying that he argued that the Egyptians were not as ignorant as Hartington claimed, and that they were opposed to being ruled by people of alien race and religion.[15] 'Abduh made the same point at

---

[11] *Ibid.*, p. 547.
[12] *Ibid.*, pp. 549–550.
[13] *Ibid.*, pp. 261–262.
[14] *Ibid.*, pp. 274, 276.
[15] 'Abduh's version is available in English in Osman Amin, *Muhammad 'Abduh*, trans. Charles Wendell (Washington, 1953), pp. 63–64.

greater length in an interview conducted by Blunt and printed in the London *Pall Mall Gazette* of August 17, 1884, in which he also said that peace would come to the Sudan only if the British left Egypt.[16] 'Abduh may have had some small effect on opinion in Great Britain, where there were people who wanted to end the British occupation of Egypt, particularly if it would bring peace to the Sudan. Other than that, his mission was of no practical importance and did not have any of the dramatic effect that Labouchere and Blunt must have hoped for.

In the fall of 1884, Blunt went to Istanbul, according to his diary entry in order "to try and urge the Sultan to take a lead in reform." On his way he stopped off again in Paris to see 'Abduh, Sanua, and Jamāl ad-Dīn.[17] Blunt reached Istanbul in October, and tried to get in touch with the Sultan. On October 19, 1884, Salīm Faris, the editor of the leading Istanbul Arabic newspaper *al-Jawā'ib*, told Blunt that he was disliked by the Sultan, who was angry at Blunt's sticking to 'Urābī after he himself had abandoned him. Also Blunt recorded, "Tewfik's envoy, Sabit Pasha, is constantly telling him that I am head of a party in England bent on restoring the Arabian Caliphate."[18]

On the next day, October 20, Blunt met a man who was to become party to schemes involving also Afghānī, Blunt, and Drummond Wolff, namely, Ismā'īl Jaudat, who had been Prefect of Police of Cairo under 'Urābī. He was now a retainer of Prince Ḥalīm, who was the candidate of the Sultan, as well as of some Egyptian nationalists, for the khedivate. The Blunts met him when they went to pay their first visit to Ḥalīm: "We were received at the door by a man whom I did not recognize, but who turned out to be Ismail Jowdat, who had been Prefect of Police for the foreigners at Cairo during the war, and who, having kept order and saved much European life there, was exiled by Malet after Tel-el-Kabir."[19] Further on in his diary entry, Blunt notes that Ismā'īl Jaudat and Muṣṭāfā Bey, 'Urābī's doctor, apparently both lived as dependents of Ḥalīm. Ḥalīm, predictably enough, expressed to Blunt the opinion that the Powers should ask the Sultan to name a new khedive.[20]

---

16 Blunt, *Gordon*, pp, 622–626.
17 *Ibid.*, pp. 284–286.
18 *Ibid.*, pp. 304–305.
19 *Ibid.*, p. 310.
20 *Ibid.*, p. 311.

Blunt convinced Ḥalim to send Ismā'īl Jaudat back to England with them in order to give evidence corroborating Blunt's charges that the Khedive Taufīq had been responsible for the massacres in Alexandria in 1882 (which had helped bring on British intervention).[21] Back in England in December 1884, Blunt was introduced by Ismā'īl Jaudat to a fellow Egyptian exile, Ibrāhīm al-Muwailihī (an associate of Afghānī's in Egypt and Paris). According to his own account, written for the Sultan in 1885, Muwailihī in 1879 had helped the then Khedive Ismā'īl to arouse Egyptian agitation against the mixed cabinet (i.e., the cabinet with European ministers) and had become Ismā'īl's private secretary on his exile from Egypt to Italy. On Ismā'īl's orders he had edited (in Paris) three issues of *al-Ittihād,* a paper favoring Ismā'īl and hostile to the Ottoman Sultan. Muwailihī claims he helped publish *al-'Urwa al-Wuthqā,* which was opposed by Ismā'īl. Ismā'īl ordered Muwailihī to put out a fourth issue of *al-Ittihād,* which Muwailihī says was kept from distribution by Jamāl ad-Dīn. But the Ottoman Embassy in Paris unjustly blamed Muwailihī for this propaganda against the Sultan and ordered his expulsion from Paris.[22] A different version of these events, saying that the fourth issue of *Ittihād* was a scheme of Afghānī's to extort money from Ismā'īl, was published in the newspaper, *Paris,* on December 3, 1884. This version emanated from an anonymous correspondent in Livorno who had known Afghānī in Paris and who writes that Ibrāhīm al-Muwailihī had been Ismā'īl's secretary for only a few months, years before Muwailihī's editing of the fourth *Ittihād* issue and his consequent expulsion from Paris at Ottoman request. The writer also claims that even the first issues of *Ittihād* were subsidized by Ḥalīm's party, and says that the fourth issue was never intended for widespread distribution but was a scheme of Afghānī's to force money out of Ismā'īl—a scheme that backfired with Muwailihī's expulsion. As noted in chapter 8 the correspondent also makes other charges against Afghānī, and says that he got his money from Ismā'īl, from General Ḥusain Pāshā at-Tunisī, who was connected with Ismā'īl, and from Blunt. Afghānī responded on December 5 to the December 3 article, but his refutation covers the personal charges made against himself rather than the points noted above, and in a rebuttal published on December 12 both the original author

21 *Ibid.,* p. 336.
22 *Documents,* pp. 41–44, doc. 164; photos 101–105.

and the editors note that the original charges were affected very little by Afghānī's answer.[23]

Afghānī must have written to General Ḥusain blaming the ex-Khedive Ismā'īl for these articles since letters from General Ḥusain from Italy to Afghānī in late 1884 and early 1885 insist that Ismā'īl is not responsible for what newspapers, and specifically *Paris*, have written against him (Ḥusain) and Afghānī. General Ḥusain says he is certain that Muwailihī is responsible, and that Muwailihī included charges against himself in these articles only in order to deceive others. General Ḥusain attacks Muwailihī as an ingrate and a thief, and asks Afghānī not to give Muwailihī any more money.[24]

Also concerning Muwailihī, *Ittihād*, and the *Paris* articles is a note sent by James Sanua in Paris to Ismā'īl Jaudat in London on December 12, 1884. Both Sanua and Jaudat were linked with Ḥalīm, and Sanua says he has just received a letter from Istanbul, presumably from or on behalf of Ḥalīm, saying that it was Ismā'īl's party who had spread the word that Muwailihī had been working on *Ittihād* on Ḥalīm's behalf. "Jules Mignon therefore expects me to keep away from Ibrāhīm Bey [Muwailihī] and from Jamāl ad-Dīn and their group, from whom we may expect only headaches," Sanua writes. He adds that he has informed Wahbī (Muwailihī's brother) that Muwailihī is going to London, and that Wahbī's letter has arrived, but he, Sanua, had not yet shown it to Jamāl ad-Dīn, with whom he has had little contact since the day that Wahbī had cursed the "imām of men" (the Sultan-Caliph). Regarding Jamāl ad-Dīn, Sanua continues, "Today the government here watches him, because he used always to be with General Ḥusain, al-Muwailihī, and Ismā'īl's party. Therefore an important man advised me not to associate with him."[25] This note was later discovered by Muwailihī, who sent a copy to Jamāl ad-Dīn to try to demonstrate Sanua's deceitfulness.

It is difficult to unravel the truth among all the charges and countercharges among Afghānī's partisans, but the most probable deduction seems to be that Ismā'il had subsidized the first three issues of *al-Ittihād*, but possibly not the fourth, and that the *Paris* articles,

---

23 The *Paris* articles are reprinted in Pakdaman, pp. 357–365. In his response (*ibid.*) Afghānī made no attempt to refute these charges. A handwritten Arabic translation of the *Paris* articles is in the Majlis Library collection (misidentified as the minutes of a congress in Livorno in *Documents*, p. 23, doc. 52).

24 Majlis Library collection, catalogued in *Documents*, p. 62, docs. 207–210.

25 Majlis Library collection, part of doc. 308 (not mentioned in the description of that document in *Documents*, p. 77).

which reflected badly on everyone, were not encouraged by Ismā'īl, Ḥalīm, or Muwailihī, but stemmed simply from a (hostile) former associate of Aghānī's, as *Paris* maintained.

Muwailihī's expulsion from France occurred late in 1884, and he wrote at least twice to Jamāl ad-Dīn shortly afterward; once from the Belgian border and once from London.[26] Although we do not have Afghānī's replies, we may guess that Afghānī advised Muwailihī how to influence Blunt and his British friends. Perhaps taking the idea from Jamāl ad-Dīn, Muwailihī in London claimed to be an agent of the Sudanese Mahdi. Blunt's diary of December 22 notes their meeting, and also the fact that Blunt did not at first know the identity of the self-styled agent:

> I had an interview with a so-called agent of the Mahdi, whom Ismail Jowdat has brought to England. There is a kind of committee here in London of Oriental sympathizers with the Mahdi, consisting of thirty persons, who meet every night at a room they have hired for the purpose. Ibrahim . . . assured me there would be no difficulty in my going to the Mahdi. . . . Mohammed Obeyd, he said, Arabi's right-hand man, is now the Mahdi's general, and of course would receive me well. He made his escape after Tel-el-Kebir to Tripoli, and thence to the Soudan. The Mahdi also knows me well by name. I should have to go by Constantinople, but arrangements would be made so as to assure me of a quick reception there. The whole thing would take just six weeks.[27]

When publishing this diary entry, Blunt adds the note: "The report of Mohammed Bey Obeyd's having escaped to the Soudan was long prevalent. But it is certain now that he was killed at Tel-el-Kebir."[28] Whether it was this report that made Muwailihī and Jamāl ad-Dīn so cavalier in giving out assurances of good treatment by the Mahdi, who was intensely suspicious of Europeans, or if it was sheer bravado, is unclear.

On January 1, 1885, Blunt noted that Ibrāhīm

> turns out to be no other than Ibrahim Bey Moelhy who was Ismail's private secretary and who was expelled from Paris by Ferry's Government a month ago in deference to the Sul-

---

26 *Documents*, p. 40, docs. 160, 161.
27 Blunt, *Gordon*, pp. 354–355.
28 *Ibid.*, p. 355.

> tan's wishes. . . . It is arranged that we are to have a conference with Jemal-ed-Din at Boulogne, and they [Jaudat and Muwailihī] explained to me the nature of the Franco-Russian-Indian Conspiracy, of which Jemal-ed-Din is the head. If the Sultan does not work with him, they say they can depose him. But he will work with them. They want to force terms of peace on England. Otherwise they say there will be a revolt in India. (N. B. [Blunt's later note]—This Ibrahim El Moelhy, brother of Abd-el-Salam Pasha El Moelhy, was a well-known character who subsequently played a variety of parts in many notable intrigues both at Yildiz and Abdin [the palaces of Istanbul and Cairo]. . . . His pretence of being an "agent of the Mahdi" had however very little reality, Jemal-ed-Din alone having influence in that direction.)[29]

Why Blunt was able to see through Muwailihī's pretense, but not Jamāl ad-Dīn's, is hard to say. Muwailihī certainly heard from Afghānī or Jaudat of Blunt's intense interest in the question of negotiations over the Sudan. It was very likely Blunt's known concern about this subject that gave Muwailihī or his associates the idea that he should present himself to Blunt as the Mahdi's agent.

Probably acting in accord with Jamāl ad-Dīn, Muwailihī was now most concerned to ingratiate himself with Sultan Abdülhamid. To this end he wrote the Sultan a letter the existence of which in Afghānī's papers shows that it was possibly a joint effort. The letter says that Muwailihī was then in London, and stresses his devotion to the Sultan. Muwailihī says he notified the Ottoman Embassy in Paris of his orders from the ex-Khedive, Ismā'īl, to publish a newspaper in Ismā'īl's behalf in advance of publication, but that the Embassy later took fright and hence wrongly blamed him when the pro-Ismā'īl words were published. In order to prove his devotion to the Sultan, Muwailihī also says that he wrote many articles in *al-'Urwa al-Wuthqā* favoring the Sultan's government. He ends by saying that he has come to London in order to serve the Sultan with pure intent.[30]

Since Muwailihī's documents directed at the Sultan with claims of influence on and writing for *al-'Urwa al-Wuthqā* were sent to Jamā ad-Dīn, it must be assumed either that these stories are true or that Jamāl ad-Dīn had agreed to Muwailihī's making such claims.

---

29 *Ibid.*, pp. 357–358.
30 *Ibid.*, pp. 40–41; doc. 162.

Afghānī may have wished to stress the utility of his newspaper to the Sultan.

Muwailihī's letter from London appealing to the Sultan, probably supported by Ismā'īl Jaudat, had remarkably quick results, considering that Muwailihī had just been expelled from France at Ottoman request. In February 1885, the head of the Sultan's privy purse confidentially sent Muwailihī a check for £50, drawn on the Ottoman Bank in London. The covering letter says that Muwailihī on receipt of this fifty pounds should come to Istanbul immediately and says that Ismā'īl Jaudat's intervention has been made known to the Sultan.[31]

According to a well-documented biography by Muwailihī's grandson, Muwailihī followed Afghānī's advice and in London edited Arabic newspapers favoring Sultan Abdülhamid. The Sultan sent Muwailihī an invitation via the Ottoman Ambassador to London to come to Istanbul. Muwailihī was surprised at this sudden change on the Sultan's part and suspected a trap. He therefore sent his son Muḥammad from England to Istanbul to learn the true situation, and he himself traveled there only some months later, after receiving reassuring information from his son.[32]

The next news comes again from Blunt's diary. According to his entry of January 3, Ḥalīm must have got word that Ismā'īl Jaudat was meddling in matters that had nothing to do with the purpose for which he had been sent to London—to provide evidence against Khedive Taufīq. Blunt records then that "Jowdat has got a letter from Halim Pasha's son, ordering him back to Constantinople, and warning him against mixing himself up with Irishmen or Hindus, as such a course might compromise the Prince."[33] Jaudat did return to Istanbul, and the first news of him there comes in March 1885.

Meanwhile, late in January Gordon's forces at Khartoum were defeated and Gordon killed, and the Liberal Government was under considerable pressure to avenge Gordon, though more sober spirits realized that this would be exceedingly difficult and that it would

31 *Ibid.*, p. 71, doc. 235. The Persian translation in the *Documents* is not an exact rendering of the Turkish original in the Majlis Library, which is summarized here

32 Biography from *ar-Risāla*, no. 250, April 15, 1938, translated in G. Widmer, special issue of *Die Welt des Islams*, III, 2 (1954), on Ibrāhīm Muwailihī. This biography also contains details on Muwailihī's expulsion from France, including journalistic opposition to his summary exile at Ottoman request.

33 Blunt, *Gordon*, p. 358.

be wiser to try to arrange a truce with the Mahdi. Beginning in February 1885, Blunt got his first indications that the Gladstone government might be interested in using him and his Muslim friends for negotiations with the Mahdi, and he immediately involved Jamāl ad-Dīn. On February 19 Blunt records:

> Labouchere sent word to say he wanted to know Ismail Jowdat's address, and I called on him to-day. He tells me Herbert Gladstone has been at him to try and find out a way of communicating with the Mahdi. . . . Herbert Gladstone is used by his father as a go-between, and communicates with the Irish through Labouchere. . . . I promised him to put the Government in communication with the Mahdi's agents whenever they like.
>
> *20th Feb.*—Labouchere writes that he has seen Herbert Gladstone again, and wants me to advise the Mahdi to constitute some one his regular agent by sending him credentials. I had already thought of doing this, and I had another long talk with him about it. The essential, he says, is that the thing should not be known, as the Government could never carry a proposal through the House to employ me in treating. But all the same they would like to treat. . . .
>
> Ibrahim Bey called again, and I told him I thought it better he should not come back to James Street [Blunt's house] for the present, as it might compromise us, that the Government were in a fair way to treat and that it would not do to frighten them. He expressed his willingness to go to Suakin on a mission if required; and perhaps some day we may use him in this way.[34]

Probably with the Sudan negotiations in mind, Blunt then went to Paris and saw Jamāl ad-Dīn. On February 25, after talking with Sanua and Jamāl ad-Dīn, Blunt recorded that he had found that dealing with the Mahdi would be more difficult since the fall of Khartoum, an event certain to raise the Mahdi's terms:

> Still, Jemal-ed-Din says distinctly that peace can be made if the English are willing, *first* to abandon the Soudan, *second*, to hand over Saukin to the Sultan, *third* to use their good offices to get the Italians out of Massowa, and *fourth*, to arrange with the Sultan for the establishment of Mohammedan Government in Egypt. The recall of Arabi would much

---

34 *Ibid.*, pp. 379–381.

> facilitate matters, but any popular Government in Egypt could be on friendly terms with Mohammed Ahmed [the Mahdi]. With regard to the method of treating Jemal-ed-Din says it is essential that the English Government should make the first move. The Mahdi could not under present circumstances send an Embassy to England, or even appoint him (Jemal-ed-Din) his *wakil* for that purpose. The Embassy must be sent by England, and all he can do is to forward it to its destination and recommend it as a *bona fide* mission. I asked him about Gordon's bible, which Mrs. Allnatt has been very anxious I should try and get back; but Jemal-ed-Din declines to hold out hopes of its restoration until peace is made. I begged him, however to try to obtain it, as if he succeeded it would be a great proof to our Government of his power. . . . When Sanua was gone he told me privately that he had thought over my proposals of negotiations with the Mahdi, and was sure it could be done. But he would have nothing to do with it unless the English Government would show its sincerity by employing me or someone else he could trust to represent them. Then he would introduce the mission, which must also be accompanied by a Mohammedan, to a man of high station in Egypt who was in a position to speak as to terms. He himself was not in such position, and he could not do more than indicate the way to others who would give the necessary introductions and safe-conducts to the English agent. It must, however, be distinctly arranged beforehand that the English Government should engage itself to protect the persons through whose agency the negotiations should be carried on. . . . He does not think it would be judicious to apply for Gordon's bible just now.[35]

On his return to London, Blunt wrote a letter to Gladstone that went further than Jamāl ad-Dīn had in indicating the latter's relations with the Mahdi. Since the British government was being pushed into foolishly aggressive statements that could come to no good, Blunt may have thought himself justified in overstating the likelihood of a negotiated peace. Blunt's letter to Gladstone of March 12 is only summarized in his book, and it is instructive to read the original in the Gladstone Papers. Blunt says that since the fall of Khartoum he has been in touch with Europe with those in communication with the Mahdi, and has ascertained that the road

[35] *Ibid.*, pp. 387–389.

of peaceful negotiation is still open "through the intermediary of these agents," who can indicate a person competent to treat the question with authority. The Mahdi cannot deal with Lord Wolseley or Sir Evelyn Baring (Cromer), whom he does not trust. Blunt goes on to list terms that might be acceptable to the Mahdi, as gleaned from his conversations, and these terms are essentially those Blunt's diary records from the mouth of Jamāl ad-Dīn. "I am further authorized to say that the services of an Arab gentleman of great political intelligence are offered, who undertakes immediately to convey either to Osman Digna's or the Mahdi's camp any explanations of the English attitude toward the Soudanese which Her Majesty's Government may desire to make." Ibrāhīm Muwailihī, whose offer to make such a trip is recorded in Blunt's diary, is intended. Blunt concludes by saying that, although he does not wish to impose his own mediation, "I still consider that my presence would materially add to its chances of success." In any case, someone must be appointed who is not considered unfriendly to Muslim interests.[36]

The minutes on this letter by Hamilton, Gladstone's private secretary, suggest that Blunt might be made use of and that the matter should be followed up. Hamilton wrote back to Blunt asking why the Mahdi, if he did not wish to deal with Wolseley and Baring, did not send his own representative or a direct communication of his views.[37] Blunt answered that the Mahdi could hardly send a man unless he had some idea of terms and was sure he would be well received, and that he was suggesting only preliminaries to negotiations. Blunt goes on:

> Perhaps under the circs: the best course to pursue might be to give safe conduct to the Arab gentleman I spoke of in my former letter and to allow him to explain matters to the Mahdi at Khartoum and arrange there for the despatch of a regular mission. It is obvious however that the English government alone can guarantee his safe passage through the English and Egyptian lines and that without some knowledge of its ideas he wd be at a great disadvantage . . . in any case his journey to Khartoum cd not but be of use. I may add that I know him to be a man of enlightened ideas and one whose influence can be trusted to be all on the side

36 Gladstone Papers, XXV (British Museum Add. MS 44, 110), Blunt to Gladstone, March 12, 1885.

37 Blunt, *Gordon*, p. 597.

> of peace, and I know that he has or had lately, complete confidence in his ability to succeed.[38]

In his minutes, Gladstone addresses Lord Hartington, saying he did not see why the Mahdi should not be allowed to make his proposals to the British Government or why "the Arab Gentleman, if his character be only certified, sh[oul]d not be allowed to carry this message to the Mahdi." Later notes say that Lord Wolseley has instructions to forward any overtures from the Mahdi, but if the Mahdi does not know this it might be possible for the Arab Gentleman to go through British lines to tell him, but the Government "would require to be satisfied as to this gentleman's character and intentions."[39] Hamilton wrote to Blunt to this effect on March 21. Blunt responded to Gladstone on March 24, saying he did not think this answer was definite enough for his contacts to proceed on, and asking for a personal interview in which he could explain his plans and the grounds for anticipating its success. He said, however, that he would convey the government's message to his contacts.[40] Gladstone's minutes say that he does not see that the message is indefinite, or what more Blunt can propose to discuss. Hamilton answered in these terms, and Blunt replied on March 31, saying that they had wanted the Arab gentleman to be in a position to explain the British government's position. He adds that he is going abroad soon and can arrange to see these people further and even arrange for them to send someone to Khartoum, but he must have more to tell them. Blunt was very careful never to name any of the Muslims involved, perhaps realizing that they might be known in an unpleasant way to the British Government. In response to Gladstone's insistence on assurances about the character and purposes of the man involved, Blunt now wrote: "With regard to the Arab Gentleman's character I am afraid you must take my word for it that he is a suitable person. He is not a soldier or a fanatic or anything else that cd be dangerous in a military sense, but a man of more than ordinary good sense and one whose education and interests as well as instincts guarantee his using his influence on the side of a civilized solution." He again asked to see Gladstone, without result.[41]

---

38 Gladstone Papers, XXV, Blunt to Hamilton, March 16, 1885.

39 *Ibid.*, minutes.

40 *Ibid.*, Blunt to Gladstone, March 24, 1885; and Blunt, *Gordon*, pp. 597–598.

41 Gladstone Papers, XXV, minutes on March 24 letter, and Blunt to Hamilton, March 31, 1885.

On April 2 Hamilton replied that the object of the government was the security of Egypt and the freedom of the Sudan, that the Mahdi had sent no communication, and if these objects were not known to the Mahdi steps could be taken to communicate them to him.[42] In response, Blunt said he would transmit this statement to the Sudanese agents, hoping that one would agree to go to communicate with the Mahdi, though there might be suspicions of British goals expressed in such general terms, and there would have to be further discussion of details before the messenger was actually sent.[43]

At this point Blunt went to Paris, and his diary of April 4 records that he read Jamāl ad-Dīn "the whole of my correspondence with Downing Street. He approved the line taken, but insists that the English Government must write a letter to the Mahdi for Ibrahim to carry. He will think the matter over, however, and decide in a day or two."[44] Another meeting between Blunt and Jamāl ad-Dīn is recorded on April 7, and its results may be seen in a letter from Blunt to Gladstone on April 8. This letter refers to Jamāl ad-Dīn, without naming him, as "the Mahdi's principal agent in Europe," and says he was satisfied with the terms of negotiation Blunt suggested to the British government (hardly a surprise, since Afghānī had originally suggested them). Blunt further reports to Gladstone that

> the Mahdi's principal agent is prepared to send the Arab gentleman as bearer of a communication stating that England's policy is one of "freedom for the Sudan and security for Egypt" [the government's phrase], and he assures me that the Mahdi will in turn despatch a mission of peace to England, which may be expected to arrive not later than September. The Arab gentleman will, moreover, if the Government is willing, arrange in the interval for an armistice, for the better treatment of captives, and for immunity for such tribes as may have joined the English arms. . . .
>
> From all I heard yesterday I am satisfied that it depends wholly now upon the Government to prolong the Mahdi's hostility, or change it into friendship; and I therefore await with much hope your answer to this letter.[45]

---

42 Blunt, *Gordon*, p. 599.
43 Gladstone Papers, XXV (*loc. cit.*), Blunt to Hamilton, April 3, 1885.
44 Blunt, *Gordon*, p. 409.
45 *Ibid.*, pp. 600–601.

To this letter Hamilton replied on April 11, indicating that Gladstone could do no more than he had, and that it was difficult for the government to deal with Blunt on matters at all related to Egypt, whose ruler Blunt openly opposed.[46] On April 13, just before returning to England, Blunt saw Jamāl ad-Dīn again, and, as Blunt's diary records: "I read him a new and unsatisfactory letter I received last night from Downing Street. He insists that the Government must write a letter to the Mahdi if they want him to treat; and he says he will come over to England if necessary to arrange about it, if only I will guarantee his not being arrested there. I told him there was no danger of arrest, but his experience in India has made him suspicious of the English Government."[47]

On April 14 Blunt wrote to Gladstone from London saying "The Mahdi's agent is ready now to send the messenger whenever it suits you to give him the necessary facilities. But he has impressed very strongly and repeatedly upon me the necessity there is of his having a *written* message in Arabic to deliver."[48] Hamilton replied saying that Gladstone could not draw a distinction between Egypt and the Sudan and hence found it difficult to communicate with Blunt on the question. He adds that the government "has received no application from any agent of the Mahdi to be allowed a pass through the British lines . . . I cannot say with what response such an application might meet."[49] Another letter from Hamilton is not printed by Blunt, but is mentioned in his diary. It reached Blunt on April 23, and Blunt saw it as giving a further opening for correspondence. Blunt consulted Muwailihī about it and records: "He tells me the French are sending a secret mission to the Mahdi, *via* Tripoli, and thinks I might hint this to Downing Street."[50] Whatever the truth of the story of a French mission, Blunt did make such a hint in a letter to Hamilton the next day, where, among other things, he said "I think you hardly appreciate the difficulty I have had in convincing these people that England cd under any possible circs: be friendly to them, and if you now hold back they will certainly make their terms with others."[51] To this Hamilton simply replied that his last note was not intended to invite further remarks, but to in-

46 *Ibid.*, p. 601.
47 *Ibid.*, p. 411.
48 *Ibid.*, p. 602.
49 *Ibid.*, p. 603.
50 *Ibid.*, p. 420.
51 Gladstone Papers, XXV (*loc. cit.*), Blunt to Hamilton, April 24, 1885.

dicate that under altered circumstances the correspondence must close.[52]

Blunt's *Gordon at Khartoum* includes several conjectures as to why Gladstone had appeared at first to encourage his mediation through his Muslim acquaintances, and had then closed the matter so firmly. One of Blunt's friends considered the whole affair "humbug" on Gladstone's part, while Blunt himself thought it was probably Cromer's influence that decided Gladstone against it. The Gladstone papers contain no decisive evidence on the point, but Blunt records that a mutual acquaintance said, "Gladstone explains his rejection of my offers of negotiation by saying he does not believe those who made them through me are really in communication with the Mahdi."[53] Though this point does not enter Gladstone's minutes on the correspondence, it may be that Gladstone had indeed figured out what appears to be the true situation—that Jamāl ad-Dīn and Muwailihī's claims of contact with the Mahdi had no basis in reality.

Jamāl ad-Dīn and the Sultan

WHILE ALL this fruitless letter writing about the Mahdi was going on, Jamāl ad-Dīn in Paris, aided by Ismā'īl Jaudat from Istanbul, was carrying out other plans designed to put himself in relations with the Ottoman Sultan. Jaudat probably reached Istanbul early in March, as Blunt records on March 25 that Ḥalīm had written to Ibrāhīm al-Muwailihī saying that Jaudat, on his arrival at Istanbul, was ordered to the Palace. "There he was kept twelve days and made to draw up a report of everything he had seen, heard, or done while in London, and then was sent home and kept there under arrest. Such is the Sultan's way."[54]

---

52 Blunt, *Gordon*, p. 603.
53 *Ibid.*, p. 436.
54 *Ibid.*, p. 405.

More important is a series of letters from Ismā'īl Jaudat in Istanbul to Afghānī in Paris included in the *Documents.* Unfortunately, as usual, only the letters *to* Afghānī are there, and we must speculate on what Afghānī was writing and saying. From the first letter included, however, it appears that Afghānī had already written to Jaudat and had some fairly clear plans in mind, which involved trying to establish relations with the Sultan. This first letter from Jaudat to Afghānī is dated March 24, 1885. Jaudat says: "The letters that you wrote to the Sultan via the post have been translated into Turkish and given to him. He asked me about you and I told him what was appropriate. The affair has reached the point that in order to bring you to Istanbul they will either send me . . . (without anyone knowing) . . . or they will send Ḥusain Efendi, the Hyderabad Consul, who is close to the Caliph, knows several languages, and is a partisan of Islamic unity."[55]

Jaudat continues that he will inform Afghānī of whatever happens regarding this matter. He says that they have got Muwailihī pardoned and invited to Istanbul, and that he has sent Muwailihī the money to come, and awaits him. Jaudat warns Afghānī not to say anything about this, for fear of Ismā'īl's intrigues. He finishes by saying that the trunk Afghānī sent by Messagerie Maritime had arrived and that it was apparently filled with books on Eastern problems.

This letter helps explain the money sent to Muwailihī in London and the request to him that he come right away. The reference to letters from Afghānī to the Sultan is also significant. Jaudat's letter suggests that Afghānī may have initiated the idea that the Sultan should bring him to Istanbul, rather than the Sultan's being the originator of this invitation, as the standard biographies state. To judge from Jaudat's letter to Afghānī, Afghānī's letters to the Sultan plus the information given him by Jaudat had interested the Sultan to the point of talking of sending someone to bring Afghānī to Istanbul.

Jaudat's next letter to Afghānī, dated April 27, 1885, says that Afghānī's letter has arrived, and that Jaudat had communicated Afghānī's ideas (to the Sultan) via a court official. The result was that Jaudat was asked to continue corresponding with Afghānī, but that Afghānī should remain in Paris for the present, since his com-

[55] *Documents,* pp. 56–57, doc. 176. Only a Persian translation from the Arabic is given.

ing to Istanbul would give rise to political suspicions. There follows an obscure reference to Afghānī's criticism of the ineffectual behavior of someone who had been sent from Istanbul to London.[56] Probably Afghānī was reflecting Blunt's criticisms of the weak conduct of the Ottoman envoy Hasan Fehmi, who had been sent to London to discuss the Egyptian question.[57]

Jaudat then continues to discuss Afghānī's letter to him. Afghānī had said that it was time to set up relations with the Afghan government, but Jaudat says that only Afghānī himself could do this because of his influence, his origins, and his many ties to the Afghans. This suggestion is an instance where Afghānī's invented background may have been embarrassing to him, though he probably found an excuse to avoid taking up the challenge. Jaudat concludes that "our brother Ibrāhīm" (Muwailihī) has been pardoned and, if he comes, work will be given him that is worthy of him.[58]

On the subject of this invitation to Muwailihī, Blunt recorded on May 13, 1885:

> Ibrahim informed me yesterday that he had received an invitation from the Sultan, conveyed to him through Jowdat, to go to Constantinople and be one of his secretaries, and he asked my advice about accepting. He said he was very afraid of what might happen, it was such a very risky thing, Court favour, I said that, if he looked to his own interest he had better go and take the chance, but that if he really had ideas of patriotism he had better stay and be ready to carry a message when required to the Mahdi. I could not advise him; he must judge for himself. He says for the present he will stay.[59]

As noted above, Muwailihī sent his son to Istanbul to assess the situation before agreeing to go himself.

On May 16, 1885, Jaudat wrote to Afghānī saying again that his last letter had been delivered to the Sultan, who was pleased and told Jaudat to write to Afghānī. He had done so on April 27, but was worried that the letter had not arrived. At the same time Jaudat had written Ibrāhīm to come to Istanbul, and his not coming caused suspicion. Afghānī should tell him not to delay in coming. The

56 *Documents*, p. 57, doc. 177.
57 Blunt, *Gordon*, p. 361.
58 *Documents*, p. 57, doc. 177.
59 Blunt, *Gordon*, p. 434.

Sultan has ordered Jaudat to correspond with Afghānī and to ask him about the conduct of the man in London (probably Hasan Fehmi).[60]

After this there is a break in the correspondence from Jaudat preserved in the *Documents* until the fall of 1885. Meanwhile, however, momentous changes were occurring in England which raised hopes of a settlement in the Sudan and, more important, of a possible evacuation of Egypt by British troops, theoretically only in temporary occupation. The Gladstone government, under severe criticism for its conduct regarding Gordon and the Sudan, and also because of Russian victories in Merv and Panjdeh in Central Asia, fell over a minor issue. In June a minority Conservative government under Lord Salisbury came in. Blunt hoped that with Randolph Churchill at the India Office and Drummond Wolff playing an important role in foreign affairs he might be able to get across his program for Arab independence, in which direction he had helped influence these two. When he learned that Salisbury was to come into office, Blunt wrote to Jamāl ad-Dīn on June 22, "begging him to hold himself in readiness to come over here should he be wanted."[61] Blunt's early talks with Churchill and Wolff seemed to justify this optimism. On June 30 and July 6 Blunt recorded conversations with them. Beginning with Churchill, he said: "Randolph is keen also to make peace with the Mahdi, which he said would be a feather in his cap before the election. And he approved the idea of Ibrahim going as forerunner to prepare my way before me. I am to talk all this over, however, with Drummond Wolff . . . and afterwards see Lord Salisbury. . . . [Wolff] asked me about the possibility of treating with the Mahdi, and I have agreed to bring Jemal-ed-Din from Paris to talk things over with him."[62] On one part of his program, Blunt was soon disillusioned, as Salisbury made it clear that the Conservative Government would go on supporting the Khedive Taufīq and not allow any new khedive, as Blunt and the Egyptian nationalists wanted.

On July 9 Blunt records: "Ibrahim has received a letter from Jemal-ed-Din hinting that, if nothing is done in Egypt in the sense we hope for from Randolph, he will go off to Afghanistan to raise up trouble against England. I have consequently written to Wolff, urging him to get Lord Salisbury to commence negotiations with

60 *Documents*, pp. 57–58, doc. 178.
61 Blunt, *Gordon*, pp. 448–449.
62 *Ibid.*, pp. 455, 457.

the Mahdi and sending him my correspondence with Downing Street."[63] Blunt wrote offering to show the correspondence so far to Salisbury, who could carry forward the interrupted plan. In a later note Blunt points out that this led to nothing, since the Mahdi died soon after (July 1885). "But for this it is probable that Lord Salisbury would have negotiated."[64]

On July 16 Blunt records a conversation with Randolph Churchill who, as Secretary of State for India, "told me he was in great trouble to know what sort of game the Amir was playing in Afghanistan, and he asked me to try and get him information. And I offered to bring Jemal-ed-Din from Paris, and talk that matter and Egypt over with him. He was much pleased at this, and said he would see him at my house."[65]

Responding to Blunt's invitation, Jamāl ad-Dīn came to England late in July 1885, as Blunt's guest. On July 22, before Jamāl ad-Dīn arrived, Blunt went to see Churchill at the India Office, and the latter promised to come to see Jamāl ad-Dīn the next day. Blunt told Churchill something of Jamāl ad-Dīn's history, and added: " 'He is in the black book . . . of every one here, and an enemy of England. But if he was not he would be of no use to us.' "[66] The next day Churchill came as promised, and Blunt gives what purports to be an exact report of their conversation. At one point, Jamāl ad-Dīn said:

> There are three reasons why the Mohammedans of India have hated you more than the Russians: Firstly, because you destroyed the Empire of Delhi; secondly, because you give no salaries to the *imams* and *muezzins* and keepers of the mosques, which the Russians are careful to do; and you have resigned the Wakaf property and do not repair the sacred buildings. . . . And, thirdly, because you give no high offices of rank in the army to Mohammedans. The Russians do this. . . . England has done more harm to us than Russia, but Russia is now more dangerous. If the Russians remain . . . at Merv still five years, there will be no more Afghanistan and no more Persia and no more Anatolia and no more India. . . . You must make an alliance with Islam, with the Afghans, the Persians, the Turks, the Egyptians, the Arabs; you must drive the Russians back out of Merv to the Caspian

63 *Ibid.*, p. 458.
64 *Ibid.*, p. 605.
65 *Ibid.*, p. 461.
66 *Ibid.*, p. 464.

> Sea. To make friends with the Mohammedans you must leave Egypt. . . . With a Mohammedan government in Egypt the Mahdi is not a danger. . . . if the Russians stay five years at Merv it will be too late; you should attack them not through Afghanistan but by the other side; then the Mollahs would preach a *jehad to* join you against the Russians.[67]

Jamāl ad-Dīn encouraged the British to declare war on Russia, and to get a Muslim *jihād* in favor of the British; while in 1887 he asked the Russians to declare war on the British, which he said would be followed by a Muslim rising in India. This might look like simple opportunism, with Afghānī encouraging whichever side he thought he could influence. In fact, however, the case seems somewhat different. It would seem that in Afghānī's thinking it was rather incidental which side the Muslims fought on as long as their sentiments for holy war could be aroused. He thought that a war between Russia and Great Britain, whose interests clashed in the Muslim world, could arm the Muslims; bring them into an alliance with whichever side seemed to promise more gains; and ultimately strengthen the Muslim position. Though the idea had elements of fantasy, it was not as wild as it might now appear: it was a time when war between England and Russia was widely anticipated and when both sides were concerned over the loyalty of their Muslim subjects. In general Jamāl ad-Dīn was hostile to British policy and tried to get help from the French and Russians. But since Blunt had given him entrée into British ruling circles, and had led him to believe that men like Churchill and Wolff might influence governmental policy in favor of the independence of Egypt, it is not surprising that Afghānī adapted his holy war vision to make the Muslims the allies of England, rather than their enemy. His making the evacuation of Egypt a prerequisite of such an alliance is also consistent with his lasting concern over this subject. Blunt reports that Churchill expressed pleasure "with the Seyyid's frankness and justness of his views."[68]

On July 30 Wolff went to Blunt's house, and told Blunt that the government would continue to support Taufīq, and that Salisbury would not consent to 'Urābī's recall to Egypt (from exile in Ceylon), which Blunt had hoped was a serious possibility. There followed a discussion between Wolff and Jamāl ad-Dīn, reported by Blunt as follows:

---

67 *Ibid.*, pp. 466–467.
68 *Ibid.*, p. 468.

> The points Wolff principally discussed with Jemal-ed-Din were as to a possible acknowledgement by the Mahdi of the Sultan's Caliphate. This Jemal-ed-Din declared to be impossible, either for the Mahdi or his successors, but they might be got to accept each other, as the Ottoman Sultan and the Sultan of Morocco had done, if Egypt were evacuated by the English and a legal Mohammedan Government restored there. There would then be no danger from the Soudanese. . . . There ensued a long discussion about the evacuation, Wolff declaring that Bismarck had announced in writing to the Foreign Office that he should approve the French entering Egypt if we abandoned it. The French would never allow Turkish troops, and it must be occupied somehow. So it would be the French. This the Seyyid refused to believe, as he knew from Ferry and others in France that nothing of the sort would happen. In the end, however, it was agreed between Wolff and the Seyyid that, if England consented to fix a date for evacuation, an arrangement with the Sultan might be come to. There followed the Slave Trade question in the Soudan. Jemal-ed-Din said it was impossible to stop the capture of idolatrous tribes in Central Africa, but the seizure and sale of Abyssinians might be prevented by the Mahdi. He could arrange that matter and commercial relations with England and Egypt. It would not be difficult to get the Sultan to consent to reasonable arrangements for Egypt, and Jemal-ed-Din would go if necessary to Constantinople—this was my suggestion—nor would it be difficult to get the Sultan to propose Arabi's return. Wolff, however, said distinctly that nothing definite could be settled till after the elections.[69]

Wolff had been appointed to a special mission to Istanbul and Egypt to try to arrange for the eventual evacuation of British troops from Egypt, if British interests could be guaranteed. Blunt had helped convince Wolff of the usefulness of taking Muslim interests into account, and this probably explains such concern as he showed in Jamāl ad-Dīn and his Egyptian friends. On August 4 Blunt records that Wolff talked with him about Jamāl ad-Dīn's going to Istanbul, but said Afghānī was too stiff in his ideas about the Mahdi's not accepting the Sultan's caliphate. He said if he wanted Jamāl ad-Dīn he would telegraph him, through his private cipher with Churchill.[70]

---

69 *Ibid.*, pp. 474–475.
70 *Ibid.*, p. 475.

On August 5 Wolff telegraphed from Portsmouth asking to see Jamāl ad-Dīn again, and they met on August 6. Blunt records the conversation, in which he also participated, as follows:

> Wolff is quite favourable to a Turco-Perso-Afghan alliance, but says he shall not be able to talk of this with the Sultan, except incidentally, as that would be the ambassador's business, but shall have to keep to Egypt. He was very anxious to know how an accord could be made between the Sultan and the Mahdi. Would the Mahdi acknowledge the Caliphate? Jemal-ed-Din said it would not be necessary to decide or even raise that point just yet. The thing the Sultan would really care for was a fixing of a limit of time for the English occupation. Wolff said that that could be done. . . . Next there was a good deal of talk as to whether Jemal-ed-Din should go to Constantinople while Wolff was there, the principal point being as to whether the Sultan would understand it rightly. Jemal-ed-Din said that the Sultan knew him only as an enemy of English policy, and, unless Wolff explained the position, he would fancy Jemal-ed-Din had come to Constantinople to counteract Wolff. Wolff, however, said that it would be difficult for him to protect Jemal-ed-Din or seem to have anything to do with him. . . . Wolff explained that he should not tell Lord Salisbury anything about the Seyyid or his arrangements with me. "The reason I am sent," he said, "is that I am ready to take responsibilities of this sort on my shoulders which other men might refuse. . . ."[71]

That Wolff really did act frequently on his own responsibility, without telling Salisbury what he was doing, is amply indicated by his later behavior in Iran from 1888 to 1890.[72]

Wolff left on his mission shortly after this conversation, and on August 12 sent a cipher telegram to Churchill, the text of which was given to Blunt, who reproduces it as follows: "I think it would be well for Jemal-ed-din Afghani to come. Have you (any objection?), [words omitted in ciphering] if involving no responsibility or complicity on my part, and if it can be done without his coming into collision with Turkish authorities. . . ."[73] On August 14 Blunt told

---

71 Blunt, *Gordon*, pp. 476–477.

72 Cf. Nikki R. Keddie, *Religion and Rebellion in Iran: The Tobacco Protest of 1891–1892* (London. 1966), pp. 35–39.

73 Blunt, *Gordon*, pp. 614, 479.

Churchill Jamāl ad-Dīn would leave at once if Wolff met certain conditions; and Blunt's diary further records:

> Randolph with his usual quickness seized the points at once, and wrote a telegram to Wolff something as follows: "Jemal-ed-Din starts for Constantinople on Sunday. He says, however, he is known to the Sultan only as the enemy of England, and it would be necessary to give the Sultan a hint that he is now our friend. He hopes also that you will not enter on the Egyptian question with the Sultan separately from the larger question of a Mohammedan alliance. With regard to this last he believes he can be of great service to you."
>
> I also saw Ibrahim and wish I had seen him before, for he is a great support to me with the Seyyid, and is bolder than he is. I am for their starting together at once, and not waiting for an answer for Wolff. One never knows what changes of mind may take place, and the ball is at our foot now and we must play with courage. My fear is lest Wolff should be scared by the telegram which the Seyyid insisted on. If I had my way, he should have started without conditions; Wolff could not refuse him protection when he arrived.[74]

As Blunt seems here to realize, a main factor holding Jamāl ad-Dīn back was fear of how he might be treated by the Sultan once he arrived, and he did not want to leave without a promise of British protection.

Blunt's fears were confirmed when, on August 15, Wolff telegraphed from Budapest saying: "From something I have heard it would be well for Jemal-ed-deen not to leave England till I can telegraph to you from Constantinople."[75] Blunt failed to persuade Churchill to allow Afghānī to start off right away and to telegraph Wolff that his message had arrived too late. In a later and fanciful note, Blunt says: "I have always been of opinion that Wolff's change of mind on this occasion caused him the success of his mission, and that its ultimate failure was due to his having commenced it on the common lines of English diplomacy without that moral support which Seyyid Jemal-ed-Din could have given him both at Constantinople and elsewhere with the secret societies."[76] On August 27

[74] *Ibid.*, p. 480.
[75] *Ibid.*, p. 615.
[76] *Ibid.*, pp. 481–482.

Churchill's private secretary, Moore, read to Blunt an extract of a letter from Wolff:

> It was to the effect that he was in such a delicate position in regard to his mission that he dared not appear to know Jemal-ed-Din. Jemal-ed-Din, he said, was opposed to the Sultan's Caliphate in the Soudan, and if he acknowledged him as a friend, the Sultan might think that he had some design on his spiritual pretensions. For this reason he dared not mention his name. This is all nonsense. The question of the Sultan's Caliphate need never be raised, and Jemal-ed-Din is not known as its opponent. On the contrary his newspaper was always loud on the Sultan's rights. The Seyyid, however, declined to go to Constantinople without some acknowledgement from Wolff, because he says it would ruin his influence everywhere if the Sultan were to shut the door in his face.[77]

One may believe in the frankness of the last avowal.

Also indicative of Jamāl ad-Dīn's efforts to ingratiate himself with Sultan Abdülhamid are two Arabic letters from London written by Afghānī's friend Muḥammad Wahbī, a brother of Ibrāhīm Muwailihī, to Shaikh Ẓāfir Madanī, one of the Sultan's leading religious advisers, whose influence went beyond religion into politics. Muḥammad Wahbī knew him, according to the information contained in these recently uncovered letters.[78]

The first and more important letter is dated August 5, 1885. In it Wahbī begins by apologizing for writing before he had an answer to an earlier letter, but says he is writing now because of important and strange events—namely Jamāl ad-Dīn al-Afghānī's coming to London and dealing with British statesmen, after he had been known for hostility to the British. Wahbī stresses Afghānī's interviews with Churchill and Wolff, saying "the great men in power visit him with respect and exaltation. On the very day of his coming, two hours after his arrival, there came to him . . . the Minister for India, Lord Churchill. . . . Now visits to him are proceeding by her important statesmen, especially Mr. Wolff, who will continue his visits." Wahbī says that Jamāl ad-Dīn is helping Muslim states and particularly the Ottoman government against the hostile policy that has hitherto been

---

77 *Ibid.*, p. 485.

78 Original Arabic letters found by Hamid Algar. The translation is mine.

followed by the British government. The entire letter is a discussion of Jamāl ad-Dīn in London, and is clearly directed toward creating a favorable attitude toward him among the Ottoman authorities. The letter also suggests that Ẓāfir Madanī himself write to Afghānī for more details. He also warns against the Wolff mission to Istanbul.

The second letter, dated August 29, notes that Shaikh Ẓāfir has not answered his letter, warns him again against Wolff, and says Jamāl ad-Dīn is still working to stop English greed in the East. Wahbī asks that the Sultan and leading Ottoman statesmen be informed of what he has written. Whether these letters were answered we do not know, but since both letters speak of lack of answers it is probable that they were not.

The complicated and ultimately fruitless affair of Jamāl ad-Dīn and the Wolff mission was not yet finished. On September 4, Blunt records: "Ibrahim Bey has received a letter from Ismail Jowdat once more pressing him to come and see the Sultan. It has been decided he shall go. The Sultan has heard of Jemal-ed-Din having seen one of the Ministers, and has sent for Ibrahim to find out what it is all about. He wants Jemal-ed-Din too, but the Seyyid says he will wait till the Sultan sends for him. For Ibrahim there will be no danger, and I will put him in communication with Wolff and let Randolph know."[79]

On September 6 Blunt records that Ibrāhīm Muwailihī had left the night before for Istanbul, whereas Jamāl ad-Dīn would stay in London. The *Documents* include translations into Persian of several subsequent letters from Ibrāhīm to London. On September 9 he wrote to Blunt's address saying he had reached Vienna, and hoped that Lord Churchill would write to Wolff as soon as possible about him; that this was very important and that it would be best if Churchill could telegraph.[80] In another letter from Vienna, postmarked September 12, Muwailihī reiterates the need for Churchill to write Wolff that "I was sent by you." It is unclear whether Blunt or Jamāl ad-Dīn was the addressee, but it was probably Blunt.[81]

Muwailihī wrote to London to his brother Muḥammad Wahbī Bey in a letter postmarked September 19, 1884, the first letter since his arrival in Istanbul. He says: "The Ottoman officials ordered me to write all I did in London, so that they would gain confidence. I am

---

[79] Blunt, *Gordon*, pp. 486–487.
[80] *Documents*, p. 36, doc. 149; Blunt, *Gordon*, p. 487.
[81] *Documents*, 36–37, doc. 150.

with Ismā'īl Bey [Jaudat] and I do not know your situation. As I perceive, the Sayyid and I will have a high position with them."[82] On September 23, Blunt recorded: "A letter has arrived from Ibrahim giving an account of himself. He is staying with Jowdat, has been to the Palace, and is to see the Sultan after Beiram. They are only angry with him for not coming before. The Sultan is sending a man to Jemal-ed-Din for consultation."[83] Blunt does not specify who the man sent by the Sultan was, but the only man from Istanbul whom he mentions as seeing Jamāl ad-Dīn after this is Münif Paşa. On September 28, Blunt records: "Munif Pasha is in London and has seen the Seyyid. He wants to see Churchill. I have written about it."[84] This was the same Münif Paşa who had been head of the Council of Education and had known Jamāl ad-Dīn during his 1869–1871 trip to Istanbul. He was now Minister of Education, having survived the change in governmental tone under Abdülhamid, and it is possible that his former relations with Jamāl ad-Dīn made him seem a good man to send to talk with him. Unfortunately there is no record of what passed between them. The *Documents* do contain three Persian letters (to Afghānī) listed as from "Muhammad Tāhir Munīf." They are written from Vichy, shortly before Münif saw Afghānī in London. The first is addressed to Paris, and dated September 5, 1885, expressing Münif's regret that he did not see Afghānī in Paris because Afghānī had gone to London. The second, addressed to London, expresses a strong desire to see Afghānī. The third, dated September 22, is in answer to a letter of the Sayyid and says Münif will come to London.[85] The subsequent correspondence from Afghānī's friends in Istanbul makes it unclear whether Münif was actually sent by the Sultan to see Afghānī.

To meet the Sultan's demands and to justify his own behavior, Muwailihī wrote a long autobiographical memorandum addressed to the Sultan shortly after his arrival in Istanbul. The first part of this memorandum is interesting for what it reveals of Muwailihī's participation in the ex-Khedive Ismā'īl's plots first to get rid of the mixed ministry in Egypt in 1879 and later to regain the khedival throne. Much of the memo concerns Jamāl ad-Dīn, and, since a copy of it was in Jamāl ad-Dīn's papers, it is reasonable to assume that Jamāl ad-Dīn

---

82 *Ibid.*, p. 37, doc. 151.
83 Blunt, *Gordon*, p. 488.
84 *Ibid.*, p. 489.
85 *Documents*, p. 33, docs. 133–135.

approved, and possibly even drafted, this part. After telling of his own relations with Ismā'īl until 1883, Muwailihī says:

> During my stay in Livorno, Sayyid Jamāl ad-Dīn al-Afghānī arrived from India in Paris. As we had been friendly during his stay in Egypt, a correspondence between us started. We agreed about the publication of the journal *al-'Urwa al-Wuthqā*. Sayyid Jamāl ad-Dīn published it in Paris, defending in it the interests of the Empire and the Muslims, urging Islamic unity under the leadership of the Commander of the Faithful. The appearance of this journal with this direction mortified the ex-Khedive, as it was opposed to his goals, thwarting his aspirations. . . . After a while Ḥusain Pāshā at-Tūnīsī . . . demanded I should edit No. 4 of the journal *al-Ittihād* [on behalf of Ismā'īl] in Paris, and assured me he would not promote its distribution and the purpose was merely to use its name. . . . Then I informed Sayyid Jamāl ad-Dīn in detail. He immediately took whatever was printed of the journal, and kept it lest any of it should be distributed.

Muwailihī goes on that Ismā'īl exculpated himself and blamed Muwailihī for publication against the Sultan, as a result of which Muwailihī was made to leave France through the influence of the Ottoman Embassy. He goes on with an exaggerated account of Afghānī's influence that may emanate from Afghānī's pen:

> Sayyid Jamāl ad-Dīn wrote to me that "it would be most appropriate for you to go to London and expose in the press the true situation, how the ex-Khedive betrayed you." I proceeded there, and met there Ismā'īl Efendi Jaudat, and I saw he was so loyal to the Sublime Porte that I felt induced to write a memorandum to this Holy Presence to secure its pleasure. Later I met Mr. Blunt and saw that his policy was directed to supporting the Porte. . . . When Sayyid Jamāl ad-Dīn learned thereof he approved of dedication to that service that may hurt the ex-Khedive, and informed me he was active therein in the East. He had some contacts with the Conservative Party in London, and I made efforts to strengthen them. Then Lord Churchill arrived from India. He had gone there with instructions of Sayyid Jamāl ad-Dīn to some Indian princes, as that trip was made by him in his private capacity. What the Lord learned of Sayyid Jamāl ad-Dīn's influence among the Muslims there strengthened

> the contacts between the Sayyid and the Conservative Party upon his arrival. . . . When [Gladstone's] cabinet fell, the new cabinet summoned Sayyid Jamal ad-Din to London [!] He wrote that he would come only if his arrival would guarantee the interests of the Muslims. Then they sent an emissary with whom he arrived. On the day he arrived, Lord Churchill visited him, then Lord Salisbury [!] Visits were exchanged between him and the other ministers. This caused a delay in my reporting to the Porte what was going on. They asked Sayyid Jamāl ad-Dīn about the ideas of the Muslims in India and Afghanistan in relation to the Russian government.

What follows consists almost entirely of purported quotations from Jamāl ad-Dīn, directed first at his British questioners, and then at the Ottoman government. Much of it tallies with Blunt's reports, and it certainly represents what Afghānī wished to convey. Afghānī is reported as advising the British ministers to secure Indian and Afghan friendships through a "religious bond," and:

> The only religious bond is to secure the pleasure of the Sublime Porte. . . . He persuaded them. This helped to set up Mr. Wolff's mission. Further he said to them: This satisfaction must be recorded, publicized among Indians and Afghans. . . . You have to transmit it orally but the time is not propitious, especially as the Russian power has its spies throughout India under various guises, and it will destroy what you are building and make your acts seem doubtful. You must have an immediate way to record the satisfaction [of the Porte] beyond doubt. I think this can be attained only if the Muslim ulama will have a committee or representation in India, in some such manner as may be agreed upon. . . . You do not have to have any apprehensions, as the Porte has no territory contiguous with India. He persuaded some of the ministers. The Sayyid suspended the further persuasion of the rest until I submit this matter to the Imperial See. He is waiting at present.

Citing what Afghānī told Wolff about Egypt, Muwailihī continued:

> The Sayyid told them: You must delimit the term of evacuation of Egypt, and without that you will not be able at all to persuade the Muslims in India and Afghanistan that you gave satisfaction to the Ottoman Empire. They said: We

> fear the French will succeed us there in Egypt, so that we are compelled to impose upon it a semi-protectorate for a while. The Sayyid said: To impose a protectorate upon Egypt out of fear of France is a pretext for France to impose a protectorate on Tripoli out of fear of Italy, and also a pretext for Austria in Ottoman domains, out of fear of Russia, and so on. . . . Furthermore, the imposition of a protectorate on Egypt kindles the Sudanese movement and is bound to cause the whole population of Egypt to join that movement. . . . Your cannons' muzzles cannot extinguish this movement, nor will arms subdue it. Only the name of the Sultan-Caliph will. On the day of his departure, Mr. Wolff came again, and had a long discussion on the subject. Mr. Wolff became convinced there should be no protectorate.
>
> Sayyid Jamāl ad-Dīn submits to the Sublime Porte that the British need the Ottoman Empire as they need to preserve their possessions in the face of the enemy. Should the British pursue a policy of giving satisfaction to the Porte, they will find no foreign power opposed to it. He submits that if an agreement is reached with the British about the timing of their evacuation of Egypt, the Sudanese problem will at once dissolve in the name of His Majesty, the Caliph, Commander of the Faithful, without recourse to arms. He will carry out this service upon receipt of the Caliph's approval thereof.[86]

Afghānī's attempt to magnify his present and potential utility to the Ottoman Sultan seems to have elicited no significant response, although Afghānī's Istanbul correspondents continued to write him for advice and generally tried to present prospects for their influence in an optimistic light.

On September 28, 1885, Muwailihī wrote to Jamāl ad-Dīn that he had presented his story, and, along with Ismā'īl Jaudat, had taken papers for delivery to the Sultan. They were now awaiting a summons from the Sultan-Caliph, although the petitions would have to be translated first. Ismā'īl Jaudat was in contact with Wolff, and wanted instructions from Afghānī on how to behave toward Wolff. Regarding others of Afghānī's former friends and disciples, Muwailihī continued: "I came across letters between Ḥalīm Pāshā and Shūbāshī and Shaikh 'Abduh and copied them for you, as enclosed; also the deceitful Abū Naẓẓāra. I found out that Muḥammad 'Abduh

86 *Ibid.*, photos 101–105.

took 80,000 francs in your name from Tunis, and Khair ad-Dīn subscribed 5,000 francs and in the same way Rustam Pāshā contributed also 5,000 francs. Khair ad-Dīn promised that he will try to procure the list. The people of Tunis paid only because of your name and your newspaper. Write us of the work you have done until now so that I can tell the Istanbul government."[87] Muwailihī ends with an appeal for money. 'Abduh's and Shūbāshī's correspondence with Ḥalīm which Muwailihī copied for Afghānī was summarized in the preceding chapter. The December 16, 1884, letter from "Abū Naẓẓāra" (Sanua) in Paris to Ismā'īl Jaudat in London, copied by Muwailihī, is summarized above in this chapter.

Further brief letters from Jaudat and Muwailihī are more obscure in their references than the above. They contain appeals for money and one says that people in Istanbul had forgotten about Wolff and England.[88]

An explication of the remark that people in Istanbul had forgotten about Wolff and British questions is found in Blunt's diary of October 7, recording a letter to him from Muwailihī, after first noting a conversation with Randolph Churchill, who

> told me something of Wolff's progress. Wolff had come to the conclusion that it was very necessary to take the Arab party at Constantinople into account, and was surprised that Ibrahim had not been to see him yet. I said he had probably been forbidden by the Sultan; and to-day a letter came from Ibrahim saying he had sent in a full report of his doings in England to the Sultan, and about myself among the rest. But the Sultan had forgotten all about Wolff and England and everything but Roumelia.[89]

On the following day, October 8, Blunt records another fanciful conversation of Jamāl ad-Dīn:

> A long talk with Jemal-ed-Din about prospects at Constantinople and about the Caliphate. He is for the Mahdi or the Mahdi's successor taking the Sultan's place, or the Sherif Own, or the Imam of Sanaa—any of these he thought might now take the lead. But Constantinople must remain the seat

[87] *Ibid.*, photos 98–99. The enclosed letters are catalogued in *Documents*, p. 77, doc. 308, where the letter from Abū Naẓẓāra (Sanua) is not identified; the originals are in the Majlis Library collection.

[88] *Ibid.*, p. 38, doc. 153; p. 38, doc. 154.

[89] Blunt, *Gordon*, p. 491.

> of the Caliphate, as Arabia or Africa would be mere places of exile. Amongst other things, he told me that it was he himself who had suggested to the Sherif el Huseyn to claim the Caliphate, but El Huseyn had said it was impossible without armed support, and the Arabs could never unite except in the name of religion. Now, Jemal-ed-Din is very anxious to be away again to the East. He will not go, he says, to Constantinople unless the Sultan sends for him, and we have agreed that if I do not win my election at Camberwell we will go together to the Imam of Sanaa in Yemen and raise the standard of the Caliphate, as I intended to do four years ago.[90]

Thus it was perhaps not mere idle suspicion when Sultan Abdülhamid was to show himself concerned that Afghānī was connected with schemes for an Arabian caliphate, and was worried that he was a partisan of the Mahdi, or, later, of rebels in the Yemen.

On October 9, 1885, the *Documents* record the first letter since May from Ismā'īl Jaudat to Afghānī. It says that Wolff had asked Jaudat what man had been sent from Istanbul to see Afghānī, but that Jaudat did not know if anyone had been sent.[91] An undated letter from Muwailihī to Afghānī apparently from the same period, says that Wolff said that someone had been sent to Afghānī to verify what Muwailihī had written. Wolff had also asked to see Muwailihī, but the latter would not go unless the Sultan gave permission. Later Muwailihī says he did see Wolff, who asked him whether he and Jaudat could go to Egypt again. Muwailihī says he will not go unless Afghānī sends him. Muwailihī concludes that he and Jaudat are awaiting orders from Afghānī, and that they are in bad need of money.[92]

Another long letter from Muwailihī, whose date appears to be October 24, 1885, deals with Muwailihī's further discussions with Wolff, and says that Wolff had now told Jaudat not to come with him to Egypt, and said Jaudat should be sent separately by the Sultan. Muwailihī's letter refers to Jamāl ad-Dīn's unjustified mistrust of them.[93] An October 24 letter from Jaudat says that the Sayyid should have confidence in their work.[94]

---

90 *Ibid.*, p. 492.

91 *Documents*, p. 58, doc. 179.

92 *Ibid.*, p. 39, doc. 158.

93 *Documents*, pp. 34–36, doc. 148. The pronouns are often unclear in this Persian translation, and the April date given in this translation must be wrong.

94 *Documents*, p. 58, doc. 180.

Despite these reports from his Istanbul friends, which were intended to be encouraging, Jamāl ad-Dīn soon decided he had had enough of England, where Blunt's diary reports, with an added later note:

> Jemal-ed-Din, who had been mysteriously absent for two or three days from James Street, turned up again this morning. He had left the house in consequence of a noisy disturbance that occurred in his room on Thursday between two of his Oriental friends, Wahbi Bey [Muwailihī's brother] and Abd-el-Rasul; they seem to have quarrelled over politics or religion and ended by beating each other over the heads with umbrellas. I had to beg them both to leave the house, and the Sayyid followed them. One must draw the line somewhere, and I have now suggested to the Seyyid that he should take up his quarters elsewhere; he has been three months with me in the house, the full term of Arab hospitality. (N.B. —this was the last I saw of the good Seyyid that year; he took huff at my treatment of his friends, and still more at the disappointment he had had in connection with Drummond Wolff's mission, and he left England a few days later in anger against everything English. . . . Jemal-ed-Din was a man of genius whose teaching exercised an influence hardly to be overrated on the Mohammedan reform movement of the last thirty years. I feel highly honoured at his having lived three months under my roof in England; but he was a wild man, wholly Asiatic and not easily tamed to European ways. . . . [95]

Jamāl ad-Dīn evidently telegraphed Muwailihī of his changed course and of his plan to leave England (from whence he intended to go to Russia via Iran). Muwailihī was less than enchanted, as he wrote back on November 9, 1885, objecting to Afghānī's planned departure and suggesting that he delay it. "The telegram arrived and it threw us into a state of dread. There is no way out for us. I expect you to wait until the 20th of the month. It is not right that you should leave us in this wild center while you travel. For your travelling, while we remain thus, will harm me and Muḥammad and that man who has no goal but to serve his people. I swear to you on your honor that you should wait until the 20th of this month. If

[95] Blunt, *Gordon*, pp. 500–501.

nothing has resulted by then the affair is with God, and our Teacher will have gained his pardon."[96] This appeal seems to have had no effect on Afghānī, and the correspondence in the *Documents* closes at this point.

What is one to make of all this complex planning and plotting? Insofar as the Mahdi is concerned, there is no evidence that Jamāl ad-Dīn had any contact with him or his followers; the evidence in the *Documents* is entirely negative as is that on the Sudanese side, according to the man who has studied the question the most exhaustively, Professor P. M. Holt.[97] Afghānī conceivably had some very indirect contacts with the Mahdi, or with former students among the Mahdi's followers, but there is no documentation even for this. It may have been Blunt's suggestion of intervention that put the idea in Afghānī's mind of claiming influence with the Mahdi.

Insofar as Blunt's use of Afghānī in relation first to Gladstone, and later to Churchill and Wolff is concerned, there seems little doubt that the question was much less important to the British statesmen involved than it seemed to Blunt and Afghānī. Both Churchill and Wolff hoped for a settlement of the Egyptian and Sudanese difficulties, and both believed, partly under Blunt's influence, that Muslim sentiments must be taken into account in these matters. But it is clear that Wolff was interested in making use of Afghānī—and probably only minor use—only as long as he thought, on the basis of Blunt's words, that this strategy would help him with the Sultan. Once he decided that this was not the case, he lost interest in Afghānī. That Wolff's dispatches from his mission make no mention of Afghānī is not decisive, since he wrote them only after he left England, and in any case he had told Blunt he was keeping this part of the affair from Salisbury. More significant is the fact that Wolff never mentions Afghānī in his long memoirs, even though he was to come into contact with him again later in Iran, and would hardly have left him out if he thought him important. What Wolff's memoirs and dispatches do indicate is that he gave importance to appeasing Muslim opinion both in Egypt and at Istanbul.

That Wolff initially took seriously the schemes and information presented to him by Blunt and by Afghānī and his friends is indicated by some of the dispatches he wrote to Salisbury shortly after reaching Istanbul. On August 23, 1885, very soon after his arrival in

---

96 *Documents*, pp. 38–39, doc. 157. Only a Persian translation is given.
97 Conversation with Professor P. M. Holt, Aug. 1965.

Istanbul, Wolff wrote home that in dealing with Egypt England must take into account "the new Pan-islamic movement which has taken possession of large numbers of those professing the Musulman religion. The chief professors and disciples of this movement are to be found amongst the Arab tribes." He says that this Pan-Islamic movement was behind 'Urabī and the Mahdi, and is much like the Pan-Slavic agitation in its political-religious mixture. He adds that the Sultan must reckon with the Pan-Islamic secret societies, many of whose Arab leaders are constant frequenters of the palace. Wolff seems not to distinguish between the Sufi fraternities, which did have leaders with influence at the palace, and the small Pan-Islamic group represented by Afghānī and his followers. Without distinguishing at all between the two, Wolff goes on to present Afghānī's scheme as that of some of the leaders of the societies who advocate "the formation of a League against Russia, of England, Turkey, Persia and Afghanistan." Still talking of Afghānī's ideas, rather than of those of large and influential societies, as Wolff seems to imagine, Wolff goes on to say that the societies repudiate the caliphate of the Sultan in the Sudan, which should be a separate and equal state like Morocco.[98] These are almost the exact terms of Afghānī's conversations with Wolff, recorded by Blunt, showing that Wolff at this point took Afghānī's opinions to represent a strong and influential body of Muslim opinion that must be taken into account in an Egyptian settlement.

On September 22 Wolff sent home a memorandum on the influential Arab shaikhs of the palace, his information emanating from an "Arab gentleman" with entrée there, probably Jaudat. He cites the views of this gentleman on the advantages of a British evacuation of Egypt:

> The Mussulman element in Egypt would in such case give not only their own support, but that of Mecca, to British policy in India. The English Government should not ignore that in the event of a war between England and Russia the whole Mohammedan element in India, Afghanistan, and Central Asia would be against England should her relations with the Ulema and Sheikhs at Cairo not be altered. In the event of a war between England and Russia, the latter may

---

[98] F.O. 78/3822 (first of two volumes on the Wolff mission), Wolff to Salisbury, no. 11, Constantinople, Aug. 23, 1885.

> obtain from some great Mohammedan Sheikh a Fetwa, and with it combat the English through the Mahommedan element.[99]

This is exactly Afghānī's line, and indicates that the information must have come from Jaudat or, less likely, the recently arrived Muwailihī. Wolff's informant presented this view as being held by some of the Arab shaikhs in important positions in the Sultan's palace. Wolff adds that though it is clear his informant is an advocate of a particular course, he himself agrees regarding the importance of Arab feeling. In the later stages of the negotiation, however, Wolff shows no sign of having retained any intense concern over this matter.

Wolff apparently made efforts in Istanbul to talk to both Jaudat and Muwailihī, but there is no reliable indication that he used them as anything other than sources of information. The one paragraph in Wolff's memoirs which appears to refer to Jaudat treats him only as a source of information on the lavish spending at the court by the ex-Khedive Ismā'īl and by Ḥalīm, who were both trying to gain the khedivate.[100]

In any case, the Wolff mission did not accomplish the evacuation of the British from Egypt, and its failure cannot be remotely ascribed, as Blunt does, to the absence of Afghānī. After an Anglo-Turkish agreement on October 24, 1885, saying that both would send commissioners to Egypt to report back to their governments, which would then consult about British withdrawal, Wolff went to Egypt with the Ottoman commissioner. The British and the Ottomans made a preliminary agreement, which would have resulted in the withdrawal of British troops. Wolff himself makes clear that Great Britain would have kept financial control in Egypt, would have had a favored position there, and would have been able to return her troops if she judged it necessary. The Sultan finally refused to ratify this agreement, under pressure from other Powers that opposed Great Britain, and the British occupation remained. Wolff in his memoirs does not conceal his satisfaction at this "failure" of his mission, and says, "Everything ultimately ended in our favour."[101] Indeed, it seems

---

99 F.O. 78/3822, Wolff to Salisbury, no. 32, Confidential, Constantinople, Sept. 22, 1885.

100 Sir Henry Drummond Wolff, *Rambling Recollections* (London, 1908), p. 308.

101 *Ibid.*, p. 288.

chimerical of Blunt and Afghānī to have looked on Wolff and Churchill as allies in the cause of Muslim liberation from Western control and conquest.

From the point of view of Jamāl ad-Dīn, the events described in this chapter provided ample material for the mythologists who could, for once, describe from the mouth of a Westerner, Blunt, the important role Jamāl ad-Dīn played in European politics. It must be admitted that Blunt gives ground for greatly exaggerating Afghānī's importance in this period. Among the points indicating his actual status for the British policy makers at this time is the fact the Foreign Office seems to have had no record at all of Afghānī's activities in London and Paris in 1885, even though they were fairly well informed about various other phases of his activity.

For the course of Jamāl ad-Dīn's life, the only real importance of these 1885 plans was that they put him in touch with Sultan Abdülhamid II, both directly through correspondence, and via what was told the Sultan about him by Jaudat, Muwailihī and perhaps Münif Paşa. Later documents emanating from the Sultan, cited below, indicate, however, that the impression he had of Afghānī was not entirely positive. Afghānī had been presenting himself on the one hand as an agent of the Mahdi, while at the same time he claimed to support the Sultan, who opposed the Mahdi. In 1885 Wolff was already saying that the Sultan thought of Afghānī as somebody who supported the Mahdi. It seems that Afghānī's offer to help the Sultan had no satisfactory response. If it had, he might not have refused to go to Istanbul when Blunt was pushing the idea. Nevertheless, it may have been in 1885 that the Sultan got the idea of making use of Afghānī, as Muwailihī's and Jaudat's letters indicate.

That Afghānī's disappointment about the Wolff mission contributed significantly to his later anti-British activities in Russia and elsewhere, as Blunt suggests, may be doubted. As noted, Afghānī's followers had already told Blunt of a certain Russo-Franco-Indian scheme of Afghānī's, and it is probable that it involved precisely the war and Indian revolt against England that Afghānī was soon to advocate in Russia.

Afghānī and his friends clearly did attach importance to the British evacuation of Egypt, and since Blunt presented an optimistic picture of the probability of this happening under the new Conservative government, it is not surprising that Afghānī suspended temporarily his anti-British activities to try to help bring the evacuation about.

Even while doing so, however, he was simultaneously pursuing other plans, and he soon turned to new arenas where he might carry them out.

The Western Woman

An unexpected aspect of Jamāl ad-Dīn's life in London and Paris has recently come to light—his love affair with a "Kathi" (Dreesen), a young German woman, whose letters and photographs are catalogued in the *Documents.* Although Afghānī's friends often note his aversion to involvements with women, there seems to have been at least one exception. Homa Pakdaman has unearthed a document in the Paris police archives relating to this woman which antedates the letters in the *Documents.* On April 28, 1885, a police officer reported that Jamāl ad-Dīn (about whom the Paris police had composed a report a year earlier) had quit his lodgings at the Hotel de Sèze as a result of an argument with the proprietor, a M. Paolini. The argument had followed Jamāl ad-Dīn's bringing "a foreigner named Catherine to sleep with him." Paolini objected, claiming that the woman was a secret German agent. Paolini told the writer that Jamāl ad-Dīn had been bothered by this woman for a long time; that she was trying to enter into "intimate relations" with him, and that Jamāl ad-Dīn had succumbed about five months before, after which he had changed from being a reserved and frugal man to a communicative and more free-spending one. Of "Catherine" the writer says, probably echoing Paolini, that she must be of Prussian origin though she says she was born in Vienna. Regarding the (not very conclusive) reasons why Paolini considered her a German spy the officer says: "It was she who made him [Jamāl ad-Dīn] resume his relations, interrupted for a long time, with a very large number of Parisian journalists; and what makes Sr. Paolini believe that she sought Sr. Jamal for interested reasons is that he is ugly, careless of his person, and in a very precarious pecuniary situation. Besides, on various occasions she showed the proprietor and diverse persons whom he knew letters and telegrams from Berlin signed by one of the secretaries of Prince Bismarck."[102]

The first letter in the *Documents* from Kathi, dated Paris, July 22, 1885, speaks of having just seen him off for London and expresses the hope of joining him there soon. The letters are written in fractured French, but the tone of adoration reminds one of that of his male disciples: "My dear Din who was everything for Kathi who loves him as nobody else in the world could love him. If I knew that it would be for long that Din left me I would not wish to live any longer but I hope that soon I can see you again, my adorable Gemal Ed Din, my God, my Everything in the world. . . . Goodnight dear Din, a thousand kisses from your Kathi who is yours body and soul."[103] The two enclosed photographs reveal an attractive blonde woman.

In a second letter from Paris on September 2, 1885, Kathi thanks Afghānī for sending 50 francs, and says that she will arrive in London on September 9, third class. "To see my dear Din I would go even 6th class."

The final two letters from Kathi date from after Jamāl ad-Dīn's departure from London, and are addressed to Bushehr, his next destination. The first, dated July 4, 1886, speaks of Jamāl ad-Dīn's having arrived in Bushehr, and says that they have been apart for three months, indicating that he left London in the early spring of 1886 and not late in 1885 as Blunt says. Kathi asks for a long letter saying Jamāl ad-Dīn will not forget her, that he will return to Europe in two years, and that she can then return with him to his country. She asks him to send her money so that she can now return to her own country, or to write Wahbī to give it to her. She says she thinks only of Jamāl ad-Dīn and dreams of him every night; she sends a thousand kisses and wishes she could really give them. "Write me very soon, dear Din, and do not forget your dear Kathi who loves and adores you and is entirely her Din's body and soul." The second letter combines information about Gladstone's electoral defeat with expressions of adoration and the hope that Jamāl ad-Dīn will soon return to Europe, and says that Wahbī has given her the return money.[104]

The *Documents* editors note that these last two letters were found sealed and it was clear that they had not been opened or read.[105] One

102 Pakdaman (pp. 339–342) reproduces the two police reports; I have seen the originals at the Préfecture de Police Archives in Paris.

103 *Documents*, pls. 66–67, photos 141–144.

104 *Ibid.*, p. 73, docs. 243–245, at the Majlis Library, Tehran.

105 *Ibid.*, p. 73, note.

may guess that Jamāl ad-Dīn in this case, as with many of his male disciples, did not entirely reciprocate the adoration directed toward him. Given the lack of further documentation, one may only speculate about the implications of this involvement, never alluded to elsewhere, for Afghānī's life and character.

If the three months' absence referred to in Kathi's July 4 letter is correct dating, Jamāl ad-Dīn must have left London in the early spring of 1886. From there he went to Bushehr in southern Iran, where he arrived in May 1886.

10

Iran to Russia: 1886–1889

Iran to Moscow: May 1886–May 1887

For Afghānī's two trips to Iran, 1886–1887 and 1889–1891, there are several eyewitness accounts, mostly in Persian. Both the *Documents* and British Foreign Office documents now supplement the published Persian accounts regarding these trips. If one accepts the dates given in the letters from "Kathi" cited in the last chapter, Afghānī left London in early spring, 1886. He reached Bushehr in May 1886.

As usual, one does not know exactly why Afghānī chose to go to a place at a particular time. Abū Turāb shipped Afghānī's books from Egypt to Bushehr late in 1882 indicating that even that long ago Afghānī had planned eventually to travel to Iran. Jamāl ad-Dīn probably had no intention of staying in Iran when he arrived there from England in 1886 but was simply passing through Bushehr, perhaps to pick up his books and papers. Persian accounts agree that it was while he was in Bushehr, and not before, that he was invited to Tehran by the Iranian Minister of Press on behalf of the Shah. He may have been planning to go from Bushehr directly to Russia. This surmise is suggested by a letter from Evelyn Baring (later Lord Cromer) in the Foreign Office records, dating from October 1886, when Afghānī was still in Iran, in which Baring says that he had heard on good authority that Afghānī had gone to Russia on the invitation of the Russian government.[1] The Baring letter indicates that

[1] F.O. 60/594, Baring to Iddesleigh, no. 242, Cairo, Oct. 23, 1886, Secret.

Afghānī's lengthened stay may have been a last-minute idea, based on a governmental invitation received only after he reached Bushehr. This interpretation receives further support from an accurate biographical note by a Persian who knew Jamāl ad-Dīn in Russia, Mīrzā Sayyid Husain Khān 'Adālat, who says: "After the stopping of '*Urwa al-Wuthqā* Sayyid Jamāl ad-Dīn set out for Petrograd, but on the urging of I'timād as-Saltaneh [the Shah's Minister of Press and Publications], Nāsir ad-Dīn Shah desired to meet him. . . ."[2]

There exists a firsthand account of Jamāl ad-Dīn's arrival in Bushehr in the form of a letter to the Persian newspaper *Kāveh* from the son of his host there. The author, Sadīd as-Saltaneh, notes that his father came to know Jamāl ad-Dīn during the latter's early stay in Bushehr on his first trip to India in the 1850's, and that on Sha'bān 16, 1303/May 20, 1886, a letter, photographed in *Kāveh*, reached his father from Jamāl ad-Dīn announcing that he was in Bushehr. The father immediately went to see Jamāl ad-Dīn at the caravanserai where he was staying and brought him home to stay as a guest. He remained in Bushehr for about six months during which time he helped educate the author of the letter, who was then a boy, and also met with other Iranians who were then in Bushehr, including Mīrzā Nasrallāh (Bihishtī) Isfahānī, later known as Malik al-Mutakallimīn, one of the foremost orators and preachers of the Iranian constitutional revolution of 1906. Another of his acquaintances there was Mīrzā Fursat Shīrāzī, who described his contact with Jamāl ad-Dīn in Bushehr in a book, in which he ascribes to ill health Jamāl ad-Dīn's several months' stay in Bushehr.[3]

The meeting in Bushehr at this time of Jamāl ad-Dīn and Malik al-Mutakallimīn is described from his father's words by the latter's son, Mahdī Malikzādeh. Malik al-Mutakallimīn was an enlightened member of the ulama, secretly a Babi of the more revolutionary Azalī branch, who was born in 1277/1860–61 in Isfahan, where he studied both theology and philosophy. According to the biography given by Malikzādeh, his father went to Mecca at the age of twenty-two, and then traveled to India on the invitation of enlightened Muslims there. There he spent two years studying new ideas, founded a school for Iranians, and wrote a book to awaken the Muslims. According to

---

[2] Luṭfallāh, appendix by Mīrzā Sayyid Ḥusain Khān 'Adālat, p. 98.

[3] Furṣat ad-Dauleh Shīrāzī, *Dīvān-i Furṣat* (Tehran, 1337/1958–59), p. 20 (henceforth called *Dīvan-i Furṣat*). On p. 17 Furṣat ad-Dauleh claims that Jamāl ad-Dīn came to Bushehr via Najd, in Arabia.

his son, his liberal ideas aroused the Isma'ilis of the Bombay area against him, and as a result the British exiled him from India. Whatever the truth about this exile, which may have some connection with his secret Babism or with even advanced ideas, it was at that point that he returned to Isfahan via Bushehr and met Afghānī in 1886.[4]

Mālikzādeh quotes his father directly on the meeting: Malik al-Mutakallimīn says that it was in Bushehr that he first met and became friendly with Afghānī, and that they carried on a correspondence until the end of Afghānī's life. Malik al-Mutakallimīn changed his prior plans to leave Bushehr to remain there for the months of Afghānī's stay, profiting, he says, from his knowledge, wisdom, and courage. He describes Afghānī's reformist and Pan-Islamic beliefs. Liberal and constitutionalist teachings ascribed to Afghānī in Bushehr are given in more detail by Fursat ad-Dauleh Shīrāzī.[5]

According to Sadīd as-Saltaneh, still a boy at the time of this visit, Jamāl ad-Dīn taught him both traditional and modern subjects, including geography and the life of Napoleon. Sadīd as-Saltaneh continues that in August 1886 a telegram arrived from I'timād as-Saltaneh to Jamāl ad-Dīn on behalf of the Shah, inviting Jamāl ad-Dīn to Tehran and including the substantial sum of 1,000 tomans from the government. In the same month Jamāl ad-Dīn set out from Bushehr for Tehran via Shiraz.

Persian sources indicate that the Shah, encouraged by his Minister of Press and Publications, I'timād as-Salteneh, wanted to see Jamāl ad-Dīn and authorized an invitation to him to come to Tehran.[6] Since I'timād as-Saltaneh probably presented Afghānī as a great intellectual and defender of Muslim states against foreign encroachments, the Shah's invitation is not particularly surprising. Afghānī's later stories, repeated by Arabic-speaking disciples, that the Shah intended to make him prime minister or that he had some other grandiose duties for him have no independent documentation. Afghānī's Arabic-speaking disciples were possibly unaware of the fact that governmental power at this time was concentrated in the hands of a chief minister, Amīn as-Sultān, who had the Shah's every con-

4 Mahdī Malikzādeh, *Tārīkh-i inqilāb-i mashrūtiyyat-i Īrān*, Vol. I (Tehran, 1328/1949–50), p. 198.

5 *Ibid.*, pp. 191–192, and *Dīvān-i Furṣat*, pp. 20–27.

6 I'timād as-Salṭaneh in *Documents*, p. 149; and 'Abbās Mīrzā Mulk Ārā', *Sharḥ-i ḥāl-i 'Abbās Mīrzā Mulk Ārā'* (the memoirs of a brother of Nāsir ad-Dīn Shāh), ed. 'Abd al-Ḥusain Navā'ī, (Tehran, 1325/1946–47), p. 111 (henceforth called Mulk Ārā').

fidence and whose position was not yet shaken by effective opposition. Though I'timād as-Saltaneh's diary shows that the Shah had some positive interest in Afghānī at first, there is no evidence of any plan to offer him an official position.

Jamāl ad-Dīn left Bushehr in August 1886, and on his way to Tehran stayed in Shiraz a few days and stopped for twenty-two days in Isfahan. Here he met Prince Zill as-Sultān, the oldest and strongest son of Nāsir ad-Dīn Shāh and governor of most of the south, and stayed with a friend of Zill as-Sultān's, Hājji Sayyāh.[7] The latter was a local landowner who had traveled extensively throughout the world whence his nickname, Sayyāh, meaning "the traveler." Hājji Sayyāh had apparently met Jamāl ad-Dīn in Egypt, and they had subsequently corresponded on the subject of *al-'Urwa al-Wuthqā*.[8] He considered himself a modernizer and had some dealings with liberals and revolutionaries, although there were some who thought that he was working primarily for the succession to the throne of Zill as-Sultān.[9] Although Zill as-Sultān was the eldest prince, he was not heir apparent because of his mother's low birth. It was probably Hājji Sayyāh who introduced Jamāl ad-Dīn to Zill as-Sultān.

Despite his justified reputation as a despotic and rapacious governor, Zill as-Sultān attracted the hopes of certain modernizers who hoped to see him gain the throne upon his father's death. He had created a somewhat modern army in Isfahan, such as existed nowhere else in the country, and, unlike his father, was favorable to Western education, at least for his own family. His strong rule appealed to some of those whose main concern was to keep Iran from falling direct prey to foreign occupation. Zill as-Sultān had cordial relations

---

7 *Documents,* p. 112, sec. 12, no. 1, transcription of letter from Hājji Abū al-Qāsim to Amīn az-Zarb, 25 Safar 1304/Nov. 23, 1886. Ḥājji Sayyāh, pp. 287–290.

8 *Documents,* p. 30, no. 112; and pl. 39, photo 87. Pakdaman, p. 123, no. 43.

9 Cf. the interrogation of Mīrzā Rizā after the assassination of Nāsir ad-Dīn Shāh, translated in E. G. Browne, *The Persian Revolution of 1905–1909* (Cambridge, 1910), p. 74: "Q. 'Amongst those persons who, on that earlier occasion [1891] notorious as your sympathisers and abettors Ḥājji Sayyāḥ appears to have been the most substantial?' A.—'No, Ḥājji Sayyāḥ is an irresolute egotist: he never rendered me any help or service, though he profited by the occasion to make the water muddy so that he might catch fish for the *Ẓillu's Sulṭān.* His idea was that perhaps this Prince might become King, and the Amīnu'd Dawla Prime Minister, and that he himself might accumulate some wealth, even as he has now nearly sixteen thousand *tūmāns'* worth of property in Maḥallāt. At this time he obtained from the *Ẓillu's Sulṭān* three thousand tūmāns, nominally for Sayyid Jamālu'd Dīn, of which he gave nine hundred *tūmāns* to the Sayyid and kept the rest himself.' "

not only with Hājji Sayyāh but also with certain other reformists. He had had at his court for some time the radical modernizers and secret Azalī Babis, Mīrzā Āqā Khān Kirmānī and Shaikh Ahmad Rūhī, later to become leading members of Jamāl ad-Dīn's Istanbul circle. Years after this stay, Mirzā Āqā Khān Kirmānī suggested in a letter to the Persian reformer Malkum Khān that he work through Zill as-Sultān, and Malkum Khān did try to do so via correspondence.[10] With this background, it is possible that Jamāl ad-Dīn was dealing with Zill as-Sultān to try for a high position and the consequent implementation of his modernizing policies if Zill as-Sultān should accede to the throne. Some Persian sources speak of an agreement between the two men, and there is evidence that Zill as-Sultān did give Jamāl ad-Dīn money. The stories that Zill as-Sultān financed Jamāl ad-Dīn's trip to Moscow in 1887 are as yet undocumented, but there is documentation in the *Documents* of money given to Jamāl ad-Dīn in Russia by his Tehran patron, Hājji Muhammad Hasan Amīn az-Zarb (i.e., Mint Master).[11]

Amīn az-Zarb, a wealthy merchant whose fortune came partly from farming the Persian mint and issuing depreciated coinage, and who was a client of the chief minister, Amīn as-Sultān, was apparently put in touch with Jamāl ad-Dīn by Hājji Sayyāh from Isfahan, Amīn az-Zarb's town of origin. The *Documents* have a letter to Amīn az-Zarb from one of his friends in Isfahan noting that Jamāl ad-Dīn after his current stay in Isfahan wanted to go to Tehran, and saying that Hājji Sayyāh wanted Amīn az-Zarb to prepare a house for Jamāl ad-Dīn there. Other documents show that I'timād as-Saltaneh was expecting to be Afghānī's host in Tehran, and it is unclear why the new arrangement was made for him to stay with Amīn az-Zarb.[12] The change evidently involved difficulties, not only angering I'timād as-Saltaneh, but also causing some confusion. There is a letter, undated, from Jamāl ad-Dīn from the shrine of Shāhzādeh 'Abd al-'Azīm outside Tehran to Amīn az-Zarb saying that in Isfahan it had been determined that Amīn az-Zarb had agreed to give him a house, and that now Jamāl ad-Dīn did not know if the house had been

---

10 Correspondence of Malkum Khān in Bibliothèque Nationale, Supplément Persan, no. 1996, Mīrzā Āqā Khān Kirmānī, letter no. 82; and letters of Malkum to Zill as-Sultān.

11 Cf. n. 9, above; *Kāveh*, II, 3 (1921), 8 n. 5; 'Adālat in Luṭfallāh, p. 98; *Documents*, photos 179–181.

12 *Documents*, p. 112, Ḥājji Sayyāḥ, p. 290, discusses the change of hosts.

obtained or where it was, and that he was awaiting an answer.[13] Despite this temporary confusion, Amīn az-Zarb did provide Afghānī hospitality during his stay in Tehran in late 1886 and 1887, as well as on his later trip in 1889–1890. Why Afghānī chose this hospitality over that of his more influential admirer, I'timād as-Saltaneh, is unclear. Perhaps he wished to be housed with a friend and not with a rival of the chief minister, Amīn as-Sultān.

The most direct accounts of Jamāl ad-Dīn's 1886–1887 stay in Tehran are in the *Documents*, particularly in the excerpts from the diary of I'timād as-Saltaneh, who claimed to be an advocate of modern and liberal ideas, although some modernizers had a low opinion of him.[14] On December 28, 1886, I'timād as-Saltaneh writes that he went for the first time to see Jamāl ad-Dīn at the home of Amīn az-Zarb. After praising Jamāl ad-Dīn's knowledge, and saying that he had come from Bushehr on the writer's invitation, I'timād as-Saltaneh says that although signing himself Afghānī Jamāl ad-Dīn now says that he comes from Sa'adābād near Hamadan. He describes Afghānī's quarters as very small, but, however much he asked Jamāl ad-Dīn to be his houseguest, Jamāl ad-Dīn refused.

The next day I'timād as-Saltaneh recounts that he was doing his translations (he used to translate orally from European newspapers for the Shah) when the Shah asked if he had seen Jamāl ad-Dīn. He replied yes, that he had seen him the day before, and spoke very highly of him. The Shah then said he had asked Hājji Muhammad Hasan (Amīn az-Zarb) to bring him for an audience. I'timād as-Saltaneh took umbrage at this since Jamāl ad-Dīn had come from Bushehr through his efforts. I'timād as-Saltaneh writes that he and Jamāl ad-Dīn had exchanged several telegrams over the visit, and now that he had come, the Shah, in order to flatter Amīn as-Sultān, had Jamāl ad-Dīn presented by Hājji Muhammad Hasan (Amīn as-Sultān's client). That Jamāl ad-Dīn and his introduction were considered matters of some importance at court is indicated by I'timād as-

13 *Documents*, photo 167.

14 The usually careful Muhammad Qazvīnī says in a note in Browne, *op. cit.*, p. 405: "Although Sayyid Jamālu'd-Din apparently thought highly of the *I'timād-u's-Salṭana*, in the opinion of others he was a charlatan and a scoundrel, ignorant, illiterate and pretentious. He could not even spell decently, and the works published in his name were written by men of learning acting under compulsion and prompted by fear of his malice." Judging from I'timād as-Saltaneh's diary, the charge of illiteracy sounds overstated. He is defended from such charges and presented as a sincere reformer in a biography in Khān Malik Sāsānī, *Siyāsatgarān-i daureh-yi Qājār* (Tehran, 1338/1959–1960).

Saltaneh's further words: "When I entered the room of the coffee-house there were there a group of those buffoons (*alwāt*) who were secretly happy that Sayyid Jamāl ad-Dīn is being presented by the Hājji and that I did not bring him. . . . I went home and wrote a sharp (*tundī*) petition to the Shah asking permission to go to the shrines"[15] [Najaf and Karbala; such a request indicated dissatisfaction].

There exist a few other Persian eyewitness accounts of this stay in Tehran. A brother of Nāsir ad-Dīn Shāh who was there at the time, 'Abbās Mīrzā Mulk Ārā, writes in his memoirs that I'timād as-Saltaneh, who was in charge of the (official) newspaper *Iran* and of writing a history of Iran, told the Shah that the presence of Jamāl ad-Dīn was necessary for writing the newspaper and the history. With the Shah's authorization I'timād as-Saltaneh telegraphed to invite Jamāl ad-Dīn to Tehran. Mulk Ārā says that during his first session with the Shah Jamāl ad-Dīn said that he was like a "sharp sword" in the Shah's hands, that he asked the Shah not to let him remain idle but to give him important work, suggesting his power be used against foreign governments. The Shah was frightened and repelled by his manner of speech and did not again grant him an audience. Amīn az-Zarb was told, Mulk Ārā continues, that Jamāl ad-Dīn "should not be so visible to the public, but the people of Tehran went in crowds to see him, and whoever his breath reached became a seeker of freedom, and he spoke so well that whoever saw him at one gathering became enchanted by him."[16] The psychologically interesting image of being a sharp sword in a leader's hand was later repeated by Afghānī to Sultan Abdülhamid in Istanbul in the 1890's.

Mulk Ārā goes on to speak of the reasons why Jamāl ad-Dīn had to leave Iran in 1887. He attributes this forced departure to the intervention of the British Minister, who harbored a grudge against Jamāl ad-Dīn over the Egyptian revolt. In fact, British documents of 1886–1887 show no British awareness of Jamāl ad-Dīn before he went to Russia, but this should not discredit the rest of Mulk Ārā's remarks, since British intervention might have been claimed by Amīn as-Sultān, who often fabricated stories to justify his actions, or even by the Shah. Jamāl ad-Dīn himself apparently also blamed the British.[17] Mulk Ārā appears on firmer ground when he says that the Shah told Amīn az-Zarb that since he, the Shah, had invited Jamāl

---

15 Diary excerpted in *Documents*, p. 149.
16 Mulk Ārā', p. 112.
17 'Adālat in Luṭfallāh, p. 98.

ad-Dīn it would not be seemly for him to expel the man directly, and asked Amīn az-Zarb to convince Jamāl ad-Dīn that it would be good for him to go abroad. Consequently Amīn az-Zarb took him to Mazanderan under the pretext of inspecting his estates, and from there Jamāl ad-Dīn went to Moscow.[18] The trips to Mazanderan and Moscow occurred in April and May, 1887.

It is already sufficiently clear from Mulk Ārā's brief story that the Shah needed no encouragement from the British to become suspicious of Jamāl ad-Dīn, with whom he broke relations very quickly. After the break Jamāl ad-Dīn apparently began to influence Tehranis in the direction of reform. The Shah, particularly in his later years, was extremely hostile to any kind of reform or westernization, and Jamāl ad-Dīn's influence in this direction very likely made him nervous. He might also have been upset if Jamāl ad-Dīn was engaging in his usual attacks on foreigners, particularly the British, with whom the Shah and Amīn as-Sultān were trying to remain in accord.

Another brief account of the 1886–1887 Iranian visit is given by Nāzim al-Islām Kirmānī, writing in the first decade of the twentieth century. He says he got his information from the following persons: Hājji Sayyāh; Āqā (Muhammad) Tabātabā'ī (a liberal Tehran mujtahid and the son of Sayyid Sādiq, whom Jamāl ad-Dīn claimed to have impressed as a child, and who came to know Jamāl ad-Dīn); and from others who knew Jamāl ad-Dīn. Kirmānī says that when Jamāl ad-Dīn's presence in Bushehr came to be known, his friends and partisans sent him telegrams and letters asking him to stay in Iran, and that the Shah invited him to Tehran and honored him greatly. Men of the ulama and government met him, and he worked both openly and secretly to awaken the Iranians. According to Kirmānī, under the leadership of Jamāl ad-Dīn "secret societies were formed and the hidden secrets were spoken."[19] Kirmānī also speaks of Jamāl ad-Dīn's outdoing certain of the ulama in debate. This story would seem to support the surmise that it was Jamāl ad-Dīn's potentially dangerous influence that turned the Shah against him.

The most intimate portrait of Jamāl ad-Dīn during this Tehran trip comes from the son of Amīn az-Zarb, Hājji Muhammad Husain Āqā, who was an adolescent when Jamāl ad-Dīn first stayed with them in 1886–1887. He tells in some detail of Afghānī's helping him to learn

---

[18] Mulk Ārā', p. 112.

[19] Nāẓim al-Islām Kirmānī, *Tārīkh-i bīdārī-yi Īrānīyān* (2d ed.; Tehran, 1945–46), pp. 61–62.

Arabic. He also says that his father had an extraordinary religious veneration for Afghānī. Then he goes on, regarding the causes for Afghānī's exile after the 1886–1887 trip: "Finally, after a period when my late father received him and took him to see Nāsir ad-Dīn Shāh, the Shah became angry at their conversations and ordered my late father that the Sayyid must be exiled." Since Amīn az-Zarb was going to oversee iron mines in Mazanderan near the Caspian Sea he asked the Shah's permission, as Afghānī was a guest, to take him honorably to Mazanderan from where they would go together to Russia, where he would tell Afghānī the situation. The Shah agreed, and it was done.[20] This story differs from Mulk Ārā's only in that the suggestion of an informal and friendly exile emanated from Amīn az-Zarb and not the Shah.

Amīn az-Zarb's adoration of Jamāl ad-Dīn, so familiar a reaction by now, is confirmed in his correspondence from this period, reprinted in the *Documents*. For example, in a letter to his brother written during Jamāl ad-Dīn's stay, Amīn az-Zarb wrote: "By the grace of the Imām of the Age . . . God has today made my lot better than that of any Sultan. His Excellency the mujtahid of the Age and the unique one of the time, Hājji Sayyid Jamāl ad-Dīn, known as Afghānī, who edited the newspaper *'Urwa al-Wuthqā* in Europe and is known as a Hanafi in religion, is staying in the house. All spiritual and bodily perfections are united in this great person and he pays special attention to Āqā Husain [the son whose memoirs are quoted above]."[21] There are other letters from Amīn az-Zarb in a similar or even more adoring tone.

It was during his 1886–1887 stay with Amīn az-Zarb that Sayyid Jamāl ad-Dīn met Mīrzā Muhammad Rizā Kirmānī, the cloak maker, who was to become one of his most devoted followers. Afghānī is said to have asked Amīn az-Zarb for a trustworthy man for his personal service, and Amīn az-Zarb apparently selected Mīrzā Rizā, who had been working for him, and transferred him to Afghānī. Afghānī must also have made some of his other important Iranian contacts during this trip, though it is unclear which men he met at this time and which during his subsequent longer stay.

In Tehran Jamāl ad-Dīn was also constantly attended by his nephew, Mīrzā Lutfallāh, who had previously tried without success

---

20 Memoirs reprinted in *Documents*, pp. 142–143.
21 *Ibid.*, pp. 116–117.

to see his uncle, not seen by him since Jamāl ad-Dīn had briefly visited Asadabad in 1865 when Lutfallāh was a child. According to Hājji Sayyāh, Jamāl ad-Dīn on arriving in Isfahan had told him that he had a sister with two sons in Asadabad, and he, Hājji Sayyāh, wrote to the elder nephew, Mīrzā Sharīf, telling of Jamāl ad-Dīn's arrival. After Jamāl ad-Dīn had already left Isfahan, Mīrzā Lutfallāh arrived there, having fruitlessly gone far out of his way. He managed to rejoin his uncle in Tehran, after Hājji Sayyāh told him where to go and telegraphed to Jamāl ad-Dīn of his nephew's coming.[22]

The *Documents* show that Jamāl ad-Dīn had sent no news to his family in Asadabad from the time he left Iran in 1866 until he published *al-'Urwa al-Wuthqā* in 1884 and sent them copies, which elicited letters from Afghānī's nephews. The elder, Mīrzā Sharīf, wrote in 1884 that his brother Lutfallāh was determined to join Afghānī in Paris and that Afghānī should write and dissuade him, which he did. Lutfallāh's own letters to Jamāl ad-Dīn that same year express total adoration and describe his many years' search to locate Jamāl ad-Dīn. He begs to join him in Paris and expresses disappointment but obedience when Afghānī's discouraging letter arrives. Lutfallāh writes that two or three years before (i.e., around 1882) the Shah had asked Sulaimān Khān [Afshār, the leading man of the Asadabad area] about Jamāl ad-Dīn, saying, "Who is this Sayyid Asadābādī?" Sulaimān Khān wrote to his son asking him to look up Jamāl ad-Dīn's name and background, and the son complied. Both nephews ask Jamāl ad-Dīn to write something against the Bahai religion, which they say is spreading rapidly in Iran. A year after this correspondence there is another letter from Lutfallāh, apparently to Abū Turāb, saying that Lutfallāh has heard nothing since Jamāl ad-Dīn's first letter and asking for information about him.[23] One may imagine that Lutfallāh was overjoyed finally to go to Tehran to see his idolized uncle, but there is no evidence that Jamāl ad-Dīn himself made any effort to see the remaining members of his family on this trip. His parents were by now dead, but at least one sister was still alive, in addition to cousins and nephews.

In Tehran, Jamāl ad-Dīn dictated a number of brief essays and articles, some of them unfinished, which were taken down both by Lutfallāh and by Amīn az-Zarb's adolescent son, Husain. Some of

---

22 Luṭfallāh, p, 40. Ḥājji Sayyāḥ, pp. 291–293.
23 *Documents*, docs. 84–95; photos 53–83.

these were apparently used as Arabic translation exercises by Husain, and it is doubtful that any of them was intended for publication. Decades after Jamāl ad-Dīn's death, however, Lutfallāh's son Sifātallāh prepared them for publication, along with Jamāl ad-Dīn's Indian articles, in the Tehran edition of *Maqalāt-i Jamāliyyeh.* The most interesting of the articles dictated in Iran is "The Suckling Baby," wherein Jamāl ad-Dīn expresses deep pessimism about the numerous passions and pitfalls that mislead most men in the world. He speaks out particularly against personal ambition, greed, and hypocrisy. In a very brief article, "On the Personal Pleasures of Human Beings," Jamāl ad-Dīn again attacks the selfishness that motivates most men, and says that true pleasure can come only when all men are in decent circumstances. Another of these brief articles, "On Pride," is directed against the baseless pride and boastfulness of Orientals.[24] The remaining Iranian articles are of less interest, and none of them is as significant as some of his earlier published articles, discussed in previous chapters.

A perceptive analysis of Jamāl ad-Dīn's 1886–1887 trip to Tehran is found in the memoirs of a man who evidently met him during that trip, the liberal and influential Minister of Posts, Amīn ad-Dauleh. He says Amīn az-Zarb (whom Amīn ad-Dauleh disliked) was attracted to men with religious reputations because of fears arising from his own dishonesty, and thus gave money and praise to Jamāl ad-Dīn. Amīn ad-Dauleh confirms that after Jamāl ad-Dīn's arrival it became known that he was from Asadabad in Iran. He says that the Shah was displeased by Afghānī's speaking of the need for reform and for the rule of law. Amīn ad-Dauleh notes that Jamāl ad-Dīn's knowledge was based mainly on a powerful memory of popular sources like newspapers and speeches rather than on profundity, but that in an ignorant country like Iran he seemed a fountain of knowledge. To his friends he spoke openly of the need for reform, awakening them to

[24] *Maqālāt-i Jamāliyyeh*, ed. Ṣifātallāh Jamālī Asadābādī, (Tehran, 1312/1933–34), pp. 1, 53–74, 149–151, 152–153. In addition to eight Indian articles, this edition contains nine others, two of which are incomplete fragments. In p. 163 n. 2 Ṣifātallāh says the articles may date from either Afghānī's first (1886–87) or second (1889–90) trip to Tehran. The use of some of these articles as translation exercises by the adolescent Ḥusain (*Documents*, p. 91) suggests they were written during the 1886–87 trip. One article, "Why Islam Became Weak," is unidentified as to time and language of original publication; Ṣifātallāh says he got it from nos. 2 and 3 of a Tehran journal, *Tazakkur.* For summaries of all of Afghānī's Persian articles, see Pakdaman, pp. 213–224; she translates "Why Islam Became Weak" on pp. 268–274.

new ideas, and news of this reached the Shah, who ordered Amīn az-Zarb to take him from Iran.

Whatever the exact mechanism, the Shah clearly expressed the wish that Jamāl ad-Dīn leave the country. Yet, apparently genuine letters between Jamāl ad-Dīn and the Shah, reprinted by Sifatallāh, indicate they parted on cordial terms.[25]

Regarding Jamāl ad-Dīn's trip to Russia, Amīn az-Zarb wrote a letter to an acquaintance on April 26, 1887, saying that after going to see his mines (in Mazanderan) he would remain in the area to finish some work, while Jamāl ad-Dīn would go first to Baku, then to Tiflis for about a week, then to Moscow for ten or fifteen days, from there to St. Petersburg for five or six months, and afterward to Paris. According to Sayyid Hasan Taqīzādeh, Jamāl ad-Dīn was the guest of a certain Muhammad 'Alī Kāshī in Vladikavkaz (now Dzaudzhikau), and then he was joined by Amīn az-Zarb who traveled with him to Moscow, where they stayed for two weeks in the house of Āqā Mīrzā Ni'matallāh Isfahānī, later Iranian consul in Moscow. (This stay together in Moscow occurred in May 1887). Taqīzādeh says, as do other Persian and British accounts cited below, that Jamāl ad-Dīn had been invited to Moscow by Katkov, the Russian chauvinist publicist and editor of the *Moscow Gazette*.[26]

From Moscow Amīn az-Zarb wrote to his patron, the chief minister Amīn as-Sultān, telling him that Jamāl ad-Dīn had been well received everywhere in the Caucasus, and praising Jamāl ad-Dīn highly.[27] Whether this letter indicates that Amīn as-Sultān, later to be hostile to Jamāl ad-Dīn, had not yet developed this antipathy, or whether it was written on Jamāl ad-Dīn's urging to try to overcome an existing hostility is uncertain. The *Documents* show that Amīn az-Zarb did indeed leave Jamāl ad-Dīn after this short Moscow stay in order to go to western Europe, but that they kept up a correspondence and that Amīn az-Zarb continued to send Jamāl ad-Dīn money during his years in Russia. Amīn az-Zarb's trip West was aimed at arranging railroad building in north Iran, and he asked Jamāl ad-Dīn to discuss this question with the Russians.[28]

---

25 The letters are translated from Ṣifātallāh, *Asnād*, pp. 51–52, in Pakdaman, p. 127. *Khāṭirāt-i siyāsī-yi Mīrzā 'Alī Khān-i Amīn ad-Dauleh*, ed. Hafez Farman-Farmaian (Tehran, 1962), p. 128.

26 *Documents*, p. 116; *Kāveh*, II, 3 (1921), 8; 'Adālat in Luṭfallāh, p. 99.

27 *Documents*, p. 120.

28 See below in this chapter; Pakdaman, p. 128; *Documents*, p. 120, and the photographed letters listed on p. 93.

British Reports on Afghānī's Activities in 1886–1887

British foreign Office and Government of India documents provide some details about Jamāl ad-Dīn's activities in Russia during the first months of his stay in 1887 and also show the actual, rather than the mythical, degree of attention given by the British to Jamāl ad-Dīn in 1886 and 1887.

The report written on Jamāl ad-Dīn's life by the Thagi and Dakaiti Department of the Government of India in 1895 showed accurate awareness of Jamāl ad-Dīn's whereabouts in the years from 1886 on, though it does not list its sources of information. Thus we find: "The next news of him was in 1886 when he went to Teheran, and on his way thither, stopped at Bushire, Shiraz and Ispahan. He found Persia too hot for his advanced ideas and was forced to leave it, when he proceeded to Russia and joined Dalip Singh and Katkoff at Moscow."[29] Despite this accurate report after the fact from India, it does not appear that the British Foreign Office was aware of Jamāl ad-Dīn's lengthened stay in Iran in 1886 and 1887. Far from following him around religiously, as some accounts would have it, the Foreign Office was under the misapprehension that Jamāl ad-Dīn had gone directly to Russia from Bushehr in 1886, a misapprehension that was probably attributable to his original plan to do exactly that. In 1886 and early 1887 the Foreign Office thus directed its inquiries about Jamāl ad-Dīn's activities to its ambassador in St. Petersburg, even though Afghānī was in Iran at the time.

On October 23, 1886, when Jamāl ad-Dīn was still in Iran, Evelyn Baring (later Lord Cromer) reported secretly from Cairo:

---

29 F.O. 60/594, "Memorandum by the General Superintendent of Thagi and Dakaiti Department, regarding Jamal-ud-Din," India Office, March 6, 1896, Confidential, p. 183.

> I have the honour to report that Hamed Ulla, son of Jemel Ullah, the native Indian Judge, who came to Egypt during Lord Northbrook's mission to examine into the state of the Egyptian legal administration, was a passenger on board the ship which brought me to Egypt, and I think it my duty to inform Your Lordship that I learned from Hamed Ulla that the well-known Gellal Eddin, who used to reside in Paris, has recently gone to St. Petersburg, whither it is supposed he was invited by order of the Russian Government.
>
> The hostility of Gellal Eddin towards England is well known and has more than once formed the subject of despatches from this country during the last few years; I would suggest, therefore, that it might be as well that Sir R. Morier [the British Ambassador to Russia] should know of the presence of the man in St. Petersburg.[30]

A copy of this dispatch was sent to Morier by the British Foreign Office, which wrote an additional note on March 2, 1887, when Afghānī was in fact still in Tehran: ". . . I have now to state to you that, according to information received from a private source, an appointment in one of the Turkestan districts has been conferred on him [Jamāl ad-Dīn]. I have to request that Y.E. write report to me should any confirmation of this rumor come to your knowledge."[31] Although Afghānī was not even in Russia, and such an appointment would in any case have been most improbable, he may in fact have been seeking such an appointment from the Russian government. This is asserted by Khān Malik Sāsānī, citing the newspaper *Qafqāz,* May 7, 1896 (presumably an article related to the assassination of Nāsir ad-Dīn Shāh, which had just occurred). Sāsānī says, after noting that one of Afghānī's aims in Russia had been to make the Russian leaders favorable to Zill as-Sultān: "He tried to obtain an office from the Russian government in Central Asia in order to propagate the Unity of Islam, but he did not succeed."[32]

As a result of the Foreign Office's second dispatch to him, Morier raised the question of Jamāl ad-Dīn with the Russian Foreign Minister, Giers, on March 21, 1887. After describing his thanks to Giers for his frank answers to inquiries regarding the Sikh pretender,

---

30 F.O. 60/594, Baring to Iddesleigh, no. 424, Cairo, Oct. 23, 1886, Secret.

31 *Ibid.*, Salisbury (?) to Morier, no. 66, March 2, 1887, Secret, Draft. See below for the source of this misinformation.

32 Sāsānī, *op. cit.*, p. 191, no. 3, citing the newspaper *Qafqāz,* May 7, 1896.

Maharaja Dalip Singh (who had also been brought to Russia by Katkov), Morier goes on:

> I thought the occasion a good one to enquire of His excellency about Jellal-ed-Din referred to in Your Lordship's despatch. . . .
>
> I said that this individual was an Arab adventurer who had edited for some time an Arab newspaper at Paris, containing the most violent attacks on Her Majesty's Government, who professed to be in intimate relations with the Mahdi and with the different religious leaders of Islam, and who was believed to have endeavoured, to the best of his ability, to promote disaffection in India. A report had reached us some time ago that he had left Paris for Russia, and a rumour had now gone forth, of which he was possibly himself the author, that he had obtained a position in the Russian administration in Turkestan.
>
> M. de Giers replied that he could not recollect ever having heard the name of Jellal-ed-Din, but that he could state very positively that no Arab had been appointed to any post in Russian Turkestan. I may add my own conviction that such an appointment would be utterly inconsistent with the official tradition and usages of Russia.[33]

Since Morier reported both the name and nationality of Jamāl ad-Dīn inaccurately, and since the latter was not even in Russia yet, one may assume that Giers's claim of ignorance on the subject was entirely genuine.

On July 20, 1887, after Jamāl ad-Dīn's May arrival in Moscow, Morier sent home a translation of a paragraph in the *Moscow Gazette*, Katkov's newspaper, announcing Jamāl ad-Dīn's arrival. Morier also said that he had instructed the British vice-consul in Moscow to inquire about the causes of Jamāl ad-Dīn's presence there. The translated passage from the *Moscow Gazette* reads:

> The Moscow Gazette of the 1/13 July 1887 announces the presence in Moscow of the Afghan Sheikh Djemal-Eddin, a native of Cabul and who passed some years in Turkey, was banished thence to Cairo, where he resided 18 years and took an active part in Arabi's insurrection. He afterwards went to Paris, and now, it would appear, is staying in Moscow. The

33 F.O. 60/594, Morier to Salisbury, no. 91, St. Petersburg, March 21, 1887.

> Sheikh is alleged to have stated that his object in visiting Russia was to make himself practically acquainted with a country on which 60.000.000 Indian Mussulmans place sole reliance, and which they hope will afford them protection and emancipate them from the detested English yoke.[34]

The plan for a Russian alliance against the British in the interest of the Indian Muslims, mentioned in other sources, here receives corroboration.

The first substantial British information about Jamāl ad-Dīn's activities in Russia comes in a report from the British vice-consul in Moscow on July 23, 1887. Since this report refers to Dalip Singh, with whom Afghānī was soon to collaborate, it is worth giving some background on this man. According to Kedourie:

> Katkov had enticed to Moscow another personage who also had a grudge against the British, and with whom Afghani collaborated in anti-British enterprises. This was Maharajah Dalip Singh (1838–1893), the last ruler of the Sikh kingdom of the Punjab. The youngest son of Ranjit Singh, the famous Sikh leader, he was one year old when his father died. Internecine struggles among his brothers and among the Sikh leaders led to his brief period of rule, before his deposition by the British at Lahore in 1849. He was given a handsome pension and eventually settled on an estate in Suffolk, having embraced Christianity and married the daughter of an Abyssinian slave and a German banker whom he met in a Presbyterian orphanage in Cairo. In the mid-1880's, he started quarreling with the India Office, demanding the restoration of his throne. He attempted to go to India, was stopped at Aden where he renounced Christianity for the Sikh religion, came back to Paris, and in 1887, patronised by Katkov, he turned up in Moscow announcing his plans for a Sikh rising and the speedy end of British rule in India. Afghani and Dalip Singh collaborated in issuing manifestoes dated from Moscow, signed, The Executive of the Indian Liberation Society, and printed and distributed with Fenian help in Paris.[35]

The British knew of Dalip Singh's presence and activities in Russia before Afghānī's and in much more detail. Since both were invited

---

[34] *Ibid.*, translation enclosed in Morier to Salisbury, no. 253, St. Petersburg, July 20, 1887, Secret.

[35] Kedourie, *Afghani*, pp. 56–57.

to Russia by Katkov and both were working for an uprising in India against the British, it was natural for the British to suppose they were connected even before there appeared any evidence to that effect. Morier had already passed easily from the subject of Dalip Singh to that of Afghānī in an interview with Giers, and the British vice-consul in Moscow, reporting on July 23, also tried to discover a connection between the two. He wrote to Morier:

> I first became aware of Djem al Eddin's appearance in this city through the "Moscow Gazette" of the 1st July (o[ld] s[tyle]) which contained an article headed the Afghan Sheikh in Moscow—giving an account of his life, and mentioning that he had arrived here from Persia.
>
> I immediately suspected that he had some connection with the Maharajah Dhuleep Singh, and at once made my inquiries, but could learn nothing about Djem al Eddin until yesterday, when I discovered that he was staying at the Hotel Royal, a third class hotel in Moscow.
>
> Since that I have ascertained that he arrived here about the 10th of May, (new style) together with the Persian Minister of Finance, Moaven el Molk, and some four or five other Persians, they all of them put up at the Hotel Slave, but only stayed there for one night, when the Minister went to stay with the Persian Consul-General here, and the others went to live among their countrymen.
>
> The Minister and his Staff soon left for Belgium, where they were bound, for the purpose of studying Railways, and also with a view to engage Belgian engineers, for the construction of railways in Persia.[36]

The correspondence summarized below between Afghānī and Amīn az-Zarb, contains references to this plan for railroad construction. Since neither Afghānī nor his biographers make any point of his having arrived in Moscow with the Iranian Finance Minister, it seems reasonable to assume that their arrival together in Moscow may have been due only to ties between Amīn az-Zarb and the Finance Minister. As Amīn az-Zarb is known also to have gone to Europe from Russia, and since his correspondence shows him to be involved in the railroad question, it seems most probable that the Persian Finance Minister's dealings were rather with Amīn az-Zarb

36 F.O. 60/594, Hornstedt to Morier, Moscow, July 23, 1887; in Morier to Salisbury, no. 257, St. Petersburg, July 26, 1887.

than with Afghānī. Amīn az-Zarb's position as a very wealthy merchant, owner of a small industrial railroad, and master of the Persian Mint made him a logical companion for the Finance Minister on such a mission, and Amīn az-Zarb was also one of the few Persians actively promoting railroad building in Iran.

Afghānī's interest in having railways built in Iran as well as in other forms of economic modernization, as long as they did not involve concessions to foreigners, is quite in character. This interest in modern technology is supported by other remarks in the vice-consul's report:

> I can give no account of the doings of Djem al Eddin from the day that he left the Hotel Slave, until just a month since when he took up his quarters at the Hotel Royal.
>
> Since he has resided at this Hotel he appears to have received no other visitors but Persian merchants living in Moscow.
>
> Accompanied by some of these he has daily visited some manufactory or other in Moscow and the vicinity and his only object seems to be the study of Russian manufactures.
>
> His evenings he mostly spends at his hotel entertaining his friends on a very modest scale. . . .
>
> He holds a Persian Passport (in French) and is therein described as Aqa Cheyck, Djem al Eddin.

Such a pasport, listing Afghānī correctly as a Persian subject, is photographed in the *Documents*.[37] After noting Afghānī's 1885 stay in England, the vice-consul concludes:

> Dhuleep Singh has taken a country house near Moscow, and I have therefore not the same opportunity to observe his movements, and feel some reserve in speaking of them, but I have not the slightest indication of any connection between the Rajah and the Aga Cheyck or that the two have ever met. I hear the Rajah blusters a good deal, he told the German Consul that within three years, there would not be an Englishman to be found in the whole of India.
>
> Alas for Dhuleep Singh, M. Katkoff is *hors de combat* and is not likely ever to show fight again.

[37] That Afghānī used Persian passports and visas—a sign of Persian birth—was known to some during his own lifetime. Two are photographed in *Documents*, photos 149, 150.

Despite the vice-consul's negative conclusions at this time about Jamal ad-Dīn's ties to Daliph Singh, such ties did develop during Jamal ad-Dīn's stay in Russia, and the Government of India learned of their joint efforts to promote a rising in India. It was in 1887, when Afghānī was in Russia, that the Government of India became most concerned about his activities, which included not only joint manifestos with Dalip Singh, but various attacks on Great Britain in the Russian newspapers. In fact, there is much more Indian documentation on him in this period than during the time he was in India in 1879–1882. The Government of India considered publishing a notice warning about Jamāl ad-Dīn but evidently decided against it.[38] Despite their annoyance with him, there is no documentary indication that either the British government or the Government of India took any steps against Jamāl ad-Dīn while he was in Iran or Russia. The Government of India's "Political and Secret Home Correspondence" contains several references to Afghānī in 1887, resulting from his anti-British activities in Russia. One file contains a clipping from an unnamed British newspaper, probably the *Times*, with a story dated St. Petersburg, August 2, 1887, reporting Jamāl ad-Dīn's presence in Moscow. Afghānī told a reporter from the *Moscow Gazette* that the revolt of the Ghilzais in Afghanistan was a result of Afghan hatred for England. He also said that the British had massacred their enemies in the last Afghan campaign.[39]

The Government of India files also have a copy of a dispatch from Morier enclosing translations of two articles in Russian newspapers written by Jamāl ad-Dīn in 1887. In the *Novoe Vremya*[39a] of August 20/September 1, 1887, is a letter from Jamāl ad-Dīn in which he criticizes the Persian government for helping the British by trying to capture an Afghan enemy of Great Britain, Ayyūb Khān, who had fled to Iran. He says that if Ayyūb Khān is turned over to the British by the Persians, Persian public opinion will see it as a sign of Russian weakness. If Ayyūb Khān returns to Afghanistan, the Afghans, who hate England, will rally around him and fight England. The English will then try to take over in Afghanistan as they have in Egypt and eventually succeed. Russia, therefore, is obliged not to remain an indifferent spectator.

---

38 Great Britain, Commonwealth Relations Office, Government of India, Foreign Department, *Political and Secret Demi-Official Correspondence*, 1887–88, vol. 2, Note of E. Neal. Sept. 6, 1887, enclosing letter on Jamāl ad-Dīn from Sir West Ridgeway.

39 *PSHC*, vol. 96 (1887), file 831.

39a New Times.

In the *Novoe Vremya* of August 15/27, 1887, was an interview with Jamāl ad-Dīn, who said he was surprised Russia had allowed English mediation in the question of delimiting the Russian-Afghan boundary. British influence in Afghanistan will grow. The British in India fear Russia and are trying to distract Russian attention elsewhere. The British always appear first as advisers and then become masters, so that even large states like Turkey and Persia become caught in their meshes. He says that the Shah has recently received from London presents, seductive promises of protection and cooperation, and invitations, which are causing him to make important concessions to the British.[40] Such criticism of the Shah by Afghānī in Russian newspapers helped to alienate the Shah and his chief minister.

On October 13, 1887, an Indian Muslim, "Aziz-ud-Din," issued a printed report for the Government of India on Afghānī, which formed the basis of the report on him made by the Thagi and Dakaiti Department in 1895. Included only in the earlier report is the following statement by Azīz ad-Dīn: "Last year, while in Burma I was informed that at the request of the Russian Government, [Jamāl ad-Dīn] went to Moscow and was to have been employed on political work in Russian Turkistan. I have learnt by the mail before last, through the same source, that he has now left Moscow, and that after having an interview with the Czar at St. Petersburg he is to go to Russian Turkistan. He is a close friend of Dalip Singh who expects a great deal of assistance from Him."[41] One may guess that Azīz ad-Dīn was the main source of the British Foreign Office's 1886 misinformation about Jamāl ad-Dīn's presence and activities in Russia.

Morier reported only once more on Jamāl ad-Dīn during the period of his Russian sojourn, and this was near the beginning of his stay in St. Petersburg, on August 27, 1887. At this time, Morier reported a long discussion on various subjects with Şakir Paşa, the Ottoman ambassador to Russia. After discussing more important subjects, the Ottoman ambassador

> mentioned that he had been informed of the presence at St. Petersburg of Jemal-ed-Din, with whose antecedents he seemed thoroughly well acquainted. He had been curious to ascertain what this literary Sheikh was about and had sent a confidential person to sound him and to say that as a

---

[40] Clippings translated in *ibid.*, vol. 97, file 938.

[41] *Ibid.*, vol. 98, file 1111. A further report from Azīz ad-Dīn is in Government of India, Foreign Department, *Secret Internal Proceedings*, May, 1888, no. 41.

> Mussulman it would be proper on his part to call on the Representative of the Caliph of Islam. He received a civil answer to the effect that Jemal-ed-Din entirely recognized the position of the Sultan as Caliph, but that he had his own political reasons for not calling on the Turkish Ambassador. Shakir, who had evidently had him very closely watched, said that he had come to Petersburg after the death of Katkow, by whom he had been attracted to Moscow, in the hope of being well received by the Russian Government but that he had been much disappointed at having failed in his attempts to see official persons, who had in a marked manner given him the cold shoulder—strangely enough however there had been one exception, that of M. Pobedonostzow [Pobedonostsev], the Proctor of the Holy Synod, who had paid him a visit and interviewed him at great length.[42]

When a copy of this dispatch reached the Government of India, the following explanatory Minute was added there: "Mr. Pobedonostow, Proctor of the Holy Synod in Russia, was the Czar's tutor and is said to exercise a great influence over the mind of his Imperial pupil. He is also known as a prominent member of the 'Katkoff' party."[43] The last point presumably explains Sayyid Jamāl ad-Dīn's success in seeing Pobedonostsev sooner than he was able to see other members of the Russian government.

Morier and the Foreign Office seem to have given up concern about Jamāl ad-Dīn at this point, as there were no further dispatches either way during the rest of Jamāl ad-Dīn's stay in Moscow. Only the Government of India retained some concern and evidently gathered later information, but this must have been considered not important enough to transmit to the Foreign Office. The information reaching the Government of India indicates that Jamāl ad-Dīn's influence in high Russian circles increased somewhat after his early disappointments reported by the Turkish Ambassador. Specifically, the Thagi and Dakaiti Department biography adds to the information in the Foreign Office letters about Jamāl ad-Dīn's activities in Russia as follows:

> . . . he proceeded to Russia and joined Dalip Singh and Katkoff at Moscow.
>
> He made a very good impression in Russian Society being

[42] F.O. 60/594, Morier to Salisbury, no. 299, St. Petersburg, Aug. 27, 1887.
[43] *PSHC*, vol. 97 (1887), file 930, Minute on Morier despatch.

> a good talker, and was soon looked upon as a great man and quite overshadowed Dalip Singh. This led to a quarrel between the two which resulted in a complete estrangement. Jamal-ud-din after this. showed up Dalip Singh in his true colours to the Russian authorities, and when questioned by M. de Giers about the Maharaja's influence in India replied that—"Dalip Singh had not even a dog with him in India, and that the rising generation knew nothing about him." Jamal-ud-din is also reported to have been connected with the Islamitic League, and while in Russia tried to start an Arabic Persian newspaper in favour of the Russian Government.[44]

Since the Thagi and Dakaiti report does not list its sources it is difficult to evaluate the last statement, not documented elsewhere, though it is not unlike Jamāl ad-Dīn to have had such an idea. The statement above, which is probably based on information later than Morier's two early dispatches, tends to confirm Jamāl ad-Dīn's reports of contacts with important Russians, including Giers and others. Since Morier's reports came from the very first months of Jamāl ad-Dīn's stays in Moscow and St. Petersburg, his negative conclusions about Jamāl ad-Dīn's contacts do not necessarily apply to a later period.

Jamāl ad-Dīn in Russia, 1887–1889 (Persian and Arabic Sources)

THE MOST complete firsthand account of Jamāl ad-Dīn's stay in Russia, which started in the spring of 1887, and continued until 1889, is by Mīrzā Sayyid Husain Khān 'Adālat, whom Jamāl ad-Dīn became friendly with and used as his interpreter in St. Petersburg. Summarizing the entire two-year stay, 'Adālat says:

[44] F.O. 60/594, "Memorandum . . . regarding Jamal-ud-Din," India Office, March 6, 1896, p. 183.

> Sayyid Jamāl ad-Dīn's relations with Katkov, who was a famous Russian newspaper editor and a close friend of the Tsar's, began during his stay in Paris. One of the reasons for the Sayyid's visit to Russia was Katkov's invitation but just as he entered Russia Katkov died and the Sayyid was forced to go alone to Petrograd to promote the fulfillment of his plan.
>
> . . . In this period the Sayyid wanted to encourage a war between Russia and England in order to create the opportunity for a revolt [in India]. But the Russians who had recently emerged from a war with the Ottomans and were in financial difficulties were not ready for any new war.
>
> Jamāl ad-Dīn repeatedly talked with Zinoviev [the head of the Asiatic Section of the Ministry of Foreign Affairs] . . . but the latter would not express support for his plan. (The exact expression of Sayyid Jamāl ad-Dīn about Zinoviev was, "Whenever I throw him in the air he lands on his feet like a cat.")
>
> Then he sought an official audience with the Tsar because he knew this question was pertinent to the affairs of India, but the Tsar was willing only to meet privately. That is why there was only one meeting with the Empress, because a private meeting with the Tsar would have been useless. Sayyid Jamāl ad-Dīn lost hope in fulfilling his plan in Russia, and in the same period the affairs of Zill as-Sultān became disturbed and he was unable to send funds to the Sayyid. That is why he was gradually left without a purpose until Nāsir ad-Dīn Shāh came to Russia on his way to Paris for the celebration of the [French] Republic [1889].[45]

Some relevant details can be added from the *Documents* about Jamāl ad-Dīn's stay in Moscow and St. Petersburg before and during the Shah's 1889 trip to western Europe via St. Petersburg. Included in the *Documents* are several letters written by Jamāl ad-Dīn to Amīn az-Zarb from Moscow and St. Petersburg. The letters are interesting mostly for the tone of moral and religious superiority and admonition which Jamāl ad-Dīn adopts and Amin az-Zarb evidently accepts. Many of them relate to financial accusations that Amīn az-Zarb made against Mīrzā Ni'matallāh, his Moscow agent and evidently the same man named as their Moscow host by *Kāveh*. These accusations may have involved Afghānī, who, in any case, adopts a tone of righteous

45 'Adālat in Luṭfallāh, pp. 99–101.

outrage and threatens Amīn az-Zarb with divine vengeance if he continues to pursue the matter. From these letters it emerges that Afghānī stayed in Moscow until mid-August, 1887. One letter from there is dated July 20, 1887, and another August 14, 1887.[46] Afghānī use Christian and not Muslim dates on these letters.

In the first of these Moscow letters Jamāl ad-Dīn, after reproaching Amīn az-Zarb for breaking some promise made in Moscow, probably involving Mīrzā Ni'matallāh, reports at the end: "I have met with Katkov. He was very happy and took it upon himself to have me meet the Tsar. I shall go after a few days. My biography was printed in the newspapers of Moscow and Petersburg, and it was also noted in the Paris newspapers by means of a telegram."[47] This confirms Jamāl ad-Dīn's hope, reported by 'Adālat, of Katkov's help in meeting the Tsar, though one cannot be certain that the commitment to this introduction was as definite as Jamāl ad-Dīn reported. The August 14 letter says Afghānī is leaving the next day (for St. Petersburg), and responds to complaints of troubles by Amīn az-Zarb. If these troubles arise from someone in a high position, says Afghānī, he will demolish that man through divine power.[48]

The first of nine letters from St. Petersburg dates from several months later, February 9, 1888. It answers certain accusations from Amīn az-Zarb that Jamāl ad-Dīn had been lying or speaking to him in allusions, rejecting such ideas indignantly, and also accuses Amīn az-Zarb of acting badly from fears, suspicions, and vain fantasies. The reference is unspecified but the financial matter of Mīrza Ni'matallāh is again mentioned. This letter and a second one to Amīn az-Zarb from St. Petersburg, dated April 30, are full of elaborately phrased exhortations using Muslim philosophical terminology and concepts on how he should regulate and reform his behavior. The April 30 letter ends with these lines: "The answer to His Excellency Amīn as-Sultān is enclosed in my letter to you which I sent to your address in Tehran. If he asks my friendship give him my greetings."[49]

The correspondence from Amīn az-Zarb to Jamāl ad-Dīn in this St. Petersburg period is also included or summarized in the *Documents,* from which it is learned that Mīrzā Ni'matallāh, Amīn az-

46 Letters listed in *Documents,* p. 93; photos 168–171.

47 *Ibid.,* photos 168–169.

48 *Ibid.,* photos 168–169.

49 *Ibid.,* photo 176. The two letters are in photos 172–176.

Zarb's agent in Moscow, was accused of falsifying accounts. In answer to Jamāl ad-Dīn's April 30 letter, Amīn az-Zarb wrote on June 4 describing further the situation of Mīrzā Ni'matallāh's accounts, and adding, at the end of the letter: "As for the situation of Mīrzā Muhammad Rizā I say that there was and is much to tell about this person. There has been in him nothing but dissimulation and trickery. Truth and sincerity have not been given him. . . . I take refuge in God from this type of men."[50] This reference to a man whose actions against the Iranian government from 1891 to 1896 showed him to be one of Jamāl ad-Dīn's most faithful revolutionary followers is one of several indications that Amīn az-Zarb had little or no idea of the more hidden and revolutionary part of Jamāl ad-Dīn's teachings regarding Iran. A later letter from Amīn az-Zarb to Jamāl ad-Dīn complains further of Mīrzā Rizā, whom Jamāl ad-Dīn defends by defining the present as the age preceding the end of the world, characterized by the depravity and corruption of those who clothe themselves as Muslims. He goes on to request a loan of 5,000 rubles.[51] Several letters from Amīn az-Zarb provide for substantial sums to be given to Jamāl ad-Dīn, and there is also some discussion about railroad building, which Amīn az-Zarb had initiated in Iran and was trying to promote further.[52]

It is apparently in answer to one of these points about railroad building that Jamāl ad-Dīn answered on November 3, saying at the end, "As for the material for the railroad, the ambassador who is in Petersburg says that Hājji Amīn [az-Zarb] has bought nothing for the railroad, and the Minister of the Interior of Russia has verified this question from Belgium. I was very surprised."[53] The reference is apparently to Amīn az-Zarb's trip to western Europe regarding one of the several abortive Iranian railroad proposals, in which Russians were involved. Jamāl ad-Dīn may have been acting as an intermediary between Amīn az-Zarb and Russian governmental figures.

The question of correspondence with Amīn as-Sultān, mentioned by Jamāl ad-Dīn in the April 30 St. Petersburg letter, is brought up again in late November in a letter from Amīn az-Zarb to a mutual

---

50 *Ibid.*, pp. 121–122.

51 *Ibid.*, photos 177–179.

52 *Ibid.*, pp. 122–124. The large sums given by Amīn az-Zarb are listed in Pakdaman, p. 130.

53 *Documents*, photo 180.

acquaintance, Muhammad Javād, who was used to transmit money and news to Jamāl ad-Dīn in Russia. Amīn az-Zarb says, "His Excellency Amīn as-Sultān has written an answer to the letter of Āqā Sayyid Jamāl ad-Dīn. I have enclosed it, please deliver it."[54]

Probably in response to the November letter Jamāl ad-Dīn wrote a long letter to Amīn as-Sultān on January 1, 1889, from St. Petersburg, and another letter on the same day to Amīn az-Zarb.[55] The letter to Amīn az-Zarb refers to a letter from Amīn as-Sultān to Jamāl ad-Dīn promising protection to Abū Turāb via the son of Hājji Sādiq Mujtahid (i.e., Muhammad Tabātabā'ī, a prominent and liberal Tehran mujtahid). The same letter thanks Amīn az-Zarb for loans of 2,000 and 5,000 rubles.

The long letter from Jamāl ad-Dīn to Amīn as-Sultān begins, after honorific greetings, by recalling a discussion they had had on the way to the shrine of 'Abd al-'Azīm, near Tehran. If Amīn as-Sultān recollects what Jamāl ad-Dīn said on that occasion and what he himself said, he will know that if someone through vain fantasies should claim that Jamāl ad-Dīn was trying to create disorder in the "world of disorder" of Iran, he would be mistaken. Some phrases later, Jamāl ad-Dīn attacks the man who published in the (official) newspaper *Iran,* some months before, the charge that Jamāl ad-Dīn's religion was money. (I'timād as-Saltaneh, whose later apology to Jamāl ad-Dīn for publishing things against him is recorded by 'Adālat, is intended.) After referring elliptically to his own attitude to the Shah and the Tsar, Jamāl ad-Dīn continues that he wishes to encourage the unbelievers (i.e., the Russians) to force those who clothe themselves as Muslims (i.e., Iran's rulers) to be Muslims in at least one part of their religion—that which concerns the rights of the public. Jamāl ad-Dīn goes on to a philosophical discussion of the bases of orderly government, saying (as he had in the "Refutation of the Materialists") that good order in kingdoms rests utimately on one of three

---

54 *Ibid.*, p. 125.

55 The letter to Amīn az-Zarb is in *Documents,* photo 181; that to Amīn as-Sultān is both photographed and transcribed into print in Ibrāhīm Ṣafā'ī. ed., *Asnād-i siyāsī-yi daurān-i Qājāriyyeh* (Tehran, 1346/1967–1968), pp. 249–255 (henceforth called Ṣafā'ī, *Asnād*). Although neither includes a year date, the year of the letter to Amīn az-Zarb is clear from the fact that Jamāl ad-Dīn's letters to Amīn az-Zarb were preserved by the latter and are given in the *Documents* in date sequence. The identity of year for the letters to Amīn as-Sultān and Amīn az-Zarb is shown by the absolute identity of headings displayed in the photographs of both letters, and by the reference of both letters to a recent letter from Amīn as-Sultan to Jamāl ad-Dīn promising favor to Abū Turāb in Tehran.

forces: either souls must by nature be so noble that they shun oppression, injustice, and transgression on rights; or men must have a comprehensive reason to restrain them from transistory self-interest and vain passions; or else they must have a very firm faith that forces everyone to observe the rules of right and justice because of his desires and fears (regarding the afterlife). When none of these three exists, disorder, corruption, and ultimately the downfall of a kingdom are inevitable. When one observes decline, it proves the prior existence of the causes of decline:

> Thus every intelligent man can judge from the weakness of Muslim governments, the ruin of their kingdoms, and the afflicted state of the Muslims that the souls of most Muslims are devoid of those threefold foundations. Therefore they consider permissible all things deserving to be shunned, and find all forbidden acts licit, and always count abominable and shameful acts as ordinary affairs. They believe calumny and lying to be intelligence and take pride in oppression and tyranny (like Ahriman, the God of evil among the Zoroastrians). They are distant from every good and are the source of all evils. For example, if someone chooses to remain distant from one of these recent Muslims, or does not greet or pay homage to him, that latter-day Muslim considers it licit to cast every sort of calumny upon that unfortunate man, and to stir up the fires of every sort of trouble; and the fire to his anger will not be quelled until he achieves the killing and the ruin of that man's family, without his regretting it in the least. Rather, he is proud of it, and is constantly saying, "Did you see what I did to so and so, and how I burned him and ruined his household, because one day he did not show respect to me, as was proper?" Of course you remember what things Sanī' ad-Dauleh [i.e., I'timād as-Saltaneh] and those like him wove and spoke about me, in order to gain a little access to Your Excellency, and they were proud of it.

Jamāl ad-Dīn continues that he had heard some months ago that calumnies about himself were being spread by a man in Tehran (I'timād as-Saltaneh). Recently Jamāl ad-Dīn heard that the same man has again published falsehoods. Since Amīn as-Sultān is also involved, Jamāl ad-Dīn wishes to explain the truth to him. Jamāl ad-Dīn then defends himself from charges that he has worked against

Amīn as-Sultān whom, he writes, "I consider the greatest man I have ever encountered. I have developed such a love in my heart for your luminous person that I do not think it could be effaced even by unkindness from you."

The reason for his own intervention with the Russian government, writes Afghānī, is that neophytes in politics have been saying and writing, as in *Akhtar* (a liberal Persian newspaper published in Istanbul) that the Shah and Amīn as-Sultān consider the Russian Government an implacable enemy of the Iranian Government. Since such statements will undoubtedly arouse Russian enmity, Jamāl ad-Dīn says he intervened with the Russians, especially on behalf of Amīn as-Sultan, and everywhere said that neither the Shah nor the men of his government had such an idea (of Russian enmity to Iran), and especially not Amīn as-Sultān.

Jamāl ad-Dīn concludes by thanking Amīn as-Sultan for his letter offering protection of Abū Turāb.

Amīn as-Sultān presented this long letter from Jamāl ad-Dīn to the Shah, along with a note of his own stating that Jamāl ad-Dīn's letter had just been brought to him from the Russian Embassy. Amīn as-Sultān wrote the Shah that Jamāl ad-Dīn's letter was deceitful and did not express his true thoughts; he added that Jamāl ad-Dīn and Hājji Sayyāh's brother, Mīrzā Ja'far, who was also then in St. Petersburg, were working on behalf of Prince Zill as-Sultān, and that Jamāl ad-Dīn and Mīrzā Ja'far had written most of the (bad) things reported in the Russian newspaper about Iran, especially some very bad things that one issue of the newspaper *Herald* had written about Amīn as-Sultān. The presumptuous goal of these men is to show that most of Iran's troubles arise from "ourselves."

After reading Jamāl ad-Dīn's letter, the Shah wrote: "I read the letter of this son of a burnt father (*pidarsūkhteh*). It is not worth two cents and has no significance. Such sons of burnt fathers, when they have fled the country, remain like vipers, and never become moderate and human. No attention should ever be paid to him, and of course you will not write him an answer. Henceforth no attention should be paid to the Russian newspapers either, with the exception that you must write an answer in Europe and give it to western European newspapers."[56]

During the Shah's visit to St. Petersburg early in the summer of

---

[56] Ṣafā'ī, *Asnād*, pp. 249–257. The full translation is in Appendix III.

1889 and afterward, Amīn as-Sultān's behavior toward Afghānī was generally hostile. As noted, Russian newspapers had evidently attributed to Afghānī statements criticizing the Iranian government for following a pro-British policy in the years 1888 and 1889, and these reports had added to preexisting suspicions of Afghānī on the part of Amīn as-Sultān and the Shah. As for I'timād as-Saltaneh's accusations against Afghānī in his newspaper, the articles have not been unearthed, but one may guess that he was writing under pressure from the Shah or his chief minister. According to Adālat's story, cited below, I'timād as-Saltaneh asked and received Jamāl ad-Dīn's forgiveness for these articles when he visited St. Petersburg with the Shah's party.

A most interesting letter from Jamāl ad-Dīn to Amīn az-Zarb dated March 27, 1889, answers unspecified accusations from Amīn az-Zarb against him, apparently related to the accusations discussed in the letter to Amīn as-Sultān. Jamāl ad-Dīn says that all he says and does is for the good of the Muslim community, and in no way has personal selfishness entered it. If the enemies of Iran deny this, Amīn az-Zarb should nonetheless acknowledge it. He says that since God knew the rightness of his deeds and ways, therefore the Ottoman government, which oppressed him, has since been severely cut down. Similarly his other persecutors, the Egyptian Khedive and the Afghan Amīr Shīr 'Alī have since been punished by God—the Khedive by the British occupation of Egypt, and Shīr 'Alī by physical destruction. He says that if Iran persists in her sins and does not repent of them, God, who has cut off the nose and ears of Iran for her past sins, will now cut off her head, and her corpse will be good for vultures and eagles. He says this in warning, and the world will soon see.

Jamāl ad-Dīn continues that many men through him have reached the rank of bey or pasha, or have got salaries, but he himself has no aim but reform and giving counsel. Only God knows what changed the Shah's heart toward him—several men who might be responsible are mentioned allusively, but the allusions are unclear. Jamāl ad-Dīn adds that if his eyes do not work for the good of all he should become blind; if his hand does not try to help the oppressed it should stop moving; and if his feet do not move on the road of freeing all the Muslim community they should be broken. This is his creed. He hopes that His Highness (Amīn as-Sultān) will work for the good of the poor, oppressed, and unfortunate Iranians.[57]

[57] *Documents,* photos 182–183.

One may well believe the sincerity of Jamāl ad-Dīn's view that he had spent his whole life working for the freedom and reform of the Muslim community without trying for personal gain. It is certainly true that he gave no thought to material luxuries and was always content to live a modest life, and also that he often risked his personal position by his bold or frank advice or activities. Although he tried to influence the powerful, it was never only influence for its own sake he wanted, but rather in order to carry out his deeply believed programs. Somewhat more special is Jamāl ad-Dīn's belief, expressed in the above letter and in the 1882 letter to Riyāḍ, that God has punished those who have oppressed him. Although one could infer that this punishment was visited on rulers because of their generally evil policies, there is also a more personal note: God is said to know the rightness of Jamāl ad-Dīn's ways and to punish especially those who do not heed him and instead persecute him.

In a letter to Amīn az-Zarb from St. Petersburg on May 10, 1889, Jamāl ad-Dīn requests the forwarding of the answer he has written to the letter of Amīn as-Sultān—whether this refers to the January 1 letter or, more likely, to a later exchange of letters, is unclear.[58]

On July 3, Jamāl ad-Dīn wrote Amīn az-Zarb describing his contacts with the members of the Shah's suite which had just visited St. Petersburg on its way to London, Paris, and other European cities. Jamāl ad-Dīn writes that at the time the Shah came to St. Petersburg, he, Jamāl ad-Dīn, left cards for all the important men in the Shah's entourage, in the European manner. As a result, Amīn ad-Dauleh, Mukhbir as-Saltaneh, and I'timād as-Saltaneh, all ministers and members of the Shah's party, set appointments for him and met with him. Jamāl ad-Dīn adds that he also wrote a letter to Amīn as-Sultān and asked him to set the time for an appointment. In the letter Jamāl ad-Dīn explained to Amīn as-Sultān that he wanted to refute with sure proofs the lies that liars had spread about him. Amīn as-Sultān kept the bearer of the letter waiting for three hours. Every half hour he emerged to attend to something and said that he would now answer the letter. Finally the bearer gave up hope and returned. Jamāl ad-Dīn adds that he had been planning to leave Russia but some important Russian friends had asked him to stay until the results of the Shah's trip to London became known, so he was now planning to stay longer.[59]

---

58 *Ibid.*, photo 184.
59 *Ibid.*, photos 186–187.

'Adālat gives further details about Jamāl ad-Dīn's contact with ministers in the Shah's suite at the time of their visit to St. Petersburg in the early summer of 1889. Adālat notes that the ambassador and officials of the Iranian Embassy at St. Petersburg were hostile to Jamāl ad-Dīn, and would not help him to see the Shah. Amīn as-Sultān, although he had been friendly to Jamāl ad-Dīn in Tehran, would not see him during this trip. I'timād as-Saltaneh, however, came respectfully to visit Jamāl ad-Dīn and asked forgiveness for the newspaper article he had written against him after Jamāl ad-Dīn left Tehran. I'timād as-Saltaneh criticized the Shah for deliberately keeping Iranians in ignorance and spoke hopelessly about Iran under Nāsir ad-Dīn Shāh.

> When I'timād as-Saltaneh left the Sayyid the latter said, "If there is one wise man who knows history in Iran it is that man." The following day in a government building [the Sayyid] met the late Mukhbir ad-Dauleh and Hājji Amīn ad-Dauleh. Since these two great men were both circumspect with regard to each other, they cautiously parried the Sayyid's questions with jokes. The Sayyid had greater confidence in Hājji Amīn ad-Dauleh than in Mukhbir ad-Dauleh. On his return he said to me that if and when these two men came to trust each other they would save Iran from her present perdition.
>
> Nāsir ad-Dīn Shāh stayed three days in Petrograd and from there headed for London. The Sayyid was very annoyed at the Shah and the courtiers over this trip, and he planned to inflict a blow on the Shah that perhaps might warn him away from his course.[60]

Recalling what Jamāl ad-Dīn had told him about the reasons for the bad policies of Amīn as-Sultān, 'Adālat says that Amīn as-Sultān

> when he was going to Shāhzādeh 'Abd al-'Azīm with the Sayyid in a droshky and the Sayyid was explaining to him perfectly the bad state of affairs [in Iran] and the outcome of the evil policy of Russia and England, confessed in a tearful state that his intimacy to the Shah came from [Amīn as-Sultān's] having no opinions. The Shah wanted to be in peace for his lifetime, and after that he did not care whether Iran

60 'Adālat in Luṭfallāh, pp. 101–102.

remained in existence or not. "Thus it is that I have passed as guilty in the eyes of the people."[61]

This droshky interview with Amīn as-Sultān is also cited in the January 1, 1889, letter from Jamāl ad-Dīn to Amīn as-Sultān. A detail such as the tears of the Amīn as-Sultān may be fanciful, from what is known of the chief minister's character. On the other hand, the words attributed to Amīn as-Sultān match so exactly his statements as often reported by the British representatives in Tehran that some credence may be given to the interview. Jamāl ad-Dīn in his public pronouncements from 1890 on never gave this (mainly accurate) picture of Amīn as-Sultān as simply carrying out the wishes of the Shah, but rather tried to show him as a strong evil influence.

Afghānī's correspondence and the 'Adālat story reveal a continuing effort by Jamāl ad-Dīn to get back in the good graces of the leading men of the Persian government, including Amīn as-Sultān. The calculated snub by Amīn as-Sultān, reported above, may have been one reason why Jamāl ad-Dīn soon began to be more direct in his attacks on the Iranian government. Also important were economic concessions made to the hated British in the years 1888 and 1890. These concessions on top of years of selfish misrule by the Iranian government were to give Jamāl ad-Dīn and others an opportunity to rally opposition to that government from 1890 on.

Russian economic and political influence in Iran had been generally growing through the 1870's and 1880's, partly as a result of the completion of Russian railroads near the Iranian border, making the transport of goods into Iran much easier and more economical. Lord Salisbury's Conservative British government wanted to create a counterweight to Russian pressure in Iran, and so sent the prominent and powerful Sir Henry Drummond Wolff as minister from 1888 until illness forced his retirement in 1890. Wolff was instructed to promote British influence and commerce, which he did in a most aggressive, and at first successful, manner. Amīn as-Sultān and Nāsir ad-Dīn Shāh were glad to have this counterweight to growing Russian pressure on Iran, and Amīn as-Sultān confided in Wolff on many questions of policy. The Iranian government conceded to him much of what he requested, starting with a paper guarantee issued by the Shah but written in fact by Wolff, of the inviolability of life and property of Persian subjects, which was never enforced. The first

61 *Ibid.*, p. 101.

important achievement by Wolff was to convince the Shah to open the Karun, Iran's only major navigable river, to the commerce of all nations in October 1888. Since the river was in the south only the British could be expected to use it, and the Russians objected to its opening. The Russians had earlier forced from the Shah a secret agreement that no transport concessions would be granted without Russian perusal, and though the Shah could point out that the opening of one of his own rivers to the ships of all countries was not technically a concession, Russian anger continued. Russian complaints were to mount when further actual concessions of a major character were made to the British, beginning with the Imperial Bank concession of 1889, giving a British company the right to build the only modern bank in Iran with a monopoly on the issuance of paper money. Some counterconcessions were forced by the Russians.[62]

Jamāl ad-Dīn, already disgusted with the Iranian government for its lack of interest in reform and aggressive independence, must now have become concerned over the Anglophile policy of the government, on the increase from the time of Wolff's arrival in 1888, and also over the renewed scramble for Western concessions in Iran, which had been somewhat in abeyance since the cancellation of the notorious and all-embracing Reuter Concession of 1872. According to 'Adālat, upon the opening of the Karun to trade, Jamāl ad-Dīn wrote an extended article in a German-language newspaper against it, pointing out that England would benefit from it and Russia would lose. This article was translated in other Russian newspapers, and helped arouse hostility to Nāsir ad-Dīn Shāh in Russia. 'Adālat, who by now was in Tiflis and so reports indirectly, says that the Shah decided it was harmful to have a man like Sayyid Jamāl ad-Dīn in Russia, and so invited him back to Iran.[63] There may in fact have been some such invitation from the Iranian government with the hope of getting Jamāl ad-Dīn away from Russia, but, as noted below, the story is both more murky and more complicated than 'Adālat's simple account.

Soon after the Shah and his party left Russia in mid-1889, Jamāl ad-Dīn also left, joining up with the Shah's party later that year at Munich. Thus, his first stay in Russia lasted about two years, from

---

[62] See Nikki R. Keddie, *Religion and Rebellion in Iran: The Tobacco Protest of 1891–1892* (London, 1966), chap. i and the sources cited therein. See also Firuz Kazemzadeh, *Russia and Britain in Persia 1864–1914* (New Haven, 1968), chap. iii.

[63] 'Adālat in Luṭfallāh, p. 102.

the spring of 1887 until mid-1889. Russian documents might tell more about this two-year stay, once they become available.

Interesting anecdotes about Jamāl ad-Dīn in St. Petersburg have been preserved in Arabic by 'Abd ar-Rashīd Ibrāhīm, a Russian-born Muslim who was in St. Petersburg during Jamāl ad-Dīn's visit. Ibrāhīm says that he first met Jamāl ad-Dīn in St. Petersburg in 1889 and was extraordinarily attracted and impressed by him. Jamāl ad-Dīn entered a discussion with one of the Muslim ulama of Russia, and when the conversation turned to the question of Islamic jurisprudence (*fiqh*), Jamāl ad-Dīn laughed and said: "Haven't you stopped being concerned with questions of *fiqh*? You will drown in a storm of contradictions." Ibrāhīm says he was dumbfounded by an alim who laughed at the books of *fiqh*. When another alim asked him whether the lands subject to Russian penetration were in the Abode of Islam or the Abode of War (*Dār al-Islām* or *Dār al-Ḥarb*), Jamāl ad-Dīn said, "How can it be *Dār al-Islām*? . . . There is no *Dār al-Islām* in the East except the defense of the Islamic caliphate; and Islam does not allow anything against that."

After describing his own vast admiration for Jamāl ad-Dīn, Ibrāhīm says that after some days Jamāl ad-Dīn expressed a desire to go to a theater, and, when Ibrāhīm suggested the opera house, Jamāl ad-Dīn asked him to reserve a box near the Tsar's box, and he did. Jamāl ad-Dīn went to the opera in the full regalia of a Muslim alim, and his appearance caused a stir. The curtain rose on a wonderful scene, but Jamāl ad-Dīn kept glancing at his watch as if he had forgotten something. Then he arose, faced toward Mecca, and said in a loud voice: "I intend to say the evening prayer: God is the Most Great!" All eyes turned toward their box in amazement, but Jamāl ad-Dīn continued to pray aloud. The Tsar, the Empress, and the princes had turned toward them and all whispered to one another. Then a Russian general entered their box and asked Ibrāhīm the meaning of all this. Sweating and dizzy, he could only answer, "Ask him after he finishes the prayer!" Both waited until the end of the prayer, and when Jamāl ad-Dīn finished praying without deviating in the slightest from the proper form, he went out into the hall and told the general (with the author translating) that the Prophet had said, "I have a time with God which has no room for King or Prophet," (a misstatement of a Muslim hadith) and asked the general to repeat his words to the Tsar. When the general told the Tsar, the latter expressed his respect for so strong and fearless a religious faith, whereas the author rebuked Jamāl ad-Dīn for embarrassing him before his friends and the Tsar. Jamāl ad-Dīn replied that he had brought the word of Islam to the Tsar, the Empress, the princes, and the ministers of Russia, and was not worried about the results.

The significance of this story was not Jamāl ad-Dīn's punctiliousness about the hour of prayer, to judge from Ibrāhīm's very next story concerning a gathering of Jamāl ad-Dīn's in Istanbul in the 1890's attended by Ibrāhīm at which Jamāl ad-Dīn refused repeatedly the entreaties of a man present who wanted to interrupt the gathering at the prayer hour so that all could say their prayers.[64] Ibrāhīm apparently accepts Afghānī's explanation that he acted in order to bring Islam to the attention of Russia's leaders, but others might conclude that he was equally concerned to bring himself to the Tsar's attention.

Although these stories have no independent confirmation, they do stem from an admirer of Afghānī's and were not invented to cast a bad light on him, and they do ring true, from what is known of his character, personality, and manner of speech and behavior.

As for the results of Jamāl ad-Dīn's Russian trip as a whole, despite his probable contacts with Giers, the talks with Zinoviev noted by 'Adālat, and the impression he may have made on Russian society, it seems clear that Afghānī failed to accomplish anything substantial during his two-year stay in Russia. As already indicated by the 'Adālat story, he was unable to convince Zinoviev to give him any encouragement in schemes involving a Russo-British war and an Indian uprising, and his influence on the cautious Giers very likely was even smaller. Through occasional newspaper articles and his talk in society he may have added his bit to the growth of anti-British feeling in Russia, particularly with reference to Iran, but this feeling was already running high because of Drummond Wolff's aggressive support of British interests, and it is doubtful that Jamāl ad-Dīn contributed anything very significant to it.

When Jamāl ad-Dīn left Russia for western Europe in the middle of 1889, he had not yet given up hope of accomplishing something through his Russian contacts, and it is now that we must try to follow him through one of the most obscure episodes of his adventurous career.

---

64 Memoirs reprinted in Anwar al-Jundī, *ash-Sharq fī fajr al-yaqẓa* (Cairo, 1966), pp. 30–33.

11

Russia to Iran: 1889–1891

FROM 1889 TO 1891 the interaction of Sayyid Jamāl ad-Dīn and the Iranian chief minister, Amīn as-Sultān, resulted in a complex web that is difficult to unravel on the basis of the words of either, since both sometimes manipulated the truth for their own purposes. Here the words of neither are taken as gospel, and an attempt is made to arrive at the most likely story for those years.

When he left Russia in mid-1889, Jamāl ad-Dīn may have gone first to Paris, and was concerned to rejoin the Shah's suite, which he succeeded in doing in Munich. The most direct and apparently unprejudiced account of what occurred in Munich is in the diary of I'timād as-Saltaneh, Iran's Minister of Press and Publications, published in the *Documents*. The following entries are relevant:

> 21 Zī al-Hijjeh, 1306 [August 18, 1889], Munich. Sayyid Jamāl ad-Dīn has come from Petersburg and came to my house; I did not see him.
>
> 22 Zī al-Hijjeh, 1306—I went to see Sayyid Jamāl ad-Dīn. He wanted to meet with the Shah and Amīn as-Sultān. . . . I sent him to the house of Amīn as-Sultān. I went to see the Shah. . . . Sayyid Jamāl ad-Dīn says: What they have attributed to me in the Russian newspapers I did not write, and I came to exonerate myself. However, he must have come for another purpose. He has seen the Shah. *Tonight he will also go for an interview with Amīn as-Sultān.*

> 24 Zi al-Hijjeh, 1306, Salzburg. . . . Among the new events are, first of all, *Amīn as-Sultān in order to flatter the Russians will bring Sayyid Jamāl ad-Dīn to Tehran.* He has also satisfied the Shah.[1] [Italics mine]

Amīn ad-Dauleh, who was with the Shah's party in Munich, also records that the Shah and Amīn as-Sultān invited Jamāl ad-Dīn to Tehran.[2] Amīn as-Sultān later denied making the invitation, but on this point it appears that Jamāl ad-Dīn and not Amīn as-Sultān was telling the truth. Before going from Munich to Tehran Afghānī returned to Russia, where he later claimed he had been sent on a mission by Amīn as-Sultān, a claim consonant with I'timād as-Saltaneh's report that Amīn as-Sultān wanted to use Jamāl ad-Dīn to flatter or appease the Russians. During this period the Russian government was angry at the Iranian government over concessions to the British and over the fact discovered by the Russians that their conversations with the Iranian government were reported to Sir Henry Drummond Wolff.[3] The Iranian rulers, and particularly Amīn as-Sultān, were looking for ways to allay Russian anger, and they may have thought to make use of Jamāl ad-Dīn, who no doubt impressed on them his influence with the Russian government.

Unfortunately, we are at present entirely dependent on Jamāl ad-Dīn's words for a description of his second Russian trip. Jamāl ad-Dīn's most complete extant description of the second Russian trip was written after the Shah had banished him from Tehran for the second time in mid-1890, when he wished to protest this and change the Shah's attitude toward him. The circumstances would prompt him to give an apologetic account. At this point, from his sanctuary near Tehran, he wrote a letter to the Shah, which was later reprinted and became the basis of accounts of his second trip to Russia.[4] The letter may be summarized as follows:

---

1 *Documents,* p. 150. After this, in what appears more like a later emendation than I'timād as-Saltaneh's real opinion in 1889, he says, "It is likely that the presence of this man will be the cause of a great disturbance in Iran which will have no benefit for the government."

2 Amīn ad-Dauleh, *Khāṭirāt-i siyāsī-yi Mīrzā 'Alī Khān-i Amīn ad-Dauleh,* ed. Hafez Farman-Farmaian (Tehran, 1962), p. 140.

3 Nikki R. Keddie, *Religion and Rebellion in Iran: The Tobacco Protest of 1891–1892* (London, 1966), chap. i, and Firuz Kazemzadeh, *Russia and Britain in Persia 1864–1914* (New Haven, 1968), chap. iii.

4 The letter, a draft of which is in the Majlis Library Collection, was first published in Nāzim al-Islām Kirmānī, *Tārikh-i bīdārī-yi Īrāniyān* (2d ed.; Tehran, 1945–46), pp. 65–67.

Jamāl ad-Dīn begins with the usual honorifics, and then says that although he was not able to see the Shah himself in Munich, he did see Amīn as-Sultān. (This contradicts I'timād as-Saltaneh's statement that Afghānī did see the Shah and must be considered a more reliable statement, as Afghānī would hardly have written to the Shah that he had not seen him if he had.) Jamāl ad-Dīn says that Amīn as-Sultān had asked him to go to St. Petersburg in order to regulate "some necessary matters," and after finishing to return to Iran. He says Amīn as-Sultān spoke with him for five hours and asked him to pacify the anger of the Russian government and newspapermen at him, Amīn as-Sultān, as he had not been able to control recent events, and that Amīn as-Sultān also relayed the statement that the recent concessions to the British—the Bank, the opening of the Karun River and its attached concessions of virtually all mining rights in Iran[5]—had been completed before his own promotion to the rank of chief minister, but that he, Amīn as-Sultān, was unfortunate enough to have their execution occur in the time of his ministry. Jamāl ad-Dīn says that Amīn as-Sultān asked that he exonerate the chief minister from responsibility before the Russian government, change their negative attitude toward him, and demonstrate his good intentions toward the Russians. Second, Amīn as-Sultān had asked him to tell Giers, the Russian Prime Minister and Foreign Minister, and Giers's advisers Zinoviev and Nikolai (?)[6], that in order to demonstrate his good intention toward the Russians he was prepared to cancel the Karun, the Bank, and the mines and return them to their former state if only the Russians would propose an easy way to do so. Jamāl ad-Dīn continues:

> I, since I knew that the success of the aims of the chief minister was the source of the Shah's satisfaction and the good of the Islamic nation, returned to Petersburg. I endeavoured to persuade to my opinion several persons whom I knew were in accord with me about Eastern politics, such as General Obruchev in the Ministry of War, and General Rikhter in the Ministry of Court, and General Ignatiev, the former Russian Minister in Istanbul, and Madam Novikov,

[5] The letter refers to these only as the bank, the mines, and the Karun; the explanation is mine.

[6] The Russian names are written in the Arabic script, and several of them are mistranscribed in the published version of the letter. This Russian name reads Y-l-n-kā-lī (or lai).

> an influential woman who is chiefly occupied with questions of Anglo-Russian relatives. In the course of two months I met twenty times with M. Giers and with his advisers.

Jamāl ad-Dīn continues that even before turning to the mission given him by Amīn as-Sultān he had tried, with the help of his supporters in Russia, to prove that the good of the Russian government in the East lay in harmony and kindness toward the Iranian government. Jamāl ad-Dīn says he had constantly pointed out the Shah's beneficence in giving over (to the Russians) the Atrek and the Turkoman lands. Then he had referred to the aims of Amīn as-Sultān, and said the latter had told him personally in Munich that he was ready, if the Russians showed a way that would not bring about war or an indemnity, to cancel the [British] Karun and Bank and mines concessions and restore the former balance among Russia, Iran, and England. Jamāl ad-Dīn says he also tried, as much as possible, to show the chief minister's good intentions regarding Russia, as he had written to him from Petersburg. Giers and his advisers afterward said they must consult with the Russian Minister of War and the Minister of Finances about the matter, and present the results of their consultations to the Tsar. Then, they said, if a way was found to solve the problem they would tell Jamāl ad-Dīn for communication to Amīn as-Sultān.

After several consultations, continues Afghānī, two policies were decided on, one for Jamāl ad-Dīn and one for Amīn as-Sultān, and Jamāl ad-Dīn was asked to communicate them to Amīn as-Sultān. If the policies were followed the problem would be solved. Jamāl ad-Dīn says he was very happy at having been able to do such a service to the Islamic government and to satisfy the chief minister.

Jamāl ad-Dīn continues that when he returned to Tehran (in November, 1889) he notified the chief minister, who placed him in the home of Amīn az-Zarb. He says he did not move from this spot for three months, except once to answer an honorable invitation to visit the Shah. In this period the chief minister did not ask what had happened in Petersburg. Jamāl ad-Dīn sent him several notes and Amīn as-Sultān promised to see him. As time passed Jamāl ad-Dīn was asked (presumably by the Russians) about the affair, and he said there had as yet been no inquiry from the chief minister, and he did not know why. When this indifference of the chief minister was made known to the Russian Ministry, after all Jamāl ad-Dīn's insistence and pleas in Petersburg, they considered the affair as trifling with them and a political trick and telegraphed the Russian Embassy in Tehran saying that Sayyid Jamāl ad-Dīn had carried out some oral commissions on behalf of the chief minister. The Russian Government said further: If the chief minister wants to enter into those questions let him talk directly and officially to the Russian Ministry in Tehran or to the Iranian Ministry in Petersburg, and from now on if Sayyid Jamāl ad-Dīn, who was given some commissions in an unofficial manner, speaks to them (the Russians) about these affairs, they would not accept it.

Jamāl ad-Dīn continues, expressing shock and amazement, that after taking such great pains, affairs finally reverted to their original bad state. The Shah, with his God-given wisdom, knew better than anyone the results of this kind of affair. When Amīn as-Sultān learned the contents of the Russian telegram, instead of expressing regret at not exploring the thoughts of the Russian ministers in this matter and listening to their answers, he told Arab Sāhib (Grigorovich, the translator of the Russian Legation), "I said nothing to Sayyid Jamāl ad-Dīn that he was to transmit to the Russian Ministry, and I did not send him to Petersburg."

Jamāl ad-Dīn goes on to say that the strangest thing of all is that the Shah should have asked him (in mid-1890) to leave Tehran for Qum, for which he cannot imagine the reason. He asks which of the services he performed in Russia is his fault, and asks the Shah not to pay attention to the idle talk of others.

This letter, written for the purpose of regaining the favor of the Shah, is the main source of information about Jamāl ad-Dīn's second stay in Russia in the autumn of 1889. It cites Amīn as-Sultān's denial that he had sent Jamāl ad-Dīn on a mission to Russia, a denial that is reiterated in other sources. What is one to conclude? Although it seems most probable that his usual mechanism of exaggerating his own role in important events was at work, and though Jamāl ad-Dīn had self-protective motives in presenting the affair as he did to the Shah, it appears likely that there is a substratum of truth in his story. The words attributed to Amīn as-Sultān in trying to exonerate himself from blame for concessions to the British in the eyes of the Russians are entirely typical of his confidential conversations reported in other documents. Also, I'timād as-Saltaneh's Munich diary indicates that Amīn as-Sultān was dealing with Jamāl ad-Dīn in order to flatter or pacify the Russians. On the other hand, Amīn as-Sultān's hostile note to the Shah about Afghānī in 1889 (cited in the last chapter) makes it unlikely that Amīn as-Sultān would entrust Afghānī with any official mission. If one were to make an educated guess about the question it might run somewhat like this: Jamāl ad-Dīn had presented himself to Amīn as-Sultān at Munich as someone who, because of his personal ties to high Russian officials, might help smooth over the current anger of the Russians at Iran's recent Anglophile policies and concessions. Amīn as-Sultān had agreed it would be useful to pacify this anger, had maintained that he personally should not be blamed by the Russians for the recent concessions, and had possibly suggested that Jamāl ad-Dīn speak to some of his Russian friends before coming to Iran. To the Russians Jamāl ad-Dīn had presented his visit as a high-level mission from Amīn as-Sultān. Meanwhile, Amīn as-Sultān had had second thoughts, perhaps becoming convinced that no good could come of dealing with Jamāl ad-Dīn, refused henceforth to see him, and denied having suggested any kind of mission. The names of the persons Jamāl ad-Dīn said he saw are credible, since his acquaintance with the two most important, Giers and Zinoviev, is documented from other sources, while the others were mostly representatives of the anti-British party with whom Jamāl ad-Dīn had contact. The words attributed to Amīn as-Sultān, that the Karun, Bank, and mines concessions could be canceled if the Russians could think of a way to do this without indemnity or war, seem plausible, for Amīn as-Sultān must have been well aware that cancellation without indemnity was impossible. He might have taken this means to indicate goodwill toward the Russians, if only they could think of a way out. Amīn as-Sultān, as British, French, and Russian documents of these years show, was much inclined to present himself to both the British and the Russians as being basically their partisan, unfortunately moved by irrevocable force of circumstances to make certain concessions to the other side.

It seems that Jamāl ad-Dīn, having exaggerated the official nature of his mission from Amīn as-Sultān to the Russian officials, proceeded to claim upon his arrival in Iran that he had an official mission from the Russian government. This claim is suggested in the first official British report of the presence of Jamāl ad-Dīn in Tehran, which was made by Sir Henry Drummond Wolff, now British Minister to Iran, shortly after Jamāl ad-Dīn's arrival, on December 20, 1889. Wolff wrote of hearing a report that I'timād as-Saltaneh was to be dismissed as Minister of Press and the "well-known Sheikh Jemaleddin" was to become the new minister. On this question, he enclosed a memorandum by his Oriental Secretary, named Churchill. The latter said that in reply to an inquiry on the above rumor Amīn as-Sultān

> said that he had not seen the sheikh since his arrival at Tehran; that Jemaluddin had written to His Excellency from the frontier informing him of his projected sojourn at Tehran; that the Amin had replied that every one was free to come to Persia who liked, no permission was required. He understood what Sheikh Jemaludin wished to intimate, that he had been trying to avoid any contact with the man, whom he stigmatized as an intriguer of the vilest type. When the Sheikh arrived at Tehran he went to stay outside the town about five miles away, at a house belonging to Haji Muhammed Hassan, Amin dar-uz-zarb, adjoining the Mint. This Haji is a dependent of the Amin-us-Sultan. From there the Sheikh wrote to the Amin-us-Sultan, saying that he was his guest, longing to pay his respects to him and awaiting his instructions. The Amin put him off by saying that he was accompanying the Shah to Jajurd and had no time.

Amīn as-Sultān then asked Grigorovich, the translator of the Russian legation, if it was true that Jamāl ad-Dīn had a mission from the Russian government. After making inquiries at St. Petersburg, Grigorovich denied it. The British Oriental Secretary, Churchill, continued: "Since this communication from the Russian Legation the Amin-us-Sultan perceives a change in the language used by Sheikh Jemaludin, who no longer advertises himself as the agent of the Russian Government to the people of Persia."[7] Churchill adds that there is no truth to the story about the dismissal of I'timād as-Saltaneh and his replacement by Jamāl ad-Dīn.

It thus seems likely that Jamāl ad-Dīn first presented himself in Russia as having a regular official mission from the Iranian government, probably exaggerating an informal discussion with Amīn as-Sultān; and then in Iran similarly inflated his informal and unofficial conversations with various members of the Russian government into an official position from the Russians. At a time when British advances loomed more menacing than Russian ones to many enlightened Iranians, and when men like Amīn ad-Dauleh and I'timād as-

---

[7] F.O. 60/502, Wolff to Salisbury, no. 231, Dec. 20, 1889. Enclosed Memorandum by Churchill, Dec. 18, 1889.

Saltaneh were working with the Russians against Amīn as-Sultān and his concessions to the British, a claim of Russian backing was not necessarily in conflict with the reforming and patriotic words of Jamāl ad-Dīn. Such a claim could have the additional benefit of rendering him a force to be reckoned with by the Iranian government, and to restrain them from treating him too harshly.

On the day after he sent home the above report by letter, Wolff telegraphed the Foreign Office, "Sheikh Jemaledeen is here. The Shah is much annoyed."[8] Since Wolff nearly always got his reports on the Shah's sentiments via Amīn as-Sultān, the report may in fact be more indicative of the latter's feelings than of the Shah's. Indeed there is no indication in the British document that Wolff had any information beyond the conversation cited above between Churchill and Amīn as-Sultān.

Correspondence between Jamāl ad-Dīn and Nāsir ad-Dīn Shāh in December, 1889, reprinted by Jamāl ad-Dīn's nephew Lutfallāh, suggests that the relations between Jamāl ad-Dīn and the Shah were not then hostile, although Jamāl ad-Dīn feared possible mistreatment. Soon after his arrival in Iran Jamāl ad-Dīn wrote to the Shah saying that, having accomplished his mission, he had arrived at the Mint (outside Tehran), but before entering Tehran and asking for an audience with the Shah he wished to be assured that the Shah's invitation was sincere, and that the Shah would not act against him, as calumniators were suggesting. The Shah answered that he had confidence in Jamāl ad-Dīn's word and his patriotism, and that he, the Shah, would keep his engagements. He asked Jamāl ad-Dīn to go to stay with the chief minister (Amīn as-Sultān) and to come for an audience in his company. Jamāl ad-Dīn replied that he did not wish to stay with the chief minister, but rather with Amīn az-Zarb, to which the Shah agreed.[9]

That Amīn as-Sultān went to great pains to have as little as possible to do with Jamāl ad-Dīn while he was in Tehran on this trip is amply documented in the *Documents*. In notebooks containing the correspondence of Amīn az-Zarb, the presence of Sayyid Jamāl ad-Dīn near Tehran is first announced at the end of November, 1889, a few weeks before Wolff reported on it. On December 3, 1889, Amīn az-Zarb wrote a letter to a friend saying that Jamāl ad-Dīn, whom

---

8 F.O. 60/594, Wolff to Salisbury, Dec. 21, 1889, Tel. no. 182.

9 This correspondence is translated from Luṭfallāh's biography in Pakdaman, pp. 319–321.

the government had invited from Russia to Iran, had become his guest near Tehran. He says that they are now awaiting a visit from Amīn as-Sultān who would either take Jamāl ad-Dīn to be his own guest, determine another host, or ask Amīn az-Zarb to be his host.[10]

From a letter written to Amīn az-Zarb, who was out of town, by his son Husain on December 7 it is learned that Amīn as-Sultān had given Jamāl ad-Dīn more hope of governmental favor and contact than he admitted to Wolff. In talking with Amīn az-Zarb's son Amīn as-Sultān seemed to think it natural that he be asked to determine Jamāl ad-Dīn's dwelling, and also felt obliged to promise a visit. In this letter the son writes that he had received a letter from Jamāl ad-Dīn who had arrived at the Mint (outside Tehran). Jamāl ad-Dīn had enclosed a letter from Amīn as-Sultān and asked Amīn az-Zarb's son to deliver it and to bring an answer. The son delivered it immediately, and Amīn as-Sultān said he must transmit it to the Shah. The son asked where Jamāl ad-Dīn should stay, and Amīn as-Sultān is quoted as saying: "Your home is the house especially for my intimates. Bring him and let your house be his lodging. I will show his letter to His Majesty. When the proper course is decided I will tell you and will also come myself." Amīn az-Zarb's son went the next day to bring Jamāl ad-Dīn to his house in town, where the guest was well received on all sides. Amīn as-Sultān had promised to come the day before but he had not come either then or the next day. Now it seemed he had gone on a trip to Jajurd and Amīn az-Zarb's son did not know when he would come.[11]

The letter to Amīn az-Zarb from his son suggests that Amīn as-Sultān had made some promises to Jamāl ad-Dīn and had assumed some responsibility for him. Otherwise he should have expressed surprise when Amīn az-Zarb's son expected him to be responsible for Jamāl ad-Dīn and to determine some course of activity for him. It seemed likely that Amīn as-Sultān, by his temporizing behavior, was trying to placate both the Russians and Jamāl ad-Dīn's influential Iranian friends, without actually having anything to do with him.

Two days later, on December 9, Amīn az-Zarb's son wrote to his father complaining that nobody in the government has visited, given

---

[10] *Documents*, p. 127, sheet 90.

[11] *Ibid.*, p. 128, sheet 100. This series of letters is listed only as being written *to* Hājii Muhammad Hasan in Mahmudabad. Their content reveals that they are from his son, Hājji Muhammad Husain, as was told me by the latter's son, Asghar Mahdavī, in Tehran, 1966.

instructions, or even asked about Jamāl ad-Dīn.[12] On December 28 he wrote again that Amīn as-Sultān has still not come to see Jamāl ad-Dīn, and described his own call on Amīn as-Sultān: "He asked how Jamāl ad-Dīn was. I said, 'Since he has not seen you, he is very sad.' He said, 'You yourself know that I am very busy, and of course will excuse me.' I said yes, and he said 'How long does he intend to stay?' I said 'However long you command.' He said no more."[13]

The Shah was now apparently less hostile to Jamāl ad-Dīn than was Amīn as-Sultān, since unlike the latter he agreed to give him an audience. It may be that the Shah's relative acceptance of Jamāl ad-Dīn at this point influenced Amīn as-Sultān's use of delaying tactics toward him rather than openly hostile ones. In any case, Amīn az-Zarb's son wrote his father on January 4, 1890, that he had gone that day to see the Shah, who had ordered Amīn as-Sultān to come to his house to see Jamāl ad-Dīn on Monday, and to bring Jamāl ad-Dīn for a royal audience on Tuesday.[14] Amīn as-Sultān failed to keep his Monday appointment with Jamāl ad-Dīn. The next day, however, the Shah gave Jamāl ad-Dīn his promised audience. Amīn az-Zarb's son reports the conversation (concerning railroads) of the Shah and Jamāl ad-Dīn.[15]

A month later, on February 8, there is another report that Amīn as-Sultān had still not come to visit, and had not even answered Jamāl ad-Dīn's latest petition.[16] The *Documents* also contain a letter from Amīn az-Zarb to Amīn as-Sultān, undated, saying that he had come to visit Amīn as-Sultān along with Sayyid Jamāl ad-Dīn. Amīn as-Sultān returned a note in the margin thanking them for the visit, asking to be excused, and saying that he would come to visit them later.[17] I'timād as-Saltaneh also noted in his diary on February 13, 1890, that he had gone to see Jamāl ad-Dīn, who said that Amīn as-Sultān had not yet seen him, and was very offended about this neglect.[18]

There is no suggestion in the *Documents* or elsewhere of further

---

12 *Ibid.*, pp. 128–129, sheet 149.

13 *Ibid.*, p. 129.

14 *Ibid.*, p. 129, sheet 201.

15 *Ibid.*, p. 130. According to Pakdaman, p. 136, the railroad discussed was one that Amīn az-Zarb wanted to build in north Iran, which Jamāl ad-Dīn had discussed with Russian authorities.

16 *Documents*, p. 130.

17 *Ibid.*, p. 110, item 1; and photograph no. 204.

18 *Ibid.*, p. 150.

contact between Jamāl ad-Dīn and Amīn as-Sultān or the Shah between February and July, when the Shah ordered Jamāl ad-Dīn to leave Tehran. By then the Shah had evidently come to share Amīn as-Sultān's antipathy, for reasons that are discussed below.

The dispatches from Sir Henry Drummond Wolff on December 20 and 21, 1889, raise not only the question of Amīn as-Sultān's and the Shah's attitudes toward Jamāl ad-Dīn, but also the rumor of his becoming Minister of Press. Two other documents imply that the question of having Jamāl ad-Dīn edit a newspaper had been discussed with the Shah. It may be this proposal that Wolff had heard of in the exaggerated and unlikely form that Jamāl ad-Dīn was to replace I'timād as-Saltaneh as Minister of Press.

The first evidence of an editorship for Jamāl ad-Dīn comes in I'timād as-Saltaneh's diary entry for December 24, 1889, parts of which, indicated by the ellipsis, are unfortunately illegible: "The Shah without introduction said: 'Why have you not brought the newspaper *Ittilā'* for me some time?' Against the wish of the chief minister the Shah . . . will not show honor to newspapers [?] and will not make Sayyid Jamāl ad-Dīn the editor of a newspaper."[19]

What seems implied is that Jamāl ad-Dīn's editorship had been suggested to the Shah, probably by I'timād as-Saltaneh, but the Shah would not accept the idea, since Amīn as-Sultān was opposed to it.

Another document concerning the proposed editorship, which also helps to explain the Shah's growing fear of Jamāl ad-Dīn, comes in a report home by the long-standing French Minister in Tehran, de Balloy, on May 27, 1896, following the assassination of the Shah by a disciple of Afghānī's. Of Sultan Abdülhamid II's refusal to extradite Jamāl ad-Dīn to Iran from Istanbul on the grounds that he was an Afghan, de Balloy says:

> In fact this individual is perfectly Persian; he was born at Saad Abad, everyone knows his family. He is a revolutionary agitator by profession. . . . When he came here in 1890 he wanted to publish a journal. The Shah and Amin es Sultan said they could allow it only if his manuscripts were censored. The first article he submitted to them was a long *factum* directed against the Christians who everywhere, in India, in Egypt, in Tunisia, and in Algeria, hold good Mus-

19 *Ibid.*, p. 150. The illegibility is of course in the original handwritten version and noted by Afshār.

> lims under the yoke. The blood of the infidels must run in order that the number of Muslims should grow and their influence increase in the world, etc. etc. The Shah, fearing that this ranter would produce some attempt against the Europeans who lived in Tehran, made him leave.[20]

Though de Balloy is probably reporting what Amīn as-Sultān told him about Jamāl ad-Dīn's exile, presenting it as having been done to protect Europeans, the contents ascribed to Jamāl ad-Dīn's first article sound typical and convincing. It is strange that this story of the proposed newspaper editorship, refused by the Shah, has not entered the published biographies, which have instead given baseless accounts of the Shah's plans for a high ministerial post for Jamāl ad-Dīn.

Quite apart from any newspaper venture, the Shah was given increasing reason in the course of 1890 to be wary of Jamāl ad-Dīn. He was very likely getting warnings from others than Amīn as-Sultān. The Persian Minister to St. Petersburg was concerned enough to report to his British counterpart Morier on the dangers of Jamāl ad-Dīn's presence in Tehran, and was likely to have reported similarly to his own government. On February 7, 1890, Morier reported:

> . . . Mirza Mahmoud Khan, my Persian colleague, has now informed me in the strictest confidence and with great anxiety lest it should appear that the information came from him, that he had reason to know that the Sheikh was at present in Persia and doing much mischief there. He knew for certain that when here the individual had been frequently in communication with Monsieur Zinovieff. He is now posing at Tehran as under the protection of Russia, and is undoubtedly trying to further Russian interests there. Mirza Mahmoud has reason to know that he was the author of the sensational telegram from Tiflis descriptive of the presentation to the Shah of a Persian Bible by Sir Henry Wolff, the consequent riot and the flight of H.M. Minister to Tabreez. It would appear that the Sheikh is a Persian subject, or at least that he was born there, of Afghan parents and my colleague is strongly of opinion that the Persian authorities should expel him without loss of time, though quietly and

20 France, Archives du Ministère des Affaires Étrangères (henceforth called A.E.) Perse, 46, 1895–1896, de Balloy to Honotaux, no. 27, May 29, 1896.

> circumspectly so that he should not have a pretext for posing as a victim and rushing into Russian arms.[21]

A copy of Morier's dispatch was sent to Wolff in Tehran, and it was apparently in response to this that Wolff reported home on April 24, 1890:

> . . . I have communicated with the Amin-es-Sultan respecting the presence of Tehran of the Sheikh Jemaluddin. The Sheikh is living at the house of Hadji Mohammed Hassan, the proprietor of the Amol railway and to a certain extent a subordinate of the Grand Vizier.
>
> His Highness said that he had seen as little as possible of the Sheikh and had instructed the Hadji to give him a hint to leave Tehran as he could gain nothing by remaining.[22]

A confidential report was sent home by Wolff on April 14, 1890, emanating from a secret informant, apparently an Iranian with access to the Russian Legation. On April 9 this man reported that various Iranian notables who were discontented with their positions were working against Amīn as-Sultān, and were counting on the arrival of the new Russian Minister [Biutzov] for their success. They were said to be inciting the Russians against Amīn as-Sultān by saying he was Anglophile. (In fact the Russians needed no such incitement, in view of Amīn as-Sultān's concessions to the British, and constant consultations with Wolff.) Among the notables who visited the Russian Legation were Sāhib-i Dīvān, (Yahyā Khān) Mushīr ad-Dauleh, and I'timād as-Saltaneh (the last two had relations with Afghānī). The informant continued:

> I hear that the Shah has invited Seyyed Jamal u din to Tehran but until now nothing has been done for him.
>
> People of all classes visit this Seyyed, he has been praising the Russians. It appears that as he despaired of the Persians he is now appealing to the Russians through Mohammed Hussein Mirza. Very likely the Russians may take some steps to obtain money for him from the Persian Government. He talks of his intentions to start for Mashad and thence to

---

21 F.O. 60/594, Morier to Salisbury, no. 40, Secret, St. Petersburg, Feb. 7, 1890. The charge about the telegram appears to be untrue.

22 F.O. 60/594, Wolff to Salisbury, no. 146, April 24, 1890.

> proceed to Sarakhs, Merv and Bokhara and afterwards to go to Russia.[23]

The informant adds that Arab Sahib (Grigorovich, the Dragoman of the Russian Legation), has spoken to Jamāl ad-Dīn and praises him very highly.

Like various Iranian notables, Jamāl ad-Dīn was probably hoping for Russian help in ending the Anglophile course of the government and its policy of concessions to England. The report also indicates that it was generally believed (probably correctly) that the Shah had invited Jamāl ad-Dīn to Iran, and one may imagine that Jamāl ad-Dīn was complaining to those who talked with him about the Shah's subsequent lack of attention. Jamāl ad-Dīn's considerable following, his eloquence, and his apparent complaints about government policy were all enough to make the government nervous about his presence in Tehran.

British documents reveal no further concern or awareness about Jamāl ad-Dīn until they were told of his expulsion from Iran in January 1891. It is possible that Wolff, who interfered frequently in Persian politics, expressed hostility to Jamāl ad-Dīn, but on the whole his dispatches demonstrate no deep concern about him and indicate Wolff's satisfaction that Amīn as-Sultān was handling the matter adequately, as no further British action was proposed or reported.

Frustrated in his efforts to influence the Iranian government directly or to edit a newspaper, Jamāl ad-Dīn did not accept the hint that he should leave the country, but instead tried to accomplish his ends in Iran by other means. In many ways the time was ripe for his influence. The misgovernment, oppression, and greed of the Shah had been growing in recent years. There was also increasing concern over the new wave of concessions to the British and counterconcessions to the Russians which had characterized the period of Wolff's ministry. Religious feeling against the infidel influx was also growing, as was economic discontent, both from merchants facing European competition and common people affected by grain speculation and hoarding, rising prices, and depreciation of the currency. There had not been in Iran such efforts at westernization from the top as had characterized Turkey and Egypt. Despite the Shah's attempt to prevent his subjects from getting educated abroad, there was some infiltration of Western ideas of governmental reform and efficiency.

---

[23] F.O. 60/511, Wolff to Salisbury, no. 124, Secret, April 14, 1890, enclosure of April 9. Muhammad Husain is the name of Muhammad Hasan's son.

During Jamāl ad-Dīn's second stay in Iran, the westernizer Malkum Khān, having been dismissed as Iranian minister to London following his improper dealings with a lottery concession, began to publish his reformist and antigovernmental newspaper, *Qānūn*, which was smuggled into Iran from London and had considerable influence. Iran was thus ready for Jamāl ad-Dīn's program. His impassioned pleas against growing foreign encroachments could appeal both to westernizers who wanted to defend Iran's independence and to traditionalists primarily concerned about infidel incursions. To the westernizers he could confide the more radical parts of his program, while to the traditional ulama and masses he could, as usual, stress the protection of Islam and the need for Islamic unity and action against the West. Jamāl ad-Dīn was also helped by the fact that at this point England appeared to be making greater encroachments on Iranian independence than did Russia, so that his anti-British orientation and claim of Russian protection would act in his favor with most Iranians. In these years, partly out of opposition to British incursions, and partly from hostility to the then Anglophile Amīn as-Sultān, even such westernizing ministers as Amīn ad-Dauleh and I'timād as-Saltaneh were working with the Russians, as was another associate of Jamāl ad-Dīn's, Yahyā Khān Mushīr ad-Dauleh, former Minister of Foreign Affairs and later Minister of Commerce and of Justice.

From Persian descriptions of Jamāl ad-Dīn's stay in Tehran from December 1889 to July 1890 it appears that during this period Jamāl ad-Dīn held secret meetings in which he put forth his aims of reform and combating autocracy. Nāzim al-Islām Kirmānī says that about fifty persons attended his sessions. He lists those who were in accord with the aims of Jamāl ad-Dīn. Some of the most important of these were: Hājji Shaikh Hādī Najmābādī, a saintly, enlightened and tolerant alim of Tehran, whose strong personal influence helped spread progressive ideas there;[24] Āqā Muhammad Tabātabā'ī, an

[24] The descriptions are mine. Of Hājji Shaikh Hādī Najmābādī, a friend of Jamāl ad-Dīn's, Mīrzā Muhammad Qazvīnī says in one of his useful notes to E. G. Browne's *The Persian Revolution of 1905–1909* (Cambridge, 1910), p. 406: "Ḥājji Shaykh Hādī Najm-ābādī was one of the most celebrated of the *'ulamā* of Ṭihrān, and the services which he rendered to the cause of liberty in Persia were almost if not quite equal to those of Sayyid Jamālu'd-Dīn, for he was a *mujtahid* of the first rank and enjoyed the confidence of gentle and simple. He was absolutely incorruptible, and never accepted a penny from anyone. Every afternoon he used to sit on the ground outside his house . . . where he received people of all classes and all faiths, statesmen and scholars, princes and poets, Sunnīs, Shī'īs, Bābīs, Armenians,

enlightened and influential mujtahid with some modern ideas—a freemason and later one of the prominent ulama leaders of the constitutional revolution; Amīn ad-Dauleh, Minister of Posts, Head of the Council of State, and chief reformist candidate for the post of prime minister; Yahyā Khān Mushīr ad-Dauleh, pro-Russian Minister of Justice and recently Foreign Minister, removed at British insistence; Zukā al-Mulk Furūghī, an enlightened nationalist poet and later newspaper editor; I'timād as-Saltaneh, Hājji Sayyāh, and Mīrzā Rizā Kirmānī.[25] In addition several lesser persons are named by Nāzim al-Islām Kirmānī who says that Jamāl ad-Dīn's apparent aim was the unity of Islam, but that he was really for republican and constitutional government, and in his sessions discussed the evils of despotism. He adds perceptively that in his secret sessions he incited his followers to enlighten the people "but after his exile from Tehran he ordered his followers to dissimulation and concealment of their goals."[26]

Amīn as-Sultān may have got wind of Jamāl ad-Din's secret gatherings, and in any case very likely tried to convince the Shah of the danger to him of Jamāl ad-Dīn's presence in Tehran. The Shah was not as yet alarmed enough to exile Jamāl ad-Dīn from the country, but did order him to the city of Qum, south of Tehran. The *Documents* include a copy of the Shah's order (*dastkhatt*), dated 23 Zū al-Qa'da 1307/July 11, 1890, which reads: "Amīn as-Sultān. It is decided that Hājji Muhammad Hasan must send Sayyid Jamāl ad-Dīn to Qum. If he is still in Tehran and has not left write to Hājji Muhammad Hasan that he must certainly send him to Qum."[27]

Persian accounts say that Jamāl ad-Dīn got prior warning of this decree, perhaps from Amīn ad-Dauleh, so that before it reached him

---

Jews, 'Alī-Ilāhīs, etc., with all of whom he discussed all sorts of topics with the utmost freedom. Though a *mujtahid,* he was at heart a freethinker, and used to cast doubts into men's minds and destroy their belief in popular superstitions, and he was instrumental in 'awakening' a large proportion of those who afterwards became the champions of Persia's liberties. . . . Sayyid Muḥammad Ṭabāṭabā'ī was originally his disciple, but afterwards denounced his opinions as heretical to his father Sayyid Ṣādiq, who publicly banned him as an infidel. This denunciation, however, so far from injuring him, actually added to his prestige and increased the number of his disciples and admirers."

[25] The list is in Kirmānī, *op. cit.,* pp. 63–64; the descriptions are mine. A different list of his disciples at this time, with no source quoted, is given in Browne, *op. cit.,* p. 10. Since the list includes Mīrzā Āqā Khān Kirmānī, who was in fact then in Istanbul, its accuracy cannot be absolute.

[26] Kirmānī, *op. cit.,* p. 64.

[27] *Documents,* p. 110.

he was able to take refuge at the Shrine of Shāhzādeh 'Abd al-'Azīm just south of Tehran.[28] In Iran, sanctuary, or *bast*, in many places, and particularly in a holy shrine, is supposed to be inviolable by the civil authorities. From his presumably impregnable position Jamāl ad-Dīn evidently began to indulge in more open attacks on the government for its selfishness, autocracy, and sale of Iran to foreign interests. He apparently stressed the need for the people to take action to end oppression. Persian sources emphasize the influence of Jamāl ad-Dīn's eloquent speeches in helping to enlighten many Persians, and say that many persons came to hear him even though their names were being recorded by agents of Amīn as-Sultān.[29] Given the existence of widespread Iranian discontent and the reactionary and shortsighted policies of the government, it is easy to believe that Jamāl ad-Dīn's eloquence fell on fertile ground. Indeed, Iran was rapidly approaching a crisis centered on the sale of the country to foreign interests, not unlike the Egyptian crisis of 1879–1882, when Jamāl ad-Dīn had also been influential.[30]

In January 1891, after Jamāl ad-Dīn had been in sanctuary for seven months, continuing to give speeches to his followers and admirers, the Shah ordered the highly unusual step of having cavalrymen violate Jamāl ad-Dīn's sanctuary, arrest him, and have him escorted in chains to the Irano-Turkish border. Persian sources attribute this act primarily to Amīn as-Sultān's convincing the Shah that Jamāl ad-Dīn's continued presence in the country was a danger to his rule. Such general motives probably entered into the Shah's decision, but both Mulk Ārā and the British documents give a more detailed story. Mulk Ārā says that one night three to four hundred leaflets were thrown in the mosques and madrasas of Tehran and sent to the Tehran ulama, leaflets said to have contained an incitement to depose the Shah. Seeing in this a scheme of Jamāl ad-Dīn, the Shah sent in cavalrymen who dragged him bodily from his sanctuary. His servant, Mīrzā Rizā, cried out that they were seizing a descendant of the Prophet and called for help, but nobody answered. Jamāl ad-Dīn was beaten and jailed before being escorted from the country.[31]

A similar, though not identical story, is told in the British doc-

---

28 Cf. Kirmānī, *op. cit.*, p. 62.
29 *Ibid.*, Luṭfallāh, pp. 48–50; and Mulk Ārā', p. 113.
30 See Keddie, *Religion and Rebellion*, chap. i.
31 Mulk Ārā', p. 113.

uments. The British were presumably kept informed of the matter chiefly by Amīn as-Sultān, who wished to make his own role appear as good as possible, but on most points the British reports seem credible. On January 12, 1891, the British chargé d'affaires, Kennedy, who took over Wolff's duties during his illness and absence, wrote home:

> . . . a few days ago, the Shah received an anonymous letter grossly abusing His Majesty for the misgovernment of Persia and more especially for having surrendered Persian interests into English hands.
>
> The Shah being convinced that the notorious Syed Jamal ud-Din was the instigator, if not the actual writer of the letter ordered that he should be at once expelled the country [*sic*] and His Majesty refused to listen to the Amin-es-Sultan's advice that this expulsion should be effected in a quiet and unostentatious manner, so as to avoid a possible disturbance, more especially as the Syed had taken "bust," or refuge, at the shrine of Shah Abdul Azim, close to Tehran.
>
> The Syed was accordingly arrested in a garden into which he had been enticed, and which, tho' not actually within the shrine boundaries, is usually considered to be a place of refuge. A slight disturbance was caused by the Syed and his supporters, who endeavoured to resist, but eventually the Syed was, after a short struggle, placed on a horse and sent off escorted by thirty sowars to Kermanshah, whence he will be banished across the Turkish Frontier.
>
> Some letters have been found in the possession of the Syed which compromise several prominent personages, the most notable of whom is the Amin-ed-Dowleh, Minister of Posts and President of the Council, who is one of the Amin-es-Sultan's chief rivals. These letters speak in terms of contempt and derision of the Shah, the Amin-es-Sultan and other Ministers. . . .
>
> P.S. January 15th. Yesterday the Amin-es-Sultan informed me that Monsieur Gregorevitch, Dragoman of the Russian Legation, had called upon him and complained that the Syed had been arrested and banished at the instigation of the British Legation. This idea which is generally current in Persian circles had been suggested to Monsieur de Bützow [the Russian Minister in Tehran] by the Amin-ed-Dowleh.
>
> The Amin-es-Sultan emphatically denied this statement, and pointed out that not only was the Syed a Persian subject,

> with whom the Shah was at liberty to deal as His Majesty saw fit, but that the fact of the Russian Legation interfering on his behalf rendered that Legation morally responsible for any evil consequences which might ensue from secret agitation which was being fomented by a dangerous conspirator.
>
> The Amin-es-Sultan informed me that M. Gregorevitch hastened to disavow any intention on the part of the Russian Minister to protect the Syed.[32]

Kennedy here speaks of a letter to the Shah rather than a leaflet or placard as being the immediate cause of Jamāl ad-Dīn's expulsion, but another dispatch from Kennedy includes a translation of an anonymous placard, recently circulated, which must be the one referred to by Mulk Ārā. The tone is entirely typical of Jamāl ad-Dīn. It is addressed to the Persian authorities. (The parenthetical notes are by the British translators.) It says that enemies of the true faith

> have found an opportunity for ruining this country and nation under various deceitful pretexts. One under the name of the Police Chief (Count Monteforte) another under the pretext of being the Director of the Customs (Monsieur Kitabgi) one calling himself instructor (General Andreini or Russian Officers) another saying he is a priest (Dr. Torrence and American Missionaries) another under the excuse of hiring the mines (English Mining Company) another of establishing a Bank (Imperial Bank of Persia) and another under the plea of having the monopoly of the tobacco trade (Major Talbot) are taking away the resources of the country and in time they will take possession of the country itself, when it will be the beginnings of your misfortunes.
>
> Before you become the slaves of the foreigners like the natives of India you may find a remedy. Your silence and endurance have caused a great surprise to the Ulema and the people. The former have always protected the religion, should you show any energy they are ready to help you. If you do not fear for the destruction of the religion you may, at least, care for your worldly affairs and fear the misfortunes of your friends, the evil speaking of historians, the curses and derision of your descendants, and the contemptuous laughter which the foreigners now cast on you.

---

[32] F.O. 60/594, Kennedy to Salisbury, no. 11, Jan. 12, 1891.

After stating that the addressed officials have caused the killing or banishment of a series of Iranian officials, who are listed, the placard continues: "and now what has become of you that you do not make any movement. As you are the officials of the Government of Islam you have to protect the religion and the Government, you are positively responsible to God. It is most abominable that 18 krores [9 million] of people should be in trouble and only a few in comfort. Having pity for the Islamic nation and in order to encourage the powerful (people) I ventured to write this paper."[33]

Some further particulars on the points discussed in Kennedy's dispatch are in the diary of I'timād as-Saltaneh, who, like many Persians, attributes to British influence Jamāl ad-Dīn's original banishment to the shrine of Shāh 'Abd al-'Azīm and states that at the time of this move that Jamāl ad-Dīn was expecting a visit from the Russian Minister. I'timād as-Saltaneh visited Jamāl ad-Dīn at least twice during his sanctuary, which tends to confirm Persian statements that prominent men continued to visit him there. On January 7, 1890, I'timād as-Saltaeh wrote:

> A new event which disgraced the government greatly is the blow which they have delivered to Sayyid Jamāl ad-Dīn. Since some letters were written to the ulama and the madrasa students on the evils of giving concessions to Europeans, of the Count [Monteforte, the Italian Police Chief] and Nā'ib as-Saltaneh [the Shah's third son, governor of Tehran], some people say that Nā'ib as-Saltaneh got ahold of these letters, gave them to the Shah, and held Sayyid Jamāl ad-Dīn responsible. The order was given for five bodyguards to take the Sayyid from 'Abd al-'Azīm and carry him toward Iraq.

I'timād as-Saltaneh notes the struggle at 'Abd al-Azīm, reporting that the Sayyid's possessions were taken from him and brought before the Shah to be plundered by his favorites. He adds that when Amīn as-Sultān heard of this, despite his opposition to Jamāl ad-Dīn, he opposed such mean treatment, took everything back, added to it some money, a horse, and some other things, and sent them to Jamāl ad-Dīn. I'timād as-Saltaneh adds, though one wonders on what authority,

33 F. O. 60/522, Kennedy to Salisbury, no. 15, Jan. 16, 1891. The parenthetical words are added by the British translator. A Persian crore is 500,000. (I have changed a few of the worst renderings of Persian, here and elsewhere in the British documents.)

that Jamāl ad-Dīn set out from Tehran despairing of the Shah but with hope in Amīn as-Sultān.[34]

It is unlikely that Amīn as-Sultān actually performed the restitution, as other documents indicate that Jamāl ad-Dīn traveled and arrived in Kermanshah with virtually nothing.[35]

On January 16, I'timād as-Saltaneh wrote that at the home of Amīn ad-Dauleh he had heard that when the Sayyid's bag was taken and brought to the Shah several letters in Amīn ad-Dauleh's handwriting had been found. He adds that Amīn ad-Dauleh was not afraid since he never wrote compromising letters. I'timād as-Saltaneh concludes, "Thank God that I have never written letters to this person. From this point of view I am glad that I was never completely intimate with him."[36] I'timād as-Saltaneh's feelings regarding his relations with Jamāl ad-Dīn had thus undergone an opportune change since the time in 1886 when he was upset because Jamāl ad-Dīn would not be his houseguest. The comment that Amīn ad-Dauleh would not write anything compromising seems to have been apt, as he apparently received no punishment for his correspondence.

On January 28 I'timād as-Saltaneh gives a plausible explanation for Amīn as-Sultān's sudden claim of generosity toward Jamāl ad-Dīn. He says: "In the afternoon 'Arab Sāhib [Grigorevich] said that when Sayyid Jamāl ad-Dīn was taken, Muhktār Khān [the governor of 'Abd al-'Azīm] said, 'This is the recompense for friends of Russia.' " Grigorevich, after hearing this, went to the house of Amīn as-Sultān and asked what his enmity was for the Russians that his servant should use such an expression. "Amīn as-Sultān became fearful, and sent money, a robe, and a horse for him, which was not on account of generosity."[37]

Further doubt is cast on Amīn as-Sultān's actual generosity toward Jamāl ad-Dīn in a dispatch from Kennedy on January 20, 1891, which says:

> . . . a few days after the banishment of the Seyed Jamal-ud-Din, the Shah fearing that the health and possibly the life of the prisoner might be endangered by a long and rough journey undertaken at a moment's notice in the depth of the winter, directed the Amin-us-Sultan to despatch a messenger

---

[34] *Documents,* p. 151.
[35] *Ibid.,* p. 151n.
[36] *Ibid.,* p. 152.
[37] *Ibid.*

> with an order to the officer commanding the escort to keep the Seyed either at Kum or at Hamadan until the weather should become milder; after which he should take his prisoner to the Turkish frontier.
>
> The Shah also desired that a friendly letter should be written to the Seyed and a present of money sent to him from His Majesty.
>
> The Amin-us-Sultan endeavoured to dissuade the Shah, but His Majesty insisted upon his wishes being carried out.
>
> His Highness informs me that he has not yet obeyed His Majesty in this matter and that he will avoid if possible doing so, as the Seyed is in the enjoyment of excellent health and there is no danger of his succumbing to the hardships of the journey and of giving rise in consequence to the public scandal which the Shah seemed to dread.[38]

This account, from a source friendly to Amīn as-Sultān, suggests that the latter's announced presents to Jamāl ad-Dīn were purely for the purpose of avoiding Russian anger and that the announcement was not accompanied by any reality of presents or restitution. The scandal that the Shah dreaded, and which Amīn as-Sultān's behavior helped abet, indeed arose. The rough treatment of Jamāl ad-Dīn during the scuffle over his arrest, the violation of sanctuary, and the long forced ride in the depth of winter, when Jamāl ad-Dīn said he was ill, were all referred to repeatedly by the victim and his followers as crimes of the Shah, Amīn as-Sultān, and Nā'ib as-Saltaneh. This event seems to have been one motive for the later dramatic actions of Jamāl ad-Dīn's follower and devoted servant, Mīrzā Rizā Kirmānī.[39]

Amīn az-Zarb, despite his ties to Amīn as-Sultān, remained generous toward Jamāl ad-Dīn. He had evidently continued to send Jamāl ad-Dīn money during his retirement to 'Abd al-'Azīm, and now tried to make life easier for him during his arrest and forced journey. On January 12, 1891, Amīn az-Zarb wrote to a friend at Qum, the first city to which Jamāl ad-Dīn was taken, telling of the latter's imminent arrival. Amīn az-Zarb said his Qum correspondent should give Jamāl ad-Dīn anything he needed and report on his condition.[40]

---

38 F.O. 60/594, Kennedy to Salisbury, no. 20, Jan. 20, 1891.
39 Cf. the interrogation of Mīrzā Rizā in Browne, *op. cit.*, pp. 70–71.
40 *Documents*, p. 131.

From Qum Jamāl ad-Dīn was taken on a hard winter's ride to Kermanshah. His stay there is described in letters to Amīn az-Zarb from a Mullā 'Alī 'Arab, who had met Jamāl ad-Dīn at the home of his correspondent. These letters from Kermanshah agree with other reports that the governor of Kermanshah treated Jamāl ad-Dīn well, having him rest honorably several days in town and sending him off honorably toward Baghdad.[41]

Two letters from Jamāl ad-Dīn to Amīn az-Zarb from Kermanshah are photographed in the *Documents*—one dated February 16, 1891, and the second eight days later. In the second and longer letter Jamāl ad-Dīn gives his first extant account of his seizure and subsequent treatment. He says that he was already ill when taken at 'Abd al-'Azīm, and that 20 *farrāsh* (royal guards) had broken into his house, where Mu'īn at-Tujjār was also a witness, and carried him off with much violence. The soldiers, he says, were afraid that the people of 'Abd al-'Azīm would protect him and pulled him off in such haste that his collar almost suffocated him and he fell to the ground. He was unconscious for four hours and when he came to he saw Mukhtār Khān, the governor of 'Abd al-'Azīm, and the Colonel, Hasan Khān Qazvīnī. He asked Mukhtār Khān for his bag in which there was some money, some letters, and some books, but Mukhtār Khān was unable to discover its whereabouts, though he promised to forward it to Jamāl ad-Dīn in Qum if possible. He was left with nothing, and delivered, sick and feverish, to five cavalrymen. Without any outer coat or covering he was driven out into the bitter cold and snow on the very arduous journey to Kermanshah, during which he experienced illness, deprivation, and discomfort of all sorts. But he says he was inwardly happy, and knew that without doubt wise Iranians would know that he had been to the highest degree steadfast in working for reform in their material and spiritual conditions. He hoped that God would make this terrible event "a cause of my victory." This letter is one of several statements from Jamāl ad-Dīn which voice a messianic and martyred tone with regard to his own role. In the letter his two chief captors are repeatedly called Shimr and 'Umar ibn Sa'd, the names of the generals who conquered and slew the great martyred Imam Husain, and others involved in his expulsion are also given the names of others responsible for killing Husain. Jamāl ad-Dīn's descriptions of his own sufferings, including severe thirst and fever, are in recollection of those of the Imam

[41] *Ibid.*, p. 106.

Husain in his final battle near Karbala. Jamāl ad-Dīn expresses the hope that his suffering will be the cause of Iran's salvation and will fill hearts with a faith that will lead to the attainment of his high goal.

Perhaps because of his ambivalent relations to Iran, the country of a childhood that he always denied when he was beyond its borders, the expulsion from Iran assumed overwhelming importance for Jamāl ad-Dīn from this time on. Although the rulers of the Ottoman Empire and Egypt had expelled him in uncomfortable circumstances, he never expressed toward them anything like the hatred that he henceforth focused on Amīn as-Sultān and, especially, Nāsir ad-Dīn Shāh. The Shah, the key figure of authority in his own denied homeland, now became an object for revenge outweighing the British, his former focus of hostility. In writing to an official like Amīn az-Zarb, Jamāl ad-Dīn would not carry his analogies to the implied point that if the military men who captured him were like the generals who defeated Husain, the Shah must be the analogue of the hated Umayyad Caliph Yazīd who gave them their orders. In later statements, however, Jamāl ad-Dīn makes it clear that it was the Shah more than his minions whom he blamed.

Jamāl ad-Dīn's letter to Amīn az-Zarb goes on to thank him for writing to friends to help him, and says he is still sick. He ends by saying that Vakīl ad-Dauleh (the governor of Kermanshah) had come to him and said that he was ready to give whatever Jamāl ad-Dīn needed of cash or horses, for which Jamāl ad-Dīn thanked him. A man in Kermanshah to whom Amīn ad-Dauleh had written to the military officer in charge to do whatever was necessary for him. He concludes with greetings of Hājji Malik, probably the Tehran Malik at-Tujjār (leader of the merchant guilds), soon to play a leading role in the Iranian tobacco protest movement.[42] A later letter from Jamāl ad-Dīn specifically sends greetings to the Malik at-Tujjār.

Letters from Amīn az-Zarb to correspondents in Kermanshah show that he instructed them to give Jamāl ad-Dīn what he needed and to bill him for it.[43] Notes from the British agent at Kermanshah, a Persian national, to the British Legation in Tehran, add a few details about Jamāl ad-Dīn's stay there.[44]

---

42 *Documents*, photos 189–191. The letter is translated in Pakdaman, pp. 321–324.

43 *Documents*, pp. 132–133.

44 F.O. 248/533 (Tehran Embassy Archive), Reports of Kermanshah Agent: Jan. 21 and Feb. 26, 1891.

Early in 1891, Jamāl ad-Dīn was escorted across the Iranian border into Ottoman Iraq. Jamāl ad-Dīn's next stop was Baghdad. Details are available in an account by a Persian, Sādiq Nash'at, who got them from Baghdad acquaintances. Nash'at states that in Kermanshah the local governor Vakīl ad-Dauleh had gone against orders by treating Jamāl ad-Dīn honorably and releasing him from jail. (That he was in jail in Kermanshah is not indicated by the other sources.) Nash'at goes on to say that nobody accompanied Jamāl ad-Dīn to Baghdad, which is corroborated by implication in the British Kermanshah agent's report. Jamāl ad-Dīn in Baghdad was both ill and in bad spirits because of the behavior of the Iranian government and he lived anonymously in a caravansarai there until an admirer, Hājji 'Abd as-Samad Isfahānī, an Iranian merchant, heard of his condition and began to care for him. That this man was Jamāl ad-Dīn's host in Baghdad is confirmed by a letter from Jamāl ad-Dīn from Baghdad to Mullā 'Alī 'Arab of Kermanshah in the *Documents*.[45]

Nash'at goes on to say that there apparently came an order from the Ottoman government to the vālī (governor) of Baghdad to find Jamāl ad-Dīn, which the vālī's agents succeeded in doing. Nash'at states that Jamāl ad-Dīn was then taken to the vālī, who, as an enlightened man, at first treated him very well. The vālī is then said to have received orders from the Ottoman government to be more strict, so he began to guard Jamāl ad-Dīn closely. At this point certain influential Persians of Baghdad, whose names are given, are said to have appealed to the Sultan for his release, after which he went to Basra.[46]

The accuracy of this story is difficult to judge. That the vālī of Baghdad was involved in surveillance of Jamāl ad-Dīn is also indicated elsewhere, but it seems that Jamāl ad-Dīn's departure from Baghdad for Basra was not a realease but an enforced move by the Ottoman government out of the city of Baghdad. Thus the British chargé d'affaires at Tehran reported on May 4, 1891, that the Turkish Ambassador in Tehran had told Amīn as-Sultān that Jamāl ad-Dīn had been "expelled from Baghdad, where his presence was objectionable and that he has gone to Bussorah."[47] The Shah was said

45 Nash'at in Luṭfallāh, p. 137; *Documents*, photo 200.

46 Nash'at in Luṭfallāh, pp. 137–138.

47 Great Britain, Commonwealth Relations Office, Government of India, Foreign Department, *Political and Secret Demi-Official Correspondence*, 121, 1891, Kennedy to Salisbury, no. 98, May 4, 1891. This dispatch should also be in the regular F.O. 60 Persia series, but I have not found it there.

to be very pleased that he had been removed (from Baghdad, a city close to Iran) and to intend asking if he could not be sent further from Iran. In fact, the Shah soon requested Afghānī's removal from Basra too.

On March 24, 1891, Mullā 'Alī 'Arab wrote from Kermanshah to Amīn az-Zarb that he had heard that Jamāl ad-Dīn had been taken forcibly from Baghdad to Basra. Mullā 'Alī 'Arab also wrote that Jamāl ad-Dīn was sending him many letters to forward to others in Iran. Possibly some of these were letters denouncing the Shah and asking for action against the government, which other sources note that he wrote from Iraq.[48]

The Ottoman government, in expelling Jamāl ad-Dīn from Baghdad, may have been partly responding to pressure from the Iranian government. In a famous letter Jamāl ad-Dīn wrote in the spring of 1891 to the leader of the Shi'i ulama in Iraq he attributed his expulsion from Baghdad to Basra to Amīn as-Sultān's pressure and desire to keep him away from the shrine cities of Iraq where he might meet with the most authoritative Shi'i religious leaders. This letter, written from Basra, gives Jamāl ad-Dīn's summary account of his treatment since the time of his seizure at 'Abd al-'Azīm and shows very well his bitterness toward Amīn as-Sultān. In it, Jamāl ad-Dīn says:

> As for my own story and what that ungrateful tyrant [Amīn as-Sultān] did to me . . . the wretch commanded me to be dragged, when I was in sanctuary in the shrine of Shāh 'Abdu'l-'Aẓīm and grievously ill, through the snow to the capital with such circumstances of disrespect, humiliation and disgrace as cannot be imagined for wickedness (and all this after I had been plundered and despoiled). Verily we belong to God and verily until Him do we return!
>
> Thereafter his miserable satellites mounted me, notwithstanding my illness, on a pack-saddle, loading me with chains, and this in the winter season, amidst the snow-drifts and bitter, icy blasts, and a company of horsemen conveyed me to Khāniqīn, guarded by an escort. And he had previously written to the *Wālī* (Turkish governor), requesting him to remove me to Baṣra, knowing well that, if he left me alone, I should come to thee, O Pontiff, and inform thee of his doings and of the state of the people [of Persia], and explain

48 *Documents,* p. 109; Nash'at in Luṭfallāh, p. 139.

> to thee what had befallen the lands of Islām through the evil deeds of this infidel. . . . [49]

Jamāl ad-Dīn was probably correct in attributing his removal to Basra to Amīn as-Sultān. The Ottoman ambassador in Tehran made a point of informing Amīn as-Sultān that the expulsion had been carried out, suggesting that Amīn as-Sultān had expressed to the Ottomans the Persian government's wish for this expulsion.

Some indication of Jamāl ad-Dīn's state of mind while in Baghdad, though not of his activities, is found in two letters he wrote from Baghdad which are photographed in the *Documents*. One, to Mullā 'Alī 'Arab, dated March 1, 1891, soon after his arrival in Baghdad, is primarily a letter of thanks. Jamāl ad-Dīn says he hopes there are many like Mullā 'Alī in the circle of Hājji (Amīn az-Zarb), who is a true servant of the nation and community (*milla* and *umma*), and promises to tell Amīn az-Zarb of his services. He says he is staying in Baghdad with 'Abd as-Samad Isfahānī.[50]

The other letter, of the same date, to Amīn az-Zarb, is most interesting. Like his February 16 letter to Amīn az-Zarb from Kermanshah it has an apocalyptic tone, claiming that God will deal with those who have so mistreated a descendant of the Prophet and predicting portentous events to occur in the near future. It compares the events of the present to the major religious events of the past, and defends Afghānī's devotion to human betterment and reform. Again Afghānī speaks of his oppressors as the killers of the Imam Husain, in this letter comparing Amīn as-Sultān to Ibn Ziyād, the governor of Kufa at the time of Husain's martyrdom, and denying that this Ibn Ziyād gave him any provisions for the journey. The relevant text reads:

> When did Ibn Ziyād show mercy to the family of the Prophet? . . . He who accuses the descendant of 'Alī of being Armenian and uncircumcised [a rumor against Afghānī spread by Amīn as-Sultān], would he provide a journey's provision for him? May the curse of God be on the liars!
>
> Yes, the events of the past and the present must parallel each other in every respect. Because the evil ones, although

[49] Letter translated in Browne, *op. cit.*, p. 20. In a personal letter from Basra in *Documents*, photo 194, Afghānī again attributes his expulsion from Basra to the "evildoers of Iran."

[50] *Documents*, photo 200.

> they may enter the world of existence in different epochs, are all from the same malevolent tree. Their deeds and their words have always been similar and alike. And the way of God in the world of creation has always been and shall remain in the same manner. Now one must await the wonders of the Divine Power.
>
> I verily performed the duty advised by religion. In travelling the path of Truth I did not allow fear and trembling, which are the behavior of a majority of people, to take hold of me. I did not remain silent in offering warnings because of vain superstitions. And the evildoers did whatever they could. Now it remains to be seen what God will do. Of course, whoever is weak of character and infirm in faith can imagine whatever he wishes, and can say whatever he wants, and can make any kind of accusation—just as was done and said long ago.
>
> But it is incumbent upon the Lord of the World to remove falsehood, affirm the truth, and to make it manifest by His conclusive proof. Yes, there have always been trials and tribulations in this path. Otherwise, how can one distinguish the impure from the pure. There has always been suffering and danger in the path of strengthening and reforming mankind. Otherwise, what would be the virtues of the reformers? Of course those people who are content with words in the realm of faith and whose heart is oblivious to the reality of faith, and who have no regard for anything but the outward forms of life in this world and its pleasures; they consider such acts as idiocy and madness. But if one day the light of reason should shine in their heart and the true and essential faith should kindle in their heart's abode, then they shall know that their opinions were nothing but utter falsehood. . . . [51]

One can imagine from this letter that Jamāl ad-Dīn in Baghdad was already considering what he might do to attack Amīn as-Sultān and the Shah, and to advance his goals of lessening foreign influence in Iran. While in Iran he had helped focus the existing discontent over the misrule of Iran and its sale to foreign governments. He had left behind many admirers, and probably a secret society, and had apparently introduced his followers to the use of secret leaflets and organizations as an effective mode of political action. Fortunately for

---

[51] *Ibid.*, photos 192–193.

his goals, Iranian discontent regarding foreign concessions was coming to a head in 1891 over a tobacco monopoly given to a British subject, and it was this issue that Jamāl ad-Dīn was able to utilize, first from Basra and then from London in 1891, to contribute something to a successful Iranian mass movement which resulted in the first popular victory and governmental defeat in modern Iran. To this story attention is now turned.

12

The Tobacco Protest of 1891–1892

OF THE series of concessions granted by the Iranian government to foreigners in the period 1888–1890, the concession of a monopoly on purchase, sale, and export of all Persian tobacco to a British subject aroused the most opposition. This concession was granted to Major G. F. Talbot in March 1890 but was at first deliberately kept secret by the Iranian government, hence not widely known in Iran. The first critical analysis of the concession that brought it to the attention of Iranians appeared in the Persian-language newspaper *Akhtar*, published in Istanbul, late in 1890 and early in 1891. From September 1890, the Russian representatives in Iran also began strong protests against the concession, and it is likely that they discussed it with their Iranian contacts. The opposition leaflets of January 1891 attributed to Jamāl ad-Dīn and responsible for his expulsion from Iran mention the tobacco concession as among many reprehensible ones, but do not focus particular attention on it. Soon thereafter, however, Iranians began to be more aroused about this concession than about any other. Beginning in late February 1891 there were a series of petitions and protests from Iranian merchants, who saw that the British-owned Imperial Tobacco Corporation of Persia's monopoly on sales would take away much of their livelihood. These protests followed the first public announcement of the concession in February, which made many Iranians aware of it for the first time.[1]

Since tobacco was an item very widely grown, sold, and exported, the foreign monopoly affected the livelihood of many Iranians. In addition, religious feeling against the handling by unbelievers of an item of intimate use probably added to the explosiveness of the issue. The flames were also fanned by growing discontent over the sale of Iran's resources to unbelievers and over increasing misrule and exploitation by the governing classes. who were backed up by England and Russia.

During his stay in Iran, Afghānī had helped to focus existing feelings against Nāsir ad-Dīn Shāh and Amīn as-Sultān, his chief minister, and to organize methods of agitation against them and their policies. Afghānī's tactic of encouraging modernizers to utilize the religiously motivated antiforeign feelings of the ulama and the masses now came to fruition.

Because of Afghānī's international reputation, he has often been given credit as the chief organizer of the successful movement against the tobacco concession. In fact, although Afghānī and his followers played a role in this movement, its chief leaders were the leading ulama of the major cities of Iran and the Shi'i shrines of Iraq, men whose influence over the Iranian population was decisive. The Shi'i ulama, whose top leaders resided outside Iran, and who were financially and ideologically independent of the government, had been increasingly alienated by the Iranian government's subservience to infidel foreigners. In the tobacco movement they were responsive to mass feeling and also gave direction to it.[2]

The antigovernmental movement was also encouraged by those who criticized the government from a more modern, reforming, and nationalist viewpoint. Among these were not only Afghānī but the newspaper *Akhtar* which had been published by Iranians in Istanbul since the 1870's. Also of some influence was the Persian journal *Qānūn* published in England by Malkum Khān, a European-educated son of an Armenian convert to Islam. In 1889 Malkum had been dismissed from his post as Iranian minister in London after the Iranian government had canceled a lottery concession he had

---

1 Nikki R. Keddie, *Religion and Rebellion in Iran: The Tobacco Protest of 1891–1892* (London, 1966), chap. ii.

2 *Ibid.*, and Hamid Algar, *Religion and State in Iran 1785–1906* (Berkeley and Los Angeles, 1969), chaps. xi, xii.

arranged and there ensued a quarrel over Malkum's sale of the concession when he knew of its cancellation. Malkum had hitherto limited his liberal writings to manuscripts with small circulation, but now began to aim his newspaper, which called for the rule of law, at a wider Iranian audience.

Qānūn, like Afghānī, attacked the Shah's and Amīn as-Sultān's concession-granting policies. In his private correspondence with leading Iranians Malkum suggested that they follow policies of opposition and reform. When one of Malkum's correspondents, Mushīr ad-Dauleh, showed the Shah such a letter in March 1891, the Shah was furious. He denounced anyone corresponding with Malkum as a traitor, asked the British government to expel Malkum and suppress *Qānūn,* and withdrew all of Malkum's Persian titles and decorations.[3] Nevertheless, the influence of Malkum as well as that of Afghānī continued to grow during 1891, when some of their words and tactical ideas bore fruit in the tobacco protest movement.

As noted, Afghānī in Iran had instructed his followers in propaganda and agitational methods, and he had continued to write to them and to prominent members of the Iranian ulama from Iraq. His influence can be seen in late March and April of 1891, when a group of his and Malkum's followers began to send anonymous hostile letters to high government officials denouncing the government's policy of concession granting and noting the evils of the tobacco concession. At the same time anonymous placards were circulated against this governmental policy in both Tehran and Tabriz. They were written very much in the orthodox, Islamic style utilized on such occasions by Afghānī, and emanated from men he had influenced while in Iran. The Shah was very upset and ordered the arrest of men found to be in secret correspondence with Malkum Khān and Afghānī, who were believed to be plotting against the government. According to information reaching the British Oriental Secretary in Tehran, T. E. Gordon, the various printed opposition leaflets came from a secret society set up in Tehran by Jamāl ad-Dīn which was exposed to the Iranian government by an informer.[4] Among those arrested in Tehran for complicity were Mīrzā Rizā Kirmānī, Afghānī's Tehran servant and disciple, and Hājji Sayyāh, Afghānī's 1886 host in Isfahan.

---

[3] F.O. 60/522, Kennedy to Salisbury, March 10, 1891, and enclosures. On Malkum's activities see Hamid Algar's forthcoming biography.

[4] Sir Thomas Edward Gordon, *Persia Revisited* (London, 1896), p. 186.

The French diplomatic documents give further details on the arrests of April 1891. On April 30 the French Minister, de Balloy, wrote home that the stripping of Malkum Khān's ranks and honors

> occurred at a time when everyone was already excited over the establishment of the tobacco regie, and it had the effect of exciting people still further. Qanun got only more vogue and the petitions demanding the suppression of the regie continued uninterrupted. I cannot say that Russia counts for nothing in this movement.
>
> A few days ago the malcontents, perhaps feeling themselves supported by this Power, had placed in the gardens of the Shah derogatory placards accusing him of selling his country to foreigners, or not occupying himself with public affairs, which he abandoned to the hands of an inexperienced favorite, of dreaming only of his pleasures, without concern for the good of his impoverished and unhappy people, and that such a state of affairs could not continue; if he did not change his conduct he would be killed.[5]

Both the criticism of the Shah and the threat of assassination are in the style of Afghānī. The dispatch continued that the Shah was very frightened and began seizing correspondence and arresting people; and arrests had now reached about thirty. Later dispatches from the French Minister report torture of some of the accused, which is also reported in some Persian sources. De Balloy also states that some of the opposition leaflets were sent in from London by Malkum Khān,[6] although other reports suggest that they were run off locally in Tehran.

In the same period—it was the holy month of Ramadan—the mullas were preaching against the sale of Iran to the infidels, and there was already the beginning of the peculiar alliance between the religious and the radical parties which was to continue so effectively throughout the tobacco movement and beyond. On April 29 the British chargé d'affaires, Kennedy, reported in detail on the situation and noted:

> Among the persons arrested is a pedlar of the name of Mirza Ali Reza. His secret correspondence proved him to be one of Seyed Jamal-ud-Din's chief Agents, and to be his mouthpiece in propagating the belief that England is an

[5] A.E., Perse, 1891, de Balloy dispatch no. 14, April 30, 1891.
[6] *Ibid.*, no. 20, May 14, 1891.

> oppressive Ruler, by whom the natives of India are cruelly used, and that it is to Russia that Persians should look for assistance and protection. . . .
>
> These occurrences, as may be supposed, have caused a good deal of excitement, more especially as they have taken place during the month of Ramazan.
>
> There appear to be two distinct and opposing causes for these disturbances.
>
> On the one hand the partisans of Malkom Khan who share his "liberal" and "reforming" views, chiefly perhaps for the purpose of attacking the Shah's Chief Minister, are trying to open the eyes of the nation to the tyrannical and corrupt form of Govt under which they are living, and to imbue the people with an idea of democratic power; on the other, the fanatical Mollahs, taking advantage of Ramazan, are preaching everywhere against the surrender of the Faithful into the hands of the Infidels. Trade of all kinds, Mines, Banks, Tobacco, Roads, are, it is said, sold to Europeans, who will gradually obtain corn land and even Mussulman women.
>
> To quote an expression used in a letter by a certain Seyed at Shiraz to the Prince Governor of Fars, and sent by the latter to the Shah: "Mussulman lambs are being devoured by European wolves."
>
> It is unfortunate that this strong feeling should have arisen just at the time the Director of the Persian Tobacco Regie has arrived at Tehran and is preparing to begin operations. . . .[7]

The names of the most important men arrested were included in the dispatch, along with the claim, probably false, that Mīrzā Rizā when arrested had with him two loaded revolvers which he declared to be destined for the Shah and Amīn as-Sultān. Enclosed in the dispatch was a translation of one of the protest letters, this one addressed to Nāsir as-Saltaneh, the chief of the court of justice at Tabriz. The "Afghānian" tone of the letter can be seen from the following excerpt:

> How could we pass the Serat . . . while we have yielded the path of the Moslems to the Infidels? How could you appear before the Prophet while you have caused such oppression on his followers? . . . These few pounds of Tobacco, which were produced with labour and which a few men with trouble used to export in order to obtain a piece of bread have been coveted and they have been granted to the infidels and forbidden to the followers of the Prophet. . . .

7 F.O. 60/522, Kennedy to Salisbury, no. 116, April 29, 1891.

> Oh great human beings, don't you know yourselves? When are you going to wake up? They have suppressed the "Akhter" who through pity used to criticize us; others are not blind. . . .
>
> It is not the fault of the Ulema who are the representatives of the Prophet, why reproach them? . . . Who is the executioner of this people? The Ministers who are the lowest of European gardeners, who have the privilege of being received in private places. . . . [8]

In another dispatch Kennedy notes the possible complicity in the movement of Afghānī's Russian Legation contact, Grigorovich. Amīn as-Sultān had claimed that "there are grave reasons for suspecting, in consequence of the confessions of some of the prisoners, that M. Gregorovitch, Oriental Secretary of the Russian Legation, has been privy to the present seditious movement.[9]

In his testimony in 1896 after the assassination of Nāsir ad-Dīn Shāh, Mīrzā Rizā denied association with the group that wrote and circulated seditious proclamations, saying that he had been tricked into writing only one protest letter by the Shah's third son and governor of Tehran. Nā'ib as-Saltaneh. He does, however, corroborate the fact that the proclamations were written and distributed by a group of Afghānī's followers:

> When Sayyid Jamālu'd-Dīn came here, some persons heard his denunciations and were moved to enthusiasm thereby, like Mīrzā 'Abdullāh the physician, Mīrzā Naṣru'llāh Khān and Mīrzā Faraju'llāh Khān. These went and wrote certain papers which they sent into the provinces, so that they came back stamped with the provincial post-marks. Mīrzā Ḥasan Khān, grandson of the *Ṣāhib-Dīwān*, enthusiastically supported this association, because he had seen the Sayyid and heard his words. Some of his associates were frying their own fish. Of these was Ḥājji Sayyaḥ, who wished to make the *Ẓillu's-Sulṭān* King and someone else [Amīn ad-Dauleh] Prime Minister.[10]

Malkum Khān was also suspected of complicity in the seditious movement, and after the initial arrests the government seized and

---

8 Enclosure in *ibid.*

9 F.O. 539/53, Kennedy to Salisbury, no. 129 (91), April 27, 1891, Most Secret.

10 E. G. Browne, *The Persian Revolution of 1905–1909* (Cambridge, 1910), p. 88. In a different translation of Mīrzā Rizā's words in "Assassinat de Nasr-ed-Dine

examined Amīn ad-Dauleh's correspondence with Malkum. According to the French Minister, Amīn ad-Dauleh was released when nothing compromising was found in his papers; but at the home of one of his secretaries was found a packet of leaflets from Malkum for distribution in the provinces.[11] Malkum's propaganda was thus supplementing that of Afghānī.

Mass protests against the tobacco concession broke out in the major cities in Iran beginning in the spring of 1891. About this time company agents began to arrive in the various cities and to post a six months' deadline for the sale of all local tobacco to the company and for the end of trade in tobacco except by merchants with authorizations from the company. When this happened the vast implications of the concession were for the first time borne home on the Iranians, many of whom depended for their livelihood in whole or in part on tobacco cultivation or trade. Although the specific form of protest varied from city to city, there were certain features common in all cities. Everywhere it was the merchants, many of whom could expect to lose their income from the tobacco trade if the concession came into force, who were the most directly affected and who took a leading part in the opposition movement. In the tobacco-growing areas the peasants were also made to believe that they would suffer heavy losses, although the company, in order to forestall opposition, declared that it would buy tobacco at prevailing rates and for cash. Along with the merchants the ulama were the group most hostile to the concession. Partly this reflected their ties to merchant families and merchants guilds and their interest in tobacco grown on their private or endowed *vaqf* land, but partly also they had their own reasons for opposition. The entry of large numbers of tobacco-company employees into Iran was seen as a wedge for un-Islamic practices and beliefs.[12] A generalized opposition to the sale of Iran to foreigners was also operative among all classes. Although in all cities the main leaders of the opposition were members of the ulama

Chah Kadjar," *Revue du monde musulmane,* XII (Dec., 1910), 593n, Mīrzā Rizā is quoted as saying, "When the Sayyid left, the meetings continued at the home of Mirza Hasan Khan, the grandson of the Sahib Divan," implying a confirmation of Gordon's account of a secret society left in operation by Jamāl ad-Dīn.

11 A.E., Perse, 1891, no. 20, May 14.

12 These religious feelings are well illustrated in an eyewitness account of the tobacco movement written by a member of the ulama, Shaikh Ḥasan Karbalā'ī, *Qarārdād-i rizhī 1890 m.,* ed. and intro. by Ibrāhīm Dihgān (Arāk, Iran, *ca.* 1955), pp. 4–14.

class, they were often acting partly as representatives of others, particularly the merchants. Russian agents, too, were apparently involved in many of the protests, but the exact extent and nature of Russian activity is difficult to determine.

From the beginning, there was some organized liaison between various cities, and Jamāl ad-Dīn's and Malkum's followers played an important role.

In April 1891, a mass protest against the tobacco concession broke out in Shiraz, a major tobacco-growing center. A leading mulla, Sayyid 'Alī Akbar, preached strongly against the concession and in late April the Shah ordered his expulsion to Karbala—an unusual step to take against a sayyid and mulla. The Sayyid was expelled in May, after which there were disturbances in Shiraz culminating in the killing of several persons by soldiers there.

The Shiraz disturbances provided an example to other cities. They also had another important result; they gave Afghānī a means to intervene directly in the situation. Sayyid 'Alī Akbar, when he left Iran, went to see Afghānī, then under surveillance at Basra, discussed matters with him, and went from there to Samarra to see the chief leader of the Shi'i ulamā, Hājji Mirzā Hasan Shīrāzī, whose directions were followed by Iranian Shi'is and who was later to become important for his *fatwā* forbidding the use of tobacco until the concession was withdrawn.[13] It was apparently on the urging of Sayyid 'Alī Akbar that Afghānī now wrote his famous letter to Shīrāzī against the concessionary policy of the Shah's government—a letter that many saw as a key factor in Shīrāzī's later boycott *fatwā*. The letter says that the Persians are being made desperate by oppression and the sale of their country to foreigners, but that they lack a leader, and are waiting for Shīrāzī to direct them. Afghānī continues, in the religious tone he used when addressing the ulama:

> Verily the King's purpose wavereth, his character is vitiated, his perceptions are failing and his heart is corrupt. He is incapable of governing the land, or managing the affairs of his people, and hath entrusted the reins of government in all things great and small to the hands of a wicked freethinker, a tyrant and usurper, who revileth the Prophets openly, and

---

[13] *Mulk Ārā'*, p. 115. This contemporary account is quoted in Mahdī Malikzādeh, *Tārīkh-i inqilāb-i mashrutiyyat-i Īrān*, Vol. I (Tehran, 1328/1949–50), p. 128.

heedeth not God's law, who accounteth as naught the religious authorities, curseth the doctors of the Law, rejecteth the pious, contemneth honourable Sayyids and treateth preachers as one would treat the vilest of mankind. Moreover since his return from the lands of the Franks he hath taken the bit between his teeth, drinks wine openly, associates with unbelievers and displays enmity towards the virtuous. Such is his private conduct; but in addition to this he hath sold to the foes of our Faith the greater part of the Persian lands and the profits accruing therefrom, to wit the mines, the ways leading thereunto, the roads connecting them with the frontiers of the country. . . . Also the river Kārūn and the guest houses which will arise on its banks . . . and the highway from Ahwāz to Ṭihrān. . . . Also the tobacco . . . with the chief centres of cultivation, the lands on which it is grown, and the dwellings of the custodians, carriers and sellers, wherever these are found. He has similarly disposed of the grapes used for making wine, and the shops, factories and wine-presses appertaining to this trade throughout the whole of Persia; and so likewise soap, candles and sugar, and the factories connected therewith. Lastly there is the Bank: and what shall cause thee to understand what is the Bank? It means the complete handing over of the reins of government to the enemy of Islām, the enslaving of the people to that enemy, the surrendering of them and of all dominion and authority into the hands of the foreign foe. . . .

Then he offered what was left to Russia as the price of her silence and acquiescence (if indeed she will consent to be silent), namely the Murdāb (lagoon) of Rasht, the rivers of Ṭabaristān, and the road from Anzalī to Khurāsān, with the houses, inns and fields appertaining thereto. But Russia turned up her nose at this offer, and declined to accept such a present; for she is bent on the annexation of Khurāsān and the occupation of Āzerbaijān and Māzandarān, unless these agreements be cancelled and these compacts rescinded —agreements, namely, which involve the entire surrender of the kingdom of Persia into the hands of that most contentious foe. Such is the first result of the policy of this madman.

In short this criminal has offered the provinces of the Persian land to auction amongst the Powers, and is selling the realms of Islām and the abodes of Muḥammad and his household (on whom be greeting and salutation) to foreigners. But by reason of the vileness of his nature and the meanness of his understanding he sells them for a paltry sum and at a wretched price. (Yea, this it is when meanness and avarice are mingled with treason and folly!)

And thou, O Proof, if thou wilt not arise to help this people, and wilt not unite them in purpose, and pluck them forth, by the power of the Holy Law, from the hands of this sinner, verily the realms of Islām will soon be under the control of foreigners, who will rule therein as they please and do what they will. . . . And thou knowest that the *'ulamā* of Persia and the people thereof with one accord (their spirits being straitened and their hearts distressed) await a word from thee wherein they shall behold their happiness and whereby their deliverance shall be effected. How then can it beseem one on whom God hath bestowed such power as this to be so chary of using it or to leave it in abeyance?

I further assure Your Eminence, speaking as one who knoweth and seeth, that the Ottoman Government will rejoice in your undertaking of this effort and will aid you therein . . .

[Amīn as-Sultān] had previously written to the *Wālī* (Turkish governor), requesting him to remove me to Baṣra, knowing well that, if he left me alone, I should come to thee. . . . For he knew for a certainty that, should I succeed in meeting thee, it would not be possible for him to continue in his office, involving as it does the ruin of the country, the destruction of the people, and the encouragement of unbelief. . . . Moreover his conduct was made more culpable and mean in that, in order to avert a general revolt and appease the popular agitation, he accused the party whom zeal for religion and patriotism had impelled to defend the sanctuary of Islām and the rights of the people of belonging to the Babi sect. . . .

Wherefore, seeing myself remote from that high presence, I refrained from uttering my complaint. . . . But when that learned leader and *mujtahid* Ḥājji Sayyid 'Alī Akbar came to Baṣra, he urged me to write to that most high Pontiff a letter setting forth these events, misfortunes and afflictions, and I hastened to obey his command, knowing that God will effect something by they hand.[14]

[14] Translated in Browne, *op. cit.*, pp. 15–21. Browne says the letter "must have been written immediately after Sayyid Jamālu-d Dīn's expulsion from Persia," but since it comes after Sayyid 'Alī Akbar's expulsion it must in fact date from about June 1891.

Several points in this letter deserve comment. First, it indicates that Afghānī and his followers had far broader aims and grievances than those centering on the tobacco concession, and indeed stress is put on the English bank, rather than on the tobacco concession. The appearance in rapid succession of the Karun and bank concessions, with the latter's monopoly on minerals, and then the compensatory concessions to the Russians were, along with the tobacco concession, causes of general discontent and apprehension of foreign control. Even when the movement became more specifically focused on tobacco, its leaders tried to force a cancellation of all concessions, not only the tobacco one.

Second, the letter indicates that Afghānī was not absolving the Russians from blame or acting in favor of their control of Iran, as some, particularly the British, seemed to think. His remarks about Russian evil designs on Iran are very strong.

Third, there is the hint of cooperation from the Ottoman Sultan, foreshadowing the period from 1892 on when the Sultan brought Afghānī to Istanbul and encouraged him and his followers to write letters to the Shi'i ulama in all countries promising gifts and favors in return for support of the Sultan's position as Caliph and leader of all Muslims.

Finally, Afghānī takes great pains to assert the religious quality of the opposition to the Shah, to deny that they have any connection with the heretical Babis, and to turn the charge of irreligion against Amīn as-Sultān and the Shah. The longer translation of the letter included in the British documents says that Amīn as-Sultān is "unquestionably a Babi."[15]

Afghānī's letter also contains an exaggerated account of the punishments inflicted on the opposition. Near the end of the letter he says:

> No doubt the Pontiff of the people hath heard what the ring-leaders of infidelity and the confederates of unbelief have done to that learned, accomplished and virtuous Ḥājji Mullā Fayẓu'llāh of Darband; and thou wilt shortly hear what these cruel miscreants did to the learned, pious and righteous *mujtahid* Ḥājji Sayyid 'Alī Akbar of Shīrāz. Thou wilt also learn what killing, beating, branding and bonds have been inflicted on the defenders of the country and their

[15] Enclosed in F.O. 60/594, Lascelles to Salisbury, no. 14, Jan. 19, 1892.

> faith. Of such victims was that virtuous youth, Mīrzā Muḥammad Riẓā of Kirmān, whom that apostate [i.e., the *Amīnu's-Sulṭān*] killed in prison, and the eminent and virtuous Ḥājji Sayyāḥ (Maḥallātī), the noble and talented Mīrzā Muḥammad 'Alī Khān, the well-proved and accomplished *I'timādu's-Salṭana* and others.[16]

Of these persons, several were among those arrested and sent to jail in Qazvin after the mailing of seditious notices in Tehran and Tabriz in the spring of 1891. None of them was in fact killed, but it was difficult to ascertain the fate of political prisoners in Iran until long after their arrest. The charges of killing of political prisoners that Jamāl ad-Dīn made at this time, and later in London, were based to a degree on stories he had actually heard. Thus the *Documents* contain a personal letter from Jamāl ad-Dīn to Mullā 'Alī 'Arab from Basra, July 22, 1891, saying that Mullā 'Alī 'Arab's letter had arrived, but that he did not write the reason for the killing of Mīrzā Muhammad Rizā. Jamāl ad-Dīn says that in Basra he has heard that Hājji Sayyāh was killed also and that Hājji (Amīn az-Zarb) was fined and many others jailed. He asks Mullā 'Alī 'Arab to write details soon and describe well what occurred in Tehran.[17]

Jamāl ad-Dīn's letter to Shirāzī also describes his own ignominious treatment. The exact influence of this letter on Shīrāzī cannot be determined, but within a few months Shīrāzī wrote to the Shah denouncing concessions to foreigners in a way rather similar to Jamāl ad-Dīn's, and later Shīrāzī called successfully for the boycott of tobacco by Iranians as long as the concession remained. It is probable that Jamāl ad-Dīn's letter helped influence Shīrāzī's decision to enter into political affairs for the first time and also that Afghānī discussed with Sayyed 'Alī Akbar the importance of such intervention by the leading *mujtahids*—Sayyid 'Alī Akbar very likely made specific oral suggestions to Shīrāzī on how he might intervene when he saw him in Samarra. The boycott *fatwā* was, however, called forth largely by appeals to Shīrāzī from many leaders of the Iranian ulama.

Jamāl ad-Dīn later in London printed his letter to Shīrāzī and distributed it widely in Iran, which added to its influence on Iranians, although it reached them only shortly before the tobacco concession

16 Browne, *op. cit.*, p. 20. Mirzā Muhammad 'Alī is presumably the follower of Afghānī of whom Browne (p. 10) says that he wrote "a work in refutation of religions (*Radd-i Madhāhib*)."

17 *Documents*, photo 201.

was canceled in January 1892. The letter was thus of considerable importance, but Arab disciples of Afghānī such as Rashīd Riḍā who would make Afghānī and his letter the major cause of the tobacco protest movement are giving him too much importance.[18] The movement had many other leaders, and was based on deep grievances among many classes of Iranians.

According to Sādiq Nash'at, who says he has firsthand information about Jamāl ad-Dīn's stay in Iraq, Afghānī wrote many letters from Basra to the ulama of Iran and of the Shi'i shrine cities in Iraq asking them to unite to save Islam and Iran from oppression and unbelief. Among those listed by Nash'at as recipients of such letters are Shīrāzī; Sayyid 'Alī Akbar; Hājji Shaikh Hādī Najmābādī (the enlightened and saintly mujtahid of Tehran); Hājji Mīrzā Hasan Āshtiyānī, the leading mujtahid of Tehran; Āqa Najafī, the leading mujtahid of Isfahan; and other mujtahids throughout Iran and the shrines. All those listed by name played leading roles in the tobacco protest. Now there is word that Afghānī also exchanged several letters with Shīrāzī.[19]

The Iranian government was concerned to remove Afghānī from any city close to Iran's borders, as proved in documents recently reproduced by Ibrāhīm Safā'ī. One of these gives a partial description of a statement by the Ottoman ambassador in Tehran, Halil Halid Bey, as transcribed by the Iranian minister of foreign affairs, Mīrzā 'Abbās Khān Qavām ad-Dauleh, without a date. The Ottoman ambassador said that he knew of Jamāl ad-Dīn's activities in Tehran and had handed over to the Iranian foreign minister one of the leaflets (attributed to Afghānī) distributed in the winter in Tehran. He had informed the vālī of Baghdad via Istanbul when Jamāl ad-Dīn was expelled; he says the Istanbul authorities were well acquainted with Jamāl ad-Dīn, and claims Jamāl ad-Dīn had *twice* been expelled from Istanbul and from Ottoman territory. The Istanbul authorities thus ordered the vālī of Baghdad to keep track of Jamāl ad-Dīn, and the vālī set spies upon him, and confiscated some money and some letters Jamāl ad-Dīn had received from Tehran, as well as letters he was sending out to various countries (referred to by Nash'at,

---

18 Browne, *op. cit.*, pp. 22–23 quotes Muhammad Rashīd (Riḍā)'s attribution of Shīrāzī's boycott *fatwā* and the cancellation of the concession to Jamāl ad-Dīn's influence alone.

19 Nash'at in Luṭfallāh, p. 139. A descendant of Shīrāzī's, Mr. Faripur, told me in Tehran, 1966, that he had found this correspondence and planned to publish it if he found time.

above.) The Ottoman ambassador continued that Jamāl ad-Dīn, from the time of his entry into Baghdad, had set about establishing ties with the Babis as well as with a disaffected Ottoman, Nusrat Paşa. Istanbul authorities ordered that the money, but not the letters, be returned to Jamāl ad-Dīn, and that he be expelled from Baghdad to Basra, that some of the Babis who remained in Baghdad be expelled to Mosul, and that Nusrat Paşa be imprisoned. The Ottoman ambassador in Tehran then asked if the Shah had any further requests regarding Jamāl ad-Dīn.

On the back of this report, the Shah wrote an order to Amīn as-Sultān saying that Basra was too close to the Iranian border. The Shah continued, "It would be much better if they expel him to Yemen, Syria, Jerusalem, or the island of Crete [all Ottoman territories]. If they give us that part of the writings seized from him that are from Iran we would be very pleased with the friendship of the Ottoman authorities."

An undated draft of a telegram from Amīn as-Sultān to the Iranian ambassador in Istanbul, Nāzim ad-Dauleh, carried out the Shah's request, reminding the ambassador that it had earlier been requested that the Ottoman government send Jamāl ad-Dīn from Baghdad to Yemen, and asking on behalf of the Shah that the Sultan now banish Jamāl ad-Dīn far from Iran's borders and forward to the Shah the writings taken from Jamāl ad-Dīn.[20]

Khān Malik Sāsānī quotes other documents in the Iranian Foreign Ministry Archives to show that the Iranian government knew of Afghānī's letter writing and activities in Basra, and asked the Ottoman government to expel him from Basra. Sāsānī also shows that the Sultan wished rather to bring Afghānī to Istanbul and keep him under surveillance. Probably in response to the telegram (reproduced by Safā'ī) from Amīn as-Sultān ordering the Iranian ambassador in Istanbul to ask the Ottoman government to expel Jamāl ad-Dīn from Basra, that ambassador wrote back as follows to Amīn as-Sultān:

> Regarding the expulsion of Shaikh Jamāl ad-Dīn discussions were held with the foreign ministry so that they should expel him from Basra and the vicinity of the Iranian border. They wrote an order entrusting it to the vālī of Basra, but the Sultan issued a decree that they should bring him and hold him in Istanbul. I told the prime minister that his stay-

[20] Ṣafā'ī, *Asnād*, pp. 259–261.

> ing in Istanbul would not be good for either government. He said: "Here he will be under surveillance"; in such a way that I understood that the Ottoman government are afraid that if they send him away he will cause trouble or even ally himself with the rebels in Yemen and be the source of revolt.[21]

This story is independently confirmed and amplified by 'Abd al-Qādir al-Maghribī, an Arab admirer of Afghānī's who knew him in Istanbul in the 1890's, from the words of men who had known Jamāl ad-Dīn in Basra. Jamāl ad-Dīn is said to have still been ill when he arrived there. When he recovered he prepared to make a trip to the Arabian peninsula, but the vālī forbade this on orders from Istanbul. Then Jamāl ad-Dīn requested permission to go to London; the first message from Istanbul authorities permitted this, and Jamāl ad-Dīn left in haste. After he left there was a telegram from Istanbul forbidding also the London trip.[22]

Jamāl ad-Dīn's plan to go to Arabia is expressed in a letter from him in Basra to Amīn az-Zarb dated June 2 (1891). The letter begins with another long discussion of his own sufferings, saying that those who enter the path of truth must accept such difficulties, as the lives of the prophets and the learned men of the past show. For those who enter this path even sufferings and checkmate are the essence of victory. Afghānī continues: "These evildoers of Iran did not allow me to remain in Baghdad. Now I am in Basra. The road to Najd and Medina and Mecca is open. The Arabs of Najd are pleading with me to go to Najd and they indicate their obedience, but consultation and consideration of these times is necessary."[23] In a postscript Jamāl ad-Dīn adds that roads to other countries are open also, and some people are requesting that he go to the West.

Ever since 1885 Sultan Abdülhamid associated Afghānī with a pet idea of Wilfrid Blunt's—the revival of an Arabian caliphate to take over the caliphal and religious claims of the Sultan. Hence Abdülhamid was not willing to have Jamāl ad-Dīn travel in Arabia, particularly since there was rebellion in the Yemen at the time. Just too late to stop Afghānī's departure the Sultan evidently realized that

---

[21] Khān Malik Sāsānī, *Siyāsatgarān-i daureh-yi Qājār* (Tehran, 1338/1959–60), p. 192, citing the Iranian Foreign Ministry archives.

[22] 'Abd al-Qādir al-Maghribī, *Jamāl ad-Dīn al-Afghānī* (Cairo, 1948), pp. 33–34, 86–87.

[23] *Documents*, photo 194.

the safest thing of all would be to bring Jamāl ad-Dīn to Istanbul, where he could be kept under surveillance. The Iranian government was not as wise, since they did not realize that the method of exile might cause them more trouble than it prevented. Just as the exile of Sayyid 'Alī Akbar had given him the opportunity to talk first to Afghānī and then to Sayyid Muhammad Hasan Shīrāzī, so Jamāl ad-Dīn's departure first from Iran to the Ottoman Empire and then from there to England did not lessen his ability to harass the Iranian rulers.

An unnamed Iranian who saw Jamāl ad-Dīn after his arrival in London reports his saying that he had escaped Basra by boat with the help of an Arab shaikh, and that it took him thirty-two days to reach London.[24]

On his way from Basra to London Afghānī evidently stopped at Port Said, as there is a letter dated September 23 from him to 'Abduh from there. It is mistakenly ascribed to Afghānī's 1882 stop there by Rashīd Riḍā, but its content and the month, September, show it must date from 1891. In it he sends greetings to various men, including Ibrāhīm al-Laqqānī and Sa'd Zaghlūl. He says he is in Port Said on his way to London and 'Abduh should answer him care of Mr. Blunt or the newspaper *Sharq wa Gharb (East and West)*.[25] He writes he has been cut off from news for seven months and does not know the location of 'Ārif (Abū Turāb), but 'Abduh should tell 'Ārif of his trip. At the end Afghānī adds greetings to the "man of pure soul and elevated zeal" Riyāḍ Pāshā.[26]

---

[24] Ṣafā'ī, *Asnād*, pp. 263–267, Notes of Mīrzā Mahmūd Khān 'Alā al-Mulk, Iranian ambassador in St. Petersburg, regarding 1891–92, reporting the words of an unnamed emissary who had heard Jamāl ad-Dīn in London.

[25] Riḍā, *Tārīkh*, p. 282. There is no Arabic paper in London with the title *Sharq wa Gharb*, and it is likely that Afghānī was referring to a bilingual Arabic-English paper that was to begin publication early in 1892, *The Eastern and Western Review*, whose Arabic title was *Ḍiyā' al-Khāfiqain* ("The Light of the Two Hemispheres"). Contrary to Riḍā and others, this paper was not edited by Afghānī but, as noted below, by Habib Anthony Salmoné, an Anglicized Arab who, the *Documents* show, knew Afghānī from his first trip to London. For Afghānī's contributions to the paper, see below.

[26] Riḍā, *Tārīkh*, p. 282. Among the points showing that this letter dates from 1891 and not 1882 are: (1) its September date, which fits only the later trip; (2) the presence in Egypt in 1891 of 'Abduh and the others referred to; (3) Afghānī's letters from Port Said in 1882 say he has sent Abū Turāb to Cairo to collect money for him, while this letter says he has lost track of Abū Turāb; (4) the 1882 letters refer to Afghānī's destination as Paris, not London, and do not refer to Blunt, whom Afghānī had not yet met, who is named in the 1891 letter.

Meanwhile, in the summer of 1891 a popular uprising against the tobacco concession had developed in the large northern Iranian city of Tabriz. Placards threatening death to Europeans and to those who cooperated with them were posted there in July. A petition was also circulated denouncing the tobacco concession in religious terms. It received several pages of signatures and greatly disturbed the Shah. People gathered arms for a planned uprising, which was only averted by a misleading telegram from the Shah promising cancellation of the concession. The concession did have to be suspended in Tabriz, and this victory for the opposition helped inspire other cities.[27]

In September 1891, right after the Tabriz disturbances, Hājji Mīrzā Hasan Shīrāzī entered the battle with a telegram of protest to the Shah from Samarra. Amin as-Sultān was convinced that even earlier, during the Tabriz disturbances, the chief mujtahid of Tabriz had been in constant communication with Shīrāzī as well as with the Russian consul general.[28] And on September 22, the Shah's French doctor, Feuvrier, noted that Shīrāzī from the shrine cities.

> who holds there all the strings of the insurrection, has written a long letter to the Shah to prove to him, Koran in hand, that the concession of any monopoly to foreigners is against the holy book. I do not believe His Majesty is much concerned with the reasoning of the mujtahid, but he knows his influence and must take account of it.
>
> The Persian consul at Baghdad has been sent to Karbala with the aim of acting on the mujtahid. It does not appear that he has succeded in modifying the convictions of the holy man.[29]

Shīrāzī's telegram to the Shah condemns the interference of foreign subjects in the internal affairs of Muslim peoples, and specifically names the English bank, the tobacco concession, and railroad concessions; and he speaks of the killing and wounding of a number of Muslims in Shiraz and the exile of Sayyid 'Alī Akbar as manifestations of the bad results of such policies. It calls for the end of all concessions, showing again that this broader aim was held by some of the leaders throughout the tobacco movement. The text of this

27 Keddie, *Religion and Rebellion*, chap. iii.

28 R.O. 60/524, Kennedy to Salisbury, no. 214, Sept. 24, 1891.

29 Dr. (Jean-Baptiste) Feuvrier, *Trois ans à la cour de Perse* (new ed.; Paris, 1906), p. 276. This book contains the most vivid eyewitness account of the tobacco movement that exists in a Western language.

telegram was later translated in one of de Balloy's dispatches. A translation from the French follows:

> Up to the present I have addressed myself only to His Majesty with wishes of happiness, but because of the various news that has reached me and which is against the rights of Religion and Government I ask permission to say: The entry of foreigners into the interior affairs of the country, their relations and trade with Muslims, the concessions such as the Bank, Tobacco Regie, Railroads, and others are, for many reasons, against the exact sense of the Koran and God's orders. These acts weaken the power of the Government and are the cause of the ruin of order in the country, and they oppress the subjects. The proof is in what has just occurred in Shiraz, where there has been disrespect for the tomb of the venerable Imamzadeh Ahmad ibn Musa, a great number of Muslims have been killed and wounded, and His Excellency Sayyid Aki Akbar chased in the grossest fashion—all this is the consequence of what I said above.
>
> It is certain that Your Majesty has not been informed of it. He who wishes only the prosperity of his subjects would have been very dissatisfied and would not have allowed today these affairs that in the future will provoke troubles and paralyze Religion and Government, which will, God forbid, lose the glorious renown acquired for many years. I have the highest confidence in the generosity of Your Majesty who, if the country's Ministers have authorized these affairs, will show the foreigners that the whole population is united to reject them, and so calm will be reestablished. I have confidence also in seeing Your Majesty grant once more his favor to the venerable personage expelled from Shiraz with so little respect and who took refuge in the holy places. The mullas will pray again for Your Majesty and confidence will be restored among the subjects. The decision is in the hands of Your Majesty.[30]

Despite the milder tone, as befitting a letter sent to the Shah, the similarity of the grievances to those outlined in Jamāl ad-Dīn's earlier letter to Shīrāzī, is striking. It would thus seem that Jamāl ad-Dīn's letter, plus what he may have conveyed to Shīrāzī personally through Sayyid 'Alī Akbar, did have an immediate effect on Shīrāzī, who, as

[30] A.E., Perse, 1891, enclosed in no. 64 of Dec. 23, 1891. The undated Persian text of this "First telegram" from Shīrāzī to the Shah is in Nāẓim al-Islām Kirmānī, *Tārīkh-i bīdārī-yi Īrāniyān* (2d ed.; Tehran, 1945–1946), p. 24.

his telegram states, had not previously addressed the Shah on political questions.

Ibrāhī Taimūrī, in a recent Persian book, gives details of the Shah's and Amīn as-Sultān's efforts, via telegrams and a personal visit of the Iranian representative at Baghdad to Shīrāzī, to change the latter's position. In the same period Shīrāzī was receiving telegrams and letters from all parts of Iran asking him to help cancel the concession, and he did not yield to any of the government's arguments. He also continued pressure for the lifting of Sayyid 'Alī Akbar's exile, in which he ultimately succeeded.[31]

The continuous telegraphic communication in this period between Shīrāzī and the leaders of the Iranian ulama, between Shīrāzī and the Shah, and among the leaders of the Iranian ulama, helped make the tobacco movement perhaps the first coordinated national movement of Iranians. This coordination was attributable partly to the introduction of the telegraph, an infidel innovation that the ulama did not scorn to use. The coordination also owed something to the introduction of new ideas and to the simultaneous impact of the growth of foreign influence in Iran. The restrictions on native banking caused by the Imperial Bank were felt quickly in several cities, while the simultaneous arrival of agents of the tobacco company who forced growers to sell to them, and in many cases behaved badly, also brought a series of immediate reactions. Russian encouragement of the opposition was also coordinated into the national movement, as was that of the leading ulama. Both Jamāl ad-Dīn and Malkum Khān helped introduce into Iran such methods as secretly posted placards and leaflets, distribution within Iran of printed propaganda from abroad, and the use of widespread correspondence and secret organizations as means of forcing the government to change its policies.

In the fall of 1891 there were major movements against the tobacco concession—in Mashhad, where the concession suffered a six-month delay, and in Isfahan, where the tactic of boycotting tobacco began. Early in December 1891, the nationwide protest reached its culmination in the beginnings of a boycott of tobacco. Then a *fatwā* was announced from Shīrāzī which read: "In the name of God, the Merciful, the Forgiving, Today the use of *tonbaku* and tobacco in any form is reckoned as war against the Imām of the Age (may God hasten

---

31 Ibrāhīm Taimūrī, *Taḥrīm-i tanbākū* (Tehran, n.d.), pp. 89–98. The texts of several telegrams are included.

his Glad Advent!)"[32] The universality of the boycott which ensued in Iran amazed outside observers, and the British Foreign Office finally began to see that it was hopeless to try to save the concession.

The telegraphic communication between Shīrāzī and the Tehran ulama was carried out via Malik at-Tujjār (chief of the merchants) in Tehran who was a close follower of Afghānī's. After the arrival of the boycott order, Malik at-Tujjār was accused by the government of forging it and was imprisoned in Qazvin in order to frighten the opposition, but popular outcry was so vehement that he had to be released.

The government tried to save the situation by suppressing only the internal monopoly of the tobacco company and letting the export monopoly continue. After this was done, the government, early in January, ordered the leader of the Tehran ulama, Āshtiyānī, either to leave the country or to break the boycott by smoking. When Āshtiyānī opted to leave Iran and his decision became known in Tehran, a large mob of Tehranis, led by mullas and sayyids, surged on the government buildings, where the unarmed crowd was fired upon by order of the Shah's third son, Prince Nā'ib as-Saltaneh. Several persons were killed, and there were threats of a further mass uprising which could be quelled only by complete cancellation of the tobacco concession.[33]

Thus an alliance of ulama, merchants, modernizers, and the city populace had for the first time in modern Iranian history engaged in a coordinated movement that shook the foundations of the government and forced it to change course. The strength of the opposition was so great that many observers doubted that either the Shah or Amīn as-Sultān could keep his position. Amīn as-Sultān was able to save himself by switching from an Anglophile to a Russophile policy and by bribing some of the leading ulama, but organized opposition to the government continued after 1892 culminating in the Iranian Constitutional Revolution of 1905–1911.

The success of the tobacco movement influenced some of the most characteristic features of the opposition movement that led to the revolution—leadership by the ulama and use of ulama leadership by the more radical opposition. Before the tobacco movement this alliance with the ulama was by no means the universal tactic of the reformist opposition, but one can see from documents of the period

32 Browne, *op. cit.*, p. 22 n. 1.

33 Keddie, *Religion and Rebellion*, chap. iii.

that the movement's success helped turn the minds of the opposition in this direction. Thus Malkum Khān, who for most of his life, even after his dismissal from government service, had appealed largely to men of the government to lead in a reform program, now began to speak of Shīrāzī and the ulama as the proper leaders of reform. And the freethinking Azalī Babi, Mīrzā Āqā Khān Kirmānī, who had often attacked the ulama violently in his works, wrote to Malkum that during the tobacco movement even the stupid ulama were won over.[34] Soon thereafter he began cooperating with Sayyid Jamāl ad-Dīn in Istanbul.

Insofar as the radical opposition was concerned, the tobacco movement was thus a decisive victory for the tactics of Jamāl ad-Dīn—tactics that might have developed in any case, but of which he was the prime exponent. What the radical opposition did from now on was more than what Malkum Khān had suggested before the tobacco movement, proving reform to be compatible with Islam. After the tobacco movement the reformers made continual attempts to keep the leading ulama involved in oppositional activity. The movement had demonstrated how the leading ulama, from their positions of relative impunity, could mobilize both the resentments and the religious feelings of the masses in a way that the reformers could never hope to duplicate on their own. Profound discontent with economic and administrative oppression, which the people saw had increased *pari passu* with the encroachments of foreigners, meant that popular reaction was bound to take a largely traditionalist and antiforeign form.

Jamāl ad-Dīn in London: 1891–1892

Jamāl ad-Dīn was able to influence the last phase of the tobacco movement and the subsequent opposition movement by printed propaganda sent from London. In the autumn of 1891 he

[34] Correspondence to Malkum Khān at the Bibliothèque Nationale, Paris, Oriental MSS, Supplément Persan, 1966, letter no. 82.

arrived in London, where he evidently stayed for some time with Malkum Khān. There he printed oppositional articles for delivery to Iran and also tried to arouse the British public against the Shah and his policies. A notice in a French newspaper of October 13, 1891, announces that Sayyid Jamāl ad-Dīn, well known in Paris for his debates with Renan, has just escaped from a prison in Basra where he was put by the Ottoman authorities at the demand of the Persian government. It says that Jamāl ad-Dīn has left for London and that "there, he will take over direction of the Persian emigrés who, wanting to introduce in Persia Western civilization, were condemned to death and only saved their lives by fleeing."[35] That Jamāl ad-Dīn was actually in jail in Basra is doubtful, as it is not mentioned in any of the Persian sources or in Afghānī's complaints about the crimes against him committed by, or because of, the Iranian government. He was under surveillance, though.

When he reached London and joined Malkum Khān, Jamāl ad-Dīn influenced and may have contributed to *Qānūn*. More important, he printed his letter to Shīrāzī and sent it to his associates in Iran for distribution. He also found opportunities right away to publish in the British newspapers statements against the Iranian government and its policies. The Persian government was immediately alarmed. The Persian minister in London, 'Alā' as-Saltaneh, tried to report on Jamāl ad-Dīn's and Malkum Khān's joint activities at this time in as reassuring a way as possible, but he had to note the harm they were doing to the Iranian government. On November 19, 1891, he wrote to Amīn as-Sultān (as translated by the British): "Malkom Khan, after his interview with Jamal ud-Din, has probably found out that the imprisonment of certain persons at Tehran has been the result of the intrigues of Jamal un-Din and not of the effects of his 'Kanoun' regarding which he always used to boast." He adds that Jamāl ad-Dīn should be grateful to escape with his life, but instead in spreading "scandalous statements in the papers." The minister says that precautions should be taken to keep other Iranians from leaving their country to join the two. He also refers to one of the orders from the Shah to Amīn as-Sultān to ask the British to expel both men from England.

A few days later, on November 23, the Persian minister reported

---

35 I saw this article in a collection of clippings about Iran at the British Bank of the Middle East (formerly the Imperial Bank of Persia) in London. The date is given on this item but not the name of the newspaper.

that Malkum and Jamāl ad-Dīn, although they consider each other rivals "and do not like each other and mostly discuss the difference of their opinions still as they know their objects to be of the same nature and are in a position and place that they require each other's approval they are mostly together." They are presenting themselves as the leaders of the Persian liberals and are hoping that after the new British elections a new Liberal Party government will help them. The Persian minister promises to work to contradict their statements.[36]

Three days later, on November 26, the minister reported (in British Embassy translation): "Under the pretence of being a Sayyed, a Mojtehed and one of the heads of the Shiah sect sent by the Olemas, the Princes the Merchants and the people of Persia to the capital of Great Britain to seek the British protection over Persia the Seyyed has made the English people believe of the great oppressions and cruelties which, in his opinion, are prevailing in that country." The minister says that Jamāl ad-Dīn has found some friends in parliament, and that he says he has come on the part of the Persian nation to ask the English government to bring the Persians under their protection and end the cruelties being practiced in Persia. He was saying that he could bring petitions from all classes to confirm him. "In order to excite the English people the Sayyed has also said that if his words are not listened to in England he will go to Russia." The minister adds that he is doing his best to frustrate the effectiveness of Jamāl ad-Dīn's statements, though without giving them too much importance.[37]

The nature of Jamāl ad-Dīn's activities in London in this period is further reported on in the British press. *Queen* of November 28, 1891, reports on a distinguished meeting held at Queen's House, London, by invitation of a Reverend and Mrs. H. R. Hawais. Malkum Khān spoke first, and the brief description of his speech indicates that it was the one later printed in the *Illustrated London News* of December 19, 1891, under the title "The Persian Crisis." The talk is significant as indicating what Malkum conceived to be his and Jamāl ad-Dīn's common program for the regeneration of Iran. Malkum began by noting that the new agitation in Iran might have the seeds of this regeneration. He goes on to say that thirty years ago, with the growing contact with Europe,

---

[36] F.O. 248/531 (British Embassy Archive, Tehran), translation of Persian Minister, London, to Amīn as-Sulṭān, Nov. 19 and Nov. 23, 1891.

[37] F.O. 248/531, same to same, Nov. 26, 1891.

> our learned people in the East conceived a great desire to know why Eastern races were not able to assimilate the European civilization. They believe they have found the reason and the remedy. As the reason had its source in a certain form of exclusive religion, so the remedy would have to be found in a modification of that religion. After much study and reflection and a frank exchange of ideas, they have succeeded in formulating a new doctrine, which, however, agrees perfectly with the essence of pure Islamic religion, while it is in perfect harmony with European civilization. With this doctrine they have begun a new propaganda everywhere, a work which has been hitherto ignored by Europe, though it begins to show some surprising fruits.
>
> No progress, no undertaking, either commercial or political, can be realized in the East without the help of religion. Religion dominates us entirely. . . . Knowing this to be the *sine qua non* of the Eastern question, our learned people sought to discover in religion the principle which had been the source of European progress.[38]

Malkum is then quoted as referring to a "new Koran," a phrase he later repudiated in a letter to the editor and which he was probably not imprudent enough to have used. He goes on to quote the sevenfold commandments of regenerated Islam, which turn out to be the same as those of Malkum's previously founded "religion of humanity," and are all based on liberal, humanistic, and progressive principles. Malkum concludes:

> The Shah has been very favourable from the beginning to these ideas, but now he is tired. He has abandoned the high functions of government into the hands of some very young and foolish people, who are more absolute than any sovereign in Europe. They have imprisoned, even tortured, many of our most distinguished people and exiled many more. Some of our Ambassadors have been disgraced; others, like myself, have prayed to be relieved of their diplomatic duties. [!]
>
> Now the cry in Persia is, "Why does not England help us?" Why does not your Minister at Teheran intervene? It was by the diplomatist's instance that the Shah issued the firman

---

[38] Malkom Khan, "The Persian Crisis," *Illustrated London News*, XCIX, 2748 (Dec. 19, 1891). (This article also appeared in the *Pall Mall Gazette*, as it was to them that he wrote on Dec. 30, 1891, repudiating the phrase "new Koran.")

> by which he guarantees security of life and property to his subjects. For the first time in history, the Mussulman people are resolved seriously to bring themselves into harmony with European civilization, and they look to England for practical sympathy. Our women in Persia, who are more highly gifted, as a rule, than our men, appeal to you for personal liberty and private honour. The best advocate of their cause, the Sheikh Djemaledin, is now in England. He is the Luther of the new Reformation, and I trust that he will persuade the English people to move their Government in our favour, and help us to establish in Persia the reign of law, which alone can regenerate our institutions.

Malkum thus introduced Jamāl ad-Dīn, who went on to deliver a speech in French, the substance of which was published in the *Contemporary Review* of February 1892 under the title, "The Reign of Terror in Persia." In this article, Jamāl ad-Dīn begins by saying that there has been no progress and no law but much terror in Persia. The nobles, who had formerly given the people some protection from autocracy, have been ruined by the Shah, who has also spread the notion that his power is backed up by England and Russia, so that people do not dare to oppose him. But people are now being driven to the point of wanting to depose such a Shah. The Shah has been promising for years to give the people some elements of law and justice, such as those that were suggested to him repeatedly by Malkum Khān. "I, Sheikh Djemal ed Din, on my return from Europe, also endeavoured to formulate the modest and reasonable aspirations of the people exactly in the same sense suggested by Malcom and approved by the Shah." But when the Shah saw his power threatened he arrested the speaker. Regarding Amīn as-Sultān's claim to have provisioned Jamāl ad-Dīn on his journey of expulsion, Afghānī continues saying that the chief minister "diligently published that I had been escorted with all honour by my own wish to the frontier; that special supplies of money and stores had been despatched after me that I might lack no comfort. Lies!—I was half naked, half starved, in chains till I escaped to Bagdad." (It is probable that Afghānī was the more truthful man here, as there is no evidence that Amīn as-Sultān actually sent provisions.)

Jamāl ad-Dīn continued by saying that three hundred of his companions were imprisoned. The actual number imprisoned in the spring was about forty, which Jamāl ad-Dīn may or may not have known. He goes on to describe the systematic misrule of Iran, the sale of office to the highest bidder, the lack of exploitation of Iran's mineral resources, and the emigration of impoverished Persians to Transcaucasia and Turkey. He adds, astutely:

> However *bizarre* it may seem, it is nevertheless a fact, that after each visit of the Shah to Europe he has increased in tyranny over his people. Probably this may be more or less due to his receptions which he received in Europe. The result is that the masses of Persia, observing that after each European tour the Shah became more intolerant and despotic, naturally ignorantly attributed their increased sufferings to European influences, and hence their dislike of Europeans became yet more intense, at the very moment when a *rapprochement* might easily have been effected, and when, more than at any previous time, Persia stood in need of the kindling and liberalising influences of wisely directed British statesmanship.[39]

Jamāl ad-Dīn went on to note that the British newspaper reports of the crisis in Iran were most misleading and says this was because they were filtered through the Imperial Bank. Implied is that since the Reuter family were the owners of the Imperial Bank concession as well as of the news agency responsible for all British reporting from Iran, the news was less than accurate. (The point about the inadequacy of British newspaper reporting is substantiated by a reading of the misleading and optimistic Reuter's reports on the tobacco struggle in the British press.)

Jamāl ad-Dīn concludes by saying that when the British minister to Iran (Wolff) had the Shah issue an order guaranteeing security of life and property to Persians the latter naturally expected British intervention to support this guarantee. But nothing was done to protest such an event as the seizure, arrest, and torture of the speaker. Jamāl ad-Dīn asks members of parliament and British pressure to insure that the Shah support his own order. He says that Persia is awaiting word from England, and if this does not come Russia is ready to take advantage of the current mood of the Persian people for her own ends.

As usual, Afghānī was capable of dealing with Western audiences

---

39 Sheikh Djemal ed Din, "The Reign of Terror in Persia, *Contemporary Review*, n.v. (Feb., 1892), 238–248. The quotation is from p. 245.

in terms quite different from those he used to mass Muslim audiences, with a stress on liberal and rational principles rather than religious ones. As usual, also, one finds him playing down his anti-British tone when addressing the British. Indeed he implies he would welcome British intervention in Iran, if only it were in order to help liberty and justice instead of to shore up the authority of the Shah, as it had been thus far.

The extent to which Afghānī's program of working with the leading ulama had won over even such a former critic of the ulama as Malkum Khān after the successes of this tactic in the tobacco movement is indicated by a letter from Malkum to the *Pall Mall Gazette,* December 30, 1891. After denying that he had ever used the term "new Koran," as reported in an earlier *Gazette* article, Malkum goes on, antedating his conversion to Afghānī's tactics:

> During more than thirty years in all my political writings my constant effort has been to show that the spirit of the true Islam is in perfect harmony with the principles of the present and coming civilisation of the world, and that the regeneration of Mahommedan countries will never be possible except by the Koran. By what authority is that liberal spirit of Islam going to be interpreted? By the authority of those learned sheikhs and eminent ulemas of Persia and of Kerbela who have formed lately, and for the first time, a national and powerful advanced party, and who are now dictating triumphantly the law of justice to the astonished Ministers of Tehran.[40]

Very much in the liberal and rationalist vein he and Malkum used when expressing their feelings to European audiences, Jamāl ad-Dīn gave an interview that was printed in the *Pall Mall Gazette* of December 19, 1891. He is here quoted as saying that Persians are more disposed toward progress than other Asian peoples and that their literary and philosophic temperament has made their Islam much more open than that of other peoples to ideas of toleration and human fraternity. But this has been checked by a terrible despotism. He continues, "Some of the highest and most distinguished people of all classes have united themselves to obtain guarantees for the security of life and property and to establish a tolerable administration. I am here in London as their representative to expose their

[40] *Pall Mall Gazette,* Dec. 30, 1891.

situation, hoping that generous and humanitarian minds will not fail to help by moral support our oppressed people." When asked how a liberal spirit can be introduced into Islam, Jamāl ad-Dīn answered: "The true spirit of the Koran is in perfect accordance with modern liberties. Disorders and fanaticism have come from additions and ignorant commentaries. Now the progress of time has shown the evil effects of past mistakes. Therefore, a learned Mussulman, well acquainted with the liberal principles of Europe, can easily convey them to his people with the authority of the Koran, without the difficulties which surround Luther." He adds that since the basis of reform must be sought in the Koran, the position of the Shi'is and the Sunnis toward reform is almost the same, but since the Shi'is regard temporal monarchies as usurpations the modification of despotism is easier among them. This regard for Shi'ism from a man who generally claimed to be a Sunni is striking.

Jamāl ad-Dīn goes on to suggest that the British should leave Egypt and India, where the British occupation has only made both local and outside Muslims hostile to Great Britain. He says that the Persians had long been pro-British, but now that British agents are supporting despotism, the Persians have become so deeply exasperated "that instead of relying on English support they are looking for other assistance."[41]

In a talk of December 19, 1891, at the National Liberal Club, Jamāl ad-Dīn stated that the tobacco agitation in Iran had been misrepresented in the British press as being of a religiously fanatical character, that it actually included demands for reforms and a legal code. He mentioned again the general Iranian desire to depose the Shah and the hope that England and Russia would not support him.[42]

How much influence these talks and articles had on British audiences is difficult to say, but the severe criticisms of government policy in the tobacco affair made by the Liberal opposition in parliamentary debates in the spring of 1892 may in part reflect the picture that Jamāl ad-Dīn was presenting of the tobacco movement—a picture radically different from the truncated story of religious reaction that alone was carried by most of the British press.[43]

---

41 *Ibid.*, Dec. 19, 1891.

42 This talk is announced in the *Manchester Guardian* of Dec. 18, 1891, and is described in a later clipping with no heading included in the clipping collection I have seen.

43 Keddie, *Religion and Rebellion*, App. VI, pp. 155–156, on the British press.

More important that his influence on British audiences was Jamāl ad-Dīn's influence in Iran. where the Shah's extreme concern over Jamāl ad-Dīn's activities provides some confirmation of his effectiveness. His activities in England also caused some consternation among the more conservative of his followers, again pointing up their impact. On December 3, 1891, Amīn az-Zarb wrote from Iran to Muhammad Javād in Moscow. He said he could not write directly from Iran to Jamāl ad-Dīn in London, and asks Muhammad Javād to write and ask how he is. He says to write that "From foolishness and imprudence Mīrzā Muhammad Rizā, who is mad, has thrown the people in the fire." He says that Mīrzā Rizā and poor Hājji Sayyāh are now in jail and are the cause of disgrace for Jamāl ad-Dīn and the people. He adds that surely Jamāl ad-Dīn's honor does not require that he write or express things which will cause shame to the Muslims. Even if Jamāl ad-Dīn has been badly treated by a certain individual, it has nothing to do with ten million Muslims.[44]

A letter from Amīn az-Zarb to Jamāl ad-Dīn, on July 26, 1892, is even more explicit in trying to stop his activities against the Iranian government. He says he had heard that Jamāl ad-Dīn had written bad things about the Shah and Amīn as-Sultān in a newspaper, but he knew these must be a forgery. He knows such a person as Jamāl ad-Dīn would not want to open the Iranian people to the reproaches of foreigners; if there are faults in Iran it is better to talk about them at home. Also, some of those attacked are innocent. Amīn az-Zarb continues that a short time ago he heard of two sheets coming into Iran regarding the crime of tobacco. He says that these sheets have made things worse, have led to misdeeds and hurt the Muslims. They seem to verify the bad things said about Jamāl ad-Dīn earlier. Amīn az-Zarb says that nobody in Iran has the power to act according to Jamāl ad-Dīn's words, but that even if they did, nothing good could result. He adds that he does not want to interfere, as he knows Jamāl ad-Dīn is the best man in the world, but he also knows the Shah and the chief minister are not at fault, and that the Shah loves his land. European ways can never come completely to Iran and never be accepted by Muslims; in Europe there is no mercy, while Muslims are completely merciful and generous. Jamāl ad-Dīn should support the Shah of Islam and not lead to destruction. If he speaks out properly the innocent Muslims now in jail will be released, but

---

44 *Documents*, pp. 133–134.

with the articles he is now writing this is impossible. Amīn az-Zarb expresses grief that people say Jamāl ad-Dīn has surrendered to Malkum Khān and works with him; but he knows it is not so. He concludes by asking Jamāl ad-Dīn to have pity on his condition and at least to write no more such papers in the future.[45]

One can imagine the pressure on Amīn az-Zarb from his superior, Amīn as-Sultān. Very likely Amīn az-Zarb had never been initiated into any of Jamāl ad-Dīn's secret plans and aims, and he was genuinely surprised at the bitter attacks on the Shah and Amīn as-Sultān. This letter had no apparent effect; Jamāl ad-Dīn went on to write even more bitter attacks, which brought about increasing complaints from the Shah to the English government against his presence and activities in London.

Further evidence of the embarrassment Jamāl ad-Dīn caused his more conservative Iranian disciples is found in the diary of I'timād as-Saltaneh. On January 22, 1892, he wrote that he went to Amīn ad-Dauleh's because two days before a package had arrived for him from London containing a printed copy of the letter Jamāl ad-Dīn had written from Basra to Shīrāzī which had moved Shīrāzī to attack the Iranian government. I'timād as-Saltaneh notes that the letter speaks entirely ill of Amīn as-Sultān, calling him an unbeliever, and says that he has sold Iran to the Europeans. He adds quite correctly that his own name is included among those arrested or exiled by the government. He continues: "Since the origin of the tobacco uprising and the *fatwā* of Shīrāzī about this question was clearly the result of this letter I could not loyally hide this letter from the Shah. . . . I found out that Amīn ad-Dauleh had also received one of these printed letters in the same post and had given it to the Shah." I'timād as-Saltaneh decided it was a good idea to give a translation (from Arabic into Persian) to the Shah, and "to translate badly that part where my name is and to present both the letter and its translation to the Shah. Afterwards I went to court with Amīn ad-Dauleh. I gave the letter to the Shah."[46]

Jamāl ad-Dīn's activities in London upset and frightened the Shah almost as soon as they began, as shown by the reference above to a request made by the Shah to Amīn as-Sultān as early as November 1891 to get the British to expel both Afghānī and Malkum. Another means taken by the Shah and Amīn as-Sultān against Jamāl ad-Dīn

45 *Ibid.*, pp. 134–136.
46 *Ibid.*, pp. 152–153.

was more unusual. It involved getting the liberal Persian newspaper *Akhtar*, published in Istanbul, to publish an article accusing Jamāl ad-Dīn of being an unbeliever. Khān Malik Sāsānī, one of the few persons who has been able to use Iranian archives, has given the background of this phenomenon in his recent biographical sketch of Afghānī.

Sāsānī says that in this period *Akhtar* had had to cease publication for a time owing to lack of funds. The Iranian ambassador to Istanbul, Asadallāh Khān Tabātabā'ī Nāzim ad-Dauleh (who replaced Malkum Khān's friend Mu'īn al-Mulk, recalled during the disturbances of the spring of 1891) on December 16, 1891, proposed to Amīn as-Sultān that it would be good to pay *Akhtar* in order to refute the articles of Jamāl ad-Dīn. Amīn as-Sultān presented Nāzim ad-Dauleh's letter to the Shah, who wrote an order on it saying it was necessary to write refuting Jamāl ad-Dīn and that a subsidy to the newspaper for this purpose would be very proper. (A photograph of Nāzim ad-Dauleh's letter and the Shah's order in its margin are included in Sāsānī's book.)[47] Sāsānī gives no more details on this story.

For the actual article in *Akhtar* one can turn to the *Documents*. The article is there called "The Letter of Excommunication (*takfīrnāmeh*) of the Newspaper *Akhtar*," though it is not likely that this title is on the printed article. The subheading, which is from the article, says "The Devil in Man's Clothing." In view of all the signs of unorthodoxy Jamāl ad-Dīn had in fact shown during his lifetime, the article itself must be considered rather unskillful, concentrating on Jamāl ad-Dīn's association with an Armenian [Malkum Khān], which might have been an important point for Ottoman Turks, but not particularly for the Persians to whom the article was addressed.

The article says that Jamāl ad-Dīn is working in London with some Armenians to cause sedition and spread lies about the great men of Iran. The authors have felt it necessary, to keep people from being misled, to show that this man is a foreigner to religion, and that he clothes himself in the garb of the ulama in order to further irreligious aims. His interior is, however, the opposite of his exterior. On his first trip to Istanbul he had been expelled for atheism and heresy, and his expulsions from Egypt and India were also tied to attacks on religion. In Iran men became aware of his heresy and atheism (*zandaqeh* and *ilhād*), and avoided him. He was expelled from Iran and then from Basra when he tried to cause trouble, and

---

[47] Khān Malik Sāsānī, *op. cit.*, pp. 205–207. The letter is photographed on p. 206.

now is working with expelled Armenians in London for seditious purposes.[48] Although the article is over two book-pages long, it has little content beyond this, and one wonders if the liberal editors, whose liberalism was clearly not untouched with venality, were not deliberately trying to write an ineffective article.

Far from being deterred by any of these attacks and warnings from Iran, Jamāl ad-Dīn continued and even intensified his campaign against Amīn as-Sultān and the Shah. A combination of personal and political feelings had convinced him that both these men must be got rid of before Iran could hope to progress. Thus, E. G. Browne reports that on his one meeting with Jamāl ad-Dīn, in the autumn of 1891 at the home of Malkum Khān, they first discussed the Babis, and then, "In the course of conversation I asked him about the state of Persia, and he answered, so far as I can recollect, that no reform was to be hoped for until six or seven heads had been cut off; 'the first,' he added, 'must be Nāṣiru'd-Dīn Shāh's, and the second the Amīnu's Sulṭān's."[49]

Leaving his assassination plans for the future, Jamāl ad-Dīn now concentrated on the possibility of having the ulama depose Nāsir ad-Dīn Shāh. This was not so fantastic an idea as it might sound, since depositions had in the past been sanctioned by ulama in certain cases. Also, the position of the Shah was profoundly shaken and that of the ulama enhanced by the tobacco movement. The rebellious wave had subsided somewhat since the tobacco victory and the bribing of some of the leading ulama by the government, but Jamāl ad-Dīn could not be expected to have known that from London. In any case, early in 1892 he sent to all the leading ulama of Iran and the shrine cities of Iraq two separate printed appeals calling on them to depose the Shah. In one he denounced the rapacity of the Shah and cited verses from the Koran favoring the deposition of unjust and unbelieving monarchs. The Shah was declared to be wringing money from the people for the tobacco indemnity, and the defeat of England was said to be of little help "because the weakness of England means the strength of Russia and the latter will seize Khorasan, when England will not dare to oppose her, being afraid of her designs on India. Only dethronement can make this misfortune pass away." The appeal argued that in an absolute monarchy only the sovereign who actually makes an engagement is bound by it. Hence if the Shah were

---

48 *Documents,* pp. 144–146.
49 Browne, *op. cit.,* p. 45.

dethroned all the disastrous contracts he had made would be canceled. It was up to the mullas to rise up and insist on the Shah's dethronement.[50]

This proclamation and a similar one calling on the ulama to save Iran from complete foreign domination by dethroning the Shah caused the Shah to communicate more of his strong complaints against Afghānī to the British. The Shah said that Jamāl ad-Dīn was guilty of the European crime of lesè majesté, and that the British should execute him or imprison him for life, "otherwise how can we believe that the English government is the protector of our Sovereignty and Our Person."[51] The new British minister in Tehran, Sir Frank Lascelles, forwarded the complaint, although he told Amīn as-Sultān that the British government could proceed only according to law. A Foreign Office minute on an earlier complaint noted, "Jamal-ed-Din is a dangerous intriguer—and has been as much opposed to England as to any other Power—But I do not see what action we can take against this paper."[52]

The Shah did not calm down, but continued to press his complaints to the British noting the violent language that Afghānī had used against him. On May 11 Lascelles noted: "It is not surprising that the Shah should deeply resent the accusations brought against him by Djemal ed Din and fear the effect which they may produce in the country; more especially as, although there may be some exaggeration of language, there can be little doubt of their substantial truth."[53] The Shah complained that Lascelles had not given an immediate answer to his demand to have Afghānī punished, and wrote to Amīn as-Sultān: "We cannot accept or admit that the British Government is Our friend or the protector of our Sovereignty and Ourselves, while they do nothing and allow such a person to write such nonsensical things and then say that England is a free country."[54]

---

[50] The two appeals are translated in F.O. 60/594, Lascelles to Salisbury, no. 82, May 11, 1892; and Mīrzā Muḥammad 'Alī Khān to Salisbury, London, June 22, 1892. A partial translation of the second is in Browne, *op. cit.*, pp. 24–27.

[51] Autograph of the Shah to Amīn as-Sulṭān, received April 28, 1892, translation enclosed in F.O. 60/594, Lascelles to Salisbury, no. 82, May 11, 1892. Some supplementary documentation of exchanges between Iranian officials and the British is found in Ṣafā'ī, *Asnād*, pt. 8.

[52] F.O. 60/594, Minute, apparently by T. H. Sanderson, on Morier to Salisbury, St. Petersburg, no. 87, April 27, 1892.

[53] *Ibid.*, Lascelles to Salisbury, no. 83, Secret, May 11, 1892.

[54] *Ibid.*, enclosed translation of Autograph of Shah in Lascelles to Salisbury, no. 86, May 12, 1892.

After a still further complaint from the Shah in May Amīn as-Sultān suggested to Lascelles that the British government at least say it would do what it could so that the Shah might retain some hope. Acting on this advice, Lord Salisbury, the British prime minister and foreign minister, decided to get an opinion from the Law Officers of the Crown stating that no action could be taken by the British, and to show the Foreign Office request and the answer to it to the Shah in order to prove that the Foreign Office had done all it could. The Law Officers reported that the facts afforded no grounds for the institution of legal proceedings by the British government, but that Sayyid Jamāl ad-Dīn could be prosecuted by the Persian minister in England. When this answer was given to the Persian minister he, naturally enough, returned it and asked if it could not be modified so that he would not be blamed for not taking proceedings against Jamāl ad-Dīn which the Law Officers said he could. In the same period, the summer of 1892, the news came that Sayyid Jamāl ad-Dīn had left England for Istanbul, much to the relief, one would imagine, of both the Foreign Office and the Persian minister in London.[55]

Further evidence of the Iranian government's concern over Jamāl ad-Dīn's activities in London is found in Persian documents. A note from the liberal minister of posts, Amīn ad-Dauleh, to the Shah some time in 1892, confirms that he has been seizing from distribution anything he recognized as coming from Jamāl ad-Dīn (presumably on orders from the Shah). He adds, however, that the government's complaints about Jamāl ad-Dīn to London, and the "exposure of his character" in the newspapers *Akhtar, Ittilā'* (Tehran), and *Kaukab-i Nāsirī* (Bombay) was unwise, as it only attracted people's attention to him. The Shah responded that Amīn ad-Dauleh should give the English and French newspapers pertinent to Jamāl ad-Dīn to Amīn as-Sultān to be translated for the Shah, and should discuss questions regarding "these two unclean persons" (Malkum and Jamāl ad-Dīn) with Amīn as-Sultān.[56]

To combat Jamāl ad-Dīn and Malkum's influence, Amīn as-Sultān also wrote a long letter to Mīrzā Hasan Shīrāzī, the chief Shi'i mujtahid in Iraq, denouncing the two as heretics or unbelievers, noting that Jamāl ad-Dīn had for many years, in Russia and Afghanistan,

---

55 *Ibid.*, series of documents from June to Sept., 1892.

56 Ṣafā'ī, *Asnād*, pp. 268–269; Amīn ad-Dauleh's report and the Shah's reply are translated in A. Albert Kudsi-Zadeh, "Iranian Politics in the Late Qājār Period: A Review," *Middle Eastern Studies*, V, 3 (Oct., 1969), 251–257, on pp. 253–254 (henceforth called Kudsi-Zadeh, "Iranian Politics").

called himself a Sunni, and claiming that he had even written in newspapers against the Shi'is. In Tehran, wrote Amīn as-Sultān Jamāl ad-Dīn had set up a secret circle of Babis and materialists and had helped lead people away from true religion. To protect religion the Shah ordered his expulsion. The printed leaflets Jamāl ad-Dīn has recently sent out slandering the government of Islam should be given no credence, and Shīrāzī should instead know the truth about this man and should inform the people about him, to protect them from his heresies.[57]

Afghānī's two printed appeals in Arabic for the Shah's deposition were sent as separate letters to the Shi'i ulama, but were also printed in an Arabic-English newspaper published in London to which Afghānī was a contributor, *The Eastern and Western Review—Ḍiyā' al-Khāfiqain* ("The Light of the Two Hemispheres"). Since he contributed an article to the first issue of this paper, he may have helped inspire its publication, but he was not the paper's editor, as the standard biographies say. The editor of the paper was listed in its later issues as H[abib] Anthony Salmoné. Salmoné was an Arabic teacher and writer who met Afghānī during his first trip to London, translated for him at least one of his talks in London, and who now printed some articles by Afghānī in his newspaper. His newspaper was generally quite favorable to British imperial policy in the East, and most of its articles show no sign of Afghānī's influence. The first issue was dated February 1892 and included an article signed S. al-Saiyid, clearly a pseudonym for Jamāl ad-Dīn in view of its contents: a description of the reign of terror and tyranny in Persia. The second issue, dated March 1892, reprints one of Jamāl ad-Dīn's two appeals to depose the Shah, saying it had been widely distributed by secret agents of the revolutionary party in Persia and that it had reached the paper via a special correspondent at Baghdad; the authorship is kept mysterious through the use only of the letter's signature as-Sayyid al-Ḥusainī, which might have been recognized by some readers, but not most. A later issue reported the receipt of a second similar appeal, which it printed in Arabic but said it would not print in English pending verification of its serious charges against the Shah, who had tried to benefit his people through introducing European enterprise.[58] This short-lived newspaper, most of whose ar-

[57] Ṣafā'ī, *Asnād*, pp. 312–319.

[58] *The Eastern and Western Review (Ḍiyā' al-Khāfiqain)*, [British Museum], Vol. I (1892) issues. The most relevant items are in nos. 1–5, and are summarized in Pakdaman, pp. 162–165.

ticles were not in tune with Afghānī's views, does not seem to have been important in spreading his influence.

Meanwhile Sultan Abdülhamid, having let Afghānī slip through his hands in 1891, was trying to attract him back to Istanbul. He conveyed an invitation first via the Ottoman ambassador in London, Rüstem Paşa, but Jamāl ad-Dīn was wary of it. The Sultan then had his chief religious confidant, the leader of an important Sufi order, Abū al-Hudā aṣ-Ṣayyadī, write to Afghānī in London. Abū al-Hudā's two letters to Jamāl ad-Dīn have remained in the papers of Malkum Khān. In the first letter Afghānī is asked how a good Muslim like himself can stand to live outside Muslim territory among infidels, and he is told that people have attributed to him articles in newspapers that harm the caliphate and the Muslim community. The Sultan wishes that such a good servant of Islam were instead helping him against aggressors, and has asked the writer to convey an invitation. Jamāl ad-Dīn should accept the invitation of Rüstem Paşa and return to live in comfort near the Caliph. The letter is dated 16 Rajab, 1309/February 15, 1892. The second letter from Abū al-Hudā says that Afghānī's answer to Rüstem Paşa has been communicated by telegraph, but despite its expressions of obedience to the Sultan it gave excuses based on what had happened to Afghānī and his companions in Iran. Afghānī has answered wrongly, the letter says, and it adds especially in his old age he should live and die among good Muslims as a religious duty. The writer promises him the protection of his brothers in religion and an easy life, close to the great Caliph.

Abū al-Hudā continues with some barely disguised threats: There have been attributed to Afghānī words harmful to the caliphate and the Sultan printed in the British newspapers. If Afghānī accepts the invitation to Istanbul he can disprove these accusations, but if he delays after this second letter he will confirm what is charged against him and will allow his Muslim brothers to write of him things that will not please him. He will be considered an enemy, after having been considered a great friend. Thus, Afghānī should surely accept and come to Istanbul.[59]

---

59 Malkum Khān papers, Bibliothèque Nationale, Supplément Persan, no. 1995, ff. 35–36. The letters are rather illegibly photographed at the end of the *Documents*, photos 216–217. Pakdaman, p. 169, translates part of the second letter as follows: "If your stay in London has no other object than the announcement of your complaints against the Iranians, that can also be done in Muslim countries. Know, O scholar, that if you do not accept this invitation, which it is your duty to accept, and if you continue to manifest so much heedlessness, you will attract to

A Turkish poet, Abdülhak Hamid, who met Jamāl ad-Dīn first in London and later in Istanbul, has left in his memoirs some further details about Jamāl ad-Dīn's invitation from London to Istanbul. Hamid says that in London Jamāl ad-Dīn used to say that Nāsir ad-Dīn Shāh was the worst of all despots, whereas Sultan Abdülhamid, even if nothing could be said for him, was at least the caliph. Jamāl ad-Dīn, continues Hamid, lived in a small, high, mansard room on the outskirts of London. Jamāl ad-Dīn was not well regarded by the pro-British Ottoman ambassador to London, Rüstem Paşa, who felt that the salvation of the Ottoman government lay in the hands of the British, whereas Jamāl ad-Dīn thought that reliance on the British was contrary to the interests of Muslim unity. After the first invitation from Abū al-Hudā, Jamāl ad-Dīn said that he could not go to Istanbul as long as he was awaiting the occurrence of a certain (unspecified) event in Tehran. Later for unknown reasons he changed his mind and said to Hamid that going to Istanbul would be a means to serve the public. Jamāl ad-Dīn added that he had no desire for a high post in Istanbul, that he hoped there to be in a condition to perform public service, and that he did not fear prison, because in the past, "they have imprisoned my person but as for my thought, it is not in their power to imprison it."[60]

Whether moved by the threats or the promises, or hopeful of finally finding that high political influence that he had grasped for only brief moments in the past, Jamāl ad-Dīn in 1892 set out for Istanbul where, ultimately against his will, he was forced to remain and to cease his lifelong wanderings.[61]

---

yourself waves of protest from all your Muslim brothers, scattered in all the near and distant territory of Islam. 'Not to execute the orders of the Sultan is to turn away from the orders of God.'

"I therefore ask you to accept the invitation of the Caliph of Islam and to come to the Seat of the Caliphate. If you come I promise you an important rank and a comfortable life."

60 Memoirs reprinted in Anwar al-Jundī, *ash-Sharq fī fajr al-yaqẓa* (Cairo, 1966), pp. 27–29.

61 It is unclear what role a letter from Afghānī some time prior to August 1892 "to a personage in Constantinople for communication to the Turkish government," appealing for an Ottoman-Afghan alliance, played in Afghānī's trip to Istanbul. After outlining the policy of alliance with Afghanistan, Jamāl ad-Dīn says, "I guarantee to Turkey the accomplishment of this achievement if she adopts my advice, listens to my counsel, and charges me with this mission. If fate favors me to be near her I will show her several useful things which my experience makes me more able than anyone else to know." Since the letter has no reference to a prior invitation, one may guess that this letter preceded the Sultan's invitations, but that Afghānī nonetheless hesitated to accept the first invitation until he had

guarantees for his position in Istanbul. The above letter from Afghānī is found, in French, in F.O. 78/4452, Hardinge to Rosebery, Ramleh, Sept. 3, 1892; reprinted in Jacob M. Landau, "Al-Afghani's Pan-Islamic Project," *Islamic Culture*, XXVI, 3 (July, 1952), 50–54; and translated into English in Nikki R. Keddie, "The Pan-Islamic Appeal: Afghani and Abdülhamid II," *Middle Eastern Studies*, III, 1 (Oct., 1966), 46–67, at pp. 65–66.

13

The Final Years: Istanbul, 1892–1897

THE COMBINATION of threats and promises emanating from the court of Sultan Abdülhamid II finally sufficed to bring Jamāl ad-Dīn back to Istanbul in the summer of 1892. Here he hoped to have a strong influence on the Sultan's Pan-Islamic policy and also to continue his bitter campaign against Nāsir ad-Dīn Shāh. These two goals were congruent, as promotion of loyalty to the Sultan-Caliph outside the Ottoman Empire could be used as a threat to the sovereignty of the Shah over his own subjects; in fact, nearly all Iranian Pan-Islamists were opponents of the Shah. Jamāl ad-Dīn probably believed that he had finally found his way into the counsels of the most important ruler in the Muslim world, to whom he could give direction in strengthening Muslim lands, and from whom he could expect a high advisory position. For a brief period he did enjoy the favor of the Sultan, although Abdülhamid brought him to Istanbul to control him as well as to make use of him. At least as early as Jamāl ad-Dīn's 1891 stay in Ottoman Iraq the Sultan was suspicious of him as one who wanted to stir up trouble among his Arabic-speaking subjects, and perhaps support Wilfrid Blunt's scheme for a new Arabian caliphate. The Sultan had therefore refused him permission to travel in Arabia in 1891 and wished even then to bring him to Istanbul largely in order to keep an eye on him. The Sultan must also have been aware of the propaganda value of having at his court and working in his behalf a man with a considerable reputation among many Muslims, and Abdülhamid was more able than any earlier host to keep his fiery guest under control.[1] Even after relations between the Sultan and Jamāl ad-Dīn had cooled, Abdülhamid was shrewd enough to keep Afghānī as a prisoner in a gilded cage instead of exiling him so that he might give free rein to his pen and plans.

Jamāl ad-Dīn later related that he arrived in Istanbul with so little baggage that it surprised the Ottoman officials who met him. He was placed in the Sultan's large guesthouse and given a monthly allowance. He evidently got to see the Sultan soon after his arrival and was at first on good terms with Shaikh Abū al-Hudā and the Sultan's other top religious advisers.[2]

The Iranian government, which had been addressing its complaints about Jamāl ad-Dīn's activities against the Shah to London, now began making complaints to Istanbul. On July 25, 1892, Amīn as-Sultān addressed a telegram to the Iranian ambassador in Istanbul, Mīrzā Asadallāh Khān Nāzim ad-Dauleh, saying that information had arrived from London that Jamāl ad-Dīn had been invited to Istanbul, where he had gone for a temporary stay, after which he would return (to London). Amīn as-Sultān asked Nāzim ad-Dauleh to find out if Jamāl ad-Dīn had in fact been invited to Istanbul and, if so, whether it was by the Sultan or by someone else. Nāzim ad-Dauleh was also asked to arrange to have Jamāl ad-Dīn imprisoned, "as was done in Baghdad and Basra, which is very necessary." Nāzim ad-Dauleh was authorized to take whatever steps were necessary to fulfill his orders, and promised a special reward if he succeeded.[3]

[1] British and Persian documents cited in this and earlier chapters reinforce the conclusion of Niyazi Berkes that the Sultan wanted Jamāl ad-Dīn in Istanbul both for prestige and because he was associated with Blunt's schemes for an Arab caliphate. Cf. Niyazi Berkes, *The Development of Secularism in Turkey* (Montreal, 1964), pp. 268–270.

[2] Khān Malik Sāsānī, *Siyāsatgarān-i daureh-yi Qājār* (Tehran, 1338/1959–60), p. 194. Wilfred S. Blunt, *My Diaries* (Single vol. ed.; London, 1932), quotes Ibrāhīm Muwailihī as telling him in Istanbul in April 1893 that Jamāl ad-Dīn "is now in high favour at Yildiz, having succeeded with Abdul Hamid by his plainspoken audacity. The Sultan has offered him all kinds of grades and decorations, but Jemal ed Din has wisely refused, and the other day, on being turned back by the master of ceremonies at one of the Bairam Court functions, Jemal ed Din pushed his way through notwithstanding, and so attracted the Sultan's notice, who sent for him and made him stand close to him behind his chair, nearer even than the Grand Eunuch. So Jemal ed Din is the man of whom to solicit favours" (p. 100).

[3] Ṣafā'ī, *Asnād*, p. 275. An English translation is in A. Albert Kudsi-Zadeh, "Iranian Politics in the Late Qājār Period: A Review," *Middle Eastern Studies*, V, 3

Nāzim ad-Dauleh telegraphed a reply on August 1, 1892, and also sent Amīn as-Sultān a longer undated letter, reporting what he had heard in Istanbul. The more complete, letter version of Nāzim ad-Dauleh's reply to Amīn as-Sultān reads:

> For some time the English government has been secretly of the opinion that they should undermine the Sultan's caliphate and dissuade people from believing in it. With this aim they have incited the Arab shaikhs and brought them to the point of revolt. The British are giving them the idea of choosing the caliph themselves and placing him in Mecca, or else recognizing the Sharīf of Mecca who is a descendant of Zaid ibn Alī. One of the means of the activity of the English was the presence of Jamāl ad-Dīn who published some articles in London encouraging and inciting the Arab shaikhs, making them stand firm in rebelliousness against the Ottoman government; and making the common people disrespectful of the Sultan, whom they recognized as the caliph of the earth. The policy which the Ottoman government followed to repel this danger was to write to their ambassador in London in order to lure and tempt Jamāl ad-Dīn and bring him to Istanbul. The ambassador according to his instructions gave him the necessary guarantees and sent him to Istanbul. Here they have made him a guest. After receiving Your Highness's telegram I spoke to the prime minister. He said: "It is impossible to imprison Sayyid Jamāl ad-Dīn. His Majesty the Sultan gave him his word, and brought him here; how can he imprison him?" I gave the Sultan a message through the prime minister. He answered: "As I see it on this matter I have done a great service to His Majesty [the Shah]. I have separated Jamāl ad-Dīn from the cursed Malkum and brought him here so that I can silence him so that he will not write or publish. As long as he is here I will be watchful that he does not write anything about Iran. Afterwards I will send him to a place and occupy him with compiling books, in order that he should abandon these ideas of his. Since I brought him here with guarantees, jailing him would be inconsistent with the dignity of the sultanate."[4]

(Oct., 1969), 251–257, on p. 254. (Kudsi-Zadeh notes [p. 257 n. 16] that Ṣafā'ī is wrong in giving 1310 as the year date for this telegram, actually sent on the last day of 1309.) My summary of this and other documents in Ṣafā'ī's book was prepared from the original Persian, before the appearance of Kudsi-Zadeh's article, reference to which was nevertheless helpful.

4 Sāsānī, *op. cit.*, pp. 193–194, quoting Archives of the Iranian Foreign Ministry.

In response to the briefer telegraphic version of the same report, which also noted the Ottoman authorities' promise to keep Jamāl ad-Dīn under police surveillance,[5] Nāsir ad-Dīn Shāh ordered Amīn as-Sultān to write the Iranian ambassador in Istanbul to say categorically to the Ottoman prime minister and the Sultan that if they gave any honor or position to Jamāl ad-Dīn after he had written nonsensical things against the Shah and ministers of Iran, it would be considered an unfriendly act and worsen relations between Iran and the Ottoman Empire. Amīn as-Sultān telegraphed Nāzim ad-Dauleh on August 3, 1892, conveying these views from the Shah to the Ottoman authorities and specifying that Nāzim ad-Dauleh must tell the Ottoman authorities in detail of Jamāl ad-Dīn's evil designs toward the Iranian government. Also, Nāzim ad-Dauleh was asked to investigate further the true reasons for the Sultan's invitation and attention to Jamāl ad-Dīn.[6]

Probably in response to these orders, the Iranian ambassador in Istanbul sent a letter to the Sultan saying that in the opinion of the Shah the Sultan had brought Jamāl ad-Dīn to Istanbul against the interests of Iran. In answer, the Sultan said: "My opinion about Sayyid Jamāl ad-Dīn is the same as the opinion of the Shah. However, in order to prevent the incitement and trouble among the Arabs that he was accomplishing at the instigation of the British I invited him and brought him here. Be confident that I will not let him say or write anything against the interests of Iran."[7]

Although the Sultan was surely giving the Iranians only the most palatable of his reasons for bringing Jamāl ad-Dīn to Istanbul, such reasons must have played a part. The Sultan evidently exacted a promise from Jamāl ad-Dīn to stop his violent public attacks on the Shah, and Jamāl ad-Dīn was not permitted while in Istanbul to publish any more against the Shah. According to Jamāl ad-Dīn's later story, conversations on the subject ended with Jamāl ad-Dīn's saying

---

[5] Ṣafā'ī, *Asnād*, pp. 276–278 photographs the original and reprints the deciphered telegram, which was written on Muḥarram 7, 1310/August 1, 1892, and sent the following day. A translation is in Kudsi-Zādeh, "Iranian Politics," pp. 254–255. Persian and English versions of the telegram are also in F.O. 248/553, Telegram from Persian Ambassador in Constantinople, Aug. 1, 1892.

[6] Ṣafā'ī, *Asnād*, pp. 279–280 photographs and prints the handwritten draft of Amīn as-Sultān's August 3 telegram. On p. 280, n. 1, Ṣafā'ī quotes the Shah's prior order to Amīn as-Sultān from p. 142 of a book entitled *Bāzīgar-i inqilāb-i Sharq*, about which he gives no additional information. Amīn as-Sultān's August 3 telegram is translated in Kudsi-Zadeh, "Iranian Politics," p. 255.

[7] Sāsānī, *op. cit.*, p. 194, citing Archives of the Iranian Foreign Ministry.

that he had intended to put the Shah in his grave, but must obey the Sultan. Hence he forgave the Shah of Iran.[8] Reports of friends as well as later events show that he continued to nurture his violent hatred of the Shah and his hopes of revenge upon him. It can well be believed that the Sultan, for all his desire to increase his foreign Muslim following, was not inclined to encourage talk of deposing or assassinating a legitimate Muslim monarch.

Although the Sultan had friendly personal consultations with Jamāl ad-Dīn in the early months of his stay, it is unclear whether Jamāl ad-Dīn was at this time given any specific duties. He was not allowed to publish anything during the whole of his stay, and his one important labor in the Sultan's behalf, writing letters to the Shi'i ulama urging them to support the Sultan's claims to the caliphate, seems to have begun only in 1894. Certainly Jamāl ad-Dīn was never given the position or influence he had hoped for.

In his first months, however, Jamāl ad-Dīn seems to have been well received by the Sultan's chief religious confidants, and also to have met the most important Iranian exiles in Istanbul. Mīrzā Āqā Khān Kirmānī, a writer and an editor of the paper *Akhtar*, who passed from Azalī Babism to radical free thought wrote to Malkum Khān of his friendship with Jamāl ad-Dīn soon after the latter's arrival. He also relayed a request from Jamāl ad-Dīn that Malkum bring out a special issue of *Qānūn* advocating the unity of Islam and directed at the ulama of Najaf and Karbala, a request with which Malkum complied.[9]

Mīrzā Āqā Khān also wrote a treatise describing an apparently genuine session in the first months of 1893 at which the Muslim religion was discussed, with Jamāl ad-Dīn taking a leading role. Those present, included the Sultan's three chief confidants, all leaders of Sufi orders—Shaikh Abū al-Hudā, Shaikh Ẓāfir (Madanī), and Aḥmad

---

[8] One of Jamāl ad-Dīn's accounts of this interview is in Shakīb Arslān's section of the Arabic translation of L. Stoddard's *The New World of Islam*, *Ḥāḍir al-'ālam al-Islāmī* (Cairo, 1343/1924–25), I, 203. Another is given by Muḥammad al-Makhzūmī, who reports from the mouth of Jamāl ad-Dīn that he finished by saying, "I accept the observation of the Caliph and I forgive Nāsir ad-Dīn Shāh." Those present were amazed that he arrogated to himself the right to forgive the Shah. Cf. Muḥammad al-Mukhzūmī, *Khāṭirāt-i Sayyid Jamāl ad-Dīn Asadābādī*, Persian trans. (Tabriz, 1949–50), p. 58. (This translation and the 2d Arabic edition [*Khāṭirāt Jamāl ad-Dīn al-Afghānī*, Damascus, 1965] are henceforth called Makhzūmī, *Khāṭirāt* [Persian] or [Arabic]).

[9] Malkum Khān correspondence, Bibliothèque Nationale, Supplément Persan, no. 1996, no. 110.

As'ad. Also present were Iranian modernizers including the treatise's author and the Shaikh ar-Ra'īs, a radical relative of the ruling Qājār dynasty. On this occasion Jamāl ad-Dīn expressed a middle view between Mīrzā Āqā Khān's criticism of theological discussion as harmful to the welfare of Muslims and those who supported such discussions. The discussion that evening centered on a work by a Shaikhi leader, one of whose treatises Jamāl ad-Dīn had copied decades before, regarding the meaning of the common phrase, "If God wills" (*In shā'a Allāh*), in view of the theological contention that everything that happens in the world is written in advance of an eternal slate. The evening's host, Yusuf Rıza Paşa, and Mīrzā Āqā Khān took the position that such phrases and discussions distracted the Muslims from practical achievements, while others among those present regarded this position as heretical. Jamāl ad-Dīn, no doubt conscious that he had to impress an audience containing both freethinkers and influential religious personages, and perhaps still favorably impressed by Shaikhi ideas, tried to reconcile the positions expressed with an explanation that implied neither total fatalism nor a rejection of traditional religious formulas. The formula "in shā'a Allāh," he said, shows the believer's recognition that God is in ultimate control of everything, and, he added, God will grant victory to those who follow what is good. Mīrzā Āqā Khān recorded his own view that Jamāl ad-Dīn's argument simply perpetuated useless theological formulas.[10]

In his first period in Istanbul, Afghānī exercised his talent for uniting people of divergent views around the goal of strengthening the Muslim world against European aggression. His own support for Sultan Abdülhamid was, as previously noted, based on the belief, voiced explicitly in 1883, that unity and strength against European encroachments had first priority for Muslims, and that reform might follow later. He won over Azalī Babis and freethinkers among his circle in Istanbul to his Pan-Islamic ideas, and they soon came to help him to propagandize for the Sultan and for Pan-Islam. As the representatives of the most powerful Islamic state, Sultan Abdülhamid had some of the same attraction for reformers who were wor-

10 Anonymous, "Controverses persanes," trans. A. L. M. Nicolas, *Revue du monde musulmane*, XXI (Dec., 1912), 238–260. Nicolas was unaware of the author of the work he translated, but reference to E. G. Browne's catalog of Persian books and manuscripts shows the work to be by Mīrzā Āqā Khān Kirmānī. The treatise is discussed in Hamid Algar's forthcoming biography of Malkum Khān and in Mangol Bayat Philipp's dissertation, "Mīrzā Āqā Khān Kirmānī: Nineteenth-Century Persian Revolutionary Thinker," University of California, Los Angeles, 1971.

ried about foreign encroachments in Muslim lands that Bismarck, Cavour, and the dynasties they supported had for German and Italian nationalists, including many with liberal and reformist backgrounds.

Among those who joined Jamāl ad-Dīn's circle during his first year there was a young Syrian student, 'Abd al-Qādir al-Maghribī, who many years later wrote his recollections of Jamāl ad-Dīn. In this book he tells of the tremendous intellectual and emotional impression that *al-'Urwa al-Wuthqā* had on him and his good friend Rashīd Riḍā when they were boys, and of his own successful determination to become a follower of the great Sayyid when he went to Istanbul in 1892–93. He also includes letters to him from Rashīd Riḍā at that time conveying the latter's admiration for Jamāl ad-Dīn.[11] Also in Jamāl ad-Dīn's circle was his old follower Ibrāhīm Muwailihī, now holding a position at the Sultan's court.

The outside world heard very little about Jamāl ad-Dīn's activities during his years in Istanbul, and the Sultan seems to have discouraged not only publication by Jamāl ad-Dīn but also any publicity about him. One of the rare pieces of information to reach any outsider came in December 1893, after Jamāl ad-Dīn persuaded the Ottoman government to invite to Istanbul the Egyptian nationalist writer, orator, and agitator, 'Abdallāh Nadīm, who knew Afghānī from his stay in Egypt. On December 22, 1893, the British ambassador wrote home responding to telegrams from Cromer in Egypt regarding Nadīm:

> I have been informed that this individual has been given a situation in the Press Bureau here. He has placed himself under the protection of Sheikh Djemaleddin, and I am told that he recently, in conjunction with this Sheikh, drew up a very inflammatory indictment against the British particularly, which it was intended to circulate at Mecca among the Indian and other pilgrims during the next pilgrimage season. The document was submitted to the Sultan, who, before giving his sanction to its distribution, consulted some of his advisers in such matters. The latter came to the conclusion that its dissemination might entail consequences the ultimate effects of which it was impossible to foresee; and they, therefore, recommended that the matter should be laid aside, at any rate for the moment.

11 'Abd al-Qādir al-Maghribī, *Jamāl ad-Dīn al-Afghānī* (Cairo, 1948), pp. 17–26, 109–114.

The Sultan acquiesced in this view, and the question has been dropped.

Abdullah Nedim, I am told, is, nevertheless, making way in the Imperial favour, under the auspices of his friendly Sheikh.[12]

Afghānī's anti-British proclivities were apparently kept in check by the Sultan during Afghānī's years in Istanbul, since there is no word of any activity or writing by him in this direction from the Istanbul stay. Jamāl ad-Dīn's Pan-Islamic ideas and his hostility to the Shah were given some rein beginning in 1894, however, when the Sultan had him lead a group of Persians and other Shi'is to write to the Shi'i ulama in favor of the Sultan's claims to the caliphate. There are several Persian accounts of this, the most complete of which stems from an Iranian, Afzal al-Mulk Kirmānī, a brother of the writer and poet, Shaikh Ahmad Rūhī. These two were close associates of Mīrzā Āqā Khān Kirmānī, and Rūhī, like Kirmānī, had been an Azalī Babi and was now a freethinker. According to Afzal al-Mulk, who was himself part of Afghānī's Iranian circle in Istanbul:

> The Ottoman Sultan . . . asked Sayyid Jamāl ad-Dīn to write to the Shi'i ulama in Iran and Iraq and call them to unity. The late Sayyid Jamāl ad-Dīn answered that this problem had great importance for Islamic states. Today the Muslims of the world were more than three hundred million, and if they believed in unity and brotherhood among themselves no government or people could prevail or excel over them. He said if he had the power of the sultanate and the necessary money . . . he could accomplish this great work with the help of a circle of patriotic (*millat parast*) intellectuals. The Ottoman Sultan gave guarantees and obligations for this. The Sayyid formed a society of Iranian and other Shi'i men of letters who were in Istanbul. This society was made up of twelve men. . . . When the Sayyid's group was formed, he spoke to it as follows: "Today the religion of Islam is like a ship whose captain is Muhammad, peace be with him, and all Muslims are passengers of this holy ship, and this unhappy ship is caught in a storm and threatened with sinking, and unbelievers and freethinkers (*ahl-i zandaqeh*) from every side have pierced this ship. What is the duty of the passengers of such a ship, threatened with sink-

[12] F.O. 78/8, Nicholson to Rosebery, Confidential, Dec. 22, 1893.

ing, and its inhabitants close to perdition? Should they first try to preserve and save this ship from the storm and from sinking, or instead bring the ship and each other to the verge of ruin through discord, personal motives, and petty disagreements?" All with one voice answered that preserving the territory of Islam and saving this holy ship was the religious duty of every Muslim.

Then the Sayyid asked all to write to every acquaintance and friend in Iran and the shrines of Iraq, in general, and in particular to the Shi'i ulama in India, Iran, the Arab lands, Balkh, and Turkestan, about the kindness and benevolence of the great Islamic Sultan toward all Muslims of whatever opinion and group they might be. If the Shi'i ulama united in this Islamic unity the Sultan would give every one of them, according to his rank, special favor and a monthly salary, and would order Ottoman officials to observe the same good conduct toward Iranians in Mecca and Medina as toward their own people, and in recognition of this great action of the Shi'i ulama and the state of Iran he would bestow on them the holy cities of Iraq . . . and about 400 letters were written in all directions, and a report of this society was given to the Ottoman Sultan. . . . After six months about 200 petitions from the Arab and Iranian Shi'i ulama with some gifts and antiques were sent to the Sultan through Sayyid Jamāl ad-Dīn. . . . The Ottoman Caliph was so happy to see these letters that he embraced the late Sayyid and kissed his face and said to him: "Since some are such fanatical Sunnis and will find a pretext to accuse me of Shi'ism, it is better that we turn over the accomplishment of this holy goal to the Prime Minister and the Sublime Porte. We will have the Şeyhülislam collaborate with us confidentially." He accepted the royal will in this matter and an imperial command went to the Sublime Porte. I was delegated to go to the holy cities of Iraq to investigate the mentality and affairs of the ulama and give a report to the Sublime Porte.[13]

The involvement of freethinkers like Ahmad Rūhī and Mīrzā Āqā Khān Kirmānī in Afghānī's Pan-Islamic movement is one of many

[13] Biography of Mīrzā Āqā Khān Kirmānī by Afẓal al-Mulk Kirmānī, prefaced to the anonymous Azalī Babi text *Hasht Bihisht* (n.p., n.d.,), trans. in Nikki R. Keddie, "Religion and Irreligion in Early Iranian Nationalism," *Comparative Studies in Society and History*, IV, 3 (April, 1962), 292–295, where the names of all those in Jamāl ad-Dīn's Persian and Shi'i circle are included. See also the letter of Shaikh Ahmad Rūhī about these activities in Pakdaman, p. 173.

indications of the largely political and secular goals of this movement. These two were probably largely motivated by hatred of the Shah and of the Iranian government, and hoped that the strengthening of the Sultan might weaken the Shah. Mīrzā Āqā Khān, although he published anonymously the most virulent attacks on Islam and on religion in general, did not fail to publish a poem excoriating Nāsir ad-Dīn Shāh as an unbeliever. And Rūhī had himself photographed leaning on a tablet that reads, "There is nothing except nature," while he had inscribed on his seal, "I am the propagandist of the Unity of Islam."[14]

Various pieces of correspondence between Afghānī's Iranian circle and the Shi'i ulama fell into the hands of the Iranian consul in Baghdad and the Iranian ambassador in Istanbul, and they reported home that Jamāl ad-Dīn and his followers were working against the Shah. On orders from Tehran, the Iranian ambassador at Istanbul began to demand the imprisonment or extradition of Jamāl ad-Dīn, Rūhī, Kirmānī, and another friend, the Iranian consul general, Mīrzā Hasan Khān Khabīr al-Mulk. One source says the latter had written to the Iraqi ulama urging them to support not only the caliphate of the Sultan but the deposition of the Shah.[15] Jamāl ad-Dīn and the others had some high protectors in Istanbul but, according to Rūhī's brother, the chief of police was bribed into pressing for their surrender to the Shah, and the Sultan issued an order that Iranians were under the control of their own ambassador (and hence should be surrendered). At the end of 1895 it was agreed that Rūhī, Kirmānī, and Khabīr al-Mulk would be sent to prison at Trabzon, near the Iranian border, and this was done. Although Jamāl ad-Dīn had broken relations with Rūhī and Kirmānī several months earlier, he now evidently appealed to the Sultan for their release. Jamāl ad-Dīn said he told the Sultan that people who had done important services for the caliphate were now being imprisoned or executed, and the Sultan replied that he had been misinformed about the prisoners and that he would order them returned (to Istanbul). Their return was delayed, however, according to Rūhī's brother because of interference by Abū al-Hudā, the police chief, and the Iranian ambassador. Then came the news of the assassination of Nāsir ad-Dīn Shāh by a disciple of Jamāl ad-Dīn's who had recently arrived in

[14] E. G. Browne, *The Persian Revolution of 1905–1909* (Cambridge, 1910), p. 93n, and p. 415; Keddie, "Religion and Irreligion," pp. 284–285. Philipp (*op. cit.*) gives more details on Mīrzā Āqā Khān Kirmānī.

[15] Sāsānī, *op. cit.*, p. 207.

Istanbul, news that was to have disastrous consequences for the men in the Trabzon prison.[16]

By 1895, Jamāl ad-Dīn's relations with the Sultan had deteriorated badly, and he was trying unsuccessfully to escape from Istanbul. In view of Jamāl ad-Dīn's repeated history of rapid proximity to those in power followed by their suspicions and hostility, the repetition of this pattern with the Sultan, who was somewhat suspicious of Afghānī from the first, is not surprising. Nevertheless, certain incidents have been cited by witnesses as crucial in ending good relations between the two, and it is typical that these incidents involved both charges of irreligion against Afghānī and indications that he was plotting with enemies of the Sultan. The accusations of irreligion stemmed primarily from Abū al-Hudā, who is recorded as objecting to some of the ideas voiced by Jamāl ad-Dīn in his presence. He learned the truth about Afghānī's country of origin and used his Iranian and presumably Shi'i background against him, calling him "The Pretended Afghan." Abū al-Hudā became a firm opponent of Afghānī's and was influential in turning the Sultan against him.[17]

The political incidents that influenced the Sultan against Afghānī involved fears or suspicions that Afghānī was intriguing with his opponents. The most important of these suspicions concerned a visit of the new Egyptian Khedive, 'Abbās Ḥilmī, to Istanbul in the summer of 1895. The young Khedive apparently asked to see Jamāl ad-Dīn and was denied permission. Then, according to Afghānī's account to his followers, 'Abbās Ḥilmī came secretly to see him, without Afghānī's having planned it, and spies followed them and falsely reported to the Sultan that they were plotting for an Arab caliphate, held or presided over by the Egyptian Khedive. Although Sultan Abdülhamid's suspicions were often without basis and may have been unjustified on this occasion as on many others, there was in fact talk among some of the Sultan's opponents of a caliphal movement in behalf of 'Abbās Ḥilmī, and it is possible Afghānī might have discussed such an idea.[18] Similar suspicions were aroused in the Sultan by Afghānī's associations with Sayyid 'Abdallāh of the

[16] *Ibid.*, pp. 207–212; Keddie, "Religion and Irreligion," pp. 294–295. A letter from Rūḥī quoted in Pakdaman, pp. 179–180, does not mention any intervention with the Sultan by Afghānī.

[17] Maghribī, *op. cit.*, pp. 35–36. Albert Hourani, *Arabic Thought in the Liberal Age* (London, 1962), p. 108.

[18] Makhzūmī, *Khāṭirāt* (2d [Arabic] ed.), pp. 74–79. On 'Abbās Ḥilmī and the caliphate see Sylvia Haim, *Arab Nationalism* (Berkeley and Los Angeles, 1962), pp. 28–29.

Hejaz, the scion of one of the two contending families for the sharifate of the Holy Cities of Mecca and Medina, who was on bad terms with the Sultan.[19] Finally, the Armenian disturbances and movements of opposition among Turkish military and religious students in 1894 and 1895 made the Sultan highly suspicious of any potential opposition. By December 1895, when Wilfrid Blunt revisited Istanbul, he found that Jamāl ad-Dīn was no longer received by the Sultan, and many sources including Blunt tell us that Jamāl ad-Dīn was constantly watched by the Sultan's spies.[20]

In 1895 Jamāl ad-Dīn made determined but unsuccessful efforts to leave the Ottoman Empire. The only document concerning him which is currently listed in the Yıldız collection (pertaining to Abdülhamid's reign) is a long petition from Jamāl ad-Dīn to the Sultan which must date from this period. It complains of the unjust calumnies directed against him by his enemies, says that he has always served the Sultan and the unity of Islam with the greatest loyalty and without thought of personal gain, and begs permission to leave the country. There is a reiteration of imagery used by Jamāl ad-Dīn in Iran; as he had said to the Shah, he says he has offered himself to the Caliph to be used as a cutting sword against his internal and external enemies, but the offer was not accepted. And, regarding accusation against him whose content is unspecified he writes:

> But what can I do against those intriguers and slanderers who have access to every heart and mind? God gives me patience! I have not the slightest doubt that these cruel Yazids and these tyrannical Shimrs like the robbers of Kufa and Damascus will continue until the last moment to weave their hundreds of intrigues against me. Of course, with the help of God it is the easiest thing for me to hang the ruses of these intrigues on their own necks like necklaces of damnation. As God Almighty has made my heart free from aspirations of rank and glory and from the love of glitter and pomp and as God Almighty has created me as I am but devoted to serve the world of Islam, it is clearly forbidden for me to waste my time with the hallucinations and futilities of base individuals. Every intelligent person will admit that your Sacred Caliphal Highness will not suffer that I lose my time and

---

19 Cf. Keddie, "Religion and Irreligion," p. 294.

20 Blunt, *My Diaries*, p. 253; Mīrzā Rizā in Browne, *op. cit.*, p. 84; Keddie, "Religion and Irreligion," pp. 294–295.

> vital energy for the undignified and trifling occupation with the calumniations of these people here, and that, consequently, You will accelerate Your gracious permission for my leaving, seeing that my departure is preferable.[21]

The reference to his new persecutors once again as the killers of the Shi'i martyr Husain, Yazīd and Shimr, is striking in a letter to the Sunni Sultan-Caliph from a man who in Istanbul was trying to prove himself an Afghan Sunni. On the other hand, it is true that Husain's killers were also anathemetized among Sunnis.

Receiving no satisfaction from the Sultan in his requests to leave, Jamāl ad-Dīn attempted to get a British passport from the British Embassy in Istanbul. On December 12, 1895, Sir Philip Currie reported home to the British prime minister and foreign minister Lord Salisbury from Istanbul:

> . . . the Sheikh Jemal-ed-Din whose history is well known to the Foreign Office, has recently made overtures to this Embassy for British Protection as an Afghan. It would appear that the Sheikh was deeply implicated in a movement among the softas hostile to the present Sultan and that his bitter enemies the Sheikhs Abal Huda and Ahmed Essad availed themselves of this to bring about his downfall. He was subjected to the strictest espionage and practically made a prisoner in his house. Under these circumstances he addressed me the letter which I have the honour to enclose herewith and also sent an Indian friend of his, Sayed Mohammed Sadik Khan, who describes himself as "Judge of the Deccan" to plead his cause. No encouragement however was given to this individual.
>
> Jemal-ed-Din then applied to Her Majesty's Consulate General and not being known there, obtained a pass describing him as a "Gentleman resident at Cabul" and proceeded to England via Vienna. [*sic*, but contradicted below] This pass is good for the voyage only and merely entitles the bearer to consular protection.
>
> The house in which Jemal-ed-Din and other Mohammedan notables are lodged by the Sultan was burnt the other day and the Sheikh availed himself of the opportunity to escape. He has not however succeeded as yet in leaving the country, though I understand he is anxious to do so.

21 Turkey, Başbakanlık Archives, Istanbul, Yildiz Collection, MS 1103. Thanks to Andreas Tietze for translating this. The entire translation is in Appendix IV.

> The Persian Ambassador claims him as a Persian subject and on the ground that he has published treasonable proclamations against the Shah, wishes to send him under guard to Tehran where he would probably be put to death.
>
> Under the circumstances I propose to take no action in the matter and without further encouraging Jemal ed Din, let him retain possession of the British passavant. I do not think it likely that the Turkish Government will hand him over to the Persians.[22]

The enclosed letter from Jamāl ad-Dīn, dated November 19, reads, in translation from the original French:

> Your Excellency:
>
> You represent a government which holds high the standard of civilization and which spreads everywhere the benefits of humanity. Your action is felt especially in the Orient, where Christians as well as Muslims have always been prey to torture and tyranny.
>
> You have always been the zealous protector of the weak who tremble under the yoke of unjust and barbarous ambitions. Convinced of your high sentiments, permit me to bring to your attention what follows:
>
> I am an Afghan (Kabul) and I depend on England. I have passed a great part of my life in the East with the sole aim of uprooting fanaticism, the worst malady of these lands, and reforming society and establishing there the benefits of tolerance. This is what I have set for myself to do.
>
> I have also stayed for a rather long period in the principal capitals of Europe, where I have had occasion to be in the society of the greatest personages, statesmen, friends of the press, and great scholars.
>
> I was in London when I received the invitation of H.I.M. the Sultan and that is how I found myself his guest. I did not think that such an invitation could ever have been prejudicial, but in coming to Constantinople I found myself faced by unworthy follies, deceits of all sorts, and plunged in a series of absurd and insignificant calumnies. Therefore I have several times asked to take leave, which has always been refused me.
>
> During these recent events, (that is to say, the Armenian question) which have obscured the situation still more, in

[22] F.O. 60/594, Currie to Salisbury, no. 923, Dec. 12, 1895.

multiplying lies and absurd calumnies, H.I.M., who seems to be submerged amidst his entourage, has let himself be influenced by certain men of his court so that a great number of innocent persons have been expelled, etc., without cause or reason.

Having come here as a guest, I have naturally been only a simple spectator of all these affairs.

H.I.M., always guided by vague suspicions suggested by his entourage, has had the police besiege my house without my having been allowed to learn the cause, and, what is more painful, is that I find myself in a doubtful situation, not knowing what will be the effect of these impressions.

I constantly find myself very restricted. Believe me, Excellency, that, although a foreigner in this land, and even having come from London as a guest of H.I.M. and on his invitation, the fact is that I have not had a moment's tranquillity.

You may hence conclude, Excellency, how many thousands of poor persons—who unhappily find themselves under the claws of executioners without conscience—cry for help. Thousands of Muslims and Christians cry out from the depths of their hearts. Save me! Save us! for as always it is chance which decides things here and not reason and justice.

I come therefore in the name of humanity to attract your attention to this state of affairs, and pray you to take into consideration my request. . . .

(Signed) Djemalledin El Husseini El Afgani[23]

It was in response to this request that the Foreign Office reviewed its own records and asked the India Office for additional information on Jamāl ad-Dīn. The result was the Thagi and Dakaiti Department biography cited above, which confirmed information reaching the Foreign Office from other sources that Jamāl ad-Dīn was born in Iran, and the collection of Foreign Office references to Jamāl ad-Dīn showing his anti-British record. The British thus had no desire to help Jamāl ad-Dīn escape.

Shakīb Arslān, who knew Jamāl ad-Dīn in his last years in Istanbul, has reported, however, that after the assassination of Nāsir ad-Dīn Shāh Afghānī sent to Fitzmaurice, the dragoman of the British Embassy, for help in getting a ship to leave Istanbul. Jamāl ad-Dīn said that Fitzmaurice had promised to do this, but "the Sultan then came to hear of it, and sent him [Afghānī] one of his chamberlains to im-

23 Enclosure in *ibid.*

plore him in the name of Islam not to seek foreign protection and thus impair the dignity of the Caliph. Zeal for Islam then inflamed Afghānī, and having already prepared his bags for the journey, he now said to Fitzmaurice that he was giving up the ideas, and let what will happen."[24] One may guess, however, that it was probably the Sultan's efficient spies more than his appeal that kept Jamāl ad-Dīn in Istanbul.

Jamāl ad-Dīn's Discourses to His Circle in Istanbul

Much of Jamāl ad-Dīn's time in Istanbul was spent in talks to a circle of disciples and acquaintances, and the content of some of these discussions has been recorded by men who were present. Two such men have recorded Jamāl ad-Dīn's Istanbul sessions at length: 'Abd al-Qādir al-Maghribī and Muhammad al-Makhzūmī. Although Westerners more frequently refer to Makhzūmī's book it should, in fact, be treated with some caution, since attributed to Jamāl ad-Dīn are anachronistic references to twentieth-century inventions and also words on twentieth-century Arab interests like Muslim socialism, and against war, which do not at all jibe with what Afghānī can be shown to have believed and said on such subjects. Where Makhzūmī was not influenced by later Arab ideology he is probably fairly reliable. Makhzūmī says he recorded the conversations in 1892–1897, but there must have been subsequent additions.[25] Maghribī, although like Makhzūmī publishing many years after the event, appears to have recorded conversations accurately and to have made no improbable ascriptions to Jamāl ad-Dīn. Most of what Makhzūmī and especially Maghribī report is consistent with what is known from other firsthand sources and interviews, and may be accepted in general outline, if not in every detail.

---

24 Shakīb Arslān, *op. cit.*, I, 204; translated in Kedourie, *Afghani*, p. 62.

25 Makhzūmī, *Khāṭirāt*, p. 1. The references to airplanes and radios are on pp. 101 and 133, although Bernard Lewis informs me *ṭayyārāt* might mean balloons.

One thing that stands out from these reports is Jamāl ad-Dīn's distorted self-view in his later years; his claims of influence on rulers are greater than ever before, and one may wonder if he entirely distinguished reality from fantasy in his stories. Entirely similar claims are also quoted directly in Western newspaper interviews in 1896, and so such claims cannot be dismissed as later writers' distortions.[26] 'Abd al-Qādir al-Maghribī reports several such exaggerated stories from Jamāl ad-Dīn: for instance, that the British were anxious to have him in an embassy to deal with the Sudanese Mahdi regarding a peace settlement; this mission, if completed, could have delivered Egypt from English domination, but it was not completed because of the Mahdi's death. Regarding Nāsir ad-Dīn Shāh, Afghānī falsely claimed that the Shah had tried to see him during his trip to St. Petersburg, but that he, Afghānī, was not interested. "Then I went to Munich and the Shah came there too, and he asked for an interview with me and I refused." Then, he said, some important personages mediated between them and brought them together and the Shah "asked me to go to his country in order to be his prime minister. I refused." Jamāl ad-Dīn continued that he told the Shah he was going to the Paris exposition, but the Shah beseeched him strongly to come to Iran and he found no way to decline the invitation. Maghribī, who had heard, on the basis of a book published by I'timād as-Saltaneh in 1889, that some people believed Jamāl ad-Dīn to be an Iranian Shi'i, now asked Jamāl ad-Dīn how he, as a well-known Sunni, could be the prime minister in Shi'i Iran. Jamāl ad-Dīn seems to have recovered immediately, saying this contradiction only proved the Shah's madness and folly.[27]

Jamāl ad-Dīn also claimed: that when he was in Russia the Tsar liked to see him and invite him to his presence; that the Tsar asked him why he hated the Shah, and Jamāl ad-Dīn reported that he guilelessly told the Tsar that he had advised the Shah to bring in a constitutional order, at which the Shah had become angry and ordered his expulsion; that the Tsar then said the Shah was correct, and turned against Jamāl ad-Dīn.[28] As already noted, the most direct evidence suggests that Jamāl ad-Dīn never met the Tsar.

Makhzūmī reports very similar stories from the mouth of Jamāl

---

[26] See especially Jamāl ad-Dīn's claims in the June 1896 interview summarized and quoted below, pp. 410–413.

[27] Maghribī, *op. cit.*, pp. 46–80.

[28] *Ibid.*, pp. 103–104.

ad-Dīn: for example, that during his stay in India before his 1869 trip to Istanbul, he attracted hundreds of people to see him, thus frightening the British government, who insisted he leave;[29] that he then went to Istanbul where Âli Paşa gave him a reception unparalleled until that time; but that the Ottoman Şeyhülislam found in his words a false excuse for his expulsion; and that then in Egypt those who were jealous of his great influence attributed to him the heretical philosophy of some of the books he discussed.[30]

Makhzūmī further reports that the Shah, during Jamāl ad-Dīn's 1886–1887 trip to Iran, made him minister of war and did nothing without his advice. Jamāl ad-Dīn wanted to move quickly to assure the Iranian people the benefits of freedom and popular rights, and he gathered around him the great and the learned men of the country. When the Shah saw how great was Jamāl ad-Dīn's influence he became fearful and began to treat him badly. Jamāl ad-Dīn then asked the Shah for permission to leave, and went to Russia where the great men of the country received him well. There follow the same stories as in Maghribī about the Tsar. There is also the story of the Shah's asking Jamāl ad-Dīn's pardon in Munich and inviting him back to Iran. There the wise and great gathered around him again, and the Shah asked him to codify the laws of Iran in accord with contemporary needs. Jamāl ad-Dīn says he drew up a fundamental law that would have made Iran a constitutional state, and the Shah was frightened, seeing that this would lessen his power. When Jamāl ad-Dīn sensed the coolness of the Shah he asked permission to go to the shrine of 'Abd al-Azīm, but the Shah was so fearful of his influence there that he sent five hundred men to seize him while he was ill. When news spread about this his friends and followers began a great movement against the government of the Shah, and much blood flowed.[31] Similarly exaggerated stories are recorded by Iranians who knew Jamāl ad-Dīn in Istanbul.

The pattern of these stories, many of which have entered the biographical literature on Afghānī, is clear enough. A series of powerful rulers, impressed by the fame and ability of Jamāl ad-Dīn, invite him to their presence and offer him a great share of power. When he tries to use this power in favor of popular and constitutional rights and of the independence of Eastern peoples the rulers become suspicious

---

29 Makhzūmī, *Khāṭirāt* (Persian), pp. 26–27.
30 *Ibid.*, pp. 28–35.
31 *Ibid.*, pp. 50–56.

and expel him. Jamāl ad-Dīn apparently even exaggerates the number of expulsions, saying that the British expelled him from India in 1869 and the Tsar from Russia in 1889, both of which seem most improbable. An interesting feature of these stories is Jamāl ad-Dīn's insistence that he was continually recommending constitutionalism to autocratic rulers. To the Shah, whom he evidently saw twice, and to the Russians what he in fact recommended was a strong anti-British policy. There is some evidence that toward the end of his life, having failed to influence rulers to implement his goals, Jamāl ad-Dīn became a more consistent advocate of constitutionalism, an idea that was gaining popularity in the Middle East. There is no stress in any of his writings or reported speeches on constitutional ideas except in Egypt in 1879, although some Iranians and Egyptians do speak of his talking to his close followers of constitutional rule and popular rights. His exchange with Khalīl Ghānim in 1883 regarding Sultan Abdülhamid, cited in chapter 9, above, shows that he then put the strengthening of Muslim states above constitutional reform, which could come later. By the 1890's, however, he may have decided that constitutional reform was a prerequisite to strengthening the Muslims. The vision he presented of himself in Istanbul was of a persecuted leader of the cause of constitutionalism. While it is true that he was persecuted by autocratic rulers, constitutionalism was not the main cause of this persecution.

Also interesting in the reports of Maghribī and Makhzūmī are Jamāl ad-Dīn's views on religion. Maghribī quotes him as saying that Muslim revival must be based on the rules of Islam and the Koran or it would not be good. He complained that recent advances by Muslims had all been in imitation of Europeans, "and this is an imitation that by its nature will drag us into admiration for foreigners; submission to them; and being content with their domination over us. The nature of Islam, which includes raising the banner of rule and mastery, will therefore change into a character of apathy and accommodation to the rule of foreigners."[32] Maghribī then asked Jamāl ad-Dīn what was the right way to achieve civilization, and Jamāl ad-Dīn answered:

> It must be a religious movement. . . . If we consider the reasons for the transformation in the condition of Europe from barbarism to civilization we see it was only the religious

[32] Maghribī, *op. cit.*, p. 95.

> movement raised and spread by Luther. This great man, when he saw that the peoples of Europe had declined and lost their vigor due to the long period that they had submitted to the heads of the church and to (religious) imitation, not based on clear reason, started that religious movement. . . . He reminded [Europeans] that they were born free, and so why were they submitting to tyrants?[33]

Jamāl ad-Dīn continued that the result of the spread of Protestantism in Europe and of its rivalry with Catholicism was that each party tried to surpass the other in strength, greatness, and civilization, and to acquire the means to progress and to superiority over its rival. From this rivalry arose modern civilization. Maghribī then said that Luther had brought religious reform, but since the Muslim religion was to be found in the Koran, and was free of change, he did not understand the meaning of a new religious movement within Islam. Jamāl ad-Dīn said that he referred to the uprooting of the incorrect understanding of Islam held by the majority of its followers. Islam has been misunderstood as discouraging striving for change, progress, and reform, and as limiting its followers to the traditional Islamic sciences. In fact, foreigners have taken over the sciences of the Muslims and developed them to strengthen themselves, leaving the Muslims behind in ignorance. The essence of Jamāl ad-Dīn's religious movement, Maghribī adds, was a return to the Koran alone, truly and freely understood.[34]

Both Maghribī and Makhzūmī give several examples of Jamāl ad-Dīn's interpretations of koranic passages to make them encompass modern scientific and political ideas, including parliamentary rule. The essence of Jamāl ad-Dīn's position on Islam is clearly adumbrated in his words cited above from Maghribī. The Muslims must not turn to pure imitation of Europeans, as this will open their countries to the acceptance of European rule. Instead, they should find the inspiration for reform and science in their own religious texts, especially the Koran. The latter, if properly interpreted, will be found to be compatible with modern values and even to predict them. The return to a single religious scripture and the rejection of later religious rules as mistaken innovations is a familiar feature not only in Protestantism but in other more recent religious reform movements throughout

---

33 *Ibid.*, pp. 95–96.
34 *Ibid.*, pp. 96–100.

the world. It has the appeal of stressing the correctness of the basic text of the religion while enabling the reformer to ignore the vast body of conservative interpretations and regulations that have helped make most traditional religions inimical to rapid social and political change. It is also true that the Koran encompassed a reforming and activist ethic that Afghānī tried to free from later fatalistic interpretations.

Maghribī reports that on another occasion Afghānī said that the people of Europe and the United States were ready to accept Islam, if its preaching were improved. Westerners now turned away from Islam because they saw the low state of the Muslims; to convert them they must be shown that most Muslims were not following the true principles of Islam. Among the greatest virtues of the Koran was that it first led the Muslims toward the truths of philosophy and to the need for rational answers to important questions. Before the Koran the Arabs were in a state of indescribable savagery, but in less than a century and a half they came to rule the known world, and to lead the world in politics, science, philosophy, the crafts, and trade. The Koran alone provided sufficient guidance for the early Muslims, and it can be sufficient for today too. The Muslims' defects come from turning from Koran's true meaning.[35]

The combined stress on the importance of rationalist philosophy and of the proper understanding of the Koran again indicated Jamāl ad-Dīn's adherence to the position of the Muslim philosophers that the proper interpretation of the Koran was a rationalist, philosophical, and scientific one, which for Jamāl ad-Dīn included modern science and political theory. The stress on the political strength of the earliest and truest Muslims reappears in a conversation reported by Maghribī where Jamāl ad-Dīn discussed the reasons he had written his treatise on the Naichirīs: "Many of the Muslims of India are stained by this unlawful innovation (*bid'a*) which the English disseminated in their land, since they saw it as the best means to reach their goal, and to strengthen their rule in India. The English found that the Islamic religion requires of its followers that they be the holders of power and sovereignty in their own countries."[36] The British thus thought that the best way to weaken the Muslims was to spread this heresy, and they opened a great madrasa to spread Naichirī teachings. (The college at Aligarh sponsored by Sayyid

---

35 *Ibid.*, pp. 57–59.
36 *Ibid.*, p. 68.

Ahmad Khān with British support is intended.) Jamāl ad-Dīn claims that when his own treatise spread in India many princes withdrew their sons from this school.[37]

Makhzūmī gives several examples of Sayyid Jamāl ad-Dīn's modernist interpretations of the Koran. Although it is in this section that one finds what appear to be anachronistic references to the radio and probably to airplanes, the more likely of these exegeses may perhaps be accepted as genuine reminiscences.

Makhzūmī quotes Jamāl ad-Dīn as saying that the Muslims have disobeyed what the Koran ordered, and done its opposite, as if the Koran had ordered them to be disunited in order to decline and disappear. Instead of seeking the true meaning of the Koran, Muslims engage in meaningless interpretations of its smallest phrases. Many of the ignorant ulama have lied against the Koran, saying that it opposed clear scientific truths. In fact, scientific truth cannot disagree with the Koran, and if it disagrees with the Koran's obvious meaning then Muslims must have recourse to spiritual exegeis (*ta'wīl*). Since modern inventions had not come into existence at the time of the Koran's revelation, it was impossible to have open reference to them. For example, had the Koran spoken of such things as railroads and electricity, people would have considered it untruthful and would have shunned it. Thus, the Koran only hinted at all that is now happening and will happen in the future, taking into account the preparedness of people's minds. Properly understood, the Koran alludes to the bases of consultative government, the duties of rulers, and the foundations of modern arts and sciences. Regarding government, the Koran gives the boundaries of the behavior of rulers, and recommends consultation with the ruled, especially in the Sura of the Ant. This sura, concerning Solomon and the Queen of Sheba, is quoted to show that when faced with a problem the queen called an assembly (*majlis*) of her people and asked their opinion on the matter. The assembly told her that they would fight Solomon if she declared war. Solomon used the winds to carry his orders like airplanes (? *ṭayyārāt*—possibly balloons), and his orders were carried with the speed of lightning, like the telegraph. Thus, the idea of rapid means of transport was recorded in the Book long before it entered the world in reality.

A koranic passage is quoted by Jamāl ad-Dīn as alluding to the

---

37 *Ibid.*, p. 69.

roundness of the earth, and another as referring to the sun's turning on its axis. The Koran also hints that the earth and the sun were once one body, and then split. Other passages are cited to show that the Koran included modern principles of economics and taxation as well as modern ideas in various sciences.[38]

Such nonliteral and sometimes forced interpretations of the Koran have a long history in Islam, particularly in the Shi'i, Sufi, and philosophical traditions that were a major part of Jamāl ad-Dīn's educational background. Such interpretations were natural means for the heterodox to use in a religious tradition that stressed that its Scripture contained the exact and immutable word of God; only by rather forced interpretation could this immutable word be made to mean something quite foreign to Muhammad's environment and background—whether Greek philosophical ideas, as with the traditional Muslim philosophers, or these plus more modern philosophy, political thought, and science, as with Jamāl ad-Dīn. Jamāl ad-Dīn may have been the first important Muslim thinker to indulge in such extensive modernist reinterpretation of koranic texts, although Ottoman and Persian rulers and statesmen in the early nineteenth century had already cited koranic texts on the duties of Muslim self-defense in order to justify modernized armies, and Muslim reformers had cited Islamic precedents. After Jamāl ad-Dīn the practice of reinterpretation of koranic texts by modernist intellectuals became very popular, and there are numerous examples in a book by al-Kawākibī, a Pan-Arabist admirer of Jamāl ad-Dīn, *Ṭabā'i' al-istibād* (the characteristics of despotism).[39]

Since Jamāl ad-Dīn said that Islam should be based on the Koran alone, and also said that the Koran could not be in contradiction with modern science, economics, and political theory, it seems clear that Jamāl ad-Dīn's famous and externally traditionalist principle of a return to the Koran and to the ways of the early Muslims meant in fact a radically modernist interpretation of Islam. Essentially Jamāl ad-Dīn was calling for an end to all traditional religious theories and interpretations that might stand in the way of Muslim unity and self-strengthening and for a modern interpretation of Islam that

---

38 Makhzūmī, *Khāṭirāt* (Arabic), pp. 99–104.

39 'Abd ar-Raḥman al-Kawākibī, *Ṭabā'i' al-istibād* (Cairo, 1889), *passim.* For earlier reinterpretations of the Koran and of Islamic precedents see especially Berkes, *op. cit.*, Şerif Mardin, *The Genesis of Young Ottoman Thought* (Princeton, 1962), and Bernard Lewis, 'Ḥurriyya," *EI*², Vol. III, fasc. 49–50, pp. 589–594.

would inculcate the virtues of national cohesion, anti-imperialism, and modern science and technology. To stress the Western provenance of some of these ideas could weaken Muslim pride and unity.

Similar conclusions arise from what Makhzūmī quotes from Jamāl ad-Dīn in refutation of the orthodox Sunni view that the door of *ijtihād* (interpretation in law and doctrine) had long been closed. When someone cited the fact that the sayings of a certain early *qāḍī* were so revered as to be almost like revelations, Jamāl ad-Dīn said that the *qāḍī* had reasoned according to the conditions of his times and had not hesitated to progress beyond the words of his predecessors. Should not men today also add to the ocean of knowledge and change their judgments according to the changed times? When others objected to Jamāl ad-Dīn that the door of *ijtihād* was closed, he denied this. The great legists and scholars of the past broadened their understanding of the Koran's meaning, but they could not fully grasp all Koran's secrets. With all their brilliant knowledge, scholarship, and effort what these scholars understood of the Koran was like a drop in the ocean compared with all the wisdom in the Koran.[40] As in one of his Persian articles, Jamāl ad-Dīn here adapted the Sufi idea of an infinity of meanings in the Koran to the modern need for a free reinterpretation of the Koran in order to prove its consonance with modern values.

Similarly pragmatic was Jamāl ad-Dīn's rejection of the Shi'i-Sunni division in Islam, as reported by Makhzūmī. Jamāl ad-Dīn said that this split had been caused by selfish kings who wanted their people ignorant and desired an excuse to launch wars to increase their territories. Thus Shi'i and Sunni rulers exaggerated the differences between their followers, while the followers shared the essential belief in the Koran and Muhammad. Today the split only divides and weakens the Muslims. Neither 'Alī [whom the Shi'is see as Muhammad's successor] nor Abū Bakr [recognized as the first caliph by the Sunnis] would approve of the wars and divisions carried out in their names.[41] The idea that selfish leaders were responsible for splits in the Muslim community had already appeared in Afghānī's writings in the 1880's.

The emphasis on unity among the Muslims as the best safeguard against further Western incursions in the East is found again and again. Jamāl ad-Dīn also states that true religion consists of two parts, worship and deeds, and the latter should lead people to work for the

40 Makhzūmī, *Khāṭirāt* (Arabic), pp. 111–112.
41 *Ibid.*, pp. 112–114.

good of their nation, and to unite in support of it with a true patriotic love.[42]

More special are the views Makhzūmī quotes from Jamāl ad-Dīn on the unity of the Muslim, Christian, and Jewish religions. Afghānī is quoted as saying that the three religions are the same in their origins and goals: Where one has a defect, another perfects it. He desired that the three should unite for human welfare. What divides their followers are errors and superstitions. Jamāl ad-Dīn continues that early in life he discovered that any man who opposes divisions and wants to enlighten people and unite them on the basis of true religion will be seen by his community as an unbeliever. Jamāl ad-Dīn goes on from this to say that he early set to work to diagnose the malady of the Orient and to find its remedy; he found that the malady was in the division and the heedlessness of Orientals. His aim became to arouse the East to an awareness of the danger from the West, to unite Easterners, and to have rulers lead people toward progress, to strengthen themselves through constitutional government, and to follow the lead of the Caliph.[43]

On another occasion, Jamāl ad-Dīn reiterated the view that Judaism, Christianity, and Islam were essentially identical (a view in part derived from the Muslim idea of the identity of the three revelations, but rarely pursued as a practical question for contemporary action). Makhzūmī then cites from Jamāl ad-Dīn the very unorthodox view that Moses, Jesus, and Muhammad were very wise sages who chose from their environment and from more ancient sources rules and sayings that they put in books, not understanding that they were from God. The three religions are divided not because of what is in their scriptures but because of some of their leaders who traffic in religion. If religious leaders are good, religion can be a beneficial remedy for most human ills. Ignorant leaders, and not the true Islamic religion, are the cause of Islamic decline. The perfect, pure religion would take the essential truth of Islam, Judaism, and Christianity. When others objected that the texts of the three religions are in contradiction: for example, Muslims and Jews support strict monotheism, while Christians believe in the Trinity, and that God had a son, Jamāl ad-Dīn replied that such apparent contradictions must be interpreted so that they disappear, as in Sufi interpretations. The contradictions are only external, or in the forms of expression. The

42 *Ibid.*, p. 88.
43 Makhzūmī, *Khāṭirāt* (Persian), pp. 76–78.

essential meaning of a text is often different from the apparent (*ẓāhir*) meaning, as the Sufis know. All three religions in fact teach the unity of God and work for human welfare.[44] There is some contradiction between this broad religious tolerance, and the equation of the three religions as having both virtues and defects, and the more public posture of Afghānī as a believer in the special virtues of Islam. If one sees the pragmatic and proto-nationalist nature of Jamāl ad-Dīn's stress on Islam, however, and also that his attacks on the West were directed not against Western or Christian values, but rather against imperialist conquest, then the apparent contradiction is comprehensible.

As was true throughout Jamāl ad-Dīn's life, there were many persons in Istanbul who heard him and accused him of heresy or even atheism. As 'Abduh had done in his apologetic biography. Makzūmī attributes these accusations to the ascription to Jamāl ad-Dīn by ignorant listeners of the opinions of the philosophers he discussed:

> The gatherings of Jamāl ad-Dīn al-Afghānī used to attract people of different faiths and diverse schools of thought. This made it necessary for him to address each person in a way suitable to his intelligence and preparedness, and to take into consideration his beliefs. He engaged in argument those who would strip God of attributes; the materialists as well as bigoted divines. He expounded the philosophers, their writings and their systems; he outlined their reasoning and conclusions.
>
> Thus opinions about him differed. Some considered him a renegade, others a religious fanatic. Many attributed to him the atheism found in some philosophical treatises. This was also the view held by common people of different sects who attended his gatherings and heard things they could not understand. Unconsciously they would transmit a distorted version of his teaching, proudly claiming to be his disciples, and to have learned their unbelief from him. . . .[45]

Maghribī also notes that there were many criticisms of Jamāl ad-Dīn's religious behavior during his last trip to Istanbul. He was accused of drinking beer, against the koranic prohibition of alcohol,

---

44 Makhzūmī, *Khāṭirāt* (Arabic), pp. 137–143.

45 *Ibid.*, pp. 118–119, translated in Sami A. Hanna, "Al-Afghāni: A Pioneer of Islamic Socialism," *Muslim World*, LVII, 1 (Jan., 1967), 25.

and Maghribī admits that he did frequent a tavern where he teased the bar girls for the amusement of his companions. Abū al-Hudā, in particular, disapproved of his religious behavior and opinions, such as his approval of an Orientalist's rearrangement of the koranic verses according to subject. Jamāl ad-Dīn in Istanbul also frequented Gypsy fortune-tellers, which was frowned on by the more orthodox.[46]

Jamāl ad-Dīn's words on the need for unity and cooperative defensive action among the Muslims were closely tied to his striving against Western imperialism and for the encouragement of nationalism among Muslims. Makhzūmī cites Jamāl ad-Dīn's words about the British, in which he stressed British patience and perseverence, in contrast with the Eastern lack of these qualities. Westerners, despite their altruistic claims, are not trying to improve life in the East or to preserve the rights of Easterners, but to prolong the denial of these rights. The Westerners say their presence in the East is needed to safeguard Christian and other minorities and to teach liberty, but these are deceptive claims. The Westerners in fact encourage divisions among tribes, peoples, and parties in the East, thus strengthening their own position. To regain their freedom Easterners need to achieve unity and a willingness to accept death in order to revive their fatherland. They need leaders who will not be frightened or dissuaded by the threats and promises of their opponents. The Westerners have insidious means for undermining Eastern strength, including weakening of the Easterners' national language and educational system. A people, Jamāl ad-Dīn added, has no community without a language, no language without a culture, no greatness without a history, and no history if there is no one to defend and revive the works of its historic men. All this depends on a patriotic education, centering on the fatherland, so that religious and tribal divisions will be overcome. Once again national unity, including even non-Muslims, is stressed along with Islamic unity; both are potential weapons for self-strengthening and against Western imperialism. Jamāl ad-Dīn's appreciation of the importance of unity to repel foreign rule and of the role of history and language in creating a united patriotism is striking.

Children, said Jamāl ad-Dīn, should be kept from those official schools where unpatriotic poison is slipped to them. Instead they should be sent to popular schools and be taught patriotism, as well

---

46 Maghribī, *op. cit.*, pp. 36–40.

as practical, technical knowledge. Westerners do not improve the customs and education of Easterners, but do the opposite.[47]

In other passages, Makhzūmī quotes Jamāl ad-Dīn at length as showing that the early Muslim Arabs had achieved the bases of many modern scientific ideas, including evolution. They also preached and practiced whatever was beneficial in the modern idea of socialism, such as generosity and the sharing of wealth, without the evils of class hatred and strife. Jamāl ad-Dīn is also quoted at length as an opponent of war, although this seems somewhat in contradiction with his earlier advocacy of various inter-European wars as an indirect means of freeing the Muslims.[48] These passages seem the most dubious in Makhzūmī's book—more in accord with twentieth-century preoccupations than with what is known of Afghānī's ideas.

Most interesting from a personal viewpoint are Afghānī' views on marriage and on women. Maghribī reports that the Sultan wanted Jamāl ad-Dīn to marry a court concubine, and assigned them a house and furnishings. Jamāl ad-Dīn refused, however, and explained it to his hearers by saying: "Man in this world is like a traveler—naked, afraid, surrounded by obstacles on all sides, and fighting to free himself of them and to be liberated. What would happen if you burdened this traveler with another who would tire him and make him fear perdition?" Also, if he got married at his age (56), people would find it strange.[49] A more detailed and striking story is in Makhzūmī, who says that when the Sultan sent someone to tell Jamāl ad-Dīn that he would send him a pretty slave girl from the Yıldız palace to marry he refused, saying that the Koran says that if a man does not think he can be just to one wife he should not marry. Jamāl ad-Dīn knew his own inability to fulfill justice to a wife, and so would rather refrain from injustice by being single than to marry and be oppressive. He added that if the Sultan insisted on his marrying he could only suspect that the Sultan wanted him to be a eunuch, and he asked the messenger to tell the Sultan that if he insisted then he, Jamāl ad-Dīn, would cut off his own organ of procreation. The messenger went away

47 Makhzūmī, *Khāṭirāt* (Arabic), pp. 80–87.

48 *Ibid.*, pp. 91–95; the reported words on socialism have been translated from Makhzūmī's book by Hanna, *op. cit.*, pp. 24–32. The translator refers to Afghānī's words as an essay and quotes Makhzūmī as writing: "The essays were written during the reign of Sultan 'Abd al-Ḥamid II between the years 1892 and 1897," but in fact Makhzūmī does not use the word "essay" and makes it clear that he is reproducing conversations, which he says he took down in those years.

49 Maghribī, *op. cit.*, pp. 62–64.

amazed at this form of refusal.[50] Psychologists might differ on the meaning of this outburst, but there is no doubt that it seemed extreme and strange to those who heard it, and would scarcely have been invented by an admirer like Makhzūmī.

From his life history it seems that Jamāl ad-Dīn's emotional affects were almost totally tied up in his own mission and in relations with men, even though these were probably not physical relations. Only the German "Kathi" is recorded as a female companion, and she seems to have initiated their relations. There are two dominant life-long patterns in his relations with men: one with the devoted disciples who gathered around him and with whom relations could be sustained as long as they retained their attitude of discipleship, and the other with the powerful rulers whom Jamāl ad-Dīn hoped to guide, but with whom relations were quickly broken. To both the Shah and the Sultan he said he wished them to use him as a cutting sword; once he turned against ruling figures, they were seen as unjust persecutors toward whom sharp action should be taken. In the passage above, marriage, one of the many means that the Sultan tried to use to control Jamāl ad-Dīn, is seen as a desire to emasculate him. The suggestion of cutting off his own sexual organ, even if not seriously intended, was sufficiently strange to amaze Jamāl ad-Dīn's hearers, and indicates at the very least the depth of Jamāl ad-Dīn's horror at the idea of taking a wife.

His own attitude to relations with women may explain Jamāl ad-Dīn's reported preference for Muslim tradition over modern Western ideas regarding the position of women, although in Egypt he had once advocated women's education. Makhzūmī reports that Jamāl ad-Dīn said that some Eastern youths were absurdly imitating Europeans on the question of women's equality. Men's faculties and endowments were in fact different from women's, and men had to support their families while women had to manage the household and raise children. If a woman leaves this sphere to compete with men in earning a living there will be a great loss to her household and children. Also, Jamāl ad-Dīn said he saw no benefit in unveiling women, and if veiling were suddenly ended it would lead to depravity and immorality. Unveiling might be acceptable only if it was not used as a means for women to escape the home. When one of his listeners pointed out that prominent women in the first period of

50 Makhzūmī, *Khāṭirāt* (Arabic), pp. 66–67.

Islam, including 'Ā'isha, Muhammad's favorite wife, entered into the battle and all other aspects of life, Jamāl ad-Dīn said that these were exceptional circumstances, and not to be taken as a rule. When others praised the status of women in the West and said that women in all cultures were once equal to men, Jamāl ad-Dīn said that that was at the time of communism of women, when men did not know their own fathers. He asked if his listeners wanted men to turn from their state of progress back to the stone age with all its evils. How can they urge women to leave the job of raising men and undertake what will turn society upside down? This would be a reversal of the law of existence; and when all were equal in the professions, who would then do women's work? The work of women was in fact more important than the professions, and the strength of woman was in her weakness. To change women's situation would be to abandon and oppose nature. Makhzūmī notes that this was one of the few subjects that Jamāl ad-Dīn disliked discussing, but he gave his views when his followers insisted.[51]

The question of the status of women is virtually the only question where Jamāl ad-Dīn reportedly stood firmly behind the current practice in the Muslim world, and refused to do what he did on most other questions—to cite, or even to accept, early Islamic examples in order to call for a modernizing change. It is probable that Jamāl ad-Dīn was reflecting his own feelings toward women in this discussion, as is further suggested by Makhzūmī's report of Jamāl ad-Dīn's untypical discomfort and reluctance to discuss the subject at all.

Shakīb Arslān ties Jamāl ad-Dīn's rejection of marriage to his disdain for all the usual passions and for money and decorations. He reports that Jamāl ad-Dīn refrained from all passions, and his only pleasures were intellectual. The Sultan tried to attract him with money, decorations, girls, and marriage and he refused them all, saying, "I have passed my life like a bird on a branch." After a Damascene had asked him why he did not marry and have children, Jamāl ad-Dīn said that the philosophical spirit had not entered the community, meaning that philosophy took no heed of progeny and lineage. According to Arslān, Jamāl ad-Dīn looked upon money as dirt and took only what he needed in order to live. He refused to accept decorations (which were common at the Sultan's court), saying, "should I be like a mule with bells on his chest?"[52] Makhzūmī sim-

51 *Ibid.*, pp. 67–74.
52 Arslān, *op. cit.*, pp. 204–207.

ilarly reports on Jāmal ad-Dīn's disdain for the ranks and decorations offered him by the Sultan, in contrast particularly with Abū al-Hudā, and cites an incident of Jamāl ad-Dīn's dividing a large sum of money given him by the Sultan with needy students, keeping only enough for his subsistence. Maghribī and some others have similar stories of Afghānī's renouncing honors and giving away money in Istanbul.[53]

Further regarding Jamāl ad-Dīn's personality, Maghribī reports that he had expected him to be entirely solemn and serious, but instead found him full of wit and humor. He records some of Jamāl ad-Dīn's jokes, several of which have a religiously skeptical flavor. His elaborate teasing of pretty bar girls to bring them first to tears and then to laughter is also reported in this context.[54] In Istanbul, as in Egypt, Jamāl ad-Dīn spent much of his time drinking tea and smoking cigarettes while discoursing to disciples and acquaintances. Until the Sultan became suspicious of him and dogged his steps with spies, he seems to have been satisfied with this existence, but after that he devoted much effort, unsuccessfully, to trying to escape from his gilded captivity. On all previous occasions Jamāl ad-Dīn had been able (or forced) to escape when he broke with those in power; now being unable to do so seems to have set him into a state partly of bitterness against the stupidity and ingratitude of Muslims, and partly of escape into exaggerated visions of his own glorious and influential past. His moods of joking alternated with those in which he criticized his fellow Muslims for stupidity, selfishness, cowardice, and failure to heed his message—as he did in an 1896 newspaper interview, quoted below, strengthening the condemnation of the Muslims in earlier letters (see Appendixes II and III).

Reports indicate that Jamāl ad-Dīn was uncommonly forward and lacking in ceremony when dealing with the Sultan, as he had often been with other rulers. It was largely this sort of unceremonious behavior that won for him in the Muslim world the reputation of being straightforward and unafraid to say what was on his mind. When Muslim sources speak of the unusual honesty and courage in Jamāl ad-Dīn's speech it is mainly his uncharacteristic lack of flattery and deference and his boldness in the face of the possible displeasure

53 Makhzūmī, *Khāṭirāt* (Arabic), pp. 62–64; Maghribī, *op. cit.*, pp. 36–37; Mīrzā Rizā testimony in Browne, *Persian Revolution*, p. 84. Anwar al-Jundī, *ash-Sharq fī fajr al-yaqẓa* (Cairo, 1966), pp. 29–33.

54 Maghribī, *op. cit.*, pp. 38–40, 47–49. Two of the skeptical stories are quoted in Kedourie, *Afghani*, p. 15.

of rulers to which they refer. The different "levels of discourse" that have been noted in Afghānī did not involve the usual practice of telling the powerful what they wished to hear, but rather speaking on different levels to a philosophic elite and a religious mass. This practice was evidently not accompanied by the almost universal deference to the powerful expected in the Muslim world—thus it is that Muslim sources can, with considerable justice, speak of Jamāl ad-Dīn as having been unusually honest and forthright, while a different kind of analysis will find him to have chosen his words to have different meanings to mass and elite audiences.[55] With Sultan Abdülhamid and his religious confidants, as previously with Nāsir ad-Dīn Shāh, this bold behavior in their presence probably played a part in Jamāl ad-Dīn's loss of favor. It also served as a model to his followers to break with the hypocrisy and deference to the powerful that custom had sanctioned.

The Assassination of Nāsir ad-Dīn Shāh

JAMĀL AD-DĪN's strong desire to accomplish the death of Nāsir ad-Dīn ever since his 1891 expulsion from Iran is recorded by several witnesses. E. G. Browne writes that in England Jamāl ad-Dīn stated that the Shah's must be the first of several Persian heads that must roll if Iran was to be regenerated. Maghribī reports Jamāl ad-Dīn's saying that while in London he had been asked via the Persian minister in London to refrain from attacking the Shah, in return for which he would be given what he desired. According to Jamāl ad-

55 Aḥmad Amīn's chapter on Jamāl ad-Dīn in *Zu'amā' al-iṣlāh fī al-'aṣr al-ḥadīth* (Cairo, 1949) argues that Jamāl ad-Dīn's blunt forthrightness proves that he could not have been irreligious as charged, or else he would have argued openly for irreligion; and 'Uthmān Amīn made a similar argument to me in Cairo in 1966. In fact, however, Jamāl ad-Dīn, while unusually blunt and direct in pressing some of his political views on the powerful, used very different lines of political and religious argument according to the audience he was addressing.

Dīn he answered, "I only want the Shah to die, his belly to be split, and him to be put in his grave."[56] Shakīb Arslān says that Jamāl ad-Dīn told him that when he came to Istanbul the Sultan, pressed by the Persian ambassador, called him in and asked him to stop attacking the Shah, and Jamāl ad-Dīn told him, "I did not intend to abandon the Shah of Persia until I put him in his grave, but after the Prince of Believers ordered me to desist I must obey him."[57] The nature of his concern is shown especially in the report of one of his Persian followers in Istanbul, Mīrzā Husain Khān Dānish Isfāhānī, who writes that he once came to see Jamāl ad-Dīn and found him pacing the room, crying out to himself. "There is no salvation except in killing, no way out except in killing," and other similar phrases, in Arabic. Jamāl ad-Dīn was so beside himself that he was completely unaware of the author's presence, and the author says that when he saw Jamāl ad-Dīn in this mad state, he left. A month later he heard of the Shah's assassination. He adds that Jamāl ad-Dīn never forgave the Shah and Amīn as-Sultān for the manner of his exile, that his eyes always became red with anger when he told about it, and that he was resolved on revenge.[58] This concentration on the killing of Nāsir ad-Dīn, which lasted several years and can be compared with Jamāl ad-Dīn's anti-British obsession, probably had some psychological basis. If it were only a question of mistreatment, Jamāl ad-Dīn would have had many other equally promising targets for vengeance, including his most recent oppressors, the Sultan and Abū al-Hudā, but there are no words attributed to Jamāl ad-Dīn about others that match his rage against the Shah. It is probable that this rage was tied in some way to Jamāl ad-Dīn's rejection of his Iranian family and homeland, and that he saw himself as the potential savior and regenerator of that homeland, thwarted by the hands of hostile figures of authority.

The most complete account of the inspiration of Nāsir ad-Dīn's assassination is found in the confession of the assassin, Jamāl ad-Dīn's faithful Iranian disciple and servant Mīrzā Rizā Kirmānī, who visited Jamāl ad-Dīn in Istanbul before killing the Shah. Mīrzā Rizā's total religious adoration of Jamāl ad-Dīn as well as the somewhat distorted picture Jamāl ad-Dīn gave him of his own position with the

---

56 Maghribī, *op. cit.*, p. 47.

57 Arslān, *op. cit.*, p. 203.

58 Mīrzā Ḥusain Khān Dānish Iṣfahānī in Mīrzā Luṭfallāh Asadābādī, ***Sharḥ-i*** *ḥāl-i Sayyid Jamāl ad-Dīn Asadābādī* (Berlin, 1926), pp. 87–88.

Sultan are especially well indicated in one long passage of Mīrzā Rizā's answers to interrogation:

> ". . . Whoever has even a little perception understands that the Sayyid stands quite apart from the men of this age. The realities of all things lie open before him; the necks of all the greatest philosophers and thinkers of Europe and all the world are bowed in obeisance to him. Not one of the wisest of the age is worthy to be his servant or his disciple. . . . Whoever appears with these signs and tokens is . . .[59] himself. The Persian Government did not appreciate his worth, and could not derive advantages and benefits from his honoured being. They banished him with contempt and disrespect. Now go and see how the Sultan of Turkey appreciates his value. When the Sayyid went from Persia to London, the Sultan telegraphed to him several times, saying, 'It is a pity that your auspicious existence should be passed far from the lands of Islām, and that the Muslims should not derive benefit from it. Come to the metropolis of Islām, let the Muslim call to prayer sound in thine ears, and let us live together.' At first the Sayyid would not consent, but at length Prince Malkom Khān and some others said to him, 'When such a King is so urgent with thee, it is surely right to go.' So the Sayyid came to Constantinople, and the Sultan gave him a lofty mansion, assigned him two hundred pounds a month for his expenses, sent him supper and luncheon from the royal kitchen, and always placed at his disposal and orders the royal horses and carriages. On that day when the Sultan invited him to the Palace of Yildiz, and kissed his face as they sat together in the steam-yacht which plies on the lake in his garden, they discoursed together; and the Sayyid undertook that in a short while he would unite all the States of Islām, draw them all towards the Caliphate, and make the Sultan the Commander of the Faithful over all the Muslims. Thus it came about that he entered into correspondence with all the Shīʿite divines of Karbalā, Najaf and all parts of Persia, and convinced them by promises, hopes and logical demonstrations that if the Muḥammadan nations would only unite, all the nations on earth could not prevail against them. . . . Just at this juncture the trouble at Sāmarrā . . . broke out. The Sultan of

---

59 Browne notes, *Persian Revolution,* p. 82n: "Omission in the original. The word *Mahdī* is probably to be understood." The reference to "signs and tokens" makes this almost certain.

> Turkey, imagining that the Shāh of Persia had specially fomented this trouble so as to disturb the Ottoman dominions, held consultations and discussions on this subject with the Sayyid. He said, 'By reason of the long duration of this reign and his venerable age, Nāṣiru'd-Dīn Shāh has acquired a power and prestige such that, if he is firm, the Shī'ite divines and the people of Persia will not move to support our ideas or accomplish our aims. We must therefore think of some plan for dealing with him personally.' Then he said to the Sayyid, 'Do whatever you can in regard to him, and be not anxious about anything.' "[60]

When asked then how he could know what was said at meetings between the Sultan and Jamāl ad-Dīn at which he was not present, Mīrzā Rizā replied that nobody was more intimate than he with the Sayyid, who kept nothing from him. Mīrzā Rizā's report is quite in keeping with Afghānī's claims about his influence with the high and mighty; the story about the Sultan's approval of the Shah's assassination would have been entirely out of character for the Sultan. A bit later in the interrogation, Mīrzā Rizā explained that the Sultan had become suspicious of Jamāl ad-Dīn owing to the intervention of "those shifty hypocrites who surround and dominate him, such as Abu'l-Hudā and the like," who aroused the Sultan's suspicions over Jamāl ad-Dīn's meeting with the Khedive of Egypt. Mīrzā Rizā goes on to quote Jamāl ad-Dīn as saying, "Alas that this man (meaning the Sultan) is mad, otherwise I would secure for him the allegiance of all the nations of Islām; but since his name is great in men's minds, this thing must be done in his name."[61]

Regarding his own history, Mīrzā Rizā related that after Jamāl ad-Dīn was expelled from Iran he, Mīrzā Rizā, was tricked by one of the Shah's sons, the Nā'ib as-Saltaneh, into writing the Shah a letter of complaint over the sale of Iran to Europeans. This letter was then used as an excuse to arrest him. During an interrogation he had unsuccessfully attempted to kill himself with a pair of scissors, and he had subsequently been imprisoned for four and a half years, during which he was badly mistreated and his wife left him, taking their children. When he was finally released he went to Istanbul to see Sayyid Jamāl ad-Dīn (whose servant and close disciple he had been during Jamāl ad-Dīn's trip to Iran). He quotes Jamāl ad-Dīn as saying

60 Translated in *ibid.*, pp. 82–83.
61 *Ibid.*, p. 84.

when he heard of Mīrzā Rizā's misfortunes: "How poor-spirited wert thou! Why didst thou not kill [one of thy tormentors]?"[62]

Upon questioning by his interrogators about Jamāl ad-Dīn, Mīrzā Rizā reiterated the story about the Sultan's telling Jamāl ad-Dīn to do whatever he wished about the Shah, and then said:

> "So when I described to the Sayyid my misfortunes, sufferings, imprisonments, and torments, he said to me, 'How poor-spirited you were, and how great was your love of life! You should have killed the tyrant. Why did you not kill him?' Now there was no tyrant except the Shāh and Prince Nā'ib as-Salṭana; and though I was thinking of the latter also, yet on that day my mind decided that it should be the Shāh. I said to myself, 'The Tree of Tyranny must be cut down at the roots, and then its branches and leaves will wither in the natural course of things.' "[63]

Mīrzā Rizā saw Jamāl ad-Dīn in Istanbul in 1895, and he testified that he left Istanbul in January 1896 and went to the shrine of 'Abd al-'Azīm outside Tehran in March 1896. He killed Nāsir ad-Dīn Shāh there with a pistol on May 1, 1896, when the Shah was visiting there in preparation for the celebration of the fiftieth (lunar year) anniversary of his accession to the throne. In his testimony, Mīrzā Rizā attributes the assassination to his desire to serve Iranian liberty and to avenge his own sufferings. Since his target was not his own tormentor, Nā'ib as-Saltaneh, but rather the Shah, is is probable that both the idea and the choice of target were Jamāl ad-Dīn's, and indeed the testimony suggests this. Regarding the Shah, Mīrzā Rizā enumerated several cases of his oppressive behavior, giving the most prominence to his treatment of Jamāl ad-Dīn:

> "For years the flood of injustice has engulfed all his subjects. What had Sayyid Jamālu'd-Dīn, that holy man and true descendant of the Prophet, done to be dragged forth with such ignominy from the sanctuary of Shāh 'Abdu'l-'Aẓīm. They tore his under-clothing, they treated him with all this ignominy, yet what had he said except the truth? . . . Does God tolerate such deeds? Are they not tyranny? Are they not oppression? If there be a discerning eye it will not

[62] *Ibid.*, p. 89.
[63] *Ibid.*, p. 92.

> fail to observe that it was in that very same place whence they dragged the Sayyid that the Shāh was shot."[64]

When asked who else was involved in the assassination, Mīrzā Rizā replied, in part:

> "You know how, when Sayyid Jamālu'd-Dīn came to this city, all the people, of every class and kind . . . came to see him and wait upon him, and how they listened to his discourses. And since all that he said was said for God and for the public good, everyone profited and was charmed by his words. Thus did he sow the seed of these high ideas in the fallow ground of men's hearts, and the people awoke and came to their senses. Now everyone holds the same views that I do; but I swear by God Most High and Almighty, who is the Creator of Sayyid Jamālu'd-Dīn and of all mankind, that no one, save myself and the Sayyid, was aware of this idea of mine or of my intention to kill the Shāh. The Sayyid is in Constantinople: do what you can to him."[65]

At another point, Mīrzā Rizā said that Jamāl ad-Dīn had suggested he kill Nā'ib as-Saltaneh,[66] but it is improbable that he gave it priority over the killing of the Shah.

The Shah's assassination caused a great stir in Iran and was one sign, as the tobacco movement was another, that the forces of despotism were not impregnable, hence it probably helped to lead Iran toward the Constitutional Revolution of 1905–1911. At the time of the killing, disturbances were avoided by Amīn as-Sultān's clever expedient of releasing news only that the Shah had been wounded; by propping up the dead Shah in a carriage for the return ride to Tehran; and by pretending to engage him in conversation on the trip. After the return to the capital, Amīn as-Sultān called on the Russian-officered Iranian Cossack brigade to police the area in order to prevent disturbances. Mīrzā Rizā was executed in August 1896, and the Russian head of the Iranian Cossack Brigade, Kosogovskii, reports on his calm until the end and his firm belief that he belonged to a very numerous party that would gain its "sublime and noble goal." Mīrzā Rizā said that he was happy to have burnt the heart of the

64 *Ibid.*, p. 71.
65 *Ibid.*, p. 73.
66 *Ibid.*, p. 75.

Shah on the very spot where the Shah had burnt the heart of his glorious master, Sayyid Jamāl ad-Dīn. Kosogovskii reports Mīrzā Rizā's conviction that he had done a noble and praiseworthy deed, and his refusal in any way to implicate anyone beyond himself and Jamāl ad-Dīn.[67]

According to Shaikh Ahmad Rūhī's brother, who was in Istanbul at the time, Jamāl ad-Dīn had refused to put up Mīrzā Rizā at his house when he came to Istanbul, but had given him money and, as he was ill, sent him to a hospital, where he stayed forty days until he was better.[68] An oral report emanating from Jamāl ad-Dīn's Christian servant in Istanbul, Jurjī Kuchī, says that Jamāl ad-Dīn told Mīrzā Rizā that since he was ill and had not long to live he could lose nothing by the great deed of killing the Shah.[69]

Very shortly after the Shah's assassination it became known that Jamāl ad-Dīn might be implicated, and as a result of the assassination there was a flurry of articles in European newspapers in May and June 1896 telling something about Jamāl ad-Dīn. This was the only significant publicity that Jamāl ad-Dīn received abroad since he had come to Istanbul. An enterprising German newspaperman managed to get to interview Jamāl ad-Dīn, and the interview, published in a Munich newspaper in June, gives another glimpse of Jamāl ad-Dīn's flights of fancy in this period. The reporter begins with a biography, originating with Jamāl ad-Dīn, which stresses his military exploits in Afghanistan, beginning at age thirteen, and notes his friendship with Prince Zill as-Sultān (who some had thought would succeed the late Shah). The biography goes on to say that the late Shah had wanted to appoint Jamāl ad-Dīn as war minister and prime minister when he was in Iran, but then became jealous of his influence. On his second trip to Iran the prime minister had seen him as a competitor and had persuaded the Shah to reject his proposed code of laws. (None of this

---

67 V. A. Kosogovskii, *Iz tegeranskogo dnevnika polkovnika V.A. Kosogovskogo* (Moscow, 1960), pp. 39–40, 61.

68 Afẕal al-Mulk Kirmānī, introduction to *Hasht bihisht*, p. *ya*.

69 R. Rustam interview, Cairo, Sept., 1966. Rustam knew Kuchī, who wrote a book about his experiences which seems to be unavailable. I have not seen it, although I have talked to persons in Egypt who have, among them Osman Amin ('Uthmān Amīn), who in his *Muhammad 'Abduh: Essai sur ses idées philosophiques et religieuses* (Cairo, 1944), lists it in his bibliography as Georges Cotchy, *Djamal Eddin al-Afghani et les mystères de Sa Majesté Impériale Abdul-Hamid II* (Cairo, n.d.). Amīn suggested to me in September 1966 that the book may have been confiscated after publication by the Ottoman authorities, with only a few copies escaping confiscation.

is substantiated by documents now available.) With regard to the claim being made by the Iranian government that Jamāl ad-Dīn should be extradited as an Iranian subject, he claimed that his earlier expulsion proved that the Shah had not considered him an Iranian, since if he had he would have arrested him, not expelled him. The reporter continues that while in London Jamāl ad-Dīn yielded to honorable and pressing invitations from the Sultan, but made it a condition that he might return to the West after having an audience with the Sultan. Now he is tossed between Abdülhamid's favors and the inimical machinations of members of the court. Although he has repeatedly asked the Sultan for permission to leave he is retained in a house in the palace area "in a kind of resplendent captivity" (the reporter's words). The reporter describes Jamāl ad-Dīn's quarters as strikingly simple, and says he spends most of his time in a roomy salon with European furnishings. When the reporter arrived Jamāl ad-Dīn was in the company of half a dozen Muslims of different nationalities. Jamāl ad-Dīn's French, in which language they conversed, is described as not fluent, but, the reporter continues, since he has impressive and picturesque gestures his meaning can be followed. His external appearance gives the impression of an extraordinary man, with his enormous head, fine features, and black, sharp eyes that penetrate his listener and reflect his shafts of thought. All this turns the visitor in his favor. His answers make one feel that he is a man used to expressing himself impetuously and fearlessly, and in the fire of his speech he sometimes rises from his chair. The author quotes Jamāl ad-Dīn as follows:

> "You have heard that they intend to expel me from here and to extradite me to Persia, accusing me of being a co-plotter in the assassination of the Shah. However, this is the work of the Persian ambassador, himself a tool of men of low mentality, and without an atom of justice and humanity, who acts on their orders, and himself lacks any consciousness of the baseness and malevolence of his own course of action. I am but a messenger of thought and truth, and do not lay hands on men. I have striven and still strive for a reform movement in the rotten Orient, where I would like to substitute law for arbitrariness, justice for tyranny, and toleration for fanaticism. I do not belong, as they have claimed, to the Babi sect, even though I do not altogether condemn them, but they are mystics with fantasies. I have always openly pro-

claimed my views and teachings, and I have had thousands of enthusiastic adherents, who are partly being persecuted, put in captivity, and loaded with chains. The entire Oriental world is so entirely rotten and incapable of hearing the truth and following it that I should wish for a flood or an earthquake to devour and bury it.[!]

"They accuse me of being involved in a conspiracy against the life of the Shah. Surely it was a good deed to kill this bloodthirsty tyrant, this Nero on the Persian throne who destroyed more than 5,000 people during his reign [and] who when he went out was preceded by the executioners in red garb, saber or axe in hand, and who nonetheless knew how to throw sand into the eyes of civilized Europe so that it did not recognize his deeds. It was well done then to kill him, for it may be a warning to others. This is the first time that a Shah has found his death not in a palace revolution but at the hand of an ordinary man, and thus for a tyrant to receive the just recompense for his deeds. As far as I personally am concerned, however, I have no part in this deed, and I do not even know whether a conspiracy of several people existed to this end. If such a conspiracy did exist it was by no means planned in my house, for it is open to all and I do nothing whatever in secret. It has been asserted that the Shah's killer is identical with a certain Mīrzā Rizā, who was my guest last winter. It is possible, but I know nothing about it. If it be true then I cannot understand how this man could have committed the deed. For after he left the French hospital in Constantinople where I had put him up he was, after all, barely able to move, since the misery of a four-year imprisonment in Persia, during which he had been cast in chains of a hundred-weight around his neck and feet, had virtually paralyzed him. His shaky hands were barely able to hold a cup of tea, and in his whole life he had so far not held a weapon. For the rest, it does not matter to me what people say about me. I am not attached to life, of whose insignificance I am only too conscious. My heart is not attached to the honors and decorations of men, and were I to be offered a million to accept a decoration, I would refuse. I desire nothing but the truth and my sole aim is to spread its light, to bring about reforms, and to have toleration prevail."[70]

---

[70] Robert Federmann, "Scheik Dejmaleddin el Afghan: Ein Lebensbild aus dem Orient," *Beilage zur Allgemeinen Zeitung* (Munich), June 24, 1896, no. 144, pp. 1–4. The author says he is giving an extract from Jamāl ad-Dīn's words, which he

The reporter adds that Jamāl ad-Dīn continued to talk at length on his last theme with unusual eloquence, like a preacher desirous of imprinting his most sacred convictions deeply on his listeners. When the reporter asked if he could print the interview, Jamāl ad-Dīn said that he desired it, knowing well he would be understood in Europe, where the truth he was trying to spread in the Orient was properly valued. The reporter concludes that the content of their talk convinced him that Jamāl ad-Dīn was a most interesting and attractive man, both prophet and warrior, inspired by noble humanitarian ideas, and having astounding knowledge and learning. One must wonder if the Sultan's splendid captivity is not designed to render innocuous this man's great influence in the Islamic world.[71]

A slightly different version of what is probably the same interview, since most of its contents are the same, was published by *Le Temps* of Paris on June 14, 1896. Herein, more fanciful details of Jamāl ad-Dīn's biography are given, as in the following:

> It was by chance that Jamal ad-Din making a round trip around Europe met his former master and friend Nasir ad-Din, who was coming from the Universal Exposition. "What are you doing here among the unbelievers," said the Shah to the scholar. "Come with me. I am carrying back from France the intention to give laws to my people; you will help me to write them." And that is how Jamal ad-Din returned to Paris in the suite of his sovereign. But while he retained his idea and publicized it in Tehran, the Shah abandoned his under the influence of a retrograde clergy. There was thus formed a constitutional party, of which Nasir ad-Din could perhaps have wished to be the head, and which included besides the masses of the people, many princes and princesses of royal blood. One of them said to Jamal ad-Din, "Shaikh, give us laws, as I, who love my horses so much, have no means to keep my intendant from stealing them from me."

After outlining Jamāl ad-Dīn's great services to the Sultan's religious program, the author goes on to quote Jamāl ad-Dīn's denial of complicity in the assassination:

---

puts in quotation marks. In the *Le Temps* interview (n. 72, below). most of whose substance is so similar that it is almost certainly based on the same interview, some of the statements are quoted with a different wording.

71 *Ibid.*, p. 4.

"You are in my house. Did you have difficulty entering it? No; it is open to everyone, without the least mystery. And it is here that they have wanted to find black plots against the life of the Shah. That makes me laugh." And he in fact laughed loudly.

"See these men, my friends"; he pointed to them one by one, presenting them with abundant formulas. "Among them not a Persian. The Persians do not come here. My relations with the assassin, what were they? It is true that I knew a certain Mirza Riza, but Mirza Riza is a very widespread title—Riza is the name of a saint which thousands of men have in Persia, and in all Islam.

"Is this Mirza Riza really the guilty man? . . . How could the former peaceful merchant use a pistol and how could the fugitive . . . deprived of the use of one leg, have gone a quarter of a kilometer on Persian soil without being recognized and seized? And would I have had the stupidity to send there with such goals a being in a state of imbecility?

"I repeat to you that, barring a miracle, the murderer of the Shah is not the Mirza Riza that they say.

"Do not take me for a guilty man who defends himself and is afraid. I am not afraid of anything, because for more than thirty years I have detested life, and it is all the same to me if I die. If you passed an hour with me you would learn to know my thought and you also would detest life."[72]

Jamāl ad-Dīn apparently never admitted participating in the Shah's assassination. To have done so would have strengthened the hand of the Iranian government in its demands for his extradition or punishment, and he was probably not as indifferent to life as he claimed.

Iranian demands for Jamāl ad-Dīn's extradition evidently began almost immediately after the May 1 assassination, as on May 4, 1896, Sir Philip Currie telegraphed from Istanbul:

Persian Ambassador informs me that there is reason to believe that assassin of Shah was an emissary of Sheikh Djelalleddin [*sic*]. He is anxious to have the latter arrested and sent to Persia. Turkish Govt on being applied to stated that the Sheikh as an Afghan claims British protection.

Persian Ambassador asserts that he is a Persian subject and

[72] *Le Temps* (Paris) June 14, 1896.

> begs me not to put any difficulty in the way of his arrest. What course would Your Lordship wish me to pursue?

After getting an opinion from the India Office that Afghānī was a Persian, Salisbury replied: "According to the latest information in the possession of the India Office the nationality of Jemal-ed-din is Persian and the question of his surrender is therefore not one which concerns us."[73]

Beginning early in May 1896 and continuing for months thereafter, the Iranian government made strenuous efforts to get the Ottoman government to allow the extradition of Jamāl ad-Dīn on the grounds that he was a Persian national and implicated in the Shah's assassination. Khān Malik Sāsānī has unearthed much of the official correspondence on this subject, which indicates that the Sultan at times gave the Iranians reason to hope that their extradition attempts would be successful. The correspondence suggests that the Sultan was alternately influenced by men favorable to Jamāl ad-Dīn, who wanted extradition denied, and his enemies, who wanted it granted.

On May 10 the Iranian ambassador in Istanbul replied to word from Amīn as-Sultān, saying that in response to his code telegram he had spoken to the English ambassador, who expected orders from London not to give British protection to Jamāl ad-Dīn. The Iranian ambassador had also continued his efforts on the subject with the Sultan. In his next letter, the Iranian ambassador wrote of his insistence that an Iranian-Ottoman agreement provided for extradition in just such cases. The ambassador next wrote that Izzet Bey, who exercised great influence on the Sultan, was protecting Jamāl ad-Dīn. On July 3, 1896, the ambassador wrote home that the Sultan had asked him to write the proofs of the complicity of Jamāl ad-Dīn in the Shah's assassination, to which he had protested that such proofs had never been customary in extradition cases. Later, the Ottoman prime minister promised him that Jamāl ad-Dīn would be delivered to Iranian authorities, but that an eight-day delay was unavoidable. In a later letter, though, the ambassador wrote that the prime minister now said that there were living in Iran close to a thousand Ottoman malefactors and that they should be extradited if Jamāl ad-Dīn was. This letter contains a marginal note by the new Shah Muzaffar ad-Dīn, to Amīn as-Sultān saying that he should impress on the Otto-

---

73 F.O. 60/594, Currie to Salisbury, Tel., no. 143, May 4, 1896; Salisbury to Currie, Tel., no. 74, May 6, 1896.

man ambassador in Iran that unless the extradition was accomplished friendship between the Ottoman and Iranian states would be impossible. The Iranian ambassador's next letter is again optimistic about extradition, but his following letter vividly describes further procrastination by the Ottomans, despite their claim that the extradition was to be carried out. The ambassador demanded definite word from the Sultan, and found out that the Ottoman ministers were meeting again to discuss the subject. Subsequent letters reveal that the procrastination of the Ottoman government was partly attributable to the intervention of Jamāl ad-Dīn's old friend Münif Paşa, now on a special mission in Tehran. The next letter from the Iranian ambassador in Istanbul, on August 21, 1896, reports in detail:

> Two telegrams came from Münif Paşa, which delayed the affair of Shaikh Jamāl, the first claiming that the interrogation of the assassin had not given any proof of the complicity of Jamāl ad-Dīn in killing the Shah. However, from the beginning I have not entered into the question of whether or not he conspired in the killing, but rather have requested his extradition because of treaties in force, without agreeing to furnish any proof or evidence.
>
> The second telegram affirms that His Majesty [the Shah] himself does not attach any great importance to this matter. It follows that they are now claiming that I am the only one to pursue Shaikh Jamāl. This is the worst thing of all.[74]

The letter goes on to request a delay in the scheduled execution of the assassin, if it is not too late, since the writer has told the Ottomans that Jamāl ad-Dīn is needed in Tehran right away to confront the assassin. The Iranian ambassador also suggests strong measures, including the stationing of troops at the frontier and repeated complaints, as well as mistreatment of the Ottoman Embassy in Tehran.

Amīn as-Sulṭān was apparently moved to firmer action at this point, as in the fall of 1896 the Iranian ambassador wrote to him:

> Having received your telegram, I consequently had a firm discussion with the prime minister and the foreign minister in the following terms: "I affirm to you, unofficially, that in case you refuse the extradition of Jamāl, the Iranian government will be constrained to break off diplomatic relations.

[74] Sāsānī, *op. cit.*, p. 218, quoting Archives of the Iranian Foreign Ministry. The earlier correspondence is on pp. 210–217.

In a case where you have violated a treaty, according to what agreement can we act in the future?"

The prime minister said that it is not proven that Jamāl is an Iranian subject. As I had written to Petersburg and Arfa' ad-Dauleh had sent firm documentation that Jamāl had been in Petersburg with an Iranian passport, and I brought and showed it, he fell silent, but said that complicity in the assassination of the Shah remained unproven.[75]

Most interesting are two cipher messages from the Iranian ambassador in Istanbul to Amīn as-Sultān written in the summer of 1896. The first is dated Muḥarram 1314/June–July 1896, and reads, "Am I authorized to incite the Iranians to assassinate Shaikh Jamāl?" In the margin of this telegram Muzaffar ad-Dīn Shāh wrote, in his own hand: "This seems wrong to me!" The second, dated 13 Rabī' al-Awwal 1314/August 22, 1896, reads: "To His Excellency the Prime Minister: The Sultan has agreed to deliver Jamāl ad-Dīn to us. He wishes him sent to Iran under surveillance and that he be imprisoned, and the people around him dispersed. Please answer this telegram as soon as possible."[76]

The affair seems to have been subsequently dropped, as there is no further correspondence recorded until December 1896 when a letter, discussed below, announced that Jamāl ad-Dīn was seriously ill.

One may surmise that Jamāl ad-Dīn was saved from execution not only by the intervention of friends but also by the Sultan's fear of having secrets of his court and his Pan-Islamic propaganda among Shi'is known to the Iranian government. The Ottoman government's claims that Jamāl ad-Dīn was an Afghan and that his complicity in the Shah's death was unproven seem more like pretexts than serious contentions.

If Jamāl ad-Dīn, who was almost surely the inspirer of the Shah's assassination, was lucky enough to escape extradition, such good fortune did not greet his three Iranian followers still imprisoned at Trabzon—Mīrzā Āqā Khān Kirmānī, Shaikh Ahmad Rūhī, and Khabīr al-Mulk. Although the Sultan had agreed months before the Shah's assassination that the three would be freed, their release had been delayed, apparently on the intervention of Abū al-Hudā; the Ottoman chief of police; and the Iranian ambassador in Istanbul. Mīrzā Rizā returned from Istanbul to Iran in the company of one of

75 *Ibid.*, p. 219.

76 *Ibid.*, pp. 217–219.

Ahmad Rūhī's brothers, but appears to have had no contact with the three luckless Iranians who were in a distant prison the whole time he was in Turkey. Nevertheless, the Iranian government used the Shah's assassination as an excuse to demand the extradition of the three, which was granted. Rūhī's other brother was in Istanbul when he heard by telegram that the three were being taken to Iran, and he reports:

> I hurried to the house of the Sayyid and showed him the telegram and asked him . . . to ask the Sultan to keep them in Ottoman territory. The Sayyid with perfect calm, after thinking a little, raised his head and said: "Supposing they took my son to be killed, and he could be saved with one word of intercession from me; I would consent to his being killed, but not to the shame of begging from an enemy. . . . Let them be taken to Iran and killed so that among their people the foundation of nobility and honor will be high."[77]

It is not certain that Jamāl ad-Dīn was really quite so cavalier with the lives of his former disciples as this makes it appear. He had intervened on their behalf before and may have known but not wished to admit that his own position with the Sultan was now so shaky that his intervention could do no good. On the other hand, there is a report from Mīrzā Husain Khān Dānish Isfahānī, an Iranian who knew Jamāl ad-Dīn in Istanbul, that after the three men were in prison and he had no hope of freeing them, he said to his guests regarding his former disciple Mīrzā Āqā Khān Kirmānī, with a voice full of hatred: "I do not understand why they took this poor man. . . . This is a very powerless and stupid man . . . what do they fear from such a man?"[78] Rūhī's brother also speaks of a period of six months before their imprisonment in which Rūhī and Kirmānī had broken off relations with Jamāl ad-Dīn. Possibly they had ceased to be his absolute disciples, like Muḥammad 'Abduh from 1885 on, and this had resulted in a break, which might help explain Jamāl ad-Dīn's reported refusal to intervene to save their lives. In any case, the three were extradited to Iran where the new crown prince and governor of Azerbaijan, the cruel Muhammad 'Alī Mīrzā, had them executed on his own orders. The Shah's assassination thus resulted

[77] Translated in Keddie, "Religion and Irreligion," p. 295.
[78] Appendix to Mīrzā Luṭfallāh Asadābādī, *op. cit.*, p. 92.

in the purging not of its instigator but of three innocent Iranian progressives.

Near the end of his life Jamāl ad-Dīn apparently wrote a letter to an unnamed Iranian friend in which he recognized his own lifelong error of having appealed to traditional rulers for reform, and expressed the wish that he had made more such appeals to the people. The letter refers to Jamāl ad-Dīn as being in prison at the time of its writing, which probably dates it from right after the Shah's assassination, when Sultan Abdülhamid is reported to have imprisoned Afghānī for a number of days. After saying that he did not fear his impending death, but only grieved that he had not lived to see the awakening of the peoples of the East, Afghānī continued:

> Would that I had sown all the seed of my ideas in the receptive ground of the people's thoughts! Well would it have been had I not wasted this fruitful and beneficent seed of mine in the salt and sterile soil of that effete Sovereignty! For what I sowed in that soil never grew, and what I planted in that brackish earth perished away. During all this time none of my well-intentioned counsels sank in the ears of the rulers of the East, whose selfishness and ignorance prevented them from accepting my words. . . . The stream of renovation flows quickly toward the East. The edifice of despotic government totters to its fall. Strive so far as you can to destroy the foundations of this despotism, not to pluck up and cast out its individual agents. . . .[79]

The optimism here expressed about the immediate future of the East is in contrast with the pessimism reported in the newspaper interviews, and one may guess that Jamāl ad-Dīn, like many other reformers, fluctuated between optimistic and pessimistic views regarding his own people.

In the last months of his life Afghānī was attacked with cancer of the jaw, which his doctor evidently attributed to his heavy cigarette smoking and tea drinking. He was operated on, probably twice, by the Sultan's surgeon, with parts of his jaw removed, but to no avail.

---

79 Translated in Browne, *Persian Revolution*, pp. 28–29. Sayyid Ḥasan Taqizādeh has doubted the authenticity of the letter, of which the original seems unavailable, and which was first reprinted in 1909–10 in Nāẓim al-Islām al-Kirmānī, *Tārīkh-i bīdārī-yi Īrāniyān* (2d ed.; Tehran, 1945–46). Homa Pakdaman is convinced of its authenticity, and both style and content tend to support its genuineness.

On December 30, 1896, the Iranian ambassador in Istanbul telegraphed home, with evident satisfaction.

> Jamāl has been attacked by cancer in a very grave manner so that there is no more hope for him. Surgeons have cut off one side of his chin along with its teeth, and he will soon die.
> The soul of the martyred Shah (may his tomb be sanctified), is finally avenged and Jamāl ad-Dīn has been punished for his acts.
> For these reasons I no longer see the necessity of continuing to demand his extradition. His death, in such conditions, and after what has happened, will make a great impression.[80]

If Iranian authorities were elated, Jamal ad-Dīn's followers in Istanbul were desolate, and one has left a vivid report of Jamāl ad-Dīn's lengthy operations and sufferings.[81]

Jamāl ad-Dīn died on March 9, 1897, evidently attended only by his Christian servant, Jurjī Kuchī. The Ottoman government buried him as quietly and with as little ceremony as possible, thus emphasizing the official disfavor that had marked his last years. At the time and subsequently it was alleged by some of Jamāl ad-Dīn's Persian and Arab followers that he was poisoned on the Sultan's orders, probably by means of a slow-acting venom injected by the Sultan's surgeon. Since Jamāl ad-Dīn's disease is attested by witnesses, and since cancer could scarcely be induced by poison, the story of poisoning is most probably part of the mythology that surrounds Jamāl ad-Dīn's life.[82]

---

80 Sāsānī, *op. cit.*, p. 219.

81 *Sirāj al-Akhbār* (Kabul), VI, 5, Oct. 14, 1916.

82 Pakdaman, pp. 188–190, accepts the story of poisoning, based primarily on Khān Malik Sāsānī's reports of conversations years after the event with two men who are reported as saying that Jamāl ad-Dīn was in excellent health until the night before his death; one story says that the Sultan's own doctor poisoned him on the day of his death. She also cites Shakīb Arslān, who knew Afghānī in his last years, but Arslān gives a very different story, admitting that Jamāl ad-Dīn had cancer and was operated on for it, but suggesting that either the Sultan's surgeon or a dentist who examined Afghānī injected poison (Arslān, *op. cit.*, pp. 204–205). Muḥammad al-Makhzūmī, who also knew Afghānī at the time, speaks of three operations for cancer, but not of poison (*op. cit.*, [Arabic], p. 39). The numerous direct reports of Jamāl ad-Dīn's cancer seem incontrovertible, and, while it is possible that the Sultan ordered a doctor to inject poison into him, it seems more likely that the Sultan, knowing that Afghānī would soon die from his illness, let nature take its course. Sāsānī's report appears tendentious, and since he published it only after the two men he quotes had died, it is impossible to check on it. The question of poisoning cannot be regarded as absolutely settled, although the fact

Jamāl ad-Dīn's last years had been characterized by increasing obscurity, restlessness, and some bitterness. Aside from the satisfaction he may have received from the inspiration of successful vengeance on the object of his greatest hatred, Nāsir ad-Dīn Shāh, Jamāl ad-Dīn must have known that he was accomplishing little in these years. Not permitted to publish anything, not allowed to leave Istanbul, his steps dogged by the Sultan's spies, Jamāl ad-Dīn was a glorified prisoner whose manifest influence was now almost limited to a small group of disciples, most of whom had as yet made no mark in the world. There is no indication that any powerful persons besides the Egyptian Khedive tried to see him in these years, and consciousness of his existence seems to have been declining among both Westerners and Easterners, with rare exceptions like Rashīd Riḍā, until news of the Shah's assassination brought a new flurry of notices. The Egyptian leaders Aḥmad Luṭfī as-Sayyid and Sa'd Zaghlūl did, however, visit him in Istanbul.

Conclusion

ALTHOUGH NEWS of Jamāl ad-Dīn's death brought some important Eastern obituary notices, especially that by Jurji Zaidān in his journal *al-Hilāl,* renewed interest in Jamāl ad-Dīn in the Muslim East was largely a posthumous affair. In the twentieth century, as the defensive and anti-imperialist mood of the Muslim world grew, and as more and more Muslim intellectuals, particularly in the Arab world, began to build up an Islamic modernist system based on special interpretations of the Koran and early Islam, the words of Jamāl ad-Dīn began to enjoy a new popularity. His anti-British and nationalist pronouncements and his reported words to his followers favoring popular or constitutional government also met certain twentieth-century needs. Thus it was that Jamāl ad-Dīn, who had few political successes and only a sporadic influence in his own

of cancer seems proven. Two eyewitness reports of Afghānī's cancer are in Jundī, *op. cit.*, pp. 30–35. The mutually contradictory nature of the different poisoning stories is noted by Sayyid Muḥsin al-Amīn and Ḥasan al-Amīn, *A'yan ash-Shī'a,* Vol. XVI (Beirut, 1963), pp. 253–255.

lifetime became, like many other men whose ideas are in some ways ahead of their times, the inspiration for many later movements. While there is little doubt that he gave priority to independence and self-strengthening for the Muslim world, his words could be cited not only by those who shared this priority, but also by those whose chief concern was to protect traditional Islamic ways and beliefs against the encroachments of modernization. The ambiguities of his own words thus left a peculiar legacy, in which Jamāl ad-Dīn is claimed as a precursor by the widest variety of persons—all the way from leftists who cite with favor his anti-imperialism and his reported vague words advocating Muslim socialism, to groups like the Muslim Brethren who want primarily to preserve Muslim traditions from Western encroachments. He foreshadowed the political activism, anti-imperialism, and reformist and revolutionary ideals of twentieth-century politically minded Muslims, and many features of recent political ideas and action in the Muslim world are adumbrated in his complex life and writing. Jamāl ad-Dīn's posthumous influence and reputation could be the subject of another new work, and can only be mentioned in passing here, since a large number of leaders and writers in many countries were affected. In the Arab world, and particularly in Egypt, his reputation continues to grow, and numerous books, mostly without any new documented content, are still published about him. Ahead of his time in his violent condemnation of British imperialism, he found numerous anti-imperialist admirers after his death—a few of whom, notably the Egyptian nationalist leader of the early twentieth century Sa'd Zaghlūl, were his former disciples. The growth of his reputation in Muslam lands was partly due to the efforts of the Islamic writer and editor Rashīd Riḍā, who reprinted many of his articles and items about him in his journal, *al-Manār*, and in his three-volume biography of his own mentor, Muḥammad 'Abduh. In some countries, notably Egypt and Afghanistan, Afghānī has become almost a mythical hero, and as is often true of such heroes, a critical view of him is disliked. Even when all the mythology is stripped away, however, we are left with a man who devoted most of his life to trying to save or liberate Muslim lands from British control, who bolstered the self-image of the Muslims regarding the Islamic past, and called for reforms to lead the way to self-strengthening and independence. In numerous ways he foreshadowed both the strengths and the weaknesses of Muslim thought and activity in the decades after his death, and Afghānī's reputation seems secure even after the legends about him are subjected to critical scrutiny. As a pioneering political writer, speaker, and activist whose influence was felt in many different Muslim countries he has no rival in his own period.

Appendixes

Appendix I summarizes the evidence proving Jamāl ad-Dīn's Iranian birth and upbringing.

Appendixes II, III, and IV are translations of letters from Afghānī to three leading governmental figures.[1]

[1] Pakdaman, Part II, contains summaries of more Afghānī correspondence and translations of other material by or concerning him.

Appendix I

Summary of the Evidence that Jamāl ad-Dīn Was Born and Raised in Iran

More detailed proofs that Jamāl ad-Dīn was born and spent his childhood in Iran than the ones given here are available in Persian works cited in this appendix, and also in the recent book by Homa Pakdaman.[1] Here I summarize briefly only the more salient points.

First, all pre-twentieth-century accounts of an Afghan birth and childhood appear to rest on Jamāl ad-Dīn's own word. Only many years after his death was there created in Afghanistan an account that differs somewhat from the 'Abduh-Zaidān story.[2] There is no inde-

---

1 Pakdaman, chap. i.

2 In view of the fact that Jamāl ad-Dīn first arrived in Afghanistan in 1866 as a foreigner this account must be considered peculiarly inventive. It emanates from a certain 'Abd ar-Rahmān Khān, was printed in the review *Kābul* (Dec., 1939–Jan., 1940), and is summarized in Ettore Rossi, "Il centenario della nascita di Gemal ud-Din al-Afghani celebrato a Kabul," *Oriente Moderno*, XX (1940), 262–265. The account gives new details about Jamāl ad-Dīn's Afghan education, and says, as do certain other biographies, that in 1863 he first supported the new Amir, Shīr 'Alī Khān, but quarreled with his vizier and went to India until he heard that A'zam Khān had come to power. Aside from other points noted in the text, the story is sufficiently disproved by the fact that Jamāl ad-Dīn went to A'zam Khān from Iran, not from India, as shown.

The earliest Afghan biography of Jamāl ad-Dīn referred to in any secondary source is in the Afghan newspaper, *Sirāj al-Akhbār*, VI, nos. 3 and 5 (1334/1916). It was found for me in Kabul by Dr. Ludwig Adamec, who confirms that it is the earliest Afghan biographical reference. Its account of Jamāl ad-Dīn's childhood is

pendent documentation for Afghanistan from family, acquaintances, and others as there is for Iran. One biography maintains Jamāl ad-Dīn's Afghan origin on the basis that the usual reason given for his claim to be an Afghan, desire to escape the jurisdiction of the Shah, could only have arisen much later than 1869, at which time he was already making this claim.[3] Yet it seems that the primary purpose of Jamāl ad-Dīn's claim that he was born in Afghanistan was his desire to present himself to the Muslim world as a Sunni rather than a Shi'i, as the Sunnis formed the majority of Muslims outside Iran, while a Muslim ethnic Persian from Iran would be recognized as almost surely a Shi'i. In this he was followed by his faithful servant, Abū Turāb "Afghānī," whose name was of Shi'i origin.[4] Abū Turāb, who was evidently a former servant of a leader of the Persian Shi'i ulama, first appeared in Afghanistan *as an Iranian* with his master in 1866.[5] Another reason, attributed by an Iranian acquaintance to Afghānī, for his claim to be an Afghan was that Afghanistan had no consulates abroad, whereas Iran did, and Iranian citizens were subject to interference and vexation from their consuls abroad.[6] To Iranians Jamāl ad-Dīn sometimes gave other explanations, and his strong denial of his Iranian homeland may also have had more personal and psychological roots.

There are Iranians who have in the past expressed doubt about Afghani's being of Iranian origin. Yet their arguments are not very weighty, the main one being the peculiarity of Afghānī's Persian style. Most Persian doubts as to Jamāl ad-Dīn's Iranian origin seem to have disappeared since the appearance of the Afshār-Mahdavī *Documents* volume with its documentation of Afghānī's Iranian family.[7]

---

essentially a translation of the 'Abduh-Zaidān story. It adds, however, that Jamāl ad-Dīn was in Istanbul before his trip to Afghanistan in the 1860's.

3 Sharīf al-Mujāhid, "Sayyid Jamāl ad-Dīn al-Afghānī: His Role in the Nineteenth-Century Muslim Awakening" (unpublished M.A. thesis, McGill University, Montreal, 1954), pp. 38 ff.

4 I am indebted to Elie Kedourie for pointing out the Shi'i name.

5 See the documents from the Afghan period cited in chapter 3; also Nāẓim al-Islām Kirmānī, *Tārīkh-i bīdārī-yi Īrāniyān* (2d ed.; Tehran, 1945–46), p. 61.

6 *Ibid.*

7 The late Sayyid Hasan Taqīzādeh told me in 1960, perhaps ironically, that he sometimes doubted Jamāl ad-Dīn was an Iranian because he was apparently a believing Muslim, and he had never known an Iranian with modernized ideas who was a real believer in Islam. Afghānī's actual religious beliefs tend to argue for rather than against an Iranian origin. In any case, Taqīzādeh became completely convinced of Jamāl ad-Din's Iranian birth since seeing the *Documents.*

All arguments in favor of Afghan birth may be regarded as demolished by the contemporary reports regarding Afghānī's years in Afghanistan done by employees of the Government of India whose content was summarized in chapter 3.

What do the British agents' investigations about this man in 1867 show about his origins? First, they show that he made no claim to be from Afghanistan, that he was known to everyone to be a foreigner, and that he was evidently unknown in Afghanistan until his entry in 1866. Second, he could not have been brought up in Afghanistan, because he was a stranger who *"talks Persian like an Irani (Persian)."* Third, he seems already to want to avoid identification as an Iranian, because he calls himself Rūmī (i.e., "from Turkey").[8] The answers are decisive not only for his non-Afghan birth but for the equally controversial question of his country of upbringing. The *Documents* record that at this time he used the name "Istanbūlī" and also show that he began to use the name "Afghānī" only after he left Afghanistan and went to Istanbul. Thus he claimed to be from Istanbul when in Afghanistan and from Afghanistan immediately thereafter when in Istanbul. In both cases, the *Documents* make it clear that he was using these place names to identify his point of origin, and not simply a country he had passed through.

Even apart from these British documents, ever since his own lifetime there has been abundant proof that Jamāl ad-Dīn was born in Iran. Most of this evidence has appeared in Persian and has, until recently, been ignored or brushed aside by most Sunni Muslims and by some Western writers. The question of his birthplace is the only element of his own account which has been subject to intensive independent scrutiny, and the evidence for Iranian birth is overwhelming. The *Documents,* for all the editors' introductory reservations, based

---

The editors of the *Documents,* like some other Iranians, seem unwilling to grant that Jamāl ad-Dīn falsified his birthplace and upbringing. A short biography has recently appeared in Tehran which still argues both on the basis of Jamāl ad-Dīn's words and his writing style that he was probably born and surely raised in Afghanistan: Ibrāhīm Ṣafā'ī, *Rahbarān-i mashrūteh* (Tehran, 1344/1965–66), chap. 1.

8 *Cabul Précis,* pp. 46–48, 65; "Cabul Diary," Dec. 1868, pp. 54 ff. and Jan., 1869, pp. 417–418. The documents are quoted at length above in chapter 3 where the proof that this was Afghānī is given. See *Documents,* p. 158, for the useful index of the various names used in Jamāl ad-Dīn and the important chronology and documents to which they refer (pp. 156–158). Some name forms and dates are not listed—whether the editors are unsure that they are Jamāl ad-Dīn's signatures or whether it is an oversight is unclear.

entirely on incomprehension of why Jamāl ad-Dīn should have claimed Afghan birth if it was not so, include several letters from members of his family in Iran, showing that Afghānī came from an Iranian family. That Jamāl ad-Dīn was an Iranian was widely known during his own lifetime in Iran, both to his own followers, to whom he sometimes spoke of his Iranian birth and of the reasons he had taken the name Afghānī, and to his opponents in the government. Both groups knew that he came from the large village of Asadabad near Hamadan in northwest Iran. His nephew, Sayyid Lutfallāh, and grandnephew, Sifātallāh Jamālī Asadābādī, have given details of his early life and established other indications of his Iranian origin, such as the fact that he described himself as an Iranian on one of his Russian visa applications. The *Documents* reproduce two of Afghānī's *Iranian* passports: one of 1871 and the other an 1889 passport from the Iranian consul general in Vienna, listing him as "sujet persan."[9]

Even before the *Documents*, with their numerous proofs of Jamāl ad-Dīn's correspondence with many members of his family in Iran, were published, Iranians had brought forth more evidence of Jamāl ad-Dīn's Iranian Shi'i background than was published in his own lifetime. Afghānī's grandnephew, Sifātallāh Jamālī Asadābādī, several years ago published and listed several documentary proofs of Jamāl ad-Dīn's Iranian background.[10] Sādiq Nash'at, in introducing his Arabic translation of the biography by Afghānī's nephew, Sayyid Lutfallāh, gives further proofs. Among these is the given name of Afghānī's father, Safdar, an Iranian Shi'i name. It is a compound of the Arabic *ṣaf* and Persian *dar* meaning "the breaker of ranks," and it is an attributive applied by Iranian Shi'i to their most revered imam, 'Alī.[11] Several of the documents presented by Lutfallāh, Sifātallāh, and Afshār and Mahdavī also show that Jamāl ad-Dīn's family was Shi'i and that he had a Shi'i education.

More convincing to some, perhaps, is the fact that the British For-

---

[9] *Ibid.*, plates 68, 69, photos 149, 150. There is apparently no evidence that Jamāl ad-Dīn ever traveled with Afghan documents—not that such documents would be decisive in any case.

[10] Ṣifātallāh, *Asnād*.

[11] Ṣādiq Nash'at and 'Abd al-Nadīm Ḥasanain, introduction to their Arabic translation of Mīrzā Luṭfallāh Khān, *Jamāl ad-Dīn al-Asadābādī al-Ma'rūf bi al-Afghānī* (Cairo, 1957), p. 11. Thanks to Homa Pakdaman for pointing out this introduction. Pakdaaman (chap. 1) lists in greater detail than I the proofs of Afghānī's Iranian and Shi'i origin which come from Persian sources.

eign Office launched an independent investigation to determine just this question of Jamāl ad-Dīn's birthplace. The Foreign Office did so in 1895, when Afghānī in Istanbul applied for British protection and a passport on the grounds that he was an Afghan subject. An American diplomat who visited Iran in 1936 also looked into the question of Afghānī's birthplace a century before. In both cases the decision, based in the Foreign Office case on considerable questioning and documentation, was that Jamāl ad-Dīn was born in Asadabad, Iran.[12] Finally, as Albert Hourani has astutely noted both in writing and conversation, Jamāl ad-Dīn's profound and early acquaintance with the Islamic philosophical tradition, especially Avicenna and Iranian Shi'i philosophers, was one that could most plausibly have come from Iranian Shi'i schools and teachers.[13] One could add—although it alone would not be decisive—the whole cast of Jamāl ad-Dīn's thought and behavior was in many ways distinctively Persian. Not only was his knowledge of Avicenna and, as his talks and writings also show, of later Iranian philosophers, including Suhrawardī "the executed" and Mullā Sadrā, typical of an educated Persian, but his agile and continual use of *kitmān* or *taqiyya,* dissimulation of his true beliefs, would also come most naturally to a Persian, whose religious education taught the need to hide one's beliefs before outsiders.

If one is convinced that Jamāl ad-Dīn was born in Iran, then he should be moved to doubt the numerous stories of childhood and

---

12 Cf. the numerous documents on the subject in the British Public Record Office volume, F.O. 60/594. This volume on Jamāl ad-Dīn was compiled from different Foreign Office files largely to decide the question of his birth and nationality. The American investigation was described to me by Elie Kedourie. Of it Sylvia Haim (*Arab Nationalism* [Berkeley and Los Angeles, 1962], p. 7 n. 4) says: 'A despatch from the United States Minister to Egypt dated March 17, 1936 (no. 883.91/1) records the researches of the Secretary of Legation, J. R. Childs, while on a visit to Persia, into the mystery of al-Afghani's origin. Childs satisfied himself, on the basis of published investigations of Persian scholars and the presence of al-Afghani's relatives in Iran, that al-Afghani was a native of Iran, and that he assumed the title of al-Afghānī in order that his Shiite origin should not violate his influence with the Sunni world of Afghanistan, Turkey, and Egypt." I have seen the original at the U.S. National Archives, Washington, D.C.

13 Albert Hourani, *Arabic Thought in the Ligeral Age: 1798–1939* (London, 1962), p. 108. I am very indebted to Mr. Hourani for his discussion of Afghānī with me in the summer of 1962 at Oxford, which, among other points, helped change my view that Afghānī was an Afghan, and suggested research in Iranian sources for information about his early years. Conservation and correspondence with Muhsin Mahdi regarding Jamāl ad-Dīn and Muslim philosophy was also most helpful.

education in Afghanistan also stemming from the 'Abduh-Zaidān source and based on tales told by Afghānī to his Sunni friends, perhaps elaborated by them.

There are several accounts, both Eastern and Western, expressing doubt about Jamāl ad-Dīn's birthplace but evince no doubt that he grew up in Afghanistan. This distinction seems to be based on the fact that the question of his birthplace has been subject to scrutiny and argument which cast doubt on Jamāl ad-Dīn's story of his birthplace, while there has not been nearly as much attention paid to his place of education, and so that part of the standard account has simply persisted. The 'Abduh-Zaidān account, as well as Jamāl ad-Dīn's words recorded by other Arab disciples, speak of an Afghan birth *and* childhood, whereas the Iranian investigations by Nāzim al-Islām Kirmānī, Sayyid Lutfallāh, and others show an Iranian birth *and* childhood. The distinction thus has no real basis either in evidence of an Afghan childhood or in the early accounts.

There does exist one report of Jamāl ad-Dīn's words in which he is said to have placed his birthplace in Iran and said that his family migrated to Afghanistan when he was a suckling baby, but this is certainly not the story he usually told. This story, reported by the Pan-Turkish Ahmed Ağayof [Ağa-oğlu] in the first issue of his newspaper, *Türk Yurdu*, is one often cited by Turks and others as saying that Afghānī told Ağayof that he was from an Azerbaijani Turkish family. This is a good example of how with Jamāl ad-Dīn distortions grow as distance from the source passes. A check on *Türk Yurdu* shows that Ağayof does not say that Jamāl ad-Dīn said his family was Turkish, but quotes him as saying: "My father and mother were originally from Marāgha, but later moved to Hamadan. I was born in Hamadan." *Ağayof* concludes that since Maragha was an Azerbaijani Turkish town, Jamāl ad-Dīn spoke Azerbaijani Turkish as his mother tongue.[14] (In reality Jamāl ad-Dīn's parents were Iranian.)

In fact, the point that Jamāl Dīn continued to speak Turkish in the Azerbaijani rather than either the Istanbuli or Central Asian fashion argues for his upbringing in northwest Iran rather than in Afghanistan, as already noted in 1921 by Sayyid Hasan Taqīzādeh in an interesting unsigned biography in *Kāveh*, a Persian journal that he edited from Berlin.[15]

---

[14] *Türk Yurdu* (Istanbul), I (1327–28/1911–12), 201. I have seen this story incorrectly cited in three Turkish books or articles and in one English one.

[15] *Kāveh* (Berlin), II, 3 (1921), 6.

The fact that when Jamāl ad-Dīn came to Afghanistan in 1866–1868 he was known to be a foreigner, previously unknown to the Afghans, and "talks Persian like an Irani [Persian]" should be sufficient to disprove an Afghan upbringing.[16] It does indeed seem to have bothered some writers how Afghānī could have received his sophisticated Islamic and philosophical education in Afghanistan in the mid-nineteenth century. There is no more evidence for an Afghan upbringing than for an Afghan birth, whereas there is considerable evidence for an Iranian and Iraqi Shi'i education.

None of this indicates that Afghānī as an adult regarded himself as a Shi'i. He was certainly genuine in his desire to end the rupture between Shi'is and Sunnis in order to build a united Muslim community. Such unity would help Muslims to regain their early power and dynamism and repel Western encroachments. In Sunni environments he used Sunni modes of expression and in Shi'i environments Shi'i ones, but his clear preference was to end the division between the two.

---

16 *Cabul Précis,* p. 47 (113).

Appendix II

Draft of an Arabic letter from Jamāl ad-Dīn to Riyaḍ Pasha in Cairo, November or December 1882.[1]

MY MASTER:

I am today in the Canal, and I am going to London, and from there to Paris. You will recognize the Truth, and you are True Justice. . . . [followed by lengthy and fulsome praise and honorifics].

I want to tell you the truth, and I say that before he acceded to the throne the Khedive [Taufīq] loved me with a true love, and I was a friend to his friends and an enemy to his enemies, and in peace with those with whom he was at peace and at war with those who opposed him. (Shaikh al-Bakrī first and Samīn Pāshā second, instigated by Ismā'īl Pāshā, both wanted to cause an uprising and bring great disaster to Egypt out of hate for the foreigners. I was then with the masons.)[2] The Khedive used to send me his secretary Kamāl Bey every day, saying, "I have only you for help." All this was with the knowledge of the Khedive, and on his request.

A group of European masons . . . under the leadership of 'Abd al-Ḥalīm Pāshā, who was the head of the Council of Masons in Cairo, did not cease supporting 'Abd al-Ḥalīm. I, out of love for the

---

[1] The translation is approximate in some places owing to the faintness and difficulty of the original draft in the Majlis Library collection.

[2] The parenthetical phrase is crossed out in the draft. Some other crossed-out phrases are not included in the translation.

Khedive, declared my enmity to them and opposed them. I and those like me quit their group, moved by love for the Khedive, and I relinquished the leadership of their lodge and left them, although they used to love me and I them, and I had been with them for many years—all this I did out of love of the Khedive. [On the side is added:] And he went to him advising and threatening him, saying, "The masons intend to assassinate you, because you are working for the continuation of the rule of this tyrant." He became afraid . . . and said he would not work for Ismā'īl in any way.

Then the European masons and their followers went to Tricou, the Consul of France, and told him that the Egyptians were for 'Abd al-Ḥalīm Pāshā's accession and desired him, and if another were chosen there would be an uprising. When this [news] reached me, I and those like me, moved by love for the Khedive, rushed to the Consul and gave lie to what they had told him, and explained to him the truth of the matter and removed the veil. All this was announced in the patriotic newspapers, and the Khedive cannot deny what I did, or my zeal, and he must recognize what I did for him.

My ex-brother masons, with whom I was on good terms, saw that I was no longer with them, and they lost confidence in the success of Ḥalīm. They accused me and associated me with the *Nihilists* one time, and to the *Socialists*[3] another, and spread lies about me, saying I aimed at killing both the Khedive and the consuls. I was a foreigner, without any army, and did not think anyone would believe such nonsense, but some did.

After the Khedive [Taufīq] took the throne, a group of masons of Ḥalīm's party went to the Khedive with this [story] to get revenge. I knew they were numerous and strong. I had written refutations of their stories in all the Egyptian Arabic- and Western-language newspapers, and I explained to the government their true aims, and I said to take action against their evil. The masons were helped by all supporters of Ḥalīm, despite their differences, and by the evil 'Uthmān Pāshā al-Maghlūb,[4] who was chief of police at that time. One of my pupils wrote against him in a newspaper (saying only that he was not sinless), and he was angry and worked with Ḥalīm's masons, slandering me and helping them. Sharīf Pāshā heard of it and stopped

---

3 Transliterated from the French forms of italicized words into Arabic script.

4 *al-Maghlūb* is a passive participle meaning "the conquered." It is a play on the man's real appellation, the active participle of the same verb, *al-Ghālib*, "the conqueror."

them. When Sharīf resigned [as prime minister] this petty man ['Uthmān Pāshā] thought I had complained of him to Sharīf, which was untrue. I learned of it only when he arrested me, when he said: Sharīf tried to dismiss me because of you." He used to lie about me to the Khedive. They convinced the Khedive I was his enemy, and desired treachery. I disregarded it, as I thought the Khedive would not forget my support, but he thought I was against him and ordered my forcible expulsion from Egypt. I did not know of it, and was taken by surprise at 2 A.M. on the sixth night of Ramadan. When I asked the reasons, one time I was told that the ulama did not want me to remain in Egypt; another time that the foreign consuls were afraid of me; and another time that Our Efendi [Taufīq] was unable to sleep for three nights from fear of me. The true hidden reason was what was recounted above regarding his opposition to those who supported Sharīf Pāshā. He ['Uthmān] said [to me]: "I exaggerated about you, but you must go to Hell, either via Iran or India." However much I sought to be sent to Istanbul or Paris or the Hijaz, he insisted on sending me to Hell. He did not even give me two days, under police guard, to sell what I could not take. He said, "We will do it for you while you are in Suez. Aḥmad Bey will do it for you." All this was from anger, without any cause but false suspicion.

Then that vile man sent me to Suez with a group of policemen. I stayed two days, and they did not let me eat. The local police chief took what money was in my pocket and in my servant's pocket, and also beads and a handkerchief, saying that Our Efendi had ordered it. After these shameful deeds, when I went to the boat and asked why I was not fed, he said this was an order. He refused to return anything to us, saying Our Efendi had ordered everything taken away, but that orders had already gone from Egypt to return my books and money before I reached Bushehr. All this came from the activity of Ḥalīm's party and their falsehood. (I told him this was a crooked Turkish policy.) I asked him: "Why not return the money taken from our pockets, so that we can leave the boat in one of these ports." He said: "No, it is against the Efendi's orders. The Efendi ordered me to take all you two have except clothing."

On top of everything, I realized that Ḥalīm's supporters would laugh, since I supported the Khedive and they knew the truth.

I ask you now, with your wisdom and justice, to ask about this of 'Abdallāh Pāshā Fikrī, Fakhrī Pāshā, Kamāl Bey (the Khedive's secretary), and Sharīf Pāshā. They all knew my faith and deeds when I was here, and my steadfastness and justice were evidence of my good faith. They knew everything about me. Then you can judge for yourself about what occurred. You will see that the members and organization of this government are bad. You will ask whether such a tyrannical, ignorant government can survive. Do you think that Yazīd, Hajjāj, and Timūr[5] are dead? They left germs that developed from one to the next. No Muslim government in these centuries is free of their legacy. They are in every country sitting on the throne of tyranny, commanding the evil and forbidding the good.[6] And if people know what justice is, intelligent people will see that the survival of this government means more and more tyranny, and less and less justice. What has just happened to the Egyptian government [i.e., the British invasion] was thus Divine Justice.

O you, justice of Cairo! If you look at things with the eye of your equity—at the disaster that reached me owing to the Egyptian government, when I was doing nothing wrong, was pure of heart, having no crime or sin; and at all the calamities that overcame me in governmental [British] India as a result of the former disasters—you will know that it was owing to a just judgment that the bloody events overcame the Egyptian government and took it by the neck. I say that heaven and earth are built on justice, and justice means retribution.[7] It makes me sorry after it makes me laugh.

As for what was written in the *Official Gazette*, the least newspaper in the world and the encyclopaedia of misdeeds, saying that the Egyptian government had discovered a secret society headed by Jamāl ad-Dīn al-Afghānī in order to ruin Religion and the World (*Dīn wa Dunyā*); calling someone an unbeliever (*takfīr*) is the arm of weak Muslims. I did not know that their ruler would use this arm in order to strengthen himself.

After paining your heart with what happened to me in Egypt, because you are the only one who cares, I will give you a summary of what happened in India:

I arrived in the port of Karachi on the day after I got the news of the murder of . . . , the British consul in Kabul, and therefore I was kept under guard the whole time and was questioned every hour.

---

5 The men named are famous in Islamic history for tyranny and/or bloodthirstiness.

6 A play on the duty of Muslims 'to command the good and forbid the evil."

7 As noted in the text, this occasion is one of several in which Afghānī sees the disasters that have overtaken rulers who opposed him as retribution for his own mistreatment.

They checked my answers, and each official sent me to another. They always asked the same questions, and did not allow me to contact anyone. But they did not take my handkerchief and beads, as was done in Egypt—until Ayyūb Khān [an anti-British Afghan leader] went to Tehran and the British calmed down about me and left me alone. (I was upset.) . . . Therefore, I went to the Deccan, still having no money. In these circumstances the bloody 'Urābī events occurred, and therefore British suspicions began again. Fearing the outbreak of uprisings in India, and believing I was an envoy on behalf of 'Urābī Pāshā to incite the Muslims against the British government, they brought me to Calcutta and were persistent in interrogating me, and every day I found myself threatened, and they made my life very difficult.

As the voice of 'Urābī grew louder, the British government increased its strictness, especially when that rash man ['Urābī] said that I was stirring up the Indian Muslims against the British until I—because of the severity of the Government toward me, the fact that they paid no attention to my answers, and their hatred toward me—asked them to send me to the Khedive. I presented this request to the Viceroy of India while he was in Simla [the summer capital], and while he had the request and I was awaiting the answer, the Government continued its harangues and rebukes until the ['Urābī] uprising ended, and they released me, but continued to watch my actions and movements night and day. When I saw that misfortunes increased every day, and that distress opened its door every hour, I considered the calamities that came in my affairs, and I know that if I returned to my land while my eyes are all tears, my voice all complaint, and my heart all fire, I would not find there any Muslim ready to sympathize with my affliction when I recounted to him my story. For Muslims . . . do not revolt against tyranny and have no pity for its victims. I therefore, even without money, have decided to travel toward lands whose inhabitants enjoy sound minds, attentive ears, and sympathetic hearts to whom I can recount how a human being is treated in the East. Thus will be extinguished the fire that so many sufferings have lit in me and my body will be freed from the burden of sufferings that have broken my heart.

I have sent to you, my master, my servant 'Ārif to collect all my books, taken from me in Egypt, trusting in your goodness. ['Ārif is] also to take several months' salary that remained unpaid [when I left Egypt]. I count on your help. I also ask you to help 'Ārif and to treat my pupils kindly, especially Shaikh Muḥammad ʻAbduh and Sayyid Ibrāhīm Laqqānī. If they behaved wrong in the [ʻUrābī] uprising, forgive them with your wide mercy, as it was only from their ignorance.

I am also sending a letter to Sharīf Pāshā and another letter to Abdallāh Pāshā Fikrī, and I call them to give testimony and greetings.

Appendix III

Persian Letter from Jamāl ad-Dīn from St. Petersburg to Amīn as-Sultān, the chief minister of Iran, January 1 [1889].[1]

[HONORIFIC GREETING.] You of course remember the conversation that occurred on the way to [the shrine of] 'Abd al-'Azīm, and what I said and what you said. Thus, if someone by vain imaginings or fantasy should claim to have divined that, had God not taken mercy, I would have set fire to the ash heap of Iran, and turned the ruins of that country upside down, and created chaos in that world of disorder—then indeed he would have erred in his divination.

I came to Iran (by Royal request) and traveled from the Persian Gulf to the Caspian Sea. When I set foot on the ship [from Iran] and shed the dust of that abode of grief from my feet, except for the gifts of Your Excellency and the hospitality of Hājji Muhammad Hasan [Amīn az-Zarb], God praise him, I did not find myself obligated for anything else. Thus, if a rude ghoul talks nonsense (as he did and wrote in the French-[language] newspaper *Iran* some months ago) and says that positively and certainly my religion and worship are the dirham and the dinar [i.e., money], undoubtedly his observation will not be heeded even among the lowest classes of humanity, not to mention the highest ranks of them. (Yes, what is a friend and

---

1 From Ṣafā'ī, *Asnād*, pp. 249–255. The letter from Amīn as Sulṭān to which this is an answer has not been unearthed. Thanks to Amin Banani for checking this translation.

what a stranger to a mad dog?) Thus we must disregard these two subjects.

I do not consider the one there [the Shah] higher than Musta'sim, the Abbasid, and the one who is here [the Tsar] I do not consider lower than Hulagu [the Mongol conqueror of Iran]. I am not in their world. Naturally, I would like to instigate all the unbelievers of the world and encourage them to force those who cover themselves with the raiment of Islam to be Muslims in at least one part of their religion which concerns the rights of the public, that is, the standard of justice and rightful law. For the rest they can be what they wish until the Day of Hellfire, because that is their private affair, and its harm accrues to themselves. I have no goal except this public goal. Thus, if a dim-witted man calls me the partisan of such-and-such, or considers me the enemy of so-and-so, the story was made up by him. The subject is complex and the details require proof. Thus, if this letter is prolonged, you will forgive me.

The order of the kingdom (i.e., the government) rests on the orderly administration of villages and towns, and their orderly administration is not achievable without a sound outlook, and the foundations of a sound outlook are the integrity of behavior and the moderation of ethics of individuals. This is the chain that connects the order of kingdoms by the firmness of its links. The firmness of behavior of its individuals and the zeal and moderation of their ways are their various foundations. Either [1] [the kingdom's individuals'] souls must by nature be so noble that they naturally shun base matters and mean things, and by nature choose to shun oppression, injustice, transgression on rights, and violence; or else [2] they must have a comprehensive reason that can, by means of comprehension of the fundamental interests of souls, restrain them from their transitory self-interest and vain passions; or else [3] [they must have] a very firm faith that forces every one of them to [observe] the rules of right and justice by means of fetters and chains of desires and fears, and makes firm the foundations of domestic relations. When one of these three exists, disorder inevitably will occur in domestic societies, and their disorder causes corruption in the order of administration of towns and villages, and corruption of the order of administration causes the pillars of the kingdom to shake, and finally will bring about its decline.

When decline becomes known, it is a decisive proof of the cause of decline. Thus every intelligent man can judge from the weakness of Muslim governments, the ruin of their kingdoms, and the afflicted state of the Muslims that most of the souls of Muslims are devoid of those threefold foundations. Therefore they consider permissible all things deserving to be shunned, and find all forbidden acts licit, and always count abominable and shameful acts as ordinary affairs. They believe calumny and lying to be intelligence, and take pride in oppression and tyranny (like Ahriman, the God of evil among the Zoroastrians). They are distant from every good and are the source of all evils. For example, if someone chooses to remain distant from one of these recent Muslims, or does not greet or pay homage to him, that latter-day Muslim considers it licit to cast every sort of calumny upon that unfortunate man and to stir up the fires of every sort of trouble; and the fire of his anger will not be quelled until he achieves the killing and ruin of that man's family, without his regretting it in the least. Rather, he is proud of it, and is constantly saying, "Did you see what I did to so-and-so, and how I burned him and ruined his household, because one day he did not show respect to me, as was proper?" Of course you remember what things Sanīʿ ad-Dauleh [Iʿtimād as-Saltaneh] and those like him wove and spoke about me in order to gain a little access to Your Excellency, and they were proud of it.

After this lengthy introduction, perhaps I may be permitted to say that the three-cornered mirror that in this country reflects the shape of Iran to the world, because of its essential shortcomings, owing to numerous fractures in it, reflects a group of inverted and disfigured forms, and since there is no opportunity in the world of politics to perform good service, one engages in lies and falsehoods. Some months ago I heard that some calumnies about me were spread in the Abode of the Caliphate [Tehran], but at that time I did not wish to exculpate myself, since in the presence of those imbued with vain imaginings, fantasies, and falsehoods to speak of purity is unwise. Recently I heard that he [Iʿtimād as-Saltaneh] has again published some untruths. Since Your Excellency is involved in it, I thought it necessary to explain the truth. I have of course been involved in some way in this present affair in what relates to public interest and general policy. But I have had absolutely no hand in what pertains to individuals—particularly pertaining to the person of Your Excellency, whom, because of your innate sense, I consider the greatest man I have ever encountered. I have developed such a love in my heart for your luminous person that I do not think it could be effaced even by unkindness from you. I myself do not know the reason and motive for this love. Since these words come from a contented heart, I believe that they are a proof of my truthfulness.

Since some neophytes in the arena of politics have been saying and writing (in *Akhtar*) that His Majesty the Shah and Your Excellency consider the Government of Russia as the implacable foe of the Government of Iran, undoubtedly this will arouse Russian rancor and enmity, and the dangerous results of that are self-evident. Therefore, I intervened everywhere, especially on behalf of Your Excellency, and everywhere I said: "Neither His Majesty the Shah, nor the statesmen in his government have this idea, especially not Amīn as-Sultān, who is too wise to be content with such false reports." In sum, because of immaturity and vanity they sowed this sinister idea in the heart of the Russians, May God deliver us.

In your letter you wrote that you will make Mīrzā Abū Turāb Sāvajī the object of your favor. Thousands of thanks and praises to you. I know that your word is absolute truth, and therefore I am confident. I hope that you will send an answer to this letter.

Greetings to you and to those who are upright in their love for you.

Your true friend, and possibly even a martyr to your friendship,

Jamāl ad-Dīn al-Husainī

Appendix IV

Undated Turkish letter from Jamāl ad-Dīn, Istanbul, to Sultan Abdülhamid, ca. 1895–96.[1]

THE GRIEF and disappointment of my heart, which was confident that the rights of Islam, which are attacked from all sides by its enemies, would in future be protected by the sacred existence of Your Majesty; and the trouble of my mind, which is occupied with achieving means of making known to the entire world my conviction that the entire Islamic world on this globe can be secure from aggression by taking recourse to Your Majesty's protection; and the fact that my eyes, which are burning to see as soon as possible Your Majesty's lucky star shine over the whole world, are now being exposed to insulting treatment—all these are circumstances that can in no way be given favorable interpretation. My person, which takes pleasure in enduring the heaviest burdens and the bitterest calamities for the sake of the well-being of Islam, cannot endure even the slightest insult. For, when a person who has generally received respect and honor all over the world because of his honest character and personal virtues is insulted at the center of the Caliphate—this the Caliphal Majesty himself can in no way condone. Because, before I had any thought of coming here and before I had seen, and been enthralled by, Your Majesty's shining face, it had already been one of my religious commitments to defend and

[1] Turkey, Başbakanlık Archives, Istanbul, Yıldız Collection, MS 1103. Thanks to Andreas Tietze for this translation.

extol both Your Imperial Highness and the Caliphal office itself. The articles that I wrote at the time of my stay in Europe for all the newspapers of Paris and of Russia as well as for the periodical *al-'Urwa al-Wuthqā* which I published myself, are strong evidence that I always revered Your Caliphal Majesty with deepest sincerity. As for the reason why I never submitted these articles which I had adorned with Your Caliphal Majesty's praise to Your Caliphal Station: it was my intention not to try like some low-minded, base-hearted ones to demonstrate a hypocritical and feigned adherence to Your Royal Person and to enhance their importance in the eyes of the Sovereign, or to impress You by means of imaginary and artificial concerns like a desert ghost. Of all these dishonest acts I wish to be free and wish to prove through my personal honor and spiritual and material virtues that I am Your sincere, faithful, and earnest well-wisher. Alas, I failed in this. I had offered my soul as to be a cutting sword like Haidar's "Zulfikar" in Your Caliphal hands to be used against internal and external enemies. But it was not accepted. When I received the Caliphal edict ordering me to submit and expound my humble opinion concerning the possibilities of a unification of (the word of) Islam, I felt happiness as if the eight gates of Paradise had been opened to me, and I wrote down a summary of my humble opinion on this subject in accordance with Your High Imperial order and submitted it to the Caliphal threshold. Since not a word concerning this matter has been uttered until now, I have unfortunately arrived at the conclusion that the project has been thrown into the corner of oblivion or that it has been burned by the fire of malice of partial and malicious persons, or its contents were misinterpreted by latter-day wise men so as to diverge from its sublime intention and it was consequently lodged among subversive literature. Not only that, when recently the correspondents of the *Times* came to see me and Mr. Garacino mentioned in my presence certain words concerning Your Caliphal Highness, which he had heard from the British ambassador, Mehmed Bey, who was present, reported faithfully to Your Caliphal Majesty both the words that Mr. Garacino had said he had heard from the British ambassador and my sincere speech in defense [of the Sultan] in response to them.

But the matter acquired the opposite character owing to certain intrigues, and, in contrast to the real facts of the matter, I seemed to have committed a sin by my fervent and sincere defense, as I could not have done better for a real and beloved son, and I was rewarded by the insult of an interrogation. Happily it became known in the end when Garacino was confronted with Mehmed Bey in the presence of Ragib Bey how I had defended with all my heart Your Caliphal Majesty's interests, and the truth became known to Your Imperial Highness. Garacino's notorious malevolence and greed, and possibly also a subversive secret instruction, and—since he is English—the enmity of the English against state and nation in general and against my person in particular were noted. Hence, Garacino, when summoned alone would—was there any doubt?—disavow his own words and would attribute his despicable utterances to someone else. Would it not have been necessary for the quick clarification of these facts to have started, as the first thing, with the confrontation that was done last? In order for me not to be subjected to the punishment of an interrogation instead of the reward of being applauded and, in order to not give new opportunities to my enemies and evil-wishers to spread the news, "Jamāl ad-Dīn has been interrogated and this and that has been done to him." The more I think of how inappropriately the matter has been handled—never can I ascribe this scandalous misprocedure to the wisdom of the Caliph, the successor of God's Prophet. But what can I do against those intriguers and slanderers who have access to every heart and mind? God give me patience! I have not the slightest doubt that these cruel Yazids and these tyrannical Shimrs like the robbers of Kufa and Damascus will continue until the last moment to weave their hundreds of intrigues against me. Of course, with the help of God it is the easiest thing for me to hang the ruses of these intrigues on their own necks like necklaces of damnation. As God Almighty has made my heart free from aspirations of rank and glory and from the love of glitter and pomp and as God Almighty has created me as I am but devoted to serve the world of Islam, it is clearly forbidden for me to waste my time with the hallucinations and futilities of base individuals. Every intelligent person will admit that Your Sacred Caliphal Highness will not suffer that I lose my time and vital energy for the undignified and trifling occupation with the calumniations of these people here, and that, consequently, You will accelerate Your gracious permission for my leaving, seeing that my departure is preferable. Since it is impossible to live among people who do not know the fear of God and who do not refrain from intrigues like fabrication, lies, incitement, in order to shun (to render fruitless) the services and acts of loyalty of those who are really and unselfishly devoted to Your Caliphal Highness—on the one hand do I know that our Lord, Your Caliphal Majesty, does not agree to these matters, on the other hand do I not wish to be the cause [for Your Majesty] thus to be bothered needlessly all the time, for I fully understand that my adversaries who are completely at agreement will not only prevent me from rendering any service to Your Caliphal Majesty but also will not be ashamed of bothering Your Majesty at all times because of me. A few days ago when certain Imperial wishes were communicated to me through Your servant Ragib Bey, You had announced to me the good news that permission for my departure was forthcoming. I therefore request that Imperial permission be given as it had been announced and that thus this humble servant without delay be made happy and grateful. For Your Majesty's perspicacity will at once admit that it has become completely impossible for me to stay here, being exposed to humiliations generated by void and fabricated rumors which are being spread every other day and which confuse the minds of people. And whenever a firman is given I shall—there can be no doubt—obey Your Majesty and come, and wherever I shall be staying abroad, I shall always be ready to satisfy the Caliph. Should Your Caliphal Highness direct Your attention to the ilk of evil-wishers and intriguers who exist here, and should You notice that their entire activity consists of base intrigues, then—I have no doubt—will You agree all the sooner to my departure. All I request from our Caliphal Majesty is that I shall receive permission to leave, the sooner the better, by the love of God so that my ears may not hear these things that are completely unheard of in the world and that my heart not be broken by these intrigues and that I may depart sincerely praying for our Caliph. I commend to God the protection of the Caliphal person, this light in the eyes of the inhabitants of the world who has been assigned by God the task of preserving the rights of God's servants (the community) from attacks.

The one who prays for You, Jamāl ad-Dīn al-Husainī

Chronology of Jamāl ad-Dīn

Probable Dates

1838–39 (1254 A.H.)	Born in Asadabad, Iran
Ca. 1848	Leaves Asadabad for Qazvin with father
Ca. 1850	Leaves Qazvin for Tehran
Ca. 1852	Leaves Tehran for holy cities (specifically Najaf in Iraq)
1856 (1272 A.H.)	To Bushehr
Beginning in 1856 or 1857	To India for between a year plus a few months and four years
1861?to 1865	Slow trip to Iran via Mecca, Iraq, and possibly Istanbul

Definite Dates

Mid-December 1865 to late spring 1866	In Tehran; probably prior trip to Asadabad
October 1866	Begins forty days in Herat, Afghanistan, arriving via Northeast Iran

December 1866–July 1867	In Qandahar
Late October 1867	Reaches Kabul after stopover in Ghazni
November 1868	Expelled from Afghanistan, leaves Kabul
December 1868	Leaves Qandahar, Afghanistan, for Bombay, India
March–April 1869	In Bombay
July 1869	To Cairo for forty days
Late summer 1869–early spring 1871	In Istanbul; expelled owing to talk in Darülfunun in November–December 1870 (Ramadan 1287)
April–May 1871 (Muḥarram 1287)	Reaches Cairo
1878–79	Writes newspaper articles and *History of Afghanistan*
August 1879	Expelled from Egypt
Late 1879 to November 1882	Reaches Bombay, then to Hyderabad, Calcutta. Publishes Persian articles and "Refutation of the Materialists"
November 1882	Leaves India
December 1882	Stopover in boat at Suez Canal; writes letters to Riyāḍ, others
January 1883	Brief stay in London; meets Wilfrid S. Blunt
Mid-January 1883–July 1885	In Paris
May 18, 1883	Publishes "Answer to Renan"
1884	Publishes *al-'Urwa al-Wuthqā*
July–November 1885	Guest at Blunt's house, London
Early spring 1886	Probable date of departure from London for Bushehr
May–August 1886	Bushehr
Late 1886	Reaches Tehran, arriving via Shiraz and Isfahan
Ca. April 1887	Leaves Iran on Shah's request; goes to Russia
May 1887	Reaches Moscow; stays some months
February 1888 (or sooner)–Mid 1889	In St. Petersburg
August 1889	In Munich, then back to Russia

November 1889	In outskirts of Tehran
December 1889–July 1890	In Tehran
July 1890–January 1891	In refuge at Shāhzādeh 'Abd al-'Azīm
January 1891	Expelled from Iran, via Kermanshah
February 1891	In Kermanshah
March 1891–summer 1891	In Baghdad and Basra, Ottoman Iraq
Autumn 1891–early summer 1892	In London
Summer 1892–March 1897	In Istanbul
March 9, 1897	Dies in Istanbul

Bibliography

In this bibliography are listed only works that have been used substantially. For a more complete and detailed bibliography, see A. Albert Kudsi-Zadeh, *Sayyid Jamāl ad-Dīn al-Afghānī: An Annotated Bibliography* (Leiden, 1970).

Items containing significant primary material or analysis of Afghānī are starred.

Unpublished Documents

Browne, Edward G. Correspondence with Mīrzā Āqā Khān Kirmānī. *Oriental Manuscripts,* vol. 60. Edward G. Browne collection. Cambridge University Library. Cambridge, England.

France. Archives du Ministère des Affaires Étrangères. Perse, 1888–*1896.

Gladstone, William Ewart. "Gladstone Papers." British Museum Add. MS. 44,110. Vol. XXV, 1885.

*Great Britain. Commonwealth Relations Office. Government of India, Foreign Department. *Narrative of Events in Cabul from the Death of Dost Mahomed to the Spring of 1872. . . . Cabul Précis 1863–74.* Simla, 1866, 1874.

*Great Britain. Commonwealth Relations Office. Government of India, Foreign Department. *Proceedings of the Government of India in the Foreign Department, Political.* Calcutta, 1869; "Cabul Diary," Feb., April, Sept.–Dec., 1868, and Jan., 1869.

*Great Britain. Commonwealth Relations Office. Government of India, Foreign Department. *Political and Secret Home Correspondence.* 1882, vol. 51, and 1887, vols. 93–98.

Great Britain. Commonwealth Relations Office. Government of India, Foreign Department. *Political and Secret Demi-Official Correspondence.* 1887–1891.

Great Britain. Public Record Office. Documents in the following series: *F.O. 60: original dispatches to and from Persia, especially *F.O. 60/594: Djemal ed-din: Proceedings of, and expulsion from Persia, 1883–1897. F.O. 65: original dispatches to and from Russia. *F.O. 78: original dispatches to and from Egypt. *F.O. 248: archives of the British Embassy in Tehran. F.O. 539: Correspondence Relating to Afghanistan, Persia and Turkestan.

*Malkum Khān Manuscripts, Bibliotheque Nationale, Paris, Supplement Persan, no. 1995 (containing two letters from Abū al-Hudā to Afghānī, 1892); Supplement Persan, no. 1996 (correspondence of Mīrzā Āqā Khān Kirmānī with Malkum Khān).

Paris. Préfecture de Police. File, "Cheik Djemal Eddin el Afghan ou Gemmal Eddin." E/116.

*Sayyid Jamāl ad-Dīn al-Afghānī's Personal Books and Papers. Majlis Library. Tehran, Iran. (Catalogued in Afshār and Madhavī, eds., *Documents;* reference given below.)

*Turkey. Başbakanlik Archives, Istanbul. Yıldız Collection. MS 1103.

United States. National Archives. Washington, D.C.

Books and Articles by Sayyid Jamāl ad-Dīn al-Afghānī

*al-Afghānī on Types of Despotic Government," trans. L. M. Kenny, *Journal of the American Oriental Society,* 86, 1 (1966) , 19–27. Trans. of "al-Ḥukūma al-istibdādiyya," *Miṣr,* II, 33 (Feb. 15, 1879); reprinted in *al-Manār,* III (Nov. 14, 1900), 601–607.

*"An Afghan on the English," *The Bee/an-Naḥla* (London; English and Arabic), Dec. 15, 1878. (Partial translation of one of Afghānī's articles in *Miṣr*).

*"Les Anglais en Égypte," *La Justice* (Paris), March 27, 1883. (Reprinted in Pakdaman, "Notes sur le séjour. . . ."; see reference below.)

"Answer to Renan" (Réponse à Renan). See *Réfutation des matérialistes.*

**Ārā' va mu'taqadāt-i Sayyid Jamāl ad-Dīn Afghānī.* Ed. Murtazā Mudarrisī Chahārdihī. Tehran 1337/1958–59. (Includes Afghānī's Persian articles and the text of the "Refutation of the Materialists.")

*Articles in *al-Baṣīr* (Paris; Arabic), nos. 66, 67, 68, 74, 75, 77, and 78 (Feb. 8, 15, 22; April 5, 12, 26; and May 3, 1883).

*Articles in *Ḍiyā' al-Khāfiqain (Eastern and Western Review)* (London), I (1892). (Arabic-English journal, at the British Museum.)

*"Falsafat at-tarbiyya" and "Falsafat aṣ-ṣinā'a." In Muḥammad Rashīd Riḍā, *Tārīkh al-ustādh al-imām ash-shaikh Muḥammad 'Abduh.* Vol. II. Cairo, 1344/1925–6, pp. 2–14. (Talks by Jamāl ad-Dīn recorded by 'Abduh).

**Ḥaqīqat-i mazhab-i naichirī va bayān-ī ḥāl-i naichiriyyān.* Hyderabad, 1298/1881. Original Persian ed. ("Refutation of the Materialists," Majlis Library, Tehran.) Another edition, Tehran, 1303/1924–25.

*"al-'Illa al-ḥaqīqiyya li sa'ādat al-insān, *Miṣr,* II, 20 (Nov. 15, 1878); also reprinted in *al-Manār,* XXIII (Jan. 28, 1922), 37–45.

*"Lettre sur l'Hindoustan," *L'Intransigeant* (Paris), April 24, 1883. (Reprinted in Kedourie, *Afghani and 'Abduh,* and in Pakdaman, "Notes sur le séjour . . . ," both cited below.)

*"Le Mahdi," *L'Intransigeant* (Paris), Dec. 8, 11, 17, 1883. (Reprinted in Kedourie, *Afghani and 'Abduh,* and in Pakdaman, "Notes sur le séjour. . . ."

**Maqālāt-i Jamāliyyeh.* Ed. Ṣifātallāh Jamālī Asadābādī. Tehran, 1312/1933–34.

**Miṣr* articles. Articles and speeches printed or referred to in *Miṣr* (Alexandria), II: 16 (Oct. ?, 1878), 20 (Nov. 15, 1878), 21 (Nov. 22, 1878), 23 (Dec. 6, 1878), 26 (Dec. 26, 1878), 28 (Jan. 9, 1879), 33 (Feb. 14, 1879), 43 April 25, 1879), and 47 (May 24, 1879).

*Articles in *Mu'allim-i shafīq* (Hyderabad), nos. 1–10, Dec., 1880–Oct., 1881. (Persian journal, in Majlis Library, Tehran.)

"Nāmeh-yi Sayyid Jamāl ad-Dīn Asadābādī," Āyandeh (Tehran), II, 5–6 (1927), 395–401. An Arabic version of this letter appeared under the title "Ra'y ḥakīm sharqī," in *al-Muqtaṭaf* (Cairo), 66, 5 (May, 1925), 493–496.

*"Pages choisies de Djamal ad-Din al-Afghani." Trans. M. Colombe, *Orient,* 21 (1962), 89–109; 22 (1962), 125–159; 23 (1962), 169–219; 24 (1962), 125–151; and 25 (1963), 141–152.

*"Pages peu connues de Djamal ad-Din al-Afghani," trans. Mehdi Hendessi, *Orient,* 6 (1958), 123–128.

**al-Radd 'ala al-dahriyyīn.* Trans. into Arabic from the Persian by Muḥammad 'Abduh [and Abū Turāb]. New ed. Cairo, 1955.

**Réfutation des matérialistes.* Trans. A.–M. Goichon. Paris, 1942. (Includes "Réponse à Renan," from *Journal des Débats,* May 18, 1883, and a partial translation of the article "Les matérialistes dans l'Inde.") See Nikki R. Keddie, *An Islamic Response to Imperialism* for an English translation of the "Refutation" and several articles.

*"The Reign of Terror in Persia," *Contemporary Review* (Feb. 1892, pp. 238–248.
*"ash-Sharq wa ash-Sharqiyyīn," *Abū Nazzāra Zarqā'* (Paris), VII, 2, Feb. 9, 1883.
*"as-Siyāsa al-injlīziyya fī al-mamālik ash-Sharqiyya" and "Asbāb al-ḥarb bi Miṣr," *al-Manār*, XXV, (March 25, 1925), 756–760. (Reprinted from
**Tatimmat al-bayān fī tārīkh al-Afghān*. Ed. 'Alī Yusūf al-Kirīdlī. Cairo, 1901.
The Bee/an-Naḥla, V, 3 [London, ca. 1883].)
*Co-authored with Muḥammad 'Abduh. *al-'Urwa al-Wuthqā*. Cairo, 1958. Originally published as a periodical in Paris, 1884. (Original ed. Public Record Office, London, F.O. 78/3682.)

Newspapers and Journals

(Unless otherwise indicated, the language of Oriental-language items is that of the country of publication.)

**Abu Naddara Zarka (Abū Nazzara Zarqā')* (Paris; Arabic), Jan., and Feb., 1883. Several issues contain items by or concerning Afghānī.
**al-Baṣīr* (Paris; Arabic), 1883.
**Basiret* (Istanbul), no. 232, 13 Ramadan 1287/Dec. 7, 1870. (In Majlis Library, Tehran.)
al-Hilāl (Cairo), 1897.
**al-Jawā'ib* (Istanbul; Arabic), no. 484, 20 Ramadan 1287/Dec. 14, 1870. (In Majlis Library, Tehran.)
Journal des Débats (Paris), 1883.
Kābul (Kabul; Persian), Dec. 1939–Jan. 1940.
**Levant Times* (Istanbul), Nov. 15, 26, Dec. 8, 10, 1870.
**al-Manār* (Cairo), Vols. I–XXXIV (1900–1934).
Manchester Guardian, Dec. 18, 1891.
**Miṣr*. (Alexandria), 1878–1879.
Le Monde Maçonnique (Paris), 1867–1882.
**Pall Mall Gazette* (London), Dec. 19, 30, 1891.
Paris, Dec. 3, 5, and 12, 1884.
**Qānūn* (London; Persian), 1890–1896. (Cambridge University Library, Cambridge, England.)
**Sirāj al-Akhbār* (Kabul; Persian), VI, nos. 3, 5 (1916).
**Le Temps* (Paris) , May 6, 7, 8, 9, 16, 26, June 14, 1896.
**The Times* (London), Aug. 30 and Sept. 8, 1879.
Türk Yurdu (Istanbul), I (1327–28/1911–12), 200–201.
**La Turquie* (Istanbul), Dec. 9, 1870.

Books in Western Languages

Abdel-Malek, Anouar. *Anthologie de la littérature arabe contemporaine.* Paris, 1965.
———. *Idéologie et renaissance nationale: L'Egypte moderne.* Paris, 1969.
*'Abduh, Muḥammad. *Rissalat al Tawhid.* Trans. B. Michel and M. Abdel Razik. Paris, 1925.
Adams, Charles C. *Islam and Modernism in Egypt.* London, 1933.
Afnan, Soheil M. *Avicenna, His Life and Works.* London, 1958.
Ahmad, Aziz. *Islamic Modernism in India and Pakistan 1857–1964.* London, 1967.
———. *Studies in Islamic Culture in the Indian Environment.* Oxford, 1964.
Ahmed, Jamal Mohammed. *The Intellectual Origins of Egyptian Nationalism.* London, 1960.
*Alexander, J. *The Truth about Egypt.* London, 1911.
Algar. Hamid. *Religion and State in Iran 1785–1906.* Berkeley and Los Angeles, 1969.
Ameer Ali, Syed. *The Spirit of Islam.* London, 1922.
Amin, Osman ('Uthmān Amīn). *Muhammad 'Abduh.* Trans. from the Arabic by Charles Wendell. Washington, D. C., 1953.
———. *Muhammad 'Abduh: Essai sur ses idées philosophiques et religieuses.* Cairo, 1944.
Anonymous. *Eminent Mussalmans.* Madras, 1926.
Averroes (Ibn Rushd). *Averroes' Tahafut al-Tahahfut.* Trans. and ed. S. van den Bergh. London, 1954.
———. *On the Harmony of Religion and Philosophy.* Trans. and ed. George F. Hourani. London, 1961.
Avery, Peter. *Modern Iran.* London, 1965.
Avicenna (Ibn Sīnā). *Avicenna on Theology.* Trans. A. J. Arberry, London, 1951.
———. Livre des directives et remarques (*Kitāb al-išārāt wa al-tanbīhāt*). Trans., intro., and notes by A.-M. Goichon. Beirut and Paris, 1951.
Baljon, J. M. S. *The Reforms and Religious Ideas of Sir Sayyid Ahmad Khan.* Leiden, 1949.
Bary, William T. de, ed. *Sources of Indian Tradition.* New York, 1958.
Bausani, Alessandro. *Persia religiosa.* Milan, 1959.
*Berkes, Niyazi. *The Development of Secularism in Turkey.* Montreal, 1964.

Binder, Leonard. *The Ideological Revolution in the Middle East.* New York, 1964.
———. *Religion and Politics in Pakistan.* Berkeley and Los Angeles, 1961.
Blunt, Wilfrid S. *Gordon at Khartoum.* London, 1912.
———. *India under Ripon.* London, 1909.
———. *My Diaries.* London, 1919–20. 2 vols. Single vol. ed., London, 1932.
———. *Secret History of the English Occupation of Egypt.* London, 1907. New ed., New York, 1922.
Brockelmann, Carl. *Geschichte der arabischen Litteratur.* Leiden, 1937–1949. Supplements II and III.
Browne, Edward G. *Materials for the Study of the Bābī Religion.* Cambridge, 1918.
*———. *The Persian Revolution 1905–1909.* Cambridge, 1910.
———. *A Traveller's Narrative: Written to Illustrate the Episode of the Bāb.* Cambridge, 1891, 2 vols.
———. *A Year among the Persians.* London, 1893.
Churchill, Winston Spencer. *Lord Randolph Churchill.* London, 1952.
Corbin, Henry. *Avicenna and the Visionary Recital.* Trans. Willard R. Trask. New York, 1960.
Cottam, Richard W. *Nationalism in Iran.* Pittsburgh, 1964.
Cromer, Lord (Evelyn Baring). *Modern Egypt.* London, 1908. 2 vols.
Curzon, George N. *Persia and the Persian Question.* London, 1892. 2 vols.
Davison, Roderic. *Reform in the Ottoman Empire, 1856–1876.* Princeton, 1963.
Douin, G. *Histoire du règne du Khédive Ismaīl.* Rome, 1933–1941. 3 vols.
Encyclopaedia of Islam. Leiden and London, 1913–1938; new ed., 1960——.
Fabunmi, L. A. *The Sudan in Anglo-Egyptian Relations, 1800–1956.* London, 1960.
al-Fārābī. *Alfarabi's Philosophy of Plato and Aristotle.* Trans. and intro. by Muhsin Mahdi. New York, 1962.
———. *Fuṣūl al-Madanī: Aphorisms of the Statesmen.* Trans., ed., intro., and notes by D. M. Dunlop. Cambridge, 1961.
Faruqi, Ziya-ul-Hasan. *The Deoband School and the Demand for Pakistan.* London, 1963.
Feuvrier, Dr. (Jean-Baptiste). *Trois ans à la cour de Perse.* New ed. Paris, 1906.
Gardet, Louis. *La Pensée religieuse d'Avicenne.* Paris, 1951.
Gendzier, Irene L. *The Practical Visions of Ya'qub Sanu'.* Cambridge, Mass., 1966.
al-Ghazālī. *The Confessions of al Ghazzali.* Trans. Claud Field. London, 1909.
Gibb, H. A. R. *Modern Trends in Islam.* Chicago, 1947.
Gobineau, Count Arthur de. *Les Religions et les philosophies dans l'Asie centrale.* 9th ed. Paris, 1957.
*Gordon, Sir Thomas Edward. *Persia Revisited.* London, 1896.
Gould, Robert F. *The History of Freemasonry.* New York, 1885–1889. 4 vols.
———. *Gould's History of Freemasonry.* Vol. IV. Rev. by Rev. Herbert Poole. London, 1951.

Greaves, Rose Louise. *Persia and the Defence of India, 1884–1892*. London, 1959.
Guizot, François Pierre Guillaume. *History of Civilization in Europe*. Trans. William Hazlitt. New York, n.d.
Habberton, William. *Anglo-Russian Relations concerning Afghanistan, 1837–1907*. Urbana, Ill., 1937.
*Haim, Sylvia, ed. *Arab Nationalism*. Berkeley and Los Angeles, 1962.
Hanna, H. B. *The Second Afghan War*. Vol. I. London, 1899.
Harris, Christina Phelps. *Nationalism and Revolution in Egypt*. The Hague, 1964.
Hartmann, Martin. *The Arabic Press of Egypt*. London, 1899.
Hodgson, M. G. S. *The Order of the Assassins*. The Hague, 1955.
Holt, P. M. *The Mahdist State in the Sudan, 1881–1898*. Oxford, 1958.
*Hourani, Albert. *Arabic Thought in the Liberal Age, 1798–1939*. London, 1962.
Hunter, W. W. *The Indian Musalmans: Are They Bound in Conscience To Rebel against the Queen?* London, 1871.
Husain, Mahmud, et al., eds. *A History of the Freedom Movement*. Vols. I and II, pts. 1 and 2. Karachi, 1957–1961.
Iqbal, Sir Muhammad. *Javid-nama*. Trans. A. J. Arberry. London, 1966.
Kazemzadeh, Firuz. *Russia and Britain in Persia 1864–1914*. New Haven, 1968.
*Keddie, Nikki R. *An Islamic Response to Imperialism: Political and Religious Writings of Sayyid Jamāl ad-Dīn "al-Afghānī."* Berkeley and Los Angeles, 1968.
*———. *Religion and Rebellion in Iran: The Tobacco Protest of 1891–92*. London, 1966.
*Kedourie, Elie. *Afghani and 'Abduh: An Essay on Religious Unbelief and Political Activism in Modern Islam*. London, 1966.
Kerr, Malcolm H. *Islamic Reform: The Political and Legal Theories of Muḥammad 'Abduh and Rashīd Riḍā*. Berkeley and Los Angeles, 1966.
Khadduri, Majid. *War and Peace in the Law of Islam*. Baltimore, 1955.
Kirkpatrick, F. A. *Lectures on the History of the 19th Century*. Cambridge, 1904.
*Kosogovskii, V. A. *Iz tegeranskogo dnevnika polkovnika V. A. Kosogovskogo*. Moscow, 1960.
*Kudsi-Zadeh, A. Albert. "The Legacy of Sayyid Jamāl al-Dīn al-Afghānī in Egypt." Unpublished Ph.D. dissertation, Indiana University. Bloomington, 1964. (Available from University Microfilms, Inc., Ann Arbor, Michigan.)
*———. *Sayyid Jamāl al-Dīn al-Afghānī: An Annotated Bibliography*. Leiden, 1970.
Lambton, Ann K. S. *Islamic Society in Persia*. London, 1954.
Landau, Jacob. *Parliaments and Parties in Egypt*. Tel Aviv, 1953.
Landes, David S. *Bankers and Pashas*. Cambridge, Mass., 1958.
Laoust, Henri. *Essai sur les doctrines sociales et politiques de Taḳī-d-Dīn Aḥmad b. Taimīya, canoniste ḥanbalite, né à Ḥarrān en 661–1262, mort à Damas en 728/1328*. Cairo, 1939.

Lasswell, Harold. *Psychopathology and Politics.* New ed. New York, 1960.
Lerner, Ralph, and Muhsin Mahdi, eds. *Medieval Political Philosophy.* Toronto, 1963.
Lewis, Bernard. *The Emergence of Modern Turkey.* London, 1961.
———. *The Middle East and the West.* London, 1964.
Long, Col. C. Chaillé. *The Three Prophets.* New York, 1884.
Lutfi al-Sayyid, Afaf. *Egypt and Cromer: A Study in Anglo-Egyptian Relations.* London, 1968.
Mackey, Albert G. *Encyclopedia of Freemasonry.* Chicago, 1929. 2 vols.
Mahdi, Muhsin. *Ibn Khaldûn's Philosophy of History.* London, 1957.
Mahomed Khan, Mir Munshi Sultan, ed. *The Life of Abdur Rahman, Amir of Afghanistan.* Vol. I. London, 1900.
Malet, Edward. *Egypt, 1879–1883.* London, 1909.
Mardin, Şerif. *The Genesis of Young Ottoman Thought.* Princeton, 1962.
Marlowe, John. *Anglo-Egyptian Relations, 1800–1953.* London, 1954.
*al-Mujāhid, Sharīf. "Sayyid Jamāl al-Dīn al-Afghānī: His Role in the Nineteenth Century Muslim Awakening." Unpublished M.A. thesis, McGill University. Montreal, 1954.
Nasr, Seyyed Hossein. *Three Muslim Sages.* Cambridge, Mass., 1964.
Nicolas, A. L. M. *Le Beyan arabe de Seyyed Ali Mohammed.* Paris, 1905.
———. *Le Beyan persan.* Paris, 1911–1914. 4 vols.
———. *Essai sur le Cheikhisme.* Paris, 1910.
———. *Seyyed Al Mohammed, dit le Bab.* Paris, 1905.
Ninet, John. *Arabi Pacha.* Berne, 1884.
Novikoff, Olga. *The M. P. for Russia: Reminiscences and Correspondence of Madame Olga Novikoff, 1878–1908.* Vol. II. London, 1909.
Ohrwalder, Father Joseph. *Ten Years' Captivity in the Mahdi's Camp.* London, 1892.
*Pakdaman, Homa. *Djamal-ed-Din Assad Abadi dit Afghani.* Paris, 1969.
Philipp, Mangol Bayat. "Mīrzā Āqā Khān Kirmānī: Nineteenth-Century Persian Revolutionary Thinker." Unpublished Ph.D. dissertation. University of California, Los Angeles, 1971.
Rahman, F. *Prophecy in Islam: Philosophy and Orthodoxy.* London, 1958.
Razi, G. H. "Religion and Politics in Iran: A Study of Social Dynamics." Unpublished Ph.D. dissertation, University of California. Berkeley, 1954.
Renan, Ernest. *L'Islamisme et la science.* Paris, 1883.
*———. *Oeuvres complètes.* Vol. I. Paris, 1947.
*Rochefort, Henri (Henri du Rochefort-Luçay). *The Adventures of My Life.* Trans. E. W. Smith and H. Rochefort. London, 1897. 2 vols.
Rodinson, Maxime. *Islam et capitalisme.* Paris, 1966.
Rosenthal, E. I. J. *Political Thought in Medieval Islam.* Cambridge, 1958.
Sabry, M. *L'empire égyptien sous Ismail et l'ingérence Anglo-Française (1863–1879).* Paris, 1933.
*———. *La genèse de l'esprit national égyptien (1863–1882).* Paris, 1924.
*Safran, Nadav. *Egypt in Search of a Political Community.* Cambridge, Mass., 1961.
Sammarco, A. *Histoire de l'Egypte moderne.* Vol. III. Cairo, 1937.

Sayyid Aḥmad Khān (Syed Ahmad Khan Bahadur). *Review on Dr. Hunter's Indian Musalmans.* Benares, 1872.
———. *Essay on the Question whether Islam has been Beneficial or Injurious to Human Society in General and to the Mosaic and Christian Dispensations.* Lahore, 1954.
Sharabi, Hisham. *Arab Intellectuals and the West: The Formative Years 1875–1914.* Baltimore, 1970.
Sharif, M. M., ed. *A History of Muslim Philosophy.* Wiesbaden, 1963, 1966. 2 vols.
Shibeika, Mekki. *British Policy in the Sudan, 1882–1902.* London, 1952.
Slatin, Rudolf C. *Fire and Sword in the Sudan.* London, 1896.
*Smith, Wilfred Cantwell. *Islam in Modern History.* Princeton, 1957.
———. *Modern Islam in India.* Lahore, 1943. Rev. ed., London, 1946.
Strauss, Leo. *Persecution and the Art of Writing.* Glencoe, Ill., 1952.
Sumner, Benedict H. *Russia and the Balkans, 1870–1880.* Oxford, 1937.
Terentyef, M. A. *Russia and England in Central Asia.* Trans. F. C. Daukes. Calcutta, 1876. 2 vols.
Tusi, Nasir ad-Din. *The Nasirean Ethics.* Trans. G. M. Wickens, London, 1964.
Vatikiotis, P. J. *The Modern History of Egypt.* London, 1969.
Von Grunebaum, G. E. *Modern Islam.* Berkeley and Los Angeles, 1962.
Walzer, Richard. *Greek into Arabic.* Oxford, 1962.
Watson, Robert Grant. *A History of Persia: From the Beginning of the Nineteenth Century to the Year 1858.* London, 1866.
Watt, W. M. *Islamic Philosophy and Theology.* Edinburgh, 1962.
Wheeler, Stephen. *The Ameer Abdur Rahman.* New York, 1895.
Wingate, Major F. R. *Mahdism and the Egyptian Sudan.* London, 1891.
Wittlin, Alma. *Abdul Hamid: The Shadow of God.* Trans. Norman Denny. London, 1940.
Wolff, Sir Henry Drummond. *Rambling Recollections.* London, 1908.
Wyllie, J. W. S. *Essays on the External Policy of India by J. W. S. Wyllie.* Ed. Sir William Wilson Hunter. London, 1875.

Articles in Western Languages

Abbott, Freeland. "The Jihād of Sayyid Aḥmad Shahīd," *Muslim World,* 52 (July, 1962), 216–222.
———. "The Transformation of the Jihād Movement," *Muslim World,* 52 (Oct., 1962), 288–295.

Adali, Hasan. "Documents pertaining to the Egyptian Question in the Yıldız Collection of the Başbakanlık Arşivi." In *Political and Social Change in Modern Egypt*. Ed. P. M. Holt. London, 1968.
*Ahmad, Aziz. "Afghānī's Indian Contacts," *Journal of the American Oriental Society*, 89, 3 (July–Sept., 1969), 476–504.
———. "An Eighteenth-Century Theory of the Caliphate," *Studia Islamica*, XXVIII (1968), 135–144.
*———. "Sayyid Ahmad Khān, Jamāl ad-Dīn al-Afghānī and Muslim India," *Studia Islamica*, XIII (1960), 55–78.
Algar, Hamid. "Malkum Khān Akhūndzāda and the Proposed Reform of the Arabic Alphabet," *Middle Eastern Studies*, V, 2 (May, 1969), 116–130.
Anonymous (Mīrzā Āqā Khān Kirmānī). "Controverses persanes," trans. A. L. M. Nicolas, *Revue du monde musulmane*, XXI (Dec. 1912), 238–260.
Auriant. "Un emir afghan, adversaire de l'Angeleterre en Orient; Djemmal ed Dine, ténébreux agitateur," *Mercure de France*, 288 (Dec. 1, 1938), 316–330.
Avicenna (Ibn Sīnā). "Ibn Sina: Treatise on the Secret of Destiny," trans. George F. Hourani, *Muslim World*, LIII, 2 (April, 1962), 138–140.
*Baidar, Abid Riza. "Jamāl al-Dīn al-Afghānī: A Bibliography of Source Materials," *International Studies*, III, 1 (July, 1961), 99–108.
Bari, M. A. "A Nineteenth-Century Muslim Reform Movement." In *Arabic and Islamic Studies in Honor of Hamilton A. R. Gibb*. Ed. George Makdisi. Leiden, 1965. Pp. 84–102.
*Basetti-Sani, G. "Sayyid Jamâl el-Dîn al-Afghânî: Saggio sul suo concetto della religione," *Orientalia Christiana Periodica*, XXV, 1–2 (1959), 5–43.
Becker, C. H. "Panislamismus," *Archiv für Religionswissenschaft*, VII (1904), 169–192.
Ben Cheneb, Saadeddine. "Études de littérature arabe moderne: I. Muḥammad al-Muwailiḥî," *Revue africaine*, LXXXIII, 3 and 4 (1939), 358–382.
Bogushevich, O. V. "Mukhammad Dzhemal' ad-Din al'-Afgani kak politicheskii deiatel'," *Kratkie Soobshcheniia Instituta Narodov Azii* (Moscow), 47 (1961), 11–20.
Browne, Edward G. "The Assassination of Nasiru'd-Din Shah," *New Review*, XIV (June, 1896), 651–659.
———. Bāb, Bābīs," In *Encyclopaedia of Religion and Ethics*. New York, 1926. Vol. II, pp. 229–308.
———. "Pan-Islamism." In *Lectures on the History of the Nineteenth Century*. Ed. F. Kirkpatrick. Cambridge, 1904. Pp. 306–330.
Caskel, Werner. "Western Impact and Islamic Civilization." In *Unity and Variety in Muslim Civilization*. Ed. G. E. von Grunebaum. Chicago, 1955. Pp. 335–360.
Corbin, Henry. "Confessions extatiques de Mīr Dāmād," *Mélanges Louis Massignon*, I (Damascus, 1956), 331–378.
———. "L'École Shaykhie en Théologie Shi'ite," École Pratique des Hautes Études, Section des Sciences Religieuses. *Annuaire 1960–1961*. Paris, 1961. Pp. 3–59.
Dawn, C. Ernest. "From Ottomanism to Arabism: The Origin of an Ideology," *Review of Politics*, XXIII 3 (July, 1961), 378–400.

*Federmann, Robert. "Scheik Djemaleddin el Afghan: Ein Lebensbild aus dem Orient," *Beilage zur Allgemeinen Zeitung* (Munich), no. 144. (June 24, 1896).

Frechtling, Louis E. "Anglo-Russian Rivalry in Eastern Turkistan, 1863–1881," *Journal of the Royal Central Asian Society*, XXVI, 3 (July, 1939), 471–489.

Gardet, Louis. "Le problème de la 'Philosophie Musulmane.' " In *Mélanges offerts à Étienne Gilson*. Paris, 1959. Pp. 261–284.

"Ghilan" [pseud.]. "Assassinat de Nasr-ed-Dine Chah Kadjar," *Revue du Monde musulmane*, XII (Dec., 1910), 592–615. (Includes a French abridgement of an account by an anonymous courtier of the Shah's assassination and a French translation of part of the record of interrogation of Mīrzā Riẓā Kirmānī.)

Gibb, H. A. R. "Studies in Contemporary Arabic Literature," *Bulletin of the School of Oriental Studies*, London, IV, 4 (1928), 745–760.

Goldziher, I. "Djamāl al-Dīn al-Afghānī," *EI*[1]. Vol. I, pp. 1008–1011.

Goldziher, I., and J. Jomier. "Djamāl al-Dīn al-Afghānī," *EI*[2]. Vol. II, pp. 416–419.

Gregorian, Vartan. "Mahmud Tarzi and Saraj-ol-Akhbar: Ideology of Nationalism and Modernization in Afghanistan," *Middle East Journal*, XXI, 3 (1967), 345–368.

Haim, Sylvia G. "Blunt and al-Kawākibī," *Oriente Moderno*, 35 (1955), 132–143.

———. "Islam and the Theory of Arab Nationalism." In *The Middle East in Transition*. Ed. Walter Z. Laqueur. New York, 1958.

Hambly, G. R. G. "Unrest in Northern India during the Vice-Royalty of Lord Mayo, 1869–72," *Journal of the Royal Central Asian Society*, 48, 1 (Jan., 1961), 37–55.

*Hanna, Sami A. "Al-Afghānī: A Pioneer of Islamic Socialism," *Muslim World*, 57, 1 (Jan., 1967) 24–32.

Hourani, Albert. "Djam'iyya," *EI*[2]. Vol. II, pp. 428–429.

Hourani, G. F. "Averroes on Good and Evil," *Studia Islamica*, XVI (1962), 13–40.

———. "Ibn-Rushd's Defense of Philosophy." In *The World of Islam*. Ed. James Kritzeck and R. Bayly Winder. London, 1960.

*Keddie, Nikki R. "Afghani in Afghanistan," *Middle Eastern Studies*, I, 4 (July, 1965), 322–349.

*———. "Islamic Philosophy and Islamic Modernism: The Case of Sayyid Jamāl ad-Dīn al-Afghānī," Iran, *Journal of the British Institute of Persian Studies*, VI (1968), 53–56.

———. "The Origins of the Religious-Radical Alliance in Iran," *Past and Present*, 34 (July, 1966), 70–80.

*———. "Pan-Islam as Proto-Nationalism," *Journal of Modern History*, 41, 1 (March, 1969), 17–28.

*———. "The Pan-Islamic Appeal: Afghani and Abdülhamid II," *Middle Eastern Studies*, III, 1 (Oct. 1966), 46–67.

*———. "Religion and Irreligion in Early Iranian Nationalism," *Comparative Studies in Society and History*, IV, 3 (April, 1962), 265–295.

*———. "Sayyid Jamal ad-Din 'al-Afghani': A Case of Posthumous Charisma?" In *Philosophers and Kings: Studies in Leadership.* Ed. Dankwart A. Rustow. New York, 1970.

*———. "Sayyid Jamāl al-Dīn al-Afghānī's first Twenty-seven Years: The Darkest Period," *Middle East Journal,* XX, 4 (Autumn, 1966), 517–533.

*———. "Symbol and Sincerity in Islam," *Studia Islamica,* XIX (1963), 27–63.

Kedourie, Elie. " 'The Elusive Jamāl al-Dīn al-Afghānī' A Comment," Muslim World, LIX, 3–4 (July–Oct., 1969), 308–314. Response to Menahem Milson, "The Elusive Jamāl al-Dīn al-Afghānī," *Muslim World,* LVIII, 4 (Oct., 1968), 295–307.

*———. "Further Light on Afghani," *Middle Eastern Studies,* I, 2 (Jan. 1965), 187–202.

*———. "Nouvelle lumière sur Afghânî et 'Abduh," *Orient,* VIII/2, 30 (1964), 37–57, VIII/3, 31 (1964), 83–106.

Key, Kerim Kami. "Jamal ad-Din al-Afghani and the Muslim Reform Movement," *Islamic Literature,* III (Oct., 1951), 5–10.

Kudsi-Zadeh, A. Albert. "Afghani and Freemasonry in Egypt." *Journal of the American Oriental Society,* in press.

*———. "Les idées d'Afghânî sur la politique coloniale des Anglais, des Français et des Russes." *Orient,* XII/ 3–4, 47–48 (1968), 197–206.

*———. "Iranian Politics in the Late Qājār Period: A Review," *Middle Eastern Studies,* V, 3 (Oct., 1969), 251–257.

*———. "Islamic Reform in Egypt: Some Observations on the Role of al-Afghānī," *The Muslim World* LXI, 1 (Jan., 1971), 1–12.

*———. "Jamal ad-Din al-Afghani: A Select List of Articles," *Middle Eastern Studies,* II, 1 (Oct., 1965), 66–72.

*———. "Jamāl al-Dīn al-Afghānī and the National Awakening of Egypt: A Reassessment of His Role," *Actes de ve Congrès d'Etudes Arabes et Islamiques, Bruxelles, 1970,* in press.

Lambton, Ann K. S. Dustūr: iv. Irān," *EI*2. Vol. II, pp. 649–657.

———. "Persian Society under the Qājārs," *Journal of the Royal Central Asian Society,* XLVIII, Pt. II (1961), 123–139.

———. "Secret Societies and the Persian Revolution of 1905–6," *St. Antony's Papers,* no. 4 (London, 1958), 43–60.

*Landau, Jacob M. "Al-Afghani's Panislamic Project," *Islamic Culture,* XXVI, 3 (July, 1952), 50–54.

———. "Prolegomena to a Study of Secret Societies in Modern Egypt," *Middle Eastern Studies,* I, 2 (Jan., 1965), 135–186.

Lee, Dwight E. "The Origins of Pan-Islamism," *American Historical Review,* 47, 2 (Jan., 1942), 278–287.

Lewis, Bernard. "Ḥasan Fehmī," *EI*2. Vol. III, fasc. 43–44, pp. 250–251.

———. "Ḥurriyya," *EI*2. Vol. III, fasc. 49–50, pp. 589–594.

———. "The Ottoman Empire in the Mid-Nineteenth Century: A Review," *Middle Eastern Studies,* I, 3 (April, 1965), 283–295.

Mackey, Albert G. "Egypt." In *Encyclopedia of Freemasonry.* Chicago, 1929. Vol. I, pp. 315–316.

Mahdi, Mohsen [Muhsin]. "Jamal al-Din al-Afghani," *Arab Journal*, IV, 2–4 (Fall, 1967), 17–22.
Malcom Khan (Malkum Khān). "Persian Civilization," *Contemporary Review*, LIX (1891), 238–244.
———. "The Persian Crisis," *Illustrated London News*, XCIX, 2748 (Dec. 19, 1891), 807.
Malik, H. "The Religious Liberalism of Sir Sayyid Aḥmad Khān," *Muslim World*, LIV, 3 (1964), 160–169.
Mardin, Şerif. "Libertarian Movements in the Ottoman Empire," *Middle East Journal*, XVI, 2 (Spring, 1962), 169–182.
Massignon, L. M. "De Jamal oud Din au Zahawi," *Revue du monde musulmane*, XII, 12 (Dec., 1910), 561–570.
*Milson, Menahem. "The Elusive Jamāl al-Dīn al-Afghānī," *Muslim World*, LVIII, 4 (Oct., 1968), 295–307.
———. "The Elusive Jamāl al-Dīn al-Afghānī," *Muslim World*, LIX, 3–4 (July–Oct. 1969), 315–316. Rejoinder to Elie Kedourie, " 'The Elusive Jamāl al-Dīn al-Afghānī' A Comment' (Reference cited above).
Minorsky, Vladimir. "Iran: Opposition, Martyrdom and Revolt." In *Unity and Variety in Muslim Civilization*. Ed. G. E. von Grunebaum, Chicago, 1955.
Muwailihī, Ibrāhīm. [Biography of his grandfather Ibrāhīm Muwailihī], from *ar-Risāla*, 249 (April 11, 1938), 617–620, and 250 (April 15, 1938), 658–662, trans. in G. Widmer, special issue of *Welt des Islams*, III/2 (1954), at pp. 60–78.
Ninet, John. "The Origin of the National Party in Egypt," *Nineteenth Century*, XII (Jan., 1883), 117–134.
*Pakdaman, Homa. "Notes sur le séjour de Djamâl al-dîn al-Afghânî en France," *Orient*, 35 (1965), 203–207.
Pérès, Henri. "Les origines d'un roman célèbre de la littérature arabe moderne: 'Ḥadīṯ 'Īsā Ibn Hišam' de Muḥammad al-Muwailiḥi," *Bulletin d'études orientales*, X (1943–1944), 101–118.
Rossi, Ettore. "Il centenario della nascita di Gemal ud-Din el-Afghani celebrato a Kabul," *Oriente Moderno*, XX, 5 (May, 1940), 262–265.
Scarcia, Gianroberto. "Kermān 1905: La 'guerra tra Šeiḫī e Bālāsarī,' " *Annali del Istituto Universitario Orientale di Napoli*, n.s., XIII (1963). 195–238.
Smith, Wilfred C. "The Ulamā' in Indian Politics." In *Politics and Society in India*. Ed. C. H. Philips. London, 1962.
Snouck Hurgronje, C. "Les confréries religieuses, la Mecque et le panislamisme," *Revue de l'histoire des religions*, 44 (1901), 262–281.
———. "Over Panislamisme," *Archives* (Haarlem, Musée Teyler), 3d ser., I (1912), 87–105.
Thornton, A. P. "Afghanistan in Anglo-Russian Diplomacy, 1869–73," *Cambridge Historical Journal*, XI, 2 (1954), 204–218.
———. "The Reopening of the Central Asian Question, 1864–69," *History*, XI, 141–143 (1956), 122–136.
Toynbee, Arnold J. "The Ineffectiveness of Panislamism." In *A Study of History*. London, 1954. Vol. VIII, pp. 692–695.

Vambery, Arminius. "Pan-Islamism," *The Nineteenth Century*, LX (Oct., 1906), 547–558.
Vatikiotis, P. J. "Muḥammad 'Abduh and the Quest for a Muslim Humanism," *Arabica* IV, 1 (Jan., 1957), 55–72.
Wirth, Albrecht. "Panislamismus," *Deutsche Rundschau*, 163 (1915), 429–440.
"X" (Sayyid Ḥasan Taqizādeh). "Le panislamisme et le panturquisme," *Revue du monde musulmane*, XXII (1913), 197–220.

Books in Arabic, Persian, Turkish, and Urdu

(Unless otherwise indicated the language is that of the country of publication.)

*'Abbās Mīrzā Mulk Ārā'. *Sharḥ-i ḥāl-i 'Abbās Mīrzā Mulk Ārā'*. Ed. 'Abd al-Ḥusain Navā'ī. Tehran, 1325/1946–47.
*'Abd al-Ghaffār, Qāẓī Muḥammad. *Āṣār-i Jamāl ad-Dīn Afghānī*. Delhi, 1940.
*'Abduh, Muḥammad. *Mudhakkirāt al-imām Muḥammad 'Abduh*. Ed. Ṭāhir aṭ-Ṭināḥī. Cairo, 1963.
*———. *Risālat al-wāridāt*. Cairo, 1925.
Abū Rayya, Maḥmūd. *Jamāl ad-Dīn al-Afghānī*. Cairo, 1961.
Afshār, Īraj. *Savād va bayāẓ*. Tehran, 1344/1965–66.
*Afshār, Iraj, and Aṣghar Mahdavī. *Documents inedits concernant Seyyed Jamāl al-Dīn Afghānī (Majmū'eh-yi asnād va madārik-i chāp nashudeh dar bāreh-yi Sayyid Jamāl ad-Dīn mashhūr bi Afghānī)*. Tehran, 1963.
*Amīn, Ahmad. *Zu'amā al-iṣlāḥ fī al-'aṣr al-ḥadīth*. Cairo. 1949.
*Amīn ad-Dauleh. *Khāṭirāt-i siyāsī-yi Mīrzā 'Alī Khān-i Amīn ad-Dauleh*. Ed. Hafez Farman-Farmaian. Tehran, 1962.
*al-Amīn, Sayyid Muḥsin and Ḥasan al-Amīn. *A'yān ash-Shī'a*. Vol. XVI Beirut, 1963.
*Anonymous (Mīrzā Āqā Khān Kirmānī and Shaikh Aḥmad Rūḥī). *Hasht Bihisht*. N.p., n.d. (An Azalī Bābī text published in Iran.) Introduction by Afẓal al-Mulk Kirmānī.
Asadābādī, Mīrzā Luṭfallāh. (Author listed as Mīrzā Luṭfallāh Khān). *Jamāl ad-Dīn al-Asadābādī al-ma'rūf bi al-Afghānī*. Arabic trans. and intro. by Ṣādiq Nash'at and 'Abd al-Nadīm Ḥasanain. Cairo, 1957.
*———. *Sharḥ-i ḥāl-i Sayyid Jamāl ad-Dīn Asadābādī*. Berlin, 1926. Rev. ed. *Sharḥ-i ḥāl va āṣār-i Sayyid Jamāl ad-Dīn Asadābādī ma'rūf bi "Afghānī."* Tabriz, 1326/1947–48.

*Asadābādī, Ṣifātallāh Jamālī. *Asnād v madārik dar bāreh-yi Irānī as-aṣl būdan-i Sayyid Jamāl ad-Dīn Asadābādī.* Tehran, n.d.
al-Bustānī, Buṭrus, ed. *Dā'irat al-ma'ārif (Encyclopedie Arabe).* Vol. V., S.v. "Bābī." Beirut, 1881.
Ergin, Osman. *Türkiye maarif tarihî.* Vol. II. Istanbul, 1939.
*Fevzi, Halil. *Suyūf al-qawāṭi'.* Istanbul, 1872.
Furṣat ad-Dauleh Shīrāzī. *Dīvān-i Furṣat.* Tehran, 1337/1958–59.
Gövsa, Ibrahim Alāettin. *Türk Meşhurlarī.* Istanbul, 1946.
Hidāyat, Mahdī Qulī Mukhbir as-Salṭaneh. *Khāṭirāt va Khaṭarāt.* Tehran, 1329/1950–51.
al-Ḥusrī, Abū Khaldūn Sāṭi'. *Mā hiya al-qaumiyya?* 2d ed. Beirut, 1963.
I'timād as-Salṭaneh, Muḥammad Ḥasan Khān. *al-Ma'āṣir va al-āṣār.* Tehran, 1889.
*al-Jundī, Anwar. *ash-Sharq fī fajr al-yaqẓa.* Cairo, 1966.
Karbalā'ī, Shaikh Ḥasan. *Qarārdād-i rizhī 1890 m.* Ed. and intro. by Ibrāhīm Dihgān. Arāk, Iran, *ca.* 1955.
al-Kawākibī, 'Abd ar-Raḥmān. *Ṭabā'i' al-istibdād.* Cairo, 1889.
*Kirmānī, Nāẓim al-Islām. *Tārīkh-i bīdārī-yi Īrāniyān.* 2d ed. Tehran, 1945–1946.
Khūgiyānī, Muḥammad Amīn. *Ḥayāt-i Sayyid Jamāl ad-Dīn Afghān.* Kabul, 1318/1939–40. Includes several of Afghānī's articles and the author's Persian translation of *Tatimmat al-bayān fī tārīkh al-Afghān.*
Luṭfī as-Sayyid, Aḥmad. *Qiṣṣa ḥayātī.* Cairo, 1962.
Madkūr, Muḥammad Salām. *Jamāl ad-Dīn al-Afghānī.* Cairo, 1937.
*al-Maghribī, 'Abd al-Qādir. *Jamāl ad-Dīn al-Afghānī.* Cairo, 1948.
Makāryūs, Shahīn Bey. *Kitāb al-ādāb al-māsūniyya.* Cairo, 1895.
*al-Makhzūmī, Muḥammad. *Khāṭirāt Jamāl ad-Dīn al-Afghānī.* Beirut, 1931. 2d ed., Damascus, 1965.
*———. *Khāṭirāt-i Sayyid Jamāl ad-Dīn Asadābādī.* Partial trans. into Persian by Murtaẓā Mudarrisī Chahārdihī. Tabriz, 1328/1949–50.
*Malikzādeh, Mahdī. *Tārīkh-i inqilāb-i mashrūtiyyat-i Irān.* Vol. I. Tehran, 1328/1949–50.
Mudarrisī Chahārdihī, Murtaẓā. *Zindigānī va falsafeh-yi ijtimā'ī va siyāsī-yi Sayyid Jamāl ad-Dīn Afghānī.* Tehran, 1334/1955–56.
al-Muwailihī, Muḥammad. *Ḥadith 'Īsā ibn Hishām.* Cairo, 1923. (Includes a letter from Afghānī.)
*Pâkalın, Mehmed Zeki. *Son sadrâzamlar ve başvekiller.* Vol. IV. Istanbul, 1944.
*Qāsim, Maḥmud. *Jamāl ad-Dīn al-Afghānī, ḥayātuhū wa falsafatuhū.* Cairo, n.d.
*Rāfī'ī, 'Abd ar-Raḥmān. *Jamāl ad-Dīn al-Afghānī.* Cairo, 1957.
Rā'īn, Ismā'īl. *Farāmūshkhāneh va Farāmāsūnrī dar Īrān.* Tehran, 1347/1968–69.
*Riḍā, Muḥammad Rashīd. *Tārīkh al-ustādh al-imām ash-shaikh Muḥammad 'Abduh.* Cairo, 1931–1947/48. 3 vols.
*Ṣafā'ī, Ibrāhīm, ed. *Asnād-i siyāsī-yi daurān-i Qājāriyyeh.* Tehran, 1346/1967–68.
———. Rahbarān-i mashrūteh. Tehran, 1344/1965–66.

*Sāsānī, Khān Malik. *Siyāsatgarān-i daureh-yi Qājār.* Tehran, 1338/1959–1960.
Sayyāḥ, Ḥājji. *Khātirāt-i Ḥājji Sayyāḥ.* Ed. Ḥamīd Sayyāḥ and Saifallāh Gulkār. Tehran, 1346/1967–68.
*Shafīq, Aḥmad. *Mudhakkirātī fī niṣf qarn.* Vol. I. Cairo, 1934.
*Shīrāzī, Furṣat ad-Dauleh. See Furṣat ad-Dauleh Shīrāzī.
Ṣifat ʿAlī Shāh, Ẓahīr ad-Dauleh. *Tārīkh-i bī durūgh.* Tehran, 1334/1955–56.
Ṭabāṭabāʾī, Muḥammad Muḥīṭ, ed. *Majmūʿeh-yi āṣār-i Mīrzā Malkum Khān.* Tehran, 1948–49.
Taimūrī, Ibrāhīm. *Taḥrīm-i tanbākū.* Tehran, n.d.
Zaidān, Jurjī. *Tarājim mashāhīr ash-Sharq.* Cairo, 1922. 2 vols.
———. *Tārīkh al-māsūniyya al-ʿāmm.* Cairo, 1889.

Articles in Arabic Persian, and Turkish

(Unless otherwise indicated, the language is that of the country of publication.)

Âkif, Mehmet. "Cemaleddin Afghani," *Sıratı Müstakim* (Istanbul), no. 90 (May 13/27, 1910), 207–208.
Amīn, ʿUthmān. "Jamāl ad-Dīn al-Afghānī," *Minbar al-Islām,* XX, 10 (March, 1963), 58–61.
———. "Jamāl ad-Dīn al-Afghānī: Afkārihi as-siyāsiyya," *Minbar al-Islām,* XX, 11 (April, 1963), 54–56.
*Arslān, Shakīb, "as-Sayyid Jamāl ad-Dīn al-Afghānī." In A. Muwaihid, trans., *Ḥāḍir al-ʿālam al-Islāmī* (L. Stoddard, *The New World of Islam*), Cairo, 1343/1924–25.
*Canib, Ali. "Cemaleddin Afghanî" *Hayat* (Ankara), III, 77 (May, 1928).
"Cemaleddin Afgani." In *Türk Ansiklopedisi.* Ankara, 1960. Vol. X, p. 143.
Goldziher, I., plus additions. "Cemâleddin Efghânî." In *Islâm Ansikolopedisi.* Istanbul, 1945. Vol. 3, pp. 81–85.
*al-Hilbāwī, Ibrāhīm. "Ahamm ḥadīth aththara fī majrā ḥayātī," *al-Hilāl,* XXXVIII, 2 (Dec., 1929), 138–140.
*Keskioğlu, Osman. "Cemâleddin Efghânî," *Ilâhiyat Fakültesi Dergisi,* X (1962), 91–102.
Muṣṭafā, Aḥmad ʿAbd ar-Raḥīm. "Afkār Jamāl ad-Dīn al-Afghānī as-siyāsiyya," *al-Majalla at-tārīkhiyya al-Miṣriyya,* IX–X (1960–62), 215–239.
*[Riḍā, Muḥammad Rashīd.] "Fātiḥa as-sana ath-thāniyya ʿashra," *al-Manār,* XII (Feb. 21, 1909), 1–15.

*[———.] "Tafsīr al-Qur'ān al-ḥakīm," *al-Manār*, XXVIII (Nov. 24, 1927), 641–656.
*[———.] "Tatimma mulakhkhaṣ sīra al-ustādh al-imām," *al-Manār*, VIII (Aug. 2, 1905), 401–416.
Sabry, Muhammad. "[A page from the history of Jamāl ad-Dīn al-Afghānī]" (in Arabic), *Revue de l'Institut des Etudes Islamiques* (Cairo), I, 1 (1958).
Taqīzādeh, Sayyid Ḥasan. "Sayyid Jamāl ad-Dīn," *Kāveh* (Berlin; Persian), n.s., II, 3 (1921), 5–11; and "Takmileh," *Kāveh*, II, 9 (1921-, 10–11.
———. "Sayyid Jamāl ad-Dīn ma'rūf bi Afghānī," *Mardān-i khudsākhteh*. Ibrāhīm Khājeh Nūrī. Tehran, 947.
Zaidān, Jurjī. "as-Sayyid Jamāl ad-Dīn al-Afghānī," *al-Hilāl*, V (March 15, 1897), 553–554.
———. "as-Sayyid Jamāl ad-Dīn al-Ḥusainī al-Afghānī," *al-Hilāl*, V (April 1, 1897), 561–571.

Index

'Abbās Ḥilmī, 383
Abbasid forces, 139
'Abd al-'Azīm, shrine, 275, 296, 328
'Abd al-Ghafūr Shāhbāz, 156
'Abdallāh, Sayyid, 383
'Abdallāh Nadīm, 101, 379–380
'Abd al-Latīf, 148, 152, 153
'Abd al-Qādir al-Jazā'irī, 187
'Abd al-Rāziq, 88
'Abd as-Samad Isfahānī, 330 332
Abdin, 238
'Abdu, Ibrāhīm, 98
'Abduh, Muḥammad, 2, 6, 7, 29, 83, 89, 90, 114, 188, 228, 233, 350, 418, 427, 432
  biography of Afghānī, by, 5, 81
  in favor of enlightened despotism, 127
Abū al-Hudā aṣ-Ṣayyadī, 215, 370, 374, 377, 382, 383, 417, 467
Abū al-Kalām Āzād, Maulānā, 155
Abū Muslim, 139, 140
Abū Naddara Zarka, newspaper, 184, 185, 186, 189, 199
Abū Naẓẓāra Zarqā', newspaper, 96
Abū Turāb, 40, 42, 45, 183, 186
'Adālat, Mīrzā Sayyid Husain Khān, 292, 294, 299
Adams, C. C., 68
Afghan war, first, 27, 41, 53
Afghan war, second, 39–42, 103
Afghānī (Sayyid Jamāl ad-Dīn "al-Afghānī")
  acquainted with modern Western knowledge, 25
  activities in India, 144
  advocate of *jihād*, 28
  advocate of science and reason, 62
  kind of "secular messiah," 142
  mass orator, 123
  and British Foreign Office, 199–205
  and assassination of Shah, 404–421
  "Answer to Renan," by, 72, 78, 194, 195
  anti-British activity in Paris, 199
  anti-British activity in Russia, 289
  approach to Islamic past, 2
  Arab disciples of, 2
  Arabic biographers on, 3
  as ideologist of Pan-Islam, 1, 180
  as Pan-Islamic emissary, 131
  as "Neo-Traditionalist," 1
  as teacher, 81–92
  as visionary leader, 80
  as Westernizer, 64
  attacks British path in education, 168
  attacks fatalism in Islam, 223
  attitude toward Christian West, 1
  belief in Hindu-Muslim unity, 206

Afghānī (*continued*)
biographies of, 6, 8
birth of, 10
British reports on activities of, 283–292
British sources about, 7
calls prophecy a craft, 72, 73
characterizes Islam, 178
childhood of, 11
chosen as hero by modern Muslims, 2
chronology of, 448–450
contributes to development of Egyptian nationalism, 128
dedicated to Westernization, 62
defends Islam and Pan-Islam, 131
defends rationalism, reform, and science, 165
disciples of, 5, 88
discourses in Istanbul, 374–388
distorts own biography, 6
effects on Egyptian disciples, 125
Egyptian period of, 84
eloquence and charisma of, 85
evidence of birth in Iran, 427–433
exchange with Ernest Renan, 189–199
expelled from Egypt, 17, 81, 123, 124
expelled from Istanbul, 2, 17, 21
favors constitutional regime, 118
final years in Istanbul, 374–388
friendly to Russians, 25
genealogy of, 12
hated Western encroachments, 87
heresy, accused of, 73
History of Afghanistan by, 56, 104
impressed by power of West, 62
in Afghanistan, 5, 37–57
in Cairo, 187
Indian articles by, 156–170
influence of India on, 22, 25, 32
in Iran, 306–334
in London, 355–371
in Paris, 144
in Russia, 291, 292–305
in service of Afghan government, 32
interested in new Western ideas, 7
Iranian childhood of, 10–17
Istanbul period, 58–80
lax in performing religious duties, 16–17
lectures by, 65, 67
letter of, to Amīn as-Sulṭān, 440–443
letter of, to Riyāḍ Pāshā, 434–439
letter of, to Sultan Abdülhamid, 444–447
"Letter on India" by, 205
"Mahdi, The," by, 206
masonic activities in Egypt, 7, 100
messianic tendencies of, 18
"Nationality and the Muslim Religion" by, 22
nationality of, 2
on Arab civilization, 192–193
on education and use of reason, 106, 107
on egoism, 176
on fanaticism, 109
on foundation of human happiness, 105, 166
on intellectual elitism, 176
on Muslim philosophical tradition, 170
on patriotism and liberty, 106
on political despotism, 107–108, 111
on prophethood and philosophy, 70
on Protestantism, 179
on social order, 172
on teaching and learning, 161
on tyranny, 109
on Urdu language, 159
on virtues produced by religion, 175
origin of, 11
Pan-Islamic writings of, from Paris, 159
Pan-Islamism of, 85
Persian, Turkish, and Arabic sources on, 4, 7
personal magnetism of, 52, 57, 86
plots against Sultan, 7
political activities of, 38, 40–57, 92–128
political goals of, in Egypt, 126–127
political view of, on masonry, 122
practices *taqiyya*, 18
"Refutation of the Materialists" by, 5, 52, 126, 129, 131, 150, 152, 156, 160, 171–181, 228
regarded as Afghan Sunni, 2
regarded as "freethinker of French type," 145
regarded as heretic and skeptic, 2
regarded as Iranian Shi'i, 2
regarded as unbeliever, 7
rejects pure traditionalism, 1
religious orthodoxy of, 2, 91
religious tolerance of, 398

Afghānī (*continued*)
revolutionary anti-British activity of, 7, 199, 289
seeks values in Islamic tradition, 1
Şeyhülislam's anathema against, 73
skeptical about positive religions, 31
strengthens Islamic countries, 61
Syrian Christian disciples of, 97
teaching method of, 91
terminology of, 174
unorthodoxy of, 2
uses place-of-origin name, "Istanbūlī," 33, 41, 54, 429
visits Tehran, 320
Afghanistan, 2, 3, 5, 7, 10, 23, 35, 37–57, 208, 250, 265
Afghans, 221
Afshār-Mahdavī *Documents*, 32, 40, 41, 42, 52, 86, 93, 100, 131, 429
Afzal al-Mulk Kirmānī, 380, 381–382
Aghūrīs, 147, 148, 167
Agronomy, 66
Ahmad, Aziz, 151, 155
Aḥmad, Muḥammad, 184, 206, 241
Aḥmad Aḥsā'ī, Shaikh, 12, 19, 20
"Treatise on the Crafts" by, 33
Ahmad Brelwī, 27
Ahmad Khān, Sayyid, 146, 148, 153, 154, 157, 167, 181, 221
al-Ahram, newspaper, 96, 98
Ahriman, 442
Akhtar, newspaper, 298, 335, 336, 377
'Alā' as-Saltaneh, 356
Albert Hall, Calcutta, 156
Alchemy, 90
Alcohol, koranic prohibition of, 398
Aleppo, 209
Alexandria, 97, 98, 101, 115, 203
Algeria, 208
Algiers, 122
'Alī Akbar, Hājji Sayyid, 342, 344, 345, 351
'Alī 'Arab, Mullā, 331
'Alī Muhammad, Sayyid, of Shiraz, 21, 192
Âli Paşa, 59, 67, 77
al-Kawākibī, 'Abd ar-Raḥmān, 395
Amīn ad-Dauleh, 300, 307, 321
Amīn as-Sultān, 273, 275, 276, 307, 415
Amīn az-Zarb, 275, 276, 282, 287, 288, 295, 309, 318
Anatolia, 250
al-'Anḥūrī, Salīm, 5, 29, 30, 84
Arab civilization, 192
Arabia, 146, 152, 262, 349
Arabian Caliphate, 151, 152
Arabic
encyclopedia, 106
journalism, 96
language, 12
translations into, 162
Aristocles, Jean, 60
Arslān, Shakīb, 387, 402, 405
As'ad, Aḥmad, 377, 378
Asadabad, 3, 11, 12, 14, 15, 32
Aslam Khān, 49
Astronomy, 66
Atheism, 83
Atrek lands, 309
Averroes, 196, 197
Avicenna (Ibn Sīnā), 18, 19, 90, 163, 196
Ayyūb Khān, 289
Azalī Babis, 21, 275, 378
A'zam Khān, 39, 40, 41, 42, 47, 48, 53, 85
Azerbaijan, 343, 418
Azerbaijani Turkish language, 11
al-Azhar, 58, 81, 83, 231
Azīz ad-Dīn, 290

Bāb (gate), 21
Babis
heretical messianic, 20
meliorist ideas of, 22
persecution and emigration of, 22
Babism
doctrine, 21
equalitarian, 21
movement, 19
popularity of messianic, 21, 22
Baghdad, 33, 34, 330
Bahaism, 21
Bālā Hisār, 53
Baluchistan, 136, 208
Bani Aun, 211
Baring, Sir Evelyn (Lord Cromer), 242, 246, 271
al-Baṣīr, newspaper, 185, 187
Basiret, newspaper, 73
Basra, 228, 330, 348
Bavānātī, Muhammad Bāqir, 23, 24
Bee an-Naḥla, The. See *an-Naḥla*, newspaper
Beirut, 186, 187
Bengal, 27

Berkes, Niyazi, 3, 59, 65, 70, 75, 77, 78, 129
Bilgrāmī 'Alī, 147
Blasphemy, 23
Blunt, Wilfrid, 148, 183, 188, 208, 229–246
  India under Ripon by, 151
  Secret History of the English Occupation by, 125
Bombay, 24, 58
Borg, Ralph, 100
British
  Afghānī's activity against, 7
  aggression in India, 130
  anti-British policy, 51
  anti-British resistance, 56
  conquest, 25, 27
  Conservative party, 229
  control in East, 155
  Foreign Office, 189, 199–205
  imperialism, 181, 220, 224
  India, 27, 28
  informants, 41, 44, 45
  Liberal party, 229
  occupation of Egypt, 130
  Parliament, 229
  policy toward Muslims, 25
  rule, pressures of, 27
  sources on Afghānī, 7
Browne, E. G., 6, 23, 404
Bukhara, 35, 42, 43, 50, 51, 136, 208
Burujird, city, 15
Bushehr, 23, 24, 271, 272, 273
Bussorah (Basra), 330
Bustānī Buṭrus, 106
Bustānī Sa'id, 187

Cabul. *See* Kabul
"Cabul Diaries," 40, 42, 43, 48, 50
Cabul Précis, 44, 49
Cairo, 58, 94, 123, 182, 203, 214
Calcutta, 24, 147, 149, 201
Caliph al-Hādī, 193
Caliphate at Mecca, 211
Caliph of Islam, 29
Candahar. *See* Qandahar
Canib, Alī, 73
Caspian Sea, 250, 251, 279
Catholic Church, 192
Catholicism, 197
Cemal Efendi, 65, 74
Censorship, 74, 108
Chamber of Deputies, 99, 113
"Cheftaky," Ali Bey. *See* Şefkati, Ali Bey
Cherif Pāshā. *See* Sharīf Pāshā
Cholera investigations by Afghānī, 13, 15
Christianity, 29, 87, 191, 192, 178
Churchill, Randolph, 229, 233, 249, 261
Communism, 177
Congress of Berlin (1878), 99, 130
Constantinople (Istanbul), 41, 67, 122
Constitutionalism, 225, 226
Cordery, 144, 199
Cossacks, 45
Council of Education, 59, 64, 80, 257
Cromer, Lord. *See* Baring, Sir Evelyn
Czar. *See* Tsar

Dār al-ḥarb, 27
Dār al-Islām, 26, 27
Darülfünun University, 62, 65, 74, 76
Dervish convents, 64
Divan of Constantinople, 209
Documentation, 3, 10, 41, 417
Dost Mahomed. *See* Dūst Muhammad Khān
Downing Street, 244, 245
Dūst Muhammad Khān, 39, 40, 52
Ḍiyā al-Khafiqain, newspaper, 350 n, 369

East, 1, 155, 170, 176
Eastern and Western Review, 369
Eastern Star Lodge, 93
Education
  modern, 60
  secularization of, 27
  traditional Iranian-Islamic, 29
Egypt, 5, 6, 7, 82–92, 181
Egyptian Army, 200, 201
Egyptian Khedivate, 209
Egyptian nationalists, 210
Egyptian National Party, 233
"Egyptian Patriotic League," 200
England, 201, 203, 249
European financial penetration, 130
European Powers, 82

al-Fārābī, 108, 163, 174
Fatalism, 223, 224
Fehmi, Hasan Efendi, 65, 67, 248
Fevzi, Halil, 68, 69, 71, 73
Fikrī, 'Abdallāh Pāshā, 182, 439
Fiqh, 78

Freemasonry in Middle East, 92
Freemasons in Egypt, 92
French occupation of Tunisia, 130, 204
Fuad Paşa, 59
Fursat Shīrazī, Mīrzā, 272
Furughī, Zukā al-Mulk, 321

Gamad ed-Din (Jamāl ad-Dīn), 117
Gamal El-Deen, 121–122
Gellal Eddin (Jamāl ad-Dīn), 284
Ghānim, Khalīl, 185
al-Ghazālī, 37, 163
Ghazni, 37, 39, 41
Giers, Nikolai, Russian Foreign Minister, 284, 287, 292, 305, 308, 309, 311
Gladstone, Herbert, 240
Gladstone, W. E., 170, 209, 229, 232
Gladstone Papers, 241
Gomashtesh Niaz Juhood, 43
Gordon, General Charles, 231, 232
Gordon, T. E., 337
Grand Orient controversy, 122
Great Britain, 206, 229, 266
Greeks, 164
Grigorovich (Gregorevitch), 310, 323

Hādī, Shaikh, 11, 12
Haidar, Mullā, 16
Haim, Sylvia, 3, 4
Hājji Sayyāh, 16, 321
Ḥalīm, Prince, 92, 96, 119, 120, 121, 209, 213
Hamadan, 3, 11, 23
Hamid, Abdülhak, 371
Hamilton, Sir Edward, 229
Hartington, Lord, 233, 243
Hejaz, 384
Herald, newspaper, 298
Herat, 35, 37, 42, 46
Heresy, 19, 20, 26
Hicks, General William, 206
Hijaz, 80
al-Hilāl, periodical, 5, 421
al-Hilbāwī, Ibrāhīm, 83
Hindu
  conquest of Muslim territory, 27
  nationalists, 154
Hindus, 27, 28
Hindustan, 43
Homeward Mail, publication, 102
Hourani, Albert, 3
Hugo, Victor, 213
Husain Hamadānī Darjuzainī, Mullā, 16
al-Ḥusainī, as-Sayyid, 369
Ḥusain Pāshā at-Tunisī, 215, 217, 218, 219, 235
Hyderabad, 6, 143, 144, 145, 146, 202, 212, 227

Ibn Bājja, 163
Ibn Khaldūn, 26, 168, 176
Ibn Sīnā. *See* Avicenna
Ibn Ziyād, 332
Ibrāhīm, 'Abd ar-Rashīd, 304
Ignatiev, General, 308
Ijāzeh, 15, 17
Ijtihād, 18, 26
Illustrated London News, 237
Imam Husain, 328, 329
Imam of Sanaa, 261
Imperial Tobacco Corporation, 335
India, 5, 16, 17, 22–32, 144–156, 208
  missionaries, activities in, 29
  British aggression in, 130
  British Government of, 43, 147, 151
  Government of, 41
  Khilāfat movement in, 26
Indian
  nationalists, 205
  trade, 44, 205
Indian Liberation Society, 286
Indian Muslims, 25, 26, 27, 28, 152, 286
Indian Muslim University, 147
Indian Mutiny, 25, 26, 47, 102, 153
Indian Pan-Islam, 155
India Office (London), 142, 202
International Muslim alliance, 28
Intransigeant, L', newspaper, 205, 206, 213
Iran, 2, 3, 7, 11, 271–282
  Babi uprisings in, 21
  Constitutional Revolution in, 409
  Cossack brigade of, 409
  Islamic philosophy taught in, 18
  Pan-Islamists in, 373
  religio-political climate in, 18, 19
  Shi'i areas of, 19
  state religion of, 18
  traditional influences of, 18
  Western impact in, 21
Isfahan, 16
Isfahānī, Mīrzā Husain Dānish, 405, 418
Isfahānī, Mīrzā Ni'matallāh, 282

Isḥāq, Adīb, 5, 7, 84, 90, 93, 100, 186
Islam
as source of modern virtues, 165
corruption in, 224
fatalism, 223
modern, 2
Shi'i branch of, 2
Sunni branch of, 2
Islamic
cultural traditions, 18
heterodoxy, 85, 92
insurrection, 208
law, 26
liberalism, 2
milla, 64
modernists, 165
nationalism, 64
philosophers, 18, 29
philosophical traditions, 87
philosophy, 18, 36, 95, 161
religion, 23
revivalism, 2
solidarity, 184
traditional disciplines, 17
traditional ideas, 1
Ismā'īl, Khedive, 82, 96, 99, 112, 114, 216
Ismā'īl Pāshā. *See* Ismā'īl, Khedive
Istanbul, 2, 6, 7, 33, 51, 82, 131, 213
I'timād as-Saltaneh, 273, 274, 276, 321
al-Ittihād, newspaper, 235, 236
Izzet Bey, 415

Jamāl ad-Dīn. *See* Afghānī
Jaudat, Ismā'īl, 215, 234, 247, 260
al-Jawā'ib, newspaper, 74, 234
Jemalledin Efendi (Jamāl ad-Dīn), 76
Jemmal-Eddin Sheikh (Jamāl ad-Dīn), 196, 197, 385
Jihād, 27, 28
Judaism, 397
Judicial institutions, 27
Jumaludin (Jamāl ad-Dīn), 49, 50, 312
Jum'a Luṭfī, 92
Justice, La, newspaper, 205

Kabul (Cabul), 37, 39, 41, 47, 285
Kalmuks, 45
Kâmil, Mahmud Efendi, 73
Karachi, 143
Karbalā, 32, 406
Karīm Khān, Muhammad, 19, 20
Karun River, 303, 308, 311
Kashgar, 137
Kāshī, Muhammad 'Alī, 282
"Kathi," 268–270, 401
Katkov, 285, 286, 287
Kāveh, newspaper, 22, 23, 272, 432
Kâzim Efendi, 74, 76
Kedourie, Elie, 3, 187, 198, 206, 286
Kermanshah, 328, 330
Khabīr al-Mulk, 382, 417
Khair ad-Dīn Pasha, 215
Khān Khalīl, 88
Khartoum, 231, 239, 242
Khedivate, 92, 120
Khilāfat movement, 26, 155
Khiva, 44, 208
Khyber Pass, 44, 45
Kokand, 136, 208
Koran, 12, 21, 392
interpretation of, 29, 87
law of, 126
levels of meaning in, 20, 164
on sovereignty of Muslims, 224
Kuchī Jurjī, 420
Kudsi-Zadeh, A. Albert, 3, 84

Lahore, 286
Landau, Jacob, 132, 139
al-Laqqānī, Ibrāhīm, 98, 183, 186
Lascelles, Sir Frank, 121, 367
Lavizon, M., 216
Lebanon, 97
Levant Times, 205
Lodge(s), masonic, 92, 120
Eastern Star in Cairo, 93, 99, 100, 120
Italian in Alexandria, 93, 100
Scottish, 122
London, 181, 183, 184, 204, 220, 228
Lutfallāh Asadābādī, 10, 11, 12, 13, 15, 21, 24, 32, 279
Luṭfi as-Sayyid, Aḥmad, 421
Lyons, Lord, 201

Madrasa, 13, 64, 146
al-Maghribī, 'Abd al-Qādir, 388, 391, 392, 393, 403
Mahadiv, 109
Mahdi, 16, 18, 140, 204, 205, 207, 208, 222, 229–246
Mahdi, Muhsin, 176
Mahdi of the Sudan, 206, 210, 229
Mahdism, 205–214
Mahmoud Khān, Mīrzā, 317
al-Makhzūmī, Muḥammad, 388, 391, 392, 394, 396, 398, 399, 400, 402

Malet, Edward B., 200, 234
Malik al-Mutakallimīn, 272, 273
Malik at-Tujjār, 329
Malikzādeh, 272
Malkum Khān, 275, 336, 337, 339
Mansur Davānaqī, 162
Maqalāt-i Jamāliyyeh, publication, 150
Mariette, Auguste, 90
Marxists, 205
Mashhad, 35
Masons of Ḥalīm's party, 119
Matātyā Café, 84
Materialists, 5, 52, 91, 168, 171, 176, 180
Mazanderan, 279, 343
Mecca, 5, 23, 24, 132
Medina, 132
Medrese, 78
Merv, 130, 250
Messianic terminology, 140
Messianism, 20, 21, 204–205
Middle East, 206
  Bahaism spreading beyond, 21
  freemasonry in, 92
  incursions by West into, 1
  traditional education in, 29
Milla, 63, 138
Mir'at al-'Ārifīn, 19
Mīr'at ash-Sharq, newspaper, 98
Mīr Bāqir, 163
Mīrza Āqā Khān Kirmānī, 377, 378, 417, 418
Mīrzā Rizā Kirmānī, 211, 279, 321, 322, 338, 346, 405–409, 412, 414
Miṣr, newspaper. 97–98, 102–104, 106–108
Miṣr al-Fatāt, newspaper, 98, 115
Miwelhy, Salim Bey. *See* al-Muwailihī, 'Abd as-Salām
Modernization, 64, 79
Moelhy Ibrahim Bey. *See* al-Muwailihī, Ibrāhīm
Monotheism, 397
Moonshee, 41
Morier, Sir Robert, 284, 287
Morocco, 208, 252
Moscow, 271, 282, 285
Moscow Gazette, 285
Mu'allim-i Shafīq, periodical, 150, 151
Muhammad 'Alī Mīrzā, Iranian crown prince, 418
Muḥammad 'Alī Pāshā, 92, 103
Muhammad Hasan, Hājji. *See* Amīn az-Zarb
Muhammad Husain Āqā, Hājji, 278
Mu'īn āl Mulk, 215
Mujāhids, 27
Mujtahid(s), 12, 13, 15, 20
  Iranian, 17
  excommunication by, 19
Mukhbir ad-Dauleh, 301
Mukhbir as-Saltaneh, 300, 308, 318
Mukhtar Khān, 328
Mulk Ārā, 271, 322
Mulla(s), 13, 16
Mullā Sadrā, 163
"Mulvi A. M.," 152
Mulvis (Ulama), 152, 153
Munich, 306, 307
Münif Efendi. *See* Münif Paşa
Münif Paşa, 60, 67, 215
Munshī, 41
Murtazā Ansārī, Shaikh, 12, 15, 16, 17
Mushīr ad-Dauleh, 318, 320, 321
Muslim Brethren, 2
Mu'īn al-Mulk, 215
Mujāhids, 27
Mujtahid(s), 12, 13, 15, 20
  Iranian, 17
  excommunication by, 19
Mukhbir ad-Dauleh, 301
Mukhbir as-Saltaneh, 300, 308, 318
Mukhtar Khān, 328
Mulk Ārā, 271, 322
Mulla(s), 13, 16
Mullā Sadrā, 163
"Mulvi A.M.," 152
Mulvis (Ulama), 152, 153
Munich, 306, 307
Münif Efendi. *See* Münif Paşa
Münif Paşa, 60, 67, 215
Munshī, 41
Murtazā Ansārī, Shaikh, 12, 15, 16, 17
Mushīr ad-Dauleh, 318, 320, 321
Muslim Brethren, 2
Muslim(s)
  and Christianity, 29
  independence, 52
  India, Shi'is in, 18
  Indians, 209
  intellectuals, 87
  modernists, 1, 2
  philosophers, 108, 164
  religious, 1, 8
  socialism, 422
  states of Central Asia, 59
  territory, Hindu conquest of, 27

Muslims (*continued*)
unity, 160, 223
universities, 62, 65, 74, 76, 81
al-Muwailihī, 'Abd as-Salām, 116, 215
al-Muwailihī, Ibrāhīm, 101, 188, 216, 227, 237, 238, 258, 259, 262, 263, 267
Muzaffar ad-Dīn Shāh, 415, 417
Mysticism, 19, 20

an-Naḥla, newspaper, 102, 144, 184, 187
Nā'ib as-Saltaneh, 407, 409
Naichirīs, 171, 172, 177
Naichiriyya, 158, 187
Najaf, city, 15, 16, 19, 20, 31
Najmābādī, Hājji Shaikh Hādī, 320
Namık Kemal, 60, 64, 130, 151
"Refutation of Renan" by, 199
Naqqāsh Salīm, 187
Nāsir ad-Dīn Shāh, 3, 6, 21, 211, 300, 301, 302, 303, 306, 307, 308, 313, 316, 319, 323, 336, 376, 389, 390, 391, 404, 405, 410, 411, 412, 413, 414, 415, 417, 419, 421
Nasīr ad-Dīn Tūsī, 18, 21, 90
Nasīr as-Saltaneh, 339
Nasrallāh Isfahānī, Mīrzā, 272
Nationalism
Arab, Turkish, and Islamic, 64
in 'Urābī's movement, 128
National Party, 112, 113, 116
Nazīm ad-Dauleh, Mīrzā Asadallāh Khān, 374, 375
Newspapers, 98, 99, 454
New York Herald, 214
Nihilism, 177
Nile River, 104, 209
Ni'matallāh, Mīrzā, 293, 294, 295
Northbrook, Lord, 284
Northwest Frontier, 27
Novikov, Madam, 308
Novoe Vremya, newspaper, 289, 290

Obeyd, Mohammed, 237
Obruchev, General, 308
Official Gazette, 437
Orient. *See* East
Oriental fanaticism, 223
Orthodoxy, 19, 20, 24
Osman Digna, 242
Ottoman
archives, 4
Bank (London), 239
Caliphate, 154
Christians, 106
constitution, 99
documents, 59
Empire, 51, 75, 79, 87, 122
Government, 138
Iraq, 12, 14, 19
Mint, 61
modernists, 177
Pan-Islamic program, 139
Sultan, 28, 59, 99, 246–268
Yearbook, 65
Oxus, 43, 44

Pain, Oliver, 213, 230, 231
Pakdaman, Homa, 3, 215
Pakistanis, 24
Pall Mall Gazette, 234, 361
Pan-Arabism, 2
Pan-Islam, 26, 60
Indian, 155
Pan-Islamic
appeal, 129–142
ideas, 59, 60
letter, 152
movement, 129
policies, 130
unity, 130
Paolini, M., 268
Paris, 144, 145, 159, 182, 183, 186, 188
Persia, 42, 287, 343
Peshawar, 42, 53
Petrograd, 272
Philosophers
Hellenized, 19
Iranian, 19, 90
Islamic, 18, 19
medieval, 29
mission, 69
Persian, 18
Philosophy
benefits of, 163
of national unity, 157
rationalist, 19, 62, 70, 73
scholastic, 78
Piedmont, 140
Pilgrimage, 80
Pobedonostsev (Pobedonostzov), M., 291
Political journalism, 96
Porte, 258, 259
Port Said, 143, 182
Predestination, 224

Prophet Muhammad, 70, 73, 79, 109, 164
Protestantism, 179
Prussia, 140
Punjab, 286

Qafqaz, newspaper, 284
Qandahar, 37, 39, 41, 42, 47, 51, 53, 57, 58
Qānūn, newspaper, 336, 337, 338
Qazvin, 12, 13, 14, 15
Queen, newspaper, 357
Qum, 328
Quraish, idols of the, 56
Qureshi, I. H., 154, 155

Ramadan, 17, 65, 66
Rao, Nana, 47
Rasūl Yār Khān, 147, 148, 154
Religion(s)
  Bahai, 21
  Christian, 191, 397
  evolutionary view of, 198
  founders of, 109
  "Fourth Pillar" of, 20
  Islamic, 23, 397
  misuse of, 109
  prophetic, 31
  rationalist interpretation of, 19
  rational reformed, 31
  reformation of, 141
  Sikh, 286
  state, 76
Renan, Ernest, 178, 180, 190, 192, 194, 195, 198, 199
Reuter Concession, 303
Revolt(s)
  against Sikhs, 27
  in Bengal, 27
  in Northwest Frontier, 27
Riḍā Muḥammad Rashīd, 2, 5, 6, 7, 83, 86, 88, 187
Rikhter, General, 308
Riyāḍ Pāshā, 81, 117, 143, 182
Rizā Qulī, Mīrzā, 16
Rochefort, Henri, 211, 213, 231
Rogay, Muhammad Alī, 143
Rūhī, Shaikh Ahmad, 379, 380, 381–382, 417, 418
Rūmī Sayyid, 41, 43
Russia, 271–282
Russian
  advance to Oxus, 44
  aggression in Central Asia, 130, 221
  archival material about Afghānī, 4
  conquest, 25, 59
  conquest of Merv, 130
  Government, 3, 42
  military advance in Bukhara, 43
Russo-Turkish War, 94, 99, 130, 151
Ruzname, newspaper, 76

Sa'adābād, 276
Sabry, M., 100
Ṣābūnjī, Louis, 84, 102, 103, 184
Sadīd as-Saltaneh, 22, 23, 272
Sādiq Tabātabā'ī, Āqā, 13, 14, 278
Safdar, Sayyid, 12, 14
Safvet Paşa, 60, 66, 67, 71
Sāhib, Arab (Grigorovich), 310
Sāhib-i Divān, 318
Saint Petersburg, 284, 290, 304
Şakir Paşa, 290
Sālār Jang, Sir, 146, 148
Salīm al-'Anḥūrī, 29, 30
Salīm an-Naqqāsh, 97, 98
Salisbury, Lord, 249, 253, 264, 302, 415
Ṣanu', Ya'qūb (James Sanua), 84
Sanua, James, 184, 190, 202
Sardārs, 55
Sāsānī, Khān Malik, 284
Sayyāh, Hājji, 16, 278, 280
Sayyid Husain (Bilgrāmī), 144–145, 199, 202–204
Scholar(s)
  Egyptian, 98
  Iranian, 16
  on Afghānī, 3, 7
  religious, 13, 147
School(s)
  secularized, set up by British, 27
  Shaikhi, 19
  usūlī, 19
Science(s)
  European, 162
  Greek, 192
  Muslim, 162
  Persian, 192
Sea of Aral, 44
Second Afghan war, 103, 104
Şefkati, Ali Bey, 216, 217, 218
Şeyhülislam, 2, 65, 68, 73, 75, 78, 390
Shāh. *See* Nāsir ad-Dīn Shāh
Shāh 'Abd al-Azīz, 27
Shahr-i Sabz, 137
Shāh Walī Allāh of Delhi, 26, 27
Shaikh Ahmad Ahsā'ī, 12, 19

Shaikh ar-Ra'īs, 378
Shaikhi
  doctrine, 21
  ideas, 20, 21
  leaders, 19
  movement, 19
  works, 19
Shaikism, 19, 20
Sharī'a, 70
Sharif of Mecca, 211
Sharīf Pāshā, 99, 113, 117, 118, 120, 182
Shawwal, 80
Shihāb ad-Dīn the Martyr, 163
Shi'i
  branch of Islam, 2, 10
  education, 15
  Iran, 28
  mahdi of, 15
  sayyids, 12
  shrine cities, 14, 16, 33
  Twelver, 12, 18
Shi'ism, 12, 15, 18, 20
Shimr, 328, 384, 385
Shīrāzī, Hājji Mīrzā Hasan, 342, 351, 356, 364
Shirvānī-Zāde, 67
Shrine cities, 15, 16, 21
Shumayyil, Shiblī, Dr., 91
Sifātallāh, 12, 14, 15, 21, 34
Sikhs, 27, 286
Sind, 208
Singh, Maharaja Dalip, 283, 285, 286, 290, 292
Skepticism, 3, 26, 31, 87
Smith, Wilfred, 155
Social classes, Babism on, 21
Socialism, 177
Sorbonne, 189
Sudan, 206, 220, 222, 234
Suez, 123, 143
Suez Canal, 82, 209
Sufi, 57
  ideas, 87
  mystics, 18, 19
  orders, 377
  views, 85
  works, 18
Sufism, 18, 26, 88, 90
Sulaiman Khān Afshār, 13, 280
Sultan, 7, 35, 246
Sultan Abdülaziz, 59, 73, 92, 120
Sultan Abdülhamid II, 87, 120, 131, 139, 184, 277, 326, 403, 406, 407, 411, 413, 415, 419, 421
Sultan Mahomed, 46
Sultan Newaz Jang, 146
Sultan of Morocco, 252
Sunni
  alim, 78
  branch of Islam, 2, 3, 8
  countries, 10, 18
  orthodox, 19
  tradition of Muslim countries, 18
  ulama, 61
Sunnism, 18
Syria, 209

Tabātabā'ī, Āqā Muhammad, 320
Tabātabā'ī, Muhīt, 16, 17, 20
Tahsin Efendi, 60, 61, 67, 71, 74
Takvim-i Vekayi, gazette, 65, 66
Talbot, Major G. F., 335
Tanzimat reform period, 59, 62, 130
Taqiyya, 18, 19
Taqīzādeh, Sayyid Hasan, 25, 282
Taqlā brothers, 96
Tashkend (Tashkent), 43
Taufīq, Khedive, 98, 100, 113, 114, 115, 116, 118, 119, 144
Tehran, 11, 13, 14, 15, 21, 32, 34, 52, 301, 307, 310, 313, 317, 318
Tel-el-Kabir, 234, 237
Tewfik Pāshā, 117
Thagi and Dakaiti Department, India, 149, 182, 283, 292, 387
Tiflis, 42
at-Tijāra, newspaper, 98
Times (London), 111, 118, 124
Tobacco Protest, 335–355
Toorkistan, 42, 44, 45
Towfiq Pāshā, Khedive. *See* Taufīq, Khedive
Traditionalism, 1
Transcaucasia, 360
Tricou, French consul, 113
Tripoli, 208, 237
Tsar, 293, 296, 304–305, 309, 389, 390
Tunis, 208
Tunisia, 130, 204
Turin, 216
Turkey, 75, 78, 125, 209, 360
Turkish Academy, 67
Turkish language, 11, 208
Turkish nationalism, 64
Turkistan, Russian, 285, 290

Turkomans, 136, 221
Turkoman steppes, 42, 309
Turks, 190
Türk Yurdu, newspaper, 432
Turquie, La, newspaper, 76
Twelfth Imam, 18, 20, 21
Twelver Shi'ism
  doctrine of, 20
  in Islam, 12, 18
  Shaikhi school of, 19
  usūlī school of, 19

Ulama, 12, 16, 17, 37, 38, 53
  authority of, 27
  conservative, 80
  Hyderabad, 147
  orthodoxy of Najaf, 20
  power of, 178
  rejection of Muslim philosophers by, 79
  teachings of, 91
Ulema corps in Turkey, 75, 78, 125, 265
'Umar ibn Sa'd, 328
Umayyads, 139
Umma, 134
Unification, German and Italian, 130
Unity
  of Indian Hindus and Muslims, 157
  of Islam, 134, 137
Universities
  Al-Azhar, 58, 81, 231
  Darülfünun, 62, 75, 76
  Indian Muslim, 147
Unorthodoxy, 5
  in Egypt, 129
  traditional forms of, 26
Upper Egypt, 221, 231
'Urābī, Aḥmad, 101, 112, 265
'Urābī government, 112, 186
'Urābī movement, 101, 118, 127, 188
Urdu language, 149, 159
al-'Urwa al-Wuthqā, newspaper, 5, 85, 132, 159, 214–228
'Uthmān Pāshā (al-Ghālib), 120, 123

Vahbi, Ismail Bey, 61
Vakīl, 45
Vakīl ad-Dauleh, 329, 330
Vaqf land, 341
Viceroy of India, 149
Vladikavkaz, 282

Wahbī, Muhammad Bey, 213, 236, 255
Wālī, 331
al-Waqā'i' al-Misriyya, gazette, 124
West
  interest of, in Afghānī, 1
  "materialist" sects in, 176
Western
  control, 182
  encroachments, 87
  knowledge, 29
  learning, 158
  liberalism, 80
  technology, 226
  woman, 268–270
Westernism, 1, 75, 87
Westernization, 25, 62, 64, 87, 130, 153
Wilson, Sir Rivers, 99
Wolff, Sir Henry Drummond, 229, 249, 302
Wolseley, Lord, 242
Wood, Sir Evelyn, 200, 201, 203

Yarkand, 138
Yazīd, Caliph, 329, 384, 385
Yemen, 262
Yıldız, 238, 406
Young Egypt
  program, 115
  society in Alexandria, 115, 127
"Young Ottomans," 60, 151

Ẓāfir, Shaikh, 377
Zaghlūl, Sa'd, 84, 187, 421, 422
Zaidān, Jurjī, 6, 68, 421, 427, 432
  Mashāhīr ash-Sharq by, 5
Zill as-Sultān, 274, 275, 298, 410
Zinoviev, Grigori, 293, 305, 308, 311
Ziyād Ibn, 332
Zoroaster, 109
Zoroastrians, 442
Zū al-Faqār Khān, Sardār, 54